HOW THE WEST BECAME ANTISEMITIC

How the West Became Antisemitic

JEWS AND THE FORMATION
OF EUROPE, 800–1500

———◆———

Ivan G. Marcus

PRINCETON UNIVERSITY PRESS
PRINCETON & OXFORD

Copyright © 2024 by Princeton University Press

Princeton University Press is committed to the protection of copyright and the intellectual property our authors entrust to us. Copyright promotes the progress and integrity of knowledge created by humans. By engaging with an authorized copy of this work, you are supporting creators and the global exchange of ideas. As this work is protected by copyright, any reproduction or distribution of it in any form for any purpose requires permission; permission requests should be sent to permissions@press.princeton.edu. Ingestion of any PUP IP for any AI purposes is strictly prohibited.

Published by Princeton University Press
41 William Street, Princeton, New Jersey 08540
99 Banbury Road, Oxford OX2 6JX

press.princeton.edu

GPSR Authorized Representative: Easy Access System Europe - Mustamäe tee 50, 10621 Tallinn, Estonia, gpsr.requests@easproject.com

All Rights Reserved

First paperback printing, 2025
Paperback ISBN 978-0-691-25822-5
Cloth ISBN 978-0-691-25820-1
ISBN (e-book) 978-0-691-25821-8
LCCN: 2024442774

British Library Cataloging-in-Publication Data is available

Editorial: Priya Nelson and Morgan Spehar
Production Editorial: Jill Harris
Jacket/Cover Design: Heather Hansen
Production: Danielle Amatucci
Publicity: Kate Hensley and Carmen Jimenez
Copyeditor: Cindy Milstein

Jacket/Cover image: Heidelberg University Library, Cod. Pal. germ. 848 (Codex Manesse) - Zürich, ca. 1300 bis ca. 1340; p.355r

This book has been composed in Miller

For Judy

Now Israel loved Joseph best of all his sons, for he was the child of his old age; and he had made him an ornamented tunic. And when his brothers saw that their father loved him more than any of his brothers, they hated him so that they could not speak a friendly word to him.

—GENESIS 37:3–4 NJPS

CONTENTS

Abbreviations · xi
A Note on Translations · xiii

1 Introduction · 1

2 Migration to the West: Following Europa · 20

3 Reforms and Right Order: The Apostolic Age and Crusade Active Martyrs · 42

4 Assertive Words: Insulting Christianity · 65

5 Offensive Gestures: Latrine Blasphemy · 87

6 Eucharistic Fantasies: Saints, Imagined Killers, and Jewish Saints · 108

7 Cultural Aesthetics: Sexual Threats, Conversions, and Imagined "Racial" Jews · 141

8 Expulsions: Imagined Jews and Real Christian Antisemites · 171

9 Antisemitisms: Medieval and Modern · 189

Acknowledgments · 201
Glossary · 203
Notes · 205
Bibliography · 249
Index · 347

ABBREVIATIONS

- B. Babylonian Talmud (Bavli)
- b. ben (son of)
- ca. circa, approximately
- CE Common or Christian Era (AD)
- col. column
- E Eidelberg, *The Jews and the Crusaders*
- EH Haverkamp, *Hebräische Berichte über die Judenverfolgungen*
- H Habermann, *Sefer Gezeirot Ashkenaz ve-Zarefat*
- Heb/Héb. Hebrew
- M. Mishnah
- MGH SS Monumenta Germaniae Historica Scriptores
- MIGNE PL Jacques Paul Migne's *Patrologia Latina* (*Patrologiae Cursus Completus. Series Latina*)
- MS manuscript
- NJPS New Jewish Publication Society of America, publisher of *Tanakh* (1985)
- NRSV New Revised Standard Version of the Bible (1989)
- R. rabbi
- r. ruled/reigned
- RHC occ., *Recueil des historiens des croisades, occidentaux*
- RSV Revised Standard Version of the Bible (1902)

SHB *Sefer Hasidim*, Bologna, 1538

SHP *Sefer Hasidim*, Parma, Biblioteca Palatina, Hebrew MS 3280

Vat. *Sefer Hasidim*, Vatican, Vatican Library, ebr. 285/26, f. 108v–127v

A NOTE ON TRANSLATIONS

TRANSLATIONS FROM THE Hebrew Bible are based on the New Jewish Publication Society of America Tanakh (1985)

Translations from the New Testament are based on either the Revised Standard Version (RSV, 1902) or the New Revised Standard Version (NRSV, 1989).

All translations of other sources are my own unless otherwise indicated.

HOW THE WEST BECAME ANTISEMITIC

CHAPTER ONE

Introduction

IN AN EPISODE of *The Marvelous Mrs. Maisel*, the protagonist's father, Abe Weissman, finds himself in possession of a consecrated host that he wants to dispose of. His son makes a suggestion, to which Abe replies, "You're going to flush the body of Christ down the toilet?!"¹ In medieval Europe, Christian authorities frequently accused Jews of committing even more insulting, antireligious acts, although they sometimes had difficulty writing about the horrifying details. In 1146, Peter the Venerable, abbot of Cluny (ca. 1092–1156), wrote to Louis VII, king of France (1137–80), to complain that it was pointless to go on a Crusade against the distant Muslims when the Jews, who were "not far away from us, but right in our midst, blaspheme, abuse, and trample on Christ and the Christian sacraments so freely and insolently and with impunity," and "use heavenly vessels for their evil uses to the disgrace of Christ and ourselves, things too horrifying to consider and detestable to mention."²

Less inhibited to offer examples of Jewish "latrine blasphemy" was the greatest of medieval popes, Innocent III (r. 1198–1216), who expressed his disgust that after Christian wet nurses employed by Jewish families took communion on Easter, "the Jews make these women pour their milk into the latrine for three days before they again give suck to the children."³

What are we to make of these and other accusations that Jews insulted Christianity by associating it with latrines? From contemporary Jewish discussions about such gestures that we will consider in detail in chapter 5, we learn that some Jews were capable of doing exactly what infuriated Christian officials.

These accusations and stories about Jews insulting Christian symbols with latrine blasphemy are not isolated examples of how Jews viewed Christianity in medieval Europe but rather are a hint about how Jews could provocatively assert themselves in Christian Europe—a story that has not been told before.[4] For medieval European history is sometimes written as though the Jews of Christian Europe were living on the moon instead of in the small towns of northern France, England, and Germany, in a region that Jews came to refer to as *Ashkenaz*, the geographic focus of this book.[5] Medieval Jewish historians have recently revised earlier narratives that saw the Jews as the victims of the Christian majority's enmity and harmful policies.[6] General historians of medieval Europe who do not work on Jewish history still tend to see the Jews as isolated in ghettos and passive victims of persecution, if they see them at all.[7] Historians of the Christian majority sometimes forget that when they speak of "everyone," they mean Christians and usually ignore their Jewish neighbors.[8] Medieval Christians could never forget their Jewish neighbors even when Jews no longer lived among them. The Jews remained a presence even in their absence.[9]

This book reexamines not only how the Christian majority understandably affected the Jewish minority but also surprisingly how the Jews—real and imagined—so challenged the Christian majority that it became a society that was religiously and culturally antisemitic in new ways between 800 and 1500. That new self-understanding remained part of European cultural identity down to the time of the Holocaust and beyond.[10]

The Jews as a Fourth Medieval Civilization

The European Middle Ages is the often-told story of the transformation of the western provinces of the Roman Empire into several new Christian political territories. A history of medieval Europe can also be related to two other contemporary medieval civilizations, Islam and Byzantium, each of which ruled over large territories including parts of what became Europe.[11] Byzantine emperors governed southern Italy and tried to recover other former Roman territories in Europe in the sixth century. Umayyad and Berber Muslims ruled significant areas of medieval Iberia, and Ottoman Muslims governed important parts of early modern southeastern Europe.

Missing from this picture of the formation of Europe is the story of a group that became more prominent over the centuries and by its assertive presence within Europe stimulated and provoked the Christian majority into reimagining its own collective identity. These were not the Muslims far off in the East or nearby in Iberia but the Jews, who like pagans and heretics lived cheek by jowl among Christians throughout Europe. They were still the bearers of the ancient religious culture out of which Christianity first developed. Survivors of the pagan and Christian Roman Empire and the Muslim conquest in the eastern Mediterranean, Jews migrated into the emerging Christian West with a unique relationship to Christianity. Once settled there, Jews usually resisted complete social assimilation through conversion.[12] A distinctive minority organized in self-governing local communities, the Jews lived closely and sometimes intimately among their Christian neighbors for centuries. The Jews were a fourth medieval civilization embedded in three other civilizations: Islam, Byzantium, and Latin Christian Europe.[13] This is the story of the Jews and the formation of Christian Europe, the West.[14]

Contrary to the widely accepted picture of Jewish history, medieval Jews were assertive agents. The Jews of the Middle Ages were convinced of their chosenness, and Christian rulers inadvertently reinforced Jewish solidarity by recognizing Jews as legal, self-governing communities, not just as individuals, if only to tax them better. The Jewish-Christian confrontation was grounded in a deep structural clash between two related religious cultures, each of which thought itself chosen and the other excluded from divine favor.[15] Given the different power dynamics, this meant that force would be a Christian option, but the Jews had resources as well, even if limited and often ineffective. Jews were assertive, not passive, even without having the option of coercive force. Acts of Jewish assertiveness directed against Christianity, in turn, increased Christian authorities' anti-Jewish views and policies. Christians reasserted their claims to divine election and tried to subject the Jews to servitude unless they converted. One effect of this confrontation between two chosen cultures was to make Christian Europe antisemitic in new ways.

In rethinking medieval Christian antisemitism, it becomes clear that the rivalry between Jews and Christians led each religious culture to create both symmetry and asymmetry in the way each created their imagined other.

The story was in part symmetrical in that each culture claimed to be the one God chose in its Bible. The Hebrew Bible and New Testament agree that it is the second or later party, not the first, that is God's chosen one, and Jews and Christians each claimed to be the second. In the Hebrew Bible, the Israelites displace the Canaanites, who are there first, and the younger sons, Isaac and Jacob, displace the elder sons, Ishmael and Esau. In the latter case, the Bible says that *the elder shall serve the younger* (Gen. 25:23). The Christian reading of those texts read the church as Isaac and Jacob, and the Jews as Ishmael and Esau, who were to serve the younger Jacob as the church.

Despite this symmetry about rival claims to being chosen, an important asymmetry developed in medieval Europe. Although most rabbinic leaders viewed their Christian neighbors as misguided and not as pagans, they still assumed that *Christianity* itself was a form of forbidden "foreign worship" (*'avodah zarah*).[16] The Christian majority, on the other hand, asserted its own spiritual election and treated *Jews* as rejected and despised pagans, and paid little attention to Judaism except as foretelling the truth of Christianity.[17] So medieval Christian antisemitism was directed at medieval *Jews*. Jewish animosity was directed at *Christianity* and its sancta that Jews associated with biblical idolatry and filth.[18]

In asserting their Jewish religious and communal chosen identity in new ways at the same time that medieval Christians were reaffirming the exclusive truth claims of Christianity, Jews collided with Christians, and the confrontation resulted in new collective identities that were shaped in part by the impact of the other. The ways Jews and Christians became aware of each other as competing claimants to biblical, covenantal chosenness played a central role in shaping the West.

The focus of this book is on cultural history and the social settings in which Jews and Christians from all levels of society interacted. To get at the mentality of ordinary Jews and Christians, we will consider carefully how they appear in written sources like saints' lives, exempla or moralistic stories, such as the hundreds found in *Sefer Hasidim* (before 1225), behavior portrayed in chronicles, and a variety of images.[19] These sources are important because they make use of everyday settings of life in contemporary Ashkenaz.

But the ways Jews and Christians regarded and treated each other in medieval Europe reflect fundamental religious assumptions about chosenness laid out in the Jewish and Christian Bibles, two very different books. In working out their differences, Jews and Christians engaged in a rivalry over chosenness in society that we can explore by studying what Peter Gay referred to as "the social history of ideas."[20]

Ancient Theological Assumptions about Chosenness

For the Jews' chosenness, the Book of Exodus foretells, *Now then, if you will obey Me faithfully and keep My covenant, you shall be My treasured possession among all the peoples. Indeed, all the earth is Mine* (Ex. 19:5). On this verse, the ancient rabbinic midrash on Exodus, *Mekhilta de Rabbi Yishmael* (third century CE Palestine), elaborates: (the phrase) *you shall be My* (means) "(if you) turn to Me and are occupied with Torah and not with other things," (then) *you shall be My treasured possession.* "Just as a man's treasured possession is precious to him, so, you will be precious to Me." The biblical passage continues: *but you shall be to Me a kingdom of priests and a holy nation* (Ex. 19:6). On the phrase, *And you shall be unto Me,* the *Mekhilta* adds, "I shall not appoint nor delegate anyone else, so to speak, to rule over you, but I myself will rule over you."[21]

The special relationship between Israel and God promised conditionally in the Book of Exodus is stated as a reality in the Book of Deutcronomy on which the early rabbis grounded their conviction of Jews as God's Chosen People for all time. The Book of Deuteronomy asserts that all of Israel is holy *now* and therefore is chosen to be God's special people: *For you are a people consecrated to the Lord your God: of all the peoples on earth the Lord your God chose you to be His treasured people* (Deut. 7:6).[22]

This choice is not based on Israel's great numbers: *It is not because you are the most numerous of peoples that the Lord set His* heart on you and chose you—indeed, you are the smallest of peoples (Deut. 7:7). Rather, it is because of Israel's holiness or dedication to God: *For you are a people consecrated to the Lord your God: the Lord your God chose you from among all other peoples on earth to be His treasured people* (Deut. 14:2). And the rabbinic midrash on Deuteronomy, *Sifrei Devarim* (third century CE Palestine), explains that Israel's holiness in the first part of the verse is the reason for its chosenness in the second part: "the holiness that is upon you has made you holy (that is, chosen)."[23] "Another interpretation of *the Lord your God chose you from among all other peoples on earth to be His treasured people* (Deut. 14:2) is, "Hence we learn that each individual (Jew) is more precious to the Holy One, blessed be He, than all the nations of the world."[24]

Medieval Jews who engaged with Christians in everyday encounters understood themselves, not Christians, as God's "treasured people," as referred to in Exodus and Deuteronomy, which they read annually in the synagogue, along with the commentary of Rashi of Troyes (d. 1105), who relied on the ancient midrash commentaries of *Mekhilta* and *Sifrei*.

Christians, for their part, also claimed to be the chosen Israel, as church father Justin Martyr (d. ca. 200) and others explained (see below), but they still developed a theological rationale for permitting Jews to live as Jews in a Christian society. Paul formulated this reason in his Letter to the Romans, and Augustine of Hippo (d. 430), the most influential of the Latin fathers, elaborated on it. It was supported by the Christian Roman legal traditions and adopted by the early popes as well. Unlike pagans, whom the church forced to convert, or heretics, who were to be exterminated, Jews who did not convert were theoretically allowed to live in a Christian society, though in a degraded or servile capacity, so that they could eventually play a divinely required role in salvation history.[25]

Paul, Justin Martyr, and Augustine of Hippo

In his letters, the earliest part of the New Testament, the apostle Paul glosses key passages of the Hebrew Bible to make his case that gentiles as well as Jews can be part of a new covenant between God and "Israel." In his Letter to the Galatians (4:21–31), he identifies the

Jews as Ishmael, the son of the "slave" Hagar, Abraham's concubine, and Jewish and gentile believers in Christ as Isaac, the son of the "free woman" Sarah, Abraham's wife (see Gen. 17 and especially Gen. 21). He further associates Hagar with Mt. Sinai, the law, and Jerusalem in this world, in contrast to the heavenly Jerusalem, the locus of Sarah's son Isaac of the spirit, including gentiles as well as Jews who accept Christ. This interpretation is part of Paul's insistence on Jewish servitude to those who accept Christ. Paul's underlying idea, the first part of the three-part structure of the imagined Jew, is that Jews should be subordinate to Christians who received the divine promise—a view summarized as the *binary of inverted hierarchy.*

Paul reinforces the biblical warrant for Jewish servitude even more explicitly in a second biblical comparison. Following the narrative about pairs of siblings in the Book of Genesis, he then distinguishes between Isaac's son Esau, the elder brother, and Jacob, also known as "Israel" (Gen. 32:29), the younger one: *though they were not yet born and had done nothing either good or bad, in order that God's purpose of election might continue, not because of works but because of his call, she was told, "The elder will serve the younger"* (Rom. 9:11–12 RSV, quoting Gen. 25:23). Paul identifies the Jews as the elder son, Esau, and gentiles and Jews who believe in Jesus as Jacob, the younger, also known as "Israel," the recipients of the covenant.[26] The rabbis identified the Jews as Jacob and Christians as Esau.[27]

In these passages, then, Paul not only reinterprets the Book of Genesis to include gentiles and Jews who believe in Jesus as recipients of the divine covenant or promise made to Abraham (Gen. 15) but also insists that in each case the Jews are the elder sibling, the one who is to serve the younger whom God preferred and to whom he gave the covenant. Jewish servitude is expected and a condition for Jewish presence in a Christian society.

Moreover, Paul assigns a special role to subservient Jews in the economy of salvation history in the future. Complementing his view that Jews are to serve those who accept Jesus in the present is his hope that the Jews can eventually become part of the New Covenant in the future. In his Letter to the Romans, he says that God has not rejected the Jews for all time: *I ask then, has God rejected his people? By no means! I myself am an Israelite, a descendant of*

Abraham, a member of the tribe of Benjamin. God has not rejected His people whom He foreknew (Rom. 11:1–2a RSV).

He then proceeds, in his parable of the wild olive tree, to present the relationship between Jews who do not accept Jesus and Jews and gentiles who do:

> *Now I am speaking to you Gentiles. Inasmuch then as I am an apostle to the Gentiles, I magnify my ministry in order to make my fellow Jews jealous, and thus save some of them . . . if the root is holy, so are the branches.*
>
> *But if some of the branches were broken off, and you, a wild olive shoot, were grafted in their place to share the richness of the olive tree, do not boast over the branches. . . . And even the others, if they do not perish in their unbelief, will be grafted in, for God has the power to graft them in again.*
>
> *For if you have been cut from what is by nature a wild olive tree, and grafted, contrary to nature, into a cultivated olive tree, how much more will these natural branches be grafted back into their own olive tree.*
>
> *Lest you be wise in your own conceits, I want you to understand this mystery; brethren: a hardening has come upon part of Israel, until the full number of the Gentiles come in, and so all Israel will be saved. . . . As regards the Gospel they are enemies of God, for your sake; but as regards election they are beloved for the sake of their forefathers* (Rom. 11:13–28 RSV).

The Jews without faith in Jesus are the natural branches, but because of their unbelief, they have been temporarily lopped off and replaced by the engrafted gentiles, comparable now to Isaac and Jacob of the promise. He makes use of a logical argument to offer hope for Jews to be regrafted back in if they accept Jesus. If gentiles, who had nothing to do with the root and are a foreign body, can be grafted onto the root, the Jews who originally were descended from the root certainly could be regrafted back on.

The conclusion to Paul's parable, Romans 11:28, was to have profound and lasting mixed consequences for medieval Jewish-Christian relations. Paul refers to Jews as both theological enemies and beloved, but for different reasons. When Paul says *"as regards the Gospel they are enemies of God,"* it is because they continue to follow the Old Covenant of the "letter" and reject the New Covenant of the "spirit" that includes gentiles and Jews with faith in Christ as chosen. In Paul's binary vision of the world, the status of the literalist, Torah-law-following, fleshly, this-worldly Jew is in polar opposition to the new dispensation of the Gospels. But *they are beloved for the sake of their forefathers.* Jews are also beloved because of their earlier election or chosenness that made them special in the age of the biblical fathers. Jews thus exist in two planes in the present: they are formerly chosen, but now are still following the letter and not the spirit, and are in that sense "enemies" to the Gospel, its antithesis.[28]

Paul's theological trope of the Jews as "enemies of God" would be transformed at the time of the First Crusade into the active social and political category of "the enemy nearby," a new stage in the Christian construction of the imagined Jew (chapter 3).

Although Paul maintains that God's covenant with Israel now includes all who accept Christ, he does not say explicitly that the church has superseded the covenant with the Jews and that the Christian Church, not the Jews, is now Israel of the covenant, but he hints at it.[29] It becomes explicit in the second century, as in the writings of the church father Justin Martyr (ca. 100–160s) in his *Dialogue with the Jew Trypho* (ca. 160 CE). A gentile born in Samaria, Justin sought to defend Christianity by interpreting Scripture properly to a Jew, and he continued the New Testament tactic of using the Hebrew Bible as the platform from which to try to win over Jews to Christianity. To reassure Christians, he added that they, and not the Jews, are Israel, the heirs of the covenant with Abraham, Isaac, and Jacob also called by that name: "We have been led to God through this crucified Christ, and we are the true spiritual Israel, and the descendants of Judah, Jacob, Isaac and Abraham, who, though uncircumcised, was approved and blessed by God because of his faith and was called the father of many nations."[30]

Medieval Jews were aware of the Christian claim, and it spurred them on to resist Christian triumphalism at times of crisis such as during the First Crusade. A Jewish chronicler in the early twelfth century has Crusaders taunting the Jews that they are no longer the Chosen People: "God has forgotten you and is no longer desirous of you since you are a stubborn nation. Instead, He has departed from you and has taken us for His portion, casting His radiance upon us."[31]

Augustine of Hippo in North Africa (former Carthage) (348–430) was the most influential author of Christian doctrine in the West, and it is his image of the Jews as blind witnesses to the truth of Christianity that turned Paul's contrast between free and slave in his Letter to the Galatians and the parable of the wild olive tree in the Letter to the Romans into theological policy.[32]

In his *Contra Faustum*, he defended the antiquity of the Old Testament with its prophecies of the truth of the New Testament from the attack of dualist Manichaeans, who denied its validity. The Jews themselves read in public the Old Testament that prophesies the coming of Jesus and the truth of Christianity even though they do not understand what they read. This proves to pagans and Christians alike that Christians have not invented the Hebrew traditions on which the church bases its claim to be the true Israel. Thus Jews unwittingly serve as "the desks (*scriniaria*) of the Christians, bearing the law and the prophets as testimony to the tenets of the church, so that we honor through the sacrament what it announces through the letter."[33]

In *The City of God*, written to defend Christianity against the taunts of pagan Romans who blamed Christian impiety for the sack of Rome in 410, Augustine interprets Psalms 59:12 [58:12] to add other reasons why Jews serve a positive role in Christian societies. *Slay them not lest they forget thy law. Scatter them in thy power and bring them down* (Ps. 59:12 [58:12]) means that it is forbidden to kill the Jews, but it is God's will that they should be dispersed and degraded to serve as blind witnesses to the truth of Christianity for Christians and others everywhere. By being scattered and subordinated in Christian society, Jews prove that God has rejected them since they killed Christ and has exiled them from their land, and this benefits the church: "For, if the Jews had remained bottled up in their own land with the evidence of their Scriptures and if they were not to be found everywhere, as the Church is, the Church would not then have them as ubiquitous witnesses of the ancient prophecies concerning Christ."[34]

Four years after he wrote *The City of God*, Augustine wrote the tract "Against the Jews." It begins with Paul's parable of the olive tree in Romans 11, and after warning Gentile Christians not to boast, tries to convince Jews of the Christian meaning of their own Scriptures. The emphasis in Augustine on a positive role for Jews in a Christian society, despite their being Christ's killers and servants to Christians, reinforced Paul's position of hopefulness in Romans. The exegesis of Psalms 59:12 [58:12] that specifically forbade Christians to kill Jews, and instead emphasized scattering and subduing them, placed a powerful theological restraint on official Christian attitudes toward Jews.[35]

Early Europe

Despite the future redemptive role early Christian theologians assigned to Jews living in a Christian society, the presence of Jews is not what usually comes to mind when we think about the making of early Christian Europe. Instead, we are supposed to think about the search for unity and law that looked back to Rome, as when Pope Leo III crowned a Germanic Frankish king, Charles the Great (Charlemagne, d. 814), "emperor of the Romans" on December 25, 800.[36] Newly formed kingdoms made up of partly Romanized and Christianized Germanic tribes took over several western Roman provinces. The Germanic kings were tied to their fighting men by bonds of loyalty according to ancient custom. Some German kings married into local Gallo-Roman, or Hispano-Roman, or Italo-Roman Christian noble families. Christianity gradually became the central religious identity, replacing pagan cults with the life of Christ and his representatives on earth as the bishops of Rome, the popes, and with attempts to approximate the Christian life in religious orders and reforms of lay behavior.

Rome, Germanic customs, and Christianity, then, combined over time to form early Europe—the West. And yet despite the fact that medieval Jews, unlike Byzantine Christian emperors or Muslim caliphs, did not exercise coercive power in any territory, the story of Europe is made more intelligible when one also looks closely at the Jews who formed a fourth medieval culture, the only religious minority that formed "infidel" communities that were permitted to live within Christian Europe itself.

Jewish and Christian Transformations

Two remarkable and lasting changes occurred during those centuries. Jews who migrated into Christian Europe from Byzantine Christian or Muslim Mediterranean lands became "Europeanized," and even Christianized, without actually becoming Christians. The Jews changed: they were not only an Eastern Roman- or Muslim-dominated culture but also an integral part of the emerging Latin Christian West. By a process of selective *inward acculturation*, they absorbed some elements of that Christian cultural environment while rejecting others.[37]

Even though they looked down on Christians and continued to view Christianity as no different from ancient paganism, Jews had to take Christianity seriously in the Christian West. They didn't have to like it, but they had to deal with it. Out of a sense of cultural competition, Jews sometimes selectively internalized and Judaized Christian motifs or practices and incorporated them into their own Jewish cultural and religious practices.

As a result, Jews now studied the Bible and Talmud with a French interpreter, Rashi of Troyes (d. 1105), who used thousands of French words to clarify the Hebrew text.[38] Now they studied the Talmud with French scholastic commentators who resolved contradictions by making distinctions, as had Peter Abelard in his theological lectures at the University of Paris.[39] Now they remembered Jewish martyrs and deceased relatives by lighting candles annually on the anniversary of their deaths or in public liturgical memorials, as did Christian monks in their monasteries.[40]

They built stone synagogues in the form of church chapter houses, and ritual baths designed by the same people who built the new local cathedrals and related buildings that they sometimes helped finance.[41] They wrote Hebrew manuscripts with bold vertical letters like the Christian scribes' Gothic script in Latin that they did not read but saw in books that were pawned as collateral for loans to Christian owners.[42] They spoke Yiddish or French based on the local tongues they learned over the centuries.[43] They wrote stories in Hebrew about romantic love as Christian writers did in Latin or French.[44] They atoned for their sins by confessing them to rabbis and asking them for penances, as did Christian sinners who confessed to their priests.[45] Jews took many of these Christianized practices with them into the Polish-Lithuanian Commonwealth and continued to adapt selectively from their Christian environments later in early modern and even modern times. Judaism had become European and even Christianized while remaining defiantly Jewish.

But the everyday contact between Jews and Christians in medieval Europe transformed the Christianizing population there as well.[46] Christians had difficulty understanding why Jews did not convert and adopt what they considered the obvious good news (gospel) of their religion. What was wrong with the Jews? Why were they so resistant to accepting the truth? To make matters worse, although Jews lacked coercive political power over Christian rulers, they actually were *assertive* in their conversations with Christian neighbors and affirmed that they, and not Christians, were God's Chosen People. They hired Christian maids and wet nurses, like aristocratic Christian nobility. They prayed loudly in their synagogues, were in positions of influence when they were creditors, and abused Christian sacred objects. All of these Jewish actions rubbed Christian authorities the wrong way, making them more resentful and antisemitic.[47]

Competing Claims of Chosenness

As the population grew in the towns of Christian Europe, Jews continued to migrate there to make a secure living in an expanding economy. Close contact with Christians was inevitable.[48] Isolation was not possible or desirable. Jews engaged in business with Christians first in trade and then also as borrowers or suppliers of credit. So much Jewish business depended on Christian clients that Jewish legal authorities permitted Jews to do business with Christians even though they considered Christianity to be a form of "foreign worship." Jews were simultaneously attracted to Christians and repelled by Christianity.

At first, Christian rulers inadvertently reinforced Jewish religious self-confidence. Since antiquity, Christian theologians had argued that there was a degraded place for Jews in a Christian society, but early medieval Christian kings treated Jews as assets for their developing economies, invited them into their realms, and issued them protective charters that exempted them from tolls and taxes. These supportive Christian policies, motivated by self-interest, and a strong Jewish sense of "chosenness" encouraged Jewish settlement in early European Christian societies.

Although Jewish migration was gradual and went on largely unrecorded, members of different Jewish regional elites later created a "useful past" in the form of foundation legends. They remembered that a great king, Charlemagne himself, was a founder of the Jewish community of Narbonne in southern France and the Jewish community of Mainz in the German Empire, the heartland of what became Ashkenazic or northern European Jewish history. The elite claims expressed a sense of supremacy of one Jewish community in the West over another there, as well as a claim to being the heir to an earlier, esteemed Jewish center in the East. But intercommunal rivalries paled before the ongoing Jewish assertion that they, and not the Christian infidels, were God's chosen (chapter 2).

Jewish assertiveness also clashed with the new Christian reform movements that emerged in the eleventh century and stimulated Jewish competition even further. Papal reformers launched a political and religious campaign to assert "right order." One goal was to affirm ecclesiastical superiority over Christian kings by insisting that only the pope should be the "head" of the Christian social "body." Right order also meant not allowing Jews to have power over Christians.

The concern for right order also dictated a new papal policy toward the recent Muslim occupation of holy sites in Jerusalem that resulted in what became the First Crusade. In 1095, reform pope Urban II called for an armed pilgrimage to the Holy Land to liberate the Church of the Holy Sepulcher from "pagan" pollution and reestablish right order there. The hysteria that the pope generated against non-Christian enemies abroad reinforced the Christian view that the Jews who lived among them now were the "enemy within." To Paul's imagined Jew as subservient to the church was added a second dimension: *the Jew as the internal enemy*.

As a result, Crusader knights and mobs attacked Jewish communities mainly in the towns of the German Empire in spring and summer 1096. Jews reacted defiantly to Crusader mob attacks by fighting invaders, bribing authorities, and even provocatively pretending to convert, only to spit in the face of their attackers, kill and be killed in the streets, and to the horror of Christian chroniclers, be driven by the cruel Crusaders to ritually kill their own children and themselves to avoid being forced into the church (chapter 3).

After peace was restored, Jewish assertiveness assumed other forms as well.

The Jews created an *imagined Christianity* that they continued to view since ancient times as a form of paganism to be avoided and derided as much as possible. And so Jews went out of their way, when safe, to insult Christian sancta by making offensive wordplays and confronting Christians informally about their beliefs, provoking Christians to defend their faith. Jews also illustrated their Hebrew books with images of knights in combat and imagined themselves to be God's true knights as they engaged in everyday informal religious debates that irritated the church, which could not stop them. Christians saw this assertiveness and perceived Jews as Goliaths going out to battle them (chapter 4).

Moreover, Jews denigrated Christian sancta by engaging in private and public gestures of contempt, such as placing Christian images or statues in their latrines. Jews found the idea that God had been inside a woman preposterous and expressed their disgust about this idea in gestures that equated Christianity with bodily elimination, the opposite of the holy in both religious cultures. As Christian lay piety began to center on the Eucharist, a group of pietist Jews developed a ritual of childhood that challenged the efficacy of "eating God" by making young boys eat Torah verses written on cakes while seated on the lap of a rabbi in the pose of a Madonna and child. This nurturing ritual for young Jewish boys also served to discourage them from being lured away to a church increasingly eager to convert them (chapter 5).

There were limits, though, as to what real Jews actually did to show their contempt for Christianity. In the mid-twelfth century, as the eucharistic ritual reenactment of the Passion became more popular and enthusiasm for a Second Crusade gripped ecclesiastical circles, the idée fixe suddenly crystallized, first among English Benedictine monks, that Jewish infidels reenacted the Passion by ritually killing young Christian boys, whom monks now treated as local martyr saints. Local competition among Benedictines in England for making new Christian saints added a new dimension to the imagined Jew, augmented during the First Crusade frenzy as the nearby enemy of Christians. The imagined "enemy within" was now thought to harm "the body of Christ" in the present too, not just in the past, by ritually killing Christians (the ritual murder accusation), ingesting the victim's blood or heart (the blood libel), stabbing the consecrated host that was understood as the real body of Christ (the host desecration accusation), and even trying to kill all Christians (the well-poisoning libel). Jews, in turn, were familiar with Christian saints and imagined that Jewish figures, like the martyr communities of 1096, were saintly Christ figures victimized by violent Christian Crusaders or other wicked people. Other Jewish holy men described how pious Jews living in a time of peace should keep away from Christians unless they were in a position of relative dominance or right order over them (chapter 6).

The idea of the body of Christ also led Jews and Christians to argue vigorously over Jewish and Christian bodies. Depending on the context, Christians considered Jews indistinguishable from Christians and therefore sexually threatening without external markers such as distinctive clothing, or in the framework of potential conversion, some Jewish physical features were thought to prevent especially an adult male Jew from becoming a sincere Christian despite baptism.

In their encounters over "cultural aesthetics," Jews sometimes conceded to Christians that older Jewish (men) were dark and even "ugly" but insisted that they alone knew the inner truth about God and that such appearances were temporary. As the church tried to protect the faithful from heretics and assertive Jews in the thirteenth century, it took more defensive measures than before to convert Jews. An important question was, Could all Jews convert sincerely to Christianity and transform themselves completely, or were there physical traits that remained, especially among older Jewish male converts, in addition to circumcision? A gender and age analysis of Jews yields important nuances about the possibility of Jewish adult male conversion.

Thus to the imagined Jew as subordinate and then feared as the enemy within, a third characteristic was added: the belief that Jewish adult men could not change by conversion, and that *their Jewish condition was permanent*. At the same time, some room was left for the possibility that Jewish boys and "the beautiful Jewish woman," a potential or actual Christian sexual partner, could convert sincerely (chapter 7).

The reform of Christian society took a new turn as town walls expanded to accommodate growing populations, and money and credit became more visible in everyday life. A Christian-renewed emphasis on apostolic poverty meant that wealth, and especially the uses to which money was put involving interest or "usury," penalized foreign Christian bankers and local Jewish merchants and suppliers of credit but undermined vulnerable Jews more. Some pious kings supported these ecclesiastical reform efforts and thought that their realms needed to be purged of the polluting sin of usury, especially before they went on a Crusade.

Since even after conversion, some Jews persisted in their Jewish practices or were thought to retain hated Jewish characteristics, kings made bargains with political rivals by forcing Jews to emigrate, despite the ancient theological rationale to retain them. The danger that authorities said the Jews posed to Christian society now outweighed the Pauline and Augustinian need to keep them inside Christendom.

But even after their expulsion, the imagined Jew remained and expanded, along with converted Jews, as a persisting feature of antisemitic European Christian culture and society. Because Paul and Augustine taught that Jews, unlike heretics, were supposed to be part of Christian society, their physical exclusion created an even greater reason than before to emphasize the presence of the imagined Jew as an inner enemy within Christian social space. In literary works in England, we see the imagined presence of the unchangeable enemy Jewish male adult featured in Geoffrey Chaucer's *Prioress's Tale*, Christopher Marlowe's *Jew of Malta*, and William Shakespeare's *Merchant of Venice* (chapter 8).

The imagined Jew, however defined, could not be expelled from Europe, because it existed in the minds of Christian Europeans and persisted for centuries there and wherever Europe spread its influence. It enabled medieval and early modern images of European antisemitism to linger and develop through the centuries until they were selectively redeployed to support new, antimodern, and pseudoscientific racial forms of Jew hatred in the late nineteenth century, becoming lethal in the twentieth. The Jews were first understood to be the enemy of the church and the body of Christ, and then became, in redefined racial categories, the enemy of the *Volk*.

Medieval antisemitism is related to its modern form. But instead of following those scholars who point to one or more stereotypes that seem to continue into modern times, this book suggests a different approach. Because medieval Christian antisemitism was built on structural assumptions about Jews and Christians in society, it contained the possibility of being translated into modern categories.

Christians had created an imagined Jew in three stages. First, Jews and Christians agreed that they lived in a binary of inverted hierarchy. Each thought that it should be above and control the other. Neither wanted to be subordinated to the other. This was an extension of the chosenness claims of both, and it meant that *power* was an important theme of difference from the Middle Ages on. Domination and resistance were the result when power was one-sided in favor of the Christian culture. But Jews were also assertive, and Christians sometimes were defensive.

Secondly, after the First Crusade and prior to each subsequent one, the structure of hierarchical power and chosenness was sharpened as Jews came to be seen as the dangerous enemy within. The many different stereotypes of the "Jew" were actually expressions of this second structural feature of the Jew as an inner enemy. The idea emerged in bursts of religious zeal created by the first Crusades, but it persisted long afterward, as did the binary of inverted hierarchy.

Third, Jewish identity, especially that of adult Jewish men, was seen as an unchangeable or permanent condition, regardless of conversion. Late medieval efforts to convert Jews in northern Europe, not just in Iberia, raised issues of "racial" permanence despite efforts to convert Jews, especially adult males.

The three factors of inverted hierarchical power, internal enemy, and permanence shaped the Christian-imagined Jew, and these Christian antisemitic assumptions could be transformed into modern antisemitism by replacing medieval attributes with modern ones that fit the three structural categories. This new interpretation builds on the insight of Robert Stacey that "we need, in short, to put the history of antisemitism squarely at the center of the history of medieval Europe if we are properly to understand either one" (chapter 9).[49]

The story begins with the realization that Europe includes the role of the Jews as a challenging cultural presence before, during, and after they actually lived there. The real and imagined movements of Jewish populations into the early medieval West coincides with the birth of Europe. Jews were present at the creation and played an active part in shaping the new Christian culture that developed there.[50] Before we consider how Christian religious reforms helped reinforce Jewish assertions of chosenness that, in turn, stimulated Christian competitive claims of its superiority, we need to see the early Jewish-Christian symbiosis that was based more on common business interests than on hierarchical claims of superiority. It serves as an instructive foil for what was to follow.

CHAPTER TWO

Migration to the West

FOLLOWING EUROPA

HOW AND WHEN did the Jews get to early Europe? Although Jews moved in and out of the various western provinces of the Roman Empire, there are few signs of Jewish settlements there in late antiquity.[1] One is reported in 321 CE in Cologne, Germany, where Jews received the right to be tax collectors—an onerous and risky way to make a living since if there were a shortfall in collections, the collector had to make up the difference from his own pocket. Though prohibited from holding power over Christian Romans, Jews were conceded this exception because of the possibility that it might ruin them.[2] It is not clear if that community was disrupted during the great population migration of late antiquity and refounded later, or if it persisted into medieval times.[3]

Local church councils and inscriptions of Jewish names on tombstones from the fifth century give us a blurry picture of the first Jews of Europe north of the Alps.[4] Jews also settled in parts of the territory that had been Gaul. In the south, Jews settled early in Narbonne, Agde, Avignon, and Arles, among other locations. In his *History of the Franks*, Gregory, bishop of Tours (539–94) refers to a number of incidents that involve individual Jews.[5]

Other Jews lived in towns in Roman and Visigothic Spain, where bishops and kings tried forcibly to convert or expel them.[6] Unlike the restrictive Visigothic kings' laws, a branch of the Germanic Franks known as the Carolingians provided security to international

Jewish merchants by means of issuing private charters of protection (*tuitio*) to them. Around 825, Charlemagne's son, Louis the Pious (d. 840), issued three such private charters to Jews who were among the international traders doing business in the Carolingian Empire. Louis granted to each protection of their lives, exemption from tolls, guarantees of religious practice, and royal justice.[7] At the same time, other international Jewish merchants from Baghdad brought rare spices and other commodities from China to the courts of Europe.[8] The Carolingian privileges provided the framework for later communal charters that local and regional political leaders issued in the German Empire, and then in Angevin England and Christian Spain, though not in the Kingdom of France.[9]

The gradual migration of Jewish families into the former western provinces of the Roman Empire where the early communities formed went largely unrecorded. In contrast, later elites attributed their communal beginnings to the decisive act of a great Christian founder, Charlemagne (d. 814). The twofold pattern of gradual beginnings by immigration, on the one hand, or "foundation legends," on the other, is instructive. Gradual migration meant that individual Jews took advantage of opportunities to better their lives as a matter of course. Creating foundation legends meant different Jewish elites invented a "useful past" to affirm their Jewish community's superiority over another in either the European "West" or the Muslim "East."

The dual tendency to be both pragmatic and defiantly assertive would also characterize how Jewish communities in Christian Europe interacted cooperatively with Christian populations and authorities from the late tenth century on. For about a hundred years, Jews and Christians did business together and formed close social bonds on a daily basis. Christians, including priests, became Jewish merchants' favored clients, lending or borrowing money to make ends meet. On rare occasions, an ecclesiastical zealot temporarily forced Jews out of a particular town.[10] For the most part, however, neither Jews nor Christians were confident or threatened enough to assert their own chosenness at the expense of the other. This early period of settlement provides a contrast to the emergence of Jewish and Christian confrontations based on rival claims to chosenness that intensified after the First Crusade (chapter 3).

It also illustrates that the Jews were organized in communities and their leaders exercised agency.

The Tenth Century: Jews Establish New Communities in the German Empire

From the late tenth century onward, Jews in the German Empire and northern France participated in the slow expansion of urban life. Following a period of invasions by the Muslims, Vikings, and Hungarians, a new era of relative stability attracted merchants from the south and east, among them Jews seeking new economic opportunities.[11] Jews settled down as international and local merchants in northern Christian lands in the episcopal market towns that were developing along major rivers.[12] In a period of immigration of many different groups, Jews were not distinctive as newcomers and would not be treated as outsiders. Jewish occupations were diversified, but a significant part of the male population was engaged in trade. From the beginning, Jews were part of the developing "commercial revolution."[13] As a result of this new migration and settlement in the tenth century, Jews and Christians interacted on a daily basis in different towns to form early Europe.

Eventually, Jewish communities of varying sizes were organized locally in towns and governed internally by local committees of elders known as "good men of the town" (*tovei ha-'ir*). Even though they had limited internal coercive power and did not rule over any territory, local Jewish leaders acted on behalf of their communities, exercised agency over their civic lives, and negotiated with Christian leaders. The Jews in medieval Europe, as elsewhere, have a political history.[14]

Between 950 and 1100, Jews lived in all the politically and economically important towns in the German Empire, where the earliest Jewish communities provide Hebrew sources of Jewish communal life. They settled early in Mainz around 950, and soon in Magdeburg, Merseburg, Prague, and Regensburg in the east, Bamberg on the Main River, Cologne, Worms, and Speyer on the Rhine farther west, and Trier on the Moselle. Although the Jewish settlements in the east reflect the early beginnings of the empire in the tenth century, Jewish demography increased in the west, along the

Rhine. This pattern reflects the shift in German politics from the base of the Saxon emperor Otto the Great base in the tenth century in the northeast, to the eleventh- and twelfth-century centers of power of the Salian and Staufen houses farther west.[15] They formed the beginnings of what became Ashkenazic or northern European Jewry, one of the major demographic and culture areas of medieval Jewry, alongside Eastern Byzantine (Romaniyot), eastern Muslim (Mizrahi), and Muslim, and later Christian, Iberian (Sephardi) communities.

Of special significance was the Qalonimos family from Lucca, Italy. As their Greek name implies, they originally hailed from southern, Greek-speaking Byzantine Italy (Magna Graecia) and ultimately from Roman Palestine. Another branch was the Abun family descended from a Rabbi Abun from Le Mans in northwestern France. Other families also came perhaps from Metz, and together they became the nuclei of the Mainz Jewish elite, the first important settlement that recorded its new beginnings.[16]

In the Rhineland, members of former Italian Jewish families quickly married Jews who had come to Germany from France. Into the newly melded local communities of a few families, Jews brought with them ancient family traditions as well as Palestinian and Babylonian lore, law, and especially customary patterns of local Jewish living (minhag). Ordinary and learned individuals alike recommended following not only ancient sacred books but also what came to be called "the custom of our ancestors" (*minhag avoteinu*), which both groups regarded as sacred, on a par with ancient texts.[17]

Among the early signs of Jewish economic activity in medieval German lands, we have a few short answers to religious questions (*responsa*) of Rabbi Qalonimos of Lucca, who seems to have moved back and forth from Italy and the Rhineland, and a significant number of others from his son, R. Meshullam ben (son of) Qalonimos, who spent some time in Germany but was based mainly in Lucca.[18]

From responsa attributed to R. Meshullam b. Qalonimos (late tenth century), probably referring to Jewish-Christian contacts in Germany, we hear that in order to sell to Christians some parts of a slaughtered cow that is not kosher for Jews to eat, a Christian butcher joins the Jewish ritual slaughterer (*shohet*), and after the shohet kills the Christian's cow properly, the Christian puts his knife on the cow's neck to help convince Christian buyers that he, and not a Jew, slaughtered the animal.[19] In another case, a Jew serves as an agent of a wealthy Christian nobleman and advises him how to lend money to Christians or other Jews.[20]

But when a Jew who owns a baking oven wants to rent it to a Christian and share the profits, the ruling is that since the Christian fires the oven on the Jewish Sabbath and Jewish holidays, it will appear that the Jew is benefiting from this forbidden work. Therefore, a Jew may not rent the oven to the Christian unless he stipulates in advance that the Christian may not fire the oven on the Jewish Sabbath or Jewish holidays.[21]

From other responsa that also reflect aspects of everyday Jewish-Christian business interactions, we learn that even in the relative peace of postinvasion early Europe, there were reasons for Jews and Christians to cooperate in an atmosphere of uneven security. We see this in one of the distinctive patterns of Jewish economic life at this time: the exclusive partnerships of a Jewish merchant with one or more Christian favored client or *ma'arufia*.[22] This term that denotes a friend should be taken seriously as a sign of close personal relations in the late tenth and early eleventh centuries, despite occasional local interruptions, as in 1007 and 1012.[23] From responsa attributed to R. Meshullam b. Qalonimos, we see that a ma'arufia can be bought like property, and more than one Jew can share a ma'arufia and divide the profits accruing from it.[24] Brothers could also jointly inherit a ma'arufia from their father.[25]

Local family customs, not authoritative shared ancient religious texts, came to play an important role in Jewish living. True, some northern French rabbinic pioneers would later travel to far-off centers in Palestine or Babylonia and even maintain contacts with the Jewish political and religious authorities in those lands or with Muslim Spain. And we also have communications between R. Meshullam b. Qalonimos and rabbinic masters (*geonim*) in Abbasid Baghdad, some of which have been found in the Cairo Geniza.[26]

But the geographic distance of Ashkenaz from other Jewish centers often gave the leaders of the Mainz community considerable room to improvise and experiment with new patterns of autonomous local governance.[27] The most important of the early rabbinic masters of Mainz was Rabbeinu (our master) Gershom b. Judah

(d. 1028), who was a merchant as well as one of the first major rabbinic scholarly figures in medieval Christian Europe. Shaping Ashkenazic rabbinic culture in northern Europe, R. Gershom functioned as a judge on matters of Jewish law, and his responsa rarely mentioned the decisions and precedents of the Babylonian rabbinic masters. Rather, he answered questions by interpreting and directly applying Talmudic, earlier Mishnaic, or even biblical passages, thereby imitating, rather than following, the geonim in the Muslim East.[28]

Of lasting significance are two decisions that he made on his own requiring a Jewish woman's consent before her husband can divorce her and forbidding male polygyny, despite its permissibility in the Hebrew Bible and Talmud. He took these measures to inhibit Jewish international traders from staying away from their families for long periods of time when they set up additional families in their places of trade abroad.[29]

R. Gershom's responsa also reflect close business dealings between Jews and Christians at different levels of society. Cases came up in which a Jew had "many priests as his exclusive customers" (ma'arufia), or a Talmud teacher taught for no remuneration and "enjoyed the exclusive custom (ma'arufia) of priests."[30] A Jew lends money against the collateral of ecclesiastical vestments used in Christian worship; a Jewish winemaker hires a Christian employee to handle barrels of wine; a Christian woman asks a Jew to buy expensive clothes for her and gives the Jew the money but asks for collateral while he is gone; and a Jew mortgages his vineyard to a Christian and agrees to pay him a fixed amount of wine each year.[31]

To be sure, there are also some signs of Christian hostility toward individual Jews in the course of doing business or just living in the same town. So, for example, Jews who were engaged in the production and sale of kosher wine for Jewish consumption might encounter a Christian putting a stone into an open barrel of wine, thereby making it prohibited "libation wine."[32] Or R. Gershom was asked about a Christian, described as "a violent man," who seized one Jew's house and sold it to another Jew.[33] And yet in another case, one Jew sues another to recover the value of his barrel of wine that Christians used to put out a fire that saved the second

Jew's house. For whatever reason, the value of the wine could not be recovered from the Christians who used the wine to extinguish the fire, but instead the plaintiff tries to recover the value of his wine from the Jew who benefited from the Christians' action.[34]

In other cases, a questioner complains about other Jews who are interfering with someone's ma'arufia monopoly, and R. Gershom points out that this means that technically, the legal restraint offered by a ma'arufia monopoly does not actually exist where they are living and that other considerations determine the outcome of the case. What might underlie such informal monopoly relationships is made clear in a third case involving a Jew and Christians, who are not identified as priests. A plaintiff who had a ma'arufia explains that this meant that he "assiduously cultivated the friendship of the latter, often lent him money at no interest, and countless times served him in various capacities."[35]

Although the complaint may be framed in formulaic language, some hint of what might be involved in these Jewish-Christian business relationships is at least suggested here. It is not possible to overhear how friendly these ties were, but from the number of complaints just in R. Gershom's responsa, it seems that close relations between Jews and Christians triggered social rivalries among Jews. There are even signs of Jewish complicity with Christians in committing crimes while ignoring Jewish communal and judicial discipline—another sign of close Jewish-Christian business relations, including the business of crime.[36]

A sign of how the social relations and legal systems of Jewish and Christian communities did work is revealed in another case that came to R. Gershom. A boat sank with Jews and valuables on board. The Jews survived, but salvaging the property on board became complicated because some Christians stole "some of the money, some of the silver, a sparkling gem, and other items and carried them off to their homes." The following day, the Jews who suffered the loss bribed local authorities to carry out a search for their stolen cargo, and much of the property was recovered. One Jew, however, who had acquired possession of some of the property in the river and sold it to a Christian, claimed that he could do so because of a Talmudic principle that "'goods engulfed in a river' were considered ownerless property."[37] R. Gershom rules that the

Talmudic principle does not apply here since the Jewish owner has clearly been making efforts to recover his lost property, and so the Jewish defendant must return the jewel to its owner.

Of special interest is the way the local Jews were successful in getting both Christian and Jewish authorities to enact judicial measures to restore the property taken either by Christian looters or the Jewish buyers of stolen property. There is no hint here of any anti-Jewish animus, that the Jews deserved what they got, or that there was any underlying enmity or even tension between members of the two communities.

We also learn how Jews were to view Christians theoretically in R. Gershom's ruling in a case in which he says *Christians* as a group are not practitioners of "foreign worship," even though *Christianity* itself was. The Talmud devotes an entire section to "foreign worship" ('avodah zarah) or Greco-Roman pagan cults, but later interpreters had to decide if the rules of separation applied to Christians or Christianity. Among these, the Mishnah (early third century CE) stipulates, "For three days before the festivals of gentiles it is prohibited to engage in business with them; to lend items to them or to borrow items from them; to lend money to them or to borrow money from them; and to repay debts owed to them or to collect repayment of debts from them."[38]

If applied to Christians, this would mean that Jews were not permitted to do business with them for three days before their religious holidays, and medieval Jews knew that almost every day was a saint's day. R. Gershom makes a distinction between Christians and Christianity, and it had the effect of condoning close business relations that already had developed in the late tenth and early eleventh centuries: "We are justified in assuming that the non-Jews among us are not worshipers of 'foreign worship.' We may therefore accept the garments of their priests as pledges, though not the actual objects of their worship; and we may transact business with them on their holidays."[39]

Close business dealings between Jews and Christians increased along with the general demographic and urban expansion in eleventh- and twelfth-century Christian Europe. As the first tiny Jewish communities grew, communal roles got more differentiated and specialized. Communal leadership assumed two overlapping but distinct forms. On the one hand, legal decisions were rendered by religious judges or rabbis, unpaid scholars who acquired expertise in custom and the written traditions of Jewish law, especially the Talmud. On the other hand, communal control over public affairs devolved on the "elders," whose authority derived from their age, wealth, family lineage, perhaps government favor, and other personal qualities, and in some cases from their Torah learning as well. The elders maintained public order, collected taxes for the Christian authorities and the support of Jewish social services, and were the liaison between the community and the Christian central and local rulers. In the period of first settlement, rabbis were merchants like most of the rest of the male Jewish community, and they were among the elders who decided public policy. Eventually—exactly when is a matter of interpretation and even definition—a paid rabbinate developed, perhaps in embryo as early as the thirteenth century and certainly by the fifteenth.[40]

Local Communal Autonomy

We also find signs of improvisation in the actions of the early communal board (*qahal*) and communal leaders (*parnasim*) contemporary with R. Gershom. They undertook to maintain law and order, supervise the weights and measures in the market, and provide for the indigent. As early as the tenth century, local communal boards enabled a Jew with a grievance to interrupt the service in the synagogue (*herem 'iqquv ha-tefillot*). As the Jewish population grew, members of the founding families tried to limit immigration and placed bans on new settlement (*herem ha-yishuv*) to prevent excessive economic competition and accompanying conflict.[41]

By the middle of the eleventh century, questions about the authority of local Jewish communal leaders arose in newer areas of settlement, like the County of Champagne. R. Judah ha-Kohen, R. Gershom's successor in Mainz as head of the rabbinic school (*yeshivah*), replied to a question that the elders of Troyes (Champagne) sent him. The case involved the community's decision to impose a six-month boycott on hiring a particular Christian maid who had been abusive to the Jewish plaintiff. In the areas of general public welfare and security, he ruled, each local community was completely autonomous. But if one Jewish community violated religious law, another community or outside religious authority could hold it accountable and impose sanctions, such as excommunication of its guilty members. Moreover, individual Jews in one community did not have the right to claim immunity from decisions reached by the elders there, even if those elders constituted a numerical minority of voting members.[42]

Rivalries existed not only among Jews. Christian leaders might assert their claim to have their own Jews to upgrade the political and economic status of their town. In 1084, when some Mainz Jews fled a fire that broke out in the Jewish quarter there, Rüdiger, the bishop of Speyer, issued them a formal charter of privileges in his town. The first community charter granted to a Jewish community in Christian Europe, it was similar to the charters of protection (*tuitio*) that Louis the Pious had issued to individual Jewish merchants over 250 years earlier. The Speyer charter extended to its new community guarantees of life, religious protection, self-government, and exemption from tolls. Just before the bishop died, he arranged for three Jewish communal leaders from Speyer to seek the confirmation of his episcopal charter from his temporal superior, German emperor Henry IV, who granted it in 1090. The Carolingian policy of royal and imperial protection of Jewish local self-rule, first developed in the German towns, became the model for Jewish communities in the regions of England, Christian Spain, and central Europe down to early modern times. It should not be surprising, then, to see that some Jews referred back to Charlemagne himself as the founder of their new community in the West. They made this claim in the form of what historians call "foundation legends."

Foundation Legends Claim Greatness in the West

Since antiquity, the very name "Europe" was connected with a move across the Mediterranean Sea from east to west, and some have even claimed that it is connected etymologically to the land of the setting sun. In Greek mythology, Europa was a Phoenician goddess for whom Zeus changed himself into a bull to seduce her. She climbed on his back, and they swam off together westward and settled in Crete.

The lure of the West affected Christians, Muslims, and Jews. We see this in the themes of a transfer of authority (*translatio imperii*) and transfer of learning (*translatio studii*) in the case of Charles the Great himself (Charlemagne, d. 814), crowned Roman emperor in 800, although there was a Byzantine empress in Constantinople at the time. And we see it in the emergence of caliphs in the Tunisian capital of Qayrawan and Iberian capital of Córdoba in the tenth century, despite the Abbasid caliph ruling in Baghdad.

Although the western Jewish communities in the former Roman provinces of Hispania, Gallia, and Germania were the result of the gradual immigration of groups of families that sought economic well-being and new opportunities, later elites wrote down stories of origin or foundation legends to ascribe communal beginnings to a crucial event and prestigious founder. In so doing, a representative of a Jewish community in Islamic Spain or Christian France or Germany was proposing either a claim of successorship to an earlier community in the East or being more important than one of its neighboring Jewish communities in the West. For a long time, historians looked askance at these foundation stories as fictions and discarded them as historically irrelevant. But more recent approaches to literary expressions of historical change provide a methodology for appreciating these Jewish stories as documenting the "collective memory" of a particular community elite that sought to justify a shift from East to West of regional Jewish communal or intellectual leadership.

The Shift from East to West in Muslim Lands

In the foundation legends written down in the late twelfth century based on earlier oral traditions, there are three claims in each story: first, a great Muslim or Christian leader established an important new Jewish community or place of learning in the West; second, it succeeded an established Jewish center in the East; and third, the new western Jewish community was superior to a rival one in the West.

Although these stories tell us about the times when they were written down, they make use of historical traditions from the time they are describing from two hundred or more years earlier as well. They point back to a renewal of either study, governance, or both as occurring in the ninth or tenth centuries and not before. They also tell us about the cultural origins of each community.

The Jewish communities of the Muslim world generated such a foundation legend to explain why central rabbinic authority in Abbasid Baghdad was being challenged by rabbinic circles in Egypt, Tunisia, and especially Córdoba in the tenth century. A rabbinic legal and philosophical figure from late twelfth-century Iberia, R. Abraham Ibn Daud (ca. 1110–80), explained a shift in Jewish culture to the west as a divine intervention in a narrative that scholars refer to as "the story of the four captives." It begins by making a broad claim about the transfer of learning from East to West: "Prior to that, it was brought about by the Lord that the income of the academies which used to come from Spain, the land of the Maghreb, Ifriqiya, Egypt, and the Holy Land was discontinued. The following were the circumstances that brought this about."[43]

In a narrative designed to explain the shifting location claimed in the introduction, Ibn Daud tells about a dramatic capture at sea of four scholars, although actually only three are named, and how especially the one who was ransomed in Córdoba rose to take the place of the local rabbinic judge. This story served to legitimize the authority of Iberian Jewish rabbinic leaders and allow them to claim themselves as successors of the geonim in Baghdad:

> The commander of a fleet, whose name was Ibn Rumahis, left Córdoba, having been sent by the Muslim king of Spain, Abd ar-Rahman an-Nasir. This commander of a mighty fleet set out to capture the ships of the Christians and the towns that were close to the coast. They sailed as far as the coast of Palestine and swung about to the Greek sea and the islands therein. [Here] they encountered a ship carrying four great scholars, who were travelling from the city of Bari to a city called Sefastin, and who were on their way to a Kallah convention. Ibn Rumahis captured the ship and took the sages prisoner. One of them was R. Hushiel, the father of Rabbenu Hananel; another was R. Moses, the father of R. Hanok, who was taken prisoner with his wife and son, R. Hanok (who at the time was but a young lad); the third was R. Shemariah b. R. Elhanan. As for the fourth, I do not know his name.

The author goes on to describe how each of the captives was sold to different Jewish communities, where they became heads of rabbinic academies: R. Shemariah in Fustat, Egypt, R. Hushiel in Qayrawan (Tunisia), and R. Moses in Córdoba, where he first disguised himself as an ignorant nobody only to displace the local rabbinic authority, R. Nathan the Pious. The story of succession then concludes:

> The community then assigned him a large stipend and honored him with costly garments and a carriage. [At that point] the commander wished to retract his sale. However, the king would not permit him to do so, for he was delighted by the fact that the Jews of his domain no longer had need of the people of Babylonia.[44]

The point of the story is to explain the shift in learning and power in the Jewish elite of Muslim Spain from allegiance to the Abbasid court in Baghdad to the court of the second Umayyad caliphate in Córdoba. It remembers this as a displacement, even though we know that geonim continued to serve in Baghdad for over two hundred years after the episodes described here.[45]

Charles the Great as Founder of Western Jewish Communities

Whereas Ibn Daud credited the Muslim Iberian caliphate with the arrival in Córdoba of a new rabbinic elite, the Jewish communities in Christian Provence and Mainz looked to the north and the mythical figure of Charlemagne as their great founder.[46] They did so to claim superiority over a nearby Jewish community as well as to assert themselves as legitimate successors to earlier Jewish political or intellectual centers that still existed in the East. In so doing, both elites appropriated Charlemagne, who himself exemplified the pattern of the transfer of empire (translatio imperii) from East to West, when Pope Leo III crowned him "emperor of the Romans" in 800. The elites of Narbonne in southern France and Mainz in the Rhineland, parallel to the mythical Europa riding on the back of Zeus to the West, claimed the backing of Charlemagne himself as their great founder.

Like Ibn Daud, who was primarily interested in showing how the Iberian Jewish elite in Christian Spain was independent of the geonim in Baghdad, the new Jewish West independent from the old

Jewish East, the two other foundation traditions also claimed to succeed the rabbinic masters of the Muslim East (geonim). But they wanted to assert their supremacy over a rival Jewish community in Europe as well.

It is likely that the appearance of the Jewish culture of northern, Christian Spain, when Ibn Daud wrote in the late twelfth century, provoked the foundation legend of nearby Narbonnese Jewry in the south of France to be written down.[47] Ibn Daud's invoking the memory of Córdoba in the tenth century constituted a challenge to Narbonnese leaders, who now claimed the venerable Charlemagne as *their* founder even earlier in the ninth century.[48]

A Hebrew account that was published as an appendix to Ibn Daud's *Sefer ha-Qabbalah* puts this as follows:

> And King Charles (Charlemagne) sent to the (Muslim) king (Caliph) in Babylonia (Baghdad) (asking him) to send him one of his Jews of royal descent. He followed his request and sent him a great and wise man whose name was Rabbi Makhir whom he settled in the metropolis of Narbonne. And when he conquered the city from the Ishmaelites (Muslims), he gave him a great area and he took a wife from the grandees of the city. When he conquered the city, he divided it into three parts. One third he gave to a ruler who was in the city named Don Aymeric; a third he gave to the governor of the city; and a third he gave to R. Makhir. He freed him and out of his love for them made favorable laws toward the Jews living in the city, as is written and sealed in a Christian charter. (It) and the seal of the King whose name is Charles are in their possession to this day.[49]

Traditions about the Jews of Narbonne and its prince (*nasi*), a title denoting a claim to descent from biblical King David, is also part of Benjamin of Tudela's travel account from the late twelfth century: "Three days further lies Narbonne.... This city contains many very wise and noble men, principally R. Calonymos son of the great and noble R. Theodoros o[f] b[lessed] m[emory], a descendant of the house of David, as proved by his pedigree."[50] The title of Jewish prince (nasi) is based on the claim of the exilarchs of Baghdad to descent from King David. In some communities, the title refers to a position of communal authority; in others, it was an honorific title.[51]

Competing with this story is another foundation legend involving Charlemagne. This time he is remembered as the founder of

Mainz Jewry. It was written down at the end of the twelfth or the beginning of the thirteenth century. Rabbi Eleazar of Worms (d. ca. 1230), author of *Sefer ha-Roqeah* (Book of the perfumer), wrote his story as a response to another neighboring Jewish communal challenge, this time from northern France.

Here is the text of the most well-known version of R. Eleazar's narrative, as preserved in his mystical *Commentary to the Prayerbook*:

> They received the esoteric traditions about the arrangement of the prayers as well as the other esoteric traditions, rabbi from rabbi, all the way back to Abu Aaron, the son of R. Samuel the Nasi, who had left Babylonia because of a certain incident, and he was therefore required to travel all over the world. He came to the land of Lombardy, to a certain city called Lucca. There he found our Rabbi Moses who composed the liturgical poem (beginning) "the fear of your awesomeness" (*eimat nora'otekha*) and he transmitted to him all of his esoteric traditions. This is Rabbi Moses bar Qalonimos, son of Rabbi Meshullam bar Rabbi Qalonimos bar Rabbi Judah.
>
> (Now Rabbi Moses) was the first who emigrated from Lombardy, he and his sons, Rabbi Qalonimos and Rabbi Yequtiel, and his relative Rabbi Itiel, as well as the rest of the people who counted. All of them were taken from Lombardy by King Charles who resettled them in Mainz. There they grew to prodigious numbers until 1096 when the Lord visited His wrath upon the holy communities. Then were we all destroyed, utterly destroyed, except for a few of our relatives who survived including Rabbi Qalonimos the Elder. He transmitted (the esoteric traditions)—as we have written—to Rabbi Eleazar Hazan of Speyer, Eleazar Hazan transmitted them to Rabbi Samuel (the) Pious and Rabbi Samuel (the) Pious transmitted them to Rabbi Judah (the) Pious. And from him did I, the insignificant one, receive the esoteric traditions about the prayers as well as the other traditions.

A second version, also derived from German pietist sources, refers to the Qalonimos family migration from Italy and contains a date that historians have pointed to as a credible fact, though a date found in a single, uncorroborated manuscript in alphanumeric shorthand (gematria) could easily contain a scribal error: "King Charles brought with him from the district of Lucca our master

Moses the Elder 849 [*tav tav mem tet*] years since the destruction of the Temple [in 68 CE = 917 CE], may it be rebuilt speedily in our day. Amen. Amen. Selah."⁵²

A third tradition about "King Charles" and R. Moses and the founding of Mainz is found in manuscripts of Eleazar's *Commentary on the Prayerbook*. The author inserted the reference to the founding of Mainz by a "King Charles" just before his comments on the morning prayer that begins and is therefore known as "Yishtabah" (Praised be [your name]). He placed the tradition about Charles there because the author was interested in the origins of the then new liturgical custom in medieval Germany of reciting the Song at the Sea (Ex. 15) in the daily morning service (*shaharit*) just before saying the prayer that begins "yishtabah." It had not been the Babylonian practice to do this, and apparently Mainz Jews were following the Babylonian custom until R. Moses b. Qalonimos arrived there from Italy and brought the custom of saying it with him.⁵³

The collective memory that Charlemagne, the most obvious meaning of "King Charles," founded the Jewish community of Mainz is consistent with a basic historical fact: all the charters of privilege given to the Jews of Ashkenaz, to individuals and communities alike, were influenced by the Carolingian model with their favorable policy toward merchants. Yet another accurate historical feature of this story emerges, namely the tendency of Charlemagne and his court to use Italian models when reforming his empire. Thus he turned to Rome for a standard for the liturgy, the Rule of St. Benedict, and canon law. Intentionally or not, the idea of Charlemagne's founding a new Jewish community in Mainz based on Italian models "remembers" this authentic Carolingian policy.⁵⁴

But there is no evidence that Jews were settled in Mainz and environs in the ninth century by Charlemagne, or even in the early tenth by another German king. They actually arrived in waves in the second half of the tenth century, and like some immigrants, a few went back and forth between their old home in Italy and new one in Germany. The foundation accounts or legends of how the earliest communities of medieval Europe were established imply that later generations were unaware of how the community was settled gradually by migrating families and were ready to create a "usable past by inventing themselves retroactively."⁵⁵

Like many other medieval European foundation legends, Rabbi Eleazar's contains a claim of a transfer of authority (translatio imperii) as well as learning (translatio studii). We see, then, that the foundation legend of Ashkenazic Judaism, based on a propagandistic use of a deep historical truth, is susceptible to an anthropological-historical reading.[56]

The Qalonimides were asserting their authority over that of the Jewish elites of northern France who had displaced earlier German Jewish rabbinic leadership in the eleventh century. It was exactly at that time that Rashi emerged as a major rabbinic figure, not in the Rhineland, where he had studied in the 1060s, but in Troyes in the County of Champagne. There his sons-in-law and grandsons developed the revolutionary methodology of Talmud analysis using dialectic, turning away from the traditions of the Rhineland based on collections of earlier custom.

Just as Rashi was emerging as a major figure in France, however, came the devastating blow of the 1096 riots in Mainz and Worms that nearly wiped out much of the Qalonimos family elite. Recall the words of Rabbi Eleazar, himself a descendant of the Qalonimos clan: "Then were we all destroyed, utterly destroyed, except for *a few of our relatives* who survived including Rabbi Qalonimos the Elder." The urgency of the narrative derives from Rabbi Eleazar's awareness that the days of German Ashkenaz were being challenged in the West—by Rashi and his descendants and students. The German Jewish citing of the Charlemagne legend is, then, part of the general German Jewish stance in its battle with the French Jewish community for authority in the post-1096 world of Christian European Jews.

In addition to these German Jewish polemical traces against northern French Judaism, the German Jewish Charlemagne legend corresponds to Christian uses of the legend of Charlemagne for similar political leverage. In the court of the German emperor Frederick Barbarossa (1122–90), the legend of Charlemagne played a major role in German imperial propaganda against the aspirations of the rising and ambitious French monarch Philip Augustus (1165–1223). Frederick had Charlemagne canonized in a state ceremony in 1165 as part of this German effort to appropriate Charlemagne for German, rather than French, political claims to compete with St. Denis, the patron of the Capetian monarchy. Significantly, we know that a relative of Rabbi Eleazar, another Rabbi Qalonimos, who was the father of the author of an important rabbinic work from late twelfth-century Germany, played a public role in the court of Frederick Barbarossa. He may well have witnessed the ceremony himself and surely was aware of the uses to which Charlemagne's memory was being put in Germany.

Ashkenazic West versus Babylonian East

There is good reason to think of the refounding of Córdoban rabbinic leadership in the tenth century as a challenge to the sitting geonim of Baghdad, a parallel to the Umayyad challenge in Córdoba to the Abbasid caliphs in Baghdad. Eleazar of Worms's traditions about the transfer of esoteric lore from Babylonia to the Rhineland claims that Ashkenazic mysticism is also a succession in the West to the venerable eastern rabbinic center in Baghdad.

The theme of eastern succession in Mainz is seen in another story that focuses on the loyalty of the Qalonimos family members to Ashkenaz despite an attempt on the part of a Babylonian Jewish leader to lure away one of its most promising rabbinic figures. Preserved in a manuscript from the thirteenth century, the story proposes a claim of German Jewish superiority over Babylonia, parallel to Ibn Daud's story of the four captives, especially the one about Iberia succeeding Babylonia.[57]

The story starts out seeming to undo the foundation of the Mainz account by threatening a brain drain from Mainz to Babylonia, with a kidnapping of Meshullam b. Qalonimos, but in the end affirms that Ashkenazic rabbinic leadership is superior to the Jewish authorities in Baghdad. Although there is no evidence of any relationship between this story and Ibn Daud's four captives, it uses a similar deus ex machina device to propel the plot. In Ibn Daud's case, a piratical capture at sea and ransom establishes three new centers of Jewish rabbinic leadership in Fustat, Qayrawan, and especially Córdoba; in the case of R. Meshullam, the kidnappers almost undo Charlemagne's establishment of the Qalonimide dynasty in Mainz by selling the grandson of the founding Qalonimide back to Babylonia! It is the story of R. Meshullam

b. Qalonimos, the grandson of the founding Qalonimide, R. Moses ben Qalonimos of Lucca.

The focus is not on immigration from Lucca but on the relationship between Mainz and the Jewish leadership in Baghdad during the Abbasid caliphate, and the dominance there of the geonim and exilarchs. The story features an official called nasi, a title we saw before in the Eleazar of Worms's legend. In several medieval Jewish communities, nasi was an honorific title that connoted descent from King David, but it usually was not an important title of actual communal leadership.

It begins with an act of violence, a kidnapping—perhaps an echo of the claim that King Charles brought R. Moses from Lucca to Mainz:

> A story about Rabbeinu Qalonimos, the father of Rabbeinu Meshullam the great, who dreamt that (his son, Meshullam) would be taken away from him. Once merchants came to the market in (R. Qalonimos') town when Rabbeinu Meshullam was fourteen years old. The merchants accosted him in the market, looked him over, grabbed him, and took him to their kingdom in far off Babylonia.[58]
>
> The merchants sent to the Nasi of Babylonia and said to him, "Do you want to acquire a Jew to serve you?" The Nasi said, "Yes." And so, he acquired (R. Meshullam) from them.[59] The Nasi was the head of the yeshivah. Rabbeinu Meshullam asked him to see to it that he tells the rest of his household to treat him well.
>
> Now the *beit midrash* (yeshiva) was next to the room where they prepared (the Nasi's) meals and (Meshullam) was in charge of that room. Rabbeinu Meshullam heard that the Nasi was in doubt about some matter of Jewish law (*halakhah*) about which the students had raised difficulties.[60]

The immigrant great scholar who disguises himself is a motif found in the Talmud in connection with Hillel, who arrives in Jerusalem from Babylonia and, while disguised, overhears mistakes being made in the Jerusalem academy of the Benei Beteira, the rabbinic elite there.[61] This tale of disguise and self-revelation is also reprised in Ibn Daud's *Sefer ha-Qabbalah* in the story of Rabbi Moses, captured at sea, who corrects Rabbi Nathan the Pious of Córdoba. Both are important stories about the transfer of study (translatio studii), and the Meshullam story follows suit, even though it is not likely that either knew about the other.

When the Nasi left his school (beit midrash), Rabbeinu Meshullam went in and wrote down the explanation in the margin, just as his father had taught him, but said nothing. When the Nasi returned, he saw the note in the margin but said nothing. Rabbeinu Meshullam did the same thing each time the Nasi did not clearly understand something. The Nasi thought that it was from G[od] m[ay He be blessed], himself that these explanatory notes were appearing in the margins of his book.

Once he told his students, "I want to be unclear (on purpose). After I leave, can one or two of you see who is editing the books?"

Two of his students said, "We want to witness what will happen." When the Nasi left, two of his students stood behind the wall and through a hole saw that it was Rabbeinu Meshullam who came in, explained the doubtful passages in the margin, and went back to his room.

When the students returned to listen to the Nasi's lesson in Jewish law, the two young men who had seen him edit the book for their teacher said, "Our teacher, your servant is greater than you in Torah learning." He asked them, "Who?" "It is the servant whom the merchants brought you from abroad who is editing your book."

He immediately sent word to the servant to come to his beit midrash and in the presence of his students he asked for his forgiveness for treating him like an ordinary servant. Then he seated him next to himself whenever he taught Jewish law.

One day he asked him, "What is the name of your father and of your grandfather?" He replied to him, "The name of my father is Our Master (*rabbana*) Qalonimos ben h[a-Rav] R[abbi] Moses from Lucca who wrote (the *piyyut* that begins) 'the fear of your awesomeness' (*eimat nora'otekha*)."[62]

The Nasi wanted him to marry his daughter, but Rabbeinu Meshullam did not want to do so without his father's permission. The Nasi said to him, "If you forgive me completely for having served me, I will give you a servant and food for the journey until you reach your father or other towns where people know you." "Good," he said.

The Nasi gave him a servant and food for the journey, and he reached Mainz. There he married a woman who was his relative's sister and had a son named Todros. And so, Rabbeinu Meshullam returned to his father, died there, and Rabbi Todros, his son, became the head of the yeshivah in Mainz.[63]

The confrontation of the great scholar whose learning is deficient and corrected by an outsider is a story told by the community of the outsider to show the coming-of-age and maturity of a relative newcomer to an established intellectual order. In this case, it is Ashkenaz over Babylonia.

These stories are arguments from the time long after the communities were gradually established in the tenth century. But it is not the case that a legend tells us only about the teller and not about the told. This story asserts the authority and coming-of-age of the Mainz Jewish elite over that of the Babylonian geonim. We saw earlier that R. Gershom b. Judah actually was independent of the geonim when he made his legal decisions. The Meshullam b. Qalonimos story reinforces the image of Ashkenaz as an independent region as well as of the Qalonimos elite within it as the intellectual leaders of that community.

As in other stories comparing one scholar to another, the virtue of having greater learning is used here to prove superiority. There is something deficient in the scholarship of the eastern ruler, and it is the visitor from the West who knows more than the local authority. We see this, too, in the "Story of the Four Captives," where the newly arrived Rabbi Moses, this time from Bari, knows more than the head of the local rabbinic school in Córdoba.[64]

Implications for the Jews in Christian Europe

The stories of rivalry over Jewish intercommunal dominance, especially in emphasizing the West against the earlier East, prefigures the even fiercer competition that ensued between different Jewish communities and the majority Christian cultures within which Jews lived. The gradual urban growth that began already in the late tenth and eleventh centuries meant that Jews and Christians would be in greater contact than before. For four generations, the population increased and both communities actively cooperated to rebuild the fragile towns of northern Europe.

Two changes occurred that would challenge those interreligious patterns of cooperation, producing new areas of confrontation and conflict. The first was the Gregorian reform, a religious reform movement that originated with a series of scholarly popes who aimed to reassert papal supremacy over Christian society. The quest for "right order" in Europe would also explode beyond it in an armed pilgrimage to rescue Jerusalem and Byzantine Christians from attack by newly converted Muslim Seljuk Turkish armies. The religious zeal that this effort aroused against enemies of Christ abroad would become a new rationale for attacking as "nearby enemies" the members of the relatively new Jewish communities in northern Europe, despite the close business relations many Jews and Christians had enjoyed over the years. The appeal to the ancient apostolic age remembered Jews not only as potential converts, as had Paul, but also as the killers of Christ whose descendants might endanger the faithful in the present. Neither the Christian nor the Jewish population would ever be the same again.

CHAPTER THREE

Reforms and Right Order

THE APOSTOLIC AGE AND CRUSADE ACTIVE MARTYRS

AS PART OF a demographic increase in the urban population of medieval Germany, Jews and Christians lived in a shared space and did business together, as reflected in the rabbinic responsa from the late tenth and early eleventh centuries. But by the middle of the eleventh century, counterforces began to emerge in the reform movement of the church, with the primary goal of reasserting the hierarchical superiority of Christianity in the world. As a result, the salient feature of the West emerges: a movement to create an ideal Christian society that is threatened by a perceived inner enemy, the Jew.[1]

The shift begins with the Gregorian Reform, initiated by Pope Leo IX (1049-54) and developed in new directions especially when Hildebrand, the future Pope Gregory VII (1073-85), was an important adviser to popes and sought to create a Christian society modeled on key values from the age of the apostles.[2] Within the reform movement, Christian writers began to express a sense of belonging to the unique religious civilization of *Christianitas* or Latin Christendom.[3] It is important to emphasize that the development of a new kind of pious Christian society was at first not concerned with Jews but was critical of a society marked by extreme violence. Efforts to reform society began in the countryside, where Jews rarely lived. The main encounters between Jews and Christians would occur after the great demographic expansion, when towns became centrally important. The pre-urban and urban stages of the formation of Europe reflect this pre-Jewish and Jewish reality.

The two phases have been described in several classic works. Marc Bloch referred to two feudal ages, the second from the middle of the eleventh century, with the emergence of merchant classes then as its defining feature.[4] Richard W. Southern called the concluding chapter of *The Making of the Middle Ages* "From Epic to Romance," a broad cultural shift from the age of aggressive aristocratic knights and local rulers to the urban life of the court and courtly poetry in growing, centralizing kingdoms.[5] Similarly, Barbara Rosenwein and Lester K. Little proposed a two-phase correlation between a tenth- and eleventh-century spirituality that was expressed by monastic "patience and prayer" in a land-dominated and violent feudal society, and a twelfth- and thirteenth-century mendicant spirituality that emphasized apostolic "poverty and preaching" in an urban context of moneymaking and commerce.[6]

The first phase sought to recover aspects of the apostolic age in rural monastic life that was detached from the rest of society. During the tenth and much of the eleventh centuries, Christian piety was expressed in the ethos of Burgundy's Benedictine house of Cluny, founded in 909, that revived the Rule of St. Benedict's emphasis on apostolic withdrawal from the world along with the absence of violence and pride, associated with the knightly class. Cluny spread its values to hundreds of Benedictine monasteries affiliated with the motherhouse.[7]

Ecclesiastical leaders also took measures to deal with the violence that continued among the fighting class outside monastic walls. Local bishops in the south and then farther north tried to limit fighting in the late tenth century by calling for the "Peace of God" (*pax dei*), to make unprotected groups such as clergy, women, pilgrims, merchants, and other travelers immune from attack.[8] In the first half of the eleventh century, advocates for the "Truce of God" (*treuga dei*) sought to limit Christian warfare to certain days of the week.

The peace movement reflected the violence that was common even after the threat from enemy foreign invaders was no more. It also meant that the society in which Jews were settling, no longer under the threat of foreign invasions, was still far from peaceful, and this violence promoted cooperation between Jews and Christian clients, including Christian merchants as well as priests and monks.[9] At the same time, paradoxically, by limiting knightly violence to certain days of the week, the church was conceding some religious approval of the fighting knights.

In the second, more urban phase, reformers attempted to improve lay society within the expanding urban walls. There was a shift in the apostolic ideal from peace to poverty too—a critique of the growth of wealth and trade. In the twelfth and thirteenth centuries, pious kings in England and France would become concerned with ending the poison of Jewish and Christian usury, especially since they saw it as polluting their lands when they were about to embark on a new sacred Crusade initiative.

Gerd Tellenbach referred to these trends toward religious reform as a "struggle for right order."[10] Different Christian institutions and religious thinkers competed to establish, legitimate, and defend the proper hierarchical structure of a Christian society.[11] Within Europe, popes vied with emperors for supremacy. At first, reform popes asserted their right to implement their prerogatives of spiritual superiority, which they derived from early collections of canon law, while German emperors appealed to a theory of sacred monarchy based on custom. To the reform pope Gregory VII, this was a struggle between custom and *veritas*—"truth" or "authenticity." As he put it, "The Lord did not say my name is custom but my name is truth."[12]

The primacy of pope or emperor was expressed symbolically in the issue of whether bishops or the emperor had the right to appoint and "invest" bishops with the signs of office—a struggle traditionally known as "the investiture controversy." Custom dictated that emperors had that right, but the series of scholarly churchmen who became popes argued that precedent and church law actually conferred that right only on bishops.[13]

The issue of right order affected how temporal and ecclesiastical rulers thought of the place of Jews in a changing Christian society, and Jews also expressed their own view of right order in relationship to the Christian majority. In so doing, each was reflecting the unspoken assumption that Esau should serve Jacob.

At first, emperors granted Jewish merchants charters of protection that offered royal support for Jewish physical security and communal self-government.[14] Medieval popes followed Pope Calixtus II (d. 1124), whose bull beginning *Sicut iudaeis* (1120) sought to guarantee the Jews physical safety and religious observances so long as they acted in a subordinate position to the Christian majority.[15]

But the Jews' usefulness to Christian kings made reform popes critical. In a letter sent in 1081 to King Alfonso VI of Castile, the early reform pope, Gregory VII (r. 1073–85), advanced the idea, already prominent in the Christian Roman Theodosian Code of 438, that the Jews needed to be politically subordinate to Christians, not hold power over them.[16] After praising the king for some reforms, the pope continued,

> But since we are bound not only to congratulate you upon the glories of your well doing but also sorrowfully to restrain you from unworthy actions, we have to enjoin upon you no longer to permit Jews in your country to rule over Christians or have power over them. For to place Christians under Jews or to subject them to their jurisdiction—what is that but to oppress the Church of God, to exalt the synagogue of Satan, and in aiming to please the enemies of Christ to throw contempt upon Christ himself?[17]

By the twelfth century, the conflict over Jewish servitude as "right order" continued to alarm popes, as when Jews hired Christian maids, including wet nurses for their children, or when they became lenders of cash, instead of borrowers, to Christians, both lay and ecclesiastical.[18]

Although it has often been observed that servitude is the norm that the church expected to impose on Jews, the resistance of Jews to this expectation in acts of assertiveness has gone relatively unnoticed. The Christian reform movement bent on subordinating assertive Jews stimulated Jewish assertiveness further. The more that urban society became Christian, the more Jews affirmed their Jewish identity and did so sometimes by insulting Christianity even as they got along with Christians in business relations. The distinctive political and religious status of the Jews, coupled with an urban demographic expansion in the eleventh and twelfth centuries that peaked only in the early fourteenth, served to increase Christian notice of them and raised concerns, especially since Jews could be assertive when they met Christians in the street or marketplace.

The place of the Jews in Christian Europe was dramatically altered in the late eleventh century as a result of a struggle between Christians and infidels, first against Muslims viewed as the enemy far away, and then extended to Jews as the enemy nearby at home. The way Jews living closely with Christians until then in the growing towns of Christian Europe became "nearby enemies" set a precedent that lasted.

"God Wills It" and the Frenzy of Divine Immanence

The call for right order within Europe between secular and ecclesiastical leaders within Latin Christendom was also reflected in the question of who should have control over Christian holy places far away in distant Palestine. The precipitating event that shook up the old status quo was the Seljuk Turks' conversion to Islam and their conquest of large parts of the Byzantine Empire in Asia Minor after the Battle of Manzikert in 1071. By 1076, they were in Jerusalem. In their religious zeal, the Seljuks prevented Christian pilgrims from visiting the Christian holy sites now under their control. A Muslim war against eastern Christians and the Turks' subsequent occupation of the Church of the Holy Sepulcher in Jerusalem led to accusations that Muslims had acted with great cruelty against Christians in the East. Both of these new realities could be viewed in the West as violations of right order, especially since many Christians continued to view Islam as a form of paganism.[19] It was about Muslims that the author of the *Song of Roland* proclaimed, "Pagans are wrong and Christians are right."[20]

Pope Gregory VII tried to launch an army of western kings and knights to redeem captives and liberate the holy places. On December 7, 1074, he wrote to German emperor Henry IV,

> Christians beyond the sea, a great part of whom are being destroyed by the heathen with unheard-of slaughter and are daily being slain like so

many sheep, have humbly sent to beg me to succor these our brethren in whatever ways I can, that the religion of Christ may not utterly perish in our time—which God forbid!

As his letter continued, Gregory was optimistic that the Eastern Church, which had split from Rome in 1054, "is seeking the fellowship of the Apostolic See," one of Gregory's reasons for wanting Henry's encouragement for "Italians and northerners . . . to take up arms against *the enemies of God* and push forward even to the sepulcher of the Lord." He concluded with his appeal to the emperor:

> If God shall grant me to begin this, I beg you for your advice and for your help according to your good pleasure. For if it shall please God that I go, I shall leave the Roman Church, under God, in your hands to guard her as a holy mother and to define her for his honor.[21]

Nothing came of this call, and the pope and emperor soon became embroiled in the investiture controversy. Underlying the ritual dispute was the fundamental issue of lay interference in episcopal appointments and the freedom of the church from imperial control.

By 1095, another reform pope, Urban II (r. 1088–99), launched the effort that Gregory VII had begun.[22] The call to send an armed pilgrimage or what became known as a "Crusade" to Jerusalem was an extension of the reform movement that began earlier in the eleventh century. The pilgrimage was to be led by knights who marked themselves with the sign of the cross—hence "Crusaders."

Although the speech that Pope Urban II made to churchmen and knights assembled at a peace council in Clermont, France, on November 27, 1095, has not been preserved, different witnesses reported what he said.[23] From the Latin accounts, it is clear that the pope did not mention the Jews, and no one would have even imagined that anyone claiming to be a Crusader would do anything but uphold the policy of all earlier popes, church fathers, and temporal rulers that Jews must not be killed or forcibly baptized but rather would be able to live and practice their religious customs and practices as in the past. But a spontaneous religious fervor emerged in that audience, and it led to a chain of events that affected many Jews who had settled in the Rhineland and central Europe just a few generations earlier.

The pope lashed out at the enemy to whip up enthusiasm among his listeners. In the version of Fulcher of Chartres, who was present at Clermont, Urban II refers to the Turks as "that wicked race" and as "a people so despised, degenerate, and enslaved by demons."[24] Robert of Reims, also possibly present, reported that Urban described "a race from the kingdom of the Persians, an accursed race, a race utterly alienated from God" that "invaded the lands of those Christians and has depopulated them by the sword, pillage and fire.... They destroy the altars, after having defiled them with their uncleanness.... What shall I say of the abominable rape of the women?" He told them to enter on the road to the Holy Sepulcher "to wrest that land from the wicked race, and subject it to yourselves."[25]

But instead of avenging these insults and outrages, Christian knights attacked one another at home and spilled each other's Christian blood. Stop these abuses and go to Jerusalem, Urban urged. Use your glorious military prowess to serve as "soldiers of Christ," he entreated, and the temporal punishment due for your sins will be remitted in return for your sacrifice and service to him. The pope promised that if French knights and barons went east to kill the enemies of the faithful, they would be able to atone for their past sins. This was a powerful message that Crusaders could interpret in unexpected ways, and it produced unanticipated consequences.[26]

In light of the fact that the pope made the speech, we might think that papal authority alone was the source behind the call to take up arms and become pilgrims to oust the Turks. But the audience assembled at Clermont understood the religious authority behind the message differently. We see this toward the end of Robert of Reims's narrative: "When Pope Urban had said these and very many similar things in his urbane discourse, he so influenced to one purpose the desires of all who were present, that they cried out, 'It is the will of God! It is the will of God!' (*Deus vult! Deus vult!*)."

The pope was so struck by this spontaneous outburst of the assembled that he interpreted it as a sign that the audience was divinely inspired then and there by the Holy Spirit itself:

> My beloved brethren, today is manifest in you what the Lord says in the Gospel, *"Where two or three are gathered together in my name there am*

I in the midst of them" [Matt. 18:20]. Unless the Lord God had been present in your spirits, all of you would not have uttered the same cry. For although the cry issued from numerous mouths, yet the origin of the cry was one. Therefore, I say to you that God, who implanted this in your breasts, has drawn it forth from you.[27]

For some, then, the authority came from the potentially uncontrollable inspiration of God that was, as even the pope himself said, known directly to the future Crusaders themselves. We may think of this as a case of *collective prophecy*, a group's claim or belief that they can directly intuit God's will independent of any institutional sources of religious authority. If, indeed, as the pope's interpretation of the passage from Matthew indicated, the spirit of God was with the knights listening to his speech, why should we be surprised if these same knights, or others who heard about the events at Clermont, should decide to go out to fight other enemies of the faithful closer to home?

As we will see, the idea of immediate revelation of God's will was also a feature of unprecedented Jewish behavior in the Rhineland acts of active martyrdom. The reward they anticipated was personal salvation. As some scholars have noted, one major figure in the anti-Jewish massacres, Emicho of Flonheim, was motivated by personal millennial fantasies, but the unprecedented behavior of Crusaders and Jewish martyrs alike was driven more by collective prophecy in general rather than by any millenarian or messianic fervor in particular.[28]

Enemies at Home

But who were the enemies of Christ? The pope was not thinking about Jews but only of Muslims as the enemies of God in his appeal to the knights of France to launch a counteroffensive in the East. In view of the religious enthusiasm the pope aroused in 1095 and his failure to indicate explicitly that the Jews should be protected, it was easy for lay knights and barons to jump to the conclusion that, on their way to Jerusalem, there might be other "enemies among us," namely the Jews of northern France and especially Germany along the Rhine. As Jonathan Riley-Smith has noted, the Christian knights who led the armies and mobs that invaded the Rhineland Jewish communities in 1096 could well confuse avenging the Jews' killing of Christ in the past with attacking the hostile Muslim Turks in the East in the present. For them, vengeance against both was part of the familiar institution of a vendetta—a blood feud to seek revenge on those who were their enemies.[29]

Contributing to the diffusion of the idea that all infidels could be viewed as enemies at home was a letter Urban wrote shortly after his rousing speech at Clermont to the counts of Besalù, Empurias, Rousillon, and Cerdaña along with their knights in the south of France and northeast Spain. His object this time was not to counter the Turks in the East but to fight the Muslim enemy in Spain. As Urban put it, there is a logical reason for Christian knights there to agree to take up arms in defense of the church:

> If the knights of other provinces have decided with one mind to go to the aid of the Asian Church and to liberate their brothers from the tyranny of the Saracens, so ought you with one mind and with our encouragement to work with greater endurance to help *a church so near you* resist the invasions of the Saracens. . . . It is no virtue to rescue Christians from Saracens in one place, only to expose them to the tyranny and oppression of the Saracens in another.[30]

In that letter, Urban differed from his predecessor, Pope Alexander II, who wrote in 1063 to Spanish bishops indicating that war was to be waged only against the Muslims in Spain, but that the Jews were to be protected: "The situation of the Jews is surely different from that of the Saracens. Against the latter who persecute Christians and drive them out of their cities and homes, one may properly fight; the former, however, are prepared to live in servitude."[31]

We will see that by the mid-twelfth century, others would disagree with the pope and argue to the contrary that Jews were worse than Saracens (see chapter 5), but for now what is of special interest is the pope's reference to nearby enemies. It did not take a great leap to go from understanding the enemies of "a church so near you" in Spain to include not only the enemy Saracens in Iberia but also all whom the church ever referred to as enemies of Christ, namely the Jews of northern Europe.

As a result of the association of Jews at home as included in the call to avenge the enemies of Christ near and far, before the army of nobles set out for the East, a mob of French and German peasants and villagers swept through the Rhineland. They understood their mission to be the liberation of the towns in their path from the infidel Jews, whose property they felt free to pillage.[32]

Jews living peacefully with Christian neighbors in Europe for three or more generations now became the hostile enemies of God by a process of association. Knights and rabble attacked Jewish communities, mainly in the upper Rhine towns of Speyer, Worms, and Mainz and the lower Rhine villages around Cologne.

The Jewish and Christian sources report acts of Christian violence directed at the civilian population with a specific intent to kill Jews or forcibly convert them.[33] Jews now transferred to themselves and Christians the binary categories of holy versus polluted that Pope Urban II had applied at Clermont to Muslims. As the twelfth century progressed, the intensity of Jewish anger and outcry for revenge increased, as measured by the anti-Christian language in the three chronicles (see chapter 4). What changed was the emergence of the imagined Jew as nearby threatening enemies of the faithful, on the one side, even as Jews continued to imagine Christianity as paganism, on the other. In this respect, the end of the eleventh century saw a distinctive shift in European Christian *attitudes* toward the Jews, and 1096 was a decisive turning point in medieval Jewish-Christian relations.[34]

There is abundant evidence that the Crusaders who attacked the Jews in Germany in spring and summer 1096 were thinking of them as nearby enemies who deserved revenge. Inspired by Crusader hysteria, some Christians took matters into their own hands and acted as though they had a divine mandate to kill Jews or force them to convert.

Jewish and Christian awareness of Crusader motives appears in several Hebrew and Latin chronicles. Some of the former put attributed speeches into the mouths of the Crusaders just before the attacks. In the three Hebrew chronicles on the riots and acts of martyrdom in 1096, the authors even put blasphemous terms of abuse about Christianity into the mouths of the Crusaders.[35] This rhetorical technique was designed to reinforce in the Jewish reader a sense of religious solidarity by expressing the author's contempt for Christian sancta, in contrast to Jewish sacrifice and martyrdom. We will look more closely at the history and range of Jewish verbal assaults on Christianity in chapter 4 and then in chapter 5 take up various Jewish gestures of contempt acted out toward Christianity, including some that associated Christian symbols with bodily excretions and latrines ("latrine blasphemy"). These verbal and especially physical acts of Jewish assertiveness, we will soon see, prompted popes to rail against the Jews' refusal to remain subordinate. Defiance of right order could result in the forfeiture of their place in a rightly ordered Christian society.

The Crusaders' Rationale

In the speeches the Hebrew chronicles attribute to the attacking Crusaders, the local Jews are considered nearby enemies deserving death because they killed Christ. According to the earliest of the Hebrew chronicles, the so-called Mainz Anonymous, written shortly after the events,

> They said to each other, "Look now, we are going to a distant country to make war against mighty kings and are endangering our lives to conquer the kingdoms which do not believe in the crucified one, when actually it is the Jews who murdered and crucified him." They stirred up hatred among us in all quarters and declared that either we accept their "abominable faith" or else they would annihilate us all, even infants and sucklings. The noblemen and common people placed an "evil symbol"—a vertical line over a horizontal one—on their garments and special hats on their heads.[36]

Another version of the speech is in the chronicle of Rabbi Eliezer bar Nathan (1090–1170), written slightly later in the early twelfth century and preserved in at least nine manuscripts:

> Now it came to pass that as they passed through the towns where Jews dwelled, they said to themselves: "Look now, we are going to seek out our 'profanity' (*tarputeinu*) [literally, "our idolatry"] and to take vengeance on the Ishmaelites for our messiah, when here are the Jews who murdered and crucified him. Let us first avenge ourselves on them and exterminate them from among the nations so that the name of Israel

will no longer be remembered or let them adopt our faith and acknowledge the 'offspring of menstrual impurity' (*ben ha-niddah*)."[37]

And near the beginning of the so-called Solomon bar Samson account, from around 1140, the longest and latest version, we find a speech close to the one in the previous chronicle:

> Now it came to pass that as they passed through the towns where Jews dwelled, they said to one another: "Look now, we are going a long way to seek out the 'profane shrine' (*beit ha-tarput*) [literally, "house of idolatry"] and to avenge ourselves on the Ishmaelites, when here, in our very midst, are the Jews—they whose forefathers murdered and crucified him for no reason. Let us first avenge ourselves on them and exterminate them from among the nations so that the name of Israel will no longer be remembered, or let them adopt our faith and acknowledge the 'offspring of menstrual impurity' (promiscuity)."[38]

A few lines after these words, in connection with a reference to the pope's speech, the same Hebrew chronicle continues:

> Why should we concern ourselves with going to war against the Ishmaelites dwelling about Jerusalem, when in our midst is a people who disrespect our god—indeed, their ancestors are those who crucified him. Why should we let them live and tolerate their dwelling among us? Let us commence by using our swords against them and then proceed upon our stray path.[39]

Here we see included as an additional reason to attack the Jews that they "disrespect our god." This addition shifts the emphasis from the past and the Passion of Christ to the present and a claim of Jewish disrespect for Christianity. This theme becomes increasingly more prominent in the twelfth century, especially in connection with propaganda for the Second Crusade.

We see this second theme reiterated in the Hebrew composition of Ovadiah the Proselyte, a former Christian whose composition written around 1100 has been preserved in the Cairo Geniza:

> [And when they were determined] to go to Jerusalem, [one said to the other], "Why are we [going to a distant land, to] our enemies, when here in our own land [and towns dwe]ll our enemies and those who

hate [our religion. Why should we leave] them with our wives?" [And an outcry was heard in the Franks' camp.]⁴⁰

This source does not mention the Passion as the reason for Christians wanting to attack the Jews but instead justifies attacking them because "they hate our religion" now. Moreover, Ovadiah fears Jews as a sexual menace. This theme does not appear in the other speeches attributed to the Crusaders.

A contemporary Latin text provides additional evidence that Crusaders were making the argument that if they were going all the way to Jerusalem to kill the enemies of God, they should first deal with the Jews, the enemies of Christ at home. In his *Autobiographie*, Abbot Guibert of Nogent (ca. 1055–1124) attributes to the people of Rouen who were about to go on Crusade the following opinion that again emphasizes the present danger rather than the Passion in the past: "After traversing great distances, we desire to attack the enemies of God in the East, although the Jews, of all races the worst foes of God, are before our eyes. That's doing our work backward."⁴¹

These Hebrew and Latin sources about the First Crusade agree that some of the knights as well as the mob thought it was only logical that if God wanted them to attack the enemy Muslims far off in Jerusalem, he certainly wanted them to kill the enemy Jews nearby.

Similarly, it was assumed that just as Pope Urban II had told the crowd at Clermont that going to Jerusalem would earn the forgiveness of earthly sins, others reasoned that "whosoever kills a Jew will receive pardon for all his sins."⁴² The mindset of the time that motivated masses to join the Crusade is captured in the idea that the world had to be purified of evil.⁴³ The argument in almost all the attributed speeches emphasizes revenge on the nearby enemy Jews.

Pope Urban II never hinted that there was a connection between his remission of earthly punishments for Christians who went on Crusade and a call to kill Jews, the enemy living nearby, to achieve the same end. On the other hand, unlike Pope Alexander II, who had explicitly written of protecting the Jew in Iberia in his letter of 1063, Urban never mentioned the Jews. Here, too, we see the consequences of a belief that Crusaders could know the will of God in a direct, unmediated way. And so if the Crusaders could equate the enemy Jews with the enemy Seljuk Turks as deserving of death, they could also imagine that their reward would be the same for killing a Jew at and home as for killing a "pagan" enemy abroad.

Jewish Actions Attempt to Restore Right Order

The search for right order was not limited to the pope inspiring Crusaders armed to fight the Turks in the East. It also appears in how Jews behaved in different communities under threat from Crusaders. The violence Christians perpetrated on the Jews as nearby enemies was actually a disruption of right order—Christians were not supposed to kill or forcibly baptize Jews—and Jews devised different ways to try to restore their proper protected place in Christian society, with varying degrees of success.[44]

As the lengthy Solomon ben Samson account indicates, when they realized the danger they were in, the leaders of Mainz Jewry elected an emergency council to go to the archbishop, the local ruler, and seek his protection, by bribery if necessary. Taking this political tack meant that Jews were willing to risk relying on their safety as theoretically guaranteed by imperial charters such as those Emperor Henry IV issued in 1090 to Speyer and Worms.[45] And it is not surprising that R. Qalonimos b. Meshullam, the local leader (*parnas*) of Mainz Jewry, "dispatched a messenger to King Henry in the Kingdom of Apulia" to secure guarantees temporarily preventing the Jews of Mainz from being harmed.[46]

At least in Mainz, Jews also met the attacks by mounting armed resistance.[47] The Mainz Anonymous puts the fighting this way:

> When the saints, the fearers of the Most High, saw the great multitude, they placed their trust in their Creator and clung to Him. They donned their armor and their weapons of war, adults and children alike, with Rabbi Qalonymos, son of Rabbi Meshullam, at their head.[48]

The account of Solomon bar Samson made use of the Mainz account but elaborated on it as follows:

> When the people of the Holy Covenant, the saints, the fearers of the Most High, saw the great multitude, a vast horde of them, as the sand upon the seashore, they clung to their Creator. They donned their armor and their weapons of war, adults and children alike, with Rabbi

Qalonymos, the son of Rabbi Meshullam, the Parnas at their head....
The Jews armed themselves in the inner court of the bishop.[49]

Thus in Mainz at least, the two chroniclers depict acts of knightly behavior of physical fighting in the streets, and only when the Jews there realized that they were overpowered and that bribing local authorities could not protect them from the invading forces did they resort to the unprecedented ritualization of violence in acts of sacrificial martyrdom, designed to prevent a fate worse than death.[50]

Knowing the Will of God

When political action or fighting in the streets failed, the Jewish narrators of the events of 1096 understood that the Jews of the Rhineland as well as the Crusaders were able to intuit the will of God directly in a form of collective prophecy. It was the Jews' awareness of God's will that made them turn away from typical political and even military acts of defense and assume that God now wanted them to carry out unprecedented acts of ritual sacrifice of their children and self-sacrificial martyrdom.[51]

We see this pattern in a story about a young man named Barukh ben Isaac, who claimed that he had heard someone crying in the synagogue.[52] It turned out, however, that no one was there: "Upon hearing this, we cried out: 'Ah, Lord God! Will you make an end of the remnant of Israel?'" Then they went and reported the occurrence to their brethren, who were concealed in the court of the count and the bishop's chambers, and all knew that this decree was of God.[53]

The other two Hebrew chronicles also claim that the Jews can know the will of God directly. For example, in R. Eliezer bar Nathan's narrative, "They hastened to fulfill the will of their Creator, not wishing to flee just to be saved for temporal life, for lovingly they accepted Heaven's judgment."[54] Similarly, in the Mainz Anonymous, the narrator assumes that the Jews know the will of God when he says, "When the people of the Sacred Covenant saw that the Heavenly decree had been issued and that the enemy had defeated them, they all cried out."[55]

In all of these First Crusade texts, we see evidence of the spontaneous religious enthusiasm that prevailed according to which it was possible for Christians and Jews to intuit the will of God. Based on this knowledge, some Crusaders killed Jews or forcibly converted them, against the norms of both church and state. Some Jews under attack thought that they had a divine mandate to try to kill a Christian, usually not possible, or instead to ritually slaughter their families and themselves as sacrifices, in unprecedented acts of defiance, to prevent any physical contact, let alone forced baptism, at the hands of their impure Christian "enemy."

It was important for the Hebrew chroniclers to present the Jewish martyrs knowing that it was the will of God that they take the lives of their families and their own. Some Jews looked back critically at what the Jewish martyrs had done. Among them is a Tosafist (Talmud glossator) who remarked in a commentary to Genesis 9:5:

> It once happened that a certain rabbi slaughtered many children during a persecution because he was afraid they would be forced to become Christians. Another rabbi there got furious with him and called him a murderer, but the first one ignored him. The (second) rabbi said, "If I am right, let the other rabbi die a horrible death." And so it happened that Christians caught (the first rabbi), skinned him alive and put sand in his wounds. Soon the persecution ended and had he not slaughtered the children they would have been saved.[56]

There was no legal precedent for the acts of ritual homicide and suicide described in the sources about the martyrdom of 1096, and some have proposed literary models such as the behavior of ancient Jerusalem Temple priests or the defenders of the Herodian fortress of Masada who took the lives of other Jews and then their own after the fall of Jerusalem in 70 CE.[57] According to those ancient literary traditions, it was even required that certain Jews take their own lives and even kill one another when it was God's will that the Temple be destroyed. The decision that their sacrifice was according to God's will followed from a sense that they could decipher it then and there.[58]

Innovative Rituals of Assertiveness

A Jewish narrator describes an innovative ceremony in which "Master Isaac the saint took his two children—his son and daughter—and led them through the courtyard at midnight into the synagogue before the Holy Ark, and there he slaughtered them, in sanctification of the Great Name, to the Sublime and Lofty God, Who has commanded us not to forsake pure fear of Him for any other belief, and to adhere to his Holy Torah with all our heart and soul. He sprinkled some of their blood on the pillars of the Holy Ark so as to evoke their memory before the One-and-Only Everlasting King. And he said, 'May this blood expiate all my transgressions!'"[59]

This act of sacrifice turns on its head the false but accepted Christian claim that a Crusader killing a Jew would avoid earthly punishment for sins. Aware of this claim, the narrator of the Hebrew account sees Jews ritually killing other Jews as an act of atonement.[60]

In the martyrologies of the Hebrew chroniclers, unlike the descriptions of political encounters preceding them, women as well as men play individualized roles.[61] For example, in the story of Rachel (of Mainz), who is described in the Mainz Anonymous and at greater length in the later Solomon bar Samson chronicle as ritually killing her four children, Rachel assumes poses that suggest associations with Mary and the Mother Church, or ecclesia, as Jeremy Cohen has pointed out. These associations, however, reinforce Jewish assertiveness of the holiness of the Jewish family and deny, without any ambivalence, the value of the Virgin Mary or Holy Mother Church.[62]

Trying to defend the unprecedented behavior of the martyrs, the Jewish narrators describe them as "Holy Things" (*qodashim*) that must not be touched by impure hands. In this way, it becomes clear that political intervention is insufficient to enable the Jews to retain their normal status of tolerated but subordinate within the Christian hierarchy. And for that reason, the Jewish narrators justify the creation of a cultic boundary, the sacrificial death of the martyrs at their own hands, to maintain the separation of Jew from Christian. Political containment of the attackers fails; ritual avoidance by means of self-inflicted sacrificial martyrdom follows.

By portraying the martyrs as sacrificing themselves, the chroniclers polemically enable the Jews to turn defeat into victory. The outcome of the narrative makes this especially clear. The Crusader mob will never get to Jerusalem. Along the way it will attack fellow Christians in Hungary and be destroyed. In noting this, the Jewish chronicler asserted how the Crusaders' wicked behavior toward the Jews was punished—a confidence not completely shared by Christian chroniclers such as Albert of Aachen, who criticized the Crusaders' attacks on Jews but was not certain whether or why God was against the Crusaders (see below).

The Jews whom the Crusader mob tried to destroy on the way to Jerusalem were even capable of symbolically rebuilding the Temple in Mainz, their own Jerusalem. As with pilgrim shrines in England or Spain, the acts of the martyrs in the Rhineland symbolically replicated another Jerusalem in Europe.[63]

In addition, Hebrew chroniclers describe Jews attacking one or more Christians, as in Mainz, where Jewish mothers "hurled stones from the window on the enemy."[64] Or "they found one of the errant ones (Crusaders) in the room, and all of them, men and women, threw stones at him till he fell dead."[65] Others acted out passively, such as when Jewish women refused to enter "the edifice of idolatry" (church) and "inhale the odor of the offending incense" and were cut down at the door.[66] In Worms, Simcha ha-Kohen was taken to a "house of idolatry" (church), where he drew a knife from his sleeve and slew a knight who was a nephew of the bishop, whereupon he was killed.[67] These acts of assertive violence toward the Christian attackers are described as active ways of provoking Jewish martyrdom.

The narrators also mention assertive acts of loyalty to Judaism by Jews crying out, "Hear, O Israel, the Lord is our God, the Lord is One" (Deut. 6:4) before and during acts of martyrdom. This gesture seems to be an innovation in 1096 and became a feature of some later Jewish martyrological behavior.[68] It served as a declaration of Jewish identity in defiance of Christianity, understood as idolatry.[69]

For example, Jews in Worms who are about to be killed by other Jews say it:

Fathers fell upon their sons, being slaughtered upon one another, and they slew one another—each man his kin, his wife and children; bridegrooms slew their betrothed, and merciful women their only children. They all accepted the divine decree wholeheartedly and, as they yielded up their souls to the Creator, cried out: *"Hear O Israel, the Lord is our God, the Lord is One."*[70]

At other times, Jews whom Christians are about to kill say it, as in Mainz: "And when the enemy was upon them, they all cried out in a great voice, with one heart and one tongue: '*Hear, O Israel, the Lord is our God, the Lord is One.*'"[71]

At still other times, Jews say it when they witness other Jews killing each other, as in the town of Wevelinghoven:

> There was a pious man there of ripe old age by the name of Rabbi Samuel, son of Yechiel. He had an only son, a handsome young man, whose appearance was like Lebanon. They fled together into the water, and the youth stretched out his neck to his father for slaughter as they stood in the waters. The father recited the benediction for Ritual Slaughter over him, and the son answered, "Amen." All those standing around them responded in a loud voice: "*Hear, O Israel, the Lord is our God, the Lord is One.*"[72]

Apart from these instances in the Hebrew narratives of someone crying out "Hear, O Israel" (*shema yisrael*), one of the Hebrew lamentations about 1096 mentions this as well. In his liturgical poem that begins "I said, look away from me, while I weep bitterly" (*amarti she'u minni, ba-bekhi amareir*), R. Qalonimos b. Judah says,

> The father subdued his compassion to be able to sacrifice his children like lambs to the slaughter, indeed he prepared the slaughter-house for his own children.... Who can hear (*yishma'*) and not weep? The son is slaughtered, and the father recites the Shema (*qorei et shema'*).[73]

Christians Also Criticize Crusader Perversion of Right Order

What especially impressed Christian as well as Jewish chroniclers were the acts of ritual slaughter and suicide in which fathers and mothers killed their own families and then themselves. The Jewish narrators extolled the martyrs as saints from whose sacrificial acts accrued a well of religious merit that others could draw on for vicarious atonement. Christian chroniclers, all clerics, criticized the Crusaders who acted cruelly and forced Jewish parents to kill their children rather than be baptized forcibly or killed. Although there may have been different motives at play in 1096, neither the murder nor the forced baptism of Jews was permitted as a legitimate policy toward Jews, whose subordinate presence was supposed to be part of right order in Christian society.

There are nearly thirty Latin chronicles that mention the events of 1096, but only a few refer to the Jews' acts of killing their families and themselves.[74] The Christian chroniclers who do mention Jews killing their families do not blame the "cruel" Jews for killing their children but instead the Crusaders for driving the Jewish parents to commit extreme acts. Killing Jews or forcibly baptizing them were sins, and this is clear in the Christian chronicles that are critical of the Crusaders, not the Jewish parents. Apart from one chronicler who criticizes Jewish behavior as motivated by the devil, the Latin evidence overwhelmingly blames the Crusaders for their sinful behavior even if they sometimes express some ambivalence about why God allowed the events to happen in the first place.[75]

We see signs of this theological uncertainty in the chronicle of Albert of Aachen, a German priest who wrote a history of the First Crusade:

> I know not whether by a judgment of the Lord, or by some error of mind, they rose in a spirit of cruelty against the Jewish people scattered throughout these cities and slaughtered them without mercy, especially in the Kingdom of Lorraine, asserting it to be the beginning of their expedition and their duty against the enemies of the Christian faith.[76]

The chronicler here expresses some doubts as to the justification for the massacre but does not doubt the Crusaders' cruelty. He continues,

> Horrible to say, mothers cut the throats of nursing children with knives and stabbed others, preferring them to perish thus by their own hands rather than to be killed by the weapons of the uncircumcised.[77]

In the end, the chronicler attributes some of the Crusaders' failure to achieve their destination to their immoral behavior toward the Jews, although here too there is some ambivalence about the Crusaders' motives but no hint at any Jewish cruelty:

> So, the hand of the Lord is believed to have been against the pilgrims, who had sinned by excessive impurity and fornication, and who had

slaughtered the exiled Jews through greed of money, rather than for the sake of God's justice, although the Jews were opposed to Christ. The Lord is a just judge and orders no one unwillingly or under compulsion, to come under the yoke of the Catholic faith.[78]

On the face of it, Albert is shocked, but not at the Jews' cruelty. Rather he blames the Christians who forced the Jewish mothers to kill their children to prevent something worse, being "killed by the weapons of the uncircumcised."[79]

Other clerical writers emphasize the horror as well and blame the Crusaders for their attacks on the Jews, regardless of whether they mention the acts of Jewish parents or not.[80] A chronicler from Trier reports,

> When in their fiery zeal (the Crusaders) approached Trier, the local Jews thought to themselves they too would experience a fate similar (to Worms and Mainz), some of them took their children and thrust the blade into their stomachs, saying that it was their obligation to bring them down to the bosom of Abraham to prevent their humiliation in the madness of the Christians. Some of their wives went out onto the bridge over the river, filled the [pockets of their] skirts and the sleeves of their clothing with rocks, and jumped into the water.[81]

Sigebertus Auctarium Acquicinense says, "Out of a zealous desire to preserve the ways of their ancestors, there were Jews who killed one another; others pretended that they were accepting the (other) faith temporarily and afterwards reverted to Judaism."[82]

The only Latin chronicle that even hints at blaming the Jews for killing each other is from the *Bernoldi Chronicon*:

> In that year [1096] in certain towns, many Jews were killed by those who were on the way to Jerusalem. And so I say: those who fled to the palace of the king and of the bishop in Speyer were able to defend themselves with great difficulty even if the bishop Johann was helping them. Afterwards he became enraged and was assuaged by the Jews' money that caused the killing of other Christians. It was similar in Worms—in order to escape the Christian persecutions, the Jews fled to the bishop. When he advised them to be baptized to save their lives, they asked (him) to delay their response and others, after they entered the bishops' living quarters, when our men were waiting for

their answer, by the influence of Satan and their hardness of heart, they killed each other.[83]

But even Bernoldi does not emphasize that Jews killed their *children* out of cruelty; he blames the Jews, and Satan, because they preferred to kill each other rather than convert. The overwhelming view of the other Latin sources is that the Crusaders were completely to blame for what happened, not the Jews.

For example, *Annales Hildesheimenses* comments on the forced baptisms and murder of the Jews:

> In their armed march to Jerusalem, countless people from parts of different nations forced Jews to be baptized and struck dead those who resisted in an immeasurable bloodbath. In Mainz, Jews were killed, men, women, and children, 1,014 in number, and the greatest part of the city was burned down. In many places, Jews were made into Christians, and they turned away from Christianity again.[84]

An important chronicle not usually considered and quoted by Benjamin Kedar in a significant study condemns the Crusaders in general for their actions:

> Jews were killed in that year [1096] in many places by the men who set out for Jerusalem. Certainly, it may seem extraordinary that this extermination was done on one day in many places with the same fervor of the spirit, although the deed is condemned by many and appraised as contrary to religion. Yet we know that it was impossible to prevent it, as many priests attempted to disrupt it by imposing excommunication and many great men by issuing threats.[85]

In addition, Ekkehard of Aura (d. 1126), a German abbot, wrote a chronicle that included details about 1096:

> There arose in those days a certain military man, a count of those lands around the Rhine named Emicho, formerly a very infamous tyrant, then however by divine revelations, it was said, called to this sort of religious profession [Crusade (or conversion of the Jews)] like another Saul, took control of 12,000 crusaders; who were led through the cities of the Rhine, Main, and Danube, and wherever they found the accursed Jews, *because of Christian zeal* they either killed them or tried to force them into the bosom of the church.[86]

William of Tyre's account expresses outrage about Crusader cruelty, without mentioning Jewish martyrs' acts of ritual killing. He refers to "innumerable bands of people on foot ... among them, indeed, some men of noble birth" who

> cruelly massacred the Jewish people in the cities and towns through which they passed, for the latter, having no reason to fear anything of the kind, took no precautions. These outrages occurred especially in the cities of Cologne and Mainz, where Count Emicho, a powerful nobleman, well known in that country, joined the pilgrim bands with a large following. He ... himself shared in the evil deeds of his followers and urged them on to crime."[87]

These Christian sources show that some clerical Christian chroniclers were aware that Jewish acts of assertive martyrdom happened in the Rhineland in 1096, but the point of nearly all of them is criticism of the Crusaders, not of the Jewish parents.[88]

In 1096, Jews and Christians acted out their assertive claims to right order in conditions that were extreme. As William Chester Jordan correctly observed, "Thus, the image of martyrdom served as a constant reminder of the fragility of social life and nurtured the spirit of resistance among the Jews to the overtures and threats of the Christians and reassured the Chosen People."[89]

After the riots, Jews continued to assert their sense of chosenness in words and acts designed to show contempt for Christianity, which they considered to be idolatry. As in the Crusader speeches inserted into the Hebrew chronicles, Jews replaced descriptive words like "church" with insults such as "abomination" to express their sense of religious superiority. Jews expressed their views about Christianity, the religion, and themselves in many different ways, among them insulting verbal challenges to Christian beliefs, blasphemous gestures, and counter rites.[90]

CHAPTER FOUR

Assertive Words

INSULTING CHRISTIANITY

THE JEWS IN medieval Europe were not just passive sufferers in "a persecuting society" but also actively expressed the "deviance" that the persecuting society sought to contain or eliminate.[1] Words and gestures made up an arsenal of Jewish assertiveness.[2] Over the course of the medieval centuries, the escalating confrontations between increasingly assertive Jews and more self-aware committed supersessionist Christians reinforced both Jewish solidarity and an intensely Christian collective identity that included new forms of Christian antisemitism. The process was dynamic and mutually reinforcing. Each culture shaped the other as its counterimage.

Jews expressed their self-confidence and contempt for Christianity in words not only when they were under attack but also when they were living peacefully with their Christian neighbors. In recounting the ways Jews asserted their loyalty to God in 1096, the Hebrew chronicles use a rhetoric of contempt when they refer to Christianity. Sometimes the terms of abuse are found in the narrator's voice; at other times, they are put into the dialogue of Jews engaged in direct verbal assault on their Christian attackers. The chroniclers' anti-Christian insults encouraged their Jewish readers to assert themselves as Jews, but they sometimes made Christians act defensively.[3]

Insulting Christianity Even When Complimenting Christians

Although most learned Jews agreed with R. Gershom of Mainz's responsum and considered Christians to be mere followers of their misguided ancestors' customs, not idolatrous pagans, the same Jewish scholars continued to view Christianity and its symbols as idolatry.[4] A French Talmud glossator who made this clear was unusually emotional in affirming, "God forbid that we should rule in a case of idolatry that one should transgress rather than die."[5]

We see this distinction in the several ways Jews insulted the symbols of Christianity even when they praised Christians for behaving in church the way Jews should behave in synagogue.[6] For example, R. Judah the Pious (d. 1217), the author of *Sefer Hasidim* (Book of the pious), criticizes Jews who gossip in a synagogue by comparing how Christians behave in church, but he replaces the word "church" with a phrase that insults Christianity: "The Christians (*goyim*) in their house of foolishness (*be-veit tiflotam*) stand respectfully (*be-tarbut*); all the more should a Jew who stands before the great King not talk nonsense in the synagogue."[7]

Similarly, R. Isaac b. Joseph of Corbeil (d. 1290), one of the great rabbinic masters of the thirteenth century, in his best-selling legal compendium *Sefer Mizvot Qatan* (The short book about the commandments), also compared how Jews pray noisily in the synagogue to Christians praying silently in church:

> We should make an *a fortiori* argument about ourselves: if Christians (*ha-goyim*), who believe in nothing stand up in their house of idolatry (*be-veit tarput shelahem*) as though mute, how much the more should we, who stand before the King of the King of Kings, the Holy One, blessed be He.[8]

The author distinguishes between something that Christians do, which he praises, and Christianity, which he finds worthless. It is the anomaly of proper behavior performed in a worthless setting that is the basis of his rebuke to his Jewish audience. There is no basis here for anyone to think that the author is praising Christians.

Insulting Jews When Complimenting Their Behavior

Christian authors also could compliment Jewish behavior that they wanted Christians to emulate. In northern Europe, the point of telling Christians to act like Jews is that one can learn how to behave even from a despised Jew. This is not the same thing as when Giovanni Boccaccio in the *Decameron* uses a Jew to serve as a positive foil for criticizing a Christian, and there is little doubt that it is sincere.[9] Even the assumption that these cases show familiarity with Jewish behavior needs to be examined. One recalls the "polemical ethnographies" of the early modern Christian Hebraists as not simply reports of observed fact when it came to describing Jewish customs and ceremonies.[10]

Thus a student of Peter Abelard (1079–1142) is quoted as praising Jews for educating all of their male children, not just those who want to be clergy, and even their daughters:

> If the Christians educate their sons, they do so not for God, but for gain, in order that the one brother, if he be a clerk, may help his father and his mother and his other brothers. They say that a clerk will have no heir and whatever he has will be ours and the other brothers.... But the Jews, out of zeal for God and love of the law, put as many sons as they have to letters, that each may understand God's law.
>
> A Jew, however poor, even if he had ten sons would put them all to letters, not for gain as Christians do, but for the understanding of God's law, and not only his sons but his daughters.[11]

This comparison needs to be looked at carefully and not taken at face value. The generalization about why Christian parents educated their children is not to be trusted, and neither is the idea that Jews "educated" all of their sons and even daughters as a general rule, even if there were exceptions (mainly in rabbinic families).

Similarly, William Langland (ca. 1332–ca. 1386) praises Jewish care for the poor in *Piers Ploughman*: "For never would a Jew see another Jew begging, if he could help it, not for all the riches in the world! ... Why cannot we Christians be as charitable with Christ's gifts as the Jews, who are truly our teachers, are with theirs?"[12] John Gower (1330–1408) in the *Vox Clamantis* also praises Jews in order to chastise Christians: "For we are so bent upon money at all hours that scarcely one festival day now remains for God. O how the Jew preserves the sacred Sabbath of the Lord, neither buying nor selling nor seeking for gain" (5.11.687–88).[13]

Richard Rex notes that Geoffrey Chaucer might have heard a sermon preached in the 1380s that included the following:

> But, as I say, the real truth seems to be that the faith of the Christians is less directed to good works than that of the Jews or the pagans. For the Jews do not do servile labor on their feast days, but the Christians commonly engage in worldly and mercantile activities on Sundays and their feast days. And whereas those days should be set aside for God and the saints alone, they in fact give them more to the flesh, the devil, and the world. The Jews do not take usury from their brethren, but the Christians do not lend money to Christians without usury. The Jews cherish the poor with gifts lest they go begging; the Christians, and especially their rich, do not take care of the poor. And even if gifts are granted, the rich escape and the poor pay the whole thing.[14]

These and other comparisons have sometimes been cited as evidence that Christians admired Jews. We should remember that these texts claim Christian familiarity with Jewish behavior that they admire and wished that their fellow Christians would emulate *despite the fact that they were Jews*. They were making the argument that if Jews, who are despised and rejected, can do X, how much the more should you who are God's elect do it? The comparison presupposes contempt for Jews even though they are praised for doing something worth imitating. The Jewish examples of assertiveness are more transparent and state explicitly the basis of the comparison. Each side praised specific behavior that a writer admired while asserting or implying its superiority over the despised other.

Verbal Insults and Blasphemy

Wordplay denigrating pagan religion is found already in the Hebrew Bible and Talmud. In both, Jews engaged in a form of verbal aggression by substituting insulting plays on words for pagan sancta that later on included Christian terms. In the Hebrew Bible, puns against pagan religion play on the sound of the name, or are based on a pattern of letters shared between the name and explanation.[15] For example, the prophet Hosea criticizes the "idolatrous" cult of the northern Israelite rebel Jeroboam by referring to the place-name of the cult Bethel (House of God) as Beit-aven (House of Sin): *"Do not come to Gilgal, do not make pilgrimages to Beth-aven. And do not swear by the Lord"* (Hos. 4:15).[16] On "Beth-aven," Rashi glosses, "This is Bethel, for Jeroboam set up the calves there," so the meaning of the substitution was known to medieval Jews who knew Rashi.

The Talmud continued this biblical way of insulting idols by replacing the name of an idol by a term that sounds like the original but undermines its meaning. For instance, if pagans call their house of worship a "house of elevation" (*beit galya*), it should be called a "house of digging" (*beit karya*); if they call it "the all-seeing eye" (*'ein kol*), it should be called the eye of a thorn (*'ein qotz*).[17]

Extending this practice from pagan to Christian terms in the Talmud, Jews denigrated the New Testament in different forms that Christians would find offensive when ecclesiastical leaders learned about them in the thirteenth century. Thus Rabbi Meir would call the Christian Gospels (Greek: *evangelion*) the "wicked folio" (*aven gilyon*); Rabbi Yohanan would call it the "sinful folio" (*'avon gilyon*).[18] In rabbinic literature, we also find puns on the name of "Mary" as "hairdresser" (*megadla sa'ar neshayya*), a riff on Mary Magdalene.[19] To mock the Christian claim that Jesus was born to a virgin (Greek: *parthenos*), the Talmud refers to him as the "son of Pantera," meaning (son of) a Roman soldier (Greek: *pantheros*).[20]

Piyyutim *and the* Nestor ha-Komer *Polemic*

During the same centuries when the Babylonian Talmud was being compiled in the Persian Empire (third to seventh centuries CE), rabbis in Christian Roman (Byzantine) Palestine were composing liturgical poems (piyyutim) that included insults directed at either pagan or Christian Rome as personified in the biblical figure of Esau. A few anti-Christian Roman references were written by Yannai and Qallir in sixth-century Byzantine Palestine.[21] As Leopold Zunz noted, ancient and especially southern Italian and German medieval piyyutim include a variety of anti-Christian terms.²² A church is called not a house of prayer (*beit tefillah*) but instead a house of foolishness (*beit tiflah*). Jesus is referred to as a stinking corpse (*peger muvas*) (Isa. 14:19) and the hanged one (*talui*), referring either to hanging and suffocating on a cross or tree, or to death by actual hanging. These verbal insults were part of a Jewish awareness of the growing Christian presence in the Land of Israel, where the building of new churches was met by the construction of new synagogues.²³

In the same spirit, we find anti-Christianity epithets in an early Jewish polemical handbook, known as *The Polemic of Nestor ha-Komer* (*Sefer Nestor ha-Komer*), written by a Christian convert to Judaism living in the East.²⁴ It was written in Judeo-Arabic and appeared in a Hebrew translation in southern France, perhaps to help Jewish refugees escaping from the persecution of the Almohads in southern Iberia adjust to living in Christian society in southern France. This text includes many insults directed against Christianity: para. 2, "their error" (*ta'utam*); para. 5, "pollution of the stomach" (*tinnuf ha-beten*); para. 28, "in the book of your error" (*be-sefer ta'utkhem*); para. 35, "in the book of their error" (*be-sefer ta'utam*); para. 51, "in the sinful scroll" (*be-'avon gilyon*); para. 68, "in the book of your error" (*be-sefer ta'utkhem*); para. 127, "in the waters of pollution" (*bi-mei ha-tzahanah*); para. 128, "in the house of your abomination" (*be-veit to'eivoteikhem*); para. 128, "sacred prostitutes" (*qedeishim*) for *qedoshim* (saints); and para. 130: "in the house of their foolishness" (*be-veit tiflatam*).²⁵

As we will soon see, this trend of verbal insult of Christian sancta continued in the later anti-Christian polemical handbooks and other Hebrew genres as well, even though the terms were limited to just a few.

Another text with only a few insulting expressions but sometimes credited with being the source of the abundant anti-Christianity insults in the 1096 chronicles is the often-copied narratives known as *Toledot Yeshu* (*Life of Jesus*). These texts mock Jesus, Mary, and Joseph in a scathing attack on the New Testament.²⁶

Especially prominent are references to Jesus as "son of a prostitute" (*ben zonah*), to which was added in some later versions "son of a menstruant" (*ben niddah*). These narratives are quoted for the first time in the Latin translations of Bishop Agobard of Lyon (r. 816–40) and his successor, Amulo (r. 841–52).[27] Agobard cites this text as part of his criticism of the court of Louis the Pious (d. 840) for the king's sympathy toward the Jews. Despite its outrageous slurs against the holy family and the Gospel accounts, this text seems not to have caused widespread alarm among Christian authorities either in the ninth century or later when Dominican Friar Raymond Martini (ca. 1220–ca. 1285) included it in his *Pugio Fidei* (*Dagger of Faith*) in the late thirteenth century.[28] It became a problem only in early modern times, when the Hebrew text appeared with a Latin translation in the massive anti-Jewish anthology *Tela Ignea Satanae* (*Satan's Flaming Arrows*), produced in 1681 by Johann Christian Wagenseil, professor in Altdorf near Nuremberg.

The Solomon bar Samson Chronicle

The variety and quantity of these negative epithets about Christianity are not evenly distributed across the sources. Despite a few references in the twenty-seven Hebrew liturgical dirges (qinot) written about 1096, the three Hebrew chronicles about the First Crusade riots are the most graphic sources documenting the Jewish state of mind in the generation of survivors from the Rhineland of the first half of the twelfth century. Although we see expressions of anti-Christian insults in different Hebrew writings before 1096, they took a quantum leap forward, especially in the twelfth-century chronicle anonymously written but known by the name of one of the sources used: Solomon bar Samson, composed around 1140.[29]

Writing in the twelfth century before 1140, the narrators of the 1096 chronicles wanted to praise the Jewish martyrs and called on God to avenge them against a religion of idolatry. This motivation produced a wide range of insults aimed at Christian sancta. The Jewish narrator was aware of the Christian claim that they were God's Chosen People and that God had rejected the Jews: "God has forgotten you and is no longer desirous of you since you are a stubborn nation. Instead, He has departed from you and has taken us for His portion, casting His radiance upon us."[30]

Anna Abulafia correctly called attention to the presence of these insults in the Hebrew chronicles, although she did not emphasize enough how they overwhelm the text compared to other medieval Jewish sources.[31] Of the earlier sources to which she pointed, Byzantine Hebrew piyyut and *Toledot Yeshu*, the latter does not contain most of the terms that appear with such intensity and frequency for the first time in the Solomon bar Samson chronicle.

And although some epithets seem to have originated in piyyut that began in Byzantine Palestine, the terms increased and developed further in southern Italy and then exploded in the Solomon bar Samson chronicle from around 1140, which contains over a hundred instances. That narrative survives in a single manuscript and shows physical signs of internal censorship.[32] The insulting language about Christianity in this and the other two Hebrew chronicles assert for Jewish readers that the Christian god was not God.[33]

Note that the terms are found in the narrator's voice and also put into the mouths of the Jews challenging Christians about to kill them—the same rhetorical device of attributing speech to protagonists that we saw in the speeches of the Crusaders who refer to the Church of the Holy Sepulcher as "the profane shrine."

In addition to crying out "*Hear, O Israel*" (*shema yisrael*) (Deut. 6:4) as a form of Jewish loyalty in the face of Christian violent pressure to convert or die (see chapter 3), individual Jews use the language of contempt toward Christianity. In the dozens of anti-Christian slurs that are found especially in the Solomon bar Samson chronicle, some are quoted as dialogue picturing Jews publicly insulting Christianity in the moment of the speaker's death: "They taunted and reviled the *errant ones* with the name of the *crucified, despicable, and abominable son of harlotry,* saying: 'In whom do you place your trust? In a *putrid corpse!*'"[34]

Another scene imagines defiant Master David, the *gabbai*, who fools Christians into thinking that he is willing to convert, only to tell them, "You are *children of whoredom*, believing as you do in a god who was *a bastard* and who *was crucified*."[35] He contrasts his belief in the "everlasting God who dwells in the lofty heavens" and concludes, "To Gehenna are you and your whoreson condemned, and to *boiling excrement* will you be consigned."[36]

The insult language that was associated with the First Crusade riots became widespread in the twelfth and thirteenth centuries.[37] Wordplays that insult Christianity are also mentioned in reference to new names Jews gave to apostates. R. Jacob b. Meir (Rabbeinu Tam, d. 1171) mentions that a Jew named Abraham (*avraham*) would be renamed Lost (*avdan*); Judah (*yehudah*) was renamed Rejected (*Yehuda[het]*).[38] Moreover, Jews used insulting terms even in bilingual Hebrew and Latin contracts with Christians who could read only the Latin parts.[39]

In the more than eighty Latin books that medieval Jews had in their possession as pawns for loans, Jewish lenders sometimes used Christian saints' dates such as "Michaelmas," written in Hebrew letters, in addition to the Hebrew date.[40] In *Sefer Hasidim*, the author advises his readers not to use the names of Christian saints, a sure sign that they did this, but to replace them instead with pejorative terms:

> It is written, *Do not mention the names of other gods; they shall not be heard on your lips* (Ex. 32:13). Right afterwards, it says, *Three times a year you shall hold a festival for Me* (Ex. 33:14). Now why did (Scripture implicitly) compare (the two)? This is to teach you that a Jew (*yisrael*) should not say to a Christian (*le-goy*), ("I will lend you so much money) until the day of the festival of idolatry" ('*ad yom eid shel 'a[vodah] z[arah]*) or "until the day of that sacred prostitute" ('*ad yom shel oto qadeish*). Instead, (a Jew) should say, ("I am lending you the money) *for so many weeks*."[41]

Although insult language can be found almost anywhere, it is not surprising to see it in Jewish texts written to attack Christianity, such as polemical writings designed not only to reply to Christian arguments based on the Hebrew Bible or Old Testament but also to belittle Christian beliefs based on the New Testament. It is found in the early anti-Christian polemic *Nestor ha-Komer* and continues in the French thirteenth-century Hebrew polemical text known as *Yosef ha-Meqaneh* (*Joseph the Zealot*) written by R. Joseph b. Nathan Official in late thirteenth-century northern France.[42] His work includes references to Christian icons with insulting slurs.[43]

The late medieval polemical handbook known as *Nizzahon Vetus*, from around 1300, refers to the New Testament several times, not as "Evangelion" but as a "sinful folio" (*avon gilayon*), as in the Talmud.[44] The author also refers to Christian saints not as "holy ones" (*qedoshim*) but rather as "sacred prostitutes" (*qedeishim*).[45] He refers to St. Peter as "Peter the ass" (*peter hamor*), a play on the biblical phrase regarding the redemption of the firstborn donkey (*peter hamor*).[46] The author also frequently renders Mary (*Maria*) by the rhyming Aramaic for feces (*hariyya*), but sometimes as "Miriam" (*miryam*).[47] In both cases, the editor cautiously translated the name as "Mary" and relegated the medieval author's offensive intent, the association of Mary with feces and latrines, to a footnote.[48] Medieval Jews liked to insult Christian sancta in this way, and for the most part they got away with it either because the Hebrew sources remained inaccessible to Christian authorities, or because texts such as *Toledot Yeshu* or the 1096 chronicles had no religious authority.

The sheer volume of anti-Christian epithets in the Solomon bar Samson chronicle is matched only later in the early thirteenth century in Judah the Pious's *Sefer Hasidim*, a book that has many anti-Christian expressions, as Mordecai Breuer indicated.[49] Writing at a time of peace and economic growth, Judah the Pious understood his small group of German pietists to be religiously superior to other Jews who did not follow the pietistic way and certainly to Christianity, which he considered a form of idolatry. There are hundreds of passages like this one:

> In a certain place where Jews were constructing a synagogue, the builder was a Christian (*goy*) who had recently built an abomination (*to'eivah*) [a church] and the builder had leftover (*ve-nish'ar*) sand and plaster that the Jews needed. The builder said to them, "I will find some that is cheap." One of the elders realized what was happening and understood that the builder wanted to sell them the plaster and sand that was left over from the (construction of the house of) idolatry ('*a[vodah] z[arah]*). The elder said to the other Jews, "It is not permitted to buy anything from them for one's own private house; how much the more does the prohibition apply to a synagogue!" Similarly, if any materials are left over after building a synagogue, it is forbidden to sell it to a builder who is constructing (a house of) idolatry (*le-'a[vodah] z[arah]*).[50]

The practice continued in Ashkenaz well into the early modern period.[51]

Debating Religion in Public

In the thirteenth century, one or more major Jewish rabbinic figures was forced to defend Judaism when attacked by a Christian convert of second rank in front of the Christian authorities. Public theatrical performances like the Paris Talmud trial of 1240 are of special interest here because Nicholas Donin, the Christian protagonist who was a former Jew, had doubts about the religious authority of the Talmud, and the Jewish community had excommunicated him. He selected Talmud passages that were or were said to be insulting to the Christian faith as reasons to either censor or destroy the Talmud. As a result, many Talmud manuscripts were publicly burned in Paris in 1242. In the event, the pope was persuaded that Jews needed the Talmud to interpret the Bible correctly, and censorship rather than additional destruction of the Talmud resulted.[52]

The Disputation of Barcelona aimed to demoralize Jews by claiming that the Talmud itself proved that Jesus was the Messiah. This represented a shift in emphasis in Christian polemics from proving the Incarnation, in the earlier Middle Ages, to arguing for the Christian truth claims about Jesus as messiah from Jewish sources.[53] This approach was sometimes used to pressure Jews to convert, though not everywhere.[54] It went beyond the ancient and early medieval Christian interpretations of the Hebrew Bible by focusing instead on the Talmud. Pablo Christiani (d. 1274), the leading protagonist in Barcelona, presented the case, and R. Moses ben Nachman (Nachmanides) (1194–1270) defended Judaism but soon departed for Palestine.

In addition, there was a second Paris debate in the 1270s conducted for the Christian side by the same Christiani who spoke at Barcelona in 1263.[55] The most effective public confrontation was in Tortosa in the Kingdom of Aragon in 1414–17, and it resulted in mass conversions of Jews and several rabbis as well.[56] Other public disputes are known from Ceuta in North Africa and Majorca, but Paris, Barcelona, and Tortosa stand out among these public performances.[57]

There is little doubt that these spectacles had some impact at the time and place where they were held, although most of the analysis of these public events tends to focus, as do studies of polemical literature in general, on the arguments and proofs offered in the different written accounts and less on the social impact these grand public events made.

Polemics about Holy Architecture

Sometimes polemics and everyday life mirrored each other. For example, the church criticized Jews for violating hierarchy by building synagogues higher than Christian buildings, as when Pope Innocent III in 1205 accused Jews of building synagogues higher than churches in France:

> They have become so insolent that at Sens they have built a new synagogue near an old Church, a good deal higher than the Church. There they celebrate the Jewish rites, not in a low tone, as they used to before they were expelled from the Kingdom, but, in accordance with their custom, with great shouting; thus, they do not hesitate to hinder divine services in that church.[58]

Polemical writings also imagined public debates between Jews and important Christian leaders to argue that the Temple in Jerusalem was more valuable than famous churches, in what we might call a "polemics of sacred architecture."

Verbal jousting over the worth or height of iconic religious buildings is seen in Jewish and Christian sources over the years in texts that describe the comparison of the Temple in Jerusalem and monumental churches, and we see signs of everyday architectural polemics in references to Jews building synagogues higher than churches in different parts of Christian Europe too.[59]

The eleventh-century Hebrew family chronicle known as *Megillat Ahimaaz* (*Scroll of Ahimaaz*), from southern Italy, describes an imaginary meeting in Constantinople between the Italian rabbi Shephatiah and the Byzantine emperor Basil. The two debate the relative monetary value of the Temple in Jerusalem compared to the Hagia Sophia that Justinian built in Constantinople in 538. This Hebrew text, which survives in a single manuscript written for family reading about an illustrious past, reflects issues that bothered Jews and Christians alike about hierarchy in religious buildings.

The substitution of religious terms of the other with insult language is meant for the benefit of the Jewish reader. We see this insult language even in quotations of reported speech attributed to Christians with power, as we did in the speeches attributed in the Hebrew First Crusade chronicles. In the debate over the relative worth of the Temple of Solomon and Justinian's great Hagia Sophia (Holy Wisdom), the author refers to church as an "impure building" and the name of the building as Wisdom (*Sophia*), without the word Holy (*Hagia*), in order to denigrate it:

> The king then conversed with Shephatiah about the Torah. He asked him regarding the construction of the Temple and of the "impure building" (*binyan ha-tum'ah*) that is called by the name "Sophia": "Which one required more funds?" inquired the king. He insisted it was the construction of Sophia, for untold wealth had gone into this one building. But R. Shephatiah's response was correct and considered: "Let the king command that Scripture be brought before him; there he will find the answer as to which structure cost more." Immediately it was done, and the king found that the funds used by David and Solomon exceeded the measure weighed out for Sophia by 120 talents of gold and an additional 500 talents of silver. Thereupon the king conceded: "R. Shephatiah has excelled me in wisdom." But Shephatiah responded and said: "My lord, Scripture has prevailed against you, not I."[60]

The words the author puts in the emperor's mouth are a Jewish response to the tradition that Justinian proclaimed after dedicating the great church: "I have bested you, Solomon."[61] Here, the Jewish writer seeks to undermine the Christian triumph by reasserting the greater value of Solomon's Temple.

A more intentionally offensive version of a polemic over sacred architecture is found in an imaginary confrontation in the anonymously written Hebrew polemical handbook *Nizzahon Vetus*. Emperor Henry and Rabbi Qalonimos of Speyer argue over the comparative cost of the Temple of Solomon and the Speyer Cathedral (*Dom*) that was completed in 1106:

> *"Moses could not enter the Tent of Meeting ... and the presence of the Lord filled the Tabernacle"* (Ex. 40:35). The evil King Henry once called Rabbi Qalonymus of Spires after the former had completed the building

of the "ugly abyss" (*ha-tehom* [= Dom] *ha-mekho'ar*) in Speyer. The king asked him, "In what way was the building of the Temple greater than this so that several books should have been written about it?"

He answered, "My lord. If you will permit me to speak and swear that you will not harm me, then I shall explain it to you."

The king replied, "I swear. You may rely on my royal faithfulness that no evil will befall you."

Rabbi Qalonymus then told him, "If you would combine the money that you have already spent with all the gold and silver remaining in your treasury you would still be unable to hire sufficient workers and craftsmen to supervise and perform the work, for it is written, *'Solomon also had seventy thousand porters and eighty thousand quarriers in the hills'* (1 Kings 5:29), and the Chronicler adds, *'with three thousand six hundred men supervising them'* (2 Chron. 2:1). Moreover, they labored eight years to build the Temple, something that you did not do for this church. And regarding the time when Solomon completed the building, see what is written:

'And the priests were not able to remain and perform the service because of the cloud, for the Presence of the Lord filled the House of the Lord' (1 Kings 8:11).

In this case, however, if one were to load a donkey with vomit and (filth) [feces] and lead him through the church, he would remain unharmed."

The king replied, "If not for my oath, I would have you decapitated."[62]

Although the imagined confrontation presents a Jewish critique of the German cathedral and contrasts the presence of the Lord in the Jerusalem Temple to "vomit and feces" in the cathedral, the Jewish community of Speyer took advantage of the materials and architecture of the Dom to design and build their own synagogue and ritual bath. In so doing, they also acted out a polemics of sacred architecture by converting building materials used for the church to build a synagogue and other sacred Jewish structures.[63] The tactic of competing with Christianity by redeploying something used in the Christian cult for Jewish benefit will also be seen in connection with the Eucharist and Jewish wet nurses in chapter 5.

Private Encounters

The social history of Jewish-Christian debating and discussing religion is not limited to a few public debates or polemical handbooks that tend to dominate the scholarly literature as well as serve as an important baseline for social history. Much more difficult is to assemble the detailed evidence for everyday meetings that occurred.[64] A dynamic religious culture war developed between Jews and Christians at different levels of society well before Christian kings tried to put an end to it by removing Jews from their lands, and as we will see, even that did not end the Christian preoccupation with the imagined Jew who existed before and remained within Christian society after Jews were forced to emigrate.

In addition to insulting verbal plays on words, directed mainly to Jewish readers, Jewish verbal assertiveness was expressed in informal conversations between Jews and Christians about religion. Every day "debates" over religion took place even though these encounters are not always easy to overhear. Jews provoked Christians to defend their religious beliefs and practices that Jews thought were of no value. We lack quantitative data as to how frequently these took place, but there is more than enough anecdotal evidence to indicate that they were real.[65]

The aggressive Jewish attack on Christian beliefs is implied, for example, in one important Christian theological defensive tract from the twelfth century and made explicit in another. As Richard Southern observed, some of the Schoolmen in Paris were motivated to use the tools of logic and dialectic to reconcile apparently contradictory authoritative Christian sources and fashion a coherent personal theology expressly because Jews questioned and challenged their Christian neighbors. These Christians then pressured the theology faculty in Paris for clear, coherent answers. In his defense of the Incarnation, the main topic of Jewish-Christian debating in the twelfth century, Anselm of Canterbury wrote his *Cur Deus Homo* to defend the Incarnation against infidels, most likely including local Jews.[66] Even before Anselm's work appeared, his student Gilbert Crispin wrote a debate to argue with a Jew about the truth of Christianity; in a prologue, he explains,[67]

> To the Rev. Father and Lord Anselm, Archbishop of the holy Church of Canterbury, his servant and son, Brother Gilbert [Crispin], proctor and servant of Westminster Abbey, wisheth prosperous continuance in this life and a blissful eternity in the future one.
>
> I send you a little work to be submitted to your fatherly-prudence. I wrote it recently putting to paper what a Jew said when formerly disputing with me against our faith in defense of his own law, and what I replied in favour of the faith against his objections. I know not where he was born, but he was educated at Mayence; he was well versed even in our law and literature, and had a mind practised in the Scriptures and in disputes against us. He often used to come to me as a friend both for business and to see me, since in certain things I was very necessary to him, and as often as we came together we would soon be talking in a friendly spirit about the Scriptures and our faith. Now on a certain day, God granted both him and me greater leisure than usual, and soon we began questioning as usual. And as his objections were consequent and logical, and as he explained with equal consequence his former objections, while our reply met his objections foot to foot and by his own confession seemed equally supported by the testimony of the Scriptures, some of the bystanders requested me to preserve our disputes as likely to be of use to others in future.[68]

Here the initiative is taken by Jews who approach the learned Christian scholar. Similarly, the Jewish convert to Christianity Judah-Hermannus describes how he initiated a debate with Rupert of Deutz.[69]

Evidence of everyday encounters is found in several sources. Christian laws and Jewish admonitions prohibited such private discussions, and exempla in Latin and Hebrew reflect their likely occurrence from the twelfth century on. The trend to meet informally and debate points of religion was common enough that it was prohibited by twelfth-century councils—an indication that it was becoming known to authorities that were trying to control this public form of debate. In contrast to the great public disputations, the evidence about everyday arguments about religion shows that the Jews often took the initiative and were a source of concern for the Christian authorities. Such encounters were considered so dangerous to the faithful that church officials repeatedly tried to prevent Christians from arguing with Jews about religion.

For example, in 1200, in an addendum to the so-called Synodical Rules of Odo in Paris, we read, "Moreover, laymen shall, under pain of excommunication, be forbidden ever to dispute with Jews about the articles of the Christian faith." The Council of Trier in 1227, canon 8, elaborated, "We furthermore decree that ignorant clergymen shall not dispute with Jews in the presence of laity." At least one other council reiterated this concern in the same decade in the Council of Tarragon in 1233: "We decree absolutely forbidding any lay person to dispute about the Catholic faith whether publicly or privately."[70] Christians and Jews feared that they might lose an informal debate and a conversion might result. William of Malmesbury (1080–1143) reported that King William Rufus joked that had a Jew prevailed at a local debate, he would have converted to Judaism himself.[71] Other Christian authorities also advised caution debating with Jews.[72]

In Hebrew sources like *Sefer Hasidim*, we find a similar prohibition from the Jewish side, and the verbal confrontations between Jewish pietists and Christians in religious debates, "polemics" in the narrow sense, were to be regulated by hierarchical considerations. This may be seen from a commentary in *Sefer Hasidim* on two adjoining, but apparently contradictory, biblical verses that require a distinction to make them understood harmonistically. Thus Proverbs 26:4 reads, *Do not answer a dullard in accord with his folly, else you will become like him*; yet, the following verse continues, *Answer a dullard in accord with his folly, else he will think himself wise*. The Talmud cites these verses as an example of a blatant contradiction and resolves it by saying that the command to answer back refers to "matters of Torah" (*ha be-divrei torah*) and the admonition not to answer back refers to "ordinary matters" (*ha be-milei de-'alma*).[73] *Sefer Hasidim*, however, goes even further in its commentary and defines precisely when a pietist is to answer back, and when not, including in "matters of Torah" such as in discussions of polemics. Jews are advised to debate with a cleric only if they are experts and will not lose the argument:

> Suppose a monk or a priest or a learned and erudite sectarian or a non-pietist Talmudist who is busy chasing after his own reputation

approaches a pietist who is not as learned; or a learned person encounters a witch to debate (*le-hitvakeiah*) Torah. If he debates them, they might persuade him to follow them. About this it is written: *Do not answer a dullard in accord with his folly, else you will become like him.*" ... Even if you are more learned than he, do not permit a less learned person to listen to your debates (*vikkuhim*) because that person might be persuaded (by your opponent) since he does not understand (which position) is the true one. But if you are so learned (*hakham*) that you are confident you will defeat your opponent (*she-tenazheihu*) ... then *Answer a dullard in accord with his folly, else he will think himself wise.*[74]

In case of formal religious discussions, the relative strength of the opponents—in other words, their hierarchical positions—is the criterion that Judah the Pious invokes to determine whether contact should take place between pietists and Christians. His reasons were practical. The danger of debating in front of a person who was susceptible to being swayed by a more astute Christian debater was real, as we see from the following exemplum in Caesarius of Heisterbach's *Dialogue on Miracles* about the conversion of "the daughter of a Jew at Louvain":

> A little while ago the daughter of a Jew at Louvain was converted to the faith in the following manner. A clerk named Rener, chaplain to the Duke of Louvain, was in the habit of going to the house of this Jew to argue with him about the Christian faith. His daughter, then a little girl, would often listen eagerly to the discussion, and would weigh, as well as her intelligence allowed, both the arguments of the Jew her father and those of his clerical opponent. And so, little by little, she became by the providence of God, imbued with the Christian faith.[75]

Among Jewish polemical texts aimed at attacking Christianity, there is one that Judah Rosenthal published that reflects Jewish confidence and assertiveness toward Christian clergy. It is between a Jew and a monk (*galah*) and deals mainly with challenges to the Incarnation. It is not a Jewish defense of Christian attacks but instead a set of arguments for Jews to use when attacking monks:

> I ALSO PROVE TO YOU that (Jesus) is not God. You say that "he rode on an ass," as it says, (*Lo, your king is coming to you* ...) *riding on an*

ass (Zach. 9:9) refers to Jesus (Matt. 21:5; John 12:15). But is it not so that when the Holy One, blessed be He, gave the Torah on Mt. Sinai to Israel, it is written, *neither shall the flocks and the herds graze (at the foot of this mountain)* (Ex. 34:3)? If he commanded the flocks and herds, that are fit for sacrifices, not to *graze at the foot of this mountain* (ibid.), how could he himself ride on an unfit animal? Say further: When the Holy One, blessed be He gave the Torah, he commanded Israel, *(Be ready for the third day,) Do not go near a woman* (Ex. 19:15) for three days. If he himself was God, how could he enter a woman? And if you reply: She was pure but the other women were impure, if so, and she really was pure, why did she sacrifice two doves to atone for her impurity (Luke 2:24)? Thus, you see for certain that (Jesus) is not God.

A REPLY TO A MONK: Why are you not circumcised? Do you imagine yourself to be better or worse than Jesus? You know that Jesus was circumcised on the eighth day after he was born (Luke 2:21), in accord with what is written in the Torah of Moses, *On the eighth day the flesh of his foreskin shall be circumcised* (Lev. 12:3). And if he answers that the water of apostasy [i.e., baptism] takes the place of circumcision, tell him that (Jesus) submerged himself in the Jordan (only) at age thirty-three. You, too, should have done both: (first) circumcision and (then) baptism. And if you say that he did the wrong thing by being circumcised, then you want to be better than your God! What kind of a God do you have if you are better than he is?

It also says in Psalms, *I said rashly, all men are liars* (Ps. 116:11). If he were a man, as you claim, he would lie. And Scripture also commands, *Man cannot be God and lie* (Num. 23:19). If so, he was not God. Why don't you believe in the God who created the heavens and the earth, the seas and the depths? And it is also written in the Torah of Moses, *If your brother, your own mother's son, entices you* (Deut. 13:7). Why does it not say, "your father's son"? Know (from this) that Moses prophesied that a Jewish son would be born about whom the nations of the world [gentiles] would claim that he had no (human) father. Everything in that biblical section was a prophesy about Jesus. And so they stoned him and hanged him on a cabbage stalk [see *Life of Jesus*].[76]

Some handbooks, like R. Nathan Official's *Sefer ha-Meqaneh* and the anonymous *Nizzahon Vetus*, were designed to prepare Jews to confront Christians with passages from the Old Testament and New Testament at the ready. David Berger offers many examples of Jews informally debating to affirm Judaism and challenge Christians in the street.[77]

And once in a while we encounter an acting-out form of a Jewish anti-Christian polemic. Such was the case of Sampson son of Samuel of Northampton, who "assumed the habit of a Friar Minor [Franciscan], preaching certain things in contempt of the Christian faith." Although his fate is not known, he combined a verbal assault on Christianity with a gesture of impersonation and appropriation that bridges the realm of words and deeds, to be discussed in chapter 5.[78]

Jewish Knights as Goliaths

The challenge of Jews to Christian theologians was also expressed metaphorically as Jews imagining themselves as Jewish knights whom Christians saw as a threat.[79] In supporting Jewish self-confidence by denigrating Christian beliefs, Jewish writers saw Christian knights as foolish people who risked their own lives for a fleeting bit of earthly pleasure or benefit. Jews imagined themselves as the true knights, serving the true God.[80] The assertive Jew was an urban dweller engaged in several activities that included private banking or moneylending, or artisanal occupations, but he also imagined himself to be an aristocratic, landed, country knight.

With the image of Jews as knights came the implication that Christians were compared to squires or servants. This reversed the correct ecclesiastical hierarchical order between Jacob and Esau in favor of the Jews as Jacob and the church as Esau.[81] Sara Offenburg has shown abundant evidence from material culture that illustrates this as well.[82]

The central importance of personal honor in *Sefer Hasidim*, a sin the author opposes as the height of irreligion, is the mirror image of the knightly code of honor to which some Jews in Ashkenaz compared themselves. As Manford Harris observed long ago, the code of love reflected in *Sefer Hasidim* overlaps with romance literature.[83] One might even see in the comparisons in *Sefer Hasidim* to Christian knights as foils for pietist virtue a critique of Jews who saw themselves as such knights and the epitome of nonpietist behavior.

Sometimes Christians wrote as though they were Davids and certain Jews were threatening them as Goliaths—armed knights in fact. In this context, consider the anonymous *Tractatus*, written in 1166, which refers to Jewish Goliaths challenging Christian Davids to engage in battle or polemics: "I am writing, then, not to extol our (faith) but rather so that we give the Jews no cause to jeer at our ignorance, they who so frequently confront us and somewhat like Goliath say, 'Give me a man, that we may fight together'" (1 Sam 17:10).[84]

Jews retold and read stories about knightly battles, and decorated their walls with romances of knights, falcons, and ladies. Christians were as aware of such representations as Jews were of Christian sculptures of ecclesia and synagoga on the facades of cathedrals. The idea that medieval Jews in Christian Europe thought of themselves as knights is not as unlikely as it first sounds.[85] Even Christian peasants could think of themselves as knights, and since Jews were in a more favorable socioeconomic position than the vast peasant population of Christian Europe, they certainly could and did.[86]

There are many examples that show how comfortable Jewish patrons were illustrating their religious texts with images of knights in battle. Rashi mentions that Jews decorated their homes with paintings with inscriptions that were not supposed to be read on the Sabbath, and they included battles and pictures about David and Goliath: "It is like people who draw on the wall strange animals or images of people doing great deeds such as the battle between David and Goliath and they write underneath: 'This is the image of such and such an animal and this is the image of so and so.'"[87] From the late Middle Ages, there is a private Jewish house in Zurich with walls painted with illustrations of the aristocratic life of falconry, and this association is another example of Jews familiar with and identifying as aristocratic knights.[88]

Another aspect of this is reflected in some Hebrew texts that have been preserved that represent Judaized versions of courtly or romance literature that deal with knightly adventures. For example, the earliest passage of preserved Yiddish is a romance fragment scratched on a roof slate found in the rubble layer of the community of Cologne from 1348.[89] The interest some Jews showed in thinking about themselves as knights and the Christian majority as servants was another sign of Jewish assertiveness that enabled Jews to resist Christian blandishments.

In the long twelfth century, from the mid-eleventh to the mid-thirteenth centuries, Christians rethought their own religious culture in new ways partly to differentiate themselves from Jews. At the same time, Jews asserted the truth of Judaism by denigrating Christianity. Each understood themselves increasingly as not the other, and in so doing, redefined themselves as a mirror image of the other they rejected.

The rabbinic view of Christianity as idolatry took different forms but focused more on its religious practices than on the people who followed it. With few exceptions, the northern rabbis considered Christianity to be idolatry and referred to Latin as the language of priests and monks. Sometimes hostile words turned into gestures of contempt that Jews acted out toward Christian sancta.

CHAPTER FIVE

Offensive Gestures

LATRINE BLASPHEMY

IN ADDITION TO using words of contempt to insult Christianity, Jews expressed their assertiveness in specific acts and gestures of disgust directed at Christian sancta. In many ways, they asserted strong religious views about the Christian other, and in so doing, acted out a challenge to Christianity. These acts included spitting at crosses, placing Christian icons in latrines, urinating or defecating on Christian symbols, and farting in a Christian setting, all of which are examples of "latrine blasphemy."[1] Such behavior was designed to insult and ridicule Christianity, which Jews equated with bodily elimination and idolatry, and by contrast assert the truth and holiness of Judaism.[2]

Both religious cultures tried to isolate the holy from bodily excretions, but the target of each culture's latrine blasphemy was different. Jews associated *Christianity* with feces; Christians did so with *Jews*.

Jewish acts of latrine blasphemy did not go unnoticed.[3] Jews were accused of putting ecclesiastical vessels, for example, into latrines. Sometimes Christian leaders had difficulty saying this explicitly. Consider again the complaint of clerics, such as Peter the Venerable's letter to Louis VII, king of France, and note Peter's assumptions about what Jews do to make them worse than Saracens:

> What good is it to pursue and persecute the enemies of the Christian faith in far and distant lands if the Jews, vile blasphemers and far

worse than the Saracens, not far away from us but right in our midst, blaspheme, abuse, and trample on Christ and the Christian sacraments so freely and insolently and with impunity?[4]

The letter goes further and accuses Jews of abusing ecclesiastical vessels that they held as pawns against loans: "They use those heavenly vessels for their evil uses, to the disgrace of Christ and ourselves, things too horrifying to consider and detestable to mention."[5]

Peter's rationale for treating Jews as nearby enemies—because they "blaspheme, abuse, and trample on Christ and the Christian sacraments" and "use heavenly vessels for their evil uses"—adds some concreteness to the argument some chroniclers offered after 1096 that the Crusaders should seek vengeance not only for the Jews' ancient crime of killing Jesus but also because they are a people "who disrespect our god" (Solomon b. Samson), "hate [our religion]" (Ovadia the Proselyte), and are "the worst foes of God" (Guibert de Nogent) (see chapter 3). But we are still not sure exactly what he is talking about.

In the late twelfth century, as Philip Augustus, king of France, was considering what to do with his Jews in the tiny royal territory around Paris that he was about to expand into the Kingdom of France, his court biographer, Rigord (ca. 1150–1209), noted that Jews were capable of latrine blasphemy.

> At that time, the Jews were afraid that their houses might be ransacked by royal officials. It happened that a certain Jew, who at the time was staying in Paris, held certain ecclesiastical objects as pledges. He had a gold cross, marked with gems, a book of the Gospels decorated with gold and precious stones in an extraordinary manner, silver cups, and other vessels. He placed them all in a sack and vilely threw it into the deep pit where he used to relieve himself (for shame!).
>
> A short time afterwards, Christians discovered the objects in that very place—God having shown the way. The objects were all returned to their own church with great joy and honor, a fifth of the debt having been paid to the lord king of all that was owed.[6]

The consequences of such behavior could be disastrous (see below).

As we saw, the most powerful of medieval popes, Innocent III, accused Jews not only of hiring Christian servants and wet nurses but also of making them express their milk into a latrine after they had taken communion on Easter.[7] We will consider this letter below in connection with how Jews looked at the Eucharist and why they associated it with latrines.

Jews, for their part, did not accuse Christians of putting Jewish ritual objects, such as Torah scrolls, into latrines. Instead, they described Christians tearing up Torah scrolls and trampling them in the mud—not the same thing.[8] Christians did associate *Jews* with feces and money, but not Jewish sancta. For example, the "Jew of Tewkesbury," from Ranulph Higden's *Polychronicon*, is a sardonic story about a Jew who falls into a latrine on his Sabbath and refuses to be rescued:

> About that time [1258] at Tewkesbury a certain Jew fell into a latrine on a Saturday but would not permit himself to be extracted, out of reverence for his Sabbath. But Richard de Clare, count of Gloucester, did not permit him to be extracted the following Sunday out of reverence for his Sabbath. And so, the Jew died.[9]

Acts of Jewish assertiveness were designed as part of a strategy not only to resist pressure to conform to Christian expectations of them but also to express outrage to Christians about their religion, to say to them that it was not a religion at all but idolatry.[10] Jews assertively insulted Christian sancta in northern Europe during most of the two hundred years of relative peace that followed the 1096 First Crusade riots. Christians accused Jews of insulting Christian sacred objects, such as those used in the liturgy or images of Jesus or Mary, by putting them into latrines. This was the most offensive act imaginable, since Jews and Christians both considered bodily elimination to be the opposite of the holy.[11]

Of course, there was always danger and concern about popular or judicial violence from leaders, but Jews also gained much by living on the edge, and that included having to calculate the risk-benefit ratio of acting out against Christian symbols that they loathed even if they were sometimes attracted to some of the ways Christians behaved.

Jewish assertiveness was partly responsible for Christian alarm and led to new efforts to contain and subordinate Jews. Two mutually exclusive religious cultures were trying to coexist, and this cultural friction made an impression on each. Christians needed certain images of the Jew to understand themselves better as their opposite; Jews, in turn, came to imagine themselves as inverted mirror images of the Christian other.[12]

"Polemic of Filth"

Judaism has an elaborate system of ritual purity and impurity that emphasizes bodily fluids related to reproduction and life-giving substances, such as blood and semen.[13] Judaism does not consider human waste products, especially feces and urine or even saliva, to be impure or generate impurity.[14] A related but separate category of practices is concerned with bodily excretion and is in opposition to the category of the holy. In Christianity, too, the category of the holy or "spirit" is viewed as the antithesis of filth and elimination of the "body."[15]

The study of bodily waste has become a new way of approaching Jewish-Christian interactions. It is an extension of "body studies," which has been used as an approach to the role of women in history and is sometimes given the term "elimination studies" but is also important for better understanding Jewish-Christian encounters in medieval society and imagination.[16]

Alexandra Cuffel discusses many of these associations in her book *Gendering Disgust* and includes how Islam fits into the larger picture of what she aptly calls the "polemic of filth." Jewish physical assertiveness assumed many forms. It is difficult to know how widespread these acts were, but the sources suggest that in their variety and distribution, we are not dealing with just a few isolated incidents.[17]

Here I would like to develop further the different Jewish and Christian associations of bodily excretions—a difference that tells us about how Jews asserted their own truth claims in relation to Christianity.[18] Jews were concerned to separate their holy activities from bodily elimination. This is typical of rabbinic literature and exaggerated in medieval Europe as in *Sefer Hasidim*, where a Torah student should not think about Torah when in the latrine or talk in a latrine in Hebrew about holy matters, or even about other matters.[19] Another exemplum supposes that a second story was added to a building where there had been a latrine. If any feces remain there, it is not proper for there to be a place of worship upstairs until it is covered over with dirt.[20]

> [Or] if a man's house has a window that faces the street in which people pass by on their way to the synagogue, neither those who sleep upstairs nor a Jew should pour urine out of the window into the street. People go to the synagogue very early in the morning, and those who walk there in the dark will not be able to take care not to become soiled by the urine on their way to the synagogue. And it is written, *Guard your foot when you go to the house of God* (Eccl. 4:17).[21]

In contrast, Jews view Christianity as bodily elimination. One reason is found in ancient Jewish sources that equate idolatry and Jesus with feces. In a rabbinic passage that considers how a pagan might be able to cancel the religious power of an idol, the Mishnah (early third century CE) proposes acts involving secretions and excretions that it assumes are the antithesis of the holy: spitting, urinating, throwing feces, and dirt: "How does (a pagan) cancel (the status of an idol as an object of worship?) . . . If he spat before (the idol), urinated before it, dragged it, threw feces at it, it is not cancelled."[22]

In the Book of Numbers, an incident is described about Israelites who are enticed by the women of Moab to follow their pagan cult known as Ba'al-Pe'or (Num. 25:1–3). The Mishnah and Talmud, followed by Rashi, all interpret the name "pe'or" from the Hebrew as meaning "to defecate," and say that the god was worshipped by followers defecating in front of or on it.[23]

The text begins by indicating ways that a pagan can "neutralize" an idol and thereby make it usable for a Jew: "How does he neutralize it? If he cut off the tip of its ear, the tip of its nose, or the tip of its finger; or if he defaced it, although there was no reduction in the mass of the material, he has neutralized it." The text continues with pagan acts that cannot neutralize an idol because they are forms of worshipping it: "When someone defecates in front of/on the idol known as Ba'al-Pe'or, he is liable to receive capital punishment, even though defecating is a degrading act, because that is the way it is worshiped."[24]

This association between worship of the idol known as Ba'al-Pe'or and feces is also stated elsewhere in the Mishnah: "One who defecates before Baʻal-Peʻor is its (form of) worship."²⁵ In addition to this classical association of pagan religion with feces, the Talmud reports that Jesus of Nazareth is in hell in boiling excrement.²⁶ These traditions reinforced the association of Christianity with both paganism and feces.

A second reason Jews developed an association of Jesus with bodily filth in acts of latrine blasphemy is as a social polemic against the Incarnation. Jewish authors express disbelief and horror that God could be inside the body of a woman. Earlier polemics going back to ancient times asked how could God be inside a filthy woman's stomach that empties into a latrine. Christianity, not Judaism, has an internal contradiction: holy should be the opposite of feces and urine, but the Incarnation puts them together. To deny the Incarnation, Jews act out by putting Jesus (and Mary) into a latrine, which is like a woman's body from which Christians say Jesus came.²⁷ We see this association of Jesus and the latrine, for example, in a Latin polemical work by Odo of Cambrai (1050–1113) in which the Jew, Leo, raises doubts about the God-Man Jesus by pointing out the absurdity of Jesus being inside "his mother's womb, surrounded by a vile fluid"—a figure that despiritualizes Jesus and Mary.²⁸

Placing Christian sancta into latrines ritualizes Jewish contempt for Christianity as the opposite of the holy. At the same time, it affirms the truth and sanctity of Judaism. Associating Christianity with bodily fluids or waste was a prominent aspect of Jewish assertiveness in the Hebrew chronicles about 1096. In one situation, R. Eliezer b. Nathan says about the Jews of Worms that "in the end they regarded the object of the enemy's veneration as no more than slime and dung (*tit ve-zo'ah*).²⁹

Latrines

Jewish rules about praying either in synagogue or at home try to isolate prayer from either ritual impurity or bodily elimination—different categories, but both to be separated from the act of praying and the holy. The marital bed that might have semen on it or clothing that might be stained with semen, a source of ritual impurity, are to be kept separate from holy activities, but small children are also a problem because they might urinate on or soil the father holding the baby during prayer.

Christian authorities accuse Jews of desecration by using latrines as places to put Christian sancta. Latrines feature prominently in stories about ritual murders, starting with Thomas of Monmouth's *Vita of William*, and this emphasis serves to contrast alleged Jewish behavior with the purity of the Eucharist. In his account of the ritual murder of William of Norwich, Thomas says that the Jews rejected putting the boy's body in their latrine because that is where the Christian authorities would look first. Using latrines for nefarious purposes was assumed to be Jewish behavior as much as their killing a young Christlike boy.[30]

Most of our Latin sources were written by clerics, and as one would expect, they expressed horror at the blasphemous ways they thought Jews behaved. A leitmotif insists on seeing Christian sancta in latrines as among the most horrifying act Jews could think of doing to achieve this reaction. It is also prominently featured in the *Chronica Maiora* of Matthew Paris. He refers to the way Hugh of Lincoln was attacked in 1255. Although Matthew actually says that Hugh was found in a well, that detail was transformed in other versions in light of Jews disposing of Christian bodies in latrines, as in the case below, and it reappears in Chaucer's *The Prioress's Tale* too (see chapter 8).[31] Matthew also describes another Jew getting away with latrine blasphemy:

> There was a quite rich Jew, Abraham by name but not in faith, who lived and had property in Berkhamstead and Wallingford. He was friendly with Earl Richard for some improper reason or other. He had a beautiful and faithful wife called Floria. In order to dishonour Christ the more, this Jew bought a nicely carved and painted statue of the blessed Virgin, as usual nursing her son at her bosom. This image the Jew set up in his latrine and, what is thoroughly dishonourable and ignominious to mention, as it were in blasphemy of the blessed Virgin, he inflicted a filthy and unmentionable thing on it, daily and nightly, and ordered his wife to do the same. Noticing this after some days, by reason of her sex, she felt sorry and, going there secretly, washed the dirt from the face of the disgracefully defiled statue. When the Jew her husband found out the truth of this, he impiously and secretly suffocated

his wife. However, these crimes were discovered and the Jew, clearly proved guilty, although there were other grounds for putting him to death, was thrust into the foulest dungeon in the Tower of London. In a bid to be freed, he promised most positively that he would prove all the Jews of England to be the basest traitors. [Text continues in the margin:] Thereupon he was accused by almost all the English Jews who tried to put him to death, but Earl Richard spoke up for him. So, the Jews, accusing him of clipping coins and other serious crimes, offered the earl a thousand marks to stop protecting him, which however the earl refused because the Jew was said to be his. This Jew Abraham then paid the king seven hundred marks so that, with the help of the earl, he could be freed from the life imprisonment to which he had been condemned.[32]

Other examples have been noted in the sources in recent studies. They seem to be everywhere.[33]

Spitting

Showing contempt by spitting has an ancient pedigree and is well documented in the Hebrew Bible and New Testament. It is ritualized in the Book of Deuteronomy, in connection with the commandment about the levirate marriage in which a brother must marry his widowed, childless sister-in-law. If the brother-in-law of the childless widow who wishes to marry him refuses (*yibbum*), *his brother's widow shall go up to him in the presence of the elders, pull the sandal off his foot, spit in his face, and make this declaration: Thus, shall be done to the man who will not build up his brother's house!* (Deut. 25:9).[34] Elsewhere in the Hebrew Bible, too, spitting in the face is a sign of humiliation, as in *They do not withhold spittle from my face* (Job 30:10).

In the New Testament, people spit on Jesus to insult him: *They spat on him* (Matt. 27:30), *and spit upon him* (Mark 10:34), *then some began to spit at him* (Mark 14:65), *spat upon him* (Mark 15:19), *and spat* (Luke 14:32). There is a contrasting curative use to saliva in the New Testament in the case when Jesus restores the sight of a blind man (Mark 8:23; cf. John 9:6), but this is not done by spitting on him.[35]

In the Mishnah, from early third-century Palestine, spitting is to be avoided in synagogues yet permitted at home, but there is an opinion of Rava (ca. 280–352 CE) in the Babylonian Talmud that one may spit in the synagogue as in one's house.[36] This issue continued to be discussed in medieval Germany, such as in *Sefer Hasidim*.[37]

Spitting on a Cross

The cross as the symbol of Christianity, like the Eucharist, can embody Jesus and was the target of Jewish gestures of abuse, like spitting or urinating, but it also could become attractive, as in the case of Yom Tov of England, who became attracted to it and committed suicide.[38]

In the 1096 Hebrew chronicles, we see spitting as a vehicle to express Jewish contempt for Christianity. So Isaac son of Elyakim was grabbed outside his house and taken to "their house of idolatry," where "he spat at them and at the object of their idolatry (i.e., a cross) and he reviled and ridiculed them" before they killed him.[39] In episodes connected with the Second Crusade, R. Ephraim of Bonn mentions the instance of a Jew named Qalonimos of Bacharach who "openly spat on the image of the crucified one and they slew him on the spot."[40] The sister of Simon ben Isaac of Würzburg was taken to a church to be baptized (literally to their "place of idolatry" so as to "profane" her), but "she sanctified the Name and spat upon the abomination (cross)."[41]

Urinating (or Trampling) on a Cross

There are other incidents that involve Jews and the cross, including individuals urinating on a cross to show contempt for Christianity. In Oxford in 1222, English chronicler Matthew Paris describes a deacon who became so involved with a Jewish woman that he converted to Judaism and showed contempt for his former religion by urinating on a cross.[42] Related is a case that also took place in Oxford, on Ascension Day in 1268, during the reign of Henry III. It is preserved in eighteenth-century historian D'Blossier Tovey's *Anglo-Judaica*, which describes a cross being paraded in town: "A certain Jew of the most consummate impudence violently snatched it from the bearer, and trod it under his feet, in token of his contempt for Christ."[43] The king became involved and forced the local Jewish community to make restitution.[44]

In mid-thirteenth-century France, R. Joseph Official refers to an incident he claimed took place between his father, R. Nathan, and a Christian count:

> Once my lord and father, Rabbi Nathan, may he rest in Paradise, was riding alongside the Count of Sens. The count got off his horse opposite a bush in order to urinate. My lord and father saw him, and he too got off his horse opposite an abomination (*to'eivah*) and urinated on it. The Count saw it and objected. (The Count) said to him, "It is not proper to do that and make the cross smell bad." My father replied, "To the contrary, *it was a foolish thing for you to do* (Genesis 31:28). (And this is why:) You urinated on a bush, on which the Holy One, Blessed be He, radiated His Presence only for salvation [i.e., the burning bush, Exodus 3:1–3]. (However,) this (abomination) [i.e., the cross], on which you (Christians) say that (the god) you fear, was defeated, stank, and rotted, it is right that you should expose yourself and eliminate all over it!"[45]

Was it safe to do this? Also writing in Hebrew for the benefit of a Jewish audience, Judah the Pious tells a story in *Sefer Hasidim* that a Jew had to be cautious when acting out views about Christianity because blasphemous gestures could be dangerous.[46]

> A (Jew) wanted to relieve himself (on or near a Christian image). His companion said to him, "They might kill you (if you do it there)." He said, "It is for the sanctification of the Name (of God)!" The other one replied, "You will have no reward but will be sinning if you jeopardize your life. Moreover, don't jeopardize your children and the other (Jewish) residents of the town. That which is written, *I should be sanctified in the midst of the children of Israel* (Lev. 22:32) refers to when gentiles are oppressing one (by threatening), 'If he doesn't do such and such, they will kill him.' It is also written, *It is for Your sake that we are killed all day long* (Ps. 44:23). But if one causes himself to be killed, about him it is written, *But for your own life-blood I will require a reckoning* (Gen. 9:5), and it is (also) written, *Preserve well your life* (Deut. 4:9)."[47]

The author counters proof texts justifying martyrdom with one admonishing against suicide. Of interest in this exemplum is not whether this kind of situation actually occurred but rather that the author thought it could happen and warned his readers to be careful and not risk sinning. Also inhibiting some pietist Jews was the ancient precedent of the scatological worship of idols, the case of Ba'al-Pe'or mentioned earlier: "Nor should one think, 'Because they used to expose themselves (to idols in antiquity), I will insult idolatry (now) by urinating or defecating on it.'"[48] There was no point in a Jew insulting a Christian "idol" by reenacting a pagan rite. But as in much of *Sefer Hasidim*, the standards the pietists held up for themselves did not jibe with what other Jews did.

Another sign of Jewish antagonism to the cross is seen in an exegetical passage embedded in a polemical handbook from late medieval Germany, the *Nizzahon Vetus*. It involves insulting a cross by sitting on it.

> The apostates say: If "there is a basis (lit., mother) to tradition," then one should consider the fact that in the verse, *Then Israel bowed at the head of the bed* (Gen. 47:31), the Hebrew word for bed (*mittah*) is written without a *yod* and can therefore be read *matteh*, which means "staff"? Consequently, it is probable that it was customary to place a cross at the head of dying men, and it was to the cross that Jacob bowed.
>
> One may answer them according to their own foolishness and say that Jacob was distraught as a result of his illness, and he therefore bowed to the cross. But when he came to his senses, he changed his mind and regretted what he has done, as it is written, *And he sat up on the bed* (or staff) (Gen. 48:2). Thus, Jacob put it under his anus.[49]

The association here of elimination and a Christian symbol is consistent with the other examples of latrine blasphemy, which were all designed to express contempt for Christianity.

Farting

As suggested by the passage from *Sefer Hasidim*, Jews were considering the option of insulting Christian symbols by associating them with bodily elimination of some kind. An example, not previously understood, involves farting as an expression of contempt. This form of acting out is shared by many cultures that seek to show agency without risk of punishment. Thus James C. Scott refers to an Ethiopian proverb, "When the great lord passes, the wise peasant bows deeply and silently farts."[50]

Scholars have been aware of how this physical act can be used in social polemics.[51] There is concern to avoid farting in sacred spaces as in the synagogue or generally as in *Sefer Hasidim*:

> And even though it says, *The remnant of Israel shall do no wrong and speak no falsehood* (Zeph. 3:13), one may say, I made a mistake... like the story about a woman whom the heads of the community approached about *halitzah* [release from the levirate marriage]. She farted. One of the men said, "What of it? *I* did it because I needed to relieve myself and I was embarrassed to go out." (He lied) so that the woman would not be embarrassed.[52]

One should also cover holy objects if one cannot avoid doing it in close proximity to them.[53]

In the Hebrew First Crusade chronicles, translators have missed two additional examples that show Jews asserting themselves by farting in moments of religious confrontation. The passages refer to Jews in Xanten and Trier. In the first,

> Natronai, son of Isaac, a wholehearted man, was also there. His acquaintances the priests had come to him throughout the entire previous day attempting to persuade him to defile himself in their evil waters, for he was a handsome man, pleasant to the sight. He threw a (branch) [melody] in their faces (*ve-zaraq zemorah be-fihem*) and said: "God forbid that I should deny God-on-High; I will trust in Him until my soul expires." He slaughtered his brother and then himself, in witness to the Oneness of the One Holy Name."[54]

In Trier,

> they then led Asher, son of Joseph, the Gabbai, outside to kill him so as to instill fear and terror in the rest so that they would acknowledge their error. Asher called out: "Who amongst you of the entire nation of the Lord—may his God be with him—will come forward: one who desires to receive and welcome the Divine Presence—and in that world which lavishes an abundance of goodness in the space of a few moments?"

A youth named Meir, the son of Samuel, spoke up and said: "Wait, I desire to accompany you to the World-that-is-All-Light, and with you I will bear witness to the Oneness of the One, Venerable, and Awesome Name—wholeheartedly and willingly." When they emerged from the door of the Palais, the crucified one was brought before them so that they would bow to him. They cast a (branch) [melody] at the abomination (*ve-hittilu zemorah 'al ha-to'eivah*), and the two pious men were slain in sanctification of the Name.[55]

Elliott Horowitz proposed that the word *zemorah*, which Shlomo Eidelberg translated as "branch," was based on the verse, *They reached the wadi Eshcol, and there they cut down a branch (zemorah) with a single cluster of grapes* (Num. 13:23). If so, the enigmatic phrase "threw a *zemorah*" might be a euphemism for the Jewish martyrs in Xanten and Trier exposing themselves and either urinating or showing a readiness to do so. Although Horowitz mentions a note by Eidelberg, "The reference is to an act of distain toward the offered baptismal rites," he neglected to quote another part of it, "After Ezekiel 8:17." The medieval interpretation of that verse holds the key to the phrase as referring to an entirely different gesture.[56] Although it is possible to imagine that the two Jewish men would take the time needed to undress to expose a circumcised penis in front of the cross, the expression means something else.

The NJPS *Tanakh* renders the verse in Ezekiel as, "And thrust the branch to their nostrils" (*ve-hinam sholehim et ha-zemorah el apam*) (Ezek. 8:17).[57] The verb in the verse, *sholehim*, is replaced in the chronicle by *shalah* or the verb *hittilu*, but the meaning is "thrust." Rashi on Ezekiel 8:17 leaves nothing to the imagination:

> Behold they send to their nose the foul odor of this "song" (*zemoruh = zemirah*), which they "sing" (*mezammerim*) with the wind emerging from their anus; i.e., this disgrace of theirs will come back to their faces.

The Hebrew *zemorah* can refer to a "branch," or "rod" as in Num. 13:23, but here it is a musical sound (*zemirah*) as in Ezekiel 8:17. The meaning is that the two men turned their back on the cross and farted, and not so silently, thereby assuring their immediate death.[58]

Jewish Awareness of the Eucharist and Mocking It

The letter of Pope Innocent III accusing Jews of making their Christian wet nurses pour their milk into the latrine after taking communion on Easter, to be discussed shortly, raises the question of how Jews viewed the Eucharist, the increasingly central rite of Christian worship. Besides formal polemics that shed light on Jewish denial of any religious meaning or truth of the doctrine of transubstantiation's belief in the real presence of Christ in the bread and wine, we get glimpses of how Jews looked at it or how Christians imagined Jews did, both in social polemics and in stories about certain gestures in everyday living.

An early Christian example is the passage in Benedictine Guibert of Nogent's *Autobiographie*, where he describes a black Mass in which a Jew mocks the sacrifice by offering semen instead of bread and wine.[59] Shortly thereafter, the Cistercian monk Caesarius of Heisterbach writes in the early thirteenth century about a Jew whose daughter became romantically involved with a local cleric, confronts the local bishop with other Jews in the church on Good Friday, and stands there struck dumb, mouth agape, as the clerics take communion. The bishop assumes that the Jews are mocking the Eucharist; their open mouths seem to the bishop to be denigrating the act of Christians receiving the wafer at the holiest moment in the year.[60]

These Christian clerical perspectives see Jews as blaspheming or mocking the Eucharist. A learned Jewish view is found in the gloss to the Talmud that deals with "foreign worship" ('avodah zarah). In his comment on the Mishnaic law that prohibits Jews from doing business with idolaters for three days before their holiday, R. Jacob b. Meir (Rabbeinu Tam, d. 1171) restricts the meaning of the text to prohibit only selling to Christians "objects used in the sacrifice" (*midei de-tiqrovet*)—that is, items used in the Mass. Here we see some awareness on the part of Rabbeinu Tam of what was involved in the Christian liturgy. The ruling means that R. Jacob considered the Eucharist to involve a form of idolatry and must be taken seriously. As Moshe Halbertal and Avishai Margalit point out, Rabbeinu Tam's interpretation permitted Jews to do business with Christians because it restricted the prohibition only to selling Christians what they needed for the eucharistic sacrifice.[61]

Jewish moneylenders regularly received valuable ecclesiastical objects such as liturgical books and chalices as collateral against loans, or as forfeited property for the nonpayment of loans. When royal biographer Rigord wrote that Jews blasphemed the church by abusing holy vessels in their care as pawns, it is not clear if there was some actual Jewish behavior behind the Christian accusation, or whether it was unsubstantiated rumor or fantasy. We do have reason to believe that Jews were familiar with Christian religious objects because religious leaders took pains to warn Jews about them.

In an unusual case from Bristol, England, in 1265, several Jews were excommunicated by ecclesiastical authorities because they "were guilty of iniquitous insults, blasphemies, and injuries and of an assault upon a chaplain . . . who had administered the holy Eucharist to a sick person in the Jewry."[62]

How medieval Jews looked at the Eucharist may also be inferred from Pope Innocent III's letter, mentioned earlier, that claims that Jews insult the Eucharist by indirectly putting it into their latrines. The case involves Jews hiring Christian wet nurses for their infants. The church continued to insist, without much success, that Jews should not hire Christian servants, including wet nurses.[63] See, for example, the council in Rouen (1074), Third Lateran Council (1179), and councils in Montpellier (1195), Paris, (1213), and Tarragona (1239). It was insulting enough for Jewish families to employ young Christian women as servants and wet nurses for their newborns, a practice associated more with aristocratic Christian households than with even middle-class Christian families.[64] This social fact aligns Jewish families that did so with aristocratic Christian domestic behavior and itself would be offensive to a reform pope. Popes railed repeatedly against this common practice. Jews were concerned that if their infants were farmed out to Christian wet nurses, they would be in danger of being killed, or if older, converted. Church authorities were equally concerned that young Christian women working for Jews in their homes would be attracted to Judaism.[65]

We hear complaints that Jews were not only hiring Christian servants including wet nurses but doing something worse too. One of the best-known illustrations of latrine blasphemy is found in *Etsi Judeos*, a letter Pope Innocent III wrote to the archbishop of Sens and bishop of Paris on July 15, 1205.[66] In it he noted that he had also written to the king of France, duke of Burgundy, and countess of Champagne to "forbid (their Jews) to have any nurses or other kinds of Christian servants in the future" on penalty of Christians not being able to have any commercial relations with their Jews.[67]

But Innocent also accused Jews of something we know about only from this letter, although it is one of several allegations that involve Jews blaspheming Christian sancta by connecting them with latrines. The text has been translated differently in the scholarly literature. Until recently, Solomon Grayzel's translation has been adopted. According to Grayzel, Innocent claimed the following:

> Thus, whenever it happens that on the day of the Lord's Resurrection [Easter] the Christian women who are nurses for the Jews, take in the body and blood of Jesus Christ, the Jews make these women pour their milk into the latrine for three days before they again give suck to the children.[68]

Here, in Grayzel's translation, the pope claims that Jewish parents prevent the Christian wet nurse from nursing their child "for three days" (*per triduum*), during which they make the wet nurse express their milk into the latrine. Only after doing this for three days are they permitted to nurse the infant again.

The pope seems to think that Jews knew about the power of the Eucharist, and they wanted to insult it so much that they were ready to starve their infants for three days. The Jews thought that the host might harm their child and were ready to act cruelly toward their own child to prevent contact.[69]

The polemical gesture attributed to the Jews, then, is twofold: they wanted to insult the Eucharist and keep it from possibly contaminating or harming their children. Whatever the understanding of the relationship between ingestion and lactation was, this interpretation means that the Jewish family wished to identify the milk as the product of the ingested host and thus associate the body of Christ with elimination into a latrine in the form of the expressed milk.[70]

Jeremy Cohen has offered a better interpretation of Innocent's letter.[71] He understands Innocent to be describing Jews making the Christian wet nurses express *some* of their milk into a latrine during the three days after they took communion, but on each of those three days after they expressed some of it into the latrine, they then did nurse the Jewish child. They were not made to wait until three days had passed to nurse the Jewish infant "again," as Grayzel translates it.

Here is the Latin as Grayzel published it: "Faciunt enim Christianas filiorum suorum nutrices, cum in die Ressurectionis Dominice illas recipere corpus et sanguinem Jesu Christi contingit, per triduum; antequam eos lactent, lac effundere in latrinam." Read simply, as Cohen does, the last nine words of the Latin say that "during three days, before they nurse the baby, they pour milk into the latrine." This seems to say that on each of three days (*triduum*), after the wet nurses have ingested the host, they pour out some milk into the latrine and then nurse the baby. This is the simple meaning of the Latin, although the words are not as clearly phrased as they could be, and Grayzel's semicolon after "triduum" should be a comma, connecting, not separating, what comes afterward. According to Cohen's interpretation, Innocent did not think that Jews withheld the milk from their children for three whole days, "nor would it attribute to the Jewish parents the presumption that the host in their nurses' bodies had become the flesh and blood of the crucified Jesus" and could contaminate their babies, and thus was not fit for their child to ingest.[72] Innocent's focus is only on the Jews insulting Christ in the host along with the outrage of Jews hiring Christian servants and wet nurses in their homes, violating right order.

Did this Jewish ritual exist? We do not know. It is possible given the widespread discussion of latrine blasphemy in the sources. There is no indication that this practice was investigated and disproven, such as the blood libel to be discussed in chapter 6. The ritualization of three days is widespread in different cultures, among them the Hebrew Bible, such as the purification for three days before the theophany at Mt. Sinai (Ex. 19) or Esther's fasting for three days (Esther 4:16), in the New Testament in the three days after the crucifixion and Jesus's rising, and Paul's fasting for three days (Acts 9:9). Three days is a common motif in folklore as well, and in some cases, it had legal consequences, as in the time Jews had to consider whether to convert. In the Hebrew story about Amnon of Mainz, he waits three days before refusing to convert, reinforced by Christian law that gave potential voluntary converts three days to decide.[73]

In contrast to the situation in Innocent III's 1205 letter, earlier in medieval Germany the Hebrew chronicle associated with Solomon bar Samson claims that

> when they had fulfilled their intention to fast three days, day and night— boy and girl, babe and suckling, along with old men—their tongues clung to their palates from thirst. Babes did not suckle at their mother's breasts before they were slaughtered. It was on the third day that they readied themselves and make haste to perform the command of their Creator and to demonstrate their love for Him even unto death![74]

This extreme situation alone justified mothers depriving their infants of food and makes the situation assumed in 1205 to be just as Cohen has suggested. Note that "per triduum" echoes the Catholic period of three days from Maunday Thursday through the Saturday before Easter, a period known as "triduum paschis." The Jewish rite of blaspheming the church, then, involved the same number of days as the holy three days of the church.

Cohen supports his interpretation that Innocent is possibly describing a Jewish rite involving the Christian wet nurses partially pouring out their milk into a latrine by referring to Caesarius of Heisterbach's exemplum where a Jewish mother is pictured trying to undo her daughter's baptism by passing her over the opening of a latrine three times.[75] This alleged rite, Cohen argues, suggests that Jews used gestures of three to insult the church in latrines. That is a definite possibility.

We also have evidence from Bernard Gui in his *Inquisitor's Manual* that Jews tried to undo the baptism of conversos or New Christians by rubbing with sand the parts of the body that had been touched by holy liquid.[76] The case of baptism, a rite that affects the surface of parts of the body, might be neutralized by acts that are done to the external body. In contrast, the Eucharist that is ingested could be negated only by eliminating it from the body—here by the wet nurse expressing the milk into the latrine, a ritualized enactment of the Talmudic tradition that Jesus is in hell in boiling excrement.

What, then, did Jews think about the Eucharist? Miri Rubin's claim that Jews thought the host was a joke is too dismissive.[77]

Jews understood that *Christians* thought it was Jesus, and treated it accordingly in order to insult and show their contempt for it, but this did not mean that they would keep it from their children.

Moreover, having the Christian wet nurse continue to feed the Jewish infant each of the three days becomes a Jewish adaptation of the Christian motif of Mary as nursing mother (*Maria Lactans*), a well-known representation of Mary as nurturing at the breast.[78] Here, however, the Jewish mother and father not only insult the Eucharist but then also turn the Christian wet nurse into a *mater lactans* by having her nurture their Jewish child with her milk, thereby reversing correct hierarchy, supporting the growth of a Jewish child with the milk of a Christian woman who has received the host.

The intention of Jews desecrating the Eucharist indirectly by making their baby's wet nurses spill some of their milk into a latrine after they take communion is one of several indications that Jews were aware of the importance Christians ascribed to the Eucharist. The attributed Jewish practice of Jews making Christian wet nurses spill out some of their milk could have been viewed correctly as an antieucharistic parody.[79] But Jews then having their wet nurses feed their babies the same three days might be viewed as a Jewish countereucharistic rite and reinforce a Jewish interpretation of Jewish-Christian hierarchy according to which the elder (the church) will serve the younger (the Jews). The latrine ceremony first neutralized the positive value that the church associated with the Eucharist. It despiritualized it by associating it with human bodily waste. Then by the Christian wet nurse feeding the baby, it made "the church" physically nurture "the synagogue." It is this reversal of correct hierarchy that bothered the pope in the first place when his letter refers to Jews inappropriately hiring Christian servants.[80]

Re-riting the Eucharist: A Jewish Countereucharistic or Conversion Rite?

Rites of latrine blasphemy were one of the ways that Jews may have insulted Christians who were now seeking communion with members of the faithful and the exclusion of others. Jews in northern Europe also developed what might be thought of as another countereucharistic rite, which involved a Jewish boy being initiated into his Hebrew letters by an elaborate set of ritual acts that included eating cakes and hard-boiled eggs on which verses from the Hebrew Bible were written.[81]

This ceremony appears in the Rhineland and northern France in the late twelfth and early thirteenth centuries, when different rabbinic authors describe it and anchor its elements in biblical verses—a sign that it was not ancient or early medieval.[82] It appeared at the same time that eucharistic piety was growing in Christian Europe, and disappeared until recent times in the late thirteenth century, perhaps because it was too similar to the Christian rite and might have made Jews concerned that it might be misinterpreted as blasphemy.

The main parts of the rite include the following. At age five or six—perhaps even as young as three—a Jewish boy living in medieval Germany or northern France might begin his formal schooling by participating in a special ritual initiation ceremony. In Germany, early on the morning of the spring festival of Shavuot (Pentecost), someone wraps him in a coat or prayer shawl (tallit) and carries him from his house to the teacher, who is either in the synagogue or at the teacher's house.[83] The boy is seated on the teacher's lap, and he shows him a tablet on which the Hebrew alphabet has been written. The teacher reads the letters first forward, then backward, and finally in symmetrically paired combinations, and encourages the boy to repeat each sequence aloud. The teacher smears honey over the letters on the tablet and tells the child to lick it off.

Cakes on which biblical verses have been written are then brought in. They must be baked by virgins from flour, honey, oil, and milk. Next come shelled hard-boiled eggs on which more verses have been inscribed. The teacher reads the words written on the cakes and eggs, and the boy imitates what he hears and then eats them both.

Although there are obvious differences between the Jewish initiation ceremony and the Eucharist, they both have in common the problem of what happens in the body to the ingested symbolic foods: the wafer of the Eucharist, and the inscribed cakes and eggs in the Jewish rite. Ecclesiastical and some Jewish writers discussed the excretion of the consecrated host or alphabet Torah cake, respectively, and the former proposed that the Eucharist is spiritualized and absorbed into the body of the faithful, and not excreted like ordinary food. In the case of the Jewish rite of passage, Judah the Pious commented that it is not proper to excrete Hebrew letters.[84] Already the rabbinic midrash on the Book of Numbers, *Sifrei Bemidbar*, contains a tradition that biblical manna, divinely provided food, was not excreted.[85]

The development of the Jewish boy's Torah initiation ceremony may also be seen, as Simha Goldin and Julie Goldstein have proposed, as a way of asserting and reinforcing Jewish identity among young Jewish boys at a time when Jewish boys especially were vulnerable to conversion to Christianity. The assertive pro-Jewish aspect of the innovative rite complements the interpretation of it as a counterritual to the Eucharist in the sense that both are affirmations of a faith community that believes it to be God's people, and the eating of the "divine food" ritualizes and literally *incorporates* that assertion.[86]

Were there limits to Jewish assertiveness? What about alleged rites that Christian authorities investigated and determined that Jews never did? How did the widespread assumption get "invented" that Jews reenacted the Passion in the present as a further expression of their behavior as inner enemies? Although the ritual murder accusation is sometimes pointed to as the beginning of the "deterioration" of European Jewish life, it should also be viewed as a time when Jews competed with Christians for making saints that embodied the truth of their own religion in contrast to that of the other.[87] Jews knew about Christian saints, and claimed that real Jews could be saints, and even compared them to Jesus.

CHAPTER SIX

Eucharistic Fantasies

SAINTS, IMAGINED KILLERS,
AND JEWISH SAINTS

ALTHOUGH JEWS ACTED out against *Christianity* in different ways, Christians began to accuse Jews of doing certain hostile acts toward *Christians* that Jews never actually did and in which even their accusers assigned them only a supporting role at first in rituals of Christian saint making. From the mid-twelfth century on, the imagined Jew understood since the First Crusade not only as Paul's subordinated other but also as the *inner enemy* began to assume new forms that Christians thought posed imminent danger to them in ways that reflect how Christians imagined themselves.[1] The first allegation was that Jews ritually reenact the Passion of Christ by crucifying a Christian boy at Easter time. It originated among Benedictine monks in England, where the focus was less on the Jews than on the body of a dead young Christian boy who was now understood to be a local martyred saint.[2]

Benedictine houses witnessed a revival of martyred Christian saints in mid-twelfth-century England. Christian saint martyrs were known and remembered from the time of the Roman persecutions in the third and early fourth centuries, but apart from the martyrs of Córdoba, in Muslim Iberia, there had been few universally remembered Christian martyrs since then.[3] Exceptions were the cults of Santiago (St. James) de Compostela and St. Thomas Becket, murdered on December 29, 1170.[4]

Benedictine writers helped spread the new idea of ritual murder even when they denied that a particular incident ever occurred or a story about one did not correspond to an actual event. The repetition of the narrative, even when it was disproven, helped create the mindset that it existed or could exist. When the conditions were right, the story could be invoked to explain the discovery of a male Christian youth's body. The death, like that of many children in the Middle Ages and today, was likely the result of physical trauma caused either by an accident or a relative's or neighbor's abuse, but now a new explanation was available that could produce a local martyr saint. Sometimes a story lacked one or more elements, such as the right time of year (Easter), or there might not even be a body, but even these cases could be made to fit the narrative that had a reality more believable that any facts that might emerge. In some situations, political rulers exploited the idea of a ritual murder, regardless of the evidence, and this could bring about devastating consequences for a Jewish community.

The emergence of the ritual murder accusation in mid-twelfth-century England has remained a puzzle. Many scholars have tried to explain its origins—so many in fact that it becomes clear that there is not enough evidence to support any one explanation. The problem is why at a specific point in time did it occur to Benedictine monks in England and other clerics in northern France, or to Crusaders setting out from Germany in the mid-twelfth century, that if a boy's mutilated body was found around Easter week or even some other time of the year, it was because Jewish men had purposefully reenacted the Passion of Jesus on a young Christian boy? Moreover, the dead body was described as performing miracles and possibly smelling sweet, both signs of sainthood. The boy, then, was understood to be a martyred saint, but to be a martyred saint, a Christian had to be killed by an infidel. In twelfth-century England, there was only one available infidel: the Jew.

Although the accusations of a ritual murder sometimes led to anti-Jewish violence on the Continent, the cases in England did not result in attacks on local Jews until 1255, with Hugh of Lincoln, over a century after they first appeared.[5] An indicator of the presence or absence of violence is who was memorialized. In the early ritual murder cases, the Christian child martyr saints were remembered, not the local Jews who were not attacked and so did not become Jewish martyrs. No Hebrew chronicle or liturgical poem remembers the fate of the Jews in Norwich who were accused of crucifying St. William in 1144, nor those of the second case, St. Harold of Gloucester in 1168 or 1167, nor those of the third, St. Robert of Bury St. Edmonds in 1181.[6] All three accusations were made in Benedictine houses, the first and the third in East Anglia, and the second farther to the southwest. Each now had a saint of its own. From the Jewish point of view, nothing had happened. This silence contrasts starkly with the liturgical poems and Hebrew chronicles that Jews wrote after the 1096 Rhineland massacres and acts of active Jewish martyrdom that accompanied them.

The absence of anti-Jewish violence in the early English cases suggests that the social context in England was not antagonism toward Jews but rather the rivalry among Benedictine houses to create a local child martyr saint.[7] How did this new idea occur to so many people at the same time?

Before the idea of a ritual murder occurred to anyone, children were found dead for a variety of reasons. Child mortality was high, estimated at anywhere from between 30 to 50 percent.[8] This meant that the death of children was commonplace enough, often due to parental neglect. We find examples in saints' lives when the power of the saint is said to have revived them.[9] In Jacobus de Voragine's *Golden Legend*, one of the most popular collections of saints' lives circulating in medieval Europe, we read that St. Elizabeth of Hungary (1207–31) revived children who were found dead:

> A schoolboy called Burchard, from the diocese of Mainz, was fishing, but carelessly fell into the river and drowned. He was pulled out after quite a while, but the body was rigid, without feeling or motion, and showed no signs of life, so he was judged to be dead by the men who had found him. Then the merits of St. Elizabeth were invoked, and, wonderful to behold, the boy was restored to life and health.
>
> A boy three and a half years old, whose name was Hugolin, of the diocese of Mainz, died on the road and his body lay rigid and lifeless. His mother carried him a distance of four Teutonic miles, imploring St. Elizabeth with all devotion, and the boy returned to life and health.

A four-year-old boy fell into a well, and a man who came to draw water noticed the body submerged and lying at the bottom. He got the boy out with some difficulty and determined that he was dead. The indications of death were the length of time the boy had been in the water, the rigidity of the body, the horrible staring eyes and gaping mouth, the blackened skin, the swollen body, and the utter absence of movement and feeling. The man therefore pronounced a vow to St. Elizabeth, invoking her help for the deceased, and the boy recovered the life he had had.

There was also a girl who fell into a river, and when she was pulled out, she was quickly restored to life by St. Elizabeth's merits.[10]

Unlike the deaths of children of both sexes, the saints in ritual murder accusations were usually boys.[11] In his lengthy Latin account, the Benedictine monk Thomas of Monmouth imagines that a group of local Jews lured a young Christian named William, twelve at the time, into a private place, where they reenacted aspects of the biblical Passion accounts and caused him suffering and death. His body was reportedly the source of miracles. As a result of publicity surrounding this ritual killing of a Christian boy, the local clerics established a memorialization of his death as a shrine, and marked the anniversary of the death with prayers for the soul and petitions for divine mercy for living sinners.[12]

Thomas of Monmouth himself knew that the new idea was not the only way to explain the body of a dead boy. In an invented speech, a prominent Jew tells his fellow Jews not to hide William's bruised body in the latrine of their rented houses. A new tenant might discover it one day and blame the Jews. Instead, they should hide it somewhere else so as not to incriminate themselves:

> I say the body should be carried away and be left exposed in a place far away from us, where—if perchance it is found—the Christians may think of it, so to speak, as a murder. And when news of the murder becomes common knowledge there is no doubt that the officers of the king's justice, to make their profit, may lend covetous ears to the false rumour. At that time when the blame has been attached to Christians, it will render us secure forever.[13]

When Thomas was writing book 1 of his *Life of St. William* in 1150, he was aware of two ways to account for the discovery of the injured body of a young boy: either the usual explanation that a Christian killed him, so that the king's officials would step in, or the new idea that Jews committed a ritual murder.

How did children dying because Christian parents abandoned or killed them, or because they accidently drowned in rivers, become the obvious occasion for a child martyr made at the hands of the only available infidel, one or more local Jews? And why did this explanation become obvious as well as spread across time and space? Why did some of these alleged incidents become politicized, as in Blois with Thibaut, count of Blois, in 1171, in France with the young King Philip Augustus in 1182, and in England with Henry III in 1255?

Moreover, while the first documented accusation based on the discovery of a body in Norwich took place around Easter, even the second incident, Harold of Gloucester, was not originally identical to Norwich regarding the date. Based on the rumor, the facts about Gloucester were doctored so that an accidental death in the Severn River in 1167 became a ritual murder in 1168 when the dates fit Easter week.[14] This suggests that the *idea* of a ritual murder existed independent of local facts from the beginning. Gloucester, in turn, made the idea of ritual murder into a pattern, not a onetime event, and it continued to circulate among Benedictines so that it was possible three years later to condemn an entire Jewish community to death in Blois without the existence of a body (see below). The idea was real; the facts were irrelevant and made to fit the idea.[15]

Thomas did not invent the ritual murder accusation, and it did not spread to the Continent via familiarity with Thomas's written account in 1150 about the death of William of Norwich, which he said took place in 1144.[16] But he did fit the death of William, probably a case of domestic violence, into the new religious paradigm of ritual murder that was becoming a common assumption around the same time in England and on the Continent, especially in Benedictine circles. He thus "documented" a case of the phenomenon for the first time. As Joe Hillaby has noted, "Transmission must have taken place within that small group of Benedictine monks with special interest in such matters. It was then seized on by powerful lay figures who realized that allegations of child martyrdom could be a useful tool in promoting their political and economic objectives."[17]

Ritual murder, then, was not so much an event as it was a shared *mentality* or assumption which spread by rumor, was then made visible or real in selective events starting with William's case. Nor did it become the default explanation for all suspicious deaths of young boys afterward. Yet it did become an explanation when useful to either Benedictine monks or Crusaders in need of a saint, or to political figures who had a local problem that a ritual murder could solve.

Würzburg and Blois

The ritual murder charge first surfaced in Norwich, England, unaccompanied by anti-Jewish violence. On the Continent, although key elements of the Norwich case were lacking, an allegation that Jews had harmed a Christian could lead to violence.

Take Würzburg. It takes place in the context of the growing religious enthusiasm for the Second Crusade. The incident occurred in February 1147, not during Holy Week, and no allegation was made that the Jews ritually crucified the victim. There was a gruesome murder involving dismemberment, not a ritual murder. How are we to make sense of the way this incident has been understood? What does it tell us about the beginnings of the ritual murder accusation and how it has been interpreted?

Two narrative sources describe the Würzburg murder. One is in R. Ephraim of Bonn's *Sefer Zekhirah (Book of Remembrance)*, and we also have a Latin source from an anonymous local chronicler, *Annales Herbipolenses*.[18] The sources do not agree about some of the details of the violent attack and counterattack in February 1147, but certain matters stand out.

R. Ephraim of Bonn's Hebrew account attributes the following to Christians there:

> On the 22nd day of the month of Adar the evil doers attacked the community of Würzburg. The enemy made false accusations in order to justify their attack upon them. They declared, "We have found a Gentile in the river whom you slew and threw there. He is thus achieving sainthood and is working miracles."[19]

An important emphasis in Ephraim's account is that the violence was instigated by "the errant ones [i.e., Crusaders] and the poorer segment of the population."[20] This is different from the English cases, where local Benedictine monks take the lead in claiming a local martyred saint at the hands of the local Jews. The emphasis on the Crusaders is also clearly stated in the *Annales*, which says "citizens and crusaders" blame the Jews. The whole story starts when "crusaders streamed into the city" in February 1147.

Ephraim's account is less detailed and graphic as to what the alleged crime was, and seems to have been received second- or thirdhand compared to the *Annales*. Ephraim states only, "They declared, 'We have found a Gentile in the river whom you slew and threw there.'"

Compare that to the *Annales*:

> The body of a man was found, cut up into many pieces. Two large pieces were discovered in the Main river, one among the mills toward the suburb called Bleicha and another toward the town of Thunegersheim. The remaining pieces were found in a ditch opposite the tower that is generally called Katzinwichus. When all the scattered pieces of the body were gathered together, it was taken to an inn within the town and there was buried in the forecourt of a church.

The details in the *Annales* about dismemberment are credible and make sense of the report later on in Ephraim's account of the condition of the Jewish victims: "On the following day, the bishop ordered that all the slaughtered saints be collected on wagons—all the choice severed limbs: hips and shoulders, thumbs of hands and feet, sanctified with holy oil, together with everything else that remained of their bodies and limbs—and buried in his garden." The dismemberment of Jewish bodies, which Ephraim did not mention earlier, seems to have been in retaliation for the dismembered Christian body whose death the Crusaders and "citizens" attributed to the local Jews.

The importance of the body parts is also related to the second claim that Ephraim says is on the minds of the Christian accusers. "Thus, the crusaders began to honor the man as if a martyr, carrying around relics of the body, and demanded that he—whom they called Theodore—should be canonized." According to Ephraim, the Christians claimed, "He is thus achieving sainthood and is working miracles." Ephraim explains the saint making of the victim as the result of the prior assumption that it was Jews who killed him and threw his body in the river. There is no mention in either the Hebrew or Latin source, however, that the Jews tried to crucify the Christian.

In Würzburg, the Crusaders are the ones interested in saint making, not the local bishop, who later resisted any move to harm the local Jews. Compared to Ephraim's laconic report about the body—"He is thus achieving sainthood and is working miracles"—the *Annales* is more detailed: "Signs were said to occur at the grave of the body. The dumb were said to speak, the blind to see, the lame to walk, and other signs of this kind."

Ephraim's reference to sainthood and miracles is one of several indications of Jewish awareness of the way Christians understood saints, and his comment also places the death and accusation of the Jews in Würzburg into the framework of Christian saint making that we find in England. But in Würzburg, there is no linkage to Easter. Nor is there any indication of the gender or age of the victim, and no mention of a ritual crucifixion. Even without all of those details, it is understood that the Jews who allegedly murdered a Christian produced a martyr saint who can make miracles, and this understanding is characteristic of the early cases in England too.

And so in different but related ways, the Würzburg and Norwich cases are part of the general rumor that Jews are responsible for killing innocent Christians who are considered martyr saints. One major difference is that in Würzburg, Crusaders passing through town, not local Benedictine monks, led to anti-Jewish violence; in Norwich, the initiative came from the local Benedictines and there was no anti-Jewish violence. It seems that the idea of a ritual murder is so bound up with saint making from the beginning that one does not need evidence of attempted crucifixion or timing around Easter to define a case, only the claim that Jews killed a Christian who could work miracles and be considered a martyr saint.

Würzburg, then, was less a ritual murder accusation than an extension of anti-Jewish violence perpetrated in the wake of a new propaganda campaign to promote the Second Crusade. We see the ideology of the Second Crusade toward the Jews in the Würzburg incident in 1147, perpetrated by Crusaders passing through the town and actively opposed to the local clerics, who not only could not defend their Jews but were almost in fear for their own lives as well. And yet it has one feature in common with the early ritual murder accusations: it involves saint making, thereby reinforcing that context in England as an important factor in imagining the ritual murder accusation in the first place.

Würzburg began to receive special attention as a ritual murder when Israel Yuval claimed in a speculative Hebrew article, later published as part of an English monograph, that Würzburg was not only a ritual murder but also the first, and may have influenced Thomas of Monmouth and the English cases. Yuval has since backed away from this extreme position of Würzburg's priority, but in his revised English version continued to maintain that it was "considered" a ritual murder: "Three facts support the assumption that the murder in Würzburg was considered a ritual one: the episode took place about a week after Purim, that is, during a period marked by high religious emotion; the corpse of the slain person worked miracles; and many Jews were killed, suggesting a collective accusation."[21]

But there is no evidence that any medieval Jews or Christians "considered" what happened in Würzburg to be a ritual murder rather than a grisly one that produced a Christian saint. Neither the Latin nor the Hebrew sources refer to a ritual murder accusation. The timing is not Easter week; the death of many Jews is unlike the English ritual murder cases, when Jews were not killed. The claim about sainthood could have linked Würzburg to the first ritual murder. The ritual murder in Norwich is associated with Easter, not "a week after Purim." Jews were not killed in the ritual murder accusations in England until 1255. It did become a special kind of murder by its association with saint making, but did anyone consider it a ritual murder? As E. M. Rose notes, before 1171 there were only two cases, not counting Würzburg—Norwich (1144/1150) and Gloucester (1168)—and the ritual murder accusation was not yet widely disseminated.[22]

By 1171, the new idea of a ritual murder was so flexible and porous that it could even be invoked in Blois without the body of a martyr saint. The case emerged in a complex political and social context. Count Thibaut V of Blois and Chartres, married to Alix, daughter of Louis VII, king of France, and his first wife, Eleanor of Aquitaine, at first was opposed to the accusation and looked for a Jewish bribe to make it go away. But a priest appeared from outside the town who insisted on testing the witness by ordeal and prevailed in proving that the event happened, despite the absence of a body. In Würzburg, it was the outsider Crusaders en route to the East who made the accusation stick despite the local clergy who opposed it. In both cases, unlike the English ritual murder accusations, Jews were put to death.

The incident and a Jewish interpretation of what transpired is recorded by R. Ephraim of Bonn:

> In the year 4931 [1171], evil appeared in France, too, and great destruction in the city of Blois, in which at that time there lived about forty Jews. It happened on that evil day, Thursday, toward evening, that the terror came upon us.
>
> A Jew, Isaac bar Eleazar, rode up to water his horse; a common soldier—may he be blotted out of the book of life—was also there watering the horse of his master. The Jew bore on his chest an untanned hide, but one of the corners had become loose and was sticking out of his coat. When, in the gloom, the soldier's horse saw the white side of the hide, it was frightened and sprang back, and it could not be brought to water.
>
> The Christian servant hastened back to his master and said "Hear, my lord, what a certain Jew did. As I rode behind him toward the river in order to give your horses a drink, I saw him throw a little Christian child, whom the Jews have killed, into the water. When I saw this, I was horrified and hastened back quickly for fear he might kill me too. Even the horse under me was so frightened by the splash of the water when he threw the child in that it would not drink." The soldier knew that his master would rejoice at the fall of the Jews, because he hated a certain Jewess influential in the city. He as much as put the following words into his master's mouth: "Now I can wreak my vengeance on that person, on that woman Pulcelina."[23]

In Blois, there was no body, but only a witness who reported that he saw something fall into the river. Moreover, the alleged crime did not take place around Easter. It was when a priest arrived and arranged for an ordeal by water that it was "determined" that local Jews had ritually killed a Christian. Because there was no body, there were no miracles, and saint making was not a factor in Blois.

It was an alleged murder accusation. Although Count Thibaut was hoping for a bribe to make the accusation go away, the clergy won, and he ordered that thirty-one or so Jews be burned. They and not a Christian boy were memorialized as Jewish martyrs. The animal hide did not become a saint.

But is Blois a ritual murder accusation? The Hebrew accounts say that the executions by burning took place on May 24, 1171. Apparently, the alleged murder took place a few days earlier, not in the Easter/Passover season at all, and no Hebrew or Latin source refers to Easter or Passover in relation to Blois.[24]

What we see in the Blois account is that the idea of sainthood was attached to Jewish as well as Christian martyr saints. R. Ephraim of Bonn ascribes attributes of sainthood to the *Jewish* martyrs that were usually associated with *Christian* saints, thereby showing that he was aware of the idea of Christian saints: "Nevertheless, they were not burnt, neither they nor those thirty-one persons. Only their souls were released by the fire; their bodies remained intact. When the Christians saw it, they were amazed and said to one another: 'Truly these are saints.'"[25]

R. Ephraim also shows that he is aware of how Christians understood what constituted a saint when he adds a bit further on in the narrative about the Jewish martyrs that "God smelled the sweet savor." A pleasing aroma is a feature of Christian saints.[26] Further awareness of Jews about Christian saints and relics is seen even in Jewish legal writings that permit oaths sworn to saints since they are not deemed to be divine.[27]

Given the political status of the temporal ruler in Blois and that his wife was the daughter of the king of France, it is not surprising that the matter was brought to the king, Louis VII, the father-in-law of Count Thibaut of Blois. In a Hebrew letter written after the Blois incident, the author expresses skepticism about the accusation in question, but from his answer it is clear that saint making was the context of at least one other accusation that Jews were involved in a Christian's death. Here, too, there is no mention of a ritual murder accusation but possibly only reference to an alleged murder:

> "For people have leveled the same accusation against the Jews of Pontoise and Janville, but, when the charges were brought before me they

were found false." Then the king told the Jews of the Pontoise incident and [Richard] who was beatified in Paris and indicated that it was completely unfounded—likewise in the present instance. "Therefore, be assured all you Jews in my land, that I harbor no such suspicions. Even if a body be discovered in the city or in the countryside, I shall say nothing to the Jews in that regard. Therefore, be not frightened over that issue."[28]

From the king's perspective, there was no legal basis for what his son-in-law had done in Blois. In Blois, there was no body and not even proof of a murder, and it did not take place around the time of Easter or Passover.[29]

Yet the Benedictine clerical perspective was very different, and some scholars have ignored the relevant sources and adopted the tendentious interpretation of Robert de Torigni (Robert de Monte [d. 1186], Benedictine abbot of Mont Saint-Michel), who made Blois into a ritual murder like Norwich and Gloucester. He also made Gloucester and Pontoise into ritual murders but did not mention Würzburg. In his *Chronicle*, he writes,

> Theobald Count of Chartres, burnt many Jews who resided at Blois, because, in order to mark their contempt to the Christians, they had crucified a child at Easter, and afterwards had put him in a sack and thrown him into the Loire. When the body was discovered, they were found guilty of the crime; whereupon (as we have stated) the count gave them up to the flames, excepting such of them as embraced the Christian faith. During the reign of king Stephen, they did the same thing at Norwich, in England, to St. William; he was buried in the cathedral church there, and many miracles are performed at his tomb. The like thing occurred at Gloucester, in the time of king Henry the second. And again; these wicked Jews perpetrated the same crime at a castle in France, called Pontisare, [Pontoise] upon St. Richard; he was conveyed to Paris, and buried in the church there, where he shines by his many [115] miracles. (These martyred persons are reported to be most liberal with their miracles about Easter-tide, if they have the opportunity) [*sic*]. [Corrected last sentence: And frequently, as was said, they (i.e., Jews) do this at Easter time, if they get the opportunity (Et frequenter, ut dicitur, faciunt hoc in tempore Paschali, si opportunitatem invenerint)].[30]

Robert's account imposes on Blois, Gloucester, and Pontoise the Norwich template of the ritual murder accusation, and even reiterates the time of the year when such ritual murders are likely to occur. This shows how the actual date of real events was irrelevant. Even the absence of a body did not matter, and so in this case, saint making was not at issue. According to de Torigni, all four cases were ritual murders that occurred at Easter time; furthermore, he alleged that Jews ritually crucified a Christian youth. Despite the absence of any factual basis, Robert asserts that Blois is to be assimilated into "a ritual murder" just like those of William of Norwich and Harold of Gloucester.[31]

These sources suggest the existence of the *idea* of a ritual murder that was widely shared in clerical, Crusader, and royal circles, even when they differed as to what happened in any particular case. It was the idea of ritual murder that came into being in the mid-twelfth century, and since it now existed, different parties for different reasons would adjust the facts to fit the idea or deny its existence altogether. It was diffused in stories, as Anthony Bale correctly emphasized.[32]

The disparity between the facts of these cases and their association with William of Norwich shows that the construct of a ritual murder was around in Benedictine circles at least as a default in some situations for explaining how a dead young Christian boy died or when a ruler needed to think there had been such a crime, as in Blois.

Although we saw that Louis VII denied that Jews were responsible for any alleged killing of Christians, the idea persisted, and his teenage son, Philip Augustus, born in 1165 (r. 1179–1223), did not follow his father on this matter.[33] In 1182, court chronicler Rigord (d. 1209) reports that Philip was persuaded that Jews not only abused ecclesiastical objects that they held as pawns but also perpetrated ritual murder and were dangerous enough to merit expelling Jews from the tiny royal domain. He repeats the allegation written by de Torigni about Jews committing a ritual murder in Pontoise on St. Richard. This clearly demonstrates how de Torigni spread the rumor that he thought had political consequences in royal France in 1182:

> Philip Augustus had often heard that the Jews who dwelt in Paris were wont every year on Easter day, or during the sacred week of our Lord's Passion, to go secretly into underground vaults and kill a Christian as a

sort of sacrifice in contempt of the Christian religion. For a long time, they had persisted in this wickedness, inspired by the devil, and in Philip's father's time, many of them had been seized and burned with fire. St. Richard [of Pontoise], whose body rests in the Church of the Holy Innocents-in-the-Field in Paris, was thus put to death and crucified by the Jews, and through martyrdom went in blessedness to God. Wherefore many miracles have been wrought by the hand of God through the prayers and intercessions of St. Richard, to the glory of God, as we have heard."[34]

Advancing de Torigni's Benedictine point of view, Rigord claims that the king expelled at least some of his Jews in 1182 in part based on his belief that Jews had ritually murdered a Christian who was considered to be a martyr saint.[35]

The examples of Blois and royal France show that a count or king might use the ritual murder idea to advance a political agenda and promote himself as a pious Christian ruler as well. The politicization of the ritual murder accusation emerges in England only in 1255 with the execution in London of nineteen Jews and the arrest of dozens more after an investigation of Jewish coin clipping, along with an additional charge of the ritual murder of St. Hugh of Lincoln under Henry III.[36]

Matthew Paris reports this case in his *Cronica Majora* as follows:

> In this same year [1255], about the time of the festival of the apostles Peter and Paul [June 29], the Jews of Lincoln stole a boy of eight years of age whose name was Hugh; and, having shut him up in a room quite out of the way, where they fed him on milk and other childish nourishment, they sent to almost all the cities of England where the Jews lived, and summoned some of their sect from each city to be present at a sacrifice to take place at Lincoln; for they had, as they stated, a boy hidden for the purpose of being crucified.[37]

The case of little Hugh was not only another example of judicial violence, like Blois or the expulsion of the Jews from France, but would also be immortalized in Chaucer's *The Prioress's Tale*, where a ritual murder, compared to that of Hugh, was transformed into a Mary story with an anti-Jewish point of view (see chapter 8).

Narratives about ritual murders continued to resurface thanks in part to de Torigni's chronicle. We see the accusation being reinvented again in the early drama that produced the story of Adam of Bristol in the mid-thirteenth century.[38]

And we also see circulating as a story without any correspondence to an alleged incident the remarkable *Cronicon* of Richard of Devizes.[39] Matthew Paris turned an accusation about a kidnapping and forced circumcision in Norwich in 1234 into a ritual murder story.[40] There were others as well.[41]

The power of the accusation derives not from facts on the ground but from the narrative idea itself that somehow formed in the minds of Benedictine clerics and spread beyond to Crusader groups en route to the Second Crusade, as in Würzburg, or was seized on by interested political parties such as Philip Augustus. Unlike his father, Louis VII, who doubted the allegations about Blois, Philip insisted on the reality of the case of Richard of Pontoise, regardless of whether knowledge of the cult was even partially responsible for Philip's expelling the Jews from his royal lands in 1182.[42]

Although each ritual murder accusation has or claims a local context, the idea was not deduced from a series of cases. Rather, it *preceded* the cases, and the cases, even if they lacked one or more key elements, were made to fit the idea.[43] This porousness shows that the binary assumption in David Nirenberg's *Communities of Violence*, which he himself rethought in *Anti-Judaism*, requires further revision. History consists not only of individual incidents that have a separate and unique history but also of *imagined patterns that can define the meaning and shape of specific events*.[44] In some sense, the event does not exist apart from the idea of a ritual murder that precedes it. Without that idea, there would only be dead bodies, not saints or ritual murder accusations. And the existence of narratives without a body (Blois) or even a real local accusation (Bristol and Winchester) reveals how relatively dependent the "facts" are in situations, even where there was a body and local incident that provoked an accusation.

Blood Libel and Ritual Cannibalism

Not only could the ritual murder charge appropriate cases of murder or imagined murder and be of use to temporal rulers for their own ends, but the very idea of the "body of Christ" could change, and with it, new ritual accusations emerge based on its different meanings.[45]

Accompanying the idea of transubstantiation and its ritualization in the eucharistic devotion, the body of Christ now came to mean the real presence of Christ. The blood and body ingested in the rite generated an imagined countereucharist of Jews ingesting the blood or heart of a Christian victim.[46] Dramatic accusations followed in the form of ritual cannibalism or the blood libel in Fulda, Germany, in 1235, which five children of a Christian butcher.[47] After an investigation, it was shown to be a false accusation. Fulda took place in December but was later connected to Passover and Easter along with allegations that the blood was needed for the holiday.[48] Other cases occurred in Valréas, France, in 1247 and with Werner of Oberwesel in 1287.[49] The most notorious case was little Simon of Trent in 1475.[50] It has been the subject of serious scholarship as well as scandalous revisionism, which has since been repudiated.[51]

The appearance of the new accusation is attested in its denial in Jewish and Christian sources at the highest level of society. In *Nizzahon Vetus*, for example, the author argues in defense that "the heretics anger us by charging that we murder the children and consume the blood."[52] Its denial was also incorporated into a saint story about Judah the Pious (d. 1217), about whom hagiographic stories were written in Hebrew and later Yiddish. In a story about an apostate and Judah the Pious, the apostate seeks to return to Judaism, but Judah refuses on the grounds that he is too wicked. When a miracle occurred and a stick began to sprout, Judah sent for him to find out what caused the miracle. The confessing apostate told him that he prevented an anti-Jewish massacre that was about to erupt because of a blood libel accusation:

> He replied that he did not do (any repentance) or speak favorably about Jews, and (I) [he] was often wicked toward them, apart from one time when he was in a large town and there also were there a large gathering of Jews [lit., people of truth and God fearers]. And they (pl.) libeled them, falsely accusing them about a certain gentile (*sheqez*) who was killed and tossed into the Jews' street and the whole town formed a mob against them to oppress and kill them and they said: "One of their

own did it"! "Let the apostate who came from them testify about them that they need blood, then they will not be able to say anything evil about us elsewhere. And our desire will be carried out by them."

They sent for the apostate and asked him if they need blood. He replied to them, "By my oath on and cursed faith in the impure [insult language for Jesus] they do not need blood." He told them how the Jews rinse (*medihim*) their meat and salt it (to extract) the blood. "The evil decree was annulled because of me." Judah the Pious said to him, "If so, I am guarantor that you will be in Paradise if you repent sincerely."[53]

We hear similar denials that Jews are capable of ingesting Christian blood from an imperial decree from Frederick II in 1236 where he reports,

> When a serious crime was imputed to the Jews of Fulda concerning the death of certain boys of the town, because of that terrible incident (!) the harsh opinion of the neighboring populace, spawned by recent misfortune, was projected against the rest of the Jews of Germany, although covert attacks were not yet in evidence.

After an investigation took place and "when their findings were published on this matter it was clear that it was not indicated in the Old or New Testament that Jews lust for the drinking of human blood. Rather precisely the opposite."[54]

In addition, two papal letters from the thirteenth century show that a more specific accusation was going around that the popes each denied. Whereas Innocent III writes a letter in 1205 in which he says that a Jew is capable of killing a Christian, the blood libel was different.[55]

On July 5, 1247, Innocent IV wrote that Jews are being persecuted because people believe that on the Passover holiday, "Jews share the heart of a murdered child."[56] In 1272, Gregory IX writes,

> Since it happens occasionally that some Christians lose their Christian children, the Jews are accused by their enemies of secretly carrying off and killing these same Christian children and of making sacrifices of the heart and blood of these very children.... And most falsely do these Christians claim that the Jews have secretly and furtively carried away these children and killed them, and that the Jews offer sacrifice

from the heart and the blood of these children, since their law in this matter precisely and expressly forbids Jews to sacrifice, eat or drink the blood, or to eat the flesh of animals having claws.[57]

Despite all of these investigations, the blood libel did not go away. It continued and proliferated into modern times and became a widely believed motive for antisemitic violence, especially in eastern Europe in early modern times and beyond.[58]

Host Desecration and Well Poisoning

A further development of the idea of the body of Christ focused on the host, which was understood in the thirteenth century as containing the real presence of the body of Christ. Beginning with Paris in 1290, we hear stories about the host desecration libel, according to which Jews were accused of acquiring consecrated hosts, often from a Christian woman, and testing or attacking them by stabbing and other procedures to cast doubt on the reality of Christian claims about the host. These stories circulated widely, and in 1298 (Rintfleisch) and again in the 1330s (Armleder) led to major outbreaks of anti-Jewish violence in the German Empire.[59]

Stories circulated about miracles involving bleeding hosts that accompanied the accusation to prove the truth of Christian beliefs and frequently ended with Jews converting.[60] In the case of the consecrated host that Jews treated like a baked wafer that they knew Christians thought was God, there is some reason to think Jews might have been involved in trying to test the host. The force of most of the stories is the miracle that the host bleeds, after which the Jew converts.

The most ambitious expansion of the idea that Jews threaten the body of Christ is the well-poisoning accusation that became important in the fourteenth century, first in association with lepers in 1321 and then with the Black Death in 1348–50, as Tzafrir Barzilay has discussed in great detail. The idea is a further expansion of the Jew as inner enemy, now understood as attacking the body of Christ in the form of all Christendom (see chapter 8).[61]

Of all these allegations, the host desecration is the only one that did not involve harming a human being. It is not surprising, then, that despite the traditional denial on the part of Jewish historians that none of these alleged events ever happened, there is some revisionist evidence that in the case of host desecration as well as insulting the cross, Jews may have acted out to insult the consecrated host if they could get one.[62]

Christian and Jewish Historical Contexts

The many different attempts to explain the ritual murder accusation demonstrate that we do not know what "caused" it. But what also needs explaining is why it was widely accepted and reiterated as soon as the first case appeared in Norwich. Historical factors making the idea plausible need to be sought, such as widely shared beliefs held in mid-twelfth-century Europe, not only in East Anglia, where the first case appeared. Taken together, these factors need to be reasonably likely to have suggested and legitimated the new idea by the time that it is first reported in the middle of the twelfth century.

If some cases are strictly a murder reinterpreted as a ritual one, as in Würzburg, or a political fantasy, as for Count Thibaut of Blois in 1171, Philip Augustus of France in 1182, and Henry III in England in 1255, the spread of the belief was accelerated by Benedictines like de Torigni, who made Blois into a ritual murder like Norwich and the other English ones even though they were not.[63] Historians need to go back and ask not only what happened in each case but also how it happened that people assumed as a default explanation at certain points in time that a damaged Christian body (or a rumor about a body that never was produced, as in Blois) was a martyr, not a victim of domestic violence. Why was this believable? Why was it assumed only some of the time?

Unlike the motivations attributed to the Christian attackers in 1096, who sought to avenge the *ancient* Passion of Christ on the nearby Jews before avenging the enemy Ishmaelites in the East, the ritual murder accusation builds implicitly on the eucharistic sacrifice as the reenactment *in the present* not only of the Last Supper, but of the Passion, especially at Easter time. Miri Rubin notes that from the twelfth century on, there is a rise in the importance of the Eucharist as contributing to the consolidation of Christian identity: "The quintessence of this claim now lay in the most powerful ritual of mediation, the eucharist, emerging as it was as a re-enactment, not merely memorial, of the central act of sacrifice which had been foretold in the Last Supper, and suffered in the Passion."[64] And David Berger considered this trend an important factor in the emergence of the new idea of the ritual murder: "The belief that the body of Jesus was regularly sacrificed in Christian ritual greatly increased Christian receptivity to the assertion that Jews sacrificed his surrogates in their own perverted fashion. Where the belief in the 'real presence' waned, the blood libel found considerably less fertile soil."[65]

Eucharistic piety and the ritual murder accusation are both understood as reenacting the Passion now, but a live Christian boy is substituted for the host and wine.[66] In the Eucharist, it is the priest, not the Jews, who offers up the sacrifice. This follows from understanding the Eucharist first as a reenactment of the Last Supper, and the priest as repeating the role of Jesus. But the further association of the Eucharist as reenacting the Passion presents the incongruity of a priest, not the Jews, as the killer of Christ. In the ritual murder idea, *Jews* reenact the Passion in the present by killing an innocent Christian boy. It restores the Jews to the reenactment of the Passion that the Eucharist dramatizes too. In creating a close Christian bond, it adds specificity to the imagined Jew as *inner enemy*, begun with the First Crusade, to include Jews ritually crucifying a Christlike saint martyr boy.[67]

Another factor was the growth of the cult of the Virgin Mary along with the more human depiction of the child Jesus and his mother. It is part of the transformation of the image of God the Father, frequently found in Romanesque church entrances, into the Christ Child, increasingly popular in the twelfth century, and the growing cult of the Virgin Mary as Mother of God and protector of children. Some of the stories about the Virgin portrayed her as saving Christian children from a cruel Jewish father, and this combination contributed to the idea that Jewish men were cruel toward Christian children. Also involved is the perception of the Christ Child in the eucharistic sacrifice.[68]

The spread of eucharistic piety and cult of the Virgin contributed to the widespread interest among Benedictines in new saints and their cults—the context for the earliest cases in England, such as Norwich, Gloucester, and Bury, and an early possible case on the

Continent in Würzburg.[69] Saint making helps explain some of the early occasions when the rumor was invoked. The popularity of the Eucharist as well as the new emphasis on Mary and the baby Jesus contributed to the mindset of a ritual murder reenacting the Passion.

Yet another factor, closer to the specific timing of its appearance in the middle of the twelfth century and present in all parts of Christian Europe, is the religious enthusiasm stirred up for a Second Crusade. In 1144, Pope Eugenius III asked Bernard of Clairvaux to preach a Second Crusade, and on March 31, 1146, Bernard preached a Crusade sermon in the Burgundian Abby of Vézelay, where King Louis VII and Queen Eleanor of Aquitaine accepted the call.

Although the religious zeal that Urban II unleashed in 1095 led only indirectly to the anti-Jewish riots in the Rhineland, it did not produce the ritual murder accusation in the late eleventh century.[70] The Crusaders' main argument for attacking local Jews in 1096 was to avenge the Passion by seeking vengeance on the Jews, the nearby enemy, before going off to fight the enemy in the East. The focus was on the past behavior of the Jews.

But in the days leading up to the Second Crusade, the Jews at home were understood as posing a more immediate threat than the far-off Muslims because of what they were doing now. We see this new emphasis on the Jewish threat in the present in the letter we considered earlier that Peter the Venerable sent to Louis VII, king of France, in 1146, and the abbot of Cluny:

> What good is it to pursue and persecute the enemies of the Christian faith in far and distant lands if the Jews, vile blasphemers and far worse than the Saracens not far away from us but right in our midst, blaspheme, abuse, and trample on Christ and the Christian sacraments so freely and insolently and with impunity?[71]

Eucharistic devotion, the cult of Mary and the Child, the Jews as nearby present danger just before the Second Crusade, and a renewed interest in local martyred saints combined to encourage Benedictine monks in northern Europe to imagine that Jews reenacted the Passion around Easter time in the form of the ritual murder of Christian boys.[72] Although there is no evidence that the idea originated at a single point and diffused from there, it must have been "obvious" to at least some people at about the same time in England and on the Continent, and spread from their circles. The idea appears quickly in France and Germany but is not appealed to in Iberia until the fifteenth century and written about there only in the sixteenth, when Jews are no longer in the Kingdom of Castile and Aragon.[73]

Explanations That Are Inspired by Jewish Practices?

Related to the possibility that Jews acted out and insulted the host or cross is the question of whether any actual Jewish practices might have led Christians to invent these different alleged attacks on the body of Christ. In minor ways, some incidents might have been triggered by Jewish religious celebrations that brought together large numbers of Jews. For example, in the case of Gloucester, our Latin source refers to Jews gathered for a circumcision feast as the time when little Harold was ritually crucified. The accusation against Hugh of Lincoln took place when Jews were gathered to celebrate a wedding.[74]

Other scholars have proposed some more regular Jewish practices, such as the annual celebration of the carnivalesque early spring holiday of Purim, in which Jews read the Book of Esther in synagogue.[75] Purim is a ritualized way to act out Jewish victory over hostile forces. It is possible to imagine the joyous Hebrew month of Adar beginning just as Ash Wednesday falls and the potentially explosive situation of Jews celebrating Purim noisily during Lent. Already the Theodosian Code (438) legislated against Jews behaving on Purim in ways that were thought to be anti-Christian.[76] A report in the fifth-century chronicle of Socrates describes an incident on Purim in which Jews ritually hanged a figure of Haman/Jesus. In medieval times, celebration of Purim in various gestures could rightly or wrongly be confused with Jewish acts of hostility toward Jesus.[77]

Cecil Roth tried to connect Jewish ritual acting out on Purim, including burning in effigy Haman figures understood sometimes as Jesus, as contributing to the new idea of ritual murder.[78] Salo Baron claimed, perhaps defensively, that this practice was not known in the Christian West.[79] This approach seems to derive from a desire to account for a Christian libel by attributing it in part at least to Christian misunderstanding of Jewish behavior. It cannot believe that Christians could have invented something so preposterous out of whole cloth.

But in fact, the whole force of the imagined Jew shows precisely the opposite tendency. The imagined Jew is the antagonistic opposite of *Christian* beliefs and rituals. Christians can imagine Jews doing things they never did precisely because Christians need an imagined Jewish other in order to see themselves as the divinely elected Christian Israel.

The assumption that something Jews actually did influenced Christians to think that Jews could commit a ritual murder was taken to new lengths by Israel Yuval in his controversial article, which continues to be cited approvingly despite the fact that all the Latin or Hebrew sources contradict it, and the fact that several scholars have shown it has no merit.[80] This is the admittedly conjectural explanation that connects the Jewish ritual homicide of Jewish children and suicides in the riots of 1096 in the Rhineland to the allegation that Jews killed Christian children in England (and Norwich, etc.). The idea is logical and assumes that those Christians who knew about the 1096 Jewish acts reasoned that if Jews were cruel enough to kill their own children, they certainly were cruel enough to kill Christian children. The motif of the cruel Jewish father is sometimes supported by references to the Mary story of the Jewish boy. The cruel Jewish father throws the Jewish son into the oven after the boy comes back from taking communion as a convert. Mary saves the boy, and the father is thrown into the oven instead.[81]

But as we saw in chapter 3, the Christian chroniclers blame the Crusaders for killing or forcibly baptizing Jews in 1096. When they mention Jewish parents killing their children or themselves, they blame the Crusaders for driving them to extreme behavior. Thus the Christian chronicles implicitly agree with the Jewish chroniclers that the martyrs are destined to share in the eternal reward of "the saints—Rabbi Akiba and his companions, pillars of the universe, who were killed in witness to His Name."[82] Despite the fact that there is no doubt that Jewish fathers and mothers killed their own children before hundreds committed suicide in 1096, the Latin sources that mention those acts were not known to those Christians who proposed or transmitted the ritual murder accusation. Thomas of Monmouth never heard of 1096, as Willis Johnson noted.[83] Thomas wrote, "It does not seem likely that Christians would have done such a thing to a Christian nor, up to a point, Jews to a Jew."[84] Thomas was right. There was no connection between Jewish martyrdom in 1096 and the invention of the ritual murder accusation. None.

Christian Guilt, Crusaders as Jews, and Jews as Jesus

Although the acts of Jewish martyrdom in 1096 involving Jews ritually killing Jewish children and themselves played no part fifty years later in the Christian imagining of the ritual murder accusation, can the same be said about the consequences of what the Christian mobs and Crusaders had done to the Jews in 1096, and were doing again in 1146? Hebrew and Latin sources hint that guilt over Christian criminal behavior toward Jews should not be ruled out as generating Christian fears about possible acts of Jewish revenge that Christian monks could have imagined included ritual murder.

Christian temporal authorities, papal and other ecclesiastical legislation and precedents all were supposed to make Jews secure, if degraded, in Christian society. And yet in 1096, Crusaders and mobs attacked and either killed innocent Jewish civilians or forced them to be baptized, against all church law and temporal privileges. Unlike the statement of Pope Alexander II in 1063, Urban II's address to the crowds at Claremont did not distinguish between the far-off Muslim enemies and nearby Jews, who should be protected because they are subservient.

In 1146, once again we learn about Christians being incited to violence against Jews before going off to fight the distant enemies of Christ in the East. In his remarkable Hebrew chronicle about twelfth-century events, *Sefer Zekirah*, R. Ephraim of Bonn describes how a renegade monk named Radulph took it on himself to preach a Second Crusade to Christians "to avenge the crucified one upon his enemies who stand before you; then go to war against the Ishmaelites."[85] In late summer 1146, Ephraim tells us that Radulph was in Cologne, and in October 1146, Bernard left Flanders for Germany to discipline him.

According to Ephraim, God stopped the persecution of the Jews when "in His great mercy and grace, He sent a decent priest, one honored and respected by all the clergy in France, named Abbé Bernard of Clairvaux, to deal with this evil person." Bernard is quoted as reprimanding Radulph that Christians are not to kill Jews, and quotes Psalm 59 [58]:12, Augustine's proof text, *Slay them not, lest my people forget*. And yet that is exactly what Christians had done in 1096, even though the pope never mentioned the Jews then as inner enemies. In 1146, it was worse because a cleric had preached it and directly incited riots.

Ephraim then quotes Bernard: "It is good that you go against the Ishmaelites, but *whosoever touches a Jew to take his life, is like one who harms Jesus himself*. My disciple Radulph, who has spoken about annihilating the Jews, has spoken in error."[86] In this remarkable attributed speech, Bernard considers Christians killing Jews to be a reversal of the Passion account. The Christian mob that Radulph has incited is compared to the biblical Jews who were responsible for killing Christ. Now the innocent Jewish victims are like Jesus. This reversal of the Passion points to Christian clerical guilt for Christians killing Jews in the mid-twelfth century.

At nearly the same time that Bernard was blaming Christian killers of Jews for criminal behavior, Thomas of Monmouth was writing the first book of his description of the ritual murder of William of Norwich. In it he has a theory as to why Jews could commit such an act on an innocent Christian boy: Jewish revenge for their suffering at Christian hands. He claims that a "former Jew who is now a monk named Theobold" told about Jewish writings that claim Jews cannot return to their homeland without shedding human blood. "For this reason, each year a Christian must be sacrificed and so *they take revenge for the injuries of Him, whose death is the reason for their exclusion from their fatherland and their exile as slaves in foreign lands*."[87]

Thomas thinks a Jewish ritual murder of a Christ figure is revenge for Jewish suffering in general—suffering that is deserved because the Jews killed Christ. Unlike Bernard, Thomas is not blaming Christians for their treatment of the Jews. But both make a similar assumption about Jews: Christians persecute them. Did this awareness contribute to some Benedictine clerics thinking that Jews were capable of avenging their suffering, justified or not, by reenacting the Passion on an innocent Christian boy?

Rabbi Jacob as a Crucified Jesus Who Lived

Thomas's story about the ritual murder accusation dovetails with Ephraim's speech attributed to Bernard in another way. Both assume that Jews killing a Christian boy or Christians killing Jews now are reenactments of the Passion. In Thomas's case, the ritual murder reenacts the Passion where the Jews kill Christ, but in Bernard's case, the Passion is reversed and guilty Christians kill innocent Christlike Jews. The same Ephraim who tells us about Bernard's speech also reports a story about another reversed reenactment of the Passion of Christ, this time involving a great rabbinic scholar. The figure of Rabbeinu Jacob, as he was usually called in Jewish sources, is an illustrious one. We have some depictions of him engaged in conversation with the Count of Troyes on biblical interpretations as he was active in the county of Champagne.[88] We see him through his work and students from northern France, Germany, and elsewhere. We see him as well bested in hagiographic stories about German Jewish pietist Samuel, the father of Judah the Pious, who travels to see Jacob or wants something of his. And we hear about him physically attacked in a story that some think historical, but that resonates as a memory of the transformation of a rabbi into a Jewish Christ figure.[89]

Here is Ephraim:

> On the second festival day of Shavuot [Pentecost], French crusaders gathered at Rameru[pt], and they came to the house of our Master Rabbi Jacob, may he live, and took all that was in his house. They ripped up a Torah scroll before his face and took him out to a field. There they argued with him about his religion and started to assault him viciously. They inflicted five wounds on his head, saying: "You are the leader of the Jews. So we shall take vengeance upon you for the crucified one and wound you the way you inflicted the five wounds on our god."[90]

Christians with crosses marked on their clothes—that is, contemporary "Crusaders"—attack Jacob, drag him from his house into the field, and impose five stigmata on him. They are about to kill him when a Christian knight intervenes and saves him with the hope that he will convert to Christianity. In this scene of a near-Passion account, a disguised Akedah, or near sacrifice of Isaac

(Gen. 22), Jacob takes on the role of Jesus and the Crusaders reenact the role of the ancient biblical "Jews" (according to John).

The Jewish story portrays Crusaders as the wild hunter Esau, in the field, in contrast to studious R. Jacob b. Meir, as the ancient rabbis imagined the biblical Jacob.[91] The ritual murder accusation reverses the associations, as in earlier church writers such as Augustine of Hippo (d. 430), who identifies Jews as violent Esau and Christians as the innocent (*tam*) Jacob.[92]

Ephraim proceeds to contrast Christianity to the Torah, which the Christians understand to be embodied in the *physical Torah scroll* as well as the *body of the rabbi*. The ripping of the Torah scrolls, as well as killing Jews, is also described repeatedly in the Hebrew narratives about 1096. The scroll is a material and symbolic attack on Judaism that is understood here incorrectly as based on the Bible, not the Talmud. As in 1096, by portraying attacks on the Torah scroll and the Jews who revere it, the Jewish narrators accurately describe Christians who mistakenly equate the two. The Jewish narrators for their part transform the objects of Christian violence into innocent victims who die or are destroyed for the truth. Where are the volumes of the Talmud that Rabbeinu Tam glossed as the great Talmud glossator? The Christians did not know yet about the Talmud. The Jewish reader appreciates the irony because Jacob is the great Talmudist and survives.

Moreover, as in the case of the English allegations of ritual murder, where a cult was established with a saint's day to mark the event of the slain boy's death or spiritual birthday, so with the report on Jacob we see an attempt to mark the occasion with an annual fast day that was not enacted but is mentioned in Ephraim's account.[93]

The near crucifixion of R. Jacob b. Meir, Rabbeinu Tam ("Our Rabbi Innocent") (1100–1171), Rashi's grandson and master Tosafist or Talmud glossator, is also about making a saint, a Jewish saint, by Christian infidels attempting to ritually crucify him. It suggests divine protection of the great rabbi too, as in the saving of Isaac, and a Jewish triumph over the whole Christian salvific idea of the crucifixion.[94]

Ephraim's account of an attack on Jacob reflects an awareness not only of the Passion accounts in the New Testament but its reenactment now as well, as is assumed in the Eucharist and ritual murder accusation that arises in the mid-twelfth century and thereafter. As in Bernard's speech, the attempted ritual murder of Jacob is a reversed Passion account: the Jew plays the role of the innocent Christlike figure, and the violent Crusaders play the role of the biblical Jewish killers of Christ.

By telling a story about the present, in which Christians attack a living Jew who substitutes for Jesus, Ephraim assumes the possibility of a *reenactment in the present of the Passion*. We find just such an assumption underlying contemporary Christian allegations like Thomas's that Jews tried to crucify an innocent Christian boy.

The appearance of these two stories at about the same time in the mid-twelfth century, one in Hebrew and one in Latin, suggests that the idea of the reenactment of the Passion of Christ was commonly held then, at least in some monastic and rabbinic circles, at a time when we know Benedictines and others were interested in identifying new innocent Christian martyr saints. The two stories show that the question of reenacting the Passion and the Jews' role as perpetrators or innocent victims was both shared and contested. Mid-twelfth-century saint making, not echoes of 1096, contextualizes the ritual murder accusations in the middle of the twelfth century, at least in England.

The fact that Jacob was not killed can be viewed as a polemical Jewish version: Jews saw the relationship between God and the Jews as superior to the Passion account. Here Jacob Tam as Jesus = Isaac is saved; God used a knight instead of a ram to intercede and redeem him. Moreover, the failed attempted ritual murder of Jacob argues that the living Jewish saint as Torah scholar is more important than the model of the crucified Christ. Jacob lives to continue to teach his students.

The idea of making martyr saints like Jesus is thus shared in these remarkable Jewish and Christian narratives from the mid-twelfth century, the very time that the ritual murder as reenactment of the Passion of Christ was read into William of Norwich's death as well as others in Benedictine houses in England, and de Torigni's chronicle spread the association to the Continent to include Blois as well as Richard of Pontoise.

In addition to the stories about Bernard and Tam in Ephraim's *Sefer Zekhirah* that portray reversals of the Passion and criticize

Christians for ritually attacking Jews as though they were Christ, there are Latin narratives that make a similar reversal. One of these, unsympathetic to the Jewish victims, is found in Richard of Devizes's *Cronicon*, in which he describes the anti-Jewish riots that broke out at the coronation of Richard I in London in 1189. Here, the author compares the slaughter of Jews as a sacrifice of a whole burnt offering (holocaust) to the sacrifice of the Son to the Father, or Eucharist. This brief narrative conflates priests with Christian murderers of Jews: "On that same coronation day, at about the hour of that solemnity in which the Son was immolated to the Father, they began in the city of London to immolate the Jews to their father, the Devil. It took them so long to celebrate this mystery that the holocaust was barely completed on the second day."[95]

This narrative resembles Ephraim's story about the Crusaders attacking Tam and also pictures Christians attacking Jews as a reversal of the Passion. Both stories portray Christians as the biblical Jews who torture and kill Jesus on the cross, now understood as Jews. Another Latin example of rewriting an attack on Jews as though it were a collective, inverted Passion is the *Passio* of Prague in 1389, which Barbara Newman has analyzed.[96]

In these stories about Jews in reverse Passion accounts, Christians and Jews show an awareness of Christian guilt for what got out of hand in 1146. Some of that sense of clerical guilt for persecuting Jews may have contributed to the belief, reflected in Thomas's theory about the ritual murder of William, that Jews were avenging the suffering that Christians imposed on them for killing Jesus.

In addition, these and other sources reveal that Jews were aware of Christian saints and how Christians invoked them by name, such as when they took an oath, and that Jews had saints of their own.[97] Martyr saints smelled good. Ephraim mentioned in connection with the Würzburg murder accusation that saints work miracles. Christian martyrs sing when they are sacrificed, and so do Jewish martyrs, as at Blois. Ephraim tells us about Bernard, actually sainted in 1174, "All the gentiles regarded this priest as one of their saints (*ki-qedoshim shelahem*)."[98] And we also have evidence that Jews in medieval Ashkenaz developed local practices of going to saints' tombs as in Worms or being buried *ad sanctos* (near the saints' graves).[99]

Jewish Saints in Medieval Germany: Shared Piety about Saints

Learned Jews like Ephraim not only knew that Christians had saints but thought Jews did too. And they did. Like the martyrs of 1096, the Jewish pietists of medieval Germany were aware of unique expressions of Jewish piety. Indeed, this awareness of alternatives to how pious Jews usually behaved stimulated them to conceptualize their religious ideal as an inward struggle, defined as the need of the pietist to make difficult choices between competing values and courses of action.[100]

In his pioneering essay about Judah the Pious and his circle, known as the pietists of medieval Germany (*hasidei ashkenaz*), Solomon Schechter referred to these writers as "Jewish Saints from Medieval Germany."[101] Over the years, the term "saints" seemed inappropriate for a group of Jews living in Christian Europe. Jewish saints? But more recently, it is becoming apparent that the term is apt. Although Jewish saints did not leave relics, they did generate awe and sanctity enough to lead to Jewish behavior that was not traditionally required by biblical or rabbinic norms. Sometimes their teachings even conflicted with the Talmud.[102]

One of the saints of medieval Germany was R. Samuel b. Qalonimos the Pious, the father of Judah the Pious of Regensburg. Samuel lived in Speyer and made his career there, but there are several saint stories about him that picture him traveling around other parts of Christian Europe.[103]

Like the Jewish martyrs of 1096, the pietists appealed to hierarchical considerations when they dealt with other Jews and especially Christians. This was especially so when the pietists discovered that there was great resistance on the part of other Jews to following their revision of traditional Judaism.[104] This resistance and the resulting isolation of the pietists, similar to how the 1096 martyrs had been viewed with horror and shunned by not only the attacking mobs but also those Christian bishops and dignitaries who had once sworn to help them, served to reinforce their group solidarity and produce a sense of the need for exclusivity. Together with their hierarchical views toward Christians, this sense of necessary exclusivity, as will now be seen in some detail, led the pietists to regard all outsiders in roughly identical, hierarchically defined terms. Although the major figures in the pietist circle spanned three generations, R. Samuel b. Qalonimos the Elder (mid-twelfth century), his younger son, Judah the Pious (d. 1217), and Judah's relative and student R. Eleazar ben Judah of Worms (d. ca. 1230), it was Judah the Pious alone, in his magnum opus *Sefer Hasidim* (Book of the pious), who articulated a socioreligious utopian program to be followed by pietists in their dealings with outsiders.[105]

In his discussion of pietist attitudes, Jacob Katz proposed that *Sefer Hasidim* assumes two distinct postures toward Christians. On the one hand, pietists are instructed to avoid contact with Christians and especially their ritual objects. On the other hand, the realities of continuous interaction with Christians in business and the domains of everyday life made such contact unavoidable. Theoretical separation and exclusiveness are contrasted to a de facto recognition that contact between pietists and Christians was inevitable.[106] Yet did the pietists always advocate separation as the ideal? The evidence points to the conclusion that the ideal itself was twofold, and consonant with variations in a hierarchical relationship between pietists and Christians. If pietist contact with Christians was from a position of relative strength or security, with the Christian subordinate to or dependent on the Jew, then there was little reason to fear undue influence, and contact was permitted. It was, however, to be avoided in the absence of a hierarchically favorable boundary, which left the pietist exposed to Christian pressures like those exercised by lay governments. The method of avoiding contact was physical separation. Thus underlying the pietist attitude toward relations with Christians was the same sense of hierarchical boundaries and right order that had shaped the responses of the 1096 martyrs.

Examples of this behavior are not hard to find. Pietists did not, for instance, object to having Christian servants in their homes, including wet nurses, since the Jew was the superior, the employer, and the Christian the inferior, the employee.[107] This was exactly why popes and other clerics were so opposed to the practice. Each was invoking right order. Similarly, a Christian might help a pietist in need of assistance to erect a *sukkah*, for the Jew would sanctify the profane structure only afterward, when while seated in the booth after the festival had commenced, they recited the appropriate blessing.[108] Once an object was sanctified, however, such as an etrog on the same holiday of Sukkot, or a garment that a pietist had used as a tallit, or a cup from which the pietist drank ritually prescribed wine with a blessing, it could not be given or sold to a Christian. As the author of *Sefer Hasidim* puts it, "I would not degrade it from its (state of) holiness," a variation on the Talmudic statement, "We may raise an object to a higher degree of holiness but not degrade it to a lower one."[109]

Again, a pietist was not to pawn a Jewish holy book (*sefer*) to obtain a loan from a Christian, even if the book remained in Jewish hands as collateral. That would be subordinating a Jewish religious object to a Christian lender.[110] And if a pietist needed to have his religious book rebound, he was to prefer a less expert Jewish craftsman over a Christian bookbinder. The Christian might use the leftover scraps of parchment for binding a Christian book, and that would violate the pietist's concept of the correct hierarchical order. On the other hand, a Christian binder could be employed if the binding were to be made from a schoolboy's writing boards, but even then, only on the condition that the pietist himself supervised the work to ensure that the scraps would not be used to bind a Christian book.[111] In a similar vein, a pietist was permitted to interpret the dreams of a Christian, for this made the Christian dependent on the pietist, but pietists were not to reveal their dreams to "people who have them," including, of course, all Christians.[112] A medical remedy was not permissible if it involved anything connected to Jesus.[113]

This cursory examination of provisions in *Sefer Hasidim* reflects the pietists' need to define "right order" by drawing social boundaries between themselves and Christians during times of peace. Jewish saints insisted on being "on top" whenever possible. This posture complemented the extreme behavior during the massacres of 1096, when Jewish martyrs acted out polemical gestures of religious defiance and superiority embodied in ritual killings of other Jews and suicides designed to avoid baptism at all costs. It is not surprising, then, that the two sources that have the most anti-Christian rhetoric, filled with insults to Christianity, are the Hebrew First Crusade chronicles and *Sefer Hasidim*. The former expresses the religious assertiveness of the Jewish martyr at war; the latter, that of the Jewish pietist at peace. But each understood

Jewish martyrs or pietists, respectively, to be in radical opposition to Christianity.

Yet another index of how Jews and Christians understood the other turned on how they regarded the appearance of Jewish and Christian bodies—a subject I refer to as *cultural aesthetics*. When it came to concerns about sexual mixing, Christian authorities thought Jews and Christians were indistinguishable from one another, but when it came to the possibility of Jews converting to Christianity, some Christians pointed to physical features, at least of older male Jews, that made complete conversion impossible despite baptism. A contextual analysis of how Christians thought Jews appeared reveals new aspects of the imagined Jew.

CHAPTER SEVEN

Cultural Aesthetics

SEXUAL THREATS, CONVERSIONS,
AND IMAGINED "RACIAL" JEWS

JEWS AND CHRISTIANS competed with each other not only over the sanctity of the few but also over cultural aesthetics, the imagined appearance of the many. Physical appearance need not be an empirical category. Depending on different contexts, Jews and Christians might seem indistinguishable from one another, if the concern was about sexual fraternization. But when it came to sincere conversions to Christianity, adult Jewish men might have or seem to retain physical features that were permanent. Which was it? Did Jews and Christians look alike? Or were there permanent physical traits that made Jewish men unchanged by baptism? Jews could be both similar and dissimilar to Christians because how Christians perceived the imagined Jew, like the ritual murder accusation, was a cultural construction, not an observation of empirical reality. The appearance of the Jew, as Denise Despres observed, is protean, not constant.[1]

At stake was how appearance related to both a standard of "beauty" and truth claims about each group's religion.[2] The appearance of the body or material things attached to the body, such as clothing, could be a stage on which each group asserted its own collective identity in relation to the oppositional other with whom it lived.

Do Clothes Make the Jew? Or, Do Jews Make the Clothes?

We have been told that in antiquity, it was not possible to tell a Jew when you saw one.[3] What was the situation in medieval Europe?[4] In some neighborhoods today, ultra- and not-so-ultra-Orthodox Jews walk about, sometimes in black pants and open-collar white, long-sleeved shirts, with long white woolen fringes hanging out of their belts, and we forget that there are no medieval illuminations that show visible ritual fringes (zizit) attached to Jewish male figures' clothing. Nor do we find medieval depictions of men with long earlocks (*pei'ot*), another commonplace today even if some hide their tresses by winding their hair around their ears to be less obvious. Similarly, male head covering, a prevalent custom but not a religious law, is not consistently found in the Middle Ages, and more attention is paid to the Jews' hat, a Christian trope, rather than to how Jews portray men's heads as covered or bare (see below).

Married Jewish women seem to be portrayed more visibly in medieval illuminations in accordance with Jewish law and custom by showing them with their hair covered, and we presume that a young woman or girl with visible tresses is unmarried. But how different would such images of Jewish women and girls be from the way married and unmarried Christian women are depicted, at least of the middle class, to which almost all Jews belonged?

The same Fourth Lateran Council that met in 1215 to require that every Christian take communion at least once a year on Easter also issued a canon to require male and female Jews (and Muslims) to wear clothing (*habitus*) that would distinguish them from Christians. The reason given is to avoid sexual contact between men and women of the different religions. Canon 68, issued on November 11, 1215, states,

> Whereas in certain provinces of the Church the difference in their clothes sets the Jews and Saracens apart from the Christians, *in certain other lands* there has arisen such confusion that no differences are noticeable. Thus it sometimes happens that by mistake Christians have intercourse with Jewish or Saracen women, and Jews or Saracens with Christian women. Therefore, lest these people, under the cover of an

error, find an excuse for the grave sin of such intercourse, we decree
that these people (Jews and Saracens) of either sex, and in all Christian
lands, and at all times, shall easily be distinguishable from the rest of
the populations by the quality of their clothes especially since such legislation is imposed upon them also by Moses.[5]

This well-known text has often been cited to argue for the lack of
differentiating features among medieval Jews, Christians, and Muslims, even though this seems far-fetched. Muslims are distinctively
dressed in medieval Christian illuminations, and one wonders if Innocent had ever seen a Muslim man or woman, or an image of either.[6]

Scholars have discussed the implementation of this canon and
how it was interpreted to require a patch of some kind added to
clothing. It varied in its enforcement in different countries as well.[7]
But what is not usually considered is an assumption underlying the
legislation. Were Jews, let alone Muslims, really indistinguishable
from Christians apart from their clothing even "in certain provinces"?[8] Leaving aside the case of Saracens, did Jewish men look
so like Christian men that clothing alone would set them apart and
prevent intimate social mixing?[9] The pope buttresses his case by
referring to the biblical law (Lev. 19:19; Deut. 22:11) that provides
that garments worn by Jews should be distinctive by not containing
mixtures of linen and wool (sha'atnez). This puts the focus of the
canon on Jews rather than Muslims, who were not concerned about
mixing linen and wool in their garments.[10]

If men are wearing clothing that conforms to the prohibition
of mixing linen and woolen fibers, is this visible to an observer?[11]
Elisheva Baumgarten has concluded that where Jewish and Christian men wore similar clothing, Jews apparently could distinguish
between those with or without forbidden mixtures in the stitching,
whereas Christians could not tell the difference.[12] Hence the canon
expresses the need for Jews and others to wear distinctive dress of
some kind. Still, some passages in *Sefer Hasidim*, the great mirror
of medieval religious and social life from early thirteenth-century
Germany, define differences in Jewish and Christian clothing that
Christians apparently can identify and that thereby endanger Jews.

Before considering these cases, note that *Sefer Hasidim* deals
with other situations that make it easy to disguise a Jew's identity:

"One man told his friend: I walked among the non-Jews wearing priestly garb until they (the non-Jews) assumed that he (the narrator) was a priest and did not harm him."[13] Another passage elaborates how one makes clothing look Christian:

> *All who see them shall recognize that they are a stock the Lord has blessed* (Isa. 61:9). How so? Israel (a Jew) should say: Even if soldiers come, they (the Jews) should not stitch crosses on their clothes nor make themselves look like priests, nor place crosses in their homes, nor shave their heads in the manner of priests and monks.[14]

It is not permitted to resort to using objects of Christian worship or wearing clerical dress even if it is effective to disguise one's identity: "But a Jew who did not apostatize, should not wear a cross or dress up as a monk or priest in order that no one recognize him. He can change his clothes but he should not shave off his beard."[15]

Sefer Hasidim also deals with other possibilities, such as a Jew disguising his identity by wearing Christian clothes:

> It once happened during a persecution that a (Jew) was wearing (Christian) clothes and escaped because (the Christians) thought he was a Christian. He asked, "Do I need atonement for wearing clothes made of forbidden mixtures?" They said to him, "Since you thought about (what you would wear) in advance, you should have bought a proper garment and mended it with yarn that was not made of flax. You need atonement." [See Lev. 19:19; Deut. 22:9–11].[16]

Could Christians detect Jewish clothes? Apparently so:

> A man is traveling in a convoy and has a change of clothing free of forbidden mixtures of threads. If he travels wearing Jewish clothes, he might cause harm to other Jews (by being taken captive for ransom). He would be indirectly responsible for harming them all. But someone who indirectly causes *good* to many is like one who did good himself.[17]

This situation assumes that Christians can tell a Jew from a Christian based on the "Jewish clothing" that lacks forbidden mixtures. In another case, a Jewish man is advised to wear a "heavy coat" made of forbidden mixtures to disguise his religious identity. Is it to hide his Jewish clothing? If so, the assumption is that Christians could identify him by his "Jewish" clothes that lack forbidden mixtures.

> A story about a pious Jew who went on a trip with a group. They said, "Wear a heavy coat so that they do not recognize you." He said, "I will not wear it because it is sewn with forbidden mixtures of thread." As a result, they caught him, and other Jews had to ransom him. The righteous man worked until he paid off (the ransom). For he said, "I caused this myself. For whoever has to go on a trip should prepare clothes made of linen (*cannibas*) or silk thread so that there will not be in it any forbidden mixture, so it is ready for him when he sets out on his journey."[18]

In an exemplum about the riots in 1096, it seems a rabbi thought he could look like a Christian just by holding a cross, but apparently his Jewish clothing gave him away:

> Two apostates were brothers. The sage looked into their ancestry to find out what could have caused this. When "the persecution" took place [in 1096], the community said, "What should we do?" The rabbi said, "Observe what I do and act likewise." He took a cross and carried it so that Christians would not kill him. But they forcibly converted him and the other townsmen anyway. That is why his children apostatized.[19]

Even if Christians could tell Jews by their clothing, the papal canon assumes otherwise. The assumption behind the new legislation to mark Jews (and Muslims) from Christians is that they are indistinguishable. It is not about facts but instead a construction of an imagined Jew who for purposes of sexual separation from Christians is presumed to look no different from them.

On Beards and Hats

Apart from clothing, *Sefer Hasidim* assumes that a beard defines adult Jewish men—that is, people who are not women, young men, or Christians:

> A story about a very beautiful Jewish woman who was going on a trip with her husband. She made a beard for herself from her girlfriend's hair and attached it to her face. Anyone who saw her would think that

she was a man and she would thus be saved from harm. This is also the same for young men who have no beard. They should wear women's clothes to save themselves from harm or Christian clothing to mislead the enemy. This is like Rabbi Meir, who put one finger into something forbidden but put a different finger in his mouth.[20]

Although there is mixed evidence about Jewish men having beards in medieval northern Europe, age has generally not been taken into account in assessing the evidence.[21] Beards and perhaps also the Jews' hat may be signs of a mature adult Jewish man, as we learn, for example, in a medieval German poem by Süsskind von Trimberg, a late thirteenth-century Jewish minnesinger or professional troubadour. The poem is preserved in the *Manesse Codex* of medieval German poetry in Heidelberg. The poet says he will retire from the court to become a Jew and "allow his beard of gray hair to grow long, henceforth will go on to live as old Jews live, his cloak shall be long, deep-shaded by a hat, he will walk in all humility."[22]

Even today, some traditional rabbis go clean-shaven until they reach the age of forty, after which they feel obligated to grow a beard.[23] An adult male being clean-shaven is attested elsewhere as having proper attire when serving in a Christian court.[24] Another issue to consider is regional differences and how Jews lined up with one ethnic community compared to another in the same region. For example, were Jews in England more likely to be clean-shaven like the Normans whose language they continued to speak?[25]

Jewish hats are also unevenly distributed in the visual sources, and the related custom of Jewish males covering their heads was slow in developing in Jewish practice. Sara Lipton's idea that the hat looks like a Christian mitre on a senior church official is to my eyes not obvious. It can also be compared to the cupola on the top of the Worms Dom towers and many other similarly shaped objects that are an even better fit than a bishop's mitre. Leaving aside the shape, its meaning as a Christian requirement, accepted by some Jewish men, seems likely to explain its origins. Andreas Lehnhertz and Hannah Teddy Schachter have proposed that Jewish men wore the hat at times of self-presentation, such as at public encounters with Christian authorities.[26]

Clothing, like a false beard, can also be used to make a Jewish woman look like a man if lives are at risk:

> Even though the Torah said, *A woman must not put on man's apparel* (Deut. 22:5), and a man should not wear a woman's dress, if enemies besieged the town, or if one is on the road and if they were to know that they were women they would violate them, they may go in male attire, even with a sword so that the others think they are men. If ten men came to attack and there were only ten Jewish men there, and there are about forty Jewish women, they should put on a sword so that the attackers think they are men and not harm them all.[27]

And clothing can disguise a Jewish woman's religious identity too:

> A Jewish woman who travels abroad and hears that Christians might violently harm her, fearing that someone might rape her, may disguise herself as a nun so that they will think she is a nun and will not rape her. If she heard that lawless Jews might harm her, she also may wear a Christian woman's clothes, say that she is a Christian woman, and tell them that if they harm her, she will scream and turn them over to the Christian authorities. She may even scream before they actually attack her to get Christians to come to her aid, even if they kill the lawless Jewish men.[28]

This passage suggests that Jewish and Christian women who were not nuns wore different clothing.

And yet there are some sources that are not clear about how distinctive Jews were. Was it possible for a Christian not to know that a man was a Jew unless he said so? On the verse, *Moses' bones were not permitted to enter the Land of Israel because he did not say, I am a Hebrew* (Ex. 2:19), *Sefer Hasidim* comments, "From this it follows that a man who hears that Christians are saying about him that he is a Christian should say, 'I am a Jew.'"[29] Similarly, Guibert de Nogent describes Jean, count of Soissons, who "sometimes acted like a Jew and at other times like a Christian." Did he change his clothes, or did Jewish and Christian men dress alike but "act" differently? How did he fool both?[30]

These and other anecdotal sources from *Sefer Hasidim* and elsewhere deal with questions about how Jews appear to Christians based mainly on clothing, and this emphasis seems to confirm Innocent III's focus on clothing—occasionally with beards—as the key marker of religious identity at least in the early thirteenth century.[31]

Although it took time to interpret and implement the canon in different countries, it was being taken seriously by the end of the thirteenth century, as in Castile's King Alfonso X's *Siete Partidas'* laws about sexual mixing. Book 24, law 9, provides the death penalty for "Jews [males] who live with Christian women" because they deserve the same penalty Christian men receive for committing adultery with a married woman, since all Christian women "are spiritually the wives of Our Lord Jesus Christ." To avoid such mixing, the law continues in book 24, law 11,

> Many crimes and outrageous things occur between Christians and Jews because they live together in cities, and dress alike; and in order to avoid the offenses and evils which take place for this reason, We deem it proper, and we order that all Jews, male and female, living in our dominions shall bear some distinguishing *mark upon their heads* so that people may plainly recognize a Jew, or a Jewess; and any Jew who does not bear such a mark shall pay for each time he is found without it ten maravedis of gold; and if he has not the means to do this he shall receive ten lashes for his offense.[32]

The earliest image we have of the implementation in England is a sketch of "Aaron the Devil."[33] Laws were passed as early as 1217 under Henry III in England, followed by the Council of Oxford in 1222, Louis IX in France in 1269, and the Iberian kingdoms in the thirteenth century, but not in the German Empire and environs until the fifteenth century.[34]

The emphasis in canon 68 and *Sefer Hasidim* on clothing that conforms to the rules of forbidden mixtures avoids explicit Christian symbols and clerical dress or grooming (tonsure) but leaves open the issue of beards on grown men. Sara Lipton has shown how so-called Jewish male signifiers such as beards or Jews' hats are distributed among Jewish and Christian figures, as in representations at Chartres, and argues that this changes only in the middle of the thirteenth century.[35] It is not clear, then, whether beards and hats mark adult Jewish males more than Jewish boys in any consistent way in light of different probabilities of converting.

Canon 68 of the Fourth Lateran Council is consistent with the visual evidence that telling a Jew from a Christian was not culturally conceded, regardless of the social realities in small face-to-face communities where everyone knew who was who. Note that all the signifiers mentioned so far can be removed: clothes, Jews' hats, and beards. None is regarded as a physical characteristic like skin or hair color, smell, unusual bleeding, or nose shape. The emphasis on clothing, including hats and beards, thus ignores a whole range of physical and aesthetic questions about how Jews and Christians appeared to or looked at the other. As we will see, this changed by the middle of the thirteenth century, at least for older Jewish men.

Before looking at this change, it is important first to consider criteria of Christian beauty. We will see that there was some agreement about what constituted beauty. We can start with a Christian idealization of physical beauty and see how Jews and Christians adapted to it, especially in the later thirteenth century and after. The ideal has implications for how Jews and Christians regarded the appearance of Jewish women and men differently. This difference will reflect how Christians thought Jewish women and men might be able to convert to Christianity, sincerely or not. Again, the issue will not be how people actually looked to others but rather how others imagined them to appear—the subject of cultural aesthetics.

Ideals of Christian Beauty

In the literary traditions of medieval France, we find examples of a well-defined aesthetic ideal for males and females. In many cases, we see beauty as a defining Christian feature that others may acquire by converting. This standard of beauty is expressed in such works as the anonymous French *Aucassin and Nicolette*, a work of parody, probably from the early thirteenth century, that portrays two ideal male and female figures engaged in a quest for love and honor. Aucassin is the noble Christian male: "He was tall and handsome and courtly, with well-formed legs and feet and body and arms. He had tightly curled blond hair and bright, laughing eyes, and a shining oval face with a proud and well-placed nose."[36]

Compare the expression of beauty of the male lover in Song of Songs 5:10–16:

> My beloved is clear-skinned and ruddy, preeminent among ten thousand. His head is finest gold; his locks are curled and black as a raven; his eyes are like doves by watercourses bathed in milk set by a brimming pool; His cheeks are like beds of spices, Banks of perfume His lips are like lilies; They drip flowing myrrh; His hands are rods of gold, Studded with beryl; His belly a tablet of ivory, Adorned with sapphires; His legs are like marble pillars Set in sockets of fine gold. He is majestic as Lebanon, Stately as the cedars; His mouth is delicious And all of him is delightful. Such is my beloved, Such is my darling, O maidens of Jerusalem!

The contrast of blond, not black, curly hair as well as ruddy skin coloring appears in Christian descriptions of beauty. In the French romance, Nicolette, a baptized Saracen, is described as "the pretty girl with golden hair."[37] And "She had blond, tightly curled hair, lively, laughing eyes, an oval face, a high, well-placed nose, lips redder than a cherry or a rose in summertime, and small white teeth."[38]

In contrast, we also have a detailed counterdescription of a male who is considered ugly:

> He was tall and looked bizarre, ugly and hideous. He had a big head, blacker than a lump of coal, and there was more than a hand's breadth between his two eyes, and he had a huge pair of cheeks and gigantic flat nose and a pair of big, wide nostrils, and a thick pair of lips redder than a grilled steak, and a set of wide teeth, yellowed and ugly.[39]

An illustration of how baptism can turn an infidel into a "beautiful" white Christian is seen in the early fourteenth-century Middle English romance *The King of Tars*. Here a Muslim sultan desires to marry a beautiful Christian princess, but her father refuses to give his consent. A war ensues, and the sultan wins. The daughter pretends to convert to Islam and gives birth to a lump. Each side prays to change the lump into a child. The Muslim fails, but the Christian priest succeeds, and as a result, the sultan converts to Christianity. When that happens, his black skin turns white.[40] This story includes both the possibility of a feigned conversion, as in the case of the Christian princess, and the transformation of skin color after conversion to Christianity.

Another illustration of this possibility, closer to home, is the exemplum from late thirteenth-century England about a French priest who "loved a certain Jewess with a mad desire." Each wanted to have sex on the other's holiday and each at first refused to do so, but in the end "was defeated." As a result, the priest's white vestments and the priest himself all became black. She converted, he repented, and his vestments and body became white.[41]

How did Christians and Jews think these ideals of beauty applied to the other and themselves? Did different contexts produce different ideas of beauty and religious truth, and how was beauty related to conversion?

Synagoga and Ecclesia

Besides the anecdotal evidence from *Sefer Hasidim*, a set of Christian representations of Jews and Christians known as synagoga and ecclesia, respectively, suggests similarities of not only dress but also facial appearance and "beauty" apart from specific symbolic differences that distinguished them. Moreover, these images seem to confirm the assumption underlying Innocent III's insistence that Jews look no different from Christians unless they wear unique external markings.

From the ninth century on, we find pairs of Passion scenes in different media in which two female figures appear. One represents the Jews to Christ's left and the other Christians to his right. Although the early examples tended to be found in luxury items seen by a limited audience, by the thirteenth century, a time of some ecclesiastical and lay efforts to convert Jews, monumental figures were added to major cathedrals, where larger audiences of Jews and Christians could easily see them.[42]

There is an inherent ambiguity in these figures, who are both females. On the one hand, they each represent Jews and Christians of both genders. On the other, they are female figures and can be read as referring to Jewish and Christian women.[43]

Setting the synagoga apart from the ecclesia is neither gender nor beauty; rather, it is an iconography of defeat and rejection that alludes to biblical Israel's defeat in her broken staff (Jer. 48:17), loss of crown (Lam. 5:16), and blindness (Lam. 5:17; cf. Matt. 23).

The church, in contrast, is clear-sighted, wears a crown, and holds a straight staff and sometimes an orb representing dominion. The synagoga also sometimes holds inverted stone tablets representing the Old Testament.

And yet in most cases, the facial features of both female figures are identical. Both are "beautiful."[44] The assumption underlying the two female faces seems to be that despite the differences in added symbolic iconography, there is a fundamental similarity between the two figures. Underlying this aesthetic similarity is Paul's parable of the wild olive tree in his Letter to the Romans, in which he proclaims that there is hope for the Jews to be regrafted back onto the trunk of the tree of Israel if they accept Christ (Rom. 11:23). That basic truth is only temporarily modified by Augustine's motif of the Jews as blind witnesses to the Christian truth.

The beauty of synagoga as well as ecclesia seems to argue that a Jew, of either sex, now may be rejected, and without power or knowledge of the truth, but they are still a *potential* Christian. Unlike blind figures in antiquity, the synagoga is blindfolded—a temporary blindness that can be remedied.[45] When the blindfold will come off, the staff will become whole and the crown restored, and the true meaning of the Old Testament will be understood as anticipating the Gospels. The Jew will become a Christian. Further support for this interpretation of high medieval synagoga is found in representations of the Jew as synagoga in apocalyptic writings where synagoga and ecclesia are portrayed identically because the Jew has converted to Christianity.[46]

This depiction of the beautiful synagoga, who is beautiful because she *can* convert to Christianity in the future, resembles the Muslim princess in *The King of Tars*. The assumption that an infidel Muslim or Jewish woman can convert to Christianity is expressed by the portrayal of the female infidel as beautiful *now*.

Jews were aware of the truth claims implicit in the appearance of the two representations, and asserted the truth of Judaism using the symbolic vocabulary of the Christian ecclesia and synagoga. We find a Jewish visual polemic of synagoga's claims against ecclesia's in a Hebrew manuscript illumination that seems to depict the protagonists of the Song of Songs as an allegory: the female figure represents Israel, and the male figure represents God. The *Levy Mahzor* contains a single figurative illumination that accompanies a liturgical poem (piyyut) based on a verse from the Song of Songs and written for the Sabbath preceding Passover. A man wearing a pointed Jewish hat faces a woman wearing both a crown and a blindfold.[47]

The image is incongruent. It seems to portray the two lovers in the Song of Songs as a Jewish man and woman, but it is not clear why the woman wears a crown topped by cross-like figures as well as a blindfold. As in many cases of Jewish inward acculturation, an earlier model in the Talmud refers to wreaths or crowns worn by Jewish brides. But there is no continuous history of this custom, and the illustrations appear for the first time when Mary is becoming increasingly important in Christian piety.[48]

This motif is a polemical adaptation of the Christian coronation of Mary, sometimes portrayed as the bride of Christ. The depiction of a crowned Jewish bride can be read as the *Levy Mahzor*'s challenge to the idea of Mary as the Virgin, similar in purpose to the 1096 Hebrew chronicle narratives of Jewish women as martyred saints who were wives and mothers of families. The image of a crowned Jewish bride also is a riposte to the synagoga depiction of the crownless Jew. Despite the political reality that the Jews have little collective power, the crowning of a bride serves to place cultural power in the institution of marriage and procreation. But what of the synagoga-like blindfold right under the crown? This seems to combine the crown of ecclesia with the blindfold of synagoga. In the *Levy Mahzor*, we have an oxymoronic image: a crowned, blindfolded woman. Is she a "synaclesia" or "ecclagoga"? Which is it?

In light of all that we have seen thus far about Jews' keen awareness of Christian images and sometimes even texts, it is highly unlikely that they were unaware of the meanings of a crowned bride who is also depicted as a synagoga figure. It is in fact inconceivable for medieval Ashkenazic Jews to think of themselves as anything other than divinely chosen over Christians. Given their tendency to transform Christian symbols into pro-Jewish ideas that can be read as an anti-Christian social polemic, it would be surprising if that is not happening here as well.

If we look at the text that the illumination accompanies, we will understand better what is at stake. The poem is based on a verse from the Song of Songs, the biblical book read in the synagogue on the festival of Passover. The verse reads, *From Lebanon come with me; from Lebanon, my bride, with me! Look down [tashuri] from Amana's peak, from the peak of Senir and Hermon* (4:8).

The poem, which also begins with the first two words of the verse "from Lebanon come with me" (*iti mi-levanon*), shortens the rest of the verse and changes the word order to read,

> From Lebanon look out with me, my bride (*kalah*),
> From Amana's peak (*mei-rosh*) look down (*tashuri*).

The lines end with the words "bride" and "look down" and include the word "head" (*rosh*), all focusing attention on the bride's head and eyes. Rashi of Troyes understood the verse to refer allegorically to the romance between God and Israel: "From the time you left here until when you return here, I am with you through all your comings and goings." And specifically on the word "tashuri," Rashi says, "When I gather together your scattered ones, you will *see* and *understand* the reward of your work from the earliest trust you put in Me, when you followed Me in the desert" (see Jer. 2:2). The central image in both the verse and piyyut is the bride's sight.

Given the emphasis on the bride's sight and understanding, it is possible to understand the female image as a twofold polemic. On the one hand, it proclaims that although the Christian world may *think* the Jews are blind to what Christians claim to be the truth, it is the *Jews* who see and understand God. The blindfold ironically represents the Jews *from a Christian perspective*, which the artist judges to be false. Jews are the true crowned bride who is God's beloved, and Jewish women are the wives of real, mortal husbands with whom they form Jewish family units. On the other hand, the crowned bride, ecclesia, is really the blind one. The crown does not belong on the head of the imitation bride, Mary, the false Christian celibate female ideal. The power of the church is illusory and temporary. God's love for Israel is eternal.

Like the Jewish comparisons to Christ in the almost crucified Rabbi Jacob that we saw in chapter 6, the image of the crowned, blindfolded bride is an internalization of Christian symbols subverted into a pro-Jewish message of triumph and turned against Christianity. A further sign of ironic symbolism is the depiction of the male groom figure, an allegorical representation of God, wearing the Jewish man's pointed hat. Both the hat and the blindfold are ironic indicators that Jews triumph over Christians despite appearances. In addition, the crowned bride alludes to the crowned Virgin in Christian iconography; Mistress Rachel in the Hebrew Crusade chronicles is associated there with Mary too. In both cases, Mary has been replaced by real Jewish women as a bride or martyred mother, respectively.[49]

The Jewish patron is making an argument to all who see it, admittedly a limited audience of cantors and members of the synagogue that commissioned it, not a public space like a cathedral facade in Paris, Reims, Strasbourg, or Bamberg, where monumental statues of synagoga and ecclesia appear for all to view. Although the church thinks of Jews as blind, here she actually wears the crown. Jews are hierarchically above Christians. Appearances are deceptive. And although the church says that Christians who are powerful know the truth, here they are really the blind ones. Christians are below Jews. The double image is a way of saying that the crown is mine and the blindfold is yours, not the opposite.

This reading means that for the Jewish patron, the church is blind despite the power of the crown. For the moment, the Jews accept the appearance of the beautiful ecclesia but deny her any claims to the truth. She is beautiful yet false.

"I Am Dark but Comely" (Song of Songs 1:5)

Iconographic images like blindfolds can be removed, as can beards, hats, or distinctive clothing, but what about skin color in distinguishing one group from another? This issue brings us closer to the question of permanent appearance as a distinguishing measure of Jews and Christians.

In the allegorical interpretations of the Song of Songs, there is the association in biblical exegesis of the female lover representing the Jewish people and the male figure as God. In this personification, the female serves to signify all Jews and also can be interpreted as embodying female Jews. In this, the figure resembles synagoga that can serve doubly to represent all Jews or only Jewish women. What does it mean that the female figure representing the Jewish people says, "I am black but beautiful"?

Rashi (d. 1105) applies the verse allegorically to the Jewish people and reads the dark appearance as a temporary state of sin, not as a permanent condition. Like sin, the skin color can become white or righteous over time, or reform. It is not a comment about a permanent attribute, although he reads having black skin now as a negative value compared to being white:

> *I am dark, but comely, O daughters of Jerusalem—Like the tents of Kedar, Like the pavilions of Solomon* (Song of Songs 1:5).
>
> *Don't stare at me because I am swarthy, Because the sun has gazed upon me. My mother's sons quarreled with me, They made me guard the vineyards; My own vineyard I did not guard* (Song of Songs 1:6).

In Jewish biblical interpretation, the figure of the beautiful but dark female in the Song of Songs asserts the real beauty of the female figure and explains why she is dark by appealing to different contingencies. Rashi notes that the apparent rejection of Israel is just that, apparent, and is partly related to Israel's past sinful status, which that like dark skin, is only temporary:

> *I am dark but comely*—You, my friends, let me not be unimportant in your eyes. Even if my husband has left me because of my blackness, for I am black because of the tanning of the sun, but I am comely with the shape of beautiful limbs. Though I am black like the tents of Kedar, which are blackened because of the rains, for they are always spread out in the wilderness, I am easily cleansed to become like the curtains of Solomon.
>
> The allegory is: The congregation of Israel says to the nations, "I am black in my deeds [i.e., sins], but I am comely by virtue of the deeds of my ancestors, and even some of my deeds are comely. If I bear the iniquity of the [golden] calf, I can offset it with the merit of the acceptance of the Torah."

Within this allegorical framing, Rashi continues to elaborate the meaning of the Jews as dark as not inborn but instead caused by climate and exposure to the sun while in exile in Egypt, or on account of an earlier sin that can be expiated by righteously following the Torah. The darkness and ugliness are presented as a negative yet temporary condition and do not undermine the inner truth and beauty of the Jew. This is so, despite potentially contrasting verses such as *Can the Cushite change his skin* (Jer. 23:13), on which Rashi has little to say.

> *Don't stare at me.* Do not look upon me disrespectfully . . .
>
> *Because I am swarthy.* For my blackness and my ugliness are not from my mother's womb, but from the sun's tanning, for that blackness can easily be whitened by staying in the shade.
>
> *My mother's sons quarreled with me.* These are the Egyptians among whom I grew up, and they went up with me in the mixed multitude. They were incensed against me with their enticement and their persuasion until *they made me guard the vineyards.* And there the sun tanned me and I became swarthy; i.e., they made me a worshiper of other gods, but *my own vineyard* [i.e., my God], which was mine from my forefathers, *I did not keep.*[50]

The argument in Rashi, commenting on a biblical verse that associates dark with beauty, leads to his explaining how dark is temporary. In later Jewish polemical handbooks containing arguments against Christianity, we find the idea that Jews, apparently women as well as men, are being accused of being dark and ugly. These Jewish sources in northern Europe start off by appearing to concede the Christians' claim, but as in Rashi, the Jewish author turns the accusation on its head and argues that appearance is not reality. R. Joseph b. Nathan Official's polemical handbook, from the second half of the thirteenth century, considered earlier in chapter 4, compares the appearance and reality between Jews and Christians to different fruit:

> *And I, in turn, have made you despicable and vile in the eyes of all the people(s)* (Mal. 2:9). An apostate said to R[abbi] Nathan, "You (Jews) are uglier than anyone else on the face of the earth! Our people are very beautiful!"
>
> He answered him: "Those (black) plums that are called 'prunels' that grow in bushes, what kind of flowers do they have?" He said to him, "White." "And what is the flower of the apple?" He said to him, "Red." He said to him, "Similarly, we too are from a pure, white seed and so our faces are black. But you are from red seed, from menstruants. For this reason, your complexion is yellowish / golden and ruddy / rosy.

There is a reason: since we are in exile, as it says in Song of Songs: *Don't stare at me because I am swarthy, because the sun has gazed upon me. My mother's sons quarreled with me, they made me guard the vineyards; my own vineyard I did not guard* (Song of Songs 1:6). But when I did guard my vineyard, I was very beautiful, as is written, *Your beauty won you fame among the nations* (Ezek. 16:14)."[51]

The passage first concedes the Christian claim that Jews are "uglier than anyone else on the face of the earth" without specifying in what that ugliness consists.[52] Only in the Jew's reply is skin color mentioned as the criterion of ugliness or beauty. By emphasizing the color of the seed as white and the skin as dark, the Jew turns the tables on the Christian and confirms that white is the inner truth, and better than external and contingent black. It is the Christian whose flower is red, associated with menstrual blood, which results in a skin color that is "yellowish / golden and ruddy / rosy." The Jew's argument goes further than claiming a white origin despite the black result. The Jew's dark complexion is temporary. Originally, Jews were beautiful but became dark-skinned because of the sun.

A second version by R. Joseph Official is found in another Hebrew manuscript. It also asserts that the difference of appearance between Jews and Christians is temporary, and uses the past, present, and future to prove the point:

If a [Christian] (*goy*) says to you: "We are so beautiful. You are not." Tell him: "Before our Temple was destroyed, we were more beautiful, as you find in Daniel when Nabuchadnezzar took Hanania, Mishael, and Azaria to serve him (?) and he did not find in his people any as handsome as they. Also, Jeremiah said in the Scroll of Lamentations: *The precious children of Zion once valued as gold* (Lam. 4:2); *those who were reared in purple* (Lam. 4:5).

"And when our Temple was destroyed, our beauty was taken away, as is also written in Lamentations: *Alas they are accounted as earthen pots* (Lam. 4:2)."

"In the future the Holy One, blessed be He, will restore beauty to us, as it says in Jeremiah: *I will build you firmly again, O Maiden Israel! Again, you shall take up your timbrels and go forth to the rhythm of the dancers* (Jer. 31:4)."[53]

The argument here is historical and contingent. Jews once were beautiful, but as a result of sin and exile they lost their beauty, as reflected in the destruction of the Temple and exile; yet once there is a restoration, it will return. The assumption is that change is possible and Jews are inherently beautiful, not ugly.

This understanding of dark skin color as temporary is also found in Christian claims that conversion to Christianity can make someone beautiful, as in the case of the Saracen king in *The King of Tars*. This assumption is consistent with the Christian representation of synagoga as beautiful too, since it assumes that she can appear to be just as beautiful as ecclesia if she removes the blindfold—that is, converts.

The assumption that the Jew's appearance differs in the present age and future messianic times is found in the early fifteenth-century polemical handbook by Rabbi Yom Tov Lipmann Mühlhausen:

> On the verse: *Their offspring shall be known among the nations, Their descendants in the midst of the peoples. All who see them shall recognize that they are a stock the Lord has blessed* (Isa. 61:9): From here we find an answer to those mockers who say that some Jews are recognizably (unattractive) as Jews. For in the days of the Messiah we will all be recognizably attractive, as is stated here.[54]

The anonymous author of the Jewish polemical handbook *Nizzahon Vetus*, written around 1300 in medieval Germany, assumes that Christians are immoral and that is why they look different from Jews. It contains a striking comment about Jews and Christians based on their physical appearance belied by their inner value. In this rewriting of Official's earlier text, we see the contrast in the question as between fair-skinned and handsome gentiles versus dark and ugly Jews:

> The heretics ask: Why are most Gentiles fair-skinned and handsome while most Jews are dark and ugly? Answer them that this is similar to a fruit; when it begins to grow it is white but when it ripens it becomes black, as is the case with sloes and plums. On the other hand, any fruit which is red at the beginning becomes lighter as it ripens, as is the case with apples and apricots. This, then, is testimony that Jews are pure of

menstrual blood so that there is no initial redness. Gentiles, however, are not careful about menstruant women and have sexual relations during menstruation. Thus, there is redness at the outset; and so, the fruit that comes out, i.e., the children, are light. One can respond further by noting that Gentiles are incontinent and have sexual relations during the day, at a time when they see the faces on attractive pictures; therefore, they give birth to children who look like those pictures, as it is written, "and the sheep conceived when they came to drink before the rods" (Gen. 30:39).[55]

This version seems to refer to Jewish and Christian men, not all Jews. Underlying this comparison is an assumption about the ideal beauty and ugliness. The association here is refined somewhat so that yellow and rosy are now referred to as "light" in contrast to black. The conclusion offers a natural explanation buttressed by the biblical precedent of Jacob's trick on Laban in getting sheep to reproduce spotted, speckled, and striped offspring by exposing them when mating to stripped branches that are white and dark (Gen. 30). The polemical passages do not refer to the Song of Songs 1:5-6 but instead to other verses, suggesting that we have different approaches to the issue of Jewish appearance compared to Christians.

All the Christian and Jewish sources so far agree that Jews appear different from Christians apart from their clothing. Rashi wants to explain how being dark is a temporary condition and does not contradict the beauty mentioned in the verse. Not tied down to explaining a verse, the polemical texts reverse the meaning of dark and ugly as external appearance as well as a temporary condition, not something essential. The synagoga, too, is beautiful but temporarily blind, the way Jews might be temporarily dark and ugly, because if they remove their blindfold—that is, convert—they will be as beautiful as Christians represented by ecclesia.[56]

The "Beautiful" Jewish Women

Did Jews internalize the Christian judgment that Jews were dark and ugly for Jewish men but not Jewish women?[57] In his study of images of medieval peasants, Paul Freedman shows how there was a gender difference between images of male and female peasants. At least until the late Middle Ages, peasant males were described often as ugly, while peasant women could be attractive and alluring. This changed in the later Middle Ages, when peasant women too were now portrayed as ugly.[58] Did a similar pattern obtain regarding Jewish men and women?

In Christian writings, apart from synagoga and ecclesia, there is a widespread assumption that Jewish women are beautiful, if only to suggest their sexual attractiveness and danger, and perhaps to mitigate Christian clerics succumbing to their lures.[59] Thus in Caesarius of Heisterbach's *Dialogue on Miracles*, we find four elaborate exempla that feature Jewish females. The two that refer to beauty involve a young Jewish women in a sexual liaison with a Christian cleric. One begins, "In a city of England there lived the daughter of a Jew, who, like many of her race, was a very beautiful girl."[60] The other opens, "In the city, I think, of Worms there lived a Jew who had a beautiful daughter."[61] It is only these two that describe a sexual encounter between a "beautiful" Jewish daughter and a Christian cleric. The other two exempla feature young Jewish girls and their conversion but say nothing about their appearance. This difference suggests that the designation of "beautiful" is meant to denote sexual availability and attractiveness independent of conversion.[62]

The motif of the beautiful Jewish woman is also found in the *Cantigas de Santa Maria* of Alfonso X, as Edna Aisenberg, Louise Mirrer, and Sara Lipton have noted.[63] And it is a theme that reappears in much of Western literature, as in the figures of Abigail in *The Jew of Malta*, Jessica in *The Merchant of Venice* (see chapter 8), and later in Rebecca in Walter Scott's *Ivanhoe*.

From Clothes to the Physical Appearance of Jews

The beautiful Jewish woman and her readiness to convert to Christianity, as in the synagoga, raises the possibility that Jewish men may be different and less likely to convert successfully. This question, in turn, will bring us to consider aspects of Jewish physical or "racial" identity along with how they may inhibit the possibility of religious conversion.

Until the mid-thirteenth century, clothes seem to make the Jew (or Christian), and the social context of papal legislation was a concern about sexual mixing. The Fourth Lateran Council canon 68 in 1215 requiring special clothing and the exempla in *Sefer Hasidim* (before 1225) along with the similarly dressed ecclesia and synagoga are concerned with clothing or symbolic iconography as indicators of religious identity, not physical features. It is assumed that Jews and Christians are otherwise indistinguishable. The imagined Jew is physically not different from the ideal of Christian beauty.

There may be inconsistent use of the Jews' hats or beards as well as the absence of physical features that begin to combine only by the second half of the thirteenth century into a profile of the adult Jew. Bernhard Blumenkranz and Sara Lipton considered many of these aesthetic issues about Jews and when they began to make an appearance in Christian art. Blumenkranz noted that there were few facial differences before the thirteenth century as, for example, in the dual images of Peter Alfonsi before and after he converted from Judaism.[64]

But from the second half of the thirteenth century, we see a different picture emerging in words and images: the aesthetics of the ugly and dark male Jew compared to the beautiful Jewish woman and the beautiful Christian man and woman. A new aesthetic standard appears, according to which one can correlate beauty and ugliness with truth and falsehood, Christian and Jew, apart from what they wear. Now what they *are* becomes as important. In addition to skin color, Jews and Christians now had views about the distinctive appearance of members of the other religious community and themselves based on physical features that Irven Resnick has aptly referred to as "marks of distinction."[65] Here, too, as Resnick and Lipton observed, there was a significant gender difference in how Christians marked the appearance of Jewish men in contrast to how they relatively ignored marking Jewish women—a subject worth exploring further.[66]

Some, though not all, physical features attributed to Jews are connected to Jewish men.[67] Although the polemical sources that refer to dark and ugly do not stipulate gender, the generalization that all Jews are dark and ugly is challenged by the strong countertradition that Jewish women are beautiful.

In one case of Christian self-representation, instead of women being depicted as blonde, there is a tradition that discusses Mary as dark haired because of her Jewish origins. Thus a Latin source by Ps. Albert refers to Mary as dark haired because Jewish:

> With respect to their innate complexion, offspring are accustomed to be like their parents, and vice versa. But we see that in many cases the race of Jews has black hair. Therefore, also our Lady, since she was the progeny of Jews.[68]

Other physical characteristics, like circumcision, are identified as male. Jewish men bleeding monthly or annually is a theme that becomes more prominent by the thirteenth century. This combines references to the guilt for deicide with efforts to feminize Jewish men. This includes the notion associated with the biblical verse *His blood be on ourselves and on our children* (Matt. 27:25), which Jacques de Vitry and Thomas de Cantimpré associated with the pseudoscientific idea that Jewish men menstruated. One of the rationales for the blood libel is connected to this idea of a male loss of blood.[69] Even when Jews thought of themselves as fighting knights in verbal encounters with Christians over their beliefs, there were efforts to make Jewish knights seem effeminate.[70] Above all, and with a persisting afterlife, the Jewish nose is gendered, and it persists as a defining male antisemitic characteristic, especially after the mid-thirteenth century down to the present.[71]

Can Jewish Men Become Christians?

Is there a causal relation between the new prominence of these physical features, especially in relation to adult male Jews, from the mid-thirteenth century on and an increase in the effort to convert Jews in northern Europe that is thought to fail? Scholars have noted the timing of the appearance of a distinctive male Jewish face but have not connected it to the mid-thirteenth-century attempt to convert Jews in northern Europe. On the one hand, certain physical attributes of Jews become just as important as clothing, hats, or beards, which could be removed or added to the body. On the other hand, there are ecclesiastical and royal efforts to convert Jews more than before, and those fail either because Jews refused to convert, or because they did, and Christians now expressed the thought that some physical condition persisted and made them still Jewish. It also is worth noting in passing that it was precisely in the second half of the thirteenth century, at least in Germany and because of the towering influence of R. Meir of Rothenburg (d. 1293), that boys under thirteen years of age and women of all ages were no longer supposed to perform ritual acts in public. The ritual Jew now became redefined as the adult Jewish male.[72] Is it a coincidence that Christian sources now begin to describe adult Jewish males as bearing distinctive physical features, as being "Jews"?

Voluntary Conversion and Its Impediments

Although it is difficult to track, voluntary conversion existed for a long time in medieval Europe except in England, where there is abundant documentation.[73] Alfred Haverkamp has proposed looking at the individual cases we know about from the German Empire and generalizing about them.[74] In France, we have anecdotal records and sporadic references, such as one in Jacob b. Meir's writings that refers to twenty cases of Jewish conversion to Christianity.[75]

In England about five hundred Jews out of a total population of five thousand might have converted before the mid-thirteenth century. England was especially interested in converting the Jews under Henry III. He founded the Domus Conversorum in 1232, a halfway house for Jewish converts to receive financial support for varying lengths of time. Royal initiatives rather than mendicants were mainly responsible, and Henry was personally involved with the lives of many new converts.[76] Despite papal policy, he took the assets of converts and offered them a home in the Domus or a monastery. Henry's approach was apparently driven more by piety than greed since it was not clear if the king benefited more from the confiscation of each convert's assets than from future taxes on those assets. The intention of conversion was to disrupt the Jew's social network from the Jewish past and provide a temporary means to enter Christian society. But like the Italian ghetto of the early sixteenth century, the Domus served to reinforce the unique status of the Jewish convert, who was not a full part of either the Jewish or the Christian community.[77]

Although there are important differences in appearance between Jewish men and women that correlate with the Christian perception of conversion, such that it was considered more likely for a Jewish woman to convert than a Jewish man, age has to be factored in as well. In some anecdotes, as in Caesarius of Heisterbach, it is young girls who are presented as attracted to Christianity and parents who confront ecclesiastical authorities to try to prevent their child from being baptized even willingly.

A group that was thought to convert easily were Jewish women, like the synagoga, but perhaps the majority of voluntary converts were young Jewish men, especially "adolescents," as William Chester Jordan pointed out. Susan Einbinder suggested that there were liturgical efforts aimed at preventing students of the Talmud from succumbing. There are several indications that Jews in medieval Europe were especially concerned about their young children in general and boys in particular.[78]

We recall that the martyrs of 1096 were motivated in large measure to kill their children rather than allow them to be baptized or even touched by Christians. Cases of successful conversion like Judah Herman's deal with the attraction and repulsion of the church, but ultimately the kindness of nuns attracted him while on a business mission for his family.[79] As noted earlier, English scholar Yom Tov was so attracted to the cross that he committed suicide on the eve of Shavuot, the same time of the year the martyrs of Mainz were attacked and killed their families in 1096—the time of the Torah's revelation.

And Simha Goldin proposed that youth ceremonies were designed to make Jewish boys in particular more attached to their Jewish identity, such as the initiation of young boys into Torah learning on Shavuot in German towns, and perhaps the early stages of the bar mitzvah ceremony marking coming-of-age at thirteen years and a day, the age of bar mitzvah, the same age Judah Herman had his first dream that enabled him to imagine himself a Christian knight.[80]

Those interested in converting Jewish men did not think they were "beautiful." Nor did they consider them likely to convert successfully. Their Jewishness could be constructed as physical, like circumcision, and therefore permanent. Jews, on the other hand, had no trouble thinking of Jewish men as handsome, thereby indicating that each religious culture saw the same people differently.[81]

Impediments to Jewish Adult Male Conversion

The ways Jews and Christians expressed their own physical identity as well as interpreted the appearance of the other raise questions about the factor of "race" in medieval Europe along with its usefulness in analyzing how Jews and Christians thought of the other. Jews argued that any ugly traits were temporary and not permanent, or that they were superficial and covered up an inner truth that belied appearances. In this denial of the permanence of physical appearances, the Jewish sources reflect how the issue of race was being debated.[82]

But in light of the perceptions Jews and Christians had of physical differences, it was not clear whether all Jews could become Christians if they wanted to. The Jews managed to live within Christian society for over two centuries without feeling any organized pressure from Christian authorities to convert. During this time, some Jews converted voluntarily or temporarily under duress, as in 1096, and then returned to the Jewish community despite the ecclesiastical prohibition of doing so.[83] This is thought to have changed in the thirteenth century, but not everywhere.[84]

Although there was ambivalence about Jewish conversion in many different circles, the thirteenth-century public disputations and forced sermons, as in England under Henry III or the Kingdom of Aragon in 1263, meant that there was some expectation that Jews could be converted, despite the policy of the popes and canonists until the sixteenth century against trying to convert Jews actively.[85]

There were dramatic instances in the late Middle Ages of significant groups that did convert. In fifteenth-century Spain, for example, influenced by the demoralization of many rabbis in Castile and the Kingdom of Aragon, hundreds and perhaps thousands voluntarily converted to Christianity, adding to the large converso communities that had emerged in the wake of the massive 1391 riots throughout the peninsula.

There was also a counterargument that Jews were not susceptible to reason because they were bestial and not fully human.[86]

Since Christianity was rational and Jews refused to be convinced, they were not rational beings and were likened to animals, and there was no need to try to convert them or debate them in public. Few remedies remained, especially after authorities were convinced that Jews presented a danger to Christian society either through the figurative poison of usury or the imminent threat of murder to the body of Christ—including the allegation of well poisoning.

The study of cultural aesthetics, how Jews and others are thought to appear physically and their cultural meanings, seems to be connected to the inability of some Jews to convert completely. The premise of conversionist activity on the part of the church was that baptism was a sacrament that was irreversible and permanent. From the days of Pope Gregory I, persuasion, not force, was supposed to be applied to the Jews by the church. But the theology of baptism assumes that the rite was effective and transformative. In an unexpected way, while the spiritual Jew might have been changed, the physical Jew remained, even as male circumcision remained a "mark of distinction." Christians and Jews resisted the implications of baptism, and one of the reasons was that certain physical features of Jewish men persisted after conversion.[87]

Rabbinic authorities, for their part, resisted the possibility that Jews who converted to Christianity ceased being Jews. They discounted the efficacy of baptism and insisted on the permanence of Jewish status. Rashi invoked the Talmudic precedent that "a Jew who sinned (by apostatizing) remained a Jew."[88] They differed, inconsistently, about the degree to which a Jew had to undergo any overt ritual act in order to reenter the Jewish community, thereby implying that some change had in fact occurred. Overwhelmingly, rabbinic law made it nearly impossible for Jews to lose their Jewish status.[89]

The editor of the Solomon bar Samson chronicle expresses one Jewish survivor's perspective about Jewish forced converts in the decade before the Second Crusade. Although most of his praise is for the saintly martyrs whose merit serves as a reservoir of atonement for survivors such as himself, he also devotes some time to praising the religious loyalty of converts who try to follow Jewish practice even while in religious captivity. However improbable as a factual description, the encomium explains what converts would have to do to remain loyal to Judaism after being converted against their will:

> It is now fitting to recount the praises of those who were forcibly converted. They risked their lives even in matters pertaining to food and drink. They slaughtered the animals they ate in accordance with Jewish ritual, extracted the forbidden fat, and inspected the meat in accordance with Rabbinic law. They did not drink prohibited wine and rarely attended church, and whenever they did go, it was under great coercion and fear, and they went with aggrieved spirits. The Gentiles themselves knew that they had not converted out of conviction but rather in fear of the errant ones, and that the Jews did not believe in the object of their reverence but remained steadfast in their reverence for the Lord and clung firmly to the Most High God, Creator of heaven and earth. In the eyes of the Gentiles they observed the Gentile Sabbath properly; but they observed God's Torah clandestinely. He who speaks evil of them, it is as though he spoke thus of the Divine Countenance.[90]

A sign of the continued Jewish identity of some converts is that Christians referred to Jewish converts as "so-and-so quondam judaeus" (so-and-so the former Jew).[91] So, too, Jews might change the names of apostates to insult them, as a reminder of past identity. Converts were sometimes discriminated against, as in the case in England of Henry of Winchester, whom Henry III knighted but whose Jewish identity continued to plague the convert.[92]

Appearances were also invoked as a reason to doubt the loss of Jewish identity even generations after conversion if the context was serious enough. The Jewish pope or antipope Anacletus II in 1130 is frequently discussed in this regard as a case in which Jewish family origins prevented a third-generation Christian from becoming pope. It was said that he "looked Jewish" despite the time elapsed since his great-grandfather Baruch-Benedict had converted.[93] This may have been a special case because of the office involved, but it raises the question of whether a Jewish man can be a true convert. In the case of the Pierleoni candidate for the papacy, the issue wasn't circumcision, an acquired Jewish male characteristic, which remained only in a first-generation male convert after his conversion.[94]

There also is disagreement about what, if any, effect conversion to Christianity had on Jews or Muslims. A significant amount of energy is spent showing that baptism not only effects spiritual change, as it should according to theological arguments, but can also change appearances that define a non-Christian, such as skin color. There are limitations, however, at least when it comes to Jewish physical traits. A similar religious-social situation had occurred in the mid-twelfth century in Muslim Spain when the Almohads refused to treat former Jews or Christians as full Muslims.[95] The sense that Jews had characteristics that were somehow immune from the efficacy of baptism and were innate became more prominent.[96]

Medievalists have investigated different aspects of how physical attributes, not religious affiliation proper, affected how identity was shaped and viewed. Specifically, the issue of race, along with attributes of skin color and other physical indicators, has been studied in material culture and literature, and medievalists are not content to leave matters of racial definitions to modern historians. It is important not to equate race only with skin color.[97]

In the early centuries when the church accepted Paul's hope that Jews would eventually convert, synagoga was depicted at least on major cathedral facades as a beautiful woman, like ecclesia, but blinded to the truth. The similarity in appearance appearance of the synagoga and ecclesia changed in the later Middle Ages, when the former became represented as undesirable types such as a lascivious or old hag—a sign that no one expected her to change, as Miri Rubin has observed.[98] Jews were Jews, something Jews had always known, but now Christian authorities were beginning to agree.

This shift in aesthetic representation reflects increasing doubt in the later Middle Ages that Jews, perhaps even Jewish women, could become sincere Christians even if they converted, and a belief that they were going to resist conversion if they could. A form of Jewish essentialism set in, as reflected in the purity of blood laws in Iberia as well as increased libels and physical attacks.[99]

A consideration of the persistence of the physical features of the Jewish male brings us to yet another change in the imagined Jew. Until now, we have seen two important components. From the Hebrew and Christian Bibles, there is the assumption of two peoples claiming chosenness and the right to be dominant—an assumption I have called the binary of inverted hierarchy. To that feature of the imagined Jew, the First Crusade added the notion of the Jew as the enemy within—a trope that developed nuance in the ritual murder and other accusations about Jews assaulting the body of Christ. Those two elements continued, and sometime in the later thirteenth century, with renewed efforts to convert Jews, we begin to see the idea that imagined Jewish male physical features persist after conversion, thereby making being Jewish *permanent and unchangeable*.

The three elements of the imagined Jew, then, come into existence *before* Jews were forced out of the principal kingdoms of western Europe in the late Middle Ages (chapter 8), and continue afterward down to modern times, when new features of antisemitism draw on and reinterpret them to form modern antisemitism (chapter 9).

CHAPTER EIGHT

Expulsions

IMAGINED JEWS AND REAL
CHRISTIAN ANTISEMITES

IT MIGHT APPEAR that as we began with the immigration of Jews from eastern Muslim and Byzantine Christian territories into western Latin Christian lands, we conclude with the forced or voluntary emigration of Jews from central Europe into the eastern territories of the Polish-Lithuanian Commonwealth and Iberian Jewry into the Ottoman Empire. But although this story about a reversal of fortune in the West has been the main narrative for some two hundred years of medieval Jewish historiography, the deeper structure is different and more interesting.

At the same time that the Jews from England and royal France were assimilating into the other Jewish communities of Ashkenazic or Iberian Jewry, the imagined Jew—first seen in the writings of Paul in the binary of inverted hierarchy, further developed during the First Crusade as the enemy within to the body of Christ, in its variations, and then again in the late Middle Ages as the unchangeable Jewish adult male convert—survived, especially in late medieval and early modern English literature. And as England expanded its empire in the nineteenth century, it spread the imagined Jew around the world. When Britannia ruled the waves, the sun never set on the imagined Jew.[1]

After a brief consideration of the forced migrations of the Jews as one of the threatening groups that was removed from the now

Christianized West, we will look at the imagined Jew who continued to be present in late medieval and early modern times, especially in English letters. As Geraldine Heng observed, "After the Expulsion of Jews from England, in the absence of real Jews of the flesh, is in fact when anti-Semitic literature exponentially increases."[2]

Why Expulsions?

The corporate expulsions of the Jews have been written about for so long as the late medieval culmination of Western anti-Jewish policies that it is difficult to realize how unusual it was for a government to expel a population beyond its borders. Governments might send individuals into exile. The ancient neo-Assyrian and early Ottoman empires forced population transfers *within* their borders, but few polities forced a group in its population to leave their borders entirely.[3]

As Benjamin Kedar pointed out, medieval western Europe was an exception for expelling whole groups from its borders. His brilliant insight as to why the West took this unusual policy is that since only the West created a moral vision of an ideal Christian society, it also posited in opposition to it an internal enemy, especially in the form of the Jews but other groups too. As a result, the West saw a dangerous enemy within where others did not and proposed a radical solution of group expulsion as a remedy that other cultures did not need to carry out.[4]

In the early Middle Ages, it was mainly zealous clerics who forced local Jews to leave various towns or kingdoms if they did not convert to Christianity, but later on, population expulsions were carried out by the temporal, not ecclesiastical, rulers, and the reasons for doing so were not explicitly religious.[5] Although King Philip Augustus of France temporarily expelled his Jews from the tiny royal French domain in 1182, the first major case of a group expulsion in medieval Europe was in 1268, when Louis IX of France expelled the Lombards, Cahorsans, and other foreign Christian moneylenders from the realm. Rowan Dorin has explained that we must place the medieval expulsions of different groups such as foreign Christian moneylenders and Jews into comparative perspectives to understand either. There was significant change over time as well as inconsistency of policies and their implementations, as in England and France.[6]

The expulsion of the Jews from European states is often connected to the problem of usury—moneylenders charging interest for a loan.[7] Scholars of the European economy have pointed out that the concern about money and lending for interest was increasingly expressed as a source of sin and danger as urbanization and increased commerce raised religious issues connected with credit that had been dormant before.

Jewish thinkers also engaged in the debate over lending at interest and argued back in defiance of the ecclesiastical interpretation that seemed to fall on ready ears. In *Milhemet Mitzvah*, a writer in southern France declared that credit was needed. Jewish thinkers in northern Europe were not of one mind on the subject. Although R. Jacob b. Meir (Rabbeinu Tam) justified Jews taking interest from Christian borrowers, *Sefer Hasidim* discussed this issue and argued against taking interest even from Christians.[8]

Because of the stereotype of Shylock as the quintessential Jewish moneylender in the Western imagination, we need to remember that not all medieval Jews were moneylenders and not all usurers were Jews.[9] In fact, the boundary between merchant and moneylender, for Jews as well as Italian Christian bankers, was often fluid.[10]

In addition to obtaining funds on demand from the Jewish community, the English kings turned to especially wealthy Jews, such as Aaron of Lincoln, for major loans. When Aaron died in 1185, he had outstanding loans of fifteen thousand pounds, the annual revenue of the royal exchequer, only part of his vast estate.[11] A Jewish woman moneylender with close ties to Henry III was Licoricia of Winchester, and there were others.[12] To protect the safety of these financial records, Jewish and Christian officials were appointed to see to it that duplicate copies of loans were drawn up and deposited in chests (*archae*). By 1200, the role of exchequer of the Jews was filled entirely by Christians, called the justices of the Jews.[13]

For several decades in the thirteenth century, Jews came to dominate the English credit market of lending against bonds from which Christian moneylenders withdrew. Memories of this unusual association between Jews and loans is part of the historical context for the image of Shylock in later English and world literature.

The question of usury, along with how different temporal and ecclesiastical rulers acted to limit or stop it among populations that they could influence or control, is fascinating as well as complicated. Generally speaking, the church was responsible for native Christian usurers; the kings had responsibility for Jews, considered natives, and foreign bankers, who were mainly Italians.

Church councils tried to curb Christian usury. This campaign could influence and reinforce royal interests in regulating foreign Christian usurers and Jews, who were under royal control. So, for example, in 1179, the Third Lateran Council made a serious effort to stop Christian usurers. Canon 25 stated,

> Nearly everywhere the crime of usury has become so firmly rooted that many, omitting other business, practice usury as if it were permitted, and in no way observe how it is forbidden in both the Old and New Testament. We therefore declare that notorious usurers should not be admitted to communion of the altar or receive Christian burial if they die in this sin. Whoever receives them or gives them Christian burial should be compelled to give back what he has received, and let him remain suspended from the performance of his office until he has made satisfaction according to the judgment of his own bishop.[14]

By 1215, the Fourth Lateran Council contained a canon that tried to limit Jews from charging immoderate usury. The position of popes and canonists, grounded in Pauline theology, was that Jews were not to be expelled from Christian society.[15]

But indirect pressure on Christian rulers through church councils was not as important as royal policies themselves, and these changed over time. In England and France, two different royal reactions to the problem of usury developed, usually justified not by church councils but rather an appeal to royal precedents.[16] Henry III made several exactions on the Jews of England in 1239, but in 1240 he issued an order arresting Siennese merchants, and then in 1240 he tried first to expel all foreign merchants and then those who were usurers—a novel assertion of royal prerogatives connecting usury as the reason for expulsion. Whereas Philip Augustus had listed usury as one of the reasons he expelled the Jews from the small royal domain in 1182, now it alone sufficed to remove an entire population from the realm, at least in theory.[17] Motives also were mixed, although by 1245 Henry assembled Italian merchants and demanded a large exaction or their expulsion. For Henry III, the primary motive to try to expel foreign usurers was mainly financial, to benefit both from their loans and fees and from their bribes to permit them to remain in England. His personal piety, real though it was, did not dictate his antiusury policy. Financial need did. Jews continued to lend and supply the king with tallages or forced payments.

A different motivation was at play in royal France. Louis IX (r. 1226–70) piously sought to purge his kingdom of evil and evildoers in preparation for a new Crusade. He generally showed public opposition to Christian usury and Jewish moneylending, as in the Ordonnance of Melun in 1230 against enforcing loans owed to Jews, but he was not bent on efficiently rooting them out. Yet in the late 1260s, in preparation for the Eighth Crusade, he showed renewed interest in limiting the two groups over which he had power: foreign usurers and Jewish moneylenders.

In 1269, Louis IX expelled foreign usurers with limited effect. His son, Philip III (r. 1270–85), issued a similar order in 1274, the same month the Second Council of Lyons promulgated the important ruling *usurarum voraginem* that provided for expelling foreign Christian usurers. Its language was heavily indebted to the order of Louis IX. Around the same time in 1274, Edward I (1272–1307) did likewise, but instead of any mention of the decree of the church council, the ruling was based on the earlier royal orders of Henry III in 1240 and 1253. Both Philip III and Henry III ordered the expulsion of foreign usurers, mainly Italian Christians, and relied on earlier royal precedents, not the ecclesiastical order, and again the decrees had limited effectiveness.

Some of the opposition to Jewish usury in England was politically motivated. The barons' rebellion of 1258 demanded an end to Jewish usury because Jews paid for royal tallages by calling in Christian loans that could also result in loss of lands held as collateral, which Christian debtors had to liquidate so that Jews could pay the king his latest assessment. In England, Henry III did not limit Jewish usury since the Jews were an important source of royal revenues.[18] In the fall, following the Second Council of Lyons's canon against usury on penalty of expulsion, Edward was cracking down on Jewish moneylenders too. More than his father, whose motives were mainly financial, Edward was principled in his opposition to Jewish usury, as is seen in his 1275 Statuto de Judeismo, which tried to put an end to Jewish usury.

In December 1289, Charles II of Anjou, nephew of Louis IX, expelled his Jews from Anjou-Maine for usury, Judaizing, and sexual relations with Christian women.[19] Although Charles cited local episcopal pressure to expel his Jews, the royal expulsions of 1290 and 1306 were grounded in political considerations, in which piety could, yet need not, play a role.

Edward I of England took measures to raise capital for a new Crusade by assessing his Jews, and that put pressure on Christian debtors.[20] Opposition to the Jews increased, and the king's decision to expel them in 1290 was a final bargain he made with the knights of the realm for a tallage of one-fifth of their movable property. The edict, now lost, was issued on July 18 and carried out on November 1. Unlike the attempts to expel foreign usurers, the expulsion of the Jews was effectively executed and Jewish assets were disposed of within three years. Thereafter, Jews who remained in England were either converts or there illegally and subject to being killed on sight. Even the chroniclers who report the expulsion did not blame the Jews and their usury but instead faulted the kings for manipulating the Jews to achieve their political goals.[21] Edward's letter issued November 5, 1290, claiming pious motives and blaming the expulsion on Jews continuing their usurious practices after 1275 was, to quote Robert Stacey, "a lie."[22]

In royal France, from the middle of the thirteenth century on, an effort was made to convert the Jews, but it failed, and the removal of the Jews was partly motivated by the goal of achieving a purified Christian polity.[23] The situation in France was also motivated by the king's need for funds to wage protracted wars. Philip IV, Louis IX's grandson, first tried to maintain his grandfather's moderate position regarding his Jews, but in 1306 he decided to arrest them, seize their property, and expel them from the realm.[24]

When some two thousand Jews who still remained in England were ordered to leave, they understandably "went home" across the Channel to Normandy or the Île-de-France. There they continued speaking the French dialect that they never forgot and became regional French Jews again. Hardly a trace remained in Jewish memory of life in England, although English Christians could not forget the Jewish presence.[25]

In 1306, Jews then had to leave the royal kingdom of France and face collective extinction over the next century, not from persecution, but from processes of cultural assimilation into other Jewish cultures.[26] In 1315, French Jews were permitted to return for a maximum of twelve years but were expelled again in 1321 after being associated with lepers and with poisoning wells in parts of France.[27]

Regardless of the motives of Edward I, Philip IV, and later French kings for expelling their Jews, as usury became the opposite of the growing ideal of apostolic poverty, the definition of the Jews as the dangerous enemy within expanded once again, this time to include the usurer, real or imagined.[28] Although Joseph Shatzmiller discussed a case from southern France in which the local Christian population was supportive of a Jewish usurer, the association of Jews and usurers was firmly planted in northern Europe and contributed to the imagined Jew of late medieval and early modern literature.[29]

The removal of Jewish communities from Christian states, an example of European medieval group exclusion, was the result of efforts to protect an ideal Christian society from perceived harmful Jewish influences.[30] The edicts leading up to the expulsions focus on the potential harm that the rulers foresaw for their Christian subjects if Jews were permitted to remain.

The texts do not mention Jews as causes of social and economic change, or as murderers, haters, avengers, or sexual predators, or as being too powerful, or as recent immigrants as reasons for removing them. They also do not refer to Jews studying Talmud instead of the Bible as a reason to expel them from Christian society as violators of an Augustinian bargain. They are much more in line with elaborating the Pauline idea in Romans that Jews are "enemies of the Gospel," as further developed into the "nearby enemy" after 1095, as elaborated in chapter 3.

But the expulsions did not create the imagined Jew in Christian minds. As we have seen, the imagined Jew was a continuously developing figure that Christian writers began to construct in antiquity. In the New Testament, Paul contrasts the son of the free Sarah, Isaac, the church, to the son of the slave Hagar, Ishmael, the Jews, and the younger son, Jacob, the church, to the elder son Esau, the Jews, of Rebecca's children. The elder serving the younger (Gen. 25:23) introduces into the imagined Jew a binary of inverted hierarchy that requires Christians to dominate Jews and Jews to serve Christians. Christians needed the dependent Jewish other, the formerly chosen, in order to regard themselves as Christians, the newly chosen. The ways Christians imagined Jews were a function of their own reciprocal or inverted self-image. The two critiques were also not symmetrical: Jews attacked Christianity as a pagan cult; Christians attacked Jews, people now constructed as enemies of Christians.[31]

Observing these patterns is sufficient to see an inverse correlation between what Christians claimed about themselves and what they imagined Jews capable of doing to and thinking about Christians. Although Jews and Christians invented each other in late antiquity by imagining an inverted virtual other who complemented their own self-image, the absence of Jews from much of medieval Europe meant that Christian Europe would now be dealing with only imagined Jews, not living ones. Before their expulsion, the imagined Jew as other served the purpose of maintaining Christian solidarity and identity. It persisted afterward in maintaining Christian society. Since it did not go away when Jews left, it formed a set of traditions that continued into modern times and played a role in the imagination of the Jew in the West.[32] The ingroup defined Jews as an out-group. Even after Jews were expelled, they continued to serve this function in Christian Europe as the self-defining other.[33]

Imagining the Imagined Jew

A few Jews managed to remain in England. Some hid and were able to maintain a clandestine existence.[34] Others who had converted observed some Jewish practices in secret. Above all, the imagined Jew persisted in the imagination of Christians for centuries, especially in England, where Jews continued to be featured in literature.

What is remarkable is that the ritual murder and blood libels, the devil and the Jews, Jewish usury, and other images persisted in

England and elsewhere in Christian Europe even when real Jews no longer were a recognizable community there. There are abundant signs of Jews in the literature and material culture produced in late medieval England, though less so in France, Germany, and Iberia.[35]

Many scholars have named and renamed the imagined Jew, including "the imagined Jew" used here, especially in late medieval English literature. Such an inventive explosion of terms reflects the serious issue of why the persisting and ever-protean image of the Jew played such a significant role in English culture.[36]

An early indication of the Jew as the product of Christian exegesis was James Parkes referring to Jews as "a theological necessity rather than a living person" in 1934.[37] Joshua Trachtenberg referred to "the mythical Jew" in 1943.[38] There was also nothing wrong with Bernard Glassman's straightforward references to "antisemitic stereotypes" or "images of the Jew" in 1975.[39]

An avalanche of new ways to describe the Jew in the Christian imagination really got started in the 1990s and is still going on. Consider Gilbert Dahan's *Les intellectuels chrétiens et les juifs* (1990); Kathleen Biddick discussed the image of the destroyed Regensburg Synagogue of 1519 in her study "Paper Jews" (1996); and Jeremy Cohen's "hermeneutical Jew," which he first brought up in 1992, acknowledges Dahan, and appears in 1999 in *Living Letters of the Law*; in his article *"Synagoga conversa"* (2004), he also proposed the notion of the "eschatological Jew," which he subsequently developed into a book (2022).[40]

Sylvia Tomasch offered a "dis-placed Jew" (1998) and useful "virtual Jew" (2000); Denise Despres's concept of the "protean Jew" (2002) emphasizes the dynamic life of the images over time.[41] Steven Kruger's *Spectral Jew* analyzes the reality of Jews who are gone and, yet are back as not so "blithe spirits" in the English imagination, and his introduction lists many of the earlier formulations. Miriamni Ara Krummel offers the idea of Jews as "legally absent, virtually present" (2011), but we should remember that the imagined Jew does not begin after the Jews were expelled but instead was there earlier.[42] In contrast to the "wandering Jew," popular only from the seventeenth century on, Kathy Lavezzo proposes the concept of the "accommodated Jew" (2017) in which the Jew is portrayed not wandering but in one location.[43] And Krummel returned with the book *The Medieval Postcolonial Jew, in and out of Time* (2022), and there is no end in sight.

The proliferation of these terms suggests not only deep scholarly interest in the subject of the Jew in late medieval and early modern English literature but also confusion about what the significance is of the presence of the Jew despite the Jews' absence for so many years.

The Jew in Late Medieval and Early Modern English Literature

Although the Jews of England and royal France assimilated into other Jewish communities and did not survive as early modern Jewish communities, the imagined Jew grew especially in English literature after 1290. Major works that refer to imagined Jews include late medieval texts like *Piers Plowman*, *Sir Gawain and the Green Knight*, and *The Book of Margery Kempe*.[44] The *Croxton Play of the Sacrament*, written in the late fifteenth century, perpetuated the allegation of the host desecration in Paris in 1290 many years after Jews were expelled.[45]

The late medieval English work that has succeeded the most in perpetuating the imagined Jew as a cruel killer of innocent Christian children is Chaucer's *The Prioress's Tale*, a short Middle English text about which a vast amount of scholarship and criticism has been written.[46] The grisly story Chaucer tells is aware of the specific ritual murder accusation in 1255 of little Hugh of Lincoln, but his narrative is invented, more generic, and transplanted far from England, and then refashioned as a Mary story in which cruel Jews are portrayed as the polar opposite of the kind Mother of God.

The scene is "in Asye, in a greet citee," where Jews live in a "Jewerye" through which runs a street "open at eyther ende" (lines 487–89).[47] A school for Christian children stands at "the ferther ende" (496).[48] A widow's child, "a litel clergeon, seven yeer of age" (503), would walk through the street to school. Along the way, he piously would kneel at an image of Mary and say his "Ave Maria" (507–8). When in school, he heard older boys singing the hymn to Mary, *Alma Redemptoris*, and he started to memorize it. An older student told him it was a prayer to Mary for help when one is about to die, and the boy learned it and sang it when going to and from school "thurghout the Juerie" (551).

Now Jews hear the boy singing about "swich sentence, which is agayn youre lawes reverence" (563-64), and conspire to kill him by slitting his throat and hiding his body in a latrine (572). When the mother realizes that her son is missing, she is distraught, and the story centers on her ordeal learning about the fate of her child. The murder becomes a saints' story when the boy continues to sing the *Alma Redemptoris* with his throat slit until a "monk" removes a "grain" from the boy's tongue, permitting him to die a saint, "his litel body sweete" (682). One of the Jews is drawn and hanged by the "provost," a symbolic resolution, since in 1255 Henry III ordered eighteen other Jews hanged and dozens more arrested.

Chaucer here mimics host desecration stories by associating the boy with the host, the "grain" that he has on his tongue and that gives him life after death. Jews typically were accused of putting hosts as well as saints' bodies into latrines, and here, in a reversal, as Susan Morrison has pointed out, the Jewerye becomes a latrine.[49] The story thus reverses the Jewish association of Christian sancta with latrines, in which Jewish latrine blasphemy puts Christ back into Mary's body, the filthy source of his birth. In *The Prioress's Tale*, the "Jewerye" becomes a latrine at one end of an "alley," representing an alimentary canal, "open at either ende" in Mary, as Merrall Price has astutely suggested.[50]

The transformation of an imagined child sacrifice, likened to Hugh's murder as told in Matthew Paris, into Chaucer's Mary story, which demonizes the Jews out to destroy any reference to or reverence for Christian sancta, can be compared to how Thomas of Monmouth refers to Jewish revenge in the allegation about Jews killing William of Norwich in 1144. Jews are portrayed as reenacting the Passion (Thomas and Chaucer) or avenging their collective suffering that resulted from the Passion (Thomas).

Early Modern Jews?

The image of the Jew as avenger of his suffering, one of several themes created in medieval Europe, is reinterpreted as a central theme in early modern times, when Jewish communities are no longer present, as in Elizabethan England.[51] Here we find elements of the imagined Jew as the reciprocal of a Christian in certain defined ways that mirror each other: in combinations of usurer, hater of

Christians, killer of Christians, consumer of Christian blood, dogs, and swine, all pointing to the supposed opposites in Christianity.[52] Christians eat pork; Jews are porcine and are nursed by pigs.[53] Christians consume the blood of Christ in the Eucharist; Jews consume the blood of Christians. Christians eat the body of Christ; Jews are cannibals and eat Christian hearts. Christians are spiritual; Jews are lustful, materialistic, and money obsessed, and so on.

Some of these images are powerfully and grotesquely depicted in the character of Barabas in Christopher Marlowe's *The Jew of Malta*, and more subtly and memorably presented as William Shakespeare's Shylock in *The Merchant of Venice*.[54] In each case, a Christian tricks a Jew (Barabas) or is thought to compete unfairly (Shylock), and the Jew then seeks personal revenge. In contrast, in his *Life* about William of Norwich, Thomas of Monmouth writes that the Jews were punished with exile because they killed Jesus and that is why they now seek revenge by selecting and crucifying an innocent Christian boy each year. The explanation is grounded in the theology of the Passion of Christ as well as Christian and Jewish history, and its alleged Jewish reenactment is based on revenge for Jewish exilic suffering.

In the early modern egomaniacal expressions of Jewish revenge in Barabas and Shylock, the motive is no longer connected to the Passion. Now the Jewish protagonists take out their revenge on *Christians*, not on symbols of *Christianity* as in the Middle Ages.[55] This is new, it is early modern, and there is no connection here between the Passion of Christ and Jewish behavior. These imagined Jews present a transition stage between the medieval and modern imagined Jew. Jews are now operating in Christian social space more than in a theological drama of competing chosenness. They are not yet transformed into a racial other.

The governor of Malta tricks Barabas out of his wealth in order to use it to save the state. Barabas is told that he must attend a meeting and give half of his wealth to ransom Malta from the Ottoman Turks. When he hesitates, the governor decrees that he has refused and thereby has forfeited his entire estate (I. i. 84–94). The cause of Barabas's revenge turns on political intrigue and international diplomacy, not theology, and is signaled by a figure representing Niccolò Machiavelli at the beginning of the play (prologue).

For Shylock, revenge centers on economic competition with the merchant Antonio, whose ships are not yet back and who borrows funds from Shylock to lend to his friend Bassanio. Shylock hates Antonio, he says, because Antonio competes unfairly by not charging interest to other Christians (I. iii. 39). Once Shylock insists on collecting the penalty in the bond of a pound of flesh as his revenge on Antonio, Portia and then the duke conspire to reduce Shylock to poverty and then force him to convert to Christianity. The trick that leads to his downfall, Portia's insisting on the letter of the bond (IV. i. 301–8), is the consequence of Shylock's act of revenge, not the cause of it, as in the case of Barabas.

As a result, instead of Jewish wealth serving the state and being rewarded, Barabas and Shylock are tricked by the state into losing their wealth and eventually either their life (Barabas) or religious identity (Shylock). Both lose their daughters and a Jewish future to Christian marriages, foretelling the end of their Jewish lines as well.

The scope of Barabas as an international merchant prince who is out for himself and loyal to no ruler is the inverse of the international Jewish courtiers like former Marrano Doña Gracia Mendes and her nephew Don Joseph Nasi who served the Ottoman sultans and were rewarded handsomely.[56] Barabas is not a small-time medieval usurer or pawnbroker but rather an early modern international merchant ("Thou are a merchant and a moneyed man" [I. ii. 53]), based in Malta, historically contested between the Christian and Muslim powers.

Shakespeare's Shylock is more modestly located in Venice, the capital of a Mediterranean naval empire, but with a limited focus on the city. Shylock's grubby Realto versus Portia's lofty Belmont contrast the low and high domains of Jewish and Christian success. His capital comes from trading abroad, but he is not a player in international realpolitik like Barabas. Neither can he be compared to the small social world of most Jewish moneylenders living in an English or Continental town in the twelfth or thirteenth century, producing mainly small consumer loans for Christian neighbors or supplying ready money for ecclesiastical or temporal rulers or vintners in need of credit to get to the next harvest.[57] The twelfth-century Jewish usurer is a local figure, even an Aaron of Lincoln; Marlowe and Shakespeare have transformed him into an international one, typical of early modern times.

The comic relief comes in part from how each overreacts when put into an impossible situation of loss and frustration instead of service. Anger and hatred ooze from Barabas, and his boasting of his killing Christians is buffoonery. He hates and is disloyal more than he is greedy. He is political and demonic, not economic, at his center. He is out to poison and kill any Christian he can, and we are not sure why. In 1945, Abba Kovner's Neqamah (Revenge) group set out with poison to kill as many Germans as possible, and we know why.[58] With Barabas it is essentially his nature. In no way is he interested in Christianity as a foreign form of worship.

Shylock tells us he hates Christians because they do not charge each other interest. This is new and fantastic, and pits imagined Christian charity against Jewish business for profit. It alludes to the biblical basis, in theory, of prohibiting loans with interest between "brothers" but not to "others," as Benjamin Nelson put it.[59] But in practice, interest was charged by Christians as well as Jewish moneylenders and bankers. So the reason for Shylock's hatred is not true to reality and is a fiction, a pose, Shakespeare's own imagined Jew.

Not only is Shylock not an accurate contemporary figure; he does not resemble the medieval Jew either. Medieval Jews hated *Christianity* as idolatry but did business with Christians, who charged exorbitant interest to other Christians. When Jews left England in 1290, Queen Eleanor took over the outstanding Jewish loans and collected them. It is not surprising that some Christians tried to get Jews readmitted to England.

Barabas and Shylock are imagined Jews not because there were no Jews to speak of in England but because such Jews never lived in England. They rage on about hatred and revenge so that Christians can monopolize mercy and love, as in Barabas being loved to death physically and Shylock spiritually with his and Jessica's conversions. There is no Christian love here for a Jew who remains a Jew.[60]

Daughters, Fathers, and Jewish Futures

The figures of Barabas and his Abigail, Shylock and Jessica—the relationship between Jewish fathers and their beautiful daughters—turn on the power of the Christian world versus the limits of Jewish wealth and cunning that are no match for it. The world of competing chosenness is gone. This is an areligious world of power politics and trickery, not religious restraint or frenzied religious enthusiasm. It also allows for some female agency for unmarried Jewish daughters, whereas before, mainly Jewish widows were able to act like men.[61]

In medieval Europe, intimate social mixing between Jews and Christians was common. We see this from the Fourth Lateran Council's canon 68 that assumes it, but also from the contemporary exempla of Caesarius of Heisterbach. In Caesarius of Heisterbach's exemplum, the Jewish father rages against the cleric who sleeps with his daughter, and in the end she converts. The father is powerless to control his daughter against the bishop. The young Jewish women are described as beautiful, suggesting foreign allure, yet serving to mitigate the cleric's weakness too.[62]

Two generations later, in a responsum of R. Meir of Rothenburg (d. 1293), a Jewish father wants revenge on his married daughter for sleeping and conceiving with a Christian while her husband is away, and asks permission to kill her. He complains that she threatens to become a Christian if she cannot have her way.[63] These sources from the thirteenth century all assume that Christian men, including clerics, fraternize with Jewish women, and young Jewish women's fathers as well as clergy and rabbis are helpless to prevent it. In these cases of Jewish-Christian sexual alliances and father-daughter dynamics, we see an earlier phase in the development of Elizabethan Jewish fathers and daughters as well as the contrast between medieval and early modern cultural contexts.

One of the consequences of the motif of Jewish fathers killing their daughters, as seen in *The Jew of Malta*, is the return of the belief that Jews ritually killed Christian boys in the past. People resorted to a logical analogy: if Jewish fathers could kill their own daughters, they surely could kill Christian boys like Hugh of Lincoln. As Livia Bitton-Jackson put it, "The Jewess in all of these works became her father's victim because of her devotion to Christianity. How much more plausible, how much more credible, was the murder of a Christian child by the same Jew?" William Prynne (1600–1669) used past ritual murder allegations as a reason not to readmit the Jews into modern England.[64]

Religion is centrally important to the medieval fathers. In the cases of Abigail and Jessica, conversion is about aversion to their fathers' behavior and moving up in the world of Christian society.

Some Jews may have converted in the Middle Ages to extricate themselves from difficult personal situations and improve their lives, but they had no doubt they were rejecting their religious heritage and moving into another religious world.[65]

With Shylock "content" to be a Christian, Jewish martyrdom or guilt over even temporary conversion, as in 1096 and beyond, is over. Unlike the medieval Jewish convert, who is still a suspected Jew, Shylock seems to succeed in crossing over, to everyone's satisfaction. But we do not really know because once Shylock converts, he literally disappears and is never seen in act 5. It is hard to imagine him ever fitting in at Belmont.

Similarly, although the themes of revenge and greed are found in medieval stories about Jews, this does not mean that Shylock was invented in the twelfth century. The issue of Jews as moneylenders or usurers is not a constant. It is "protean," in Denise Despres's term. Although Jews played a visible role, they were not the main suppliers of credit, and laws were passed to restrict Christian foreign bankers, as at the Third Lateran Council, or expel them before they were applied to Jewish moneylenders.

Shylock is an anachronism, and the audience would have found his role incongruous and perhaps even comic.[66] Sephardim in Venice were merchants; Jewish moneylenders were usually small fry and relatively poor. This imagined Jew, placed far from England in "Venice," is portrayed not as a petty lender or pawnbroker but instead as an international merchant prince. In the early seventeenth century, the merchant was more likely to be a former Portuguese Jew or Marrano in Italy.[67] Shakespeare wrote the *Merchant* knowing about real Marrano merchants in England and asks the audience to laugh at an imagined Jewish usurer on the stage. And so when Portia in disguise asks, "Who is the merchant, who the Jew?" (IV. i. 170), it might occur to some in the audience to think, "Both."[68]

It is easy to hate moneylenders as a rule, and offering a counterexample of one that Jews defended does not dent the stereotype except to make us remember that it is a stereotype and not an accurate portrayal of Jews at any particular time.[69] But Shylock does not put greed above revenge and hatred of a Christian. He wants his pound of flesh, his bond, the letter of the law, regardless of how much others are ready to pay him to ransom Antonio. He claims, as

William Chester Jordan suggests, that unless his bond is honored, there is no law and order, no civilization in England. It's not about Christian mercy.

The Jew is a comic medieval anachronism. The reason is that Shakespeare's audience was antisemitic toward the medieval Jew. Is he human? He appears to be, but maybe we know that he really is not.[70] The antisemitic audience could think Portia's mercy speech as well as Shylock's own humanity speech funny if the audience assumed that Jews were not human or rational. Or they could agree that of course a Jew bleeds if "pricked" in the meaning of sodomized or suffering from hemorrhoids, or even is like a woman and menstruates.[71] Shylock can be a comic figure not only because he converts at the end (happy ending) but also because the audience has fixed ideas about Jews that Shakespeare is playing off. Shylock is more interested in revenge than money. He keeps turning down more and more money and insisting on his bond, the pound of flesh. Would the audience think this absurdly funny since he is a Jew?[72] The audience knows he is greedy, but the pound of flesh is more important. If the play is seen in light of the audience's assumptions about Jews, all the more reason to trick him into acting counter to expectations.

The revenging and greedy Jew were not as important in medieval European religious cultures as on the Elizabethan stage. Marlowe invented Barabas; Shakespeare created Shylock. By the time of the Elizabethan dramatists, the earlier religious rivalry between Jews and Christians over chosenness was no longer the main issue, and this changed everything. By the nineteenth century, of course, the world changed again.

It remained a lasting feature of Christian Europe beyond Elizabethan England, for example, when a converted Jew and Iberian Catholic, Dr. Roderigo Lopez, was arrested, tortured, and executed for trying to poison the queen.[73] We see it in Marlowe's *The Jew of Malta* and Shakespeare's Shylock. In German lands, Martin Luther attacked Jews for their usurious practices harmful to the peasants, as did writers like the Abbé Gregoire in revolutionary France. Jonathan Frankel and Magda Teter have shown that more blood libel accusations are reported in modern times in eastern Europe than in all of medieval history. Even the Ottoman Empire reported a groundswell of cases.[74]

The Jews of England (and France) disappeared, but the antisemitic imagined Jew persisted in English literature and influenced the world into the nineteenth, twentieth, and twenty-first centuries. Chapter 9 concludes with a new approach to the problem of the relationship between medieval and modern antisemitisms. It focuses on the by now familiar three-part shared *structure* that made it possible for modern antisemitic content to build on and transform the antisemitic medieval imagined Jew into the modern antisemitic one.

CHAPTER NINE

Antisemitisms

MEDIEVAL AND MODERN

ANTISEMITISMS, OR FORMS of Jew hatred, existed before Wilhelm Marr coined the term in the 1870s.[1] Did medieval Christian Jew hatred contribute to its modern, racial expression in the Holocaust or Shoah?[2] This debate has been especially lively among historians as well as medieval literary scholars and art historians. As awareness of the Holocaust grew, medieval scholars were encouraged to look at premodern cases of anti-Jewish violence in new ways.[3] Sometimes, looking back from the Holocaust, scholars were tempted to redefine medieval antisemitism *as* anti-Jewish violence even though it includes much more.[4]

The discussion has usually adopted one of two basic approaches. The teleological view sees a causal connection between medieval and modern forms of Jew hatred. Proponents include Jules Isaac, James Parkes, Joshua Trachtenberg, Léon Poliakov, and more recently, Robert Chazan and Gavin Langmuir.[5] Modern historians sometimes argue that the term "antisemitism" is appropriate only for the modern era because it came into currency in the 1880s. But attempts to limit the term to modern racist ideologies, while technically justifiable, has the disadvantage of suggesting a complete discontinuity between premodern and modern Jew hatred.

Resisting the teleological position, it has been argued that medieval episodes of antisemitism need to be looked at on a case-by-case basis and not necessarily with the assumption that they lead to a modern form. This is the "contextual" understanding of anti-Jewish behavior before modern times. The leading formulator is David Nirenberg, whose influential book *Communities of Violence* set out to upend the teleological trend while reinterpreting the possible cultural meaning of medieval violence.[6] But the cases he cites from southern France and Iberia of ritualized and symbolic violence as a potentially stabilizing rather than destructive force are not contrary evidence of a relationship between medieval and modern Jew hatred since it is the ongoing antagonism to the Jews in northern Europe, especially the German Empire, that might be the most likely candidate for medieval influences on modern German, lethal antisemitism.[7]

Then, in a remarkable volte-face and deft sleight of hand, Nirenberg adopted a modified teleological approach himself in his book *Anti-Judaism*, in which he proposed continuity from antiquity into modern times, not of Jew hatred but "anti-Judaism," which he redefined as the West's hostility to all victimized groups, whom he renamed "imaginary Jews." This move still leaves open the question, addressed here, of how medieval Christian anti-Jewish thinking and behavior is related to real Jews and modern antisemitism, if at all.[8]

Scholars like Hannah Arendt, who resisted using the term "antisemitism" for premodern Jew hatred, contended that the medieval centuries were thoroughly religious in assumptions and institutions, whereas modern antisemitism is grounded in assumptions that include secularism, nationalism, ideologies such as socialism and liberalism, and the pseudoscience of racist scientific assumptions about Jews.

We see this neat, almost Pauline dichotomy in Arendt's confident distinction that

> anti-semitism, a secular nineteenth-century ideology—which in name, though not in argument, was unknown before the 1870s—and religious Jew-hatred, inspired by the mutually hostile antagonism of two conflicting creeds, are obviously not the same; and even the extent to which the former derives its argument and emotional appeal from the latter is open to question.[9]

But this raises the problem, Why did modern antisemitism target the Jews in the first place? And as we have seen, there are issues of race that are now being studied in medieval society as well as in modern times (chapter 8).

Those who want to insist on a basic difference between religious or premodern and modern racial Jew hatred have used the alternative term "anti-Judaism," not in the sense Nirenberg uses it about all criticized groups in general, but defined in various ways about Jews and Judaism in particular.[10] Gilbert Dahan, Jeremy Cohen, and Anna Abulafia, for example, have tended to use it in analysis of Christian theological traditions about Judaism and Jews.[11] That term focuses attention on the hatred of Jews in the Middle Ages based on Christianity derived from theological writings, and not race. This usage can also suggest a discontinuity between religious anti-Jewish thought and later lethal, racial antisemitism.

Using "anti-Judaism" when one refers to anti-Jewish hatred is at best misleading. The problem of "anti-Judaism" is that Christianity is not opposed to Judaism so much as to *Jews* who practice it, and Christians need Judaism and the Old Testament to tell the truth of the coming of Jesus. So, for example, Michael Jones discusses anti-Jewish motifs in literary works and can refer to Marlowe's Barabas as "anti-Judaic."[12] What can that mean? Or in an otherwise excellent study of demography in the German Empire, medieval historian Michael Toch refers to "popular anti-Judaism" apparently because he is unwilling to use the word "antisemitism" before the nineteenth century.[13] He is in good company since Salo Baron resisted doing so as well and referred to Trachtenberg's *The Devil and the Jews* as illustrating irrational "anti-Judaism."[14] In such cases, medieval or early modern antisemitism would be better.

Among medievalists who have used "anti-Judaism," the most controversial is Langmuir, whose work defined the term in a way that has not been widely accepted. Langmuir used "anti-Judaism" to refer to Christian religious criticism of Judaism as it was practiced, based on what Jews actually did as Jews. In contrast, he defined "antisemitism" not necessarily as a modern movement but instead as any attack on what he called irrational or chimerical anti-Jewish behavior that Jews never actually did. After making this distinction, he then posited continuity between twelfth-century "antisemitism" and what came later. Langmuir tried to square the circle by arguing first for contexts regarding the cases before the twelfth century and a teleological approach from the twelfth century on.[15]

Langmuir's view is not only fundamentally anachronistic but also potentially apologetic because his "anti-Judaism" relieves the church of any responsibility for his "antisemitism."[16] His approach was also colored by social psychological arguments that medieval Christians had doubts about such doctrines as transubstantiation and "projected" those doubts onto Jews as attackers of the consecrated host, for example.[17] In actuality, assertive Jews' criticism of Christianity led some Christians to have doubts in the first place and then react defensively, as Richard Southern noted (see chapter 4). This is the opposite of Langmuir's psychosocial model, which pictures Jews as passive victims of Christian doubt projected onto Jews as imagined aggressors. Moreover, Langmuir's use of social psychological explanations and other scholars' reference to Christian "anxiety" or "social anxiety" as an explanation for anti-Jewish behavior impose unempirical theoretical constructs on the data and are usually unverifiable.[18]

Other scholars have also offered explanations for the terms they use. In his study that argues for continuity between medieval and modern forms of Jew hatred, largely through stereotypes and folklore, Chazan discusses briefly the terms "anti-Judaism," which he correctly sees as obscuring the object of Judaism or Jews, and "antisemitism," which he unfortunately reserves only for modern racist forms. Yet in 2016, he returned to the subject and decided to use the term "anti-Judaism" despite its potentially exculpatory implications.[19] This still left him without a term to refer to premodern anti-Jewish hatred.[20] Chazan discounted the use of "antisemitism" for medieval Jew hatred, and this has influenced others to do so as well.[21]

In a cogent critique of Langmuir, Chazan correctly points to the methodological difficulty "in assessing the psychological motivations of past individuals or groups" but then inconsistently refers to "the level of anxiety aroused by these anti-Jewish motifs," which he thinks can be deciphered.[22] For his part, Robert Stacey challenged the psychosocial criteria that Langmuir invoked to distinguish between "anti-Judaism" and "antisemitism."[23] What was considered irrational *in the twelfth century*? As Abulafia has argued, the revival of rationalism in the cathedral schools in the renaissance of the twelfth century understood Jews as lacking reason and in some cases being no different from animals. For that reason, some Christians thought that Jews were capable of doing anything.[24]

Other scholars have tried to follow Langmuir's periodization without his theoretical distinctions. Guy Stroumsa uses "anti-Judaism" and "anti-Semitism" to distinguish medieval from modern, based on Langmuir.[25] Andrew Gow compares anti-Judaism, or "opposition to Jewish religious tenets and doctrines," and "antisemitic" as not predicated on a specific aversion to the Jewish faith, of which most medieval Christians had little or no knowledge, but he does not limit the latter to the twelfth or any century.[26] David Berger reviewed the long history of anti-Jewish sentiments in the West and uses "medieval anti-Semitism," which makes good sense.[27]

Recently, medievalists in literary studies as well as art and material culture have taken up racial studies and explored ways in which the attribution of physical characteristics to different groups in medieval societies is present.[28] This nuancing of race before modern "racism" also casts doubt on the salient distinction between religious premodern and racist modern forms of Jew hatred regardless of what it is called. And so the remarkable increase of interest in anti-Jewish sentiment by scholars of medieval literature, especially English, and art historians has loosened the barriers to terminological precision that historians have tended to be troubled by so as to distinguish between anti-Judaism and antisemitism. Louise O. Fradenburg's study of *The Prioress's Tale* is one of dozens of examples that use "anti-semitism," however spelled, as the most useful term to refer to Jew hatred.[29] Once we broaden the definition of antisemitism to go beyond violence and refer to any kind of anti-Jewish sentiment, and get over the technical issue of when the term was coined, we open up new possibilities for a more nuanced understanding of different kinds of anti-Jewish cultures and can reconsider how they are related to one another.[30]

From this brief review it is clear that there is no consensus about terms, and instead a variety of usages that either distinguish between some anti-Jewish writings and acts as "anti-Judaism" versus others that are referred to as "antisemitism," or modified forms of "antisemitism" such as ancient, medieval, and modern, or religious versus racist or some other distinction to privilege the modern racist form associated in particular with the Nazi regime and Holocaust.

Stereotypes: Medieval and Modern Differences?

In exploring the possible diachronic or continuous aspects of anti-Jewish motifs and politics from medieval into modern times, some scholars have pointed to images or "stereotypes"—a term taken from the study of prejudice.[31] A vivid example of this approach was seen in 1995 in an exhibition in the Vienna City Hall of visualizations of medieval Jews compared to Nazi uses of those images in the publication *Der Stürmer* and the volume *Die Macht der Bilder*.[32]

As Jonathan Adams and Cordelia Hess have observed, there is an archive of antisemitic tropes that can be drawn on in different periods.[33] Some motifs and images from the medieval stereotypes persist, adding to the modern ones a religious and venerable Christian pedigree. Alex Novikoff points to medieval sources of modern stereotypes in modern antisemitism: Jews are antiquated and stubborn, blind and irrational, the enemy of Christians and cannibalistic, greedy moneylenders, physically deficient, less than human, and a menace to society. But this is misleading since, as Richard S. Levy notes, modern antisemitism is concerned above all with "the rise of the Jews," their power real and imagined, and this was not a major concern in the Middle Ages.[34]

The appeal to stereotypes can provide a useful approach to relating medieval and modern antisemitisms, but there are pitfalls to be avoided. For example, Chazan's claim that Shylock was "unthinkable before the mid-twelfth century" implies that there is a close resemblance between the medieval Jewish moneylender and Shakespeare's imagined Jew.[35] But Barabas and Shylock are portrayed as great Jewish haters of Christians. Medieval Jews hate Christianity as "foreign worship" ('avodah zarah) because Jews thought it was paganism. They tried to get along with Christians, do business, follow the laws, pay taxes, and mind their own business, even though Jews thought of Christians as benighted followers of an ancient, biblically proscribed pagan cult that was worthy of contempt.

So Marlowe and Shakespeare got it wrong. Or better, they created their own version of the medieval imagined Jew as inner enemy who hates Christians, and in the case of Barabas goes around poisoning them. Modern scholars like Chazan have read these Renaissance Jews back into the Middle Ages and assumed that imagined medieval Jews created Barabas and Shylock. In some ways, it is the other way around. Like the ghetto that was invented in the sixteenth century in Venice (1516) and then Rome (1555) but retrojected back into the Middle Ages when there were voluntary Jewish quarters, not ghettos, Shylock has been so powerful as an imagined Jew that he has been read back into the Middle Ages and assumed to be the moneylender then. In fact, those Jews who engaged in credit were often small-time pawnbrokers compared to the large Christian merchant banking houses of the "Lombards" (chapter 8).

The same problem of anachronism that makes Shylock a weak case for arguing for the influence of medieval Jewish stereotypes on modern forms of antisemitism also weakens part of Chazan's contention that Jewish power and danger are found in common in medieval stereotypes and modern antisemitic accusations. Chazan points out that from the mid-twelfth century on, new Jewish stereotypes emerge of the Jew causing harm from financial dealings, expressing blasphemy to Christian symbols, and posing danger by killing Christians. These stereotypes share an understanding of the Jew as *powerful and harmful* to Christianity, and that shared feature contributed to modern forms of antisemitism: "All these new elements [of modern antisemitism] were, however, absorbed into the broad ideational framework of the hostile and powerful Jew that emerged in the mid-twelfth century in northern Europe."[36]

This argument has the advantage of recognizing that despite the differences between medieval and modern stereotypes of the Jews, there was influence of the former on the latter. It is true that the Jew as harmful and dangerous did emerge in medieval Europe and became part of the imagined Jew that persisted into modern times, yet that began, as we have seen in chapter 3, not in the mid-twelfth century but rather at the end of the eleventh with the disaster of the First Crusade riots, when Jews became the inner enemy.[37]

Less relevant, though, is the claim about power, a major component of modern antisemitism. The idea of the modern "rise of the Jews" along with issues of Jewish power and a quest for world domination is qualitatively different from any of the images of the imagined Jew that resonated in medieval Christian society. In Thomas of Monmouth's narrative about the alleged ritual murder of William of Norwich, he imagined an annual meeting of Jewish leaders at Narbonne, not to take over the world, but to pick a victim of ritual murder to end the exile of the Jews. It is hardly equivalent to the *Protocols of the Elders of Zion*.[38]

Given the variety of accusations in the medieval record, reducing them to Jewish power as well as hatred is a retrojection into the medieval period of modern antisemitism. And so the argument will seem valid that the medieval version contributed to the modern because, in fact, it is the modern definition that was used to selectively define anachronistically the medieval forms. Without the religious competition for chosenness, modern antisemitism is qualitatively discontinuous from its medieval predecessors. Something other than shared stereotypes enabled medieval Christian antisemitism to develop into its modern form.

From Medieval to Modern Antisemitisms

A focus on stereotypes risks anachronism. Instead, we should consider a different approach that will help us understand how medieval Jewish antisemitism is both different from its modern form and contributed to it. This is the three-part structure that medieval and modern antisemitism share, even though the former has religious content and the latter is defined in modern terms. Christian culture created this structure as the scaffolding of its imagined Jew. Each of the three parts could be transformed into modern equivalents that would become modern antisemitism.

The first part of the structure was the idea of the binary of inverted hierarchy in Christian society—an extension of the rivalry between Jews and Christians over divine chosenness. It meant that Christians, like Jews, thought that they should be above the other, and the other should serve them. Neither wanted to be subordinated to the other. But each side needed the other to mirror its own identity in an inverted form.

The cultural binary of two inverted hierarchies is found already in the Hebrew and Christian Bibles between Israel and the Canaanite and other idolatrous peoples as well as in the writings of Paul about Israel of the flesh and spirit. This meant that Christian power was an important theme of difference from the Middle Ages on. Christian domination and Jewish resistance were the result when power was one-sided in favor of the Christian culture. But resistance is misleading. Jews were also assertive, and Christians could be defensive as well. The agency derived from both sides. Each fed the other even when Jews were no longer permitted to live legally in a territory.

The structure of inverted hierarchy based on chosenness was sharpened after the First Crusade and at each subsequent one, when Jews were seen as inner enemies of Christians. This was an intermittent emergency view rather than a continuous one like the factor of chosenness or hierarchy. This too was a medieval addition to antisemitism that continued and changed. The Jews as internal enemy is largely a product of the First Crusade and succeeding Crusades, even if the New Testament and church leaders provide literary support.

The imagined Jew as the nearby enemy was extended to include poisonous usury, threatened murder, conspiracy to commit an annual ritual murder on an innocent Christian boy, ingesting Christian blood, blaspheming Christian sancta in latrines and harming the consecrated host, and poisoning the wells of Europe to kill off the Christians of Europe. The imagined Jew is motivated by hatred and revenge toward Christians—Barabas and Shylock combined. These images of the imagined Jew persisted after Jews were expelled and the Jew remained in Christian societies as the imagined other.

The third factor was that Jewish identity is a permanent condition, regardless of conversion or other factors, especially of adult Jewish men. Late medieval efforts to convert Jews in northern Europe, not just Iberia's purity of blood laws, raised issues of "racial" permanence, especially the ability of Jewish men to resist conversion either by force or voluntarily. The permanence of Jewish men as Jews becomes clear as conversion efforts accelerated from the thirteenth century on.

These three interlocking structural factors contributed to Christian antisemitic assumptions about Jews more than any stereotypes, and they persisted into modern times, when binary right order, inner danger, and unchangeability were translated into modern and racial terms.

The asymmetry observed throughout this book that Jews hated Christianity, not Christians, and Christians hated Jews, not Judaism, enabled the three-part structure of medieval antisemitism to become modern antisemitism. Both are expressions of Christian hatred of Jews, not of Judaism. This made it possible to hate Jews first for religious reasons and eventually for racial ones.

Christians hated Jews because they were supposed to be religiously subordinate but often were assertive and not servile; Christians thought that Jews were the inner enemy; and Christians believed that male Jews were unable to convert. This three-part structure of Christian antisemitism is about Jews, not Judaism.

And it is because Jews are the subject of the three-part structure of medieval antisemitism that modern antisemitism is about Jews too; the change from an age of religion to a modern secular age did not interrupt the force of the structure of antisemitism. Had Christian antisemitism been about Judaism, and not Jews, modern secularization might have ended it. Instead, it got worse.

Implications for Today

The three-part structure of antisemitism also accounts for contemporary antisemitism toward Jews in the United States. The binary of inverted hierarchy means that Jews are hated when they are not properly subordinate to a group that thinks it is superior. Jews are successful and "white," and are assimilating into the white Christian majority.[39] That is exactly when groups of white supremacists resist Jews as their equals since they are supposed to be below the self-perceived waning white majority. Jews were stigmatized with racial antisemitism after 1871, when German Jews were fully emancipated legally and became like Christian Germans.[40] So American Jews would be among those groups attacked precisely when they became socially indistinguishable from the white nativist communities.

Secondly, Jews are read as the enemy within and therefore dangerous, and need to be contained or eliminated.

And third, nativist groups adopt racial antisemitism and assume that being Jewish is a permanent condition and cannot change. Because of increased intermarriage, Jews become even more threatening since a racial essentialism is attached to their Jewishness.

For these reasons, there is little hope that diaspora Jews will cease to be victims of some forms of antisemitism so long as they threaten the binary of inverted hierarchical expectations of groups that refuse to accept a liberal political egalitarian inclusiveness as the social norm. There is every reason to be concerned that postmodern forms of nationalism and nativism recycle the medieval structure of antisemitism that developed for the first time in Christian Europe.

Unfortunately, just as Europe has proven again and again that it is a resilient culture that can survive devastating world wars in the twentieth century, its antisemitic culture has also proven resilient and transportable to other cultures, such as American nativism, which adapted the European antisemitic model for its own purposes. Awareness of the deep structure of antisemitism, derived from medieval Christian Europe, does not mean that it is coterminous with the West, but it does mean that not recognizing it will prevent any measure taken against it from succeeding. Put positively, if the West is to overcome color racism or antisemitism, it has to be aware of the history of each.

ACKNOWLEDGMENTS

THIS BOOK WAS begun with the help of a John Simon Guggenheim Memorial Foundation Fellowship, and I want to thank the foundation for its confidence in me. At a critical moment, I received encouragement from Natalie Zemon Davis, whose work has inspired me and so many others.

My thanks to Yale University's generous policy of triennial leaves and other research support that enabled me to finish the book. The ability to scan and acquire books from Yale's Sterling Memorial Library during the COVID years made working off campus a possibility.

Colleagues with whom I discussed some or all of this book include Elisheva Baumgarten, Jeremy Cohen, Judah Galinsky, Elisabeth Hollender, Elliott Horowitz z"l, Ephraim Kanarfogel, Daniel Lasker, Ahuva Liberles, David Nirenberg, Ephraim Shoham-Steiner, and David Sorkin.

Some of the ideas developed here were first explored in the essay "A Jewish-Christian Symbiosis: The Culture of Early Ashkenaz," published in David Biale's *Cultures of the Jews* (Schocken, 2002), and I want to thank him again for making that possible.

Sahar Segal, Esq., was helpful as my research assistant when she was a Yale College undergraduate, and analyzed and summarized earlier research on the issue of how Jews thought about gentiles—an earlier framing of this book.

I shared versions of chapters with students in my Yale seminar in spring 2023, including undergraduate students Zara Ashford, Rachel Brown, and Tasha Dambacher, and graduate students Jacob Romm and Lola Shehu.

My appreciation to Princeton University Press for publishing this book, which started with conversations many years ago with Fred Appel and Brigitta van Rheinberg but underwent reimagining until it reached its present form. My thanks to Eric Crahan and Priya Nelson, to Morgan Spehar and Emma Wagh for their assistance, and to the staff of the Press for their help in transforming the manuscript into a book.

GLOSSARY

Ashkenaz The biblical name (Gen. 10:3 and Jer. 51:27) associated in the Middle Ages with the Jews of central Europe, northern France, and England, and later also with eastern European Jewry and their descendants
'avodah zarah "Foreign worship," ancient term for pagan religion
beit midrash A school of Jewish study
communion The Eucharist celebrated with bread and wine
converso (f. *conversa*) A former Jew converted to Christianity
etrog A fragrant citron used to celebrate the festival of Sukkot
Eucharist The wafer and wine used to celebrate communion
exemplum (pl. *exempla*) A story used to teach a religious lesson
gabbai Synagogue or community official who might be in charge of the synagogue services or collect taxes for internal social services
gaon (pl. *geonim*) Rabbinic masters in Baghdad under Islamic rule
gematria Word associations based on Hebrew letters' numerical values
halakhah Jewish law, usually understood as the "path" (*halokh*), but possibly derived from the tax (*halakh*) in Ezra 7:24 (Saul Lieberman)
hasid Jew who is especially pious or a pietist who follows especially demanding rules of Jewish behavior
hasidei ashkenaz The Jewish pietists of medieval Germany who formed a small elite circle around Judah the Pious (d. 1217) and existed for about three generations
herem excommunication imposed on Jews who did not conform to local norms
host The unleavened wafer used in the Roman Church to celebrate the Eucharist
Incarnation The belief that God was made human in the life and death of Jesus
ma'arufia Friendly client; exclusive Christian client for a Jewish merchant or banker in medieval Ashkenaz
midrash Interpretations of Scripture
minhag Custom, as opposed to written law
minhag avoteinu Custom of our ancestors, referring to family or ancient practices
Mishnah The first compilation of rabbinic traditions produced in early third century CE Palestine
nasi Prince or possible descendant of King David, but used also as a title of honor in medieval Jewish communities
parnas (pl. *parnasim*) Local leader of northern European Jewish community
pei'ot Male earlocks grown to avoid haircutting prohibited in Lev. 19:27
piyyut (pl. *piyyutim*) Original, improvised prayers that began in Byzantine Palestine and were especially important in medieval Ashkenaz
qahal The leaders of a Jewish community in medieval Europe
qinot Liturgical dirges that mark times of tragedy in Jewish experience

responsum (pl. *responsa*) Answers to questions put to rabbinic authorities

rosh ha-golah Head of the Exile or exilarch. A regional leader in ancient and medieval Babylonia and Persia

Sepharad Hebrew name for medieval Iberia (Ovad. 20)

sha'atnez Forbidden mixture of wool and linen in cloth or thread based on Lev. 19:19 and Deut. 22:11

sukkah A temporary booth erected for the festival of tabernacles

Sukkot Festival of tabernacles

tallages Arbitrary taxes levied by a lord or king in medieval England

tallit A four-cornered prayer shawl requiring ritual fringes (zizit) at each corner

translatio imperii Transfer of authority from East to West

translatio studii Transfer of studies from East to West

transubstantiation The belief in the real presence of the body and blood of Christ in the Eucharist

yeshivah Place of study of Jewish traditions and texts

zizit Ritual fringes of a tallit based on Deut. 22:12

NOTES

Chapter 1. Introduction

1. *The Marvelous Mrs. Maisel*, season 4, episode 7, aired March 11, 2022, on Amazon Prime, 22.13 min.

2. Peter the Venerable, *Letters of Peter the Venerable*, no. 130, 1:328. English translation in Cohen, *Living Letters*, 247. See Friedman, "Anatomy of Anti-Semitism"; Price, "Medieval Antisemitism," 179.

3. Grayzel, *Church and the Jews*, 1:114.

4. Jews asserting themselves under medieval Christian rulers can be compared, despite significant differences, to the behavior of groups studied in Scott, *Domination and the Arts of Resistance*; Bhabha, *Location of Culture*.

5. The name "Ashkenaz" is biblical (Gen. 10:3 and Jer. 51:27) but gets associated with the German Empire and northern France and England by the twelfth century. See Aslanov, "Juxtaposition of Ashkenaz / Tsarfat."

6. The understanding of Jewish history as defined by "suffering and learning" goes back to the classic multivolume annotated German synthesis of Heinrich Graetz, *Geschichte der Juden*, translated into Hebrew, with notes, and into a more popular version in English without notes in six volumes as *History of the Jews*. In 1928, Salo Baron published "Ghetto and Emancipation" as a counternarrative that criticized what he called the "lachrymose" conception of Jewish history. Baron's attempt to resist viewing Jewish history as a history of persecution still recognized that the assertive behavior of Jewish martyrs shaped Ashkenazic culture. See Baron, *Jewish Community*, and volume 4 of his magisterial *Social and Religious History of the Jews*, in which he still named a chapter "The Age of Crusades." For Jewish political activity, see Elazar, *Kinship and Consent*, which pioneered the field of a Jewish political tradition; Walzer, Lorberbaum, and Zohar, *Jewish Political Tradition*. On the integration of medieval Jews and Christians in early Europe, see Marcus, *Rituals of Childhood*; Marcus, "Jewish-Christian Symbiosis," introduction; Elukin, *Living Together, Living Apart*.

7. Among the recent surveys of medieval Europe that mention Jews, much attention is still paid to their persecution. See Fried, *Middle Ages*, 160, 287–89; Wickham, *Medieval Europe*, 206–7; Rosenwein, *Short History of the Middle Ages*, 170–71, 229–30, 250–52. The best general history of medieval Europe that engages seriously with Jewish history is Jordan, *Europe in the High Middle Ages*.

8. See Langmuir, "Majority History and Post-Biblical Jews," reprinted in his *Toward a History of Anti-Semitism*, 21–41; Jordan, "Jewish Studies and the Medieval Historian," 15. In the first century CE, Jewish historian Josephus Flavius, in his *Contra Apionem*, argued against those claiming that Jews did not have a history because the Greek historians did not mention them. See Knox, introduction, 6–7, to Robert Fagles's translation of the *Iliad*.

9. For the formulation, see Krummel, *Crafting Jewishness in Medieval England*. On the growing literature and terminology on what I am referring to generically here as "the imagined Jew," see chapter 8. For a virtuoso performance of the presence of the imagined Jew, called the "imaginary Jew," in the West, see Nirenberg, *Anti-Judaism*.

10. See Marcus, "Forum on David Nirenberg." For a useful review of the historiography on medieval antisemitism, see Barzilay, "Ha-Musag 'Antisheimiyut'" (with English abstract).

11. See Lopez, *Birth of Europe*; Geanakoplos, *Medieval Western Civilization and the Byzantine and Islamic Worlds*; Rosenwein, *Short History of the Middle Ages*. None of these multicivilization surveys understands the Jews in Europe as a historical culture and society with living communities, elites, and histories of their own engaged over the centuries with the Christian majority culture as well as with the Muslim and Byzantine empires.

12. Jewish conversion to Christianity in medieval Europe has become a subject of renewed historical interest. See chapter 7.

13. For the history of the Jews in Muslim lands, see Goitein, *Mediterranean Society*; Lewis, *Jews of Islam*. For the Jews in Byzantium, see Starr, *Jews in the Byzantine Empire*; Sharf, *Byzantine Jewry*; Bowman, *Jews of Byzantium 1204–1453*; Bonfil et al., *Jews in Byzantium*. For a comparison between the Jews in Muslim and Christian (mainly Latin) lands, see Cohen, *Under Crescent and Cross*, which tends to valorize differences, real though they were. On the bias for the Jewish experience in Muslim Spain (Sepharad) over that of northern Europe (Ashkenaz), see Marcus, "Sephardic Mystique"; Schorsch, "Myth of Sephardic Supremacy"; Marcus, "Jewish-Christian Symbiosis."

14. This argument does not preclude other ways in which a confrontation with Islam helped define a sense of Christian solidarity. See Erdmann, *Origin of the Idea of Crusade*; Kedar, *Crusade and Mission*; Tolan, *Saracens*; Koenig, *Arabic-Islamic Views of the Latin West*, 3–4; Nirenberg, "Epilogue," 227–32; Cohen, "Muslim Connection."

15. For an early (1948) proponent of the view that Jewish vigor was behind early Christian antisemitism (his term, applied to the fifth century CE), see Simon, *Verus Israel*, reprinted as Simon, "Christian Antisemitism," 164, cited in Gow, *Red Jews*, 53. See also Beker, *Chosen*. The role assertive Jewish behavior played in motivating Christian attitudes and policies toward them has sometimes been downplayed or dismissed for fear of blaming the victims. See, for example, Chazan, "Deteriorating Image," 224–25; Berger, "Crusades," 19, which claims that what Jews did could not possibly account for how Christians treated them. This correct observation results in discounting *all* Jewish behavior because of invented false Christian allegations. But the issue is, how did what Jews likely did to assert their own sense of religious superiority influence how Christians viewed *themselves*, and in turn, how they then treated the Jews? See also Cuffel, *Gendering Disgust*, 3; Marcus, "Israeli Medieval Jewish Historiography," 273–74.

16. See Katz, *Exclusiveness and Tolerance*. See also, especially, Halbertal and Margalit, *Idolatry*, 211. *Sefer Hasidim* and possibly some works influenced by its author, R. Judah the Pious, seem to view Christians themselves as practitioners of foreign

worship ('avodah zarah) or idolatry. See SHP, 19, 24, cited in Biale, *Eros and the Jews*, 76. The reason offered for the practice in Ashkenaz that Jews should not mourn the death of their children who convert to Christianity is that had they lived, they would have worshipped idols. See Isaac b. Moses of Vienna (a student of Judah the Pious), *Sefer Or Zarua* 2:428, in Urbach, *Ba'alei ha-Tosafot*, 82n12, 112; Levin, "Jewish Conversion to Christianity," 101. Halbertal and Margalit do not deal with *Sefer Hasidim* or the views of the Jewish pietists of medieval Germany (hasidei ashkenaz). The pietists' view that Christians as well as Christianity are idolatrous requires Halbertal and Margalit to modify their otherwise helpful paradigm.

17. On Jews as idolators, despite St. Augustine's denial, see Lipton, *Images of Intolerance*, 40–41. This continuing association fits the model of Christianity as Israel that succeeded the biblical Canaanites, now understood as the persisting Jews.

18. The imagined Jew has undergone significant development. See chapter 8. For Christian views that Jews and Muslims are pagans, see Camille, *Gothic Idol*, which does not deal with the Jewish view of Christianity as idolatry. For an earlier formulation of how medieval Jews and Christians regarded each other, see Katz, *Exclusiveness and Tolerance*, 3–4. Katz's pioneering book, which I read as an undergraduate, was the inspiration to embark on the study of Jews and Christians in medieval Europe.

19. Judah b. Samuel, *Sefer Hasidim*; other versions. See Marcus, *Sefer Hasidim and the Ashkenazic Book*. *Sefer Hasidim* is a book of religious teachings that includes hundreds of exempla that make use of everyday situations.

20. Moshe Greenberg referred to the Hebrew Bible as a "pre-Jewish" book. See Greenberg, *'Al ha-Miqra ve-'al ha-Yahadut*, 143. During the first two centuries CE, it became both a Jewish and a Christian book. On the social history of ideas, see Gay, *Party of Humanity*, x.

21. *Mekhilta de-Rabbi Yishmael*, ed. Horowitz-Rabin, 208; *Mekhilta de-Rabbi Ishmael*, ed. Lauterbach, Tractate Ba-Hodesh, parasha 2, 2:204, with a slight change in the translation.

22. On holiness, see Deut. 14:2, 21, 26:19, 28:9. On Israel's chosenness, see also Deut. 10:15, 14:2; Weinfeld, *Deuteronomy*, especially 227–32. See also Beker, *Chosen*.

23. *Sifrei Devarim*, pisqa 97, 158; *Sifre*, 145, pisqa 97, 432n1; *Sifrei Devarim*, 158, in the last three lines of commentary to line 16, suggests that these comments were additions that were meant to be critical of the Christian Church's claims to being chosen.

24. The teaching is derived from the singular form in the phrase "chose *you*" (*u-ve-kha bahar*), suggesting the value of each individual Jew. *Sifre*, pisqa 97, 432n2.

25. On the theology of the papacy, see Stow, "Hatred of the Jews," 83; Stow, "Church and the Jews." On Christian Roman law and the Theodosian Code of 438, see Linder, *Jews in the Legal Sources*.

26. Letter to the Romans 9. In his "Sermon on Jacob and Esau," Augustine elaborated Paul's binary view of the biblical patriarchs: "So that Jacob . . . stands for the Christian people. He is the younger son, you see, because Esau is the Jewish people." Quoted in Marcus and Saperstein, *Jews in Christian Europe*, 33.

27. For the rabbis on Esau and Jacob, see *Midrash Bereishit Rabbah* 63:7; Rashi on Gen. 25:23; Thräde, "Jakob und Esau"; Cohen, "Esau as Symbol"; Bakhos,

"Figuring (out) Esau." For medieval illuminations warning Jews about Esau, see Offenberg, "Beauty and the Beast."

28. On the Pauline binary of body versus spirit in Galatians, see Cohen, *Living Letters*, 6–9; Stow, "Church and the Jews"; Stow, *Alienated Minority*, 10–12; Nirenberg, "Epilogue," 221; Nirenberg, *Anti-Judaism*, 59–60. On Jews as enemies versus beloved in Rom. 11:28, see Narin van Court, "Critical Apertures," 2. For the consequences of Paul's dichotomy of body and spirit as a history of the West, see Nirenberg, *Anti-Judaism*.

29. Cohen, "Supersessionism"; Carroll, *Constantine's Sword*; Pelikan, *Christian Tradition*, 1:11–27. On Paul, see especially Gager, *Reinventing Paul*; Sanders, *Paul and Palestinian Judaism*; Boyarin, *A Radical Jew*.

30. Justin Martyr, *Dialogue with Trypho*, 164. On Justin, see Rokeah, *Justin Martyr and the Jews*. Melito of Sardis was a Christian contemporary who also advocated Christian supersessionism. See Cohen, *Living Letters*, 9–11.

31. See the Hebrew chronicle of Solomon bar Samson, EH, 609; H, 27; E, 25 (bottom). For an introduction to the three Hebrew chronicles on the 1096 First Crusade riots and martyrs, see the abbreviations and chapter 3.

32. On Augustine, see Blumenkranz, *Judenpredigt Augustins*; Cohen, *Living Letters*, especially 24–65; Fredriksen, *Augustine and the Jews*. Augustine's key writings about Jews are his *Enarrationes in Psalmos*, *Contra Faustum Manichaeum*, and *De civitate dei*. In addition to referring to Jews as "desks" (*scrinaria*), in his *Sermo* (5.5, CCSL 41:56) Augustine employs such similes as "guardians" (*custodes*) of (what are now) Christian books, "librarians" (*librarii*), and "servants" (*capsarii*), specifically referring to the elder servant or slave (i.e., the Jew) tasked with carrying the books of the master's free children (i.e., the Christian) to school but never themselves entering the classroom. See Cohen, *Living Letters*, 36. In his address to Jews in Rome's Tempio Maggiore on April 13, 1989, para. 4, Pope John Paul II said, "You are our dearly beloved brothers and, in a certain way, it could be said that you are our elder brothers."

33. Cohen, *Living Letters*, 29.

34. Augustine, *City of God*, book 18, chapter 46.

35. See Parkes, *Conflict*; Reuther, *Faith and Fratricide*; Efroymson, "Patristic Connection." On Augustine, see Cohen, *Living Letters*.

36. See Hay, *Europe*; Pagden, *Idea of Europe*.

37. For the notion of inward acculturation, see Marcus, *Rituals of Childhood*, introduction, now slightly modified to reflect choosing some and ignoring other features of the surrounding culture, in Marcus, *Sefer Hasidim and the Ashkenazic Book*, introduction.

38. On Rashi's *le'azim*, see Shereshevsky, *Rashi*.

39. On the Talmud glossators or Tosafists and their dialectical method, see Urbach, *Ba'alei Ha-Tosafot*; Soloveitchik, "Dialectics, Scholasticism, and the Origins of the Tosafot." On a possible relationship between the method of the Tosafists and the Christian scholastic scholars of northern France, see Kanarfogel, *Intellectual History*, 102–10.

40. Memorials or cults of the dead deserve further comparative study. See Marcus, *Jewish Life Cycle*, 221–44; Marcus, "Jewish-Christian Symbiosis," 463–65.

41. See SHP, 1630, translated in chapter 4. On the history of the medieval European synagogue, see Krautheimer, *Mittelalterliche Synagogen*, especially 64; Wischnitzer, *Architecture of the European Synagogue*; Krinsky, *Synagogues of Europe*; Paulus, *Architektur*. An uncanny experience confirmed this similarity in 1990, while at a conference held on Rashi in Troyes, France. Colleagues and I, including the late Vivian Mann, drove to Vézelay, in nearby Burgundy, and approached the chapter house attached to the abbey. I said to my companions, "Inside you will find a rectangular space divided by two interior columns just like the Worms synagogue." And it was so. On the structure of the Worms synagogue, see Shalev-Eyni, "Reconstructing Jerusalem." On ritual bath styles, see Bodner, "Romanesque beyond Christianity." For an assertive example of a wealthy English Jew, Aaron of Lincoln, boasting that he financed an ecclesiastical window and shrine to St. Alban, see Lavezzo, "Minster and the Privy," 363.

42. See Sirat, "Looking at Latin Books," especially 14–15; Isserles, "Les parallèles esthétiques."

43. Banitt, "Une langue phantôme"; Aslanov, "Juxtaposition of Ashkenaz / Tsarfat"; Kiwitt and Dörr, "Judeo-French."

44. On romances, see Einbinder, "Signs of Romance"; Gruenbaum, "Learning from the Vernacular"; SHB, 142; Leviant, *King Artus*.

45. On Jews confessing to other Jews, see Marcus, *Piety and Society*, 75–86; Fishman, "Penitential System of Hasidei Ashkenaz"; Marcus, *Sefer Hasidim and the Ashkenazic Book*, 41–42.

46. The contributions approach to Jews and the West, fashionable in the 1930s as in Cecil Roth's *Jewish Contribution to Civilization* (1938), had an apologetic function. Beyond Jews teaching the *Hebraica Veritas* to Victorine monks in Paris, discussed by Beryl Smalley in *The Study of the Bible in the Middle Ages*, are less well-known areas such as Isserles and Nothaft, "Calendars beyond Borders." These contacts still remain largely unexplored.

47. For the usefulness of the term antisemitic, see chapter 9.

48. Lopez, *Commercial Revolution*; Little, *Religious Poverty*; Toch, *Economic History of European Jews*.

49. Stacey, "History, Religion, and Medieval Antisemitism," 101. See also Adams and Hess, *Medieval Roots of Antisemitism*.

50. Shapiro, "Écriture judaïque."

Chapter 2. Migration to the West: Following Europa

1. See Roth, *Dark Ages*; Linder, *Jews in the Legal Sources*; Applebaum, "Were There Jews in Roman Britain?" Did some Gallo-Romans convert to Judaism in late antiquity? See Bautier, "L'origine des populations juives de la France médiévale," cited in Iogna-Pratt, *Order and Exclusion*, 316n154.

2. See Theodosian Code, 16.8.3; Bachrach, *Jews in Barbarian Europe*, 18, no. 9; Linder, *Jews in the Legal Sources*.

3. See Shoham-Steiner and Hollender, "Beyond the Rabbinic Paradigm," 241. The renewal of archaeological excavations of the Jewish quarter in downtown Cologne stirred up a scandal in recent years. See Schütte, *Von der Ausgrabung zum Museum*.

4. See the summary in Stow, *Alienated Minority*; Roth, *Dark Ages*. See also the sources in Linder, *Jews in the Legal Sources*.

5. See Gregory of Tours, *History of the Franks*; Blumenkranz, "Premiers témoinages"; Roth, *Dark Ages*.

6. On the Visigoths, see Linder, *Jews in the Legal Sources*; Albert, "Un nouvel examen"; Katz, *Jews in the Visigothic Kingdoms*; Bachrach, "Reassessment of Visigothic Jewish Policy"; Stocking, *Bishops, Councils, and Consensus*.

7. For Louis the Pious's Jewish merchant charters, see Linder, *Jews in the Legal Sources*, 333–39. See also Bachrach, *Jews in Barbarian Europe*, 68–71.

8. For Ibn Khuradadhbih, see Lopez and Raymond, *Medieval Trade in the Mediterranean World*, 31–33. On the Radhanites, see Rabinowitz, *Jewish Merchant Adventurers*; Gil, "Radhanite Merchants."

9. For these charters, see Bachrach, *Jews in Barbarian Europe*, 68–71. On France not having any charters, see Marcus, "Why Did Medieval Northern French Jewry (*Zarfat*) Disappear"?

10. See Kedar, "Expulsion," 168–69.

11. See Bloch, *Feudal Society*.

12. For the Jews of Muslim Spain, see Ashtor, *Jews in Moslem Spain*; Gerber, *Jews of Spain*. On the German lands, see Haverkamp, "Beginning of Jewish Life."

13. See Toch, *Economic History of European Jews*.

14. See Walzer, Lorberbaum, and Zohar, *Jewish Political Tradition*; Baron, *Jewish Community*.

15. See Toch, "Formation of a Diaspora," 57, 71–72.

16. See Grossman, *Hakhmei Ashkenaz*, 27–78. A rabbinic chain of tradition derived from Rhenish sources suggests the pattern of general migration. See Luria, *She'eilot u-Teshuvot*, no. 29, translated in Marcus, *Piety and Society*, 64.

17. On the history and culture of Ashkenaz, see Güdemann, *Geschichte des Erziehungswesens*; Berliner, *Aus dem Leben der deutschen Juden*; Blumenkranz, *Juifs et chrétiens dans le monde occidentale*; Roth, *Dark Ages*; Stow, *Alienated Minority*; Cohen, *Under Crescent and Cross*; Grossman, *Hakhmei Ashkenaz*; Grossman, *Hakhmei Zarfat*; Toch, *Juden im mittelalterlichen Reich*; Marcus, "Jewish-Christian Symbiosis"; Baumgarten, *Practicing Piety*.

18. See Grossman, *Hakhmei Ashkenaz*, 27–78.

19. Isaac b. Moses of Vienna, *Sefer Or Zarua*, vol. 1, no. 478 (end), f. 70a, col. B; Agus, *Urban Civilization*, 750.

20. Ginzberg, *Ginzei Schechter*, no. 23, 1:220; Agus, *Urban Civilization*, 320.

21. Cassell, *Teshuvot Geonim Qadmonim*, no. 123, 36a; Agus, *Urban Civilization*, no. 118, 380; based on M. 'Avodah Zarah 1:9; B. 'Avodah Zarah 21a.

22. For the term, see Steiner, "'Iqvot Leshoniyim."

23. On the local urban expulsions of Jews, see Baron, *Social and Religious History of the Jews*, vol. 4; Kedar, "Expulsion," 168–69.

24. See, for example, Cassell, *Teshuvot Geonim Qadmonim*, no. 151; Agus, *Urban Civilization*, 195.

25. Müller, *Teshuvot Geonei Mizrah u-Ma'arav*, no. 174; Agus, *Urban Civilization*, 158.

26. Grossman, *Hakhmei Ashkenaz*, 56–57.

27. See Grossman, "Ties of the Jews of Ashkenaz to the Land of Israel."

28. See Marx, "Rabbenu Gershom"; Grossman, *Hakhmei Ashkenaz*, 106–74; Grossman, "Historical Background to the Ordinances on Family Affairs"; Eidelberg, *Teshuvot Rabbeinu Gershom*; Brody, *Geonim of Babylonia*.

29. See Grossman, *Hakhmei Ashkenaz*, 133–49; Grossman, *Pious and Rebellious*, 70–79.

30. Müller, *Teshuvot Hakhmei Zarfat ve-Lotir*, no. 87, 88b; no. 67, 162; Eidelberg, *Teshuvot*, 68, 159; Agus, *Urban Civilization*, 206–7.

31. Eidelberg, *Teshuvot*, no. 21, 75; Eidelberg, *Teshuvot*, no. 23, 79, Agus, *Urban Civilization*, 750–52; Eidelberg, *Teshuvot*, no. 24, 81; Eidelberg, *Teshuvot*, nos. 27–28, 89–91.

32. Eidelberg, *Teshuvot*, no. 23; Agus, *Urban Civilization*, 750.

33. R. Meir b. Barukh of Rothenburg, *She'eilot u-Teshuvot*, no. 660; Agus, *Urban Civilization*, 752.

34. Eidelberg, *Teshuvot*, no. 75, 171–72; Agus, *Urban Civilization*, 754.

35. Müller, *Teshuvot Hakhmei Zarfat ve-Lotir*, 88c; Eidelberg, *Teshuvot*, no. 69, 161; Agus, *Urban Civilization*, 210.

36. See Grossman, "'Avaryanim, ve-Alammim"; Shoham-Steiner, *Jews and Crime*. Neither deals with Jewish crimes committed or alleged to have been committed against Christians.

37. The original is found, for example, in Eidelberg, *Teshuvot*, no. 67, 154–55. The translation is based on Agus, *Urban Civilization*, 70–71, with modifications. The Talmudic precedent is from B. Bava Mezi'a 22a.

38. M. 'Avodah Zarah 1:1.

39. Eidelberg, *Teshuvot*, no. 21, 75; Agus, *Urban Civilization*, 352–54. On this important responsum and its distinction between Christians and Christianity, see Katz, *Exclusiveness and Tolerance*, 44–45. On R. Yohanan bar Nappaha's (third century, Sephoris) statement about gentiles in B. Hullin 13b, see Blidstein, "R. Yohanan, Idolatry, and Public Privilege." The statement reads: "Gentiles outside the Land of Israel are not idolators but only follow the customs of their ancestors." See the distinctions in Halbertal and Margalit, *Idolatry*, 211. Their clarification explains what is illustrated by but not so deftly articulated in Katz, *Exclusiveness and Tolerance*, the first to explore in depth the implications of the Ashkenazic rabbinic view about Christianity and Christians. Katz correctly distinguishes between the dominant medieval rabbinic view that Christians are not idolators but that Christianity remains "foreign worship," a position that I have explored further in this book.

40. On the emergence of the paid rabbinate in Ashkenaz, see Schwarzfuchs, *Études sur l'origine et le développement du rabbinat*; Yuval, *Hakhamim be-Doram*, 11–15. Compare the evidence from southern France and the Crown of Aragon in the early fourteenth century in Shatzmiller, "Rabbi Isaac Ha-Cohen of Manosque."

41. On herem ha-yishuv, see Rabinowitz, *Herem Hayyishub*; Schwarzfuchs, "Hishtalsheluto shel Herem ha-Yishuv."

42. Grossman, *Hakhmei Ashkenaz*, 189–95.

43. Cohen, *Sefer ha-Qabbalah*, 63.

44. Cohen, *Sefer ha-Qabbalah*, 64, 66.

45. Asher, *Itinerary of Rabbi Benjamin of Tudela*, 100–101.

46. Graboïs, "Demuto ha-Agadit shel Karl ha-Gadol."

47. Cohen, "Nasi of Narbonne"; Zuckerman, *Jewish Princedom in Feudal France*.

48. Cohen, "Nasi of Narbonne," 57.

49. Neubauer, *Mediaeval Jewish Chronicles*, 1:82.

50. Asher, *Itinerary of Rabbi Benjamin of Tudela*, 32.

51. Franklin, "Cultivating Roots"; Franklin, *This Noble House*; Gil, "Exilarchate." For the title nasi, which was held by Hasdai Ibn Shaprut, according to Ibn Daud, in tenth-century Muslim Spain, see Cohen, *Sefer ha-Qabbalah*, 136.

52. Luria, *She'eilot U-Teshuvot*, no. 29, cited in Grossman, *Hakhmei Ashkenaz*, 31. This genealogical text derives from Rhineland traditions about the German Jewish pietist family and contains other unique elements, such as the story about why R. Judah the Pious migrated from Speyer to Regensburg. See Marcus, *Sefer Hasidim and the Ashkenazic Book*.

53. See Grossman, *Hakhmei Ashkenaz*, 33, which quotes the text from Moscow-Günzburg Hebrew MS 119, MS Paris, Bibliothèque Nationale de France, héb. 646.

54. On Carolingian reform of the monasteries based on the Rule of St. Benedict, see Vauchez, *Spirituality*, 22.

55. For foundation legends in eastern Europe, see Bar-Itzhak, *Jewish Poland*, 113–32.

56. Bonfil, "Tra due mondi."

57. The resemblance prompted Sara Zfatman to suggest that Rabbenu Meshullam was the unnamed fourth captive in Ibn Daud's tale, but there is no evidence of any connection. See Zfatman, *Rosh va-Rishon*, 445.

58. National Library of Israel, Jerusalem, Hebrew MS 3182 [#39]; Zfatman, *Rosh va-Rishon*, 441–42; Grossman, *Hakhmei Ashkenaz*, 55–58.

59. The story hints at the Joseph saga (Gen. 37) in which merchants buy Joseph and take him to Egypt, where he rises to great heights in a foreign land, yet Meshullam will rise not through dreams but rather rabbinic expert learning and exchange his rise in one eastern diaspora Jewish community in favor of returning home to another exilic "home diaspora," Mainz, read in Ashkenaz as Jerusalem since the 1096 sacrificial acts of martyrdom. The story reaffirms Mainz as Jerusalem as an Ashkenazic trope against the Babylonian East (and the Sephardic claim to its succession), but without any direct allusion to Iberia, pace Zfatman's attractive speculation.

60. Compare the story about R. Ephraim of Regensburg's error teaching Judah's son in Marcus, *Sefer Hasidim and the Ashkenazic Book*, 67–69, to the story about a disguised R. Samuel visiting Rabbeinu Tam in Bibliothèque Nationale de France, MS Paris, héb. 772, and compare these to the odd story about R. Samuel, who had to learn something himself from three "qadarim" found in a cycle of stories about R. Samuel in

Goethe University, Frankfurt am Main, Universitätsbibliothek, Hebrew MS, Octavo 35; Zfatman, *Shivhei Rabbi Shmuel ve-Rabbi Yehudah Hasid.*

61. B. Pesahim 66a.

62. On King Charles and R. Qalonimos, see Bibliothèque Nationale de France, MS Paris, héb. 772. See also Grossmann, *Hakhmei Ashkenaz*, 27–44.

63. See Yassif, *Me'ah Sippurim Haser Ehad*; Zfatman, *Rosh va-Rishon*; Grossman, *Hakhmei Ashkenaz*.

64. It also is the theme of an encounter story between R. Samuel and the greatest of the Talmud Tosafists, R. Jacob b. Meir or Rabbeinu Tam (d. 1171). See Marcus, "History, Story, and Collective Memory," 375–79. It has the elements of the hero's disguise and later recognition by the dependent party—in this case, R. Jacob Tam.

Chapter 3. Reforms and Right Order: The Apostolic Age and Crusade Active Martyrs

1. See Kedar, "Expulsion." This binary approach explains why it was Western Christian state powers that forced their Jewish and other populations to leave their boundaries in the later Middle Ages. See chapter 8; Jordan, *French Monarchy*, 256.

2. See Vauchez, *Spirituality*, 66–68; Constable, "Renewal and Reform in Religious Life," especially 38.

3. See Hay, *Europe*, 16–36; Iogna-Pratt, *Order and Exclusion*, 21–22; Moore, "Heresy, Repression and Social Change."

4. Bloch, *Feudal Society*, 59–71.

5. Southern, *Making of the Middle Ages.*

6. See Rosenwein and Little, "Social Meaning."

7. See Cowdrey, *Cluniacs and the Gregorian Reform*; Iogna-Pratt, *Order and Exclusion.*

8. On the Peace of God, see Head and Landes, *Peace of God.*

9. On the Peace of God and Truce of God, see Cowdrey, "Peace and the Truce of God"; Vauchez, *Spirituality*, 69–72; Rosenwein, "Feudal War and Monastic Peace," 155–57.

10. Tellenbach, *Church, State and Christian Society*, 1. See also Davis, "Women on Top"; Jordan, "Jews on Top."

11. On the orders in society, see Fichtenau, *Living in the Tenth Century*; Duby, *Three Orders*; Constable, "Orders of Society." See also Duby, *Knight, the Lady and the Priest*, especially 182–83, which emphasizes hierarchy as central in Gregorian policies. On the transition to Christianitas, see Iogna-Pratt, *Order and Exclusion.*

12. See *Epistolae Vagantes of Pope Gregory VII*, 151, cited in Lipton, *Dark Mirror*, 299n130, and quoted in Vauchez, *Spirituality*, 82. See also Constable, "Renewal and Reform," 58.

13. On the investiture controversy, see Laudage, *Gregorianische Reform und Investiturstreit*; Blumenthal, *The Investiture Controversy.*

14. See Parkes, *Jew in the Medieval Community*, 155–206; Baron, *Jewish Community*; Walzer, Lorberbaum, and Zohar, *Jewish Political Tradition*. Cf. Goitein, *Mediterranean Society*, vol. 2, *The Community.*

15. Synan, *Popes and the Jews in the Middle Ages*; Grayzel, *Church and the Jews*; Grayzel, "Papal Bull Sicut Judaeis"; Stow, "Hatred of the Jews"; Rist, *Popes and Jews*.
16. On the Theodosian Code and the Jews, see Linder, *Jews in the Legal Sources*.
17. Emerton, *Correspondence of Pope Gregory VII*, 177-78.
18. Church councils repeatedly and ineffectively tried to prohibit Jews from hiring Christian wet nurses in their homes. See Irish, *Jews and Christians*, 183-84; Baumgarten, *Mothers and Children*, 128-48. For more on Jews and Christian wet nurses, see chapter 5.
19. On the Christian view of Islam as paganism, mainly because Muslims prayed to Mecca, where the former pagan shrine of the Kaaba was located, see Daniel, *Islam and the West*; Southern, *Western Views of Islam*; Camile, *Gothic Idol*.
20. For the line, see Bédier, *Chanson de Roland*, laisse 79.
21. Emerton, *Correspondence of Pope Gregory VII*, 57, 58.
22. See Erdmann, *Origin of the Idea of Crusade*; Mayer, *Crusades*, 9-42; Peters, *First Crusade*, xi-xix.
23. On the speech, see Munro, "Speech of Pope Urban II at Clermont"; Vauchez, *Spirituality*, 72.
24. Quoted in Peters, *First Crusade*, 53.
25. Robert the Monk, quoted in Peters, *First Crusade*, 27, 28.
26. On the development of the idea of a holy or just war in Christian history, see Erdmann, *Origin of the Idea of Crusade*. Erdmann's influential book played down Urban II's direct and unexpected significance in shaping the idea of the Crusade and attributed it instead to earlier canonists. For convincing arguments that the Urban speech was the main factor that suddenly created the new idea of the Crusade, see Gilchrist, "Erdmann Thesis and the Canon Law." For the argument that Urban's goal was not, as Erdmann would have it, mainly to aid Byzantine Christians but rather to liberate Jerusalem from the beginning, see Riley-Smith, *Crusades: A Short History*, 6-8. The Hebrew chronicles understand the importance of the Crusade and Jerusalem and counter with a construction of Mainz as Jerusalem Temple. See Marcus, "Politics to Martyrdom."
27. Roberti Monachi, *Historia Iherosolimitana*, lib. I, cap. 1-2, in RHC, occ., 3:727-30; English translation in Riley-Smith and Riley-Smith, *Crusades*, 44.
28. For an emphasis on millennial zeal, see Chazan, "'Let Not a Remnant or a Residue Escape'"; Cohn, *Pursuit of the Millennium*. Norman Cohn's book is derived from Paul Alphondéry, who learned about Emicho of Flonheim as a millennial figure from the German translation of the Hebrew 1096 sources in the 1930s. See Kedar, "Emicho of Flonheim"; Gabriele, "Against the Enemies of Christ." See too Langmuir, "Transformation," 362n5; Stow, "Conversion," 916n17.
29. Riley-Smith, "First Crusade," especially 66-72.
30. Kehr, *Papsturkunden in Spanien*, 287-88; English in Riley-Smith and Riley-Smith, *Crusades*, 40.
31. See Liebeschütz, "Crusading Movement," 107. For the letter of Pope Alexander II to the Spanish bishops, see Simonsohn, *Apostolic See and the Jews*, no. 37, 35-36: "Dispar nimirum est Judaeorum et Sarracenorum causa. In illos enim, qui christianos

persequuntur et ex urbibus et propriis sedibus pellunt, juste pugnatur; hi vero ubique parati sunt servire." English in Chazan, *Church, State, and Jew*, 100. See also Rowe, *Jew*, 25.

32. As Iris Shagrir and Netta Amir have noted, there seems to be no visual record in Jewish or Christian art of the anti-Jewish Crusader riots of 1096. On the 1096 episode in Metz, depicted in the nineteenth century, see Shagrir and Amir, "Persecution of the Jews." On ideological approaches to the texts in the nineteenth century, see Roemer, "Turning Defeat into Victory."

33. On motivation of the Crusaders in the 1096 riots, see Kedar, "Emicho of Flonheim"; Kedar, "Forcible Baptisms of 1096"; Stow, "Conversion." In "Destruction or Conversion," David Malkiel has argued that the main goal of the Crusaders was to kill Jews out of revenge for the crucifixion and not convert them, so that the Jews did not have a choice. In the Hebrew and Latin chronicles, however, the narrators make it clear that the martyrs thought they were killing their families to avoid their children being baptized. They may have been wrong, but the Hebrew sources and some of the Latin ones claim that the Jews thought they were avoiding something worse than death and acted on this belief. See especially Kedar, "Forcible Baptisms of 1096"; Lotter, "Tod oder Taufe"; Chazan, "'Let Not a Remnant or a Residue Escape,'" 299n23.

34. On 1096 as a turning point, see Blumenkranz, "Relations between Jews and Christians in the Eleventh Century," 41; Stacey, "History, Religion, and Medieval Antisemitism," 101; Jordan, *French Monarchy*, 19. On the motif of the enemy within, cf. Pagels, *Origin of Satan*.

35. Each of the two anonymous Hebrew accounts survives in a single manuscript. For the manuscripts of R. Eliezer ben Nathan's narrative, see David, "Zikhronot," 195–97. Former Breslau no. 189 is now in the Beinecke Rare Book and Manuscript Library, Yale University, New Haven, CT. The standard Hebrew edition now is EH, which provides both a synoptic and continuous Hebrew edition of the three texts and translations into German; Roos, *"God Wants It!,"* does so in English. References will be to the Hebrew texts in EH, the more available Hebrew edition of H, and the complete translation of E. On these texts, see Chazan, "Hebrew First-Crusade Chronicles"; Chazan, "Hebrew First-Crusade Chronicles: Further Reflections"; Marcus, "Politics to Martyrdom"; Cohen, *Sanctifying the Name of God*; Marcus, Review of *European Jewry*; Cohen, Review of *European Jewry*; Chazan, "Facticity of Medieval Narrative"; Chazan, *God, Humanity, and History*, 138–39.

36. EH, 539; H, 93; E, 99.

37. EH, 561; H, 72; E, 80. The insult terms for Christian sancta are discussed in chapter 4. For *tarput* as idolatry, see M. 'Avodah Zarah 2:3.

38. EH, 615; H, 24; E, 22; Marcus, "Politics to Martyrdom." Cf. Chazan, "Anti-Semitism," 340. See Marcus, "Jewish-Christian Symbiosis," 469n57: the manuscript, former London Rabbinic Court [Beit Din] MS 28 f. 151r, reads "niddah" (menstruation).

39. EH, 609; H, 27; E, 26.

40. See Goitein, "Obadiah, a Norman Proselyte." For the quotations, see Scheiber, "Ein aus arabischer Gefangenschaft," 170.

41. Guibert de Nogent, *De vita sua*, lib. 2, cap. 5, in *Recueil des historiens des Gauls et de la France*, ed. M. Bouquet, 12:240: "Cum ante oculos nostros sint Judei, quibus inimicitior existat gens nulla Dei." For the translation, see Benton, *Self and Society*, 134–35; Archambault, *Monk's Confession*; Guibert of Nogent, *Monodies*.

42. EH, 539; H, 94; E, 100.

43. Vauchez, *Spirituality*, 107; Cohn, *Pursuit of the Millennium*; Flori, *La première croisade*.

44. See Marcus, "Politics to Martyrdom."

45. On these charters, see Schiffmann, "Die Urkunden für die Juden von Speyer 1090 und Worms 1157."

46. EH, 611; H, 26–27; E, 25.

47. See Davis, "Rites of Violence"; Marcus, "Politics to Martyrdom."

48. EH, 317; H, 99–100; E, 108.

49. EH, 317; H, 30; E, 30.

50. On how Mainz was different from the other communities, see Chazan, *European Jewry and the First Crusade*, 309n21. On Jews and weapons, see Magin, "'Waffenrecht' und 'Waffenverbot' für Juden im Mittelalter," cited in EH, 317. Mainz was the target of Emicho of Flonheim too, as noted in Stow, "Conversion." On Emicho, see also Gabriele, "Against the Enemies of Christ."

51. See Marcus, "Politics to Martyrdom"; Marcus, "Medieval Jewish Prophecy." Although the narrative structure of a political phase, followed by a martyrological one, is most pronounced in the narrative attributed to Solomon bar Samson, it is also found in the Mainz Anonymous. See the political phase for Worms in EH, 535; H, 96; E, 103. See the political phase for Mainz in EH, 531–27; H, 98–100; E, 105–6. The martyrological phase follows for Worms in EH, 535–31; H, 96–97; E, 103–5. The martyrological phase follows for Mainz in EH, 525–19; H, 101–4; E, 106–14. In each case, the turning point between the two stages is the Jews' awareness that it is the will of God that they die as martyrs. Cf. Chazan, *European Jewry and the First Crusade*, 308–9n21.

52. EH, 607; H, 28; E, 27–28. Compare the episode in the Latin and Hebrew chronicles of how Christians interpreted the behavior of a goose as an omen portending it was the will of God that they go on a Crusade. See Albertus Aquensis, *Historia Hierosolymitana / Liber Primus Christianae Expeditionis*, lib. 1, cap. 30, in RHC, occ., 4:295; Guibert de Nogent, *Gesta per Francos*, lib. 1, cap 32, in RHC, occ., 4:251; EH, 607, 531; H, 28, 98; E, 27, 106.

53. EH, 607; H, 28–29; E, 27–28 (quotation on E, 28).

54. EH, 553; H, 75; E, 83.

55. EH, 527; H, 100; E, 109.

56. See *Da'at Zeqeinim*, f. 4b to Genesis 9:5.

57. See especially Grossman, "Shorashav," 105–19. On the unprecedented character of the martyrs' behavior, see Soloveitchik, "Religious Law and Change"; Soloveitchik, "Halakhah, Hermeneutics, and Martyrdom in Medieval Ashkenaz."

58. See Baer, "Mavo," 4; Grossman, "Shorashav," 102–5; Goodblatt, "Suicide in the Sanctuary"; Franke, "Crusades and Medieval Anti-Judaism"; Bronstein, "Crusades

and the Jews"; Hiestand, "Juden und Christen in der Kreuzzugspropaganda"; Simms, "Unspeakable Agony of Kiddush Ha-shem."

59. EH, 591; H, 37 [end]; E, 40–41.

60. The Hebrew is phrased in the language of a formal benediction ("asher zivvanu beli lehamir yir'ato ha-tehorah"). See Haim Hillel Ben-Sasson's comment that "medieval Jewish prayerbooks include, in addition to the benedictions for bread and drink, a benediction to be recited by a Jew before killing himself and his children." Ben-Sasson, *Peraqim be-Toledot ha-Yehudim*, 179. This formula appears again in EH, 597; H, 34; E, 36. See also Avramson, "Nusah Berakhah 'al Qedushat ha-Shem."

61. EH, 597; H, 34; E, 35–36; Marcus, "Politics to Martyrdom," 45.

62. The Mainz Anonymous text is in EH, 425, 523; H 101-2; E, 111–12. The Solomon bar Samson version is in EH, 497, 595; H, 34; E, 35–36. On this twice-told episode, see Marcus, "Representation of Reality"; Marcus, "Jewish-Christian Symbiosis," 469–70. Cf. Cohen, *Sanctifying the Name of God*, 127–29, which reads ambivalence instead of assertive triumphalism in this story. This view is picked up uncritically in Boyarin, *Christian Jew*, 160–61. Cohen's reading is forced. It was in the self-interest of the chroniclers, who survived by temporarily converting to Christianity, to exaggerate the piety of the martyrs and not impute to them any ambivalence or negative overtones. For another case in which he and I disagree regarding Ashkenazic assertiveness or doubt, see Cohen, *Sanctifying the Name of God*, 130–41, especially 178n10.

63. See Marcus, "Politics to Martyrdom"; Chazan, *European Jewry and the First Crusade*, 132–36, which refers to a Jewish "Counter-Crusade" that reinforces the idea; Turner and Turner, *Image and Pilgrimage in Christian Culture*, 168–70. Regarding Worms, see Shalev-Eyni, "Reconstructing Jerusalem."

64. For Solomon bar Samson's account, see EH, 597; H, 33; E, 35. For the Mainz Anonymous account, see EH, 525; H, 101; E, 111.

65. For Solomon bar Samson's account, see EH, 595; H, 35; E, 37. For the Mainz Anonymous account, see EH, 521; H, 103; E, 113.

66. EH, 589; H, 38; E, 42.

67. For Eliezer bar Nathan's account, see EH, 557; H, 74; E, 82. For a more detailed version, see Mainz Anonymous, E, 104. It is not in the Solomon bar Samson account. See E, 163n14.

68. See Marcus, "Performative Midrash."

69. For a cogent discussion of Jewish agency expressed in post-1096 liturgical poetry compared to treatments of the imagined Jew in Chaucer, see Weinhouse, "Faith and Fantasy."

70. EH, 613; H, 25; E, 23. Paralleled in EH, 557; H, 73; E, 81. In another parallel, there is no mention of the Shema: EH, 535; H, 96; E, 103.

71. EH, 699, 553; H, 33, 75; E, 34, 83.

72. EH, 553; H, 77; E. 86. The parallel (EH, 575; H, 45; E, 52) omits the reaction and calling out "*shema yisrael*." In Xanten, Jews who observe a Jew committing suicide say "*shema yisrael*." See EH, 547; H, 78; E, 88.

73. Goldschmidt, *Seder ha-Qinot*, 107. The translation is modified from Rosenfeld, *Authorized Kinot*, 140.

74. See Haverkamp, "What Did the Christians Know?," 60.

75. The Christian chroniclers' emphasis on Crusader cruelty, not that of Jewish parents, in 1096 totally refutes the speculative claim by Israel Yuval that there was an influence of Jewish behavior in 1096 on the fantasy of the ritual murder accusation in the mid-twelfth century. See chapter 6.

76. Peters, *First Crusade*, 110; Albert of Aachen, *Historia Ierosolimitana*, ed. Edgington, 50 (Latin) and 51 (English). See also the related *Chronicon* of Richard of Poitiers, cited in Stow, "Conversion," 915n13.

77. Peters, *First Crusade*, 110; Albert of Aachen, *Historia Ierosolimitana*, ed. Edgington, 52 (Latin) and 53 (English). See also Lohrmann, "Albert von Aachen," especially 138–40.

78. Peters, *First Crusade*, 111; Albert of Aachen, *Historia Ierosolimitana*, ed. Edgington, 58 (Latin) and 59 (English). On Crusader motives, see Kedar, "Crusade Historians."

79. Peters, *First Crusade*, 110; Albert of Aachen, *Historia Ierosolimitana*, ed. Edgington, 52 (Latin) and 53 (English).

80. *Annales Wiziburgenses*, in MGH SS, 2:246; *Sigeberti Chronica*, in MGH SS, 6:367; *Annalisto Saxo*, in MGH SS, 6:729; William of Tyre, *Historia Rerum in Partibus Transmarinis Gestarum*, in RHC, 1:66–68.

81. *Gesta treverorum*, in MGH SS, 8:190–91.

82. *Sigebertus Auctarium Acquicinense*, in MGH, SS 6:394.

83. Bernold of Constance, *Bernoldi Chronicon*, in MGH SS, rerum Germanicarum N.S., 14:529, based on St. Blasien, Schaffhausen, in MGH SS, 5:464–65: "diabolo et propria duricia persuadente, se ipsos interfecerunt" (465).

84. *Annales Hildesheimenses*, in MGH SS, Scriptores rerum Germanicarum, 8:49–50.

85. Hugo, abbas Flaviniacensis, *Chronicon*, in MGH SS, 8:474. Translation in Kedar, "Crusade Historians," 20–21.

86. Ekkehard of Aura [Chronica Recensio 1, 146], *Ekkehardi Chronicon Universale*, in MGH SS, 6:208.

87. William of Tyre, *Chronicon*, in MGH SS, 1:29, 1:156; William of Tyre, *Historia Rerum in Partibus Transmarinis Gestarum*, in RHC, 1–4, 1:66–67. English translation: *William of Tyre, History of Deeds Done beyond the Sea*, 1:113. See also Baraz, *Medieval Cruelty*, 78.

88. Kedar, "Forcible Baptisms of 1096," 295, which quotes additional chronicles, including *Annales Sancti Disibodi*, in MGH SS, 17:16.

89. Jordan, *French Monarchy*, 22.

90. Jewish words used to show contempt for Christianity have been referred to as "cacaphemisms." See Elliott Horowitz's neologism in *Reckless Rites*, 157. Shoham-Steiner, *Jews and Crime*, 78, 324n86, 324n87, refers to them as "dysphemisms," a nineteenth-century coinage. It is better to refer to them as "insults" or use other actual English words to describe efforts to blaspheme Christian sancta.

Chapter 4. Assertive Words: Insulting Christianity

1. Cf. Moore, *Formation of a Persecuting Society*.
2. Schmitt, *Raison des gestes dans l'Occident médiéval*.
3. See Lasker, "Impact of the Crusades," 25.
4. For the distinction in R. Gershom's responsum about the status of Christians and Christianity, see chapter 2.
5. The text reads, "*Has ve-shalom she-nifsoq 'avodah zarah ya'avor ve-al yeihareig.*" Tosafot 'Avodah Zarah 54a, *ha be-tzina*, cited in Katz, *Exclusiveness and Tolerance*, 83–84; Berger, "Jacob Katz," 57.
6. Levine, "Why Praise Jews?" Saperstein, "Christians and Jews," does not emphasize enough the Christian assumption of contempt for Jews as the basis of the a fortiori argument in favor of emulating something specific that Jews do. The Talmud contains stories praising the behavior of pagans, such as the one about Dama ben Netina, who lost a fortune because he did not want to disturb his father by waking him. See B. Qiddushin 30a; cf. SHP, 924.
7. SHP, 159, 184, 1075. See also SHP, 1589, cited in Saperstein, "Jews and Christians," 243, but as SHP, 1189 (omitting one *tav* = 400), ed. Jehuda Wistinetzki, who corrects or misreads "beit tiflatam" (house of their foolishness, i.e., a church) in the Parma manuscript as "beit tefillatam" (house of their prayer) (389).
8. Isaac b. Joseph of Corbeil, *Sefer Mizvot Qatan*, para. 12 (end), 1:90. On the book's extraordinary popularity generated by the author himself, see Galinsky, "Significance of Form." On *tarput* as idolatry, see M. 'Avodah Zarah 2:3 and the related biblical *terafim* in Genesis 31:34. My thanks to Judith R. Marcus for the second reference which led me to the first one.
9. Boccaccio, *Decameron*, First Day, Stories Two and Three, 37–44.
10. See Deutsch, *Judaism in Christian Eyes*.
11. See Landgraf, *Commentarius Cantabrigienis in Epistolas Pauli e Schola Petri Abelardi*, 2:434. English translation in Smalley, *Study of the Bible in the Middle Ages*, 78, quoted in Kanarfogel, *Jewish Education and Society*, 16n5. See also Saperstein, "Jews and Christians," 239–40; Southern, *Medieval Humanism and Other Studies*, 11.
12. Langland, *Piers Ploughman*, ix, 145, quoted in Rosenthal, "Margerie Kempe and Medieval Anti-Judaic Ideology," 410n4.
13. Narin van Court, "Hermeneutics of Supersession," 82n29.
14. Devlin, *Sermons of Thomas Brinton, Bishop of Rochester*, 2:411, quoted in Rex, "Chaucer and the Jews," 115n26; Narin van Court, "Hermeneutics of Supersession," 82. See also Herskovits, *Positive Image of the Jew in the "Comedia."*
15. On biblical puns and wordplay, see Rendsburg, "Word Play in Biblical Hebrew"; Rendsburg, "Wordplay in the Bible"; Greenblatt, "Wordplay, Hebrew."
16. See Handel, "Israel among the Nations," 63.
17. B. 'Avodah Zarah 46a.
18. B. Shabbat 116a (bottom); Lasker and Stroumsa, *Polemic of Nestor*, 1:30.
19. B. Shabbat 104b (uncensored).
20. B. Shabbat 104b, cited in Bar-Asher Siegal, "Mocking of Jesus."

21. For insults about Esau in Yannai, see Cuffel, *Gendering Disgust*, 272nn35–36. On possible anti-Byzantine polemics in the Hebrew piyyut of Yannai and Qallir, but especially in Aramaic poetry, see Van Bekkum, "Anti-Christian Polemics"; Münz-Manor, "Carnivalesque Ambivalence and the Christian Other."

22. Zunz, *Die Synagogale Poesie des Mittelalters*, 465–70. See Irshai, "Confronting a Christian Empire."

23. See Levine, *Ancient Synagogue*; Bonfil et al., *Jews in Byzantium*; Talgam, *Mosaics of Faith*.

24. Lasker and Stroumsa, *Polemic of Nestor*; Rembaum, "Influence of *Sefer Nestor HaKomer* on Medieval Jewish Polemics"; Limor, "Yahadut Mitbonenet be-Nazrut."

25. See Lasker and Stroumsa, *Polemic of Nestor*, 1:123; Hebrew texts, 2:107, 127. Note that this term appears in the Hebrew *Nestor*, but not in the original Judeo-Arabic.

26. See Meerson and Schäfer, *Toledot Yeshu: The Life Story of Jesus*.

27. See Schäfer, "Agobard's and Amulo's *Toledot Yeshu*."

28. On Martini and the Jews, see Bonfil, "Demutah shel ha-Yahadut."

29. On the dirges (qinot) for 1096 presented in Hebrew with a German translation, commentary, and introductions, see Fraenkel, Gross, and Lehnhardt, *Hebräische liturgische Poesie*. Although the Solomon bar Samson chronicle is the longest and last of the three, and thus one would expect more epithets in it than in the shorter texts, fewer than half as many *in parallel passages* are found in the Mainz Anonymous, the earliest of the three chronicles. Eliezer b. Nathan's account, written second, has a mere thirteen, and they are only in the narratives, not in the piyyutim that he added in his account that was copied several times. This suggests that Jewish anti-Christian animus about 1096 grew more intense during the first half of the twelfth century. On the dating of the three Hebrew accounts, see EH, introduction; Roos, *"God Wants It!,"* introduction.

30. EH, 609; H, 27; E, 25.

31. Abulafia, "Invectives."

32. Some of the epithets about Jesus were scratched out in the parchment and nearly impossible to read even under a portable ultraviolet light that I brought with me when I examined it in the office of the London Bet Din, stored in an office supplies cabinet, before a private collector subsequently purchased it at auction.

33. See Berger, *Jewish-Christian Debate*, 213–14 and notes, 331–32; Halbertal and Margalit, *Idolatry*, 111.

34. EH, 597; H, 33–34; E, 35.

35. EH, 593; H, 36; E, 38.

36. EH, 593; H, 36; E, 38. A second version is in the Mainz Anonymous, in EH, 521; H, 104; E, 114. The reference to Jesus in boiling excrement is from the uncensored Talmud B. Gittin 57a.

37. For example, in SHP, 1352, the term for the Church of the Holy Sepulchre is "pit" or "latrine" (*shuhah*), as discussed in Shatzmiller, "Doctors and Medical Practice," 588n13, translated on 593. A Christian woman brings a stone to cure a Jewish woman's child, but she refuses to use it because it comes from "the pit" (*shuhah* = latrine), a slur for the Church of the Holy Sepulchre in Jerusalem, and it is part of the stone

in which Jesus (so MS Parma itself, omitted in the printed Wistinetzki edition), was buried (*she-nitman*), following Joseph Shatzmiller's emendation instead of "became impure" (*she-nitma'*). The Church of the Resurrection, known as the *anastasis*, was referred to in Arabic after the Crusades as *al-Qumama* ("the heap of dung") instead of *al-Qiyama* (the Church of the Resurrection). See Gabrieli, *Arab Historians of the Crusades*, 148n1, quoting Imad al-Din al-Isfahani (d. 1201). For several Muslim sources that use this replacement term regularly, see also Le Strange, *Palestine under the Moslems*, 202–9. Both references cited in Smith, *To Take Place*, 76. For latrine blasphemy involving gestures, see chapter 5.

38. See Jacob b. Meir, *Sefer ha-Yashar*, para. 25, cited in Katz, *Exclusiveness and Tolerance*, 73; Goldstein, "Children of the Sacred Covenant," 151.

39. For curses in loan documents (*shetarot*), see Stein, "Development of the Jewish Law on Interest," 39. See also Wiedl, "Anti-Jewish Polemics," 62–63; Irish, *Jews and Christians in Medieval Castile*, 221–61.

40. See Sirat, "Notes sur la circulation des livres entre juifs et chrétiens au Moyen Age"; Olszowy-Schlanger, "Juifs et chrétiens à Troyes au Moyen Age."

41. SHP, 1348; SHB, 427. See also Rashi on Exodus 23:13. *Do not mention* (means, Do not say,) "Stay with me on the day of such and such an idol" (that is, on a saint's day or another Christian holiday).

42. On Joseph Official, see Lasker, *Jewish Philosophical Polemics*, 14, 173n14.

43. Joseph b. Nathan Official, *Yosef ha-Meqaneh*. For *hariyya*, 49, 65; other pages plus two [119, 129] not listed in index.

44. Berger, *Jewish-Christian Debate*; see, for example, paras. 145, 154.

45. Berger, *Jewish-Christian Debate*; see, for example, para. 217.

46. Berger, *Jewish-Christian Debate*; see, for example, para. 207. See also SHP, 191, 193.

47. Berger, *Jewish-Christian Debate*, paras. 145, 167, 179, 186, 200, 205, 208, 220, 224.

48. On David Berger's self-censorship regarding translating a scatological substitute for the Virgin Mary, see Cuffel, *Gendering Disgust*, 2.

49. On the German Jewish pietist circle (hasidei ashkenaz) and Christians, see chapter 6.

50. SHP. 1630. For a list of anti-Christian insults, especially in *Sefer Hasidim*, see Breuer, *Sefer Nizzahon Yashan*, 194. For most of these passages, search under "goy" (meaning "Christian") in the online Princeton University *Sefer Hasidim* Database.

51. Deutsch, "Jewish Anti-Christian Invectives and Christian Awareness."

52. For translations of the Paris trial, see *Trial of the Talmud, 1240*; Cohen, *Friars and the Jews*, 60–76.

53. See Chazan, *Barcelona and Beyond*; Cohen, *Friars and the Jews*, 108–27.

54. See Berger, "Mission to the Jews"; Irish, *Jews and Christians in Medieval Castile*.

55. Shatzmiller, *La deuxième controverse de Paris*.

56. Maccoby, *Judaism on Trial*, 82–94, 168–215.

57. See Limor, *Die Disputationen zu Ceuta (1179) und Mallorca (1286)*.

58. Grayzel, *Church and the Jews*, no. 14, 1:106–7.

59. For several examples, see Ben-Sasson, *Peraqim be-Toledot ha-Yehudim*, 247–49.

60. Bonfil, *History and Folklore*, 262-63.

61. Pseudo-Kodinos, *Narratio de aedificatione templi sanctae sophiae*, 1:105, cited in Smith, *To Take Place*, 83.

62. Berger, *Jewish-Christian Debate*, 41, 68-69. The translation cleans up the Hebrew and substitutes "ugly church" for "ugly abyss" (*tehom*)—the latter a play on the German *Dom* (cathedral)—and "filth" for "dung" (*zo'ah*). It is more accurately translated in Ben-Sasson, *History of the Jewish People*, 554-55. On this source, see Shyovitz, *Remembrance of His Wonders*, 197. Note that in the Siena Palio horse race, run twice during each summer, the town districts take their horse into the local parish church, and if the horse defecates in the church, this is taken as a good omen and the jockey steps in it. See Handelman, "Palio of Sienna," 125.

63. See Krautheimer, *Mittelalterliche Synagogen*; Krinsky, *Synagogues of Europe*; Wischnitzer, *Architecture of the European Synagogue*. Speyer architecture in relation to the Dom from a personal communication with Dr. Günter Stein. The Jewish pietists who opposed doing this, as in SHP, 1630, were ignored.

64. Abulafia, "Eleventh-Century Exchange of Letters." Evidence for everyday Jewish insults toward Christianity is implicit in an invented ritual murder account about Adam of Bristol from England in the thirteenth century. See Stacey, "Adam of Bristol," 11: "Christian perceptions of Jews as blasphemers may sometimes have been rooted in real knowledge of the ways some Jews spoke and acted toward Christians when they thought it safe to do so."

65. A good number of examples are found in Berger, "Mission to the Jews," 586-91. See also Richard, *Sex, Dissidence, and Damnation*, 95.

66. See Southern, *Medieval Humanism and Other Studies*, 11; Southern, *St. Anselm and His Biographer*, 88-90.

67. For the prologue, see Gilbert Crispin, *Disputatio Iudei et Christiani*, 13-16, 27-28. See also Gilbert Crispin, "Disputatio Judei et Christiani," 9; Berger, "Gilbert Crispin"; Southern, "St. Anselm and Gilbert Crispin, Abbot of Westminster"; Southern, *Saint Anselm and His Biographer*, 89-95; Cohen, *Living Letters*, 180-85.

68. The English translation is based on Jacobs, *Jews of Angevin England*, 7-12, with modifications.

69. Herman-Judah, *Hermanus quondam Judaeus*, 77; Herman-Judah, "Translation," 81.

70. Grayzel, *Church and the Jews*, 1:300-301, 1:318-19, 1:324-25.

71. William of Malmesbury, *Gesta regum Anglorum, atque Historia*, Novella 4:317; 2:500, cited in Resnick, *Marks of Distinction*, 41n104.

72. For other references, see Resnick, *Marks of Distinction*, 42-43.

73. B. Shabbat 30b.

74. SHP, 811.

75. Caesarius of Heisterbach, *Dialogus miraculorum*, 2:25, ed. Strange, 1:95-96; English translation from Caesarius of Heisterbach, *Dialogue on Miracles*, trans. Scott and Bland, 107-9. Reprinted in Marcus and Saperstein, *Jews in Christian Europe*, 123; Caesarius of Heisterbach, *Dialogue on Miracles*, trans. Pepin, 186.

76. The text exists in at least two forms. The shorter one, translated in part here, is from MS Paris, Bibliothèque Nationale de France, héb. 1408, and was published in

Rosenthal, *Mehqarim u-Meqorot*, 1:368–72. Rosenthal planned to publish the longer one from Oxford, Bodleian Library, Oppenheim Collection, MS 757; Neubauer 2289, f. 30–58, at the end of his edition of *Yosef ha-Meqaneh*, but did not do so.

77. Berger, "Mission to the Jews," 590–91. The signs of Jewish confidence and assertiveness are especially prominent in northern Europe.

Lasker, Daniel J. "Joseph ben Nathan's *Sefer Yosef ha-Mekanné*, and the Jewish Critique of Christianity," 118 and notes.

78. See Boyarin, *Christian Jew*, 15–20.

79. The Jews as knights is also discussed in Jacobs, *Jews of Angevin England*, 260–61. The theme of medieval Jews as knights was first called to my attention by Emily Taitz in her Jewish Theological Seminary PhD dissertation, which was published as *The Jews of Medieval France: The Community of Champagne*.

80. Oehme, *Knight without Boundaries*; Lampert-Weissig, "Why Is This Knight Different from All Other Knights?"; Marcus, "Why Is This Knight Different?"; Friedman, "Masculine Attributes of the Other"; Levinson, *"Va-Yigdelu ha-Ne'arim"*; Rosenzweig, "Jewish Knight"; Rosen, "Love and Race"; Valles, "Judaized Romance and Romanticized Judaization"; Rovang, "Hebraizing Arthurian Romance"; Warnock, "Arthurian Tradition in Hebrew and Yiddish"; Gruenbaum, "Learning from the Vernacular"; Jacobi, "Jewish Hawking in Medieval France."

81. Friedman, "Masculine Attributes of the Other"; Levinson, *"Va-Yigdelu ha-Ne'arim."*

82. Offenberg, "Jacob the Knight"; Offenberg, "Jewish Knight."

83. Harris, "Concept of Love in *Sefer Hasidim*."

84. *Tractatus adversus Judaeum*, quoted in Güdemann, *Geschichte des Erziehungswesens*, 1:18–19. On the David and Goliath motif as part of Jewish and Christian polemical awareness, see Rashi on B. Shabbat 149a; Sed-Rajna, "Illustrations of the Kaufman Mishneh Torah," 66, 76.

85. Marcus, "Hierarchies, Religious Boundaries," 23n15.

86. See Freedman, *Images of the Medieval Peasant*; Baron, "Ghetto and Emancipation."

87. B. Shabbat 149a.

88. On falcons and Jews, see Jacobi, "Jewish Hawking in Medieval France"; Shatzmiller, *Cultural Exchange*, 61–72.

89. For the Cologne slate with a Romance story, see Timm, "Neu entdeckter literarischer Text."

Chapter 5. Offensive Gestures: Latrine Blasphemy

1. On the use of latrines as both private (as in "privy") and polluting, see Lavezzo, *Accommodated Jew*, 114–17ff.

2. The study of disgust has become a perspective through which to study the other. See Miller, *Anatomy of Disgust*; Cuffell, *Gendering Disgust*; Shyovitz, *Remembrance of His Wonders*; Price, "Medieval Antisemitism"; Bayless, *Sin and Filth*. See also Marcus, "Jewish-Christian Symbiosis," 478–84.

3. See the beginning of the introduction. Another example of Jews acting assertively is from *Siete Partidas*. *Siete Partidas*, 7.24.2: "We heard that in some places the Jews reenacted derisively—and continue to do so—on Good Friday the Passion of Our Lord"; *Siete Partidas*, 7.24.11: "Many errors and offensive acts occur." Carpenter, *Alfonso X and the Jews*, 29, 36.

4. Peter the Venerable, *Letters of Peter the Venerable*, no. 130, 1:328; English translation in Cohen, *Living Letters*, 247.

5. Peter the Venerable, *Letters of Peter the Venerable*, no. 130, 1:328; Price, "Medieval Antisemitism," 179.

6. See Delaborde, *Oeuvres de Rigord*, 1:14, 27 (my translation). See also *Deeds of Philip Augustus*, 59; Stow, *Jewish Dogs*, 185.

7. See the beginning of the introduction and below. See also *Etsi Judeos*, in Grayzel, *Church and the Jews*, 1:114–15.

8. The 1096 Hebrew narratives portray Crusaders doing this and not putting them into latrines (chapter 3). We see the same when two Crusaders attack R. Jacob b. Meir (chapter 6).

9. Bale, *Jew in the Medieval Book*, 31, 191n34, translated from San Marino, Huntington Library, MS HM, 132, f. 272r (Higden's holograph); Price, "Medieval Antisemitism," 185; Bayless, *Sin and Filth*; Bale, *Jew in the Medieval Book*, 27–55.

10. See Price, "Medieval Antisemitism," 186: "But interestingly, there is no Jewish text that accuses Christians of scatological or other bodily defilement: the traffic on this is entirely one-way." For an example of a Jew seeing Jesus on the cross as an idol, see Herman-Judah, *Hermanus quondam Judaeus*, 75; translation as Herman-Judah, "Translation," 80. See also Lipton, *Dark Mirror*, 117, 121; Lipton, "Sweet Lean of His Head." Katz, *Exclusiveness and Tolerance*, 89–90, points to words and acts of contempt by Christians and Jews toward the other's religious symbols. He advanced the discussion by indicating that Jews acted out against Christianity, but he did not note the asymmetry in how each attacked the other. Christians tearing Torah scrolls and trampling them in the mud is not the same register as farting, spitting, urinating, and putting Jesus and Mary in latrines as part of latrine blasphemy. Katz does not translate the verbal insults but instead refers his English readers to the Hebrew text in H, 35, 53, 76, 102–3.

11. See especially Price, "Medieval Antisemitism"; Morrison, *Excrement in the Late Middle Ages*. In the 1970s, Jewish Theological Seminary professor Saul Lieberman kept his volumes of Christian theology upside down in bookcases nearest to the toilet in his office suite. To isolate Talmud volumes from the cross, Jewish Theological Seminary professor Haim Zalman Dimitrovsky cautioned his former PhD student, Daniel Boyarin, not to bring the Talmud or other Torah books into rented office space at Union Theological Seminary, across the street from Jewish Theological Seminary, because the office doorknobs there were part of a decorative brass cross. He didn't, and I had a private office when I was there. Cf. SHP, 663: "If a Christian made a cross on a bowl or cup or on other utensils, one should not use them while the cross is on them, but he should scratch it off."

12. See Bonfil, *Jewish Life in Renaissance Italy*, xi: "A history 'seen from the inside' is obviously not a history of isolation. Rather, it is the history of a coming to

awareness of the Self in the act of specular reflection in the Other, by which I mean a reflection of oneself in the other as in a mirror."

13. On Jewish purity, see Neusner, *Idea of Purity*; Klawans, *Impurity and Sin*; Hayes, *Gentile Impurities*; Birenboim, "Parzah Tum'ah be-Yisrael"; Cohen, "Menstruants and the Sacred," 274–76. On medieval Jewish men and women in the synagogue and purity laws, see Baumgarten, *Practicing Piety*, 21–50, which does not deal with filth and bodily elimination in contrast to the holy.

14. For these categories, see Douglas, *Purity and Danger*. For the category of disgust, see Miller, *Anatomy of Disgust*; Cuffell, *Gendering Disgust*; Morrison, *Excrement in the Late Middle Ages*. Behind some of these studies is the work of Julia Kristeva, as in *Powers of Horror*. On the fact that the Book of Deuteronomy 23:10–15 already associates but does not equate urination and defecation with a nocturnal emission, see Cohen, "Menstruants and the Sacred," 276.

15. Neis, "Their Backs toward the Temple," argues that the rabbinic rules for the profane are the inverse of their prayer rules of holiness. So for Jews to juxtapose Christian sancta with latrines or near elimination is to negate the holiness of the other and equate them with feces—the opposite of Jewish and the holy. On the Jewish issues, see also Schofer, *Confronting Vulnerability*. Cf. Bayless, *Sin and Filth*, which does not apply the Jewish categories of impurities versus bodily elimination.

16. Eilberg-Schwartz, *People of the Body*; Bynum, *Fragmentation and Redemption*; Shyovitz, *Remembrance of His Wonders*. Cf. Coudert, "Sewers, Cesspools and Privies," which underplays medieval use of latrines.

17. Cuffel, *Gendering Disgust*, 7.

18. For Jews, excrement, and latrines, see Price, "Medieval Antisemitism"; Bayless, *Sin and Filth*; Cohen, "Innocent III," 127.

19. SHP, 771; SHB, 954. Compare the story told by the thirteenth-century Italian chronicler Salimbene de Adam, whom the devil criticized for praising God while sitting in the latrine. Quoted in Bayless, *Sin and Filth*, 1–2; SHP, 799; SHB, 998. An exception is SHP, 38: "If a man is in the bathhouse or in the latrine and sees a woman passing by outside, he should think about Torah and not about a woman. For words of Torah were given (to us) in order to purify the heart and as a remedy for the evil impulse."

20. SHP, 537.

21. SHP, 540; SIIB, 819. For a summary of rabbinic law, see R. Moses b. Maimon (Maimonides), *Book of Love*. On avoiding urinating within four cubits of where one prays, see, for example, B. Megillah 27b. On Jews concerned with latrines and cleanliness, see Morrison, *Excrement in the Late Middle Ages*, 38.

22. M. 'Avodah Zarah 4:5. On making a latrine out of a former place of idolatry, see M. 'Avodah Zarah 3:7; B. 'Avodah Zarah 47b. On latrines and pagans, see Cuffel, *Gendering Disgust*, 54–55.

23. See M. Sanhedrin 7:6, B. Sanhedrin 60b; Rashi on Num. 25:3.

24. M. Sanhedrin 7:6. See also B. Sanhedrin 106a.

25. M. Sanhedrin, 7:6. See also B. Sanhedrin 106a.

26. B. Gittin 57a (in the uncensored Talmud).

27. On the Incarnation, see Lasker, *Jewish Philosophical Polemics*, 105-34; Cuffel, *Gendering Disgust*, 58-83, especially 70, 117-30; Morrison, *Excrement in the Late Middle Ages*, 45-47.

28. See Odo of Tournai, "Disputation," 95; Resnick, "Odo of Tournai"; Shyovitz, *Remembrance of His Wonders*, 194-202; Price, "Medieval Antisemitism," 185-86; Berger, *Jewish-Christian Debate*, 350-54.

29. EH, 557; H, 73; E, 81.

30. Thomas of Monmouth, *Life and Miracles*, book I:6, 25-26; Thomas of Monmouth, *Life and Passion*, 19-20; Bale, "Fictions of Judaism," 135-39.

31. See Langmuir, "Knight's Tale," especially 245-47.

32. Matthew Paris, *Matthaeus Parisiensis Chronica Maiora*, 2:14-15. On the fictionalization of the incident, see Bale, "Fictions of Judaism," 136, which refers to other examples of Jews and latrines, such as the story of Adam of Bristol; see Stacey, "Adam of Bristol."

33. See Marcus, "Jewish-Christian Symbiosis," 478-84; Shyovitz, *A Remembrance of His Wonders*, 194-204. Grayzel, *Church and the Jews*, 1:109, refers to Jews killing a Christian and putting the body into a latrine on January 3, 1205. For the story of Adam of Bristol and a latrine, see chapter 6. See below for the claim Jews made that their Christian wet nurses spill milk into a latrine after they take communion. On *The Prioress's Tale*, see Morrison, *Excrement in the Late Middle Ages*, 87; chapter 8.

34. On the procedure for spitting in front of the brother-in-law and not in his face, see M. Yevamot 12:3.

35. On the curative tradition about saliva and a selective discussion of modern restrictions on spitting, see Gonzalez-Crussi, *Body Fantastic*, 73-84.

36. M. Berakhot 9:5. For Rava, see B. Berakhot 63a; Ehrlich, *Nonverbal Language of Prayer*, 164-69. On spitting, see Ehrlich, *Nonverbal Language of Prayer*, 131, 146n31, 164, 166-69, 206, 239, 241, 245.

37. On someone who wants to avoid spitting in synagogue all the time, see SHP, 421[a]; SHB, 253.

38. Shoham-Steiner, "Vitam finivit infelicem"; Horowitz, *Reckless Rites*, 154-55; Goldstein, "Children of the Sacred Covenant," 207-8. On Yom Tov, see Weissman, *Final Judgement*, 205. On Judah the Pious approving suicide as a valid penance, see Spitzer, "She'eilot u-Teshuvot Rabbeinu Yehudah he-Hasid." Such attraction in a case of insanity is an exception compared to the overwhelming instances of aversion Jews in Ashkenaz expressed toward Christian sancta. Cf. Jean, Count of Soissons, in Guibert de Nogent, *Autobiographie*, III:16, translated in Benton, *Self and Society*, 210: "He acted sometimes like a Jew and sometimes like a Christian and the Jews thought he was insane"; Archambault, *Monk's Confession*; Guibert of Nogent, *Monodies*. On crossing categories as dangerous, see Douglas, *Purity and Danger*.

39. EH, 579; H, 44; E, 50. For Eliezer b. Nathan's account, see EH, 551; H, 77; E, 85; Shatzmiller, "Mi-Giluyehah shel ha-Antisheimiyut."

40. *Sefer Zekhirah*, in H, 118; E, 125; Price, "Medieval Antisemitism," 178; Cluse, "Stories of Breaking and Taking the Cross," 438-39.

41. *Sefer Zekhirah*, in H, 119; E, 127; Price, "Medieval Antisemitism," 178. For the argument that the Oxford 1268 Ascension Day incident may have been connected to Crusade enthusiasm in England, see Cluse, "Stories of Breaking and Taking the Cross." On medieval Jewish attitudes and gestures toward the cross, see Katz, *Exclusiveness and Toleration*, 27; Shatzmiller, "Mi-Giluyehah shel ha-Antisheimiyut"; Cluse, "Stories of Breaking and Taking the Cross"; Hames, "Urinating on the Cross"; Horowitz, "Jews and the Cross"; Horowitz, "Medieval Jews Face the Cross"; Horowitz, *Reckless Rites*.

42. For the text by Matthew Paris, see Maitland, "Deacon and the Jewess," 385-406; Horowitz, *Reckless Rites*, 167-68, which quotes Maitland's translation; Price, "Medieval Antisemitism," 178; Cluse, "Stories of Breaking and Taking the Cross." Maitland translated the act with the euphemism "he defiled the cross" and in a footnote provided in Latin: "et minxit super crucem" ("and he urinated on the cross"). Compare the case of Robert of Reading, who in 1275 became a Jew and married a Jewess, discussed in Boyarin, *Christian Jew*, 213-14.

43. Tovey, *Anglo-Judaica*, 168, quoted in Horowitz, *Reckless Rites*, 170, with earlier references at 170n70.

44. See Horowitz, *Reckless Rites*, 172.

45. Joseph b. Nathan Official, *Yosef ha-Meqaneh*, 14. On the observations on the relationship between host desecration charges and other accusations of Jewish acts of desecration, see Lotter, "Hostienfrevel und Blutwunderfälschung." Yuval, "Ha-Neqam ve-ha-Qelalah," 52n77, properly endorses Lotter's position that not every accusation that Jews desecrated Christian sancta should automatically be rejected as unfounded.

46. Price, "Medieval Antisemitism," 179; Marcus, "Jewish-Christian Symbiosis," 480; Horowitz, *Reckless Rites*, 166.

47. SHP, 1365.

48. SHP, 1348; SHB, 427.

49. Berger, *Jewish-Christian Debate*, 26, 59. Berger, "Mission to the Jews," 589, translates the last phrase as "Jacob sat on a cross," which is explained as "a delicate paraphrase of the original" (589n63).

50. Scott, *Domination and the Arts of Resistance*, v.

51. See Allan, *On Farting*. Morrison, *Excrement in the Late Middle Ages*, 67, refers to Chaucer's *The Miller's Tale* as "the most famous fart in English (if not world) literature."

52. SHP, 115 (end).

53. SHP, 685.

54. EH, 569; H, 49; E, 57-58.

55. EH, 477; H, 55; E, 65.

56. Price, "Medieval Antisemitism," 178, refers to "thrust a rod" as meaning urinating on a cross, following Horowitz, "Jews and the Cross"; Horowitz, *Reckless Rites*, 163-67.

57. Greenberg, *Ezekiel 1-20*, 165, translates the enigmatic phrase "reach the vine-branch to their noses" but on 173 refers to B. Yoma 77a, which quotes the phrase *whose backs were to the Lord's Temple* (Ezek. 8:16) to mean they would uncover themselves

and defecate downward. Moshe Greenberg mentions that medievals interpreted the gesture as "breaking wind" or referring to some phallic rite. See Neis, "Their Backs toward the Temple."

58. Cf. the film *Monty Python and the Holy Grail*: "I fart in your general direction."

59. Gibert de Nogent, *Autobiographie*, 1:26, translated in Benton, *Self and Society*, 115; Archambault, *Monk's Confession*; Guibert of Nogent, *Monodies*.

60. Caesarius of Heisterbach, *Dialogus miraculorum*, 2:23.

61. Halbertal and Margalit, *Idolatry*, 211; Tosafot to B. 'Avodah Zarah 2a, s.v. *asur*, on which see Katz, *Exclusiveness and Tolerance*, 24-36.

62. See Jordan, "Christian Excommunication of the Jews," 34.

63. For latrines along with a look at wet nurses of different religions, see Winer, *Women, Wealth, and Community in Perpignan*, 149-56. For a canon from the 1213 Council of Paris prohibiting Christian women from serving as wet nurses to Jewish babies, which clearly was being ignored, see See Grayzel, *Church and the Jews*, 1:115, 1:307; Winer, "Conscripting the Breast"; *Siete Partidas*, 7.24.8: "No Jew shall dare to have in his house Christian servants . . . to bathe together with Christians," in Carpenter, *Alfonso X and the Jews*, 34.

64. Newman, *Growing Up in the Middle Ages*, 48. On wet nurses, see Baumgarten, *Mothers and Children*, 119-53; Fildes, *Wet Nursing*.

65. Tosafot, 'Avodah Zara 26a, s.v. "Ovedet kokhavim menikah benah shel Yisrael." For a translation, see Baumgarten, *Mothers and Children*, 140; Goldstein, "Children of the Sacred Covenant," 80.

66. Grayzel, *Church and the Jews*, 1:114-17; Simonsohn, *Apostolic See and the Jews*, no. 82, 87.

67. Grayzel, *Church and the Jews*, 1:117; Morrison, *Excrement in the Late Middle Ages*, 85. Tolan, "Of Milk and Blood," claims that the change was designed to protect Christian purity. See Price, "Medieval Antisemitism," 186-87; Baumgarten, *Mothers and Children*, chapter 4, especially 136-37. Cf. Chazan, "Innocent III and the Jews," which discusses the papal letter, but omits the allegation about Christian wet nurses.

68. Grayzel, *Church and the Jews*, 1:114.

69. On the Eucharist, "believing it to be black magic that would gravely harm their offspring by way of the nurses' milk," see, for example, Stow, "Hatred of the Jews," 82. For agreement with Grayzel's reading, see Price, "Medieval Antisemitism," 186.

70. Wood, "Doctor's Dilemma," 719: "As St. Isidore of Seville had explained the connection early in the seventh century: '*Lac* (milk) derives its name from its color, because it is a white liquor . . . and its nature is changed from blood; for after the birth whatever blood has not yet been spent in the nourishing of the womb flows by a natural passage to the breasts, and whitening by their virtue, receives the quality of milk.'"

71. Cohen, "Innocent III."

72. Cohen, "Innocent III," 125.

73. See Marcus, "Pious Community and Doubt," 31-32.

74. EH, 573; H, 47; E, 54.

75. Caesarius of Heisterbach, *Dialogus miraculorum*, 2:26; Perez, "Next-Door Neighbors," 326-27.

76. See Yerushalmi, "Inquisition and the Jews of France."

77. Rubin, *Gentile Tales*, 93–103. As she observes in her summary, "From the Jewish perspective, as we have seen, there is a total rejection of the possibility of divine presence in the eucharist, and the host is treated more as a perplexing joke" (99).

78. See Warner, *Alone of All Her Sex*, 192–205; Rubin, *Mother of God*, 211–13; Dorger, "Studies in the Image of the Madonna Lactans." See also Matthew Paris, *Matthaeus Parisiensis Chronica Maiora*, for the story about Abraham of Berkhamstead placing a painted statue of nursing Mary into a latrine.

79. Cohen, "Innocent III," 125–26.

80. Stow, "Cruel Jewish Father." The *Siete Partidas* illustrates how Jews are not subordinate enough. See Lipton, "Where Are the Gothic Jewish Women?," 174n66.

81. See Marcus, *Rituals of Childhood*. For the texts, see Marcus, "Honey Cakes and Torah."

82. Marcus, *Rituals of Childhood*, 29.

83. In northern France, the ceremony took place whenever the child reached his fifth birthday at any time of the year. See Marcus, *Rituals of Childhood*, 32–33.

84. Jacques de Vitry claimed that it is not turned into waste but instead absorbed by the body as spiritualized matter. See Rubin, *Corpus Christi*, 37–38; Marcus, *Rituals of Childhood*, 114; Morrison, *Excrement in the Late Middle Ages*, 79–80. Judah the Pious opposed excreting holy letters. See Marcus, *Rituals of Childhood*.

85. *Sifrei Be-Midbar*, Baha'alotekha, sec. 88, 87; B. Yoma 75b; Swartz, "Like the Ministering Angels," 159.

86. On the initiation to Torah as a means by which Jewish boys were socialized into a Jewish identity that included a belief in the superiority of the Jewish community as compared to any other group, see Goldin, *Yihud ve-ha-Yahad*, 44–66; Goldin, "'Pen Yavo'u ha-'Areilim Halalu'"; Levin, "Jewish Conversion to Christianity," 119. Einbinder, *Beautiful Death*, 17–39, discusses martyrdom piyyutim directed at adolescent Tosafist students to discourage their attraction to Christianity. On adolescent boys converting, see Goldstein, "Children of the Sacred Covenant," 91–92; Jordan, "Adolescence and Conversion." Cf. Sherwood, "Rebellious Youth and Pliant Children."

87. See Chazan, "Deteriorating Image."

Chapter 6. Eucharistic Fantasies: Saints, Imagined Killers, and Jewish Saints

1. See, for example, Chazan, *Medieval Stereotypes*, 47–51, 60. Anthony Bale's point that the imagined Jew developed *before* the expulsion of real Jews from England in 1290 is important to keep in mind. Bale, *Jew in the Medieval Book*, 15–16.

2. On child saints, see especially Wasyliw, *Martyrdom, Murder, and Magic*.

3. On ancient Christian martyrs, see Frend, *Martyrdom and Persecution in the Early Church*. On the martyrs of Córdoba, see Coope, *Martyrs of Córdoba*.

4. On St. Thomas's cult, see Barlow, *Thomas Becket*. On Santiago de Compostela, see Dunn and Davidson, *Pilgrimage to Compostela*.

5. Israel Yuval's idea that Würzburg was a ritual murder is not supported by his assumption that anti-Jewish violence is present in ritual murder accusations; before 1255 in England, there was no such violence. Blois in 1171 is even less a ritual murder than Würzburg since there was no body. See Yuval, *Two Nations*, 169.

6. On Harold of Gloucester, see Hillaby, "Ritual-Child-Murder Accusation." On Robert of Bury, see Bale, "House Devil, Town Saint," 186. For the brief passage about Robert, see Jocelin of Brakelond, *Chronicle of the Abbey of Bury St. Edmunds*, 15; the original is in Arnold, *Memorials of Saint Edmund's Abbey*, 223, both cited in Bale, "House Devil, Town Saint," 202n4.

7. See Bale, "Fictions of Judaism," 133; Wasyliw, *Martyrdom, Murder, and Magic*.

8. The high rate of child mortality contributed to the heightened concern of parents when the ritual murder accusation got underway, but it hardly explains why only a tiny percentage of the cases were made into ritual murders. Cf. Schultz, "Blood Libel." On the high mortality numbers, see Hanawalt, "Medievalists and the Study of Childhood," 453.

9. Boswell, *Kindness of Strangers*.

10. Jacob of Voragine, *Golden Legend*, 2:315, in St. Elizabeth, no. 168. On St. Elizabeth, see Burke, "Sister in the World."

11. There were accusations about Jews killing a woman in Boppard in 1179 and Speyer in 1196, with collective punishment exacted on each Jewish community, but there is no mention of their sainthood or the body working miracles as is the case with the male victims. See H, 126 (a boat near Boppard), 131–32 (Speyer).

12. See the translation of Miri Rubin. On the early cases, see Langmuir, "L'Absence d'accusation de meurtre rituel"; Lotter, "Innocens et virgo et martyr"; McCulloh, "Jewish Ritual Murder"; Johnson, *Blood Libel*, 40–41; Cohen, "Flow of Blood," especially 40–65; Vauchez, *Spirituality*, 151; Rokéah, "State, the Church, and the Jews," 104–11, which points to apostates as helping spread the rumor. See also David Strang's theory of "diffusion studies" in Strang and Soule, "Diffusion in Organizations and Social Movements," adopted in Dorin, "Banishing Usury," 11, regarding the spread of expulsion as a royal policy that became "contagious." The same could be said about the spread of the idea of ritual murder accusations from the mid-twelfth century on.

13. Thomas of Monmouth, *Life and Miracles*, book I:6, 25–26; Thomas of Monmouth, *Life and Passion*, 19–20.

14. Hillaby, "Ritual-Child-Murder Accusation," 77.

15. Hillaby, "Ritual-Child-Murder Accusation."

16. See McCulloh, "Jewish Ritual Murder." Yuval, *Two Nations*, 170, correctly raises the question of why it was widely believed. For a discussion of the historiography on William, including Yuval, see Johnson, *Blood Libel*, but on Yuval's (and my) thesis connecting the ritual murder accusation to the 1096 Jewish martyrs, see below.

17. Hillaby, "Ritual-Child-Murder Accusation," 99. See also Bale, "Fictions of Judaism," 131, 133.

18. See *Annales Herbipolenses*, MGH SS, 16:3–4; English translation in Chazan, *Medieval Stereotypes*, 61–62.

19. H, 119–20; E, 127.

20. H, 119–20; E, 127.

21. Yuval, *Two Nations*, 169.

22. Rose, *Murder*, 151; cf. Chazan, "Blois Incident of 1171," 16.

23. Ephraim of Bonn, *Sefer ha-Zekhirah*, in Marcus, *Jew in the Medieval World*, 1938. On Pulcelina, see Chazan, "Blois Incident of 1171"; Rose, *Murder*, 158–70. On Alfonso VIII and a liaison with a Jewish woman from Toledo, cf. Nirenberg, "Deviant Politics and Jewish Love."

24. Chazan, "Blois Incident of 1171," 16–17, notes that at Blois there was no body.

25. Marcus and Saperstein, *Jews in Christian Europe*, 95. Jacob Rader Marcus also titled Blois a "ritual murder."

26. Marcus and Saperstein, *Jews in Christian Europe*, 96; Evans, "Scent of a Martyr." See also the story about the pious sinner that ends with the observation that the dead person being asked about in heaven smelled sweet, a sign of his being a saint. SHP, 1556, in Stern and Mirsky, *Rabbinic Fantasies*, no. 10, 229–30.

27. Galinsky, "Gishot Shonot."

28. Chazan, *Church, State, and Jew*, 115–16, where "Robert" should be "Richard," as in the Latin sources. Shatzmiller, "Jews, Pilgrimage and the Christian Cult of Saints," 342, renders the name "Pons Richard." The Hebrew in Habermann's version of the unique manuscript, formerly London, Jews College, then London, Beit Din, now in private hands, is R Y Y R T, probably a distortion of "RI[ch]aRDus" for the proposed original Hebrew [RYY[K]RT], where the kaf dropped out by haplography to the similar looking letter, resh.

29. See Neyrinck, "Richard of Pontoise." On the etching of Richard of Pontoise in the *Nuremberg Chronicle* and Hermann Schedel's claim that it was the reason Jews were expelled, see Teter, *Blood Libel*, 15.

30. Robert de Torigni, *Chronicle*, 250–51, English in Stevenson, *Chronicles of Robert de Monte*, 114–15; McCulloh, "Jewish Ritual Murder," 718. On Robert's tendency to augment ritual murder accounts, see Goldstein, "Children of the Sacred Covenant," 131n253.

31. On de Torigni making things up, and regarding his inventing a legend to support pilgrimage to Rocamadour, see Vauchez, *Spirituality*, 148–49. See also Hillaby, "Ritual-Child-Murder Accusation," 98–99.

32. Bale, "Fictions of Judaism," 131.

33. On the political motives of Philip Augustus in promoting the cult of Richard of Pontoise, see Rose, "Royal Power and Ritual Murder." On economic motives, see Hillaby, "Ritual-Child-Murder Accusation." Neither sees the ritual murder accusation as the main motive for his expelling the Jews—an explanation found in clerical sources like Rigord.

34. Delaborde, *Oeuvres de Rigord*, 1:5; translated in *Deeds of Philip Augustus*, 51–52; Marcus and Saperstein, *Jews in Christian Europe*, 99.

35. Jordan, *French Monarchy*, 30–32. In addition to the belief that Jews ritually killed Richard of Pontoise, there was a rumor about another case in the royal city of Orleans. See Rose, "Royal Power and Ritual Murder."

36. Langmuir, "Knight's Tale."

37. Matthew Paris, *English History*, 3:138–40.

38. On Adam of Bristol, see Cluse, "Fabula ineptissima"; Stacey, "Adam of Bristol"; Bale, "Fictions of Judaism," 136; Hames, "Limits of Conversion."

39. Appleby, *Cronicon Richardi Divisensis*. Bale, "Richard of Devizes," 59, sees the *Cronicon*'s description of the coronation riots of 1189 as portraying Christians as the Jews at the Passion and Jews as Jesus-like victims, keeping them inside the body, to be "excreted" later. See also Bale, "Fictions of Judaism," 133–34. On Richard, see Mentgen, "Richard of Devizes und die Juden"; Allin, "Richard of Devizes." Partner, *Serious Entertainments*, 176, analyzes the *Cronicon* as a failed Jerusalem Crusade and makes Winchester the Jerusalem of the Jews. Is it a coincidence that the Hebrew Solomon bar Samson chronicle, from around 1140, sees the Crusaders failing to reach Jerusalem and views Mainz as Jerusalem? See Marcus, "Politics to Martyrdom," 49–51.

40. Matthew Paris, *Matthaeus Parisiensis Chronica Maiora*, 4:30; Stacey, "King Henry III and the Jews," 125; Lipman, *Jews of Medieval Norwich*; Tartakoff, *Conversion, Circumcision*, 47–69; Boyarin, *Christian Jew*, 20–27, 233–37.

41. See Abulafia, *Christian-Jewish Relations*, 167–92; Langmuir's references in "Knight's Tale," 240–42; Chazan, *Medieval Stereotypes*, 54–57. Iberia was different. See Weissberger, "Motherhood and Ritual Murder."

42. See Jordan, *French Monarchy*, 31–32; Rose, "Royal Power and Ritual Murder."

43. See especially Bale, "Richard of Devizes," 68–69.

44. We see a similar historical dynamic at work later in the way a papal letter prohibiting Christians from lending money at interest could be transformed over time into a measure that was applied to Jewish moneylenders and contributed to their removal from Christian Europe despite a theological basis for the retention of Jews. See Dorin, *No Return*. In the accusations leveled against different groups during the Black Death, we also see how an idea that a hostile group can threaten the body of Christ by poisoning wells can spread from group to group and change over time. Barzilay, *Poisoned Wells*, 38–97.

45. See Stacey, "Ritual Crucifixion to Host Desecration"; Dundes, *Blood Libel Legend*; Arieti, "Magical Thinking."

46. On the belief in cannibalism and its sources, see Gow, *Red Jews*, 49–50; Langmuir, "Ritual Cannibalism."

47. See *Annales Erphordenses*, 31, cited in Ocker, "Ritual Murder," 183. There are earlier references to Jews eating a victim's heart or ripping it out of the body, but these show only that the idea was already present in the 1190s, as in the fictive account of Richard of Devizes in Winchester or William the Breton's reworking of Rigord regarding Pontoise in 1255, where Matthew Paris does not mention this at all. There is, then, some overlap of the ritual murder and blood libel accusations, but Fulda still is significant as the first clear, documented public case of the latter. See, however, the claims in Abulafia, *Christian-Jewish Relations*, 178–79.

48. Langmuir, "Ritual Cannibalism."

49. Vauchez, "Antisémitisme et canonisation populaire." On Werner, see Mentgen, "Ritualmordaffäre."

50. A separate Hebrew version of the allegation was copied into the last page of the manuscript of *Sefer Hasidim*, known as Former Boesky, JTS 46, and is in private hands.

51. Hsia, *Trent 1475*; Schultz, "Blood Libel"; Johnson, *Blood Libel*, 129–64.
52. Berger, *Jewish-Christian Debate*, sec. 244, 229.
53. Yassif, *Me'ah Sippurim Haser Ehad*, a collection of Hebrew legends based on Jerusalem, National Library of Israel Hebrew Manuscript 3281, no. 31, elaborated in Yiddish in Gaster, *Ma'aseh Book*, no. 178.
54. Chazan, *Church, State, and Jew*, 125. On the imperial decision, see Diestelkamp, "Der Vorwurf des Ritualmordes."
55. Innocent III, *Etsi non*, January 16, 1205, in Grayzel, *Church and the Jews*, 1:109.
56. Grayzel, *Church and the Jews*, 1:271.
57. Marcus and Saperstein, *Jews in Christian Europe*, 150–51.
58. Teter, *Blood Libel*; Frankel, *Damascus Affair*; Avrutin, Dekel-Chen, and Weinberg, *Ritual Murder in Russia*. See Barnai, "Blood Libels"; Hacker, "'Alilot Dam Neged Yehudim."
59. Rubin, "Imagining the Jew"; Rubin, *Gentile Tales*, 48–55; Merback, *Pilgrimage and Pogrom*.
60. Rubin, *Gentile Tales*.
61. Barzilay, *Poisoned Wells*; Benedictow, *Black Death 1346–1353*.
62. Berger, "Crusades to Blood Libels," 30; Saperstein, "Medieval Christians and Jews"; Chazan, *In the Year 1096*, 143–46; Horowitz, *Reckless Rites*, 172–74; Baron, *Social and Religious History of the Jews*, 11:165, cited in Horowitz, *Reckless Rites*. For an incident of Jews who broke into a church, see Rokéah, "Jewish Church-Robbers," 348; Rubin, *Gentile Tales*, 34.
63. Langmuir, "L'Absence d'accusation de meurtre rituel," refers to de Torigni as spreading the ritual murder idea in France.
64. Rubin, "Desecration of the Host," 46–47.
65. Berger, "Crusades to Blood Libel," 30–31.
66. Panxhi, "Hoc est corpus meum." For an emphasis on the ritual murder as reenacting the crucifixion, see Shahar, "Inspecting the Pious Body."
67. Berger, "Mission to the Jews"; Berger, "Anti-Semitism"; Baraz, *Medieval Cruelty*, 78.
68. Despres, "Mary and the Eucharist," 384. See also Rubin, *Gentile Tales*, 7–39; Goldstein, "Children of the Sacred Covenant," 110; MacLehose, *A Tender Age*. On Marian devotion, see Jordan, "Marian Devotion"; Levin, "Jewish Conversion to Christianity," 200–204; Sinanoglou, "Christ Child as Sacrifice"; Blumenkranz, "Juden und Jüdischen"; Ihnat, *Mother of Mercy*, 138–81.
69. Bale, "Fictions of Judaism." See especially Wasyliw, *Martyrdom, Murder, and Magic*, 107–20.
70. Even so, the author of the Hebrew chronicle blamed the riots on Satan as the pope. See EH, 609; H, 27; E, 26.
71. Peter the Venerable, *Letters of Peter the Venerable*, 1:328; English translation in Cohen, *Living Letters*, 247.
72. Bale, "Fictions of Judaism," 131, points to the Benedictine rivalry for saints' stories from the twelfth century on.

73. On the "Little Boy of La Guardia," see Weissberger, "Motherhood and Ritual Murder." As in Blois, there was no body.

74. For Gloucester, see Hillaby, "Ritual-Child-Murder Accusation," 80. In 1255, there was a gathering of Jews to celebrate a wedding. On the association between circumcision and the blood libel during the Middle Ages, see Gross, "Blood Libel," 171–74; Tartakoff, *Conversion, Circumcision*.

75. See Horowitz, *Reckless Rites*; Gribetz, "Hanged and Crucified."

76. Theodosian Code 16.8.18 (May 29, 408), in Linder, *Jews in Roman Imperial Legislation*, 236–38; Chazan, *Church, State, and Jew*, 305–6 (Brie/Bray); Horowitz, "Rite to Be Reckless."

77. Kogman-Appel, "Tree of Death"; Aronius, *Regesten*, no. 330, 148–49, cited in Ocker, "Ritual Murder," 187n102, which refers to an incident in Cologne from a chronicle about a Jew who was baptized who claimed Jews had a custom of crucifying a wax Jesus figure on Good Friday. Julius Aronius connects this idea to a custom of hanging a wax figure of Haman on Purim, but he does not refer to ritual murder.

78. Roth, "Feast of Purim." But see Langmuir, "Historiographic Crucifixion," 119–21.

79. Baron, *Social and Religious History of the Jews*, 4:139, 308n61.

80. Although Yuval developed the idea in directions that led to enormous resonance in the scholarly literature and beyond, the article started with a brief footnote that I wrote in 1986 followed by further reiterations. See Marcus, "Hierarchies," 24–25n27; Marcus, *Rituals of Childhood*, 100–101, cited in Goldstein, "Children of the Sacred Covenant," 4. Supporters of Yuval's development of my erroneous speculation include McCulloh, "Jewish Ritual Murder," 738n161; Cohen, "Flow of Blood," 40n60; Haverkamp, "Jews in Christian Europe," 176. See also Johnson, *Blood Libel*, 91–128; Alexiun, "Origins of the Blood Libel"; Goldstein, "Children of the Sacred Covenant," 134. For scholars who have refuted his arguments, see Chazan, *Medieval Stereotypes*, 75–76; Berger, "Crusades to Blood Libels," 31–37; Marcus, "Jewish-Christian Symbiosis," 505–6n2; Marcus, "Israeli Medieval Jewish Historiography," 273–77.

81. Ihnat, "Our Sister Is Little."

82. See EH, 601, 569, 519; H, 31, 49, 104; E, 31, 56, 115.

83. See Johnson, "Before the Blood Libel," 60–61.

84. Thomas of Monmouth, *Life and Passion*, 19. Thomas of Monmouth, *Life and Miracles*, 24–25, book 1:6: "Non enim verisimile videtur quod aut christiani de christiano, aut judei talia fieri aliquatenus voluisset de judeo."

85. H, 115; E, 122. On the crusading spirit as a factor, see Jordan, *French Monarchy*, 146.

86. H, 116; E, 122; Berger, "Attitude of St. Bernard of Clairvaux." On Bernard and Peter the Venerable, see Chazan, "Twelfth-Century Perceptions of the Jews." On Bernard and crusading, see Cohen, "Witnesses of Our Redemption"; Friedman, "Anatomy of Anti-Semitism."

87. Thomas of Monmouth, *Life and Passion*, 2:11, 61.

88. See Reiner, "Bible and Politics."

89. For a biography of Rabbeinu Tam as a rabbinic scholar, see Reiner, *Rabbeinu Tam*.

90. H, 121; E, 130. For Jewish awareness of the five stigmata, cf. Berger, *Jewish-Christian Dialogue*, sec. 54, 78.

91. See Marcus, "Jews and Christians Imagining the Other"; Marcus, "Jewish-Christian Symbiosis," 493–95.

92. See Augustine, "Sermon on Jacob and Esau," quoted in Marcus and Saperstein, *Jews in Christian Europe*, 33.

93. See Wachtel, "Ritual and Liturgical Commemoration."

94. On Rabbeinu Tam's attack, see Trachtenberg, *Devil and the Jews*, 244n24, which takes it as an event that occurred in 1147.

95. Bale, "Richard of Devizes," 59.

96. See Newman, "Passion of the Jews of Prague"; Rubin, *Gentile Tales*, 135–40.

97. Galinsky, "Gishot Shonot": "In our age everyone swears upon the saints, but does not understand them to be Divine" (Tosafot B. Sanhedrin, 63b, asur le-adam). See also Shoham-Steiner, "Jews and Healing"; Steiner, "For a Prayer in That Place"; Shatzmiller, "Jews, Pilgrimage, and the Christian Cult of Saints."

98. *Sefer Zekhirah*, in H, 116; E, 122.

99. See Raspe, "Sacred Space." See the Worms custom of annually reciting dirges in the cemetery on the anniversary of the two attacks on the community in 1096, f. 44c of *Ma'aravot . . . Wirmaisa*, f. 44c. See also Shoham-Steiner, "For a prayer in That Place"; Shoham-Steiner, "Jews and Healing"; Galinsky, "Gishon Shonot."

100. For narratives that deal with boundary situations, see Marcus, "Narrative Fantasies in *Sefer Hasidim*." For cycles of Jewish saints lives, see Zfatman, *Shivhei Rabbi Shmuel ve-Rabbi Yehudah Hasid*.

101. Schechter, "Jewish Saints." See Raspe, "Jewish Saints."

102. See Kahana, "Meqorot ha-Yeda.'"

103. See Marcus, *Sefer Hasidim and the Ashkenazic Book*, chapter 3.

104. Marcus, *Piety and Society*, 87–106. For the hagiographic stories about Samuel and Judah, see Yassif, *Me'ah Sippurim Haser Ehad*; Zfatman, *Shivhei Rabbi Shmuel ve-Rabbi Yehudah Hasid*; Shoham-Steiner, "Clinging to a Jewish Saint."

105. Marcus, *Piety and Society*, 55–106.

106. Katz, *Exclusiveness and Tolerance*, 93–105.

107. SHP, 159, 184, 1075. Cf. the prohibition of Christians to serve in Jewish homes in Grayzel, *Church and the Jews*, 1:25, nos. 14, 15, 29, 69.

108. SHP, para. 1539.

109. SHP, para. 1635, 1636. Cf. the rabbinic expression "ma'alin be-qodesh ve-ein moridin" (one may raise something ordinary to holiness but should not degrade something holy) in B. Berakhot 28a; B. Yoma 12b; B. Shabbat 21b. Christians prohibited pawning church objects and vestments to Jews for similar hierarchical reasons. See, for example, Grayzel, *Church and the Jews*, 1:34, nos. 4, 14, 23.

110. SHP, 689.

111. SHP, 681–82.

112. SHP, 389, 387. See also SHP, 632 (end), 1248.

113. Shatzmiller, "Doctors and Medical Practice."

Chapter 7. Cultural Aesthetics: Sexual Threats, Conversions, and Imagined "Racial" Jews

1. Despres, "Protean Jew."
2. On the "aesthetics of ugliness," which suggested the important theme in Jewish and Christian representations developed here, cf. Mazzotta, *Dante's Vision*, 140, 237. The term "cultural aesthetics" has recently been used to refer to artistic developments in different cultures, not the way it is used here.
3. See Cohen, "Those Who Say They Are Jews"; Fine, "How Do You Know a Jew When You See One?"
4. Cf. Hotchkiss, *Clothes Make the Man*.
5. For Fourth Lateran Council, canon 68, see Grayzel, *Church and the Jews*, 1:309. England was the first to interpret and enforce it. See Tolan, "First Imposition of a Badge."
6. For images of Muslim men in Christian sources, see Camille, *Gothic Idol*. For a Jewish source with depictions of Ishmaelites who take Joseph to Egypt dressed as Muslim men, cf. *Golden Haggadah*. On conversion and the *Golden Haggadah*, see Harris, "Polemical Images in the *Golden Haggadah*." Muslim men are also portrayed in *Song of Roland* manuscripts wearing white cloth wrapped around their heads as turbans.
7. On the interpretation of "clothing" as a patch of some kind, see Kisch, "Yellow Badge"; Robert, *Les signes d'infamie au moyen âge*; Cutler, "Innocent III"; Sansy, "Marquer la différence." Cf. Hunt, *Governance of the Consuming Passions*, which argues that sumptuary laws proliferated in early modern cities because of anxiety over being able to recognize people.
8. One must also be careful not to try too hard to correlate different imagined Jews with features of "real" Jews regarding skin color. See Lipton, "Jew's Face," 265.
9. See Resnick, "Medieval Roots," 249. The issue of appearance and difference has been studied by Sander Gilman and Sara Lipton regarding the Jewish nose. See Gilman, *Jew's Body*, 169–93; Lipton, "What's in a Nose?" Renaissance Jewish women were set apart with earrings according to Owen-Hughes, "Distinguishing Signs," but otherwise were not as differentiated as Jewish men. In both "Visages du judaisme" and "'Al Mashma'uyot ha-Zaqan," Elliott Horowitz does not consider the age of Jewish men in many of the sources.
10. Resnick, "Jews' Badge," 67, thinks that Fourth Lateran Council canon 68 refers to zizit, not sha'atnez, but special Jewish dress applies in the canon to men and women, as does sha'atnez, whereas zizit affects only Jewish men.
11. See Baumgarten, *Practicing Piety*, 173–76.
12. On canon 68 as well as clothing and beards, but not skin color, noses, hair color, or smell, as distinguishing physical features of Jews in Christian sources, see Baumgarten, *Practicing Piety*, chapter 5.
13. SHP, 259, translated in Baumgarten, *Practicing Piety*, 185. See also references to dressing in SHP, 202, 260, 1922, translated in Baumgarten, *Practicing Piety*, 278n96.
14. SHP, 260; Baumgarten, *Practicing Piety*, 188.
15. SHP, 202; SHB, 199; Baumgarten, *Practicing Piety*, chapter 5.

16. SHP, 203; SHB, 199; Baumgarten, *Practicing Piety*, 189.

17. SHP, 204; SHB, 199. Cf. Baumgarten, *Practicing Piety*, 189, which argues that Christians could not detect Jewish clothing that avoided mixed threads forbidden by the law of sha'atnez.

18. SHP, 205, SHB, 199. See Tosafot to B. Yoma, 71b: "What we call 'qanabus' is 'pishtan' [= flax = linen]."

19. SHP, 1922; Baumgarten, *Practicing Piety*, 184.

20. SHP, 207; SHB, 201. The reference is to B. 'Avodah Zarah 18b.

21. For a discussion of the evidence about Jews and beards, see Abrahams, *Jewish Life*, 283–84; Horowitz, "'Al Mashma'uyot ha-Zaqan" (and bibliography there); Baumgarten, *Practicing Piety*, 176–83; Lipton, *Dark Mirror* (see index under "Beards.") See also SHP, 902, a story about a Jewish captive who pulls out his (facial) hair to disguise his Jewish identity.

22. For the German text, see Kisch, "Yellow Badge," 99, 136–37n6. On the six poems attributed to him in the *Manesse Codex*, see Gerhardt, *Süsskind von Trimberg*.

23. This was the practice of David Weiss Halivni, for example, professor of Talmud at the Jewish Theological Seminary in New York City, and then at Bar Ilan University and Hebrew University of Jerusalem in Israel. In all the early faculty pictures, he is clean-shaven and grew a beard only after he turned forty. How far back this custom goes needs further study.

24. See a story from *Sefer ha-Gan* (fourteenth century) about Judah the Pious objecting to a rich Jew in Speyer who used to cut off his beard with scissors, translated in Marcus, *Sefer Hasidim and the Ashkenazic Book*, 60–61. See also Baumgarten, *Practicing Piety*, 180–82. On a German court Jew trimming his beard when mourning, see *Sefer ha-Asufot*, former Hebrew MS Montefiore 115 (now owned by David Feinberg, New York City), f. 162r: "R. permitted courtiers to trim their beards after mourning only seven days [instead of letting it grow for thirty days] because they cannot go to the king's court unkempt [the text reads *menuval*, literally, "disgusting," misread as "*mi-Toul* (!)," in Güdemann, *Geschichte des Erziehungswesens*, 1:24n2, which read the letters *nun vav* as a *tet*.]

25. On differences of hair in England, see Cohen, "Flow of Blood," 34n35. On medieval Europe in general, see Constable, introduction.

26. On the Jews' hat, see Baumgarten, *Practicing Piety*, 176–78; Lipton, *Dark Mirror*, 16–24; Mellinkoff, *Antisemitic Hate Signs*, 31–34. See also Lehnhertz and Schachter, "Jews' Hat in Medieval Ashkenaz." My appreciation to the two authors for providing a prepublication copy of their manuscript.

27. SHP, 206; SHB, 200.

28. SHP, 261; Marcus, "Jewish-Christian Symbiosis," 486–87. For another translation, cf. Baumgarten, *Practicing Piety*, 186.

29. SHP, 258; Vat. 285 [41].

30. See Guibert de Nogent, *Autobiographie*, 3:16, translated in Benton, *Self and Society*, 210; Archambault, *Monk's Confession*; Guibert of Nogent, *Monodies*. See also Kanarfogel, *Brothers from Afar*, 63–65; Lipton, *Dark Mirror*, 160; Tartakoff, "Testing Boundaries."

31. On clothing and 1215, see Constable, *Live Like a Moor*, 15–62 ("Clothing and Appearance").

32. Constable, *Medieval Iberia*, 272.

33. For the image of "Aaron son of the Devil," see Trachtenberg, *Devil and the Jews*, 27.

34. For England and France, see Kisch, "Yellow Badge," especially 105–6.

35. Lipton, *Dark Mirrors*, 171–99.

36. Sturges, *Aucassin and Nicolette*, 7.

37. Sturges, *Aucassin and Nicolette*, 13. See also Sturges, *Aucassin and Nicolette*, 37, 49, 59.

38. Sturges, *Aucassin and Nicolette*, 31.

39. Sturges, *Aucassin and Nicolette*, 55.

40. Perryman, *King of Tars*, 42–50. On the category of "religion-race," see Resnick, *Marks of Distinction*, 295; Heng, *Empire of Magic*, 226–37. For other examples of skin change after conversion, see Hahn, "Difference the Middle Ages Makes."

41. For the text and translation, see Boyarin, *Christian Jew*, 243–44. For a discussion about the text, see Boyarin, *Christian Jew*, 216–18.

42. Rowe, *Jew*; Schreckenberg, *Jews in Christian Art*, 31–66; Seiferth, *Synagogue and Church*; Blumenkranz, *Le juif médiéval*; Lipton, *Dark Mirror*, 42. For some theological associations of the pair, see Schlauch, "Allegory."

43. On synagoga as both representative of Jews in general and female Jews in particular, see Lipton, "Temple Is My Body," 132.

44. Seiferth, *Synagogue and Church*; Blumenkranz; *Le juif médiéval*; Schreckenberg, *Jews in Christian Art*, 31–66. Rowe, *Jew*, chapters 2 and 6, 83, argues that synagoga's beauty is an indication that Jews are an integral part of Christian society, but this evades the issue of her potential Jewish conversion, which justifies the visual equation. On beautiful synagoga, see Resnick, *Marks of Distinction*, 65, notes.

45. Barasch, *Blindness*, 78–90, cited in Rubin, "*Ecclesia* and *Synagoga*," 72.

46. See Cohen, "*Synagoga Conversa*"; Ihnat, "Our Sister Is Little"; Monroe, "Fair and Friendly, Sweet and Beautiful."

47. *Levy Mahzor*, Hamburg, Staats- und Universitätsbibliothek, Hebrew MS Levy 37, folio 169v. The image accompanies the piyyut by Benjamin b. Zerah, "Iti milevanon," and features two lovers seated next to each other on a pedestal.

48. The following is based on Marcus, "Jewish-Christian Symbiosis," 496–99; Feuchtwanger-Sarig, "Coronation," especially figure 1 from the *Leipzig Mahzor*, f. 64v; Shalev-Eyni "Iconography of Love"; Shalev-Eyni, "Iti mi-Levanon Kallah"; Shalev-Eyni, "Panehah ha-Enoshiyot," especially 160n70; Offenberg, "Staging the Blindfold Bride."

49. On Rachel as Mary, see Cohen, *Sanctifying the Name of God*, 120–27; Marcus, "Representation of Reality," 37–48.

50. For Rashi's text on the Song of Songs, see Rosenthal, "Peirush Rashi 'al Shir ha-Shirim"; Marcus, "Song of Songs."

51. Joseph b. Nathan Official, *Yosef ha-Meqaneh*, para. 104, 95.

52. On physical ugliness or beauty as a sign of religious truth or falsehood, see Haverkamp, "Baptized Jews in German Lands," 270, which refers to a story parallel

to one in Caesarius of Heisterbach about a beautiful Jewish girl who has an affair with a cleric.

53. Oxford, Bodleian Library, Oppenheim Collection, MS 757 (Neubauer 2289), part 6, 50-51ff, quoted in Joseph b. Nathan Official, *Yosef ha-Meqaneh*, para. 104, 95n1.

54. Mühlhausen, *Sefer ha-Nizzahon*, para. 239, 134; Resnick, *Marks of Distinction*, 293.

55. See Gen. 30:38-39; Berger, *Jewish-Christian Debate*, sec. 238, notes.

56. On the conversion of Jewish women as more likely than that of men, see Haverkamp, "Baptized Jews in German Lands," 262; Levin, "Jewish Conversion to Christianity," 210.

57. See Lipton, "Where Are the Gothic Jewish Women?"; Lipton, *Dark Mirror*, 201-37; Resnick, *Marks of Distinction*, 301. See also Boyarin, *Christian Jew*.

58. Freedman, *Images of the Medieval Peasant*, 169.

59. Lampert, "'O My Daughter!'"; Lipton, "Where Are the Gothic Jewish Women?," 157: "As an abbot of the monastery of Saint Victor-de-Paris warned, 'a woman's beauty can make even a wise man apostatize.' This warning is concretized in an image in the *Rothschild Canticles* (c. 1320) that depicts a beautiful woman enticing a man away from veneration of the crucifix."

60. Caesarius of Heisterbach, *Dialogus miraculorum*, 2:23. For the conversion of Rachel of Louvain, see Haverkamp, "Baptized Jews in German Lands," 269-73; Levin, "Jewish Conversion to Christianity," 218.

61. Caesarius of Heisterbach, *Dialogus miraculorum*, 2:24.

62. Lipton, "Where Are the Gothic Jewish Women?," 157. See also Bale, "Female 'Jewish' Libido in Medieval Culture"; Bitton, "Jewess as a Fictional Sex Symbol."

63. Aizenberg, "Judía muy Fermosa"; Mirrer, "Beautiful Jewess"; Lipton, "Where Are the Gothic Jewish Women?"

64. Blumenkranz, *Le juif médiéval*, 19-30; Lipton, *Dark Mirror*, 16-24.

65. Resnick, *Marks of Distinction*, 249.

66. On sexualized Jewish females as "beautiful," see Resnick, *Marks of Distinction*, 300; Bale, "Female 'Jewish' Libido in Medieval Culture"; Mirrer, "Beautiful Jewess"; Lampert, "'O My Daughter!'"; Aizenberg, "Judía muy fermosa"; Gilman, "Salome, Syphilis."

67. Shagrir and Amir, "Persecution of the Jews," 414n35: "Signaling male, rather than female, figures as Jewish is not uncommon. Visual cues that imply the Jewish identity of women tend to be subtle and indirect." See also Lipton, "Where Are the Gothic Jewish Women?," especially 142-43, cited in Shagrir and Amir, "Persecution of the Jews."

68. Resnick, "Ps.-Albert the Great," 239n93; Resnick, *Marks of Distinction*, 292, which refers to Ps. Albert the Great: "Secundum complexionem innatam soboles solent assimilari parentibus, et e contra; sed videmus, quod genus Judaeorum ut in pluribus habet nigros capillos, ergo et Domina nostra cum fuit de progenie Judaeorum." Source: Ps. Albert, Mariale or *Quaestiones super Evangelium*, 19.2.5, ed. Borgnet, 44. This is also discussed in Lipton, "What's in a Nose?," 202n21. On the theme

of skin color and beauty, Madeline Caviness has observed that "white man" in skin color emerges in mid-thirteenth-century France under Louis IX. See Caviness, "Self-Invention of the Whiteman."

69. Trachtenberg, *Devil and the Jews*, 50–51; Resnick, "Medieval Roots"; Johnson, "Myth of Jewish Male Menses"; Katz, "Shylock's Gender." On Thomas de Cantimpré (1201–72), see Cohen, "Flow of Blood," 42n64. The idea that Jewish males bleed annually, especially at Easter or monthly, may have originated from or been justified by Jacques de Vitry (ca. 1160–1240), who interprets *His blood be on ourselves and our children* (Matt. 27:25) to mean that Jewish men require Christian blood to survive, either from a living Christian or Christ's blood. See Johnson, "Myth of Jewish Male Menses"; Resnick, *Marks of Distinction*, 249–50.

70. Kruger, "Becoming Christian, Becoming Male?," discusses this and other beliefs about "feminizing" Jewish men. See also Kruger, "Conversion and Medieval Sexual, Religious, and Racial Categories."

71. Gilman, "Jewish Nose"; Lipton, "What's in a Nose?"; Mellinkoff, *Antisemitic Hate Signs*, 23–26. For medieval clerks' sketches of Jews in thirteenth-century English public records, Rokéah, "Drawings of Jewish Interest." See also Blumenkranz, *Le juif médiéval*, 32. For thirteenth-century Iberian sources on Jewish noses, see Mirrer, "Jew's Body."

72. Baumgarten, *Mothers and Children*, 186–87; Marcus, *Rituals of Childhood*, 121–22.

73. The literature has grown considerably since Jonathan Elukin wrote in 1994, "There are only a handful of articles on the nature of Jewish conversion to Christianity." See Elukin, "Eternal Jew in Medieval Europe," 211n453. Among these studies are the following: Stacey, "Conversion of Jews to Christianity"; Tartakoff, *Christian and Jew*; Szpiech, *Conversion and Narrative*; Endelman, *Leaving the Jewish Fold*; Tartakoff, "Conversion and Return to Judaism"; Fox and Yisraeli, *Contesting Inter-Religious Conversion;* Kanarfogel, *Brothers from Afar*; Kruger, "Conversion"; Utterback, "*Conversi* Revert"; Nirenberg, "Conversion, Sex, and Segregation"; Sherwood, "Rebellious Youth and Pliant Children"; Sherwood, "Jewish Conversion"; Malkiel, "Jews and Apostates in Medieval Europe"; Nirenberg, "Mass Conversion"; Simonsohn, "Some Well-Known Jewish Converts"; Abulafia, "Twelfth-Century Christian Expectations"; Chazan, *Medieval Jewry in Northern France*, 145; Baron, *Social and Religious History of the Jews*, 10:60; Levin, "Jewish Conversion to Christianity," 88–95. On the larger issue of individual Jews converting and Christian resistance and acceptance, see Tartakoff, "Testing Boundaries." On the problem of the Jewish male not being able to convert completely, see Kruger, *Spectral Jew*, 168.

74. Haverkamp, "Baptized Jews in German Lands," 267.

75. Jacob b. Meir, *Sefer ha-Yashar*, para. 25, 45.

76. See Stacey, "King Henry III and the Jews," 121–24; Stacey, "Conversion of Jews to Christianity," 268–69; Fogle, "Domus Conversorum"; Fogle, *King's Converts*. For a case of a Jewish woman and son who appealed to Edward I for economic support, Alice of Worcester, see Boyarin, *Christian Jew*, 97–104. For her two letters and Edward's reply, see Boyarin, *Christian Jew*, 240–42.

77. Stacey, "Conversion of Jews to Christianity," 264.

78. Sherwood, "Rebellious Youth and Pliant Children," argues that young adults converted more than boys, but the category of *adolescentia* included both. The Jewish concern about children converting, especially boys, and safeguards taken to prevent it, does not depend on the actual demographics, which are impressionistic at best. On ages of youths in Latin and Hebrew sources, see Levinson, *"Va-Yigdelu ha-Ne'arim,"* chapter 1.

79. Herman-Judah, *Hermanus quondam Judaeus*, 107–8; Herman-Judah, "Translation," 100–101.

80. Jordan, "Adolescence and Conversion," 84–87.

81. See, for example, SHP, 1113.

82. Elukin, "Jew to Christian?"; Elukin, "Discovery of the Self"; Tartakoff, "Testing Boundaries"; Tartakoff, "Conversion and Return to Judaism"; Fox and Yisraeli, *Contesting Inter-Religious Conversion*; Kanarfogel, *Brothers from Afar*.

83. See Tartakoff, "Conversion and Return to Judaism"; Kanarfogel, *Brothers from Afar*.

84. See especially Berger, "Mission to the Jews"; Berger, "Review of Jeremy Cohen"; Chazan, *Daggers of Faith*.

85. Conversion was not a papal initiative except in millennial times, such as in the sixteenth century with Paul IV. See Stow, "Hatred of the Jews," 85, 89n54. Irish, *Jews and Christians in Medieval Castile*, and Vose, *Dominicans, Muslims, and Jews*, both emphasize the Christian audiences of mendicant efforts, rather than converting Jews. Cf. Cohen, *Friars and the Jews*. The purpose of the Barcelona debate, usually viewed as directed at converting Jews, was more likely directed at Christian education. See Vose, *Friars and the Jews*. Cf. Chazan, *Barcelona and Beyond*; Berger, "Mission to the Jews."

86. Abulafia, *Christians and Jews in the Twelfth-Century Renaissance*. For a discussion of Peter the Venerable, see Abulafia, *Christians and Jews in the Twelfth-Century Renaissance*, 87–88.

87. Bale, "Fictions of Judaism," 137: "The real villain is the Jewish male; the Jewish women are considered more pliant, more easily brought to the faith." See also Abramson, "Ready Hatred"; Lipton, "Where Are the Gothic Jewish Women?," 139–77.

88. B. Sanhedrin 44a.

89. Kanarfogel, *Brothers from Afar*. On converted Jews remaining Jews, see B. Sanhedrin 44a: "Rabba bar Zavda: *yisrael af 'al pi she-hata yisrael*." Rabba bar Zavda: even though he sinned, he is still Israel. As they say, "A myrtle among thorns is still a myrtle and is called a myrtle" (*asa de-qa'i beinei hilfi, asa shemei ve-asa qaru lei*). This is based on the figure of Achan in the Book of Joshua and the phrase from Josh. 7:11 "Israel sinned," which in Hebrew reverses the word order to "sinned, Israel" (*hata yisrael*), interpreted to mean he sinned by apostatizing and he was still Israel—that is, a Jew.

90. EH, 48; H, 57; E, 68.

91. See, for example, Herman-Judah, *Hermanus quondam Judaeus*.

92. Elukin, "Jew to Christian," 174–75.

93. Resnick, "Race"; Stroll, *Jewish Pope*; Graboïs, "Mi-Sin'at Yisrael 'Teologit' le Sin'at Yisrael 'Giz'it'"; Iogna-Pratt, *Order and Exclusion*, 318–20. See Ziegler, "Physiognomy," 198. See also Levin, "Jewish Conversion to Christianity." On the Hebrew story about a Jew who became pope, reverted to Judaism, and then martyred himself, see Raspe, *Jüdische Hagiographie*, 242–322; Bamberger, *Ha-Apifiyor ha-Yehudi*.

94. In the contested papal election of 1130, the campaign against the Pierleoni candidate included Bernard of Clairvaux, who referred to him as "the offspring of a Jew." See Resnick, *Marks of Distinction*, 277.

95. Ben-Sasson, "Le-Zeihutam shel Anusum."

96. Resnick, *Marks of Distinction*, 268–319; Elukin, "Jew to Christian?" On social resistance to staying converted, see Stacey, "Conversion of Jews to Christianity," which looks at the 1280s' "great fear" about Jews relapsing who were forcibly baptized. On Jews influencing converts to Judaize, see the papal letter *Turbato corde*, Clement IV, July 27, 1267, in Grayzel, *Church and the Jews*, 2:102–4; *Nimis in partibus*, Honorius IV, November 30, 1286, in Grayzel, *Church and the Jews*, 2:157–62. See also Tartakoff, "Conversion and Return to Judaism."

97. Kim, "Reframing Race"; Hahn, "Difference the Middle Ages Makes"; Bartlett, "Illustrating Ethnicity in the Middle Ages"; Heng, "Invention of Race in the European Middle Ages I"; Heng, "The Invention of Race in the European Middle Ages II"; Cohen, "Race"; Kaplan, *Figuring Racism in Medieval Christianity*. Kaplan skillfully addresses notions of hereditary inferiority and the Christian doctrine of Jewish perpetual servitude. See also Heng, *Invention of Race*, 27–31; Kruger, *Spectral Jew*, 67–109.

98. Lipton, "Temple Is My Body"; Rubin, "*Ecclesia* and *Synagoga*," 72–80, especially 75, 80, on a loss of confidence that conversion was possible. On changes in synagoga in the late Middle Ages, see Rubin, "*Ecclesia* and *Synagoga*."

99. On the purity of blood laws, see Yerushalmi, *Antisemitism*; Nirenberg, "Was There Race before Modernity?"

Chapter 8. Expulsions: Imagined Jews and Real Christian Antisemites

1. See, for example, Darwin, *Empire Project*; Hyam, *Understanding the British Empire*. For the process of English national self-definition and Jews, see, for example, Shapiro, *Shakespeare and the Jews*.

2. Heng, "England's Dead Boys," 59.

3. On Assyrian population removals, see Frahm, *Assyria*, 146–50; Valk, "Crime and Punishment." For the Ottoman policy, see Murphy, "Sürgün."

4. Kedar, "Expulsion." For an argument that the conversos undermined the binary of Jew and Christian in medieval Iberia, see Nirenberg, "Enmity and Assimilation."

5. Kedar, "Expulsion," 168–70.

6. Dorin, *No Return*, 96–102, 4–19.

7. Nelson, *Idea of Usury*; Noonan, *Scholastic Analysis of Usury*.

8. See R. Meir b. Simon, *Sefer Milhemet Mitzvah* (Parma, Biblioteca Palatina, Hebrew MS De Rossi 2749); Chazan, "Political Themes in the *Milhemet Mitzvah*"; Chazan, *Church, State, and Jew*, 199; source by Jacob b. Meir (Rabbeinu Tam) in Satlow, *Judaism and the Economy*; Cronbach, "Social Thinking in the *Sefer Hasidim*," 3–5.

9. See Mell, *Myth of the Medieval Jewish Moneylender*; Toch, *Economic History of European Jews*; Dorin, *No Return*, 39–40.

10. On merchant banking and moneylending, see Dorin, *No Return*, 11–12, 100–101, 189–90.

11. Dorin, *No Return*, 63–64.

12. See Bartlet, "Three Jewish Businesswomen"; Boyarin, *Christian Jew*, 117–43; Stacey, "1240–60"; Jordan, "Jews on Top"; Baskin, "Dolce of Worms"; Einbinder, "Pucellina of Blois."

13. Berman Brown and McCartney, "Exchequer of the Jews Revisited," 307.

14. Tanner, *Decrees of the Ecumenical Councils*, 1:223.

15. See Stow, "Church and the Jews." For a general discussion of the medieval church's teachings on the Jews and the canonical injunctions in particular, see Stow, *Alienated Minority*, 242–73.

16. On Edward I's campaign against Jewish usury, see Brand, "Jews and the Law in England." On France, see Jordan, *French Monarchy*, 93–176.

17. Dorin, *No Return*, 83–85. The following detailed section on English and French policies toward Jewish and foreign moneylenders in the two kingdoms is based in large part on this important revisionist work.

18. Stacey, "King Henry III and the Jews."

19. Chazan, *Church, State, and Jew*, 313–17; Jordan, *French Monarchy*, 182; Stow, *Alienated Minority*, 297.

20. Koyama, "Political Economy of Expulsion"; Mundill, "Clandestine Crypto-Camouflaged Usurer or Legal Merchant?"

21. Menache, "Faith, Myth, and Politics."

22. Stacey, "Anti-Semitism," 177.

23. Jordan, *French Monarchy*, 256; Kedar, "Expulsion."

24. Jordan, "Administering Expulsion"; Balasse, *1306*; Schwarzfuchs, "Expulsion of the Jews from France"; Jordan, *French Monarchy*, 200–202, which states that it was done in secret and so there is no public record.

25. Although it is important to recover the literary legacy of medieval English Jews, the poems of Elijah of Norwich survived only in manuscripts, not in the liturgy. See Einbinder, "Meir b. Elijah of Norwich," 147–49.

26. Blumenkranz, "En 1306"; Marcus, "Why Did Medieval Northern French Jewry (*Zarfat*) Disappear?" On the 1321 expulsion and well poisoning, see Barzilay, *Poisoned Wells*, 71–97.

27. See Barzilay, *Poisoned Wells*. They were allowed to return once more in 1359 and finally expelled in 1394. Jordan, "Home Again"; Brown, "Philip V, Charles IV, and the Jews of France."

28. On the new emphasis on poverty from the twelfth century on, see Little, "Pride Goes before Avarice"; Vauchez, *Spirituality*, 110, 112–14.

29. Shatzmiller, *Shylock Revisited*. On this fascinating case study, see Jordan, "Review of Shatzmiller." As in the cases discussed in David Nirenberg's *Communities of Violence*, also from the south, there were trends in northern Europe that were different and long-lasting, and the southern exceptionalism did not influence the northern patterns.

30. Kedar, "Expulsion."

31. On the different targets of Protestants, who destroyed Catholic icons and symbols, and Catholics, who killed Protestants, cf. Davis, "Rites of Violence." This is similar to medieval Jews attacking Christian sancta and Christians attacking Jews.

32. The role of the imagined Jew as the generic object of criticism in the West is the subject of Nirenberg, *Anti-Judaism*.

33. Kedar, "Expulsion." See Erikson, *Wayward Puritans*.

34. Shapiro, *Shakespeare and the Jews*, 1–42.

35. See, among others, Johnson and Blurton, "Virtual Jews and Figural Criticism"; Akbari, "Placing the Jews in Late Medieval English Literature"; Krummel and Pugh, *Jews in Medieval England*; Lavezzo, *Accommodated Jew*. In other medieval literature besides English, see Tomasch, "Judecca, Dante's Satan, and the *Dis*-placed Jew," 243n6; Boulton, "Anti-Jewish Attitudes in Medieval French Literature," which shows that there was a growing negative view about Jews in vernacular French literature in the late twelfth century a hundred years before the expulsion of 1306; Herman, "Note on Medieval Anti-Judaism"; Gaunt, *Retelling the Tale*; Martin, *Representations of Jews*.

36. For a recent compilation of these terms, see Boyarin, *Christian Jew*, 246n10.

37. Parkes, *Conflict*, 166.

38. Trachtenberg, *Devil and the Jews*, 216.

39. Glassman, *Antisemitic Stereotypes without Jews*.

40. For the priority of Dahan, see Dahan, *Les intellectuels chrétiens et les juifs au Moyen Age*, 585; Cohen, *Living Letters*, 2–3n3. For Cohen's book, see Cohen, *Salvation of Israel*.

41. See Tomasch, "Judecca, Dante's Satan, and the *Dis*-placed Jew"; Tomasch, "Postcolonial Chaucer and the Virtual Jew." For an example of Despres's "protean Jew," see Bale, *Jew in the Medieval Book*, 23–53, on the changing exempla about the Jew of Tewkesbury who falls into a latrine on the Sabbath.

42. Krummel, *Crafting Jewishness in Medieval England*. Several of the constructs mentioned here are also listed in Heng, "England's Dead Boys," 60n14.

43. Lavezzo, *Accommodated Jew*, 4.

44. On *Piers*, especially how the B version was changed into the C version and de-Judaized, see Narin van Court, "Critical Apertures"; Lewis, "Jews, the Others, of Piers Plowman; Morrison, *Excrement in the Late Middle Ages*, 61. Langland, *Piers Ploughman*, 19:143–45, says that Jews compare Christ buried to dung being collected at night. On *Sir Gawain*, see Cox, *The Judaic Other*. On *Margery Kempe*, see Rosenthal, "Margerie Kempe and Medieval Anti-Judaic Ideology."

45. For *Croxton Play of the Sacrament*, see Beckwith, "Ritual, Church, and Theater," on *Croxton* acting out the polarity between the Christian body and the Jew: "It was through the absent presence of the Jew that history and identity in Bury could

be given the impression of concordance, stability, and wholeness." See also Lavezzo, *Accommodated Jew*, 135–71; Jones, "Place of the Jews."

46. See, among others, Delany, *Chaucer and the Jews*, especially the chapters by Rose, Jordan, Tomasch, Despres, and Bale; Patterson, "Living Witnesses of Our Redemption"; Johnson, "Antisemitism and the Purposes of Historicism"; Fradenberg, "Criticism, Anti-Semitism, and the Prioress's Tale"; Gaynor, "He Says, She Says"; Lavezzo, "Minster and the Privy"; Kelly, "'Prioress's Tale' in Context"; Hirsh, "Reopening the 'Prioress's Tale'"; Dahood, "Punishment of the Jews"; Archer, "Structure of Anti-Semitism"; Ridley, *Prioress and the Critics*; Alexander, "Madame Englyntine"; Zitter, "Anti-Semitism"; Frank, "Miracles of the Virgin"; Heng, "England's Dead Boys"; Kruger, "Bodies of Jews"; Lampert-Weissig, "Chaucer's Pardoner."

47. The text is taken from Chaucer, *Riverside Chaucer*, and references are to line numbers in this edition.

48. For an interpretation that focuses on the location of "Asie" as connoting a contemporary medieval Muslim context for the tale, see Delany, *Chaucer and the Jews*, 43–57.

49. Morrison, *Excrement in the Late Middle Ages*, 82–88. See Lavezzo, *Accommodated Jew*, 117, which notes that the only home mentioned is the Christian's, whereas the Jewry is associated with a privy.

50. Price, "Medieval Antisemitism," 182–83.

51. For a good bibliography on the imagined Jew as well as the *Merchant of Venice* and other texts into the seventeenth century along with the readmission of the Jews to England, see Wise, "Cursed Companions."

52. On Jews and dogs, see Stow, *Jewish Dogs*.

53. On Jews and pigs, see Shachar, *Judensau*; Fabre-Vassas, *Singular Beast*.

54. Marlowe, *Jew of Malta*; Shakespeare, *Merchant of Venice*.

55. For Chaucer and English identity, see Tomasch, "Postcolonial Chaucer and the Virtual Jew," 69–85; Gaynor, "He Says, She Says." On Shakespeare and Marlowe, see especially Shapiro, *Shakespeare and the Jews*; Gross, *Shylock*; Smith, "Was Shylock Jewish?"; Hall, "Guess Who's Coming to Dinner?"; Thurn, "Economic and Ideological Exchange"; Hirsch, "Counterfeit Professions"; Lavezzo, *Accommodated Jew*, 172–210; Arieti, "Magical Thinking"; Adelman, *Blood Relations*; Nirenberg, "Shakespeare's Jewish Questions"; Greenblatt, "Marlowe, Marx, and Antisemitism"; Kaplan, *Merchant of Venice*; Shoulson, *Fictions of Conversion*. On Marlowe, see Bitton-Jackson, *Madonna or Courtesan?*, 28–30, 34–35. Cf. Nirenberg, "Figures of Thought"; Lavezzo, *Accommodated Jew*, 172–210.

56. On Doña Gracia Mendes and her nephew, see Birnbaum, *Long Journey*; Brooks, *Woman Who Defied Kings*.

57. Jordan, "Jews on Top."

58. Porat, *Fall of a Sparrow*; Porat, *Nakam*.

59. Nelson, *Idea of Usury*.

60. For Shylock the Jew "refusing to be either the Scriptural Jew or the demonic usurer," see Despres, "Protean Jew," 160. See more generically, Alter, "Who Is Shylock?" On Jews converting and remaining Jews, see Kruger, *Spectral Jew*, 168.

61. Brown, "Mediaeval Prototypes."
62. See Caesarius of Heisterbach, *Dialogus miraculorum*, 2:23.
63. See Meir b. Barukh of Rothenburg, *She'eilot u-Teshuvot Maharam*, no. 310; English summary in Agus, *Rabbi Meir of Rothenburg*, part 2, 283–85. Cf. Caesarius of Heisterbach, *Dialogus miraculorum*, 2:24, in which a baby expected to be the Jewish messiah is a daughter and a Jewish relative kills it.
64. Bitton-Jackson, *Madonna or Courtesan?*, chapter 2, 35–36. See also Lavezzo, *Accommodated Jew*, 211–47.
65. See Tartakoff, *Between Christian and Jew*.
66. Karp, "Antisemitism"; Lindemann and Levy, *Antisemitism*, 95.
67. Bonfil, "Aliens Within."
68. Adelman, *Blood Relations*.
69. See Shatzmiller, *Shylock Revisited*; Jordan, "Review of Shatzmiller."
70. Alter, "Who Is Shylock?"
71. See Katz, "Shylock's Gender."
72. The idea was suggested by Vienna Scott in a Yale College seminar in fall 2020.
73. On Lopez, see Shapiro, *Shakespeare and the Jews*, 73.
74. On the proliferation of modern "blood libels" in eastern Europe, see Frankel, *Damascus Affair*; Teter, *Blood Libel*. In the Ottoman Empire, see Barnai, "Blood Libels"; Hacker, "'Alilot Dam Neged Yehudim."

Chapter 9. Antisemitisms: Medieval and Modern

1. Zimmermann, *Wilhelm Marr*. As Bale, "Fictions of Judaism," 129, notes, "The term is admittedly a modern one applied retrospectively, but the fact that the label did not exist does not mean that antisemitism was absent; it simply had not yet been categorized."
2. Adams and Hess, *Medieval Roots of Antisemitism*; Chazan, *Medieval Stereotypes*. Engel, "Away from a Definition of Antisemitism"; Barzilay, "Ha-Musag 'Antisheimiyut'"; Berger, "Gilgulei ha-Musag 'Antisheimiyut.'"
3. Spiegel, "Memory and History."
4. For works that assume that "toleration" and violent "persecution" are the underlying variables in medieval Jewish-Christian history, see Abulafia, *Religious Violence*; Berger, "Anti-Semitism"; Berger, "Crusades to Blood Libels." See also Chazan, *Medieval Stereotypes*, 6, which argues that the 1096 massacres were not part of a widespread pattern of violence and therefore not a definitive turning point. But anti-Jewish violence per se does not define medieval antisemitism.
5. Some of the authors who argue for continuity are Parkes, *Conflict*; Parkes, *Jew in the Medieval Community*; Isaac, *Teaching of Contempt*; Trachtenberg, *Devil and the Jews*; Poliakov, *History of Antisemitism*; Cohn, *Warrant for Genocide*; Langmuir, "Anti-Judaism"; Chazan, *Medieval Stereotypes*; Chazan, *Anti-Judaism to Anti-Semitism*, vi–xvi.

6. Nirenberg, *Communities of Violence*, introduction.
7. See Marcus, "Forum on David Nirenberg."
8. Marmursztejn, "La hantise de la téléologie."
9. Arendt, "Preface to Part One: Antisemitism," xi.
10. See Favret-Saada, "Fuzzy Distinction."
11. Cohen, *Friars and the Jews*, 16, uses "anti-Judaism" but does not define it. Cohen, *Living Letters*, 8, 13, uses "medieval antisemitism" but then "Christian anti-Judaism."
12. Jones, "Place of the Jews," 344.
13. Toch, "Formation of a Diaspora," 77.
14. Baron, *Social and Religious History of the Jews*, 4:308n62.
15. Langmuir, "Anti-Judaism as the Necessary Preparation," especially 388.
16. Stacey, "Antisemitism," 164, agrees with Langmuir's term "medieval anti-Semitism" but has reservations about his approach.
17. For critiques of Langmuir, see especially Chazan, *Medieval Stereotypes*, 131–34; Chazan, *Anti-Judaism to Anti-Semitism*, viii–x; Berger, "Crusades to Blood Libel," 14–16; Abulafia, *Christians and Jews in Dispute*, 135; Stacey, "History, Religion, and Medieval Antisemitism," 95–101.
18. Little, *Religious Poverty*, 56. Lester Little acknowledges the influence of Langmuir's pioneering study "Anti-Judaism as the Necessary Preparation," 388. On "anxiety" in historical analysis, see Hunt, "Anxiety and Social Explanation."
19. Chazan, *Anti-Judaism to Anti-Semitism*, viii.
20. Chazan, *Medieval Stereotypes*, 125–29.
21. See Lampert-Weissig, "Race, Periodicity, and the (Neo-) Middle Ages," 396n11, which refers to Chazan's influential entry "Antisemitism" in the *Dictionary of the Middle Ages* (1985) and gives reasons why this allows the church to exculpate itself from charges of modern "antisemitism," an unintended consequence of avoiding a modified version of "antisemitism" for medieval Christian Jew hatred.
22. Chazan, *Medieval Stereotypes*, 133. See also Chazan, *Medieval Stereotypes*, 129–43.
23. Stacey, "Anti-Semitism"; Stacey, "History, Religion, and Medieval Antisemitism," 100–101.
24. Abulafia, "Twelfth-Century Renaissance Theology," cited approvingly in Berger, "Crusades to Blood Libels," 30n11. See also Abulafia, *Christians and Jews in the Twelfth Century Renaissance*.
25. Stroumsa, "Anti-Judaism to Anti-Semitism?," 2n5.
26. Gow, *Red Jews*, 2.
27. See Berger, "Anti-Semitism," 5; Berger, "Crusades to Blood Libel," 28. See his definition of anti-Semitism in Berger, "Anti-Semitism," 3, which enables him to use the same term modified by ancient, medieval, or modern times.
28. Hsy and Orlemanski, "Race and Medieval Studies."
29. Fradenberg, "Criticism, Anti-Semitism, and the Prioress's Tale."
30. Bale, "Fictions of Judaism," 129: "Throughout this chapter 'antisemitism' will be my preferred term." See also, among others, Price, "Medieval Antisemitism";

Resnick, *Marks of Distinction*, 1–12; Stacey, "Jewish Lending," 100–101 ("antisemitism"); Heil, "'Antijudaismus' und 'Antisemitismus'"; Kruger, "Anti-Judaism and Anti-Semitism"; Ocker, "Anti-Judaism and Anti-Semitism."

31. Alport, *Nature of Prejudice*. Scholarship that emphasized medieval stereotypes includes Trachtenberg, *Devil and the Jews*; Glassman, *Antisemitic Stereotypes without Jews*; Felsenstein, *Anti-Semitic Stereotypes*; Chazan, *Medieval Stereotypes*.

32. See Klamper and Jüdisches Museum der Stadt Wien, *Macht der Bilder*.

33. Adams and Hess, *Medieval Roots of Antisemitism*, 4.

34. Novikoff, "Middle Ages," 76; Levy, "Political Antisemitism," 125. Others have argued that modern antisemitism derives from associating the Jews with modernity itself. This precludes any significant medieval Christian influence. For example, Fritz Stern emphasizes that modern antisemitism was an antimodern movement, grounded in a racial pseudobiological theory. It was based on the idea of the Jew as the avatar of the modern. None of that can be the result of a medieval factor, except by selecting the Jew in the first place as the target of hatred. But now the reason is different. See Stern, *Politics of Cultural Despair*. Jacob Katz argues that the writings of seventeenth-century Eisenmenger on the Jews focused on the defect of Judaism as having a double standard of morality for Jews and Christians, something one hardly ever finds in the medieval sources, but that does appear in modern antisemitism claims of Jews as haters of non-Jews. See Katz, *From Prejudice to Destruction*.

35. Chazan, *Medieval Stereotypes*, 139.

36. Chazan, *Medieval Stereotypes*, 133, 140.

37. Stacey also criticized Langmuir for not going back to the late eleventh century and the First Crusade, and instead emphasizing the mid-twelfth century when the ritual murder accusation began. See Langmuir, "Anti-Judaism to Anti-Semitism"; Stacey, "History, Religion, and Medieval Antisemitism."

38. On the *Protocols*, see Landes and Katz, *Paranoid Apocalypse*.

39. On Jews becoming "white," see Brodkin, *How Jews Became White Folks*; Jacobson, *Whiteness of a Different Color*.

40. On Jewish political citizenship in the German Empire, see Sorkin, *Jewish Emancipation*.

BIBLIOGRAPHY

Abrahams, Israel. *Jewish Life in the Middle Ages*. 1896. Reprinted, New York: Atheneum, 1975.

Abramson, Henry. "A Ready Hatred: Depictions of the Jewish Woman in Medieval Anti-Semitic Art and Caricature." *Proceedings of the American Academy for Jewish Research* 62 (1996): 1–18.

Abulafia, Anna Sapir. "Bodies in the Jewish-Christian Debate." In *Medieval Religion: New Approaches*, edited by Constance H. Berman, 347–62. New York: Routledge, 2005.

———. *Christian-Jewish Relations 1000–1300: Jews in the Service of Medieval Christendom*. New York: Pearson Longman, 2011.

———. *Christians and Jews in Dispute: Disputational Literature and the Rise of Anti-Judaism in the West (c. 1000–1150)*. Aldershot, UK: Ashgate, 1998.

———. *Christians and Jews in the Twelfth-Century Renaissance*. New York: Routledge, 1995.

———. "An Eleventh-Century Exchange of Letters between a Christian and a Jew." *Journal of Medieval History* 7 (1981): 153–74.

———. "From Northern Europe to Southern Europe and from the General to the Particular: Recent Research on Jewish-Christian Co-existence in Medieval Europe." *Journal of Medieval History* 23, no. 2 (1997): 179–90.

———. "The Ideology of Reform and Changing Ideas concerning Jews in the Works of Rupert of Deutz and Hermannus Quondam Iudeus." *Jewish History* 7, no. 1 (1993): 43–63.

———. "Invectives against Christianity in the Hebrew Chronicles of the First Crusade." In *Crusade and Settlement: Papers Read at the First Conference of the Society for the Study of the Crusades and the Latin East and Presented to R. C. Smail*, edited by Peter W. Edbury, 66–72. Cardiff: Cardiff University Press, 1985.

———, ed. *Religious Violence between Christians and Jews: Medieval Roots, Modern Perspectives*. London: Palgrave, 2002.

———. "Twelfth-Century Christian Expectations of Jewish Conversion: A Case Study of Peter of Blois." *Ashkenas* 8 (1998): 45–70.

———. "Twelfth-Century Renaissance Theology and the Jews." In *From Witness to Witchcraft: Jews and Judaism in Medieval Christian Thought*, edited by Jeremy Cohen, 128–32. Wiesbaden: Harrassowitz, 1996.

———. "Walter of Châtillon: A Twelfth-Century Poet's Engagement with Jews." *Journal of Medieval History* 31 (2005): 265–86.

Adams, Jeremy du Quesnay. "Ideology and Requirements of 'Citizenship' in Visigothic Spain: The Case of the Judei." *Societas* 2 (1972): 317–33.

Adams, Jonathan, and Jussi Hanska, eds. *The Jewish-Christian Encounter in Medieval Preaching*. Research in Medieval Studies 6. New York: Routledge, 2015.

Adams, Jonathan, and Cordelia Hess, eds. *The Medieval Roots of Antisemitism: Continuities and Discontinuities from the Middle Ages to the Present Day.* New York: Routledge, 2018.

Adams, Robert. "Chaucer's 'New Rachel' and the Theological Roots of Medieval Anti-Semitism." *Bulletin of the John Rylands University Library of Manchester* 77, no. 3 (1995): 9–18.

Adelman, Janet. *Blood Relations: Christian and Jew in the Merchant of Venice.* Chicago: University of Chicago Press, 2008.

Agus, Irving A. *The Heroic Age of Franco-German Jewry.* New York: Yeshiva University Press, 1969.

———, ed. *Rabbi Meir of Rothenberg.* 2 vols. New York: Yeshiva University Press, 1947.

———, ed. *Urban Civilization in Pre-Crusade Europe.* 2 vols. New York: Yeshiva University Press, 1968.

Aizenberg, Edna. "'Una Judía muy Fermosa': The Jewess as Sex Object in Medieval Spanish Literature and Lore." *La Corónica* 12, no. 2 (1984): 187–94.

Akbari, Suzanne Conklin. *Idols in the East: European Representations of Islam and the Orient, 1100–1450.* Ithaca, NY: Cornell University Press, 2009.

———. "The Non-Christians of Piers Plowman." In *Piers Plowman,* edited by Andrew Cole and Andres Galloway, 160–76. Cambridge: Cambridge University Press, 2014.

———. "Placing the Jews in Late Medieval English Literature." In *Orientalism and the Jews,* edited by Ivan Davidson Kalmar and Derek J. Penslar, 32–50. Walthan, MA: Brandeis University Press, 2005.

Albert, Bat-Sheva. "De fide catholica contra Judaeos d'Isidore de Séville: La polémique anti-judäique dans l'Espagne de VII siècle." *Revue des études juives* 141 (1982): 289–316.

———. "Isidore of Seville: His Attitude toward Judaism and His Impact on Early Canon Law." *Jewish Quarterly Review* 80, no. 1–2 (1990): 207–20.

———. "Un nouvel examen de la politique anti-juive wisigothique." *Revue des études juives* 135, no. 3 (1976): 3–29.

Albert of Aachen. *Historia Ierosolimitana: History of the Journey to Jerusalem.* Edited and translated by Susan B. Edgington. Oxford: Clarendon Press, 2007.

Alexander, Philip S. "Madame Englyntine, Geoffrey Chaucer and the Problem of Medieval Anti-Semitism." *Bulletin of the John Rylands Library of Manchester* 74 (1992): 109–20.

———. "'The Parting of the Ways' from the Perspective of Rabbinic Judaism." In *Jews and Christians: The Parting of the Ways A. D. 70 to 135,* edited by James D. G. Dunn, 1–25. Tübingen: Mohr Siebeck, 1992.

Alexiun, Natalia. "The Origins of the Blood Libel: Israel Yuval's Article 'Vengeance and Damnation, Blood and Defamation; From Jewish Martyrdom to Blood Libel Accusation' and the Response Thereto." *Scripta Judaica Cracoviensia* 1 (2002): 21–28.

Alfonsi, Petrus. *The Disciplina Clericalis of Petrus Alfonsi.* Translated and edited by Eberhard Hermes. Berkeley: University of California Press, 1970.

Allan, Valerie. *On Farting: Language and Laughter in the Middle Ages.* New York: Palgrave Macmillan, 2007.

Allin, Patricia. "Richard of Devizes and the Alleged Martyrdom of a Boy at Wincester." *Transactions and Miscellanies: Jewish Historical Society of England* 27 (1978-80): 32-39.
Almog, Shmuel, ed. *Antisemitism through the Ages*. Translated by Nathan H. Reisner. New York: Pergamon Press, 1988.
Alport, Gordon. *The Nature of Prejudice*. Cambridge, MA: Addison-Wesley Pub. Co., 1954.
Alter, Robert. "Who Is Shylock?" *Commentary* 96, no. 1 (July 1993): 29-34.
Ambrose of Milan. *Political Letters and Speeches*. Edited by J.H.W.G. Liebeschuetz with the assistance of Carole Hill. Liverpool: Liverpool University Press, 2005.
Aminoff, Irit. *Esav Ahi, Avi Edom ve-Romi: 'Iyyun bi-Meqorot ha-Talmud ve-ha-Midrash shel Eretz Yisrael bi-Tequfat ha-Tannaim ve-ha-Amoraim*. Jerusalem: Reuven Mass, 2015.
Anchel, Robert. "The Early History of the Jewish Quarters in Paris." *Jewish Social Studies* 2, no. 1 (January 1940): 45-60.
Anderson, George L. *The Legend of the Wandering Jew*. 1965. Reprinted, Providence, RI: Brown University Press, 1991.
Angerstorfer, Andreas. "Jüdische Reaktionen auf die mittelalterlichen Blutbeschuldigungen vom 13. bis zum 16. Jahrhundert." In *Die Legende vom Ritualmord*, edited by Rainer Erb, 133-77. Berlin: Metropol, 1993.
Annales Erphordenses. Anno 1220-54. MGH SS. Hannover: Hahn, 1859.
Annales Herbipolenses. MGH SS. Hannover: Reichsinstitut für ältere deutsche Geschichtskunde, 1826-.
Annales Hildesheimenses, ed. Georg Waitz, in MGH SS, Scriptores rerum Germanicarum (Hannover, 1848), 8:49-50.
Annales Wiziburgenses. MGH SS. Hannover: Hahn, 1829.
Applebaum, Shimon. "Were There Jews in Roman Britain?" *Transactions of the Jewish Historical Society of England* 17 (1951-52): 189-205.
Appleby, J. T. *Cronicon Richardi Divisensis de Tempore Regis Richardi Primi*. London: Nelson, 1963.
Archambault, Paul J., trans. *A Monk's Confession: The Memoirs of Guibert of Nogent*. University Park: Penn State University Press, 1996.
Archer, John. "The Structure of Anti-Semitism in the 'Prioress's Tale.'" *Chaucer Studies* 19, no. 1 (1984): 46-54.
Arendt, Hannah. "Preface to Part One: Antisemitism." In *The Origins of Totalitarianism*, xi-xvi. 1951. Reprinted, New York: Schocken Books, 2004.
Arieti, James A. "Magical Thinking in Medieval Anti-Semitism: Usury and the Blood Libel." *Mediterranean Studies* 24, no. 2 (2016): 193-218.
Armstrong, Guyda, and Ian N. Woods, eds. *Christianizing Peoples and Converting Individuals*. Turnhout: Brepols, 2000.
Arnold, T., ed. *The Memorials of Saint Edmund's Abbey*. Vol. 1. London: Eyre and Spottiswode, 1890.
Aronius, Julius. *Regesten zur Geschichte der Juden im fränkischen und deutschen Reiche bis zum Jahre 1273*. Edited and translated by Albert Dresdner and Ludwig

Lewinski. Auftrage der Historischen Commission für Geschichte der Juden in Deutschland. Berlin: L. Simion, 1902.

Asher, A., trans. and ed. *The Itinerary of Rabbi Benjamin of Tudela*. London: A. Asher and Co., 1840.

Ashtor, Eliyahu. *The Jews of Moslem Spain*. Translated by Aaron Klein and Jenny Machlowitz Klein. 3 vols. Philadelphia: Jewish Publication Society, 1973–84.

Asiedu, F.B.A. "Anselm and the Unbelievers: Pagans, Jews and Christians in the *Cur Deus Homo*." *Theological Studies* 62, no. 3 (September 2001): 530–48.

Aslanov, Cyril. "The Juxtaposition of Ashkenaz / Tsarfat vs. Sepharad / Provence Reassessed—A Linguistic Approach." *Simon Dubnov Institute Yearbook* 8 (2009): 49–65.

Assis, Yom Tov, et al., eds. *Yehudim mul ha-Zelav: Gezeirot Tatnu be-Historiah u-ve-Historiographiah*. Jerusalem: Magnes, 2000.

Augustine of Hippo. *The City of God*. Translated by Marcus Dods. New York: Modern Library, 1950.

———. *Contra Faustum Manichaeum*. In Migne PL 42, cols. 173–518.

———. *De Civitate Dei*. Edited by B. Dombard and A. Kalb. Corpus Christianorum Series Latina 47–48. Turnhout: Brepols, 1955.

———. *Enarrationes in Psalmos I-L*. Edited by Eligius Dekkers and Johannes Fraipont. Corpus Christianorum Series Latina 38–40. Turnhout: Brepols, 1956.

Avramson, Shraga. "Nusah Berakhah 'al Qedushat ha-Shem." *Torah She-be-'al Peh* 14 (1972): 156–64.

Avrutin, Eugene M., Jonathan Dekel-Chen, and Robert Weinberg, eds. *Ritual Murder in Russia, Eastern Europe, and Beyond*. Bloomington: Indiana University Press, 2017.

Babcock, Emily A., and August C. Krey, trans. *William of Tyre, A History of Deeds Done beyond the Sea*. New York: Columbia University Press, 1943.

Bachrach, Bernard S., ed. *Jews in Barbarian Europe*. Lawrence, KS: Coronado Press, 1977.

———. "A Reassessment of Visigothic Jewish Policy, 589–711." *American Historical Review* 78 (1973): 11–34.

Baer, Yitzhak. "Mavo." In *Sefer Gezeirot Ashkenaz ve-Zarefat*, by Abraham Meir Habermann. Jerusalem: Ofir, 1946.

———. "Rashi ve-ha-Metzi'ut ha-Historit shel Zemano." *Tarbiz* 22 (1950): 320–32.

Bagby, Albert. "The Jew in the Cantigas of Alfonso X, El Sabio." *Speculum* 46, no. 4 (1981): 681–84.

Bakhos, Carol. "Figuring (out) Esau: The Rabbis and Their Others." *Journal of Jewish Studies* 58, no. 2 (Autumn 2007): 250–62.

———. *Ishmael on the Border: Rabbinic Portrayals of the First Arab*. Albany: SUNY Press, 2006.

Balasse, Céline. *1306: L'expulsion des Juifs du royaume de France*. Brussels: De Boeck Université, 2008.

Bale, Anthony. "Afterword: Violence, Memory, and the Traumatic Middle Ages." In *Christians and Jews in Angevin England: The York Massacre of 1190, Narratives and Contents*, edited by Sarah Rees-Jones and Sethina Watson, 294–304. Rochester, NY: Boydell & Brewer, 2013.

———. "Christian Anti-Semitism and Intermedial Experience in Late Medieval England." In *The Religions of the Book: Christian Perceptions, 1400–1660*, edited by Matthew Dimmock and Andrew Hadfield, 23–44. London: Palgrave Macmillan, 2008.

———. *Feeling Persecuted: Christians, Jews, and Images of Violence in the Middle Ages*. London: Reaktion, 2010.

———. "The Female 'Jewish' Libido in Medieval Culture." In *A Search for the Erotic in Medieval Britain*, edited by Amanda Hopkins and Cory Rushton, 94–104. Cambridge, UK: Brewer, 2007.

———. "Fictions of Judaism in England before 1200." In *The Jews in Medieval Britain: Historical, Literary and Archaeological Perspectives*, edited by Patricia Skinner, 129–44. Woodbridge, UK: Boydell Press, 2003.

———. "Framing Antisemitic *Exempla*: Locating the Jew of Tewkesbury." *Mediaevalia* 20 (2001): 19–47.

———. "'House Devil, Town Saint': Antisemitism and Hagiography in Medieval Suffolk." In *Chaucer and the Jews: Sources, Contexts, Meanings*, edited by Sheila Delany, 185–210. New York: Routledge, 2002.

———. *The Jew in the Medieval Book: English Antisemitisms, 1350–1500*. Cambridge: Cambridge University Press, 2006.

———. "Richard of Devizes and Fictions of Judaism." *Jewish Culture and History* 3, no. 2 (June 2000): 55–72.

Bamberger, Yosef. *Ha-Apifiyor ha-Yehudi*. Ramat Gan: Bar Ilan University Press, 2009.

Banitt, Menahem. "Une langue phantôme: Judéo-français." *Revue de linguistique romane* 27, no. 107–8 (July–December 1963): 245–94.

Barasch, Moshe. *Blindness: The History of a Mental Image in Western Thought*. London: Routledge, 2001.

Bar-Asher Siegal, Michal. "Mocking of Jesus: III. Judaism." In *Encyclopedia of the Bible and Its Reception*, edited by Dale C. Alison Jr. et al., 19:526–27. Berlin: Walter de Gruyter, 2021.

Baraz, Daniel. *Medieval Cruelty: Changing Perceptions, Late Antiquity to the Early Modern Period*. Ithaca, NY: Cornell University Press, 2003.

Barber, Malcolm. "Lepers, Jews and Moslems: The Plot to Overthrow Christendom in 1321." *History* 81 (1996): 319–42.

Barbizat, Michael D. *Burning Bodies: Communities, Eschatology, and Punishment of Heresy in the Middle Ages*. Ithaca, NY: Cornell University Press, 2018.

Barbu, Daniel. "The Case about Jesus: (Counter-) History and Casuistry in Toledot Yeshu." In *A Historical Approach to Casuistry: Norms and Exceptions in a Comparative Perspective*, edited by Carlo Ginzburg and Lucio Biasioro, 65–97. London: Bloomsbury Academic, 2019.

———. "Voltaire and the Toledoth Yeshu." In *Infancy Gospels: Stories and Identities*, edited by Claire Clivaz et al., 617–27. Tübingen: Mohr Siebeck, 2011.

Barbu, Daniel, and Yaacov Deutsch, eds. *"Toledot Yeshu" in Context*. Tübingen: Mohr Siebeck, 2020.

Bar-Ilan, Meir. "Meqomah shel Tefillat 'Aleinu le-Shabei'ah." *Da'at* 43 (1999): 5-24.

Bar-Itzhak, Haya. *Jewish Poland—Legends of Origin: Ethnopoetics and Legendary Chronicles*. Detroit: Wayne State University Press, 2001.

Barlow, Frank. *Thomas Becket*. London: Weidenfeld and Nicolson, 1986.

Barnai, Jacob. "'Blood Libels' in the Ottoman Empire of the Fifteenth to Nineteenth Centuries." In *Antisemitism through the Ages*, edited by Shmuel Almog, 189-94. Oxford: Pergamon Press, 1988.

Baron, Salo W. "Ghetto and Emancipation." *Menorah Journal* (1928). Reprinted in *The Menorah Treasury: Harvest of Half a Century*, edited by Leo W. Schwarz, 50-63. Philadelphia: Jewish Publication Society, 1964.

———. *The Jewish Community, Its History and Structure to the American Revolution*. 3 vols. Philadelphia: Jewish Publication Society, 1942.

———. *A Social and Religious History of the Jews*. New York: Columbia University Press, 1952-93.

Bartlet, Suzanne. "Three Jewish Businesswomen in Thirteenth-Century Winchester." *Jewish Culture and History* 3, no. 2 (2000): 31-54.

Bartlett, Robert. "Illustrating Ethnicity in the Middle Ages." In *The Origins of Racism in the West*, edited by Miriam Eliav Feldon, Benjamin Isaac, and Joseph Ziegler, 132-56. Cambridge: Cambridge University Press, 2009.

———. "Medieval and Modern Concepts of Race and Ethnicity." *Journal of Medieval and Early Modern Studies* 31 (2001): 39-56.

———. "Symbolic Meanings of Hair in the Middle Ages." *Transactions of the Royal Historical Society*, 6th series, no. 4 (1994): 43-60.

Barzilay, Tzafrir. "Early Accusations of Well Poisoning against Jews: Medieval Reality or Historiographical Fiction?" *Medieval Encounters* 22, no. 5 (November, 2016): 517-39.

———. "Ha-Musag 'Antisheimiyut' ke-Qateigoriah le-Heiqer ha-Historiah shel ha-Yehudim bimei ha-Beinayim." *Zion* 85, no. 1-4 (2020): 195-207.

———. *Poisoned Wells: Accusations, Persecution, and Minorities in Medieval Europe, 1321-1422*. Philadelphia: University of Pennsylvania Press, 2022.

———. "Well-Poisoning Accusations in Medieval Europe: 1250-1500." PhD diss., Columbia University, 2017.

Barzilay, Tzafrir, Eyal Levinson, and Elisheva Baumgarten, eds. *Jewish Daily Life in Medieval Northern Europe, 1080-1350: A Sourcebook*. Kalamazoo: Michigan Institute Publications, Western Michigan University, 2022.

Baskin, Judith R. "Dolce of Worms: The Lives and Deaths of an Exemplary Medieval Jewish Woman and Her Daughters." In *Judaism in Practice: From the Middle Ages through the Early Modern Period*, edited by Lawrence Fine, 429-37. Princeton, NJ: Princeton University Press, 2001.

———. "Jewish Women in Ashkenaz." In *Late Medieval Jewish Identities: Iberia and Beyond*, edited by Carmen Caballero-Navas and Esperanza Alfonso, 79-90. New York: Palgrave Macmillan, 2010.

Battenberg, Friedrich. *Das Europäische Zeitalter der Juden*. 2 vols. in 1. Darmstadt: Wissenschaftliche Buchgesellschaft, 1990.

Baumgarten, Albert I. "Justinian and the Jews." In *Rabbi Joseph H. Lookstein Memorial Volume*, edited by Leo Sandman, 37–44. New York: Ktav, 1980.

Baumgarten, Elisheva. "Circumcision and Baptism: Development of a Jewish Ritual in Christian Europe." In *The Covenant of Circumcision: New Perspectives on an Ancient Jewish Rite*, edited by Elizabeth Wyner Mark, 114–27. Waltham, MA: Brandeis University Press, 2003.

———. "Minority Dress Codes and the Law: A Jewish-Christian Comparison." In *Religious Minorities in Christian, Jewish and Muslim Law (5th–15th Centuries)*, edited by John Tolan, 288–99. Turnhout: Brepols, 2017.

———. *Mothers and Children: Jewish Family Life in Medieval Europe*. Princeton, NJ: Princeton University Press, 2007.

———. "Mothers and Ma'asim: Maternal Roles in Medieval Hebrew Tales." In *Images of Mothers in Jewish Culture*, edited by Jane Kanarek and Marjorie Lehmann, 345–57. London: Littman Library of Jewish Civilization, 2017.

———. *Practicing Piety in Medieval Ashkenaz*. Philadelphia: University of Pennsylvania Press, 2014.

———. "Prier à part? Le genre dans les synagogues ashkénazes médiévales (XIIIe–XIVe siècles)." *Clio* 44 (2017): 43–62.

———. "Seeking Signs? Jews, Christians, and Proof by Fire in Medieval Germany and in Northern France." In *New Perspectives on Jewish-Christian Relations: Essays in Honor of David Berger*, edited by Elisheva Carlebach and Jacob J. Schacter, 205–25. Leiden: Brill, 2012.

———. "'A Separate People?' Some Directions for Comparative Research on Medieval Women." *Journal of Medieval History* 34 (2008): 212–28.

———. "Space and Place in Medieval Ashkenaz: An Everyday Perspective." *Jewish Studies Quarterly* 28, no. 3 (2021): 245–58.

Baumgarten, Elisheva, and Judah D. Galinsky, eds. *Jews and Christians in Thirteenth-Century France*. New York: Palgrave Macmillan, 2015.

Baumgarten, Elisheva, Ruth Mazo Karras, and Katelyn Mesler, eds. *Entangled Histories: Knowledge, Authority, and Jewish Culture in the Thirteenth Century*. Philadelphia: University of Pennsylvania Press, 2017.

Baumgarten, Elisheva, and Ido Noy, eds. *In and Out, Between and Beyond: Jewish Daily Life in Medieval Europe*. Jerusalem: Beyond the Elite, 2021.

Bautier, Robert-Henri. "L'origine des populations juives de la France médiévale: constatations et hypothèses de recherche." In *La catalogna et la France méridionale*, edited by Dominique Iogna-Prat et al., 306–16. Barcelona: Generalitat de Catalunya, Departament de Cultura, 1991.

Bayless, Martha. *Parody in the Middle Ages—The Latin Tradition*. Ann Arbor: University of Michigan Press, 1996.

———. *Sin and Filth in Medieval Culture: The Devil in the Latrine*. New York: Routledge, 2012.

———. "The Story of the Fallen Jew in the Iconography of Jewish Unbelief." *Viator* 34 (2003): 142–56.

Beckwith, Sarah. *Christ's Body: Identity, Culture and Society in Late Medieval Writings*. London: Routledge, 1993.

———. "Ritual, Church, and Theater: Medieval Dramas of the Sacramental Body." In *Culture and History, 1350-1660: Essays in English Communities, Identities, and Writings*, edited by David Aers, 65-89. Detroit: Wayne State University Press, 1992.

———. *Signifying God, Social Relation and Social Act in the York Corpus Christi Plays.* Chicago: University of Chicago Press, 2001.

Bédier, Joseph. *Le Chanson de Roland.* Paris: Piazza, 1947.

Bedos-Rezak, Brigitte Miriam. "Were Jews Made in the Image of God? Christian Perspectives and Jewish Existence in Medieval Europe." In *Studies in Medieval Jewish Intellectual and Social History: Festschrift in Honour of Robert Chazan*, edited by David Engel, Lawrence H. Schiffman, and Elliot R. Wolfson, 63-95. Supplements to the *Journal of Jewish Thought* 15. Leiden: Brill, 2012.

———. *When Ego Was Imago: Signs of Identity in the Middle Ages.* Leiden: Brill, 2011.

Beker, Avi. *The Chosen: The History of an Idea, and the Anatomy of an Obsession.* New York: Palgrave Macmillan, 2008.

Bell, Dean Philip. *Sacred Communities: Jewish and Christian Identities in Fifteenth-Century Germany.* Leiden: Brill, 2001.

Ben-Amos, Dan. "Jewish Folk-Literature." *Oral Tradition* 14, no. 1 (1999): 140-274.

Benbassa, Esther, and J.- C. Attias. *The Jew and the Other.* Ithaca, NY: Cornell University Press, 2004.

Benedictow, Ole J. *The Black Death 1346-1353: The Complete History.* Woodbridge, UK: Boydell Press, 2004.

Ben-Eliyahu, Eyal, Yehuda Cohen, and Fergus Millar, eds. *Handbook of Jewish Literature from Late Antiquity, 135-700 CE.* Oxford: Oxford University Press, 2013.

Benin, Stephen. "Matthew Paris and the Jews." *Proceedings of the Tenth World Congress of Jewish Studies*, part B (History of the Jewish People), 2:61-68 [English pages]. Jerusalem: World Congress of Jewish Studies, 1990.

Ben-Sasson, Haim Hillel. *A History of the Jewish People.* Cambridge, MA: Harvard University Press, 1976.

———. *Peraqim be-Toledot ha-Yehudim bimei ha-Beinayim.* Tel Aviv: Am Oved, 1958.

Ben-Sasson, Menahem. "Le-Zeihutam shel Anusum: 'Iyyun be-Hishtamdut bi-Tequfat al-Muhadun." *Pe'amim* 42 (Winter 1990): 16-37.

Ben-Shalom, Ram. "Between Official and Private Dispute: The Case of Christian Spain and Provence in the Late Middle Ages." *AJS Review* 27, no. 1 (April 2003): 23-72.

Ben-Shalom, Ram, Orah Limor, and Oded Irshay, eds. *"Ve-Rav Ya'avod Za'ir" Mitusim u-Semalim bein Yahadut ve-Nazrut: Shai le-Yisrael Ya'aqov Yuval.* Jerusalem: Carmel, 2022.

Benton, John F. "Clio and Venus: An Historical View of Medieval Love." In *The Meaning of Courtly Love*, edited by F. X. Newman, 19-42. Albany: SUNY Press, 1969.

———. ed. *Self and Society in Medieval France: The Memoirs of Abbot Guibert of Nogent.* Toronto: University of Toronto Press, 1984.

Benveniste, Henriette-Rika. "The Body as the Locus of the Supernatural Power in Guibert de Nogent's Autobiography." *Social Science Tribune.* Special issue, *History and Social Sciences: Sexuality and Power* 44 (2005): 33-47.

———. "Fierté, désespoir et mémoire: les récits juives de la première croisade." *Médiévales* 45 (1998): 125-40.

———. "On the Language of Conversion: Visigothic Spain Revisited." *Historien* 6 (2006): 88–96.

Benveniste, Henriette-Rika, and Giorgios Plakotos. "Converting Bodies, Embodying Conversion: The Production of Religious Identities in Late Medieval and Early Modern Europe." In *Contesting Inter-Religious Conversion in the Medieval World*, edited by Yaniv Fox and Yosi Yisraeli, 245–67. New York: Routledge, 2017.

Berek, Peter. "The Jew as Renaissance Man." *Renaissance Quarterly* 51, no. 1 (Spring 1998): 128–62.

Berger, David. "Anti-Semitism: An Overview." In *History and Hate: The Dimensions of Antisemitim*, edited by David Berger, 3–14. Philadelphia: Jewish Publication Society, 1986. Reprinted in David Berger, *Persecution, Polemic, and Dialogue: Essays in Jewish-Christian Relations*. Boston: Academic Studies Press, 2010.

———. "The Attitude of St. Bernard of Clairvaux toward the Jews." *Proceedings of the American Academy for Jewish Research* 40 (1972): 89–108. Reprinted in David Berger, *Persecution, Polemic, and Dialogue: Essays in Jewish-Christian Relations*. Boston: Academic Studies Press, 2010.

———. *Cultures in Collision and Conversation*. Boston: Academic Studies Press, 2011.

———. "From Crusades to Blood Libels to Expulsions: Some New Approaches to Medieval Antisemitism." *Second Annual Lecture of the Victor J. Selmanowitz Chair of Jewish History*, 1–29. New York: Touro College, 1997. Reprinted in David Berger, *Persecution, Polemic, and Dialogue: Essays in Jewish-Christian Relations*. Boston: Academic Studies Press, 2010.

———. "Gilbert Crispin, Alan of Lille, and Jacob ben Reuven: A Study in the Transmission of Medieval Polemic." *Speculum* 49 (1974): 37–47.

———. "Gilgulei ha-Musag 'Antisheimiyut': Teguvah le-Ma'amaro shel David Engel." *Zion* 85, no. 1–4 (2020): 363–73.

———, ed. *History and Hate*. Philadelphia: Jewish Publication Society, 1986.

———. "Jacob Katz on Jews and Christians in the Middle Ages." In *The Pride of Jacob: Essays on Jacob Katz and His Work*, edited by Jay M. Harris, 41–63. Cambridge, MA: Harvard University Press, 2002. Reprinted in David Berger, *Persecution, Polemic, and Dialogue: Essays in Jewish-Christian Relations*. Boston: Academic Studies Press, 2010.

———, ed. and trans. *The Jewish-Christian Debate in the High Middle Ages: A Critical Edition of the Nizzahon Vetus*. Philadelphia; Jewish Publication Society, 1979.

———. "Jews, Gentiles, and the Modern Egalitarian Ethos: Some Tentative Thoughts." In *Formulating Responses in an Egalitarian Age*, edited by Marc D. Stern, 83–108. Lanham, MD: Rowman and Littlefield, 2005.

———. "Mission to the Jews and Jewish-Christian Contacts in the Polemical Literature of the High Middle Age." *American Historical Review* 91, no. 3 (June 1986): 576–91.

———. "On the Image and Destiny of the Gentiles in Ashkenaz Polemical Literature." Reprinted in David Berger, *Persecution, Polemic, and Dialogue: Essays in Jewish-Christian Relations*. Boston: Academic Studies Press, 2010.

———. "On the Uses of History in Medieval Jewish Polemic against Christianity: The Search for the Historical Jesus." In *Jewish History and Jewish Memory: Essays in*

Honor of Yosef Hayim Yerushalmi, edited by Elisheva Carlebach, John M. Efron, and David N. Myers, 25–39. Waltham, MA: Brandeis University Press, 1998.

———. *Persecution, Polemic, and Dialogue: Essays in Jewish-Christian Relations*. Boston: Academic Studies Press, 2010.

———. "Review of Jeremy Cohen, *The Friars and the Jews*." *American Historical Review* 88 (1983): 93.

Berkowitz, Beth. "The Limits of 'Their Laws.'" *Jewish Quarterly Review* 99, no. 1 (2009): 121–57.

Berliner, Abraham. *Aus dem Leben der deutschen Juden im Mittelalter*. Berlin: M. Poppelauer, 1900.

Berman Brown, Reva, and Sean McCartney. "The Exchequer of the Jews Revisited: The Operation and Effect of the *Scaccarium Judeorum*." *Medieval History Journal* 8, no. 2 (2005): 267–72.

———. "Living in Limbo: The Experience of Jewish Converts in Medieval England." In *Christianizing Peoples and Converting Individuals*, edited by Guyda Armstrong and Ian N. Wood, 169–91. Turnhout: Brepols, 2000.

Bestul, Thomas. *Texts of the Passion: Latin Devotional Literature and Medieval Society*. Philadelphia: University of Pennsylvania Press, 1996.

Bethencourt, Francisco. *Racisms: From the Crusades to the Twentieth Century*. Princeton, NJ: Princeton Univerity Press, 2013.

Bhabha, Homi K. *The Location of Culture*. New York: Routledge, 1994. Reprinted, with a new preface by the author, 2004.

Biale, David. *Blood and Belief: The Circulation of a Symbol between Jews and Christians*. Berkeley: University of California Press, 2007.

———. *Eros and the Jews: From Biblical Israel to Contemporary America*. Berkeley: University of California Press, 1997.

———. *Power and Powerlessness in Jewish History*. New York: Schocken Books, 1986.

Bibring, Tovi. "A Medieval Hebrew French-Kiss: Analyzing the Love Story of Sahar and Kima by Ya'akov ben El'azar through Courtly Love Ideals." *Jewish Quarterly Review* 109, no. 1 (2019): 24–37.

———. "'Would That My Words Were Inscribed': Berachiah ha-Naqdan's *Mishlei Shualim* and European Fable Traditions." In *Latin into Hebrew: Texts and Studies*, edited by Resianne Fontaine and Gad Freudenthal, 1:309–31. Leiden: Brill, 2013.

Biddick, Kathleen. "Paper Jews: Inscription/Ethnicity/Ethnography." *Art Bulletin* 78 (1996): 594–621.

———. *The Typological Imaginary: Circumcision, Technology, History*. Philadelphia: University of Pennsylvania Press, 2003.

Bildhauer, Bettina. "Blood, Jews and Monsters in Medieval Culture." In *The Monstrous Middle Ages*, edited by Battina Bildhauer and Robert Mills, 75–96. Toronto: University of Toronto Press, 2003.

Biller, Peter. "Black Women in Medieval Scientific Thought." *Micrologus* 13 (2005): 477–92.

———. "Proto-Racial Thought in Medieval Science." In *The Origins of Racism in the West*, edited by Miriam Eliav-Feldon, Benjamin Isaac, and Joseph Ziegler, 157–80. Cambridge: Cambridge University Press, 2009.

———. "A 'Scientific' View of Jews in Paris around 1300." *Micrologus* 9 (2001): 137–68.

———. "Views of Jews from Paris around 1300: Christian or 'Scientific?'" *Studies in Church History* 29 (1992): 92–99.

Birenboim, Hannan. "'Parzah Tum'ah be-Yisrael': Ha-Haqpadah 'al Taharah bimei Bayit Sheini." PhD diss., Hebrew University of Jerusalem, 2006.

Birnbaum, Marianna D. *The Long Journey of Gracia Mendes*. New York: Central European University Press, 2003.

Bitton, Livia E. "The Jewess as a Fictional Sex Symbol." *Bucknell Review* 21, no. 1 (Spring 1973): 63–86.

Bitton-Jackson, Livia E. *Madonna or Courtesan? The Jewish Woman in Christian Literature*. New York: Seabury Press, 1982.

Blank, Debra Reed, ed. *The Experience of Jewish Liturgy: Studies Dedicated to Menahem Schmelzer*. Leiden: Brill, 2011.

Blidstein, Gerald J. "R. Yohanan, Idolatry, and Public Privilege." *Journal for the Study of Judaism* 5, no. 2 (1974): 154–61.

———. "Rabbinic Legislation on Idolatry, Tractate Abodah Zarah, Chapter 1." PhD diss., Yeshiva University, 1968.

Bloch, Marc. *Feudal Society*. Translated by L. A. Manyon. Chicago: University of Chicago Press, 1961.

Bloch, R. Howard. "Critical Communities and the Shape of the Medievalist's Desire: A Response to Judith Ferster and Louise Fradenburg." *Exemplaria* 2 (1990): 203–20.

Blumenkranz, Bernhard. *Les auteurs chrétiens latins du moyen âge*. Paris: Mouton, 1963.

———. "Du nouveau sur Bodo-Eléazar?" In *Juifs et chrétiens: patristique et moyen âge*, 35–42. London: Variorum Reprints, 1977.

———. "En 1306: chemins d'un exil." *Evidences* 12 (1962): 17–23.

———. "Germany: 843–1096." In *Dark Ages: Jews in Christian Europe, 711–1096*, edited by Cecil Roth, 2:162–74. New Brunswick, NJ: Rutgers University Press, 1966.

———. *Juden und Judentum in der mittelalterlichen Kunst*. Stuttgart: W. Kohlhammer, 1965.

———. "Juden und Jüdischen in Christlichen Wunderzählungen." *Theologische Zeitschrift* 10 (1954): 417–46.

———. *Judenpredigt Augustins, ein Beitrag zur Geschichte der jüdisch-christlichen Beziehungen in den ersten Jahrhunderten*. Basel: Helbing & Lichtenhahn, 1946.

———. "Jüdische und Christliche Konvertiten im Jüdisch-Christlichen Religionsgespräch im Mittelalter." In *Judentum im Mittelalter: Beiträge zum Christlich-Jüdischen Gespräch*, edited by Paul Wilpert, 264–82. Berlin: Walter de Gruyter, 1966.

———. *Le juif médiéval au miroir de l'art chrétien*. Paris: Études Augustiniennes, 1966.

———. *Juifs et chrétiens dans le monde occidentale*. Paris: Mouton, 1960.

———. "Un pamphlet juif médio-latin de polémique antichrétienne." *Revue d'histoire et de philosophie religieuses* 34, no. 4 (1954): 401–13.

———. "Premiers témoignages épigraphiques sur les juifs en France." In *Salo Wittmayer Baron Jubilee Volume*, edited by Saul Lieberman, 1:229-35. 3 vols. New York: American Academy for Jewish Research, 1974.

———. "Relations between Jews and Christians in the Eleventh Century." In *The Dignity of the Despised of the Earth*, edited by Jacques Pohier and Dietmar Mieth, 40-48. New York: Seabury Press, 1979.

———. "The Roman Church and the Jews." In *Esssential Papers on Judaism and Christianity in Conflict*, edited by Jeremy Cohen, 193-230. New York: NYU Press, 1991.

Blumenkranz, Bernhard, and Dominique Bozo. "Synagoga méconnue, synagoga inconnue." *Revue des études juives* 125 (1966): 35-49.

Blumenthal, Uta-Renate. *The Investiture Controversy: Church and Monarchy from the Ninth to the Twelfth Century*. Philadelphia: University of Pennsylvania Press, 1988.

Blurton, Heather. *Inventing William of Norwich: Thomas of Monmouth, Antisemitism, and Literary Culture, 1150-1200*. Philadelphia: University of Pennsylvania Press, 2022.

———. "The Language of the Liturgy in the Life and Miracles of William of Norwich." *Speculum* 90, no. 4 (2015): 1053-75.

Blurton, Heather, and Hannah Johnson. *The Critics and the Prioress: Criticism, Antisemitism and Chaucer's Prioress's Tale*. Ann Arbor: University of Michigan Press, 2017.

Bobichon, Philippe. "Citations latines de la tradition chrétienne dans la littérature hébraïque de controverse avec le christianisme (Xe-XVe s.)." In *Latin-into-Hebrew: Texts and Studies*. Vol. 1, *Studies*, edited by Resianne Fontaine and Gad Freudenthal, 349-88. Leiden: Brill, 2013.

Boccaccio, Giovanni. *Decameron*. Edited by Vittore Branca. Turin: Einaudi, 1980.

———. *The Decameron*. Translated by G. H. McWilliam. 2nd ed. New York: Penguin Books, 1995.

Bodner, Neta. "Romanesque beyond Christianity: Jewish Ritual Baths in Germany in the Twelfth and Thirteenth Centuries." *Jewish Studies Quarterly* 28 (2021): 369-87.

Bohak, Gideon. "Catching a Thief: The Jewish Trials of a Christian Ordeal." *Jewish Studies Quarterly* 13 (2006): 344-62.

Bokobza, Hervé Elie. *L'autre: l'image de l'étranger dans le judaïsme*. Paris: Oeuvre, 2009.

Bonet, Honoré. *Medieval Muslims, Christians, and Jews in Dialogue: The Apparicion Maistre Jehan de Meun of Honorat Bovet*, parallel text edition with Old French and modern English translated by Michael Hanly. Tempe: Arizona Center for Medieval and Renaissance Studies, 2005.

Bonfil, Robert. "Aliens Within: The Jews and Anti-Judaism." In *Handbook of European History, 1400-1600: Late Middle Ages, Renaissance, and Reformation*, edited by Thomas A. Brady Jr., Heiko A. Oberman, and James D. Tracy, 263-97. Leiden: Brill, 1994.

———. "Can Medieval Storytelling Help Us Understand Midrash?" In *The Midrashic Imagination: Jewish Exegesis, Thought, and History*, edited by Michael Fishbane, 228-54. Albany: SUNY Press, 1993.

———. "Change in the Cultural Patterns of a Jewish Society in Crisis: Italian Jewry at the Close of the Sixteenth Century." *Jewish History* 3 (1988): 11–30.

———. "Changing Mentalities of Italian Jews and the Baroque." *Italia* 11 (1994): 61–79.

———. "Demutah shel ha-Yahadut be-Sifro shel Raymond Martini's *Pugio Fidei*." *Tarbiz* 40 (1971): 360–75.

———. "The Devil and the Jews in the Christian Consciousness of the Middle Ages." In *Antisemitism through the Ages*, edited by Shmuel Almog, 91–98. New York: Pergamon Press, 1988.

———. *History and Folklore in a Medieval Jewish Chronicle: The Family Chronicle of Ahima'az ben Paltiel*. Leiden: Brill, 2007.

———. *Jewish Life in Renaissance Italy*. Translated by Anthony Oldcorn. Berkeley: University of California Press, 1994.

———. "Tra due mondi: prospettive di ricerca sulla storia culturale degli Ebrei dell'Italia meridionale nell'alto Medioevo." *Italia Judaica* 1 (1983): 135–58.

Bonfil, Robert, et al., eds. *Jews in Byzantium: Dialectics of Minority and Majority Cultures*. Leiden: Brill, 2012.

Borst, Otto. *Alltagsleben im Mittelalter*. Frankfurt am Main: Suhrkamp, 1983.

Bossy, John. "The Mass as a Social Institution 1200–1700." *Past and Present* 100 (August 1983): 29–61.

Boswell, John. *The Kindness of Strangers: The Abandonment of Children in Western Europe from Late Antiquity to the Renaissance*. Chicago: University of Chicago Press, 1998.

Bouchard, Constance Brittain. *"Every Valley Shall Be Exalted": The Discourse of Opposites in Twelfth-Century Thought*. Ithaca, NY: Cornell University Press, 2003.

Boulton, Maureen. "Anti-Jewish Attitudes in Medieval French Literature." In *Jews and Christians in Twelfth-Century Europe*, edited by Michael A. Signer and John Van Engen, 234–54. Notre Dame, IN: Notre Dame University Press, 2001.

———, trans. *Piety and Persecution in the French Texts of England*. Vol. 420. Medieval and Renaissance Texts and Studies. Tempe: Arizona Center for Medieval and Renaissance Studies, 2013.

Bowman, Steven. *The Jews of Byzantium 1204–1453*. Tuscaloosa: University of Alabama Press, 1985.

Boyarin, Adrienne Williams. *The Christian Jew and the Unmarked Jewess*. Philadelphia: University of Pennsylvania Press, 2021.

———. *Miracles of the Virgin in Medieval England: Law and Jewishness in Marian Legends*. Cambridge, UK: D. S. Brewer, 2010.

Boyarin, Daniel. *A Radical Jew: Paul and the Politics of Identity*. Berkeley: University of California Press, 1997.

———. "The Subversion of the Jews: Moses's Veil and the Hermeneutics of Supersession." *Diacritics* 23, no. 2 (1993): 16–35.

Boyd, Beverly. *The Prioress's Tale, Variorum edition of the works of Geoffrey Chaucer*. Vol. 2. Part 20:27–50. Norman: University of Oklahoma Press, 1987.

Boynton, Susan, and Diane J. Reilly, eds. *The Practice of the Bible in the Middle Ages: Production, Reception, and Performance in Western Christianity*. New York: Columbia University Press, 2011.

Bradshaw, P. F., and L. A. Hoffman. *Passover and Easter: Origin and History to Modern Times*. Notre Dame, IN: University of Notre Dame Press, 1999.

Brain, J. L. "Male Menstruation in History and Anthropology." *Journal of Psychohistory* 15 (1988): 311–23.

Brand, Paul. "Jews and the Law in England, 1275–90." *English Historical Review* 115 (2000): 1138–58.

Brann, Ross. *Power in the Portrayal: Representations of Jews and Muslims in Eleventh- and Twelfth-Century Islamic Spain*. Princeton, NJ: Princeton University Press, 2002.

Braun, Manuel, and Cornelia Herberichs, eds. *Gewalt im Mittelalter: Realitäten—Imaginationen*. Munich: Fink, 2005.

Braude, Benjamin. "The Sons of Noah and the Construction of Ethnic and Geographical Identities in the Medieval and Early Modern Periods." *William and Mary Quarterly* 54 (1997): 103–42.

Bremer, Ernst, et al., eds. *Language of Religion—Language of the People: Medieval Judaism, Christianity and Islam*. Mittelalter Studien 11. Munich: Fink, 2006.

Breuer, Mordechai. "Nashim be-Qiddush ha-Shem." In *Yehudim mul ha-Zelav: Gezeirot Tatnu be-Historiah u-ve-Historiographiah*, edited by Yom Tov Assis et al., 141–49. Jerusalem: Magnes, 2000.

——, ed. *Sefer Nizzahon Yashan*. Ramat Gan: Bar-Ilan University Press, 1978.

Brodkin, Karen. *How Jews Became White Folks and What That Says about Race in America*. New Brunswick, NJ: Rutgers University Press, 1998.

Brody, Robert. *The Geonim of Babylonia and the Shaping of Medieval Jewish Culture*. New Haven, CT: Yale University Press, 1998.

Bronstein, J. "The Crusades and the Jews: Some Reflections on the 1096 Massacre." *History Compass* 5, no. 4 (2007): 1268–79.

Brooks, Andrée. *The Woman Who Defied Kings: The Life and Times of Doña Gracia Nasi*. St. Paul, MN: Paragon House, 2002.

Browe, Peter. "Die Hostienschandungen der Juden im Mittelalter." *Römische Quartalsschrift für christliche Altertumskunde* 34 (1926): 167–98.

Brown, Beatrice D. "Mediaeval Prototypes of Lorenzo and Jessica." *Modern Language Notes* 44, no. 4 (April 1929): 227–32.

Brown, Elizabeth A. R. "Philip V, Charles IV, and the Jews of France: The Alleged Expulsion of 1322." *Speculum* 66, no. 2 (April 1991): 294–329.

Brown, Jeremy Philip. "Distilling Depths from Darkness: Forgiveness and Repentance in Medieval Iberian Jewish Mysticism (12th–13th Centuries)." PhD diss., New York University, 2015.

Brown, Peter. "Society and the Supernatural: A Medieval Change." *Daedalus* 104, no. 2 (Spring 1975): 133–51.

Brugger, Eveline, and Birgit Wiegl, eds. *Ein Thema—Zwei Perspektiven. Juden und Christen in Mittelalter und Frühneuzeit*. Innsbruck: Studien Verlag, 2007.

Brundage, James A. "Intermarriage between Christians and Jews in Medieval Canon Law." *Jewish History* 3, no. 1 (1988): 25-40.

Buc, Philippe. *Dangers of Ritual: Between Early Medieval Texts and Social Scientific Theory*. Princeton, NJ: Princeton University Press, 2001.

———. *Holy War, Martyrdom and Terror: Christianity, Violence and the West*. Philadelphia: University of Pennsylvania Press, 2015.

Buc, Philippe, Martha Keil, and John Tolan, eds. *Jews and Christians in Medieval Europe: The Historiographical Legacy of Bernhard Blumenkranz*. Religion and Law in Medieval Christian and Muslim Societies 7. Turnhout: Brepols, 2016.

Burgard, Friedhelm, Alfred Haverkamp, and Gerd Mentgen, eds. *Judenvertreibungen in Mittelalter und früher Neuzeit*. Hannover: Hahnsche Verlag, 1999.

Burke, Linda. "A Sister in the World: St. Elizabeth of Hungary in the Golden Legend." *Hungarian Historical Review* 5, no. 3 (2016): 509-35.

Burns, Joshua Ezra. *Christian Schism in Jewish History and Jewish Memory*. New York: Cambridge University Press, 2016.

Bush, Jonathan. "'You're Gonna Miss Me When I'm Gone': Early Modern Common Law Discourse and the Case of the Jews." *Wisconsin Law Review* 11 (1993): 1225-85.

Bushnell, Nelson. "The Wandering Jew and the Pardoner's Tale." *Studies in Philology* 28 (1931): 450-60.

Buttaroni, Susanne, and Stanislaw Musiel, eds. *Ritual Murder Legend in European History*. Kraków: Association for Cultural Initiatives, 2003.

Bynum, Caroline Walker. *Dissimilar Similitudes: Devotional Objects in Late Medieval Europe*. Brooklyn: Zone Books, 2020.

———. *Fragmentation and Redemption*. Brooklyn: Zone Books, 2012.

———. "The Presence of Objects: Medieval Anti-Judaism in Modern Germany." In *Dissimilar Similitudes: Devotional Objects in Late Medieval Europe*, 149-81. Brooklyn: Zone Books, 2020.

———. "Why All the Fuss about the Body? A Medievalist's Perspective." *Critical Inquiry* 22 (1995): 1-33.

———. *Wonderful Blood: Theology and Practice in Late Medieval Germany and Beyond*. Philadelphia: University of Pennsylvania Press, 2007.

Caballero-Navas, Carmen, and Esperanza Alfonso, eds. *Late Medieval Jewish Identities: Iberia and Beyond*. New York: Palgrave Macmillan, 2010.

Cabaniss, Alan. "Bodo-Eleazar: A Famous Jewish Convert." *Jewish Quarterly Review* 43, no. 4 (April 1953): 313-28.

Caesarius of Heisterbach. *Dialogus miraculorum*. Edited by Josephus Strange. 2 vols. Cologne: H. Lembertz, 1851.

———. *Dialogue on Miracles*. Translated by Ronald E. Pepin. 2 vols. Collegeville, MN: Liturgical Press, 2023.

———. *Dialogue on Miracles*. Edited and translated by H. von E. Scott and C. C. Swinton Bland. New York: Harcourt, Brace., 1929.

Cahn, Walter. "The Expulsion of the Jews as History and Allegory in Painting and Sculpture of the Twelfth and Thirteenth Centuries." In *Jews and Christians in Twelfth-Century Europe*, edited by Michael A. Singer and John Van Engen, 94–109. Notre Dame, IN: University of Notre Dame Press, 2001.

Camille, Michael. *The Gothic Idol: Ideology and Image-Making in Medieval Art*. Cambridge: Cambridge University Press, 1989.

Camporesi, Piero. *Juice of Life: Symbolic and Magic Significance of Blood*. Translated by Robert R. Barr. New York: Continuum, 1995.

Caputo, Nina, and Mitchell B. Hart, eds. *On the Word of a Jew: Religion, Reliability and the Dynamics of Trust*. Bloomington: Indiana University Press, 2019.

Carlebach, Elisheva. *Between History and Hope: Jewish Messianism in Ashkenaz and Sepharad: Third Annual Lecture of the Victor J. Selmanowitz Chair of Jewish History (May 17, 1998)*. New York: Touro College, 1998.

Carlebach, Elisheva, and Jacob J. Schacter, eds. *New Perspectives on Jewish-Christian Relations: In Honor of David Berger*. Leiden: Brill, 2012.

Carpenter, Dwayne E., ed. *Alfonso X and the Jews: An Edition of and Commentary on Siete Partidas 7.24 "De los judíos."* Berkeley: University of California Press, 1986.

Carroll, James. *Constantine's Sword: The Church and the Jews, A History*. Boston: Houghton Mifflin, 2001.

Cassell, David, ed. *Teshuvot Geonim Qadmonim*. Berlin: Fridlendershe Bukhdrukerai, [1848].

Castaño, Javier, Talya Fishman, and Ephraim Kanarfogel, eds. *Regional Identities and Cultures of Medieval Jews*. London: Littman Library of Jewish Civilization, 2018.

Caviness, Madeline. "From the Self-Invention of the Whiteman to *The Good, the Bad, and the Ugly*." *Different Visions: A Journal of New Perspectives on Medieval Art* 1 (2008): 1–33.

Chaucer, Geoffrey. *The Riverside Chaucer*. Edited by Larry D. Benson. 3rd ed. Boston: Houghton Mifflin, 1987.

Chazan, Robert. "Antisemitism." In *Dictionary of the Middle Ages*, edited by Joseph R. Strayer, 1:338–42. New York: Charles Scribner's and Sons, 1982.

——. "An Ashkenazic Anti-Christian Treatise." *Journal of Jewish Studies* 34 (1983): 63–72.

——. *Barcelona and Beyond: The Disputation of 1263 and Its Aftermath*. Berkeley: University of California Press, 1992.

——. "The Blois Incident of 1171: A Study in Inter-Communal Orgnization." *Proceedings of the American Academy for Jewish Research* 36 (1968): 13–31.

——, ed. and trans. *Church, State, and Jew in the Middle Ages*. New York: Behrman House, 1980.

——. *Daggers of Faith: Thirteenth-Century Christian Missionizing and Jewish Response*. Berkeley: University of California Press, 1989.

——. "The Deteriorating Image of the Jews—Twelfth and Thirteenth Centuries." In *Christendom and Its Discontents: Exclusion, Persecution, and Rebellion 1000–1500*, edited by Scott L. Waugh and Peter D. Diehl, 220–33. Cambridge: Cambridge University Press, 1996.

———. *European Jewry and the First Crusade*. Berkeley: University of California Press, 1987.

———. "The Facticity of Medieval Narrative: A Case Study of the Hebrew First Crusade Narratives." *AJS Review* 16 (1991): 31–56.

———. *Fashioning Jewish Identity in Medieval Western Christendom*. Cambridge: Cambridge University Press, 2004.

———. *From Anti-Judaism to Anti-Semitism: Ancient and Medieval Christian Constructions of Jewish History*. Cambridge: Cambridge University Press, 2016.

———. *God, Humanity, and History: The Hebrew First Crusade Narratives*. Berkeley: University of California Press, 2000.

———. "The Hebrew First-Crusade Chronicles." *Revue des études juives* 133 (1974): 235–54.

———. "The Hebrew First-Crusade Chronicles: Further Reflections." *AJS Review* 3 (1978): 79–98.

———. *In the Year 1096*. Philadelphia: Jewish Publication Society, 1996.

———. "Jerusalem as Christian Symbol during the First Crusade: Jewish Awareness and Response." In *Jerusalem: Its Sanctity and Centrality to Judaism, Christianity, and Islam*, edited by Lee I. Levine, 382–92. New York: Continuum, 1999.

———. *The Jews of Medieval Western Christendom, 1000–1500*. Cambridge: Cambridge University Press, 2006.

———. "'Let Not a Remnant or a Residue Escape': Millenarian Enthusiasm in the First Crusade." *Speculum* 84 (2009): 289–313.

———. *Medieval Jewry in Northern France*. Baltimore: Johns Hopkins University Press, 1973.

———. *Medieval Stereotypes and Modern Antisemitism*. Berkeley: University of California Press, 1997.

———. "Medieval Western Christendom." In *The Cambridge Companion to Antisemitism*, edited by Steven T. Katz, 158–75. Cambridge: Cambridge University Press, 2022.

———. "Political Themes in the *Milhemet Mitzvah*" (Parma 2749). In *Les Juifs au regard de l'histoire: mélanges en l'honneur de Bernhard Blumenkranz*, 169–84. Paris, Picard, 1985.

———. "Pope Innocent III and the Jews." In *Pope Innocent III and His World*, edited by John C. Moore, 187–204. Aldershot, UK: Ashgate, 1999.

———. "R. Ephraim of Bonn's *Sefer Zechirah*." *Revue des Études Juives* 132 (1973): 119–26.

———. *Reassessing Jewish Life in Medieval Europe*. Cambridge: Cambridge University Press, 2010.

———. *Refugees or Migrants: Pre-Modern Jewish Population Movement*. New Haven, CT: Yale University Press, 2018.

———. "1007–1012: Initial Crisis for Northern European Jewry." *Proceedings of the American Academy for Jewish Research* 38–39 (1970–71): 101–17.

———. "Twelfth-Century Perceptions of the Jews: A Case Study of Bernard of Clairvaux and Peter the Venerable." In *From Witness to Witchcraft: Jews and Judaism in*

Medieval Thought, edited by Jeremy Cohen, 187–201. Wolfenbütteler Mittelalter-Studien 11. Wiesbaden: Harrassowitz, 1996.

———. "Undermining the Jewish Sense of Future: Alfonso of Valladolid and the New Christian Missionizing." In *Christians, Muslims, and Jews in Medieval and Early Modern Spain*, edited by Mark D. Meyerson and Edward D. English, 179–94. Notre Dame, IN: University of Notre Dame Press, 1999.

Chernick, Michael. "Marie de France in the Synagogue." *Exemplaria* 19 (2007): 183–205.

Cluse, Christoph. "Betrügerische 'Konvertiten' und ihre Erzählungen im Mittelalter." In *Konversion in Räumen jüdischer Geschichte*, edited by Martin Przybilski and Karsten Schapkow, 21–48. Wiesbaden: Harrassowitz, 2014.

———. "Between Martyrdom and Apostasy: Doubt and Self-Definition in Twelfth-Century Ashkenaz." *Journal of Medieval and Early Modern Studies* 29, no. 3 (Fall 1999): 431–71.

———. "'Fabula ineptissima': die Ritualmordlegende um Adam von Bristol nach der Handschrift London, British Library, Harley 957." *Aschkenas* 5 (1995): 293–330.

———. "Jewish Moneylending in Dominican Preaching." In *Dominikaner und Juden: Personen, Konflikte und Perspektiven vom 13. bis zum 20. Jahrhundert/Dominicans and Jews: Personalities, Conflicts, and Perspectives from the 13th to the 20th Century*, edited by Elias H. Füllenbach and Gianfranco Miletto, 195–230. Berlin: Walter de Gruyter, 2015.

———. "The Jews of Ashkenaz: Topographies of Memory." In *Rostros Judíos del Occidente Medieval*, 137–66. XLV Semana Internacional de Estudios Medievales. Navarre: Gobierno de Navarra, 2018.

———, ed. *The Jews of Europe in the Middle Ages (Tenth to Fifteenth Centuries): Proceedings of the International Symposium Held at Speyer, 20–25 October 2002*. Turnhout: Brepols, 2004.

———, ed. *Medieval Ashkenaz: Papers in Honour of Alfred Haverkamp Presented at the 17th World Congress of Jewish Studies, Jerusalem, 2017*. Forschungen zur Geschichte der Juden. Abteilung A: Abhandlungen, Band 31. Wiesbaden: Harrassowitz Verlag, 2021.

———. "Stories of Breaking and Taking the Cross: A Possible Context for the Oxford Incident of 1268." *Revue d'Histoire Ecclésiastique* 90 (1995): 396–442.

Cluse, Christoph, Alfred Haverkamp, and Israel Jacob Yuval, eds. *Jüdische Gemeinden und ihr christlicher Kontext in kuturräumlich vergleichender Betrachtungen*. Hannover: Hahnsche Buchhandlung, 2003.

Cohen, Gerson D. "Esau as Symbol in Early Medieval Thought." In *Jewish Medieval and Renaissance Studies*, edited by Alexander Altmann, 19–48. Cambridge, MA: Harvard University Press, 1967.

———. *Sefer ha-Qabbalah = The Book of Tradition by R. Abraham Ibn Daud*. Philadelphia: Jewish Publication Society, 1967.

———. *Studies in the Variety of Rabbinic Cultures*. Philadelphia: Jewish Publication Society of America, 1991.

Cohen, Jeffrey Jerome. "The Flow of Blood in Medieval Norwich." *Speculum* 79, no. 1 (January 2004): 26–65.

———. *Monster Theory: Reading Culture*. Minneapolis: University of Minnesota Press, 1996.

———. "On Saracen Enjoyment: Some Fantasies of Race in Late Medieval France and England." *Journal of Medieval and Early Modern Studies* 31, no. 1 (2001): 113–46.

———, ed. *The Post-Colonial Middle Ages*. New York: St. Martin's Press, 2000.

———. "Race." In *A Handbook of Middle English Studies*, edited by Marian Turner, 109–22. Chichester, UK: Wiley Blackwell, 2013.

Cohen, Jeremy. "Alterity and Self-Legitimation: The Jew as Other in Classical and Medieval Christianity." In *The Jew as Legitimation: Jewish-Gentile Relations beyond Antisemitism and Philosemitism*, edited by David J. Wertheim, 33–45. London: Palgrave Macmillan, 2017.

———. "Between Martyrdom and Apostasy: Doubt and Self-Definition in Twelfth-Century Ashkenaz." *Journal of Medieval and Early Modern Studies* 29, no. 3 (Fall 1999): 431–71.

———. *Christ Killers: The Jews and the Passion from the Bible to the Big Screen*. Oxford: Oxford University Press, 2007.

———. "Christian Theology and Papal Policy in the Middle Ages." In *The Cambridge Companion to Antisemitism*, edited by Steven T. Katz, 176–93. Cambridge: Cambridge University Press, 2022.

———, ed. *Essential Papers on Judaism and Christianity in Conflict*. New York: NYU Press, 1991.

———. *The Friars and the Jews: The Evolution of Medieval Anti-Judaism*. Ithaca, NY: Cornell University Press, 1982.

———, ed. *From Witness to Witchcraft: Jews and Judaism in Medieval Christian Thought*. Wiesbaden: Harrassowitz, 1996.

———. *A Historian in Exile: Shlomo Ibn Verga, "Shevet Yehudah" and the Jewish-Christian Encounter*. Philadelphia: University of Pennsylvania Press, 2016.

———. "Innocent III, Christian Wet Nurses, and Jews: A Misunderstanding and Its Impact." *Jewish Quarterly Review* 107, no. 1 (Winter 2017): 113–28.

———. "The Jews as the Killers of Christ in the Latin Tradition, from Augustine to the Friars." *Traditio* 39 (1983): 1–27.

———. *Living Letters of the Law: Ideas of the Jew in Medieval Christianity*. Berkeley: University of California Press, 1999.

———. "The Mentality of the Medieval Jewish Apostate: Peter Alfonsi, Hermann of Cologne, and Pablo Christiani." In *Jewish Apostasy in the Modern World*, edited by Todd M. Endelman, 20–47. New York: Holmes and Meier, 1987.

———. "The Muslim Connection, or, On the Changing Role of the Jew in High Medieval Theology." In *From Witness to Witchcraft: Jews and Judaism in Medieval Christian Thought*, edited by Jeremy Cohen, 141–62. Wolfenbütteler Mittelalter-Studien 11. Wiesbaden: Harrassowitz, 1996.

———. "The Nasi of Narbonne: A Problem in Medieval Historiography." *AJS Review* (1977): 45–76.

———. "Profiat Duran's *The Reproach of the Gentiles* and the Development of Jewish Anti-Christian Polemic." In *Shlomo Simonsohn Jubilee Volume: Studies on the History of the Jews in the Middle Ages and Renaissance Period*, edited by Daniel Carpi et al., 71–85. Tel Aviv: Tel Aviv University, Faculty of Humanities, Chaim Rosenberg School of Jewish Studies, 1993.

———. Review of *European Jewry and the First Crusade* by Robert Chazan. *American Historical Review* 93 (1988): 1031–32.

———. "Revisiting Augustine's Doctrine of Jewish Witness: Review Article. *Journal of Religion* 89, no. 4 (October 2009): 564–78.

———. *The Salvation of Israel: Jews in Christian Eschatology from Paul to the Puritans*. Ithaca, NY: Cornell University Press, 2022.

———. *Sanctifying the Name of God: Jewish Martyrs and Jewish Memories of the First Crusade*. Philadelphia: University of Pennsylvania Press, 2004.

———. "'Slay Them Not': Augustine and the Jews in Modern Scholarship." *Medieval Encounters* 4 (1998): 78–92.

———. "Supersessionism, the Epistle to the Romans, Thomas Aquinas, and the Jews of the Eschaton." *Journal of Ecumenical Studies* 53, no. 4 (Fall 2017): 527–53.

———. "*Synagoga conversa*: Honororius Augustodunensis, the Song of Songs, and Christianity's 'Eschatological Jew.'" *Speculum* 79 (2004): 309–40.

———. "A 1096 Complex? Constructing the First Crusade in Jewish Historical Memory, Medieval and Modern." In *Jews and Christians in Twelfth-Century Europe*, edited by Michael A. Signer and John Van Engen, 9–26. Notre Dame, IN: Notre Dame University Press, 2001.

———. "Towards a Functional Classification of Jewish Anti-Christian Polemic in the High Middle Ages." In *Religionsgespräche im Mittelalter*, edited by Bernard Lewis and Friedrich Niewöhner, 93–114. Wolfenbütteler Mittelalter-Studien 4. Wiesbaden: Harrassowitz Verlag, 1992.

———. "'Witnesses of Our Redemption': The Jews in the Crusading Theology of Bernard of Clairvaux." In *Medieval Studies: In Honour of Avrom Saltman*, edited by BatSheva Albert et al., 67–81. Ramat Gan: Bar-Ilan University Press, 1995.

Cohen, Mark R. *Under Crescent and Cross: The Jews in the Middle Ages*. Princeton, NJ: Princeton University Press, 1994. 2nd ed., 2008.

Cohen, Samuel K. "The Black Death and the Burning of Jews." *Past and Present* 196 (August 2007): 3–36.

Cohen, Shaye J. D. "Menstruants and the Sacred in Judaism and Christianity." In *Women's History and Ancient History*, edited by Sarah B. Pomeroy, 273–99. Chapel Hill: University of North Carolina Press, 1991.

———. "'Those Who Say They Are Jews and Are Not': How Do You Know a Jew in Antiquity When You See One?" In *Diasporas in Antiquity*, edited by Shaye J. D. Cohen and Ernest S. Frerichs, 1–45. Providence, RI: Brown Judaic Studies, 1993.

———. "The Ways That Parted: Jews, Christians, and Jewish-Christians ca. 100–159 CE." In *Jews and Christians in the First and Second Centuries: The Interbellum 70-132 CE*, edited by Joshua Schwartz and Peter J. Tomson, 307–39. Leiden: Brill, 2018.

Cohn, Norman. *Europe's Inner Demons: An Enquiry Inspired by the Great Witch-Hunt.* New York: Basic Books, 1975.
———. *The Pursuit of the Millennium.* Fairlawn, NJ: Essential Books, 1957.
———. *Warrant for Genocide: the Myth of the Jewish World Conspiracy and the Protocols of the Elders of Zion.* New York: Harper and Row, 1966.
Colley, Linda. "Britishness and Otherness: An Argument." *Journal of British Studies* 31, no. 4 (October 1992): 309–29.
Constable, Giles. Introduction to *Apologia de Barbis*, by Burchard of Bellevaux. In *Apologiae duae*, edited by R. B. C. Huygens, 47–130. Corpus Christianorum, Continuatio Mediaevalis, 62. Turnhout: Brepols, 1985.
———. "The Orders of Society." In *Three Studies in Medieval Religious and Social Thought: The Interpretation of Mary and Martha, the Ideal of the Imitation of Christ, the Orders of Society*, 249–360. Cambridge: Cambridge University Press, 1995.
———. *The Reformation of the Twelfth Century.* Cambridge: Cambridge University Press, 1998.
———. "Renewal and Reform in Religious Life: Concepts and Realities." In *Renaissance and Renewal in the Twelfth Century*, edited by Robert L. Benson and Giles Constable, 37–67. Cambridge, MA: Harvard University Press, 1982.
Constable, Olivia Remie. *To Live Like a Moor: Christian Perceptions of Muslim Identity in Medieval and Early Modern Spain.* Edited by Robin Vose. Philadelphia: University of Pennsylvania Press, 2018.
———, ed. *Medieval Iberia: Readings from Christian, Muslim, and Jewish Sources.* Philadelphia: University of Pennsylvania Press, 1997. 2nd edition, 2012.
Coope, Jessica A. *The Martyrs of Córdoba: Community and Family Conflict in an Age of Mass Conversion.* Lincoln: University of Nebraska Press, 1995.
Coudert, Allison P. "Sewers, Cesspools and Privies: Waste as Reality and Metaphor in Pre-Modern Europe." In *Urban Space in the Middle Ages and the Early Modern Age*, edited by Albrecht Classen, 713–33. Berlin: Walter de Gruyter, 2009.
Coulet, Noël. "De l'intégration à l'exclusion: La place des juifs dans les cérémonies d'entrée solennelle au Moyen Age." *Annales. Histoire, Sciences Sociales* 34, no. 4 (August 1979): 672–83.
Cowdrey, H.E.J. *The Cluniacs and the Gregorian Reform.* Oxford: Oxford University Press, 1970.
———. "The Peace and the Truce of God in the Eleventh Century." *Past and Present* 46 (February 1970): 42–67.
———. "Unions and Confraternity Cluny." *Journal of Ecclesiastical History* 16 (1956): 152–62.
Cox, Catherine S. *The Judaic Other in Dante, the Gawain Poet, and Chaucer.* Gainesville: University of Florida Press, 2005.
Crasnow, Ellman, and Bente Elsworth, trans. *Into the Light: The Medieval Hebrew Poetry of Meir of Norwich.* Norwich, UK: East Publishing., 2013.
Cronbach, Abraham. "Social Thinking in the *Sefer Hasidim*." *Hebrew Union College Annual* 22 (1949): 1–147.

Cuffel, Alexandra. "Between Epic Entertainment and Polemical Exegesis: Jesus as Antihero in *Toledot Yeshu*." In *Medieval Exegesis and Religious Difference: Commentary, Conflict, and Community in the Premodern Mediterranean*, edited by Ryan Szpiech, 155–70. New York: Fordham University Press, 2015.
———. *Gendering Disgust in Medieval Religious Polemic*. Notre Dame, IN: Notre Dame University Press, 2007.
———. "Ibn Sahula's *Meshal ha-Qadmoni* as a Restorative Polemic." *Journal of Medieval Iberian Studies* 3, no. 2 (2011): 165–86.
Cutler, Allan Harris. "Innocent III and the Distinctive Clothing of Jews and Muslims." *Studies in Medieval Culture* 3 (1970): 92–116.
Cutler, Allan Harris, and Helen Elmquist Cutler. *The Jew as Ally of the Muslim: Medieval Roots of Anti-Semitism*. Notre Dame, IN: Notre Dame University Press, 1986.
Da'at Zeqeinim. Livorno, 1783.
Dahan, Gilbert. "Bernhard de Clairvaux et les Juifs." *Archives Juives* 23 (1987): 59–64.
———. *The Christian Polemic against the Jews in the Middle Ages*. Translated by Jodi Gladding. Notre Dame, IN: University of Notre Dame Press, 1998.
———. *Les intellectuels chrétiens et les juifs au Moyen Age*. Paris: Cerf, 1990.
———. "Les juifs dans les *Miracles* de Gautier de Coincy." *Archives Juives* 16 (1980): 41–49, 59–68.
———. "Saint Anselme, les juifs, le Judaïsme." In *Les mutations socio-culturelles au tournant des XIe–XIIe siècles*, edited by Ramond Doreville, 521–34. Paris: Éditions du Centre national de la recherche scientifique, 1984.
Dahood, Roger. "English Historical Narratives of Jewish Child-Murder, Chaucer's *Prioress's Tale*, and the Date of Chaucer's Unknown Source." *Studies in the Age of Chaucer* 31 (2009): 125–40.
———. "The Punishment of the Jews, Hugh of Lincoln, and the Question of Satire in Chaucer's *Prioress's Tale*." *Viator: Medieval Renaissance Studies* 36 (2005): 456–91.
Daniel, Norman. *Islam and the West: The Making of an Image*. Edinburgh: Edinburgh University Press, 1960.
Darwin, John. *The Empire Project: The Rise and Fall of the British World-System, 1830–1970*. Cambridge: Cambridge University Press, 2011.
Dasberg, Lea. *Untersuchungen über die Entwertung des Judenstatus im 11. Jahrhundert*. Paris: Mouton, 1965.
David, Avraham. "Zikhronot ve-he'arot 'al gezeirot tatnu—bi-defus u-ve-khitvei yad 'ivriyim." In *Yehudim mul ha-Zelav: Gezeirot Tatnu be-Historiah u-ve-Historiographiah*, edited by Yom Tov Assis et al., 193–205. Jerusalem: Magnes, 2000.
Davies, W. D. "Paul: From the Jewish Point of View." In *The Cambridge History of Judaism*. Vol. 3, *The Early Roman Period*, edited by William Horbury, W. D. Davies, and John Sturdy, 678–730. Cambridge: Cambridge University Press, 1999.
Davies, W. D., and E. P. Sanders, "Jesus: From the Jewish Point of View." In *The Cambridge History of Judaism*. Vol. 3, *The Early Roman Period*, edited by William Horbury, W. D. Davies, and John Sturdy, 618–77. Cambridge: Cambridge University Press, 1999.

Davis, Natalie Zemon. "The Rites of Violence." In *Society and Culture in Early Modern France*, 152–87. Stanford, CA: Stanford University Press, 1975.

———. *Society and Culture in Early Modern France*. Stanford, CA: Stanford University Press, 1975.

———. "Women on Top." In *Society and Culture in Early Modern France*, 124–51. Stanford, CA: Stanford University Press, 1975.

Decker, Sara Ifft, ed. *Jewish Women in the Medieval World, 500–1500 CE*. New York: Routledge, 2022.

Decter, Jonathan. *Iberian Jewish Memory: Between Al-Andalus and Christian Europe*. Bloomington: Indiana University Press, 2007.

The Deeds of Philip Augustus: An English Translation of Rigord's Gesta Phillipi Augusti. Translated by Larry F. Field. Edited by M. Cecilia Gaposchkin and Sean L. Field. Ithaca, NY: Cornell University Press, 2022.

Dejoux, Marie. "Gouvernement et pénitence. Les enquêtes de réparation des usures juives de Louis IX (1247–1270)." *Annales. Histoire, Sciences Sociales* 69 (2014): 849–74.

Delaborde, H.-François, ed. *Oeuvres de Rigord et de Guillaume Le Breton: 492–1404, historiens de Philippe-Auguste*. 2 vols. Paris: Librairie Renouard, H. Loones, successeur, 1882–85.

de Lange, Nicolas R. M. *Origen and the Jews: Studies in Jewish-Christian Relations in Third-Century Palestine*. Cambridge: Cambridge University Press, 1976.

Delany, Sheila, ed. *Chaucer and the Jews: Sources, Contexts, Meanings*. New York: Routledge, 2002.

Despres, Denise L. "Adolescence and Sanctity: The Life and Passion of Saint William of Norwich." *Journal of Religion* 90 (2010): 33–62.

———. "Cultic Anti-Judaism and Chaucer's Litel Clergeon." *Modern Philology* 91, no. 4 (May 1994): 413–27.

———. "Immaculate Flesh and the Social Body: Mary and the Jew." *Jewish History* 12, no. 1 (Spring 1998): 47–69.

———. "Mary and the Eucharist: Cultic Anti-Judaism in Some Fourteenth-Century English Devotional Manuscripts." In *From Witness to Witchcraft: Jews and Judaism in Medieval Christian Thought*, edited by Jeremy Cohen, 375–401. Wiesbaden: Otto Harrassowitz, 1996.

———. "The Protean Jew in the Vernon Manuscript." In *Chaucer and the Jews: Sources, Contexts, Meanings*, edited by Sheila Delany, 145–64. New York: Routledge, 2002.

Dessen, Alan. "The Elizabethan Stage Jew and the Christian Example: Gerontus, Barabas, and Shylock." *Modern Language Quarterly* 35 (1974): 231–45.

Deutsch, Yaacov. "'Eiduyot 'al Nusah Qadum shel 'Toledot Yeshu.'" *Tarbiz* 69, no. 2 (2000): 177–97.

———. "Jewish Anti-Christian Invectives and Christian Awareness: An Unstudied Form of Interaction in the Early Modern Period." *Leo Baeck Institute Year Book* 55 (2010): 41–61.

———. *Judaism in Christian Eyes: Ethnographic Descriptions of Jews and Judaism in Early Modern Europe*. Translated by Avi Aronsky. Oxford: Oxford University Press, 2012.

———. "Toledot Yeshu be-'Einayim Nozriyot: Tefuzato shel ha-Hibbur ve-ha-Teguvot eilav bimei ha-Beinayim u-ve-Reishit ha-'Eit ha-Hadashah." Master's thesis, Hebrew University of Jerusalem, 1997.

Devlin, Sister Mary Aquinas, ed. *The Sermons of Thomas Brinton, Bishop of Rochester (1373–1389)*. 2 vols. London: Royal Historical Society, 1954.

de Weever, Jacqueline. *Sheba's Daughters: Whitening and Demonizing the Saracen Woman in Medieval French Epic*. New York: Garland, 1998.

Diemling, Maria. "Navigating Christian Space: Jews and Christian Images in Early Modern German Lands." *Jewish Culture and History* 12, no. 3 (November 2010): 397–410.

Diemling, Maria, and Giuseppe Veltri, eds. *The Jewish Body: Corporeality, Society, and Identity in the Renaissance and Early Modern Period*. Leiden: Brill, 2009.

Diestelkamp, Bernhard. "Der Vorwurf des Ritualmordes gegen Juden vor dem Hofgericht Kaiser Friedrichs II. im Jahr 1236." In *Religiöse Divianz*, edited by Dieter Simon, 19–39. Frankfurt am Main: Vittorio Klostermann, 1990.

Di Segni, Ricardo. *Il Vangelo del Ghetto*. Rome: Newton and Compton, 1985.

Dobson, R[ichard] B[arrie]. *The Jews of Medieval York and the Massacre of March 1190*. Borthwick Papers, 45. York: St. Anthony's Press, 1974.

———. "Medieval York Jewry Reconsidered." *Jewish Culture and History* 3, no. 2 (June 2000): 7–20.

Doerfler, Maria. "Ambrose's Jews: The Creation of Judaism and Heterodox Christianity in Ambrose of Milan's *Expositio evangelii secundum Lucam*." *Church History* 80, no. 4 (December 2011): 749–72.

Dorger, Cecelia M. "Studies in the Image of the Madonna Lactans in Late Medieval and Renaissance Italy." PhD diss., University of Louisville, 2012.

Dorin, Rowin William. "Banishing Usury: The Expulsion of Foreign Moneylenders in Medieval Europe, 1200–1450." PhD diss., Harvard Universiy, 2015.

———. *No Return*. Princeton, NJ: Princeton University Press, 2023.

———. "'Once the Jews Have Been Expelled': Intent and Interpretation in Late Medieval Canon Law." *Law and History Review* 34, no. 2 (May 2016): 335–62.

Douglas, Mary. *Purity and Danger: An Analysis of Concepts of Pollution and Taboo*. New York: Praeger, 1966.

Drews, Wolfram. "Jews as Pagans? Polemical Definition of Identity in Visigothic Spain." *Early Medieval Europe* 11, no. 3 (2002): 189–207.

———. *The Unknown Neighbor: The Jew in the Thought of Isidore of Seville*. Leiden: Brill, 2006.

Duby, Georges. *The Knight, the Lady and the Priest*. Translated by Barbara Bray. New York: Pantheon, 1983.

———. *The Three Orders: Feudal Society Imagined*. Translated by Arthur Goldhammer. Chicago: University of Chicago Press, 1980.

Dundes, Alan, ed. *The Blood Libel Legend: A Casebook in Anti-Semitic Folklore*. Madison: University of Wisconsin Press, 1991.

Dunn, James D. G. *Jews and Christians: The Parting of the Ways AD 70–135*. Tübingen: Mohr-Siebeck, 1992.

Dunn, Maryjane, and Linda Kay Davidson, eds. *Pilgrimage to Compostela in the Middle Ages*. New York: Garland Publishing, 1996.

Edbury, Peter W. *Crusade and Settlement: Papers Read at the First Conference of the Society for the Study of the Crusades and the Latin East and Presented to R. C. Smail*. Cardiff: Cardiff University Press, 1983.

Edwards, John. "The Beginnings of a Scientific Theory of Race? Spain, 1450–1600." In *From Iberia to Diaspora: Studies in Sephardic History and Culture*, edited by Yedida K. Stillman and Norman A. Stillman, 179–96. Leiden: Brill, 1999.

———. "The Church and the Jews in English Medieval Towns." In *The Church in the Medieval Town*, edited by T. R. Slater and Gervase Rosser, 43–54. Aldershot, UK: Ashgate, 1998.

———. *The Jews in Christian Europe, 1400–1700*. London: Routledge, 1991.

Efroymson, D. P. "The Patristic Connection." In *Anti-Semitism and the Foundations of Christianity*, edited by A. T. Davis, 98–117. Mahwah, NJ: Paulist Press, 1979.

Ehrlich, Uri. *The Nonverbal Language of Prayer: A New Approach of [sic] Jewish Liturgy*. Tübingen: Mohr Siebeck, 2004.

Ehrlich, Uri, and Ruth Langer. "The Earliest Texts of Birkat Haminim." *Hebrew Union College Annual* 76 (2005): 63–112.

Ehrman, Albert. "The Origins of the Ritual Murder Accusation and Blood Libel." *Tradition: A Journal of Orthodox Jewish Thought* 15: 4 (Spring 1976): 83–90.

Eidelberg, Shlomo, ed. and trans. *The Jews and the Crusaders: The Hebrew Chronicles of the First and Second Crusades*. Madison: University of Wisconsin Press, 1977.

———. "'Maarufia' in Rabbenu Gershom's Responsa." *Historia Judaica* 15 (1953): 59–66.

———. *Teshuvot Rabbeinu Gershom Meor Ha-Golah*. New York: Yeshiva University Press, 1956.

Eilberg-Schwartz, Howard. *People of the Body*. Albany: SUNY Press, 1992.

Einbinder, Susan L. *After the Black Death: Plague and Commemoration among Iberian Jews*. Philadelphia: University of Pennsylvania Press, 2018.

———. *Beautiful Death: Jewish Poetry and Martyrdom in Medieval France*. Princeton, NJ: Princeton University Press, 2002.

———. "Meir b. Elijah of Norwich: Persecution and Poetry among Medieval English Jews." *Journal of Medieval History* 26, no. 2 (2000): 145–62.

———. *No Place of Rest: Jewish Literature, Expulsion, and the Memory of Medieval France*. Philadelphia: University of Pennsylvania Press, 2009.

———. "Pucellina of Blois: Romantic Myths and Narrative Conventions." *Jewish History* 12 (1998): 29–46.

———. Review of *Two Nations in Your Womb: Perceptions of Jews and Christians in Late Antiquity and the Middle Ages* by Israel Jacob Yuval. *Speculum* 82, no. 3 (2007): 780–81.

———. "Signs of Romance: Hebrew Prose and the Twelfth-Century Renaissance." In *Jews and Christians in Twelfth-Century Europe*, edited by Michael Signer and Jon Van Engen, 221–33. Notre Dame, IN: Notre Dame University Press, 2000.

———. "'Your Words Are the Truth': Rabbi Qalonymous and the Archbishop Ruthard of Mainz." *Speculum* 93, no. 1 (January 2018): 91–100.

Eisenberg, Saadia R. "Reading Medieval Religious Disputation: The 1240 'Debate' between Rabbi Yehiel of Paris and Friar Nicholas Donin." PhD diss., University of Michigan, 2008.

Elazar, Daniel. *Kinship and Consent: Jewish Political Tradition and Its Contemporary Uses.* 2nd ed. London: Routledge, 1997. First published 1983.

Elbaum, Yaakov. "'Al Shenei Tiqqunei-Nusah bi-Tefillat 'Aleinu.'" *Tarbiz* 42, no. 1-2 (1973): 204-8.

Elbogan, Ismar. *Jewish Liturgy: A Comprehensive History.* Translated by Raymond P. Scheindlin. Philadelphia: Jewish Publication Society of America, 1993.

Eliav-Feldman, Miriam, Benjamin Isaac, and Joseph Ziegler, eds. *The Origins of Racism in the West.* Cambridge: Cambridge University Press, 2009.

Elliot, Dyan. *Fallen Bodies: Pollution, Sexuality and Demonology in the Middle Ages.* Philadelphia: University of Pennsylvania Press, 1999.

Elman, Yaakov. "Meiri and the Non-Jew: A Comparative Investigation." In *New Perspectives on Jewish-Christian Relations in Honor of David Berger*, edited by Elisheva Carlebach and Jacob J. Schacter, 265-96. Leiden: Brill, 2012.

Elukin, Jonathan M. "The Discovery of the Self: Jews and Conversion in the Twelfth Century." In *Jews and Christians in Twelfth-Century Europe*, edited by Michael A. Signer and Jon Van Engen, 63-76. Notre Dame, IN: University of Notre Dame Press, 2001.

———. "The Eternal Jew in Medieval Europe." PhD diss., Princeton University, 1993.

———. "From Jew to Christian? Conversion and Perceptions of Immutability in Medieval Europe." In *Varieties of Religious Conversion in the Middle Ages*, edited by James Muldoon, 171-90. Gainesville: University Press of Florida, 1997.

———. *Living Together, Living Apart: Rethinking Jewish-Christian Relations in the Middle Ages.* Princeton, NJ: Princeton University Press, 2007.

Elyada, Aya. *A Goy Who Speaks Yiddish: Christians and Jewish Language in Early Modern Germany.* Stanford, CA: Stanford University Press, 2012.

Emerton, Ephraim, ed. *The Correspondence of Pope Gregory VII.* New York: Columbia University Press, 1932.

Emery, Richard. *The Jews of Perpignan in the Thirteenth Century: An Economic Study Based on Notarial Records.* New York: Columbia University Press, 1959.

Endelman, Todd. *Leaving the Jewish Fold: Conversion and Radical Assimilation in Modern Jewish History.* Princeton, NJ: Princeton University Press, 2015.

Engel, David. "Away from a Definition of Antisemitism: An Essay in the Semantics of Historical Description." In *Rethinking European Jewish History*, edited by Jeremy Cohen and Moshe Rosman, 30-53. Oxford: Littman Library of Jewish Civilization, 2009.

———. "Gilgul ha-Musag 'Antisheimiyut' ve-ha-Shimush Bo ke-Qateigoriah Kolelet." *Zion* 85, no. 1-4 (2020): 29-55.

Eph'al, I. "Ishmael and 'Arab(s)': A Transformation of Ethnological Terms." *Journal of Near Eastern Studies* 35 (1976): 225-31.

Ephraim, Michelle. *Reading Jewish Women on the Elizabethan Stage.* New York: Routledge, 2008.

Epistolae Vagantes of Pope Gregory VII. Edited by H.E.J. Cowdrey. Oxford: Clarendon Press, 1972.

Epstein, Marc Michael. *Dreams of Subversion in Medieval Jewish Art and Literature.* University Park: Penn State University Press, 1997.

———. "Representations of the Jewish Image: Three New Contributions." *AJS Review* 26 (2002): 327–40.

Erb, Rainer, ed. *Die Legende vom Ritualmord: Zur Geschichte der Blutbeschuldigung gegen Juden, Dokumente, Texte, Materialen 6.* Berlin: Metropol, 1993.

———. "Die Ritualmordlegende von den Anfängen bis ins 20. Jahrhundert." In *Ritual Murder Legend in European History,* edited by Susanna Buttaroni and Stanisław Musiał, 10–20. Kraków: Association for Cultural Initiatives, 2003.

Erdmann, Carl. *Origin of the Idea of Crusade.* Translated from the 1935 German edition by Marshall W. Baldwin and Walter Goffart. Princeton, NJ: Princeton University Press, 1977.

Erikson, Kai T. *The Wayward Puritans: A Study in Social Deviance.* New York: Wiley, 1966.

Eshed, Avital Davidovich, and Moshe Halbertal. "Bein Iyyum le-Iyyun: Hitmodedut im Miniyut ha-Goy be-Ashkenaz bi-mei ha-Beinayim." *Zion* 83, no. 3 (2023): 331–70.

Evans, Suzanne. "Scent of a Martyr." *Numen* 49, no. 2 (2002) 193–211.

Fabre-Vassas, Claudine. *The Singular Beast: Jews, Christians, and the Pig.* Translated by Carol Folk. New York: Columbia University Press, 1997.

Fagles, Robert, trans. *Homer, The Iliad.* Introduction and notes by Bernard Knox. New York: Penguin Books, 1990.

Favret-Saada, Jeanne. "A Fuzzy Distinction: Anti-Judaism and Anti-Semitism (An Excerpt from *Le Judaisme et ses Juifs*)." *HAU: Journal of Ethnographic Theory* 4, no. 3 (Winter 2014). https://doi.org/10.14318/hau4.3.021.

Felsenstein, Frank. *Anti-Semitic Stereotypes.* Baltimore: Johns Hopkins University Press, 1996.

Ferster, Judith. "'Your Praise Is Performed by Men and Children': Language and Gender in the Prioress's Prologue and Tale." *Exemplaria* 2 (1990): 150–68.

Feuchtwanger-Sarig, Naomi. "The Coronation of the Virgin and of the Bride." *Jewish Art* 12–13 (1986–87): 213–24.

Fichtenau, Heinrich. *Living in the Tenth Century: Mentalities and Social Orders.* Translated by Patrick Geary. Chicago: University of Chicago Press, 1991.

Fidora, Alexander, Harvey J. Hames, and Yossef Schwartz, eds. *Latin-into-Hebrew.* Vol. 2, *Texts.* Leiden: Brill, 2013.

Fildes, Valerie. *Wet Nursing: A History from Antiquity to the Present.* Oxford: Basil Blackwell, 1988.

Fine, Steven. "How Do You Know a Jew When You See One? Reflections on Jewish Costume in the Roman World." In *Fashioning Jews: Clothing, Culture, and Commerce,* edited by Leonard J. Greenspoon, 19–28. Studies in Jewish Civilization 24. West Lafayette, IN: Purdue Univerity Press, 2013.

———. *Jews, Christians and Polytheists in the Ancient Synagogue: Cultural Interaction during the Greco-Roman Period.* London: Routledge, 1999.

Finkielkraut, Alain. *The Imaginary Jew*. Translated by Kevin O'Neill and David Suchoff. Lincoln: University of Nebraska Press, 1994.

Finucane, R. C. *Miracles and Pilgrims: Popular Beliefs in Medieval England*. London: J. M. Dent and Sons Ltd., 1997.

Firestone, Reuven. "The Medieval Islamic World and the Jews." In *The Cambridge Companion to Antisemitism*, edited by Steven T. Katz, 137–57. Cambridge: Cambridge University Press, 2022.

Fisher, Eugene J. "The Influence of Jewish Liturgical Spirituality on Christian Traditions: Some Observations." In *Spirituality and Prayer: Jewish and Christian Understandings*, edited by Leon Klenicki and Gabe Huck, 139–47. New York: Paulist Press, 1983.

Fishman, Talya. "The Penitential System of Hasidei Ashkenaz and the Problem of Cultural Boundaries." *Journal of Jewish Thought and Philosophy* 8 (1999): 201–29.

Flint, Valerie. "The Saint and the Operation of the Law: Reflexions upon the Miracles of St. Thomas of Cantilupe." In *Belief and Culture in the Middle Ages: Studies Presented to Henry Mayr-Harting*, edited by Richard Gameson and Henrietta Leyser, 342–57. Oxford: Oxford University Press, 2001.

Flori, Jean. *La première croisade: l'occident chrétien contre l'Islam*. Historique 107. Brussels: Complex, 1997.

Fogle, Lauren. "The Domus Conversorum: The Personal Interest of Henry III." *Jewish Historical Studies* 41 (2007): 1–7.

———. "Jewish Converts to Christianity in Medieval London." PhD diss., University of London, 2005.

———. *The King's Converts: Jewish Conversion in Medieval London*. Blanham, UK: Lexington Books, 2019.

Folner, Margaretha. "On Marrying and Divorcing a Demon: Marriage and Divorce Themes in the Jewish, Christian and Pagan World." In *Religious Stories in Transformation: Conflict, Revision, and Reception*, edited by Alberdina Houtman et al., 275–99. Leiden: Brill, 2016.

Fonrobert, Charlotte Elisheva, and Vered Shemtov. "Jewish Conceptions and Practices of Space." *Jewish Social Studies* 11, no. 3 (2005): 1–8.

Fontaine, Resianne, and Gad Freudenthal, eds. *Latin-into-Hebrew: Texts and Studies*. Vol. 1, *Studies*. Leiden: Brill, 2013.

Fossier, Robert. *The Axe and the Oath: Ordinary Life in the Middle Ages*. Translated by Lydia G. Cochrane. Princeton, NJ: Princeton University Press, 2010.

Fox, Robin Lane. *Pagans and Christians*. San Francisco: HarperCollins, 1988.

Fox, Yaniv, and Yosi Yisraeli, eds. *Contesting Inter-Religious Conversion in the Medieval World*. New York: Routledge, 2017.

Fradenberg, Louise O. "Criticism, Antisemitism, and the Prioress's Tale." *Exemplaria* 1 (1989): 69–115.

Fraenkel, Avraham, Abraham Gross, and Peter Lehnhardt, eds. *Hebräische liturgische Poesie zu den Judenverfolgungen während des Ersten Kreuzzugs*. Monumenta Germaniae Historica–Hebräische Texte aus dem mittelalterlichen Deutschland 3. Weisbaden: Harrassowitz, 2016.

Frahm, Eckart. *Assyria: The Rise and Fall of the World's First Empire*. New York: Basic Books, 2023.

Frakes, Jerold C., trans. *Early Yiddish Epic*. Syracuse, NY: Syracuse University Press, 2014.

———. *The Emergence of Early Yiddish Literature: Cultural Translation in Ashkenaz*. Bloomington: Indiana University Press, 2017.

Fram, Edward. "Perception and Reception of Repentant Apostates in Medieval Ashkenaz and Premodern Poland." *AJS Review* 21, no. 2 (November 1996): 299–339.

Frank, Robert Worth. "The Miracles of the Virgin, Medieval Anti-Semitism and the Prioress's Tale." In *The Wisdom of Poetry: Essays in Early English Literature in Honor of Morton W. Bloomfield*, edited by Larry D. Benson and Siegfried Wenzel, 177–88. Kalamazoo: Medieval Institute Publications, Western Michigan University, 1982.

Franke, D. P. "The Crusades and Medieval Anti-Judaism: Cause or Consequence?" In *Seven Myths of the Crusades*, edited by Alfred Andrea and Andrew Holt, 48–69. Cambridge, MA: Harvard University Press, 2015.

Frankel, Jonathan. *The Damascus Affair: "Ritual Murder," Politics, and the Jews in 1840*. Cambridge: Cambridge University Press, 1997.

Franklin, Arnold E. "Cultivating Roots: The Promotion of Exilarchal Ties to David in the Middle Ages." *AJS Review* 29, no. 1 (April, 2005): 91–110.

———. *This Noble House: Jewish Descendants of King David in the Medieval Islamic East*. Philadelphia: University of Pennsylvania Press, 2013.

František, Graus. *Pest-Geissler-Judenmord. Das 14. Jahrhundert als Krisenzeit*. Veroffentlichungen des Max-Planck-Instituts fur Geschichte 86. Gottingen: Vandenhoeck und Ruprecht, 1987.

Frassetto, Michael, ed. *Christian Attitudes toward the Jews in the Middle Ages: A Casebook*. New York: Routledge, 2007.

———. "Heretics and Jews in the Writings of Adémar of Chabannes and the Origins of Medieval Anti-Semitism." *Church History* 71 (2002): 1–15.

Frederickson, George. *Racism: A Short History*. Princeton, NJ: Princeton University Press, 2002.

Fredriksen, Paula. *Augustine and the Jews: A Christian Defense of Jews and Judaism*. New York: Doubleday, 2008.

Fredriksen, Paula, and Oded Irshai. "Christian Anti-Judaism: Polemics and Policies." In *The Cambridge History of Judaism IV: The Late Roman-Rabbinic Period*, edited by Steven T. Katz, 977–1034. Cambridge: Cambridge University Press, 2006.

———. "Include Me Out: Tertullian, the Rabbis, and the Graeco-Roman City." In *Identité à travers l'éthique*, edited by K. Berthelot, R. Naiweld, and D. Stoeki ben Ezra, 117–32. Turnhout: Brepols, 2015.

Freedman, Charles. *Holy Bones, Holy Dust: How Relics Shaped the History of Medieval Europe*. New Haven, CT: Yale University Press, 2011.

Freedman, Paul. *Images of the Medieval Peasant*. Stanford, CA: Stanford University Press, 1999.

———. "The Medieval 'Other': The Middle Ages as 'Other.'" In *Marvels, Monsters, and Miracles: Studies in the Medieval and the Early Modern Imagination*, edited by

Timothy S. Jones and David A. Sprunger, 1–24. Kalamazoo: Medieval Institute Publications, Western Michigan University, 1999.

———. "The Representation of Medieval Peasants as Bestial and as Human." In *The Human/Animal Boundary: Historical Perspectives*, edited by Angela N. H. Creager and William C. Jordan, 29–49. Rochester, NY: University of Rochester Press, 2002.

Freedman, Paul, and Gabrielle Spiegel. "Medievalisms Old and New: The Rediscovery of Alterity in North American Medieval Studies." *American Historical Review* 103, no. 3 (March–June 1998): 677–704.

Frend, W.H.C. *Martyrdom and Persecution in the Early Church: A Study of Conflict from the Maccabees to Donatus*. New York: NYU Press, 1967.

Freud, Sigmund. *Civilization and Its Discontents*. Translated and edited by James Strachey. New York: W. W. Norton, 1961.

Freudenthal, Gad, ed. *Science in Medieval Jewish Cultures*. Cambridge: Cambridge University Press, 2012.

Frey, P. *Corpus Inscriptionum Judaecarum*. Vol. 1. Rome, 1936.

Fried, Johannes. *The Middle Ages*. Translated by Peter Lewis. Cambridge, MA: Harvard University Press, 2015.

Friedlander, Saul. *Nazi Germany and the Jews: The Years of Persecution, 1933–1939*. New York: HarperCollins, 1997.

———. *The Years of Extermination: Nazi Germany and the Jews, 1939–1945*. New York: HarperCollins, 2007.

Friedman, Albert B. "The 'Prioress's Tale' and Chaucer's Anti-Semitism." *Chaucer Review* 9, no. 2 (1974): 118–29.

Friedman, Jerome. "Jewish Conversion, the Spanish Pure Blood Laws and Reformation: A Revisionist View of Racial and Religious Antisemitism." *Sixteenth Century Journal* 18, no. 1 (1987): 3–30.

———. "The Reformation in Alien Eyes: Jewish Perceptions of Christian Troubles." *Sixteenth Century Journal* 14, no. 1 (1983): 23–40.

Friedman, John, Jean Connell Hoff, and Robert Chazan, eds. *The Trial of the Talmud: Paris, 1240*. Toronto: Pontifical Institute of Mediaeval Studies, 2012.

Friedman, John Block. *Monstrous Races in Medieval Art and Thought*. Cambridge, MA: Harvard University Press, 1981.

Friedman, Lee M. *Robert Grosseteste and the Jews*. Cambridge, MA: Harvard University Press, 1934.

Friedman, Yvonne. "An Anatomy of Anti-Semitism: Peter the Venerable's Letter to Louis VII, King of France (1146)." In *Bar-Ilan Studies in History* 1, edited by Pinhas Artzi, 87–102. Ramat Gan: Bar-Ilan University Press, 1978.

———. "Masculine Attributes of the Other: The Shared Knightly Model." In *Crusading and Masculinities*, edited by Natasha R. Hodgson, Katherine J. Lewis, and Matthew M. Mesley, 89–99. New York: Routledge, 2020.

———. "Peter the Venerable: A Humanist of the Twelfth Century or an Anti-Semite?" *Proceedings of the Seventh World Congress of Jewish Studies*, 1–8. Jerusalem, 1981.

Friess, Steve. "When 'Holocaust' Became 'The Holocaust': An Etymological Mystery." *New Republic*, May 18, 2015.

Frizzell, Lawrence, and J. Frank Henderson. "Jews and Judaism in the Medieval Latin Liturgy." In *The Liturgy of the Medieval Church*, edited by Thomas J. Hefferson and E. Ann Matter, 187–214. Kalamazoo: Consortium for the Teaching of the Middle Ages, Medieval Institute Publications, Western Michigan University, 2001.

Frojmovic, Eva, ed. *Imagining the Self, Imagining the Other: Visual Representations and Jewish-Christian Dynamics in the Middle Ages and Early Modern Period.* Leiden: Brill, 2002.

Frojmovic, Eva, and Michael Marc Epstein. "No Graven Image: Permitted Depictions, Forbidden Depictions, and Creative Solutions." In *Skies of Parchment, Seas of Ink: Jewish Illuminated Manuscripts*, edited by Michael Marc Epstein, 89–104. Princeton, NJ: Princeton University Press, 2015.

Fulbert of Chartres. *Tractatus contra Judaeos*. Migne PL 141. Paris: J. P. Migne, 1853.

Funkenstein, Amos. "Anti-Jewish Propaganda: Pagan, Christian and Modern." *Jerusalem Quarterly* 19 (1981): 56–72.

———. "Basic Types of Christian Anti-Jewish Polemics in the Later Middle Ages." *Viator* 2 (1971): 373–82.

———. "Ha-Temurot be-Vikuah ha-Dat she-Bein Yehudim la-Nozrim ba-Meah ha-12." *Zion* 33, no. 3–4: (1968): 125–44.

———. *Perceptions of Jewish History*. Berkeley: University of California Press, 1993.

Furst, Rachel. "Captivity, Conversion, and Community Identity: Sexual Angst and Religious Crisis in Frankfurt, 1241." *Jewish History* 22 (2008): 179–221.

———. "A Return to Credibility? The Rehabilitation of Repentant Apostates in Medieval Ashkenaz." In *On the Word of a Jew: Religion, Reliability and the Dynamics of Trust*, edited by Nina Caputo and Mitchell Hart, 201–21. Bloomington: Indiana University Press, 2019.

Gabbard, Glen O. "On Hate in Love Relationships: The Narcissism of Minor Differences Revisited." *Psychoanalytic Quarterly* 62, no. 2 (April 1993): 229–38.

Gabriele, Matthew. "Against the Enemies of Christ: The Role of Count Emicho in the Anti-Jewish Violence of the First Crusade. In *Christian Attitudes toward the Jews in the Middle Ages: A Casebook*, edited by Michael Frassetto, 61–82. New York: Routledge, 2007.

Gabrieli, Francesco, ed. *Arab Historians of the Crusades*. Translated by E. J. Costello. Berkeley: University of California Press, 1969.

Gafni, Isaiah M. "How Babylonia Became 'Zion': Shifting Identities in Late Antiquity." In *Jewish Identities in Antiquity: Studies in Memory of Menahem Stern*, edited by Lee I. Levine and Daniel R. Schwartz, 333–48. Tübingen: Mohr Siebeck, 2009.

Gager, John. *The Origins of Antisemitism: Attitudes toward Judaism in Pagan and Christian Antiquity*. Oxford: Oxford University Press, 1985.

———. *Reinventing Paul*. Oxford: Oxford University Press, 2000.

Galinsky, Judah. "Gishot Shonot le-Tofa'at Moftei ha-Qedoshim ha-Nozriim ba-Sifrut ha-Rabbanit Bimei ha-Beinayim." In *Ta-Shema: Mehqarim Be-Mada'ei ha-Yahadut Le-Zikhro shel Yisrael M. Ta-Shema*, edited by Avraham (Rami) Reiner et al., 195–219. Alon Shevut: Tevunot Mikhlelet Herzog, 2011.

———. "The Significance of Form: R. Moses of Coucy's Reading Audience and His *Sefer ha-Mizvot*." *AJS Review* 35, no. 2 (November 2011): 293–321.

Gaster, Moses, ed. *Ma'aseh Book*. 1934. Reprinted, Philadelphia: Jewish Publication Society of America, 1981.

Gaston, Lloyd. *Paul and the Torah*. Vancouver: University of British Columbia Press, 1987.

Gaunt, Simon. *Retelling the Tale: An Introduction to French Medieval Literature*. London: Duckworth, 2001.

Gay, Peter. *The Party of Humanity: Essays on the French Enlightenment*. New York: Knopf, 1964.

Gayk, Shannon. "'To Wondre upon This Thyng': Chaucer's *Prioress's Tale*." *Exemplaria* 22, no. 2 (2010): 138–56.

Gaynor, Stephanie. "He Says, She Says: Subjectivity and the Discourse of the Other in the *Prioress's Portrait* and *Tale*." *Medieval Encounters* 5, no. 3 (1999): 375–90.

G. Cambrensis. *Itinerarium Cambrie*. In *Giraldi Cambrensis Opera*, edited by J. F. Dimock, vol. 2, chap. xiii. London, 1868.

Geanakoplos, Deno. *Medieval Western Civilization and the Byzantine and Islamic Worlds: Interaction of Three Cultures*. Lexington, MA: D. C. Heath, 1979.

Geary, Patrick. "Ethnic Identity as a Situational Construct in the Early Middle Ages." *Mitteilungen der anthropologischen Gesellschaft in Wien* 113 (1983): 15–26.

Gerber, Jane S. *Jews of Spain: A History of the Sephardic Experience*. New York: Free Press, 1992.

Gerhardt, Dietrich. *Süsskind von Trimberg. Berichtigungen zu einer Erinnerung*. Lang, Bern: Lang, 1997.

Gershenzon, Shoshanna, and Jane Litman. "The Bloody 'Hands of Compassionate Women': Portrayals of Heroic Women in the Hebrew Crusade Chronicles." In *Crisis and Reaction: The Hero in Jewish History*, edited by Menahem Mor, 73–91. Omaha: Creighton University Press, 1995.

Gervase of Canterbury. *Opera Historica*. Edited by William Stubbs. London: Longman, 1879.

Gil, Moshe. "The Exilarchate." In *The Jews of Medieval Islam: Community, Society, and Identity*, edited by Daniel Frank, 33–66. Leiden: Brill, 1995.

———. "The Radhanite Merchants and the Land of Radhan." *Journal of the Social and Economic History of the Orient* 17, no. 3 (September 1974): 299–328.

Gilbert Crispin. *Disputatio Iudei et Christiani*. Edited by Bernhard Blumenkranz. Utrecht, 1956.

———. "Disputatio Judei et Christiani." In *The Works of Gilbert Crispin, Abbot of Westminster*, edited by Anna Sapir Abulafia and G. R. Evans. London: British Academy by Oxford University Press, 1986.

———. *The Works of Gilbert Crispin* (Auctores Britannici Medii Aevi). Edited by Anna Sapir Abulafia and G. R. Evans. Oxford: Oxford University Press, 1986.

Gilchrist, John. "The Erdmann Thesis and the Canon Law, 1083–1141." In *Crusade and Settlement*, edited by Peter W. Edbury, 37–45. Cardiff: Cardiff University Press, 1985.

Gilman, Sander. "The Jewish Nose." In *The Jew's Body*, 169–94. New York: Routledge, 1991.
———. *The Jew's Body*. New York: Routledge, 1991.
———. "Salome, Syphilis, Sarah Bernhardt, and the Modern Jewess." In *The Jew in the Text: Modernity and the Construction of Identity*, edited by Linda Nochlin and Tamar Garb, 97–120. London: Thames and Hudson, 1995.
Gilman, Sander, and Steven T. Katz, eds. *Anti-Semitism in Times of Crisis*. New York: NYU Press, 1991.
Ginio, Alisa Meyuhas. "Geirush ha-Yehudim mi-Mamlekhet Zarefat ba-Me'ah ha-14 ve-Liqho be-'Einei Alonso (Alfonso) de Espina Ba'al ha-Hibbur 'Mezudat ha-Emunah.'" *Michael* 12 (1991): 67–82.
———. "Self-Perception and Images of the Judeoconversos in Fifteenth-Century Spain and Portugal." *Tel Aviver Jahrbuch für deutsche Geschichte* 22 (1993): 127–52.
Ginzberg, Louis, ed. *Ginzei Schechter*. 3 vols. New York: Jewish Theological Seminary, 1928–29.
Ginzburg, Carlo. *The Cheese and the Worms*. Translated by John Tedeschi and Anne Tedeschi. Baltimore: Johns Hopkins University Press, 1992.
———. *Ecstasies: Deciphering the Witches' Sabbath*. Translated by Raymond Rosenthal. Edited by Gregory Elliot. London: Hutchinson Radius, 1998.
Glassman, Bernard. *Antisemitic Stereotypes without Jews: Images of the Jew in England, 1290–1700*. Detroit: Wayne State University Press, 1975.
Goetz, Hans-Werner. *Leben im Mittelalter vom 7. Bis zum 13. Jahrhundert*. 1986. Reprinted, Munich: C. H. Beck, 2002. English, *Life in the Middle Ages: From the Seventh to the Thirteenth Century*. Translated by Albert Wimmer. Edited by Steve Rowan. Notre Dame, IN: University of Notre Dame Press, 1993.
Goitein, Shlomo Dov. *A Mediterranean Society: The Jewish Communities of the Arab World as Portrayed in the Documents of the Cairo Geniza*. 6 vols. Berkeley: University of California Press, 1967–93.
———. "Obadiah, a Norman Proselyte." *Journal of Jewish Studies* 4 (1953): 74–84.
Golb, Norman. "The Autograph Memoirs of Obadiah the Proselyte of Oppido Lucano, and the Epistle of Barukh B. Isaac of Aleppo." Paper prepared for the Convegno internazionale di Studi Giovanni—Obadiah da Oppido: proselito, viaggiatore e musicista dell'età normanna, Oppido Lucano (Basilicata), March 28–30, 2004.
———. "The Rabbinic Master Jacob Tam and Events of the Second Crusade at Reims." *Crusades* 9 (2010): 63–67.
Gold, Leonard Singer, ed. *A Sign and a Witness: 2000 Years of Hebrew Books and Illuminated Manuscripts*. Oxford: Oxford University Press, 1988.
Goldenberg, Robert. *The Nations That Know Thee Not: Ancient Jewish Attitudes toward Other Religions*. Sheffield: Sheffield Academic Press, 1997.
Goldin, Simha. *Apostasy and Jewish Identity in High Middle Ages Northern Europe: "Are You Still My Brother?"* Manchester: Manchester University Press, 2014.
———. *Jewish Women in Europe in the Middle Ages: A Quiet Revolution*. Manchester: Manchester University Press, 2011.

———. "'Pen Yavo'u ha-'Areilim Halalu ve-Yitpesum Hayyim va-yehi Mequyamim be-Ta'atutam." In *Eros, Erusin, ve-Isurim*, edited by Israel Bartal and Isaiah Gafni, 97–100, 117–18. Jerusalem: Merkaz Zalman Shazar, 1998.

———. "The Role of Ceremonies in the Socialization Process: The Case of Jewish Communities in Northern France and Germany in the Middle Ages." *Archives de Sciences Sociales des Religions* 95 (1996): 163–78.

———. "The Socialization for Kiddush ha-Shem among Medieval Jews." *Journal of Medieval History* 23, no. 2 (1997): 117–38.

———. *The Ways of Jewish Martyrdom*. Translated by Yigal Levin. Edited by C. Michael Copeland. Turnhout: Brepols, 2008.

———. *Yihud ve-ha-Yahad*. Tel Aviv: Ha-Kibbutz Hameyuhad, 1997.

Goldschmidt, Daniel, ed. *Seder ha-Qinot le-Tish'ah be-Av ke-Minhag Polin u-Qehillot ha-Ashkenazim be-Erez Yisrael*. Jerusalem: Mosad ha-Rav Kook, 1968.

Goldstein, Julie B. "'Children of the Sacred Covenant': Imagining Martyrdom in Twelfth-Century Ashkenaz." PhD diss., New York University, 2014.

Goldstein, Morris. *Jesus in the Jewish Tradition*. New York: Macmillan, 1950.

Goldy, Charlotte Newman. "A Jew of Oxford: Using the Dramatic to Understand the Mundane in Anglo-Norman Towns." In *Writing Medieval Women's Lives*, edited by Charlotte Newman Goldy and Amy Livingstone, 227–45. New York: Palgrave Macmillan, 2012.

———. "A Thirteenth-Century Anglo-Jewish Woman Crossing Boundaries: Visible and Invisible." *Journal of Medieval History* 34 (2008): 130–45.

Göller, Karl Heinz. "Sir Hugh of Lincoln: From History to Nursery Rhyme." https://core.ac.uk/reader/11555372, 17–31.

Gonzalez-Crussi, Frank. *The Body Fantastic*. Cambridge, MA: MIT Press, 2021.

Goodblatt, David. "Suicide in the Sanctuary: Traditions on Priestly Martyrdom." *Journal of Jewish Studies* 46 (1995): 10–29.

Goodwin, Deborah L. "Herbert of Bosham and the Horizons of Twelfth-Century Exegesis." *Traditio* 58 (December 2003): 133–73.

———. "Nothing in Our Histories: Postcolonial Criticism and the Twelfth-Century Jewish-Christian Encounter." *Medieval Encounters* 15 (2009): 35–65.

———. *"Take Hold of the Robe of a Jew": Herbert of Bosham's Christian Hebraism*. Leiden: Brill, 2006.

Gow, Andrew Colin. *The Red Jews: Antisemitism in an Apocalyptic Age, 1200–1600*. Leiden: Brill, 1995.

Graboïs, Aryeh. "Demuto ha-Agadit shel Karl ha-Gadol bi-Meqorot ha-'Ivriyyim shel Yemei ha-Beinayim." *Tarbiz* 36 (1966): 22–58.

———. "The Hebraica Veritas and Jewish-Christian Intellectual Relations in the Twelfth Century." *Speculum* 50 (1975): 613–34.

———. "Mi-Sin'at Yisrael 'Teologit' le Sin'at Yisrael 'Giz'it': Pulmus he-Apifyor 'ha-Yehudi' ba-Me'ah ha-12." *Zion* 47 (1982): 1–17.

Graetz, Heinrich. *Divrei Yemei Yisrael*. Translated and edited by Saul Phinehas Rabbinowitz. 9 vols. Warsaw, 1891–1908. Reprinted, Jerusalem: Makor, 1972.

———. *Geschichte der Juden von den ältesten Zeiten bis auf die Gegenwart / aus dem Quellen neu bearb*. 11 vols. Leipzig: O. Leiner, 1870–97.

———. *History of the Jews*. 6 vols. Philadelphia: Jewish Publication Society, 1967.
Grayzel, Solomon, ed. and trans. *The Church and the Jews in the XIIIth Century*. Vol. 1. Revised ed. New York: Hermon Press, 1966.
———, ed. and trans. *The Church and the Jews in the XIIIth Century*. Vol. 2 (1254–1314). Edited and arranged with additional notes by Kenneth R. Stow. New York: Jewish Theological Seminary of America Press, 1989.
———. "The Confession of a Medieval Jewish Convert." *Historia Judaica* 17 (1955): 89–120.
———. "The Jews and Roman Law." *Jewish Quarterly Review* 59 (1968): 93–117.
———. "The Papal Bull Sicut Judaeis." In *Studies and Essays in Honor of Abraham A. Neuman*, edited by Meir Ben-Horin, Bernard D. Weinryb, and Solomon Zeitlin, 143–280. Leiden: Brill, 1962.
Greatrex, Joan. "Monastic Charity for Jewish Converts: The Requisition of Corrodies by Henry III." In *Christianity and Judaism: Studies in Church History* 29, edited by Diana Wood, 133–43. Oxford: Blackwell, 1992.
Green, Monica. H. "Conversing with the Minority: Relations among Jewish Christian and Muslim Women in the High Middle Ages." *Journal of Medieval History* 34 (2008): 105–18.
Green, Monica H., and Daniel Lord Smail. "The Trial of Floret d'Ays (1403): Jews, Christians, and Obstetrics in Later Medieval Marseilles." *Journal of Medieval History* 34 (2008): 185–211.
Greenberg, Moshe. *'Al ha-Miqra ve-'al ha-Yahadut: Qovets Ketavim*. Edited by Avraham Shapira. Tel Aviv: Am Oved, 1984.
———. *Ezekiel, 1–20*. Anchor Yale Bible Commentaries. New Haven, CT: Yale University Press, 1983.
Greenblatt, Rachel L. "Temple to Town Hall: Sacred and Secular in Prague's Hall Town." In *Layered Landscapes: Early Modern Religious Space across Faiths and Cultures*, edited by Eric Nelson and Jonathan Wright, 43–60. New York: Routledge, 2017.
Greenblatt, Stephen J. "Filthy Rites." *Daedalus* 111 (1982): 1–16. Reprinted in Stephen J. Greenblatt, *Learning to Curse: Essays in Early Modern Culture*. New York: Routledge, 1990.
———. *Learning to Curse: Essays in Early Modern Culture*. New York: Routledge, 1990.
———. "Marlowe, Marx, and Antisemitism." *Critical Inquiry* 5, no. 2 (Winter 1978): 291–307. Reprinted in Stephen J. Greenblatt, *Learning to Curse: Essays in Early Modern Culture*. New York: Routledge, 1990.
———. "Wordplay, Hebrew." In *Anchor Yale Bible Dictionary, Volume 6: Si–Z*, edited by David Noel Freedman, 968–71. New Haven, CT: Yale University Press, 1992.
Gregory of Tours. *The History of the Franks*. Translated by Lewis Thorpe. Baltimore: Penguin, 1974.
Greilsammer, Myriam. *L'usurier chrétien, un Juif métaphorique? Histoire de l'exclusion des prêteurs lombards (XIIIe–XVIIe siècle)*. Rennes: Presses universitaires de Rennes, 2012.
Gribetz, Sarit Kattan. "Hanged and Crucified: The Book of Esther and Toledot Yeshu." In *Toledot Yeshu ("The Life Story of Jesus") Revisited: A Princeton Conference,*

edited by Peter Schäfer, Michael Meerson, and Yaacov Deutsch, 159–80. Tübingen: Mohr Siebeck, 2001.

Gross, Abraham. "The Blood Libel and the Blood of Circumcision: An Ashkenazi Custom That Disappeared in the Middle Ages." *Jewish Quarterly Review* 86 (July–October 1995): 171–74.

Gross, John. *Shylock: A Legend and Its Legacy*. New York: Simon and Schuster, 1994.

Grossman, Avraham. "'Avaryanim, ve-Alammim ba-Hevrah ha-Yehudit be-Ashkenaz ha-Qedumah ve-Hashpa'atam 'al Sidrei ha-Din." *Shenaton ha-Mishpat ha-'Ivri shel ha-Makhon le-Heiqer ha-Mishpat ha-'Ivri* 8 (1981): 135–52.

———. *Hakhmei Ashkenaz ha-Rishonim*. Jerusalem: Magnes Press, 1981.

———. *Hakhmei Zarfat ha-Rishonim*. Jerusalem: Magnes Press, 1995.

———. "The Historical Background to the Ordinances on Family Affairs Attributed to Rabbenu Gershom Me'or ha-Golah (Light of the Exile)." In *Jewish History, Essays in Honour of C. Abramsky*, edited by Ada Rapoport-Albert and Steven J. Zipperstein, 3–23. London: Peter Halban, 1988.

———. "Peirush Rashi li-Tehillim ve-ha-Pulmos ha-Yehudi-ha-Notzri." In *Mehkarim ba-Mikra'u-ve-Hinnukh Muggashim le-Prof. Moshe Ahrend*, edited by Dov Rappel, 59–74. Jerusalem: Touro College, 1996.

———. *Pious and Rebellious: Jewish Women in Medieval Europe*. Waltham, MA: Brandeis University Press, 2004.

———. "Shorashav shel Qiddush ha-Shem be-Ashkenaz ha-Qedumah." In *Qedushat ha-Hayim ve-Heiruf ha-Nefesh*, edited by Isaiah Gafni and Eliezer Ravitzki, 99–130. Jerusalem: Merkaz Zalman Shazar, 1992.

———. "The Ties of the Jews of Ashkenaz to the Land of Israel." In *Vision and Conflict in the Holy Land*, edited by Richard I. Cohen, 78–101. New York: St. Martin's Press, 1985.

Grözinger, Karl E. "Die erzählerische Kultur der SchUM-Städten—Zur Einführung." In *Jüdische Kultur in den SchUM-Städten*, edited by Karl E. Grözinger, 15–20. Jüdische Kultur, Band 26. Wiesbaden: Harrassowitz, 2014.

Grübel, Monika, and Peter Honnen, eds. *Jiddisch im Rheinland auf den Spuren der Sprachen der Juden*. Essen: Klartext, 2013.

Gruenbaum, Caroline. "Learning from the Vernacular: Non-Jewish Influence and Didacticism in Medieval Hebrew Narrative from Northern Europe." PhD diss., New York University, 2019.

Güdemann, Moritz. *Geschichte des Erziehungswesens und der Cultur der abendländischen Juden*. 3 vols. 1880–88. Reprinted, Amsterdam: Philo Press, 1966.

Guerkan, S. Layla. *The Jews as a Chosen People: Tradition and Transformation*. London: Routledge, 2009.

Guibert de Nogent. *Autobiographie*. Edited by Edmond-René Labande. Paris: Société d'Édition 'Les Belles Lettres,' 1981.

———. *Tractatus de incarnatione contra judaeos*. Migne PL, vol. 156, col. 489–528. Paris: J. P. Migne, 1853.

———. *Monodies and On the Relics of Saints: The Autobiography and a Manifesto of a French Monk from the Time of the Crusades*. Translated by Joseph McAlhany and Jay Rubenstein. New York: Penguin, 2011.

Gurjewitsch, Aaron J. *Stumme Zeugen des Mittelalters. Weltbild und Kultur der einfachen Menschen*. Cologne: Böhlau, 1997.

Gutmann, Joseph. *Hebrew Manuscript Painting*. New York: G. Braziller, 1978.

Gvaryahu, Amit. "A New Reading of the Three Dialogues in Mishnah Avodah Zarah." *Jewish Studies Quarterly* 19 (2012): 207–29.

Habermann, Abraham Meir. *Sefer Gezeirot Ashkenaz ve-Zarefat*. Jerusalem: Ofir, 1946.

———. "Shirat ha-ḥol shel yehudé ashkenaz ve-tsarfat." *Moznayim* 5 (1957): 403–8.

Hacker, Joseph. "'Alilot Dam Neged Yehudim ba-Imperiah ha-Ottomanit ba-Me'ot ha-15-17." In *Rav Ya'avod Za'ir: Mitusim u-Semalim bein Yahadut ve-Nazrut, Shai le-Yisrael Ya'aqov Yuval*, edited by Ram Ben-Shalom, Ora Limor, and Oded Irshai, 413–30. Jerusalem: Carmel, 2021.

Hacohen, Malachi Haim. *Jacob and Esau: Jewish European History between Nation and Empire*. Cambridge: Cambridge University Press, 2019.

Hahn, Thomas. "The Difference the Middle Ages Makes: Color and Race before the Modern World." *Journal of Medieval and Early Modern Studies* 31 (2001): 1–37.

Halamish, Moshe. "Nusah Qadum shel 'aleinu le-shabeah." *Sinai* 110 (1992): 262–65.

Halbach, Evan John. "Old Tales, New Renditions: The Foundations and Development of Anti-Semitic Ritual Murder Libels with Emphasis on a Shift in Centrality from Crucifixion to Blood Motifs in Late Medieval and Early Modern German Contexts." UND Scholarly Commons, 2016.

Halbertal, Moshe, and Avishai Margalit. *Idolatry*. Translated by Naomi Goldblum. Cambridge, MA: Harvard University Press, 1994.

Hall, Kim F. "Guess Who's Coming to Dinner? Colonization and Miscegenation in 'The Merchant of Venice.'" *Renaissance Drama* 23 (1992): 87–111.

Hames, Harvey J. "The Limits of Conversion: Ritual Murder and the Virgin Mary in the Account of Adam of Bristol." *Journal of Medieval History* 33 (2007): 43–59.

———. "Urinating on the Cross: Christianity as Seen in the Sefer Yoseph ha-Mekaneh (ca. 1260) and in Light of Paris 1240." In *Ritus Infidelium: Miradas interconfesionales sobre las practicas religiosas en la Edad Media*, edited by José Martínez Gázquez and John Victor Tolan, 209–20. Madrid: Casa de Velázquez, 2013.

Hamilton, Sarah, and Andrew Spicer. "Defining the Holy: The Delineation of Sacred Space." In *Defining the Holy: Sacred Space in Medieval and Early Modern Europe*, edited by Andrew Spicer and Sarah Hamilton, 1–23. Aldershot, UK: Ashgate, 2005.

Hanawalt, Barbara. "Medievalists and the Study of Childhood." *Speculum* 77 (2002): 440–59.

Handel, Ronald S. "Israel among the Nations: Biblical Culture in the Ancient Near East." In *Cultures of the Jews*, edited by David Biale, 42–75. New York: Schocken Books, 2002.

Handelman, Don. "The Palio of Sienna." In *Models and Mirrors: Towards an Anthropology of Public Events*, edited by Don Handelman, 116–35. Cambridge: Cambridge University Press, 1990.

Hannaford, Ivan. *Race: A History of an Idea in the West.* Baltimore: Johns Hopkins University Press, 1996.
Harkins, Franklin T., ed. *Transforming Relations: Essays on Jews and Christians throughout History in Honor of Michael A. Signer.* Notre Dame, IN: University of Notre Dame Press, 2010.
Harrington, Carolyne. "Diet, Defecation, and the Devil: Disgust and the Pagan Past." In *Medieval Obscenities,* edited by Nicola McDonald, 138–55. Woodbridge, UK: Boydell and Brewer, 2006.
Harris, Julie. "Polemical Images in the *Golden Haggadah* (British Library Add. MS 27210)." *Medieval Encounters* 12, no. 2–3 (2002): 105–22.
Harris, Monford. "The Concept of Love in *Sefer Hasidim.*" *Jewish Quarterly Review* 50 (1959): 13–44.
Harris, Robert A. "Rashi and the 'Messianic' Psalms." In *Birkat Shalom: Studies in the Bible, Ancient Near Eastern Literature . . . Shalom M. Paul,* edited by Chaim Cohen et al., 2:845–62. Winona Lake, IN: Eisenbrauns, 2008.
Hart, Mitchell B. *Jewish Blood: Reality and Metaphor in History, Religion, and Culture.* New York: Routledge, 2009.
Hasan-Rokem, Galit. "Homo viator et narrans judaicus: Medieval Jewish Voices in the European Narrative of the Wandering Jew." In *Europäische Ethnologie und Folklore im internationalen Kontext: Festschrift für Leander Petzoldt,* edited by Ingo Schneider, 93–102. Frankfurt am Main: Peter Lang, 1999.
Hasan-Rokem, Galit, and Alan Dundes, eds. *The Wandering Jew: Essays in the Interpretation of a Christian Legend.* Bloomington: University of Indiana Press, 1986.
Hassig, Debra. *The Mark of the Beast: The Medieval Bestiary in Art, Life and Literature.* New York: Garland and Francis, 1999.
———. *Medieval Bestiaries: Text, Image, Ideology.* Cambridge: Cambridge University Press, 1995.
Haverkamp, Alfred. "Baptized Jews in German Lands during the Twelfth Century." In *Jews and Christians in Twelfth Century Europe,* edited by Michael A. Signer and John Van Engen, 255–310. Notre Dame, IN: University of Notre Dame Press, 2001.
———. "The Beginning of Jewish Life North of the Alps with Comparative Glances at Italy (ca. 900–1100)." In *"Diversi Angoli di Visuale" fra storia medievale e storia degli ebrei, in recordo di Michaele Luzzati,* edited by Anna Maria Pult Quaglia and Alessandra Veronese, 85–102. Atti del convegno, Pisa 1–3 febbraio 2016. Pisa: Pacini Editore, 2016.
———, ed. *Juden und Christen zur Zeit der Kreuzzüge.* Sigmaringen: Jan Thorbecke, 1999.
———, ed. *Zur Geschichte der Juden im Deutschland des Späten Mittelalters und der Frühen Neuzeit.* Stuttgart: Anton Hiersemann, 1981.
Haverkamp, Alfred, Friedhelm Burgard, and Gerd Mentgen, eds. *Judenvertreibungen in Mittelalter und früher Neuzeit.* Hannover: Hahnsche Verlag, 1999.
Haverkamp, Eva, ed. *Hebräische Berichte über die Judenverfolgungen während des Ersten Kreuzzugs.* Monumenta Germaniae Historica, Hebräische Texte aus dem Mittelalterlichen Deutschland. Vol. 1. Hannover: Hahnsche Buchhandlung, 2005.

———. "Jews in Christian Europe: Ashkenaz in the Middle Ages." In *The Wiley-Blackwell History of Jews and Judaism*, edited by Alan T. Levenson, 169–206. Chichester, UK: Blackwell, 2012.

———. "Martyrs in Rivalry: The 1096 Jewish Martyrs and the Thebean Legion." *Jewish History* 23 (2009): 319–42.

———. "What Did the Christians Know? Latin Reports on the Persecutions of the Jews in 1096." *Crusades* 7 (2008): 59–86.

Hawkins, Sherman. "Chaucer's Prioress and the Sacrifice of Praise." *Journal of English and Germanic Philology* 63, no. 4 (October 1964): 599–624.

Hay, Denys. *Europe: The Emergence of an Idea*. Edinburgh: Edinburgh University Press, 1968.

Hayden, R. M. "Intersecting Religioscapes: A Comparative Approach to Trajectories of Change, Scale, and Competitive Sharing of Religious Spaces." *Journal of the American Academy of Religion* 81 (2013): 399–426.

Hayes, Christine E. "The Complicated Goy in Classical Rabbinic Sources." In *Perceiving the Other in Ancient Judaism and Early Christianity*, edited by Michal Bar-Asher Siegal, Wolfgang Grünstäudl, and Matthew Thiessen, 147–67. Tübingen: Mohr Siebeck, 2017.

———. *Gentile Impurities and Jewish Identities: Intermarriage and Conversion from the Bible to the Talmud*. Oxford: Oxford University Press, 2002.

———. "The 'Other' in Rabbinic Literature." In *Cambridge Companion to the Talmud and Rabbinic Literature*, edited by Martin Jaffee and Charlotte Fonrobert, 243–69. Cambridge: Cambridge University Press, 2007.

———. "Were the Noahide Commandments Formulated at Yavne? Tosefta Avoda Zara 8:4–9 in Cultural and Historical Context." In *Jews and Christians in the First and Second Centuries: The Interbellum 70–132 CE*, edited by Joshua Schwartz and Peter J. Tomson, 225–64. Leiden: Brill, 2018.

Hayes, Dawn Marie. *Body and Sacred Place in Medieval Europe, 1100–1389*. New York: Routledge, 2009.

Head, Thomas, and Richard Landes, eds. *The Peace of God: Social Violence and Religious Response in France around the Year 1000*. Ithaca, NY: Cornell University Press, 1992.

Heil, Johannes. "'Antijudaismus' und 'Antisemitismus': Begriffe als Bedeutungsträger." *Jahrbuch für Antisemitismusforschung* 6 (1997): 92–114.

———. "'Deep Enmity' and/or 'Close Ties'? Jews and Christians before 1096: Sources, Hermeneutics, and Writing History in 1096." *Jewish Studies Quarterly* 9, no. 3 (2002): 259–306.

Heng, Geraldine. *Empire of Magic: Medieval Romance and the Politics of Cultural Fantasy*. New York: Columbia University Press, 2003.

———. *England and the Jews: How Religion and Violence Created the First Racial State in the West*. Cambridge: Cambridge University Press, 2018.

———. "England's Dead Boys: Telling Tales of Jewish-Christian Relations before and after the First European Expulsion of the Jews." *MLN Comparative Literature Issue: De Theoria: Early Modern Essays in Memory of Eugene Vance* 127, no. 5 (December 2012): 54–85.

———. *The Invention of Race in the European Middle Ages*. Cambridge: Cambridge University Press, 2018.

———. "The Invention of Race in the European Middle Ages I: Race Studies, Modernity, and the Middle Ages." *Literature Compass* 8, no. 5 (2011): 258–74.

———. "The Invention of Race in the European Middle Ages II: Locations of Medieval Race." *Literature Compass* 8, no. 5 (2011): 275–93.

———. "Jews, Saracens, 'Black Men,' Tartars: England in a World of Racial Difference." In *A Companion to Medieval English Literature and Culture, c. 1350–c. 1500*, edited by Peter Brown, 247–69. Oxford: Blackwell, 2007.

Herford, R. Travers. *Christianity in Talmud and Midrash*. 1903. Reprinted, New York: Ktav, 1975.

Hering Torres, Max S., María Elena Martínez, and David Nirenberg, eds. *Race and Blood in the Iberian World*. Berlin: Lit, 2012.

Herman, Gerald. "Note on Medieval Anti-Judaism as Reflected in the Chansons de Geste." *Annuale médiévale* 14 (1973): 63–73.

Herman-Judah. *Hermanus quondam Judaeus: Opusculum de conversione sua*. Edited by Gerlinde Niemeier. Monumenta Germaniae Historica, Quellen zur Geistesgeschichte des Mittelalters, IV. Weimar: H. Böhlaus Nachfolger, 1963.

———. "A Translation of Herman-Judah's *Short Account of His Own Conversion*." In *Conversion and Text: The Cases of Augustine of Hippo, Herman-Judah, and Constantine Tsatsos*, by Karl F. Morrison, 76–113. Charlottesville: University of Virginia Press, 1992.

Herskovits, Andrew. *The Positive Image of the Jew in the "Comedia."* New York: Peter Lang, 2005.

Herskowitz, William K. "Judaeo-Christian Dialogue in Provence as Reflected in 'Milhemet Mitzva' of R. Meir Hameili." PhD diss., Yeshiva University, 1974.

Herzig, Arno. *Jüdische Geschichte in Deutschland: von den Anfängen bis zur Gegenwart*. Munich: Beck, 1997.

Heschel, Susannah. *The Aryan Jesus: Christian Theologians and the Bible in Nazi Germany*. Princeton, NJ: Princeton University Press, 2008.

Hezser, Catherine. "Dirt and Garbage in the Ancient Jewish Religious Imagination and in Daily Life." In *Envisioning Judaism: Studies in Honor of Peter Schäfer on the Occasion of His Seventieth Birthday*, edited by Ra'anan S. Boustan et al., 107–28. Tübingen: Mohr Siebeck, 2013.

Hiestand, Rudolf. "Juden und Christen in der Kreuzzugspropaganda und bei den Kreuzzugspredigern." In *Juden und Christen zur Zeit der Kreuzzüge*, edited by Alfred Haverkamp, 153–208. Sigmaringen: Jan Thorbecke, 1999.

Hillaby, Joe. "The Ritual-Child-Murder Accusation: Its Dissemination and Harold of Gloucester." *Jewish Historical Studies* 34 (1994–96): 69–109.

Hilsch, Peter. "Die *Bekehrungsschrift* des Hermannus quondam Judaeus und die Frage über ihrer Authentizität." *Deutsches Archiv für Forschung des Mittelalters* 66 (2010): 69–91.

Hirsch, Brett D. "Counterfeit Professions: Jewish Daughters and the Drama of Failed Conversion in Marlowe's The Jew of Malta and Shakespeare's The Merchant of Venice." *Early Modern Literary Studies* 19, no. 4 (2009): 1–37.

Hirsh, John C. "Reopening the 'Prioress's Tale.'" *Chaucer Review* 10, no. 1 (1974): 30–45.
Hoffmann, Richard C. "Outsiders by Birth and Blood: Racist Ideologies and Realities around the Periphery of Medieval Culture." *Studies in Medieval and Renaissance History* 6 (1983): 14–27.
Hollender, Elisabeth. "Zur Reaction auf Gewalt im hebräischen Dichtungen des Mittelalters." In *Gewalt im Mittelalter: Realitäten—Imaginationen*, edited by Manuel Braun and Cornelia Herberichs, 203–24. Munich: Fink, 2005.
Holmes, Colin. "The Ritual Murder Accusation in Medieval Britain." *Ethnic and Racial Studies* 4, no. 3 (1981): 265–88.
Holmes, Urban Tigner, Jr. *Daily Living in the Twelfth Century: Based on the Observations of Alexander Neckam in London and Paris*. Madison: University of Wisconsin Press, 1952.
Hood, John Y. B. *Aquinas and the Jews*. Philadelphia: University of Pennsylvania Press, 1995.
Horbury, William. "Antichrist among Jews and Gentiles." In *Jews in a Graeco-Roman World*, edited by Martin Goodman, 113–33. Oxford: Oxford University Press, 1998.
———. "A Critical Examination of the 'Toledoth Jeshu.'" PhD diss., Cambridge University, 1970.
———. *Jews and Christians in Contact and Controversy*. Edinburgh: T and T Clark, 1998.
Horowitz, [Elliott] Elimelekh. "'Al Mashma'uyot ha-Zaqan Bi-Qehillot Yisrael: Ba-Mizrah u-ve-Eiropa bimei ha-Beinayim u-va-'Eit ha-Hadashah." *Pe'amim* 59 (1994): 124–48.
———. "'Ha-Tzlav ha-Doqer' Vi-yhudei Eiropa bimei ha-Beinayim." In *Yehudim Mul ha-Tzlav: Gezeirot Tatnu be-Historiah u-ve-Historiografiah*, edited by Yom Tov Assis et al., 118–40. Jerusalem: Merkaz Zalman Shazar, 2000.
———. "The Jews and the Cross in the Middle Ages: Towards a Reappraisal." In *Philosemitism, Antisemitism, and "the Jews": Perspectives from the Middle Ages to the Twentieth Century*, edited by Tony Kushner and Nadia Valman, 115–31. Aldershot, UK: Ashgate, 2004.
———. *Reckless Rites: Purim and the Legacy of Jewish Violence*. Princeton, NJ: Princeton University Press, 2008.
———. "The Rite to Be Reckless: On the Perpetration and Interpretation of Purim Violence." *Poetics Today* 15 (1994): 9–29.
———. "Visages du judaisme: De la barbe en monde juif et de l'élaboration de ses significations." *Annales. Histoires, Sciences Sociales* 49, no. 5 (1994): 1065–90.
Hotchkiss, Valerie R. *Clothes Make the Man: Female Cross-dressing in Medieval Europe*. New York: Routledge, 2012.
Hovav, Yamima. *'Alamot Aheivukha: Hayyei ha-Dat ve-ha-Ruah shel Nashim ba-Hevrah ha-Ashkenazit be-Reishit ha-'Eit ha-Hadashah*. Jerusalem: Carmel/ Merkaz Dinur, 2009.
Hoyer, Siegfried. "Die Armlederbewegung—ein Bauernaufstand 1336/1339." *Zeitsschrift für Geschichtswissenschaft* 13 (1965): 74–89.
Hoyle, Victoria. "The Bonds That Bind: Moneylending between Anglo-Jewish and Christian Women in the Plea Rolls of the Exchequer of the Jews, 1218–1280." *Journal of Medieval History* 34, no. 2 (2008): 119–29.

Hsia, Ronnie Po-Chia. *The Myth of Ritual Murder: Jews and Magic in Reformation Germany*. New Haven, CT: Yale University Press, 1988.
———. *Trent 1475: Stories of a Ritual Murder Trial*. New Haven, CT: Yale University Press, 1992.
Hsia, R. Po-Chia, and Hartmut Lehmann, eds. *In and Out of the Ghetto: Jewish-Gentile Relations in Late Medieval and Early Modern Germany*. Cambridge: Cambridge University Press, 1995.
Hsy, Jonathan, and Julie Orlemanski. "Race and Medieval Studies: A Partial Bibliography." *Postmedieval: A Journal of Medieval Cultural Studies* 8 (2017): 500–31.
Huffman, Joseph. *Family, Commerce and Religion in London and Cologne: Anglo-German Emigrants, c. 1000–c. 1300*. Cambridge: Cambridge University Press, 1998.
Hugo, abbas Flaviniacensis. *Chronicon*. Edited by Georg Heinrich Pertz. In MGH SS (Hannover, 1848), 8:474.
Hultin, Jeremy F. *The Ethics of Obscene Speech in Early Christianity and Its Environment* (Novum Testamentum, Supplements). Leiden: Brill, 2008.
Hunnisett, R. F. *The Medieval Coroner*. Cambridge: Cambridge University Press, 1962.
Hunt, Alan. "Anxiety and Social Explanation: Some Anxieties about Anxiety." *Journal of Social History* 32, no. 3 (Spring 1999): 509–28.
———. *Governance of the Consuming Passions: A History of Sumptuary Law*. Basingstoke, UK: Macmillan Press, 1996.
Hunter, G. K. "The Theology of Marlowe's *The Jew of Malta*." *Journal of the Warburg and Courtauld Institutes* 27 (1964): 211–40.
Hvidt, Niels Christian. *Christian Prophecy, the Post-Biblical Tradition*. Oxford: Oxford University Press, 2007.
Hyam, Ronald. *Understanding the British Empire*. Cambridge: Cambridge University Press, 2010.
Idelson-Shein, Iris. *Difference of a Different Kind: Jewish Constructions of Race during the Long Eighteenth Century*. Philadelphia: University of Pennsylvania Press, 2014.
Idelson-Shein, Iris, and Christian Wiese, eds. *Monsters and Monstrosity in Jewish History from the Middle Ages to Modernity*. London: Bloomsbury Academic, 2019.
Ihnat, Kati. "Early Evidence for the Cult of Anne in Twelfth-Century England." *Traditio* 69 (2014): 1–44.
———. "Getting the Punchline: Deciphering Anti-Jewish Humour in Anglo-Norman England." *Journal of Medieval History* 38, no. 4 (December 2012): 408–23.
———. "The Martyrs of Córdoba: Debates around a Curious Case of Medieval Martyrdom." *History Compass* 18, no. 1 (January 2020). http://doi.org/10.1111/hic3.12603.
———. "Mary as Bride in the Old Hispanic Office: Liturgical and Theological Trends." *Medieval Studies* 78 (2016): 65–123.
———. *Mother of Mercy, Bane of the Jews: Devotion to the Virgin Mary in Anglo-Norman England*. Princeton, NJ: Princeton University Press, 2016.
———. "'Our Sister Is Little and Has No Breasts': Mary and the Jews in the Sermons of Honorius Augustodunensis." In *The Jewish-Christian Encounter in Medieval Preaching*, edited by Jonathan Adams and Jussi Hanska, 119–38. New York: Routledge, 2014.

———. "Staging the Jew: Drama and Identity in Twelfth-Century Laon." In *Monasteries on the Borders of Medieval Europe: Conflict and Cultural Interaction*, edited by Emilia Jamroziak and Karen Stöber, 237–62. Turnhout: Brepols, 2013.

Iogna-Pratt, Dominique. *Order and Exclusion: Cluny and Christendom Face Heresy, Judaism, and Islam*. Translated by G. R. Edwards. Ithaca, NY: Cornell University Press, 2002.

Irish, Maya Soifer. "The Castilian Monarchy and the Jews (Eleventh to Thirteenth Centuries)." In *Center and Periphery: Studies on Power in the Medieval World in Honor of William Chester Jordan*, edited by Katherine L. Jansen, G. Geltner, and Ann E. Lester, 39–49. Leiden: Brill, 2013.

———. *Jews and Christians in Medieval Castile: Tradition, Coexistence, and Change*. Washington, DC: Catholic University of America Press, 2016.

Irshai, Oded. "Confronting a Christian Empire: Jewish Culture in the World of Byzantium." In *Cultures of the Jews: A New History*, edited by David Biale, 180–220. New York: Schocken Books, 2002.

Isaac, Benjamin. "The Ancient Mediterranean and the Pre-Christian Era." In *Antisemitism: A History*, edited by Albert S. Lindemann and Richard S. Levy, 34–46. Oxford: Oxford University Press, 2010.

Isaac, Jules. *The Teaching of Contempt: Christian Roots of Anti-Semitism*. Translated by Helen Weaver. New York: McGraw Hill Book Co., 1965.

Isaac b. Joseph of Corbeil. *Sefer Mizvot Qatan*. Edited by Yitzhaq Yaaqov Har ha-Shoshanim Rosenberg. 3 vols. Jerusalem: Y. Y. Har ha-Shoshanim, 1981.

Isaac b. Moses of Vienna. *Sefer Or Zarua*. 4 vols. in 2. Vol. 1, Zhitomir, 1862. Vol. 2, Jerusalem, 1887.

Israel, Jonathan. *Empires and Entrepots: The Dutch, the Spanish Monarchy and the Jews, 1585–1713*. London: Humbleton, 1990.

Isserles, Justine. "Les parallèles esthétiques des manuscrits hébreux ashkénazes de type liturgico-légal et des manuscrits latins et vernaculaires médiévaux." In *Manuscrits hébreux et arabes: mélanges en l'honneur de Colette Sirat*, edited by Nicholas de Lange and Judith Olszowy-Schlanger, 77–113. Turnhout: Brepols, 2014.

Isserles, Justine, and P. Nothaft. "Calendars beyond Borders: Exchange of Calendrical Knowledge between Jews and Christians in Medieval Western Europe (12th–15th c.)." *Medieval Encounters* 20 (2014): 1–37.

Jacob b. Meir. *Sefer ha-Yashar*. Berlin: B. Herts, 1923.

Jacob b. Reuven. *Milhamot Ha-Shem*. Edited by Yehudah Rosenthal. Jerusalem: Mosad Ha-Rav Kook, 1965.

Jacobi, Leor. "Jewish Hawking in Medieval France: Falconry, Rabbenu Tam, and the Tosafists." *Oqimta* 1 (2013): 421–504.

Jacobs, Joseph. *Jewish Contributions to Civilization: An Estimate*. Philadelphia: Jewish Publication Sociey, 1919.

———. *The Jews of Angevin England: Documents and Records from Latin and Hebrew Sources Printed and Manuscript for the First Time Collected and Translated*. London: Putnam, 1893.

———. "St. William of Norwich." *Jewish Quarterly Review* 9 (1897): 748–55.

Jacobson, Matthew Frye. *Whiteness of a Different Color: European Immigrants and the Alchemy of Race.* Cambridge, MA: Harvard University Press, 1999.

Jacobus de Voragine. *The Golden Legend: Readings on the Saints.* Translated by William Granger Ryan. 2 vols. Princeton, NJ: Princeton University Press, 1993.

Jaeger, Stephen. "Pessimism in the Twelfth-Century 'Renaissance.'" *Speculum* 78, no. 4 (October 2003): 1151–83.

James, Mervin. "Ritual, Drama and Social Body in the Late Medieval Town." *Past and Present* 98 (1983): 3–29.

Jansen, Katherine L., G. Geltner, and Ann E. Lester, eds. *Center and Periphery: Studies on Power in the Medieval World in Honor of William Chester Jordan.* Leiden: Brill, 2013.

Jocelin of Brakelond. *Chronicle of the Abbey of Bury St. Edmunds.* Translated and edited by Diana Greenaway and Jane Sayers. Oxford: Oxford University Press, 1989.

Johnson, Hannah R. "Antisemitism and the Purposes of Historicism: Antisemitism and Art in Chaucer's Prioress's Tale." In *Middle English Literature: Criticism and Debate*, edited by D. Vance Smith and Holly Crocker, 192–200. New York: Routledge, 2014.

———. *Blood Libel: The Ritual Murder Accusation at the Limit of Jewish History.* Ann Arbor: University of Michigan Press, 2012.

———. "Massacre and Memory: Ethics and Method in Recent Scholarship on Jewish Martyrdom." In *Christians and Jews in Angevin England: The York Massacre of 1190, Narratives and Contexts*, edited by Sarah Reese Jones and Sethina Watson, 261–77. Rochester, NY: Boydell Press, 2013.

Johnson, Hannah, and Heather Blurton. "Virtual Jews and Figural Criticism: Recent Scholarship on the Idea of the Jew in Recent Culture." *Philological Quarterly* 92, no. 1 (2013): 115–30.

Johnson, Willis. "Before the Blood Libel: Jews in Christian Exegesis after the Massacres of 1096." Master's thesis, Cambridge University, 1994.

———. "Between Christians and Jews: The Formation of Anti-Jewish Stereotypes in Medieval England." PhD diss., University of California, Berkeley, 1997.

———. "The Myth of Jewish Male Menses." *Journal of Medieval History* 24 (1998): 273–95.

———. "Textual Sources for the Study of Jewish Currency Crimes in Thirteenth-Century England." *British Numismatic Journal* 66 (1996): 21–32.

Jones, Michael. "'The Place of the Jews': Anti-Judaism and Theatricality in Medieval Culture." *Exemplaria* 12 (2000): 327–59.

Jones, Sarah Rees, and Sethina Watson, eds. *Christians and Jews in Angevin England: The York Massacre of 1190, Narratives and Contexts.* Rochester, NY: Boydell Press, 2013.

Jones, W. R. "The Image of the Barbarian in Medieval Europe." *Comparative Studies in Society and History* 13 (1971): 376–407.

Jordan, William Chester. "A travers le regard des enfants." *Provence historique* 37 (1987): 531–43.

———. "Administering Expulsion in 1306." *Jewish Studies Quarterly* 15 (2008): 241–50.
———. "Adolescence and Conversion in the Middle Ages: A Research Agenda." In *Jews and Christians in Twelfth-Century Europe*, edited by Michael A. Signer and John Van Engen, 77–93. Notre Dame, IN: University of Notre Dame Press, 2001.
———. "Approaches to the Court Scene in the Bond Story: Equity and Mercy or Reason and Nature?" *Shakespeare Quarterly* (1982): 49–59.
———. "Christian Excommunication of the Jews in the Middle Ages: A Restatement of the Issues." *Jewish History* 1 (1986): 31–38.
———. *Europe in the High Middle Ages*. London: Penguin, 2002.
———. *The French Monarchy and the Jews: From Philip Augustus to the Last Capetians*. Philadelphia: University of Pennsylvania Press, 1989.
———. "Home Again: The Jews in the Kingdom of France, 1315–1322." In *The Stranger in Medieval Society*, edited by F.R.P. Akehurst and Stephanie Cain Van D'Elden, 27–45. Minneapolis: University of Minnesota Press, 1997.
———. "Jew and Serf in Medieval France Revisited." In *Jews, Christians and Muslims in Medieval and Early Modern Times: A Festschrift in Honor of Mark R. Cohen*, edited by Arnold Franklin et al., 248–56. Leiden: Brill, 2014.
———. "Jewish Studies and the Medieval Historian." *Exemplaria* 12 (2000): 7–20.
———. "Jews on Top: Women and the Availability of Consumption Loans in Northern France in the Mid-Thirteenth Century." *Journal of Jewish Studies* 29, no. 1 (Spring 1978): 39–56.
———. "John of Garland on the Jews." *Journal of Medieval History* 48, no. 4 (2022): 478–95.
———. "Learning about Jews in the Classroom: A Thirteenth-Century Witness, UCLA Library, Rouse MS 17." In *Envisioning Judaism: Studies in Honor of Peter Schäfer on the Occasion of His Seventieth Birthday*, edited by Ra'anan S. Boustan et al., 1247–60. Tübingen: Mohr Siebeck, 2013.
———. "Marian Devotion and the Talmud Trial of 1240." In *Religionsgespräche im Mittelalter*, edited by Bernard Lewis and Friedrich Niewohner, 61–76. Wolfebütteler Mittelalter-Studien 4. Wiesbaden: Harrassowitz, 1994.
———. "The Pardoner's Holy Jew." In *Chaucer and the Jews: Sources, Contexts, Meanings*, edited by Sheila Delany, 25–42. New York: Routledge, 2002.
———. "Problems of the Meat Market of Béziers, 1240–1247, a Question of Anti-Semitism." *Revue des Études Juives* 135 (1976): 31–49.
———. "Review of Shatzmiller, *Shylock Reconsidered*." *Jewish Quarterly Review* 82, no. 1–2 (July–October 1991): 221–23.
———. "Why Race?" *Journal of Medieval and Early Modern Studies* 31 (2001): 165–73.
Joseph b. Nathan Official. *Yosef ha-Meqaneh*. Edited by Judah Rosenthal. Jerusalem: Mekize Nirdamim, 1970.
Joseph Kimhi. *The Book of the Covenant*. Translated and edited by Frank Talmage. Toronto: Pontifical Institute of Mediaeval Studies, 1972.
———. *Sefer ha-Brit. Viquah Radaq 'im ha-Nazrut*. Edited by Ephraim [Frank] Talmage. Jerusalem: Mosad Bialik, 1974.
Judah b. Samuel, the Pious or Pietist (*he-hasid*). *Sefer Hasidim* [Book of the pious], Parma, Biblioteca Palatina, Heb. MS 3280 (De Rossi, 1133), reproduced in a

facsimile edition, with Hebrew introduction by Ivan G. Marcus (Jerusalem: Merkaz Dinur, 1985) (SHP). This text was published for the first time, with many errors of transcription, by Jehuda Wistinetzki (Berlin: M. A. Wahrmann, 1891), and again with an introduction by Jacob Freimann (Frankfurt am Main: Johen Kelner, 1924). The first edition of a shorter version was published in Bologna, 1538 (SHB). See Marcus, *Sefer Hasidim and the Ashkenazic Book*.

Jung, Jacqueline. "The Passion, the Jews, and the Crisis of the Individual." In *Beyond the Yellow Badge: Anti-Judaism and Antisemitism in Medieval and Early Modern Visual Culture*, edited by Mitchell Merback, 145–78. Leiden: Brill, 2007.

Juster, Jean. "The Legal Condition of the Jews under the Visigothic Kings." *Israel Law Review* 11 (1976): 259–87, 391–414, 563–90.

Justin Martyr. *Dialogue with Trypho*. In *Writings of Saint Justin Martyr*, translated by Thomas B. Falls, 139–366. Washington, DC: Catholic University of America Press, 1948.

Jütte, Robert, and Elizabeth Bredeck. *The Jewish Body: A History*. Philadelphia: University of Pennsylvania Press, 2020.

Kahana, Maoz. "Meqorot ha-Yeda' u-Temurot ha-Zeman: Zava'at R.Yehudah he-Hasid be-'eit ha-Hadashah." In *Samhut Ruhanit: Ma'avaqim 'al Koah Tarbuti ba-Hagut ha-Yehudit*, edited by Howard Kreissel, Boaz Huss, and Uri Ehrlich, 223–62. Beer Sheva: Ben-Gurion University Press, 2009.

———. "Old Prophesies, Multiple Modernities: The Stormy Afterlife of a Medieval Pietist in Early Modern Ashkenaz." *Jewish History* 34 (2021): 233–58.

Kalmin, Richard. "Christians and Heretics in Rabbinic Literature in Late Antiquity." *Harvard Theological Review* 87, no. 2 (April 1994): 155–69.

Kanarfogel, Ephraim. "'Al Nushah u-Meqorah shel Tefillat Av ha-Rahamim," *Yeshurun* 27 (2012): 871–78.

———. *Brothers from Afar: Rabbinic Approaches to Apostasy and Reversion in Medieval Europe*. Detroit: Wayne State University Press, 2021.

———. "Changing Attitudes toward Apostates in Tosafist Literature: Twelfth-Early Thirteenth Centuries." In *New Perspectives on Jewish-Christian Relations in Honor of David Berger*, edited by Elisheva Carlebach and Jacob J. Schacter, 297–327. Leiden: Brill, 2012.

———. "From Germany to Northern France and Back Again: A Tale of Two Tosafist Centres." In *Regional Identities and Cultures of Medieval Jews*, edited by Javier Castaño, Talya Fishman, and Ephraim Kanarfogel, 149–71. London: Littman Library of Jewish Civilization, 2018.

———. "The Image of Christians in Medieval Ashkenazic Rabbinic Literature." In *Jews and Christians in Thirteenth-Century France*, edited by Elisheva Baumgarten and Judah D. Galinsky, 156–67. New York: Palgrave Macmillan, 2015.

———. *Intellectual History and Rabbinic Culture of Medieval Ashkenaz*. Detroit: Wayne State University Press, 2013.

———. *Jewish Education and Society in the High Middle Ages*. Detroit: Wayne State University Press, 1992.

———. "Nesu'ot Meshummadot she-Hazru: Heteran li-Bnei Zugan ha-Yehudi veha-Nokhri lefi Meqorot Zefon Zarefat ve-Ashkenaz Bimei ha-Benayim." *Halakhah u-Mishpat: Sefer ha-Zikkaron li-Menahem Elon*, edited by A. Edrei et al., 593–606. Jerusalem: Hebrew University, 2018.

———. "Rabbinic Attitudes toward Nonobservance in the Medieval Period." In *Jewish Tradition and the Non-Traditional Jew*, edited by J. J. Schacter, 3–35. Northvale, NJ: Jason Aronson, 1992.

———. "Returning Apostates and Their Marital Partners in Medieval Ashkenaz." In *Contesting Inter-Religious Conversion in the Medieval World*, edited by Yaniv Fox and Yosi Yisraeli, 160–76. New York: Routledge, 2017.

Kaplan, M. Lindsay. *Figuring Racism in Medieval Christianity*. Oxford: Oxford University Press, 2018.

———. "The Jewish Body in Black and White in Medieval and Early Modern England." *Philological Quarterly* 92, no. 1 (Winter 2013): 41–65.

———. *The Merchant of Venice: The State of Play*. Syracuse, NY: Syracuse University Press, 2020.

Karp, Jonathan. "Antisemitism in the Age of Mercantilism." In *Antisemitism: A History*, edited by Albert S. Lindemann and Richard S. Levy, 94–106. Oxford: Oxford University Press, 2010.

Karras, Ruth Mazo. "The Aerial Battle in the *Toledot Yeshu* and Sodomy in the Late Middle Ages." *Medieval Encounters* 19 (2013): 493–533.

———. "Separating the Men from the Goats: Masculinity, Civilization, and Identity Formation in the Medieval University." In *Conflicted Identities and Multiple Masculinities: Men in the Medieval West*, edited by Jacqueline Murray, 189–214. New York: Garland, 1999.

Katz, David S. "Shylock's Gender: Jewish Male Menstruation in Early Modern England." *Review of English Studies* 50 (November 1999): 440–62.

Katz, Jacob. *Exclusiveness and Tolerance: Studies in Jewish-Gentile Relations in Medieval and Modern Times*. London: Oxford University Press, 1961.

———. *From Prejudice to Destruction: Anti-Semitism, 1700–1933*. Cambridge, MA: Harvard University Press, 1980.

———. "Yisrael af 'al pi she hata yisrael.'" *Tarbiz* 27, no. 2–3 (1958): 203–17.

Katz, Shimon, and Yitzhak Katz, eds. *Quntres le-Mal'ot Hesronot ha-Shas*. Königsberg, 1860.

Katz, Solomon. *The Jews in the Visigothic Kingdoms of Spain and Gaul*. Cambridge, MA: Medieval Academy of America, 1937.

———. "Pope Gregory the Great and the Jews." *Jewish Quarterly Review* 24, no. 3 (1933): 113–36.

Katz, Steven T. "The Rabbinic Response to Christianity." *Cambridge History of Judaism*. Vol. 4, *The Late Roman-Rabbinic Period*, edited by Steven T. Katz, 259–98. Cambridge: Cambridge University Press, 2006.

Katznelson, Ira I. "'To Give Counsel and to Consent': Why the King (Edward I) Expelled His Jews (in 1290)." In *Preferences and Situations*, edited by Ira I. Katznelson and Barry R. Weingast, 88–126. New York: Russell Sage Foundation, 2005.

Kay, Sarah. *Courtly Contradiction: The Emergence of the Literary Object in the Twelfth Century*. Stanford, CA: Stanford University Press, 2001.

Kay, Sarah, and Miri Rubin, eds. *Framing Medieval Bodies*. Manchester: Manchester University Press, 1994.

Kedar, Benjamin Z. *Crusade and Mission: European Approaches toward the Muslims*. Princeton, NJ: Princeton University Press, 1988.

———. "Crusade Historians and the Massacres of 1096." *Jewish History* 12, no. 2 (Fall 1998): 11–31.

———. *Crusaders and Franks: Studies in the History of the Crusades and in the Frankish Levant*. London: Routledge, 2016.

———. "Emicho of Flonheim and the Apocalypse Motif in the 1096 Massacres: Between Paul Alphondéry and Alphonse Dupront." In *Conflict and Religious Conversation in Latin Christendom: Studies in Honor of Ora Limor*, edited by Israel Jacob Yuval and Ram Ben-Shalom, 87–98. Turnhout: Brepols, 2014.

———. "Expulsion as an Issue of World History." *Journal of World History* 7 (1996): 165–80.

———. "The Forcible Baptisms of 1096: History and Historiography." In *Forschungen zur Reichs-, Papst- und Landesgeschichte, Peter Herde zum 65. Geburtstag*, edited by Karl Borchardt and Enno Bünz, 1:187–200. Stuttgart: Hiersemann, 1998.

Kehr, Paul. *Papsturkunden in Spanien*. Vol. 1, *Katalonien*. Berlin: Weidmannsche Buchhandlung, 1926.

Keil, Martha. "Christliche Zeugen vor Jüdischen Gerichten: ein unbeachteter Aspekt christlich-jüdischer Begegnung im spätmittelalterlichen Aschkenas." *Mitteilungen des Instituts für Österreichische Geschichtsforschung* 117, no. 3–4 (2009): 272–85.

———. "Orte der jüdischen Öffentlichkeit. Judenviertel, Synagoga, Friedhof." In *Ein Thema—Zwei Perspektiven. Juden und Christen in Mittelalter und Frühneuzeit*, edited by Eveline Brugger and Birgit Wiegl, 170–86. Innsbruck: Studien Verlag, 2007.

———. "'Und wenn sie die Heilige Sprache nich verstehen . . .' Versönungs- und Bußrituale deutscher Jüdinnen und Juden im Spätmittelalter." In *Language of Religion—Language of the People: Medieval Judaism, Christianity and Islam*, edited by Ernst Bremer and Susanne Röhl, 171–89. Mittelalter Studien 11. Munich: Fink, 2006.

Keil, Martha, and John V. Tolan, eds. *Jews and Christians in Medieval Europe*. Turnhout: Brepols, 2016.

Kelly, Henry Ansgar. "'The Prioress's Tale' in Context: Good and Bad Reports of Non-Christians in Fourteenth-Century England." *Studies in Medieval and Renaissance History* 18, no. 3 (2006): 71–129.

Kessler, Herbert L., and David Nirenberg, eds. *Judaism and Christian Art: Aesthetic Anxieties from the Catacombs to Colonialism*. Philadelphia: University of Pennsylvania Press, 2011.

Kidd, Colin. *The Forging of Races: Race and Scripture in the Protestant Atlantic World: 1600–2000*. Cambridge: Cambridge University Press, 2006.

Kim, Dorothy. "Reframing Race and Jewish/Christian Relations in the Middle Ages." *Transversal* 13, no. 1 (2015): 52–64.

Kimmelman, Reuven. "Rabbi Yohanan and Origen on the Song of Songs: A Third-Century Jewish-Christian Disputation." *Harvard Theological Review* 73 (1980): 567–95.

Kirschenbaum, Aaron. "Jewish and Christian Theories of Usury in the Middle Ages." *Jewish Quarterly Review* 75, no. 3 (January 1985): 270–98.

Kisch, Guido. *The Jews in Medieval Germany: A Study of Their Legal and Social Status*. Chicago: University of Chicago Press, 1949.

———. "The Yellow Badge in History." *Historia Judaica* 4 (1942): 89–146.

Kiwitt, Marc, and Stephen Dörr. "Judeo-French." In *Handbook of Jewish Languages*, edited by Lily Kahn and Aaron D. Rubin, 138–77. Leiden: Brill, 2017.

Klamper, Elisabeth, and Jüdisches Museum der Stadt Wien, eds. *Die Macht der Bilder: antisemitische Vorurteile und Mythe*. Vienna: Picus, 1995.

Klaniczay, Gábor. "Fashionable Beards and Heretic Rags." In *The Uses of Supernatural Power: The Transformation of Popular Religion in Medieval and Early Modern Europe*, edited by Gábor Klaniczay, 51–78. Cambridge, UK: Polity Press, 1990.

Klausner, Theodor. *A Short History of the Western Liturgy*. Oxford: Oxford University Press, 1969.

Klawans, Jonathan. *Impurity and Sin in Ancient Judaism*. Oxford: Oxford University Press, 2000.

Kleinberg, Aviad. "A XIIIth Century Struggle over Custody: The Case of Catherine of Parc-aux-Dames." *Bulletin of Medieval Canon Law* 20 (1990): 51–67.

Knott, Kim. *The Location of Religion: A Spacial Analysis*. London: Equinox, 2005.

Koenig. Daniel G. *Arabic-Islamic Views of the Latin West: Tracing the Emergence of Medieval Europe*. Oxford: Oxford University Press, 2015.

Koestler, Arthur. *The Thirteenth Tribe: The Khazar Empire and Its Heritage*. New York: Popular Library, 1976.

Kogman-Appel, Katrin. "Coping with Christian Pictorial Sources: What Did Jewish Miniaturists Not Paint?" *Speculum* 75 (2000): 816–58.

———. "The Tree of Death and the Tree of Life: The Hanging of Haman in Medieval Jewish Manuscript Painting." In *The Image and the Word: Essays in Honor of John Pummer*, edited by Colum Hourihane, 187–208. University Park: Penn State University, 2005.

Kogman-Appel, Katrin, and Mati Meyer, eds. *Between Judaism and Christianity: Art Historical Essays in Honor of Elisheva (Elisabeth) Revel-Neher*. Leiden: Brill, 2009.

Kohn, Roger. *Les juifs du France du nord dans la seconde moitier du XIVe siècle*. Louvain: E. Peeters, 1988.

Koopmans, Rachel. *Wonderful to Relate: Miracle Stories and Miracle Collecting in High Medieval England*. Philadelphia: University of Pennsylvania Press, 2010.

Kostick, Conor. *The Social Structure of the First Crusade*. Leiden: Brill, 2008.

Koyama, Mark. "The Political Economy of Expulsion: The Regulation of Jewish Money Lending in Medieval England." *Constitutional Political Economy* 21 (2010): 374–406.

Kraus, Henry. *The Living Theatre of Medieval Art*. Bloomington: Indiana University Press, 1967.

Krauss, Samuel. *The Jewish-Christian Controversy: From Earliest Times to 1789*. Vol. 1, *History*. Edited and revised by William Horbury. Tübingen: Mohr Siebeck, 1995.

———. *Das Leben Jesu nach Jüdischen Quellen*. 1902. Reprint. New York: Classic Reprint Series, 2018.

Krautheimer, Richard. *Batei Keneset bimei ha-Beinayim*. Jerusalem: Mosad Bialik, 1994.
——. *Mittelalterliche Synagogen*. Berlin: Frankfurter Verlags-Anstalt, 1927.
Krey, August C. *The First Crusade: The Accounts of Eyewitnesses and Participants*. Princeton, NJ: Princeton University Press, 1921.
Kriegel, Maurice. *Les Juifs à la fin du Moyen Age dans l'Europe méditerranéenne*. Paris: Hachette, 1979.
Krinsky, Carol Herselle. *Synagogues of Europe*. Cambridge, MA: MIT Press, 1985.
Kristeva, Julia. *Powers of Horror: An Essay on Abjection*. Translated by Leon S. Roudiez. New York: Columbia University Press, 1982.
Kroemer, James. "Vanquish the Haughty and Spare the Subjected: A Study of Bernard of Clairvaux's Position on Muslims and Jews." *Medieval Encounters* 18 (2012): 55–92.
Kruger, Steven F. "Anti-Judaism and Anti-Semitism and the Structures in Chaucerian Thought." In *Oxford Handbook to Chaucer*, edited by Suzanne Conklin Akhbari, 146–65. Oxford: Oxford University Press, 2020.
——. "Becoming Christian, Becoming Male?" In *Becoming Male in the Middle Ages*, edited by J. J. Cohen and Bonnie Wheeler, 22–41. New York: Garland, 1997.
——. "The Bodies of Jews in the Late Middle Ages." In *The Idea of Medieval Literature: New Essays on Chaucer and Medieval Culture in Honor of Donald R. Howard*, edited by James M. Dean and Christian K. Zacher, 301–23. Newark: University of Delaware Press, 1992.
——. "Conversion and Medieval Sexual, Religious, and Racial Categories." In *Constructing Medieval Sexuality*, edited by Karma Lochrie, Peggy McCracken, and James A. Schultz, 158–79. Minneapolis: University of Minnesota Press, 1997.
——. *Dreaming in the Middle Ages*. Cambridge: Cambridge University Press, 1992.
——. "Medieval Christian (Dis)identifications: Muslims and Jews in Guibert de Nogent." *New Literary History* 28 (1997): 185–203.
——. *The Spectral Jew: Conversion and Embodiment in Medieval Europe*. Minneapolis: University of Minnesota Press, 2005.
——. "The Times of Conversion." *Philological Quarterly* 92, no. 1 (2013): 19–39.
Krummel, Miriamne Ara. *Crafting Jewishness in Medieval England: Legally Absent, Virtually Present*. London: Palgrave Macmillan, 2011.
——. "'Him Jesus, That Jew!'—Representing Jewishness in the York Plays." In *Jews in Medieval Christendom*, edited by Kristine T. Utterback, 287–312. Leiden: Brill, 2013.
——. "Jewish Culture in Medieval England." In *Handbook of Medieval Culture: Fundamental Aspects and Conditions of the European Middle Ages*, edited by Albrecht Classen, 2:772–93. Berlin: Walter de Gruyter, 2015.
——. *The Medieval Postcolonial Jew, in and out of Time*. Ann Arbor: University of Michigan Press, 2022.
——. "The Pardoner, the Prioress, Sir Thopas, and the Monk: Semitic Discourse and the Jew(s)." In *The Canterbury Tales Revisited—21st Century Interpretations*, edited by Kathleen A. Bishop, 88–109. Newcastle: Cambridge Scholars, 2008.

———. "The Ritual Murder Accusation as Medieval Invention: Linking Libels and Boy Martyrs." In *The Medieval Roots of Antisemitism: Continuities and Discontinuities from the Middle Ages to the Present Day*, edited by Jonathan Adams and Cordelia Hess, 243–56. New York: Routledge, 2018.

———. "The Semitisms of Medieval English Literature." *Literature Compass* 1 (2003): 1–12.

Krummel, Miriamne Ara, and Tison Pugh, eds. *Jews in Medieval England: Teaching Representations of the "Other."* London: Palgrave Macmillan, 2019.

Kulp-Hill, Kathleen, trans. *Songs of Holy Mary by Alfonso X, the Wise: A Translation of the Cantigas de Santa Maria*. MRTS, vol. 173. Tempe: Arizona State University, 2000.

Kushelevsky, Rella. "Jews Reading Arthurian Romances from the Middle Ages: The Reception of Chrétien de Troyes' *Yvain, The Knight of the Lion*, Based on MS JTS Rab. 1164." *AJS Review* 42, no. 2 (November 2018): 381–401.

Lackner, Jacob. "Violent Men and Malleable Women: Gender and Jewish Conversion to Christianity in Medieval Sermon Exempla." *Nashim: A Journal of Jewish Women's Studies and Gender Issues* 30 (2016): 24–47.

Ladner, Gerhard B. "Aspects of Patristic Anti-Judaism." *Viator* 2 (1971): 355–64.

Ladurie, Emmanuel Le Roy. *Montaillou: The Promised Land of Error*. Translated by Barbara Bray. New York: Vintage Books, 1979.

Lampert, Lisa. *Gender and Jewish Difference from Paul to Shakespeare*. Philadelphia: University of Pennsylvania Press, 2004.

———. "The Once and Future Jew: The 'Croxton Play of the Sacrament,' Little Robert of Bury, and Historical Memory." *Jewish History* 15, no. 3 (2001): 235–55.

Lampert-Weissig, Lisa. "Chaucer's Pardoner and the Jews." *Exemplaria* 28, no. 4 (2016): 337–60.

———. *Medieval Literature and Postcolonial Studies*. Edinburgh: Edinburgh University Press, 2010.

———. "'O My Daughter!' 'Die Schöne Judin' und 'Der Neue Jude' in Hermann Sinsheimer's Maria Nunnez." *German Quarterly* 71, no. 3 (Summer 1998): 254–70.

———. "Race, Periodicity, and the (Neo-) Middle Ages." *Modern Language Quarterly* 65 (2004): 391–421.

———. "The Transnational Wandering Jew and the Medieval English Nation." *Literature Compass* 13 (2016): 771–83.

———. "The Wandering Jew as Relic." *English Language Notes* 53, no. 2 (2015): 83–96.

———. "Why Is This Knight Different from All Other Knights? Jews, Anti-Semitism, and the Old French Grail Narratives." *Journal of English and German Philology* 106, no. 2 (April 2007): 224–47.

———. "'You Had to Have Been There': The Importance of Place in Teaching Jewish History and Literature." In *Jews in Medieval England: Teaching Representations of the "Other,"* edited by Miriamne Ara Krummel and Tison Pugh, 245–60. London: Palgrave Macmillan, 2019.

Landes, Richard, and Steven T. Katz, eds. *The Paranoid Apocalypse: A Hundred-Year Retrospective on the Protocols of the Elders of Zion*. New York: NYU Press, 2012.

Landgraf, Artur, ed. *Commentarius Cantabrigiensis in Epistolas Pauli e Schola Petri Abelardi.* 4 vols. Notre Dame, IN: University of Notre Dame, 1937–45.

Langer, Ruth. "The Censorship of Aleinu in Ashkenaz and Its Aftermath." In *The Experience of Jewish Liturgy: Studies Dedicated to Menahem Schmelzer,* edited by Debra Reed Blank, 147–66. Leiden: Brill, 2011.

———. *Cursing the Christians? A History of the Birkat HaMinim.* New York: Oxford University Press, 2011.

———. "Mapping Medieval Liturgical Rites: A Methodological Proposal." In *Jewish Prayer: New Perspectives,* edited by Uri Ehrlich, 30–70. Beer-Sheva: Ben-Gurion University of the Negev Press, 2016.

Langland, William. *Piers Ploughman.* Translated by J. F. Goodridge. New York: Penguin, 1960.

———. *Piers Plowman: An Alliterative Verse Translation.* Translated by E. Talbot Donaldson. Edited by Elizabeth D. Kirk and Judith H. Anderson. New York: W. W. Norton, 1990.

Langmuir, Gavin. "L'Absence d'accusation de meurtre rituel à l'ouest du Rhône." In *Juifs et judaisme de Languedoc,* edited by M-H Vicaire and Bernhard Blumenkranz, 247–49. Toulouse: Edouard Privat, 1977.

———. "Anti-Judaism as the Necessary Preparation for Antisemitism." *Traditio* 2 (1971): 382–89. Reprinted in Gavin Langmuir, *Toward a Definition of Antisemitism.* Berkeley: University of California Press, 1990.

———. "Historiographic Crucifixion." In *Les Juifs au regard de l'histoire: Mélanges en l'honneur de Bernhard Blumenkranz,* edited by Gilbert Dahan, 109–27. Paris: Picard, 1985. Reprinted in Gavin Langmuir, *Toward a Definition of Antisemitism.* Berkeley: University of California Press, 1990.

———. *History, Religion and Antisemitism.* Berkeley: University of California Press, 1990.

———. "'Judei Nostri' and the Beginning of Capetian Legislation." *Traditio* 16 (1960): 203–69. Reprinted in Gavin Langmuir, *Toward a Definition of Antisemitism,* 137–66. Berkeley: University of California Press, 1990.

———. "The Knight's Tale of Young Hugh of Lincoln." *Speculum* 47 (1972): 459–82. Reprinted in Gavin Langmuir, *Toward a Definition of Antisemitism.* Berkeley: University of California Press, 1990.

———. "Majority History and Post-Biblical Jews." *Journal of the History of Ideas* 27, no. 3 (July–September 1966): 343–64. Reprinted in Gavin Langmuir, *Toward a Definition of Antisemitism.* Berkeley: University of California Press, 1990.

———. "Review of Robert Chazan, *Medieval Stereotypes and Modern Antisemitism.*" *Jewish Quarterly Review* 89, no. 1–2 (July–October 1998): 213–16.

———. "Ritual Cannibalism." In *Toward a Definition of Antisemitism,* 263–81. Berkeley: University of California Press, 1990.

———. "Thomas of Monmouth: Detector of Ritual Murder." *Speculum* 59 (1984): 820–46. Reprinted in Gavin Langmuir, *Toward a Definition of Antisemitism.* Berkeley: University of California Press, 1990.

———. *Toward a Definition of Antisemitism.* Berkeley: University of California Press, 1990.

———. "The Transformation of Anti-Judaism." Original title, "From Ambrose of Milan to Emicho of Leiningen: The Transformation of Hostility against Jews in Northern Christendom." In *Gli ebrei nell'alto medioevo*, vol. 26, *Spoleto*, 313–68. Settimane del Centro italiano di studi sull'alto medioevo, 1980. Reprinted in Gavin Langmuir, *Toward a Definition of Antisemitism*. Berkeley: University of California Press, 1990.

Laqueur, Walter. *The Changing Face of Anti-Semitism from Ancient Times to the Present Day*. Oxford: Oxford University Press, 2006.

Lasker, Daniel J. "The Impact of the Crusades on the Jewish-Christian Debate." *Jewish History* 13, no. 2 (1999): 23–36.

———. "Jewish-Christian Polemics at the Turning Point: Jewish Evidence from the Twelfth Century." *Harvard Theological Review* 89, no. 2 (1989): 161–73.

———. "The Jewish Critique of Christianity—in Search of a New Narrative." *Studies in Jewish-Christian Relations* 6 (2011): 1–9.

———. "Jewish Knowledge of Christianity in the Twelfth and Thirteenth Centuries." In *Studies in Medieval Jewish Intellectual and Social History: Festschrift in Honor of Robert Chazan*, edited by David Engel, Lawrence Schiffman, and Elliot Wolfson, 97–109. Leiden: Brill, 2012.

———. *Jewish Philosophical Polemics against Christianity in the Middle Ages*. 2nd ed. with a new introduction. London: Littman Library Jewish Civilization, 2007.

———. "Joseph ben Nathan's *Sefer Yosef ha-Mekanné* and the Jewish Critique of Christianity." In *Jews and Christians in Thirteenth-Century France*, edited by Elisheva Baumgarten and Judah D. Galinsky, 113–22. New York: Palgrave Macmillan, 2015.

———. "Rashi and Maimonides on Christianity." In *Between Rashi and Maimonides: Themes in Medieval Jewish Thought, Literature, and Exegesis*, edited by Ephraim Kanarfogel and Moshe Sokolow, 3–21. New York: Yeshiva University Press, 2010.

———. "Saadia Gaon on Christianity and Islam." In *The Jews of Medieval Islam: Community, Society, and Identity: Proceedings of an International Conference Held by the Institute of Jewish Studies, University College London, 1992*, edited by Daniel Frank, 165–77. Leiden: Brill, 1995.

———. "Tradition and Innovation in Maimonides' Attitudes toward Other Religions." In *Maimonides after 800 Years: Essays on Maimonides and His Influence*, edited by Jay M. Harris, 167–82. Cambridge, MA: Harvard University Press, 2007.

Lasker, Daniel J., and Sarah Stroumsa, eds. and trans. *The Polemic of Nestor the Priest*. 2 vols. Jerusalem: Makhon Ben-Zvi, 1996.

———, eds. *Pulmus Nestor ha-Komer*. Jerusalem: Makhon Ben-Zvi, 1996.

Latteri, Natalie E. "Playing the Whore: Illicit Union and the Biblical Typology of Promiscuity in the *Toledot Yeshu* Tradition." *Shofar* 33, no. 2 (2015): 87–102.

Laudage, Johannes. *Gregorianische Reform und Investiturstreit, Erträge der Forschung*. Darmstadt: Wissenschaftliche Buchgesellschaft, 1993.

Lauterbach, Jacob Z. "The Attitude of the Jew towards the Non-Jew." *CCAR Yearbook* 31 (1921): 186–233.

———. "Jesus in the Talmud." In *Rabbinic Essays*, 473–570. Cincinnati: Hebrew Union College Press, 1951.

Lavezzo, Kathy. *The Accommodated Jew: English Antisemitism from Bede to Milton.* Ithaca, NY: Cornell University Press, 2016.

———. "The Minster and the Privy: Rereading the Prioress's Tale." *PMLA* 126, no. 2 (March 2011): 363–82.

———. "New Work in Medieval Studies." *Philological Quarterly* 87, no. 1–2 (2008): 1–192.

———. "Shifting Geographies of Antisemitism: Mapping Jew and Christian in Thomas of Monmouth's *Life and Miracles of St. William of Norwich.*" In *Mapping Medieval Geographies: Geographical Encounters in the Latin West and Beyond, 300–1600*, edited by Keith D. Lilley, 250–70. Cambridge: Cambridge University Press, 2013.

Le Goff, Jacques. *In Search of Sacred Time: Jacob Voragine and the Goldin Legend.* Translated by Lydia C. Lochrane. Princeton, NJ: Princeton University Press, 2014.

———. *Your Money or Your Life: Economy and Religion in the Middle Ages.* Translated by Patricia Ranum. New York: Zone Books, 1988.

Lehman, Manfred. "Remazim le-'Oto ha-Ish' u-le-Muhamad be-Feirusheihem shel Hasidei Ashkenaz." *Sinai* 87 (1980): 34–40.

Lehnertz, Andreas, and Hannah Teddy Schachter. "The Jews' Hat in Medieval Ashkenaz: Formal Attire for Everyday Men?" *Images* 16 (2023): 1–19.

Le Strange, Guy. *Palestine under the Moslems: A Description of Syria and the Holy Land from A.D. 650 to 1500.* London: Legare Street Press, 2022.

Levenson, Jon D. *Inheriting Abraham: The Legacy of the Patriarch in Judaism, Christianity and Islam.* Princeton, NJ: Princeton University Press, 2012.

Leviant, Curt., ed. *King Artus: A Hebrew Arthurian Romance of 1279.* New York: Ktav, 1969.

Levin, Chaviva. "Constructing Memories of Martyrdom: Contrasting Portrayals of Martyrdom in the Hebrew Narratives of the First and Second Crusade." In *Remembering the Crusades: Myth, Magic and Identity*, edited by Nicholas Paulmand and Suzanne Yaeger, 50–68. Baltimore: Johns Hopkins University Press, 2012.

———. "Jewish Conversion to Christianity in Medieval Northern Europe Encountered and Imagined, 1100–1300." PhD diss., New York University, 2006.

———. "Portrayal of Christians in Ephraim of Bonn's Sefer Zekhirah: An Alternate [sic] Ashkenazic Voice." *Journal of Jewish Studies* 65, no. 1 (Spring 2014): 129–47.

Levine, Lee I. *The Ancient Synagogue: The First Thousand Years.* New Haven, CT: Yale University Press, 2000.

Levine, Robert. "Why Praise Jews? Satire and History in the Middle Ages." *Journal of Medieval History* 12, no. 4 (1986): 291–96.

Levinson, Eyal. "'She-Megadelin Balorin ve-Loveshin Bigdei Parashin': Bahurim Yehudim be-Ashkenaz Bimei ha-Beinayim—Bein Gavriyut Rabbanit le-Gavriyut Abbirit." *Chidushim: Studies in the History of German and Central European Jewry* 21 (2019): 14–46.

———. *"Va-Yigdelu ha-Ne'arim": Migdar u-Miniyut Be-Ashkenaz bimei ha-Beinayim.* Jerusalem: Merkaz Zalman Shazar and Leo Baeck Institute, 2022.

Levy, Richard S. "Political Antisemitism in Germany and Austria, 1848–1914." In *Antisemitism: A History*, edited by Albert S. Lindemann and Richard S. Levy, 121–35. Oxford: Oxford University Press, 2010.

Lewis, Bernard. *The Jews of Islam*. Princeton, NJ: Princeton University Press, 1984. With a new introduction by Mark R. Cohen, 2014.

Lewis, Bernard, and Friedhelm Niewöhner, eds. *Religionsgespräche im Mittelalter*. Wiesbaden: Harrassowitz, 1992.

Lewis, David A. "The Jews, the Others, of Piers Plowman." Humanities Commons, 2005. http://dx.doi.org/10.17613/M69681.

Liberles Noiman, Ahuva. "Believing or Belonging: Religious Conversion, Family Life, and the Jewish Community in Late Medieval German Lands." PhD diss., Hebrew University of Jerusalem, 2020.

Lichtenstein, Aaron. *The Seven Laws of Noah*. 2nd ed. New York: Rabbi Jacob Joseph School Press, 1981.

Lieber, Laura. "'You Have Skirted This Hill Long Enough': The Tension between Rhetoric and History in a Byzantine Piyyut." *Hebrew Union College Annual* 80 (2008): 63–114.

Liebeschütz, Hans. "The Crusading Movement and Its Attitude towards Jewry." *Journal of Jewish Studies* 10 (1959): 97–111. Reprinted in Jeremy Cohen, ed., *Essential Papers on Judaism and Christianity in Conflict*. New York: NYU Press, 1991.

———. "The Significance of Judaism in Peter Abelard's Dialogus." *Journal of Jewish Studies* 12 (1961): 1–18.

———. *Synagoga und Ecclesia: Religionsgeschichtliche Studien über die Auseinandersetzung der Kirche mit dem Judentum im Hochmittelalter*. Heidelberg: Lambert Schneider, 1983.

Lifschitz-Golden, Manya. *Les juifs dans la littérature française du moyen âge, mystères, miracles, chroniques*. New York: Columbia University Press, 1935. Reprinted, Geneva: Slatkine, 1977.

Lilley, Keith D. "Cities of God? Medieval Urban Forms and Their Christian Symbolism." *Transactions of the Institute of British Geographers* 29 (2004): 296–313.

———. *City and Cosmos: The Sacred World through Urban Form*. London: Reaktion Books, 2009.

———, ed. *Mapping Medieval Geographies: Geographical Encounters in the Latin West and Beyond, 300–1600*. Cambridge: Cambridge University Press, 2013.

Limor Ora, ed. *Bein Yehudim le-Nozrim: Yehudim ve-Nozrim be-Ma'arav Eiropa 'ad Reishit ha 'eit ha-Hadashah*. 5 vols. Tel Aviv: Ha-Universitah ha-Petuhah, 1993–98.

———. "Christians and Jews." In *The Cambridge History of Christianity: Christianity in Western Europe: c. 1100–c. 1500*, edited by Miri Rubin and Walter Simons, 4:135–48. Cambridge: Cambridge University Press, 2009.

———, ed. *Die Disputationen zu Ceuta (1179) und Mallorca (1286): Zwei antijüdische Schriften aus dem mittelalterlichen Genua*. Munich: Monumenta Germaniae Historica, 1994.

———. "Mary and the Jews: Story, Controversy, and Testimony." *Historien* 6 (2006): 55–71.

———. "Qedushah Nozrit—Samhut Yehudit." *Qatedra* 80 (1996): 31–62.

———. "Yahadut Mitbonenet be-Nazrut: Pulmus Nestor ha-Komer ve-Toledot Yeshu." *Pe'amim* 75 (1998): 109–28.

Limor, Ora, and Guy G. Stroumsa, eds. *Contra Iudaeos: Ancient and Medieval Polemics between Christians and Jews*. Tübingen: Mohr Siebeck, 1996.
Lindemann, Albert S. *Esau's Tears: Modern Anti-Semitism and the Rise of the Jews*. Cambridge: Cambridge University Press, 1997.
Lindemann, Albert S., and Richard S. Levy, eds. *Antisemitism: A History*. Oxford: Oxford University Press, 2010.
Linder, Amnon. "Ecclesia and Synagoga in the Medieval Myth of Constantine the Great." *Revue belge de philologie et d'histoire* 54 (1976): 1019–60.
———, ed. and trans. *The Jews in Roman Imperial Legislation*. Detroit: Wayne State University Press, 1987.
———, ed. and trans. *The Jews in the Legal Sources of the Early Middle Ages*. Detroit: Wayne State University Press, 1997.
———. "'The Jews Too Were Not Absent . . . Carrying Moses's Law on Their Shoulders': The Ritual Encounter of Pope and Jews from the Middle Ages to Modern Times." *Jewish Quarterly Review* 99, no. 3 (Summer 2009): 323–95.
Lipman, V. D. *The Jews of Medieval Norwich*. Cambridge, UK: Heffer and Sons, 1967.
Lipton, Sara. *Dark Mirror: The Medieval Origins of Anti-Jewish Iconography*. New York: Henry Holt and Co., 2014.
———. "Images and Objects as Sources for Medieval History." In *Understanding Medieval Primary Sources*, edited by J. T. Rosenthal, 225–42. New York: Routledge, 2012.
———. *Images of Intolerance: The Representation of Jews and Judaism in the Bible Moralisée*. Berkeley: University of California Press, 1999.
———. "The Jew's Face: Vision, Knowledge, and Identity in Medieval Anti-Jewish Caricature." In *Late Medieval Jewish Identities: Iberia and Beyond*, edited by Carmin Caballero-Navas and Esperanza Alfonso, 259–85. New York: Palgrave, 2010.
———. "'The Sweet Lean of His Head': Writing about Looking at the Crucifix in the High Middle Ages." *Speculum* 80, no. 4 (October 2005): 1172–208.
———. "The Temple Is My Body: Gender, Carnality, and Synagoga in the Bible Moralisée." In *Imagining the Self, Imagining the Other: Visual Representation and Jewish-Christian Dynamics in the Middle Ages and Early Modern Period*, edited by Eva Frojmovic, 129–63. Leiden: Brill, 2002.
———. "What's in a Nose? The Origins, Development, and Influence of a Medieval Anti-Jewish Caricature." In *The Medieval Roots of Antisemitism: Continuities and Discontinuities from the Middle Ages to the Present Day*, edited by Jonathan Adams and Cordelia Hess, 183–203. New York: Routledge, 2018.
———. "Where Are the Gothic Jewish Women? On the Non-Iconography of Jewess in the Cantigas de Santa Maria." *Jewish History* 22 (2008): 139–77.
Liss, Hanna. *Creating Fictional Worlds: Peshat Exegesis and Narrativity in Rashbam's Commentary on the Torah*. Leiden: Brill, 2011.
Little, Lester K. "The Function of the Jews in the Commercial Revolution." In *Centro di studi sulla spiritualità medievale (Todi, Italy): Povertà et ricchezza nella spiritualità dei secoli XI e XII 15–18 ottobre 1967*, 271–87. Todi: Presso l'Accademia Tudertina, 1969.

———. "The Jews in Christian Europe." In *Religious Poverty and the Profit Economy in Medieval Europe*, 42–57. Ithaca, NY: Cornell University Press, 1978. Reprinted as "The Jews in Christian Europe," in *Essential Papers on Judaism and Christianity in Conflict*, edited by Jeremy Cohen, 276–97. New York: NYU Press, 1991.

———. "Pride Goes before Avarice: Social Change and the Vices in Latin Christendom." *American Historical Review* 76 (1971): 16–49.

———. *Religious Poverty and the Profit Economy in Medieval Europe*. Ithaca, NY: Cornell University Press, 1978.

Lockshin, Martin I. "Translation as Polemic: The Case of Toledot Yeshu." In *Minhah le-Nahum: Biblical and Other Studies Presented to Nahum M. Sarna in Honour of His 70th Birthday*, edited by Marc Brettler and Michael Fishbane, 226–41. Sheffield: JSOT Press, 1993.

Loewe, Raphael. "Gentiles as Seen by Jews after CE 70." In *The Cambridge History of Judaism*. Vol. 3, *The Early Roman Period*, edited by William Horbury, W. D. Davies, and Johnn Sturdy, 250–66. Cambridge: Cambridge University Press, 1999.

Logan, F. Donald. "Thirteen London Jews and Conversion to Christianity: Problems of Apostasy in the 1280s." *Bulletin of the Institute of Historical Research* 45 (1972): 214–29.

Lohrmann, Dietrich. "Albert von Aachen und die Judenprogrome des Jahres 1096." *Zeitschrift des Aachener Geschichtsvereins* 100 (1995–96): 129–51.

Lopez, Robert S. *The Birth of Europe*. New York: M. Evans, 1967.

———. *The Commercial Revolution of the Middle Ages, 950–1350*. Englewood Cliffs, NJ: Prentice Hall, 1971.

Lopez, Robert S., and Irving W. Raymond, eds. *Medieval Trade in the Mediterranean World*. New York: Columbia University Press, 1955.

Lotter, Friedrich. "Hostienfrevel und Blutwunderfälschung bei den Judenverfolgungen von 1298 ('Rintfleisch') und 1336–1338 ('Armleder')." In *Fälschungen im Mittelalter* 5 (= *Monumenta Gemaniae Historica* 33, no. 5), 533–83. Hannover: Hahnsche Buchhandlung, 1988.

———. "Innocens et virgo et martyr: Thomas von Monmouth und die Verbreitung der Ritualmordlegende im Hochmittelalter." In *Die Legende vom Ritualmord: Zur Geschichte der Blutbeschuldigung gegen Juden*, edited by Rainer Erb, 25–72. Berlin: Metropol, 1993.

———. "Das Judenbild im volkstümlichen Erzählgut dominikanischer Exempelliteratur um 1300: Die 'Historiae memorabiles des Rudolf von Schlettsta.'" In *Herrschaft, Kirche, Kultur. Beiträge zur Geschichte des Mittelatlers. Festschrift für Friedrich Prinz zu seinem 65. Geburtstage*, edited by Georg Jenal with Stephanie Haarländer, 431–45. Monographien z. Geschichte des Mittelalters, 37. Stuttgart: Georg Jenal, 1993.

———. "Die Judenverfolgungen des 'König Rintfleisch' in Franken um 1298. Die endgültige Wende in den christlich-jüdischen Beziehungen im deutschen Reich des Mittelalters." *Zeitschrift für Historische Forschung* 15, no. 4 (1988): 385–422.

———. "The Position of the Jews in Early Cistercian Exegesis and Preaching." In *From Witness to Witchcraft: Jews and Judaism in Medieval Christian Thought*, edited by Jeremy Cohen, 163–86. Wiesbaden: Harrassowitz, 1996.

———. "'Tod oder Taufe': Das Problem der Zwangstaufen während des ersten Kreuzzugs." In *Juden und Kristen zur Zeit der Kreuzzüge*, edited by Alfred Haverkamp, 107–52. Sigmaringen: Jan Thorbecke Verlag, 1999.

Lourie, Elena. "A Plot Which Failed? The Case of the Corpse Found in the Jewish Call of Barcelona (1301)." *Mediterranean Historical Review* 1, no. 2 (1986): 187–220.

Luria, Shlomo (Maharshal). *She'eilot u-Teshuvot (Responsa)*. Lublin, 1599.

Ma'aravot, Yotzrot ve-Zulatot u-Selichot.... Wirmaisa. Frankfurt am Main: Johann Kellner, [1714].

Maccoby, Hyam. *Judaism on Trial: Jewish-Christian Disputations in the Middle Ages*. Rutherford, NJ: Fairleigh Dickenson University Press, 1982.

Machinist, Peter. "Outsiders or Insiders: The Biblical View of Emergent Israel and Its Contexts." In *The Other in Jewish Thought and History: Constructions of Jewish Culture and Identity*, edited by Lawrence J. Silberstein and Robert L. Cohn, 35–60. New York: NYU Press.

MacLehose, William F. *A Tender Age: Cultural Anxieties over the Child in the Twelfth and Thirteenth Centuries*. New York: Columbia University Press, 2009.

Magin, Christine. "'Waffenrecht' und 'Waffenverbot' für Juden im Mittelalter—zu einem Mythos der Forschungsgeschichte." *Aschkenas* 13 (2003): 17–33.

Maier, Johann. *Fremdes und Fremde in der Jüdischen Tradition und im Sefär Chasidim: 4 "Arye Maimon-Vortrag" an der Universität Trier, 7. November 2001*. Trier: Kliomedia, 2002.

Maitland, F. W. "The Deacon and the Jewess; or, Apostasy at Common Law." *Transactions (Jewish Historical Society of England)* 6 (1908–10): 260–76. Reprinted in F. W. Maitland, *Roman Canon Law in the Church of England*, 158–79. London, 1898.

Malkiel, David. "Destruction or Conversion, Intention and Reaction, Crusaders and Jews, 1096." *Jewish History* 15 (2001): 257–80.

———. "Infanticide in Passover Iconography." *Journal of the Warburg and Courtauld Institutes* 56 (1993): 85–99.

———. "Jewish-Christian Relations in Europe 840–1096." *Journal of Medieval History* 29, no. 1 (2003): 55–83.

———. "Jews and Apostates in Medieval Europe—Boundaries Real and Imagined." *Past and Present* 194 (February 2007): 3–34.

———. *Reconstructing Ashkenaz: The Human Face of Franco-German Jewry 1000–1250*. Stanford, CA: Stanford University Press, 2009.

———. "Vestiges of Conflict in the Hebrew Crusade Chronicles." *Journal of Jewish Studies* 52, no. 2 (2001): 323–40.

Maloney, Robert P. "Early Conciliar Legislation on Usury: A Contribution to the Study of Christian Moral Thought." *Recherches de théologie ancienne et médiévale* 39 (1972): 145–57.

———. "The Teaching of the Fathers on Usury: An Historical Study on the Development of Christian Thinking." *Vigiliae Christianae* 27 (1973): 241–65.

Mandel, Jerome. "'Boy' as Devil in Chaucer." *Papers on Language and Literature: A Journal for Scholars and Critics of Language and Literature* 11 (1975): 407–11.

Mann, Vivian B., Jerrilyn D. Dodds, and Thomas F. Glick, eds. *Convivencia: Jews, Muslims, and Christians in Medieval Spain*. New York: George Braziller in association with the Jewish Museum, 1992.

Manuel, Frank E. *The Broken Staff: Judaism through Christian Eyes*. Cambridge, MA: Harvard University Press, 1992.

———. "The Use and Abuse of Psychology in History." *Daedalus* 100, no. 1 (Winter 1971): 187–213.

Marcus, Ivan G. "Forum on David Nirenberg, *Anti-Judaism: The Western Tradition*." *Jewish History* 28 (2014): 190–94.

———. "From Politics to Martyrdom: Shifting Paradigms in the Hebrew Narratives of the 1096 Crusade Riots." *Prooftexts* 2 (1982): 40–52.

———. "Hierarchies, Religious Boundaries and Jewish Spirituality in Medieval Germany." *Jewish History* 1, no. 2 (Fall 1986): 7–26.

———. "History, Story, and Collective Memory: Narrativity in Early Ashkenazic Culture." *Prooftexts* 10, no. 3 (Fall 1990): 365–88.

———. "Honey Cakes and Torah: A Jewish Boy Learns His Letters." In *Judaism in Practice: From the Middle Ages through the Early Modern Period*, edited by Lawrence Fine, 115–30. Princeton, NJ: Princeton University Press, 2001.

———. "The Image of the Jews in the Exempla of Caesarius of Heisterbach." In *From Witness to Witchcraft: Jews and Judaism in Medieval Christian Thought*, edited by Jeremy Cohen, 247–56. Wiesbaden: Harrassowitz, 1996.

———. "Israeli Medieval Jewish Historiography: From Nationalist Positivism to New Cultural and Social Histories." *Jewish Studies Quarterly* 17 (2010): 244–85.

———. "A Jewish-Christian Symbiosis: The Culture of Early Ashkenaz." In *Cultures of the Jews*, edited by David Biale, 449–516. New York: Schocken Books, 2002.

———. *The Jewish Life Cycle: Rites of Passage from Biblical to Modern Times*. Seattle: University of Washington Press, 2004.

———. "The Jewish Minority Experience in Medieval Spain." *Response* 40 (1981): 59–71.

———. "Jews and Christians Imagining the Other in Medieval Europe." *Prooftexts* 15, no. 3 (September 1995): 209–26.

———. "Judeo-Latin." *Dictionary of the Middle Ages*, edited by Joseph R. Strayer, 7:176–77. New York: Scribner and Sons, 1985.

———. "On Medieval Jewish Prophecy: From 'Deus Vult' to 'The Will of the Creator.'" In *From Strength to Strength: Essays in Honor of Shaye J. D. Cohen*, edited by Michael L. Satlow, 599–610. Providence, RI: Brown Judaica Series, 2018.

———. "Mi-'Deus Vult' ve-'ad 'Rezon ha-Borei': Idiologiyot Datiot Qizoniot u-Mezi'ut Historit bi-Shenat Tatnu ve-Ezel Hasidei Ashkenaz." In *Yehudim mul ha-Zelav: Gezeirot Tatnu be-Historiah u-ve-Historiografiah*, edited by Yom Tov Assis et al., 92–100. Jerusalem: Magnes Press, 2000.

———. "Narrative Fantasies in *Sefer Hasidim*." In *Rabbinic Fantasies: Imaginative Narratives from Classical Hebrew Literatures*, edited by David Stern and Mark Mirsky, 215–38. New Haven, CT: Yale University Press, 1998.

———. "Performative Midrash in the Memory of Ashkenazi Matryrs." In *Midrash Unbound: Transformations and Innovations*, edited by Michael Fidhbane and Joanna Weinberg, 197–209. Oxford: Littman Library of Jewish Civilization, 2013.

———. *Piety and Society: The Jewish Pietists of Medieval Germany*. Leiden: Brill, 1981.

———. "A Pious Community and Doubt: Jewish Martyrdom among Northern European Jewry and the Story of Rabbi Amnon of Mainz." In *Essays on Hebrew Literature in Honor of Avraham Holtz*, edited by Zvia Ben-Yosef Ginor, 21–46. New York: Jewish Theological Seminary, 2003.

———. "The Representation of Reality in the Sources of the 1096 Anti-Jewish First Crusade Riots." *Jewish History* 13, no. 2 (Fall 1999): 37–48.

———. Review of *European Jewry and the First Crusade*, by Robert Chazan. *Speculum* 64, no. 3 (July 1989): 685–88.

———. *Rituals of Childhood: Jewish Culture and Acculturation in the Middle Ages*. New Haven, CT: Yale University Press, 1996.

———. *Sefer Hasidim and the Ashkenazic Book in Medieval Europe*. Philadelphia: University of Pennsylvania Press, 2018.

———. "The Sephardic Mystique." *Orim* 1, no. 1 (Autumn 1985): 35–53.

———. "The Song of Songs in German Hasidism and the School of Rashi: A Preliminary Comparison." In *Frank Talmage Memorial Volume*, edited by Barry Walfish, 1:181–89. Haifa: Haifa University Press, 1993.

———. "Why Did Medieval Northern French Jewry (*Zarfat*) Disappear?" In *Jews, Christians, and Muslims in Medieval and Early Modern Times: A Festschrift in Honor of Mark R. Cohen*, edited by Arnold E. Franklin et al., 99–117. Leiden: Brill, 2013.

———. "Why Is This Knight Different? A Jewish Self-Representation in Medieval Europe." In *Tov Elem: Memory, Community and Gender in Medieval and Early Modern Jewish Societies: Studies in Honor of Robert Bonfil*, edited by Roni Weinstein, Elisheva Baumgarten, and Amnon Raz-Krakotzkin, 139–52. Jerusalem: Mosad Bialik, 2011.

Marcus, Jacob Rader, ed. *The Jew in the Medieval World: A Source Book, 315–1791*. Cincinnati: Sinai Press, 1938.

Marcus, Jacob Rader, and Marc Saperstein, eds. *The Jews in Christian Europe: A Source Book, 315–1791*. Pittsburgh: Pittsburgh University Press, 2015.

Marks, Jonathan D. "Rousseau's Use of the Jewish Example." *Review of Politics* 72 (2010): 463–81.

Markus, Robert A. "How on Earth Could Places Become Holy? Origins of the Christian Idea of Holy Places." *Journal of Early Christian Studies* 2, no. 3 (1994): 257–71.

———. "The Jews as a Hermeneutical Device: The Inner Life of a Gregorian Topos." In *Gregory the Great: A Symposium*, edited by John C. Cavadini, 1–15. Notre Dame, IN: University of Notre Dame Press, 1995.

Marlowe, Christopher. *The Jew of Malta*. Edited by James R. Simeon. New York: W. W. Norton, 1994.

Marmursztejn, Elsa. *Baptême forcé des enfants juifs: question scolastique, enjeu politique, échos contemporains*. Paris: Les Belles Lettres, 2016.

———. "La hantise de la téléologie dans l'historiographie médiévale de l'hostilité antijuive." *Revue d'histoire moderne et contemporaine* 62, no. 2–3 (2015): 15–39.

Martène, Edmond, and Ursin Durand, eds. *Thesaurus Novus Anecdotorum*. 5 vols. Paris, 1717.

Martin, John D. *Representations of Jews in Late Medieval and Early Modern German Literature*. Studies in German Jewish History 5. Oxford: Peter Lang, 2004.

Marx, Alexander. "Rabbenu Gershom, Light of the Exile." In *Essays in Jewish Biography*, 39–60. Philadelphia: Jewish Publication Society, 1947.

Marx, Dalia. "The Morning Ritual in the Talmud." *Hebrew Union College Annual* 77 (2007): 103–29.

Matteoni, Francesca. "The Jew, the Blood, and the Body in Late Medieval and Early Modern Europe." *Folklore* 119 (2008): 182–200.

Mattes, Barbara. *Jüdisches Alltagsleben in einer Mittelalterliche Stadt: Responsa von Rabbi Meir von Rothenburg*. Berlin: Walter de Gruyter, 2003.

Matthew Paris. *English History*. Translated by J. A. Giles. 3 vols. London: Henry G. Bohn, 1854.

———. *Matthaeus Parisiensis Chronica Maiora*. Edited by Henry R. Luard. 7 vols. Rolls Series 57. London: HM Stationary Office, 1880.

Mayer, Hans Eberhard. *The Crusades*. Oxford: Oxford University Press, 1972.

Mazzotta, Giuseppe. *Dante's Vision and the Circle of Knowledge*. Princeton, NJ: Princeton University Press, 1993.

McComish, Jane. "The Medieval Jewish Cemetery at Jewbury, York." *Jewish Culture and History* 3, no. 2 (2000): 21–30.

McCracken, Peggy. *The Curse of Eve, the Wound of the Hero: Blood, Gender, and Medieval Literature*. Philadelphia: University of Pennsylvania Press, 2003.

McCulloh, John M. "Jewish Ritual Murder: Thomas of Monmouth and the Early Dissemination of the Myth." *Speculum* 72, no. 3 (July 1997): 698–74.

———. "Thomas of Monmouth, Life and Passion of St. William of Norwich, Originally Translated by Augustus Jessopp and Montague Rhodes James." In *Medieval Hagiography: An Anthology*, edited by Thomas Head, 523–24. New York: Garland Publishing, Inc., 2000.

McGinn, Bernard. "Portraying Antichrist in the Middle Ages." In *The Use and Abuse of Eschatology in the Middle Ages*, edited by Werner Verbeke, D. Verhelst, and Andries Welkenhuysen, 1–48. Leuven: Leuven University Press, 1988.

McMichael, Steven J., and Susan Myers, eds. *Friars and Jews in the Middle Ages and Renaissance*. Leiden: Brill, 2004.

Mechoulan, Stéphane. "The Expulsion of the Jews from France in 1306: A Modern Fiscal Analysis." *Journal of European Economic History* 33 (2004): 555–84.

Meerson, Michael, and Peter Schäfer, eds. and trans., with the collaboration of Yaacov Deutsch, David Grossberg, Avigail Manekin, and Adina Yoffie. *Toledot Yeshu: The Life Story of Jesus*. 2 vols. Tübingen: Mohr Siebeck, 2014.

Meir b. Barukh of Rothenburg. *She'eilot u-Teshuvot Maharam*. Prague, 1608. Reprinted, Lemberg, 1860.

Mekhilta de-Rabbi Ishmael. Translated and edited by Jacob Z. Lauterbach. 3 vols. Philadelphia: Jewish Publication Society, 1933.

Mekhilta de-Rabbi Yishma'el. Edited by Hayim Shaul Horovitz and Yisrael Avraham Rabin. Jerusalem: Wahrmann, 1970.

Mell, Julie L. "Cultural Meanings of Money in Medieval Ashkenaz: On Gift, Profit, and Value in Medieval Judaism and Christianity." *Jewish History* 28, no. 2 (2014): 125–58.

———. "Jews and Money." In *The Cambridge Companion to Antisemitism*, edited by Steven T. Katz, 213–31. Cambridge: Cambridge University Press, 2022.

———. *The Myth of the Medieval Jewish Moneylender*. 2 vols. Palgrave Studies in Intellectual and Cultural History. New York: Palgrave, 2017–18.

Mellinkoff, Ruth. *Antisemitic Hate Signs in Hebrew Illuminated Manuscripts from Medieval Germany*. Jerusalem: Center for Jewish Art, 1999.

———. *Averting Demons: The Protective Power of Medieval Visual Motifs and Themes*. 2 vols. Eugene, OR: Wipf and Stock, 2004.

———. *The Mark of Cain*. Berkeley: University of California Press, 1981.

———. *Outcasts: Signs of Otherness in Northern European Art of the Late Middle Ages*. 2 vols. Berkeley: University of California Press, 1993.

———. "Riding Backwards: Theme of Humiliation and Symbol of Evil." *Viator* 4 (1973): 153–76.

Menache, Sophia. "Faith, Myth, and Politics: The Stereotype of the Jews and Their Expulsion from England and France." *Jewish Quarterly Review* 75, no. 4 (1985): 351–74.

———. "The King, the Church, and the Jews: Some Considerations on the Expulsions from England and France." *Journal of Medieval History* 13 (1987): 223–36.

———. "Matthew Paris' Attitudes toward Anglo-Jewry." *Journal of Medieval History* 23, no. 2 (1997): 139–62.

———. "Tartars, Jews, Saracens and the Jewish-Mongol 'Plot' of 1241." *History* 81 (1996): 319–42.

Mentgen, Gerd. "Die Ritualmordaffäre um den 'Guten Werner' von Oberwesel und ihre Folgen." *Jahrbuch für Westdeutsche Landesgeschichte* 21 (1995): 159–98.

———. "Hivvazrutah shel ha-Bedutah 'al 'Alilat ha-Dam." *Zion* 59 (1994): 343–49.

———. "Richard of Devizes und die Juden: Ein Beitrag zur Interpretation seiner 'Gesta Richardi.'" *Kairos* 30–31 (1989): 95–104.

Merback, Mitchell B., ed. *Beyond the Yellow Badge: Anti-Judaism and Antisemitism in Medieval and Early Modern Visual Culture*. Leiden: Brill, 2008.

———. *Pilgrimage and Pogrom: Violence, Memory, and Visual Culture in the Host-Miracle Shrines of Germany and Austria*. Chicago: University of Chicago Press, 2012.

Mesler, Katelyn. "Legends of Jewish Sorcery: Reputations and Representations in Late Antique and Medieval Europe." PhD diss., Northwestern University, 2012.

Metzger, Thérèse, and Mendel Metzger, eds. *Jewish Life in the Middle Ages: Illuminated Hebrew Manuscripts of the Thirteenth to the Sixteenth Centuries*. New York: Alpine, 1982.

Midrash Bereishit Rabba. Edited by J. Theodor and C. Alberk. 3 vols. 1903–29. Reprinted, Jerusalem: Wahrmann, 1965.

Miller, Debra Jo. "The Development of the Ritual Murder Accusation in the Twelfth and Thirteenth Centuries and Its Relationship to the Changing Attitudes of Christians to Jews." Master's thesis, Cambridge University, 1991.

Miller, Fergus. "Hagar, Ishmael, Josephus, and the Origins of Islam." *Journal of Jewish Studies* 44 (1993): 23–45.

Miller, William Ian. *The Anatomy of Disgust.* Cambridge, MA: Harvard University Press, 1997.

Milton, Gregory B. "Christian and Jewish Lenders: Religious Identity and the Extension of Credit." *Viator* 37 (2006): 301–18.

Minty, Mary. "Judengasse to Christian Quarter: The Phenomenon of the Converted Synagogue in the Late Medieval and Early Modern Holy Roman Empire." In *Popular Religion in Germany and Central Europe, 1400–1800*, edited by Bob Scribner and Trevor Johnson, 58–86. New York: St. Martin's Press, 1996.

———. "Qiddush ha-Shem be-'Einei Nozrim be-Germania bimei ha-Beinayim." *Zion* 59 (1994): 233–66.

———. "Responses to Medieval Ashkenazi Martyrdom (Kiddush ha-Shem) in Late Medieval Christian Sources." *Jahrbuch für Antisemitismusforschung* 4 (1995): 13–38.

Mirrer, Louise. "The Beautiful Jewess: Marisaltos in Alfonso X's *Cantiga* 107." In *Women, Jews, and Muslims in the Texts of Reconquest Castile.* Ann Arbor: University of Michigan Press, 1996.

———. The Jew's Body in Medieval Iberian Literary Portraits and Miniatures: Examples from the Cantigas de Santa Maria and the Cantar de Mio Cid." *Shofar* 12, no. 3 (1994): 17–30.

———. "Representing 'Other' Men: Muslims, Jews, and Masculine Ideals in Medieval Epic and Ballads." In *Medieval Masculinities: Regarding Men in the Middle Ages*, edited by Clare A. Lees, with Thelma Fenster and Jo Ann McNamara, 169–86. Minneapolis: University of Minnesota Press, 1994.

Modder, Montague Frank. *The Jew in the Literature of England.* Philadelphia: Jewish Publication Society, 1939.

Möhring, Hannes. "Graf Emicho und die Judenverfolgung von 1096." *Rheinische Vierteljahresblätter* 56 (1992): 97–111.

Monroe, Elizabeth. "'Fair and Friendly, Sweet and Beautiful': Hopes for Conversion in Synagoga's Song of Songs Imagery." In *Beyond the Yellow Badge: Anti-Judaism and Antisemitism in Medieval and Early Modern Visual Culture*, edited by Mitchell J. Merback, 33–62. Leiden: Brill, 2007.

Moore, R. I. *The First European Revolution c. 870–1215.* Oxford: Blackwell, 2000.

———. *The Formation of a Persecuting Society: Power and Deviance in Western Europe 950–1250.* Oxford: Oxford University Press, 1987.

———. "Heresy, Repression and Social Change in the Age of Gregorian Reform." In *Christendom and Its Discontents: Exclusion, Persecution, and Rebellion 1000–1500*, edited by Scott L. Waugh and Peter D. Diehl, 9–46. Cambridge: Cambridge University Press, 1996.

———. "Making Enemies: Latin Christendom in the Age of Reform." *Historien* 6 (2006): 48–54.

Moorhead, John. *Ambrose: Church and Society in the Late Roman World*. London: Routledge, 1999.

Morin, Edgar. *Rumour in Orléans*. Translated by Peter Green. London: Blond, 1971.

Morrison, Karl F. *Conversion and Text*. Charlottesville: University Press of Virginia, 1992.

———, ed. *Understanding Conversion*. Charlottesville: University Press of Virginia, 1992.

Morrison, Susan Signe. *Excrement in the Late Middle Ages: Sacred Filth and Chaucer's Fecopoetics*. New York: Palgrave Macmillan, 2008.

Moses b. Maimon (Maimonides). *The Book of Love*. Yale Judaica Series. New Haven, CT: Yale University Press, 2004.

Moskin, Carmel. "Tadmit ha-Goy be-Sifrut Yehudei Germania ba-Mei'ot 12–13." Master's thesis, University of Haifa, 1982.

Mühlhausen, Yom Tov Lipmann. *Sefer ha-Nizzahon*. Nuremberg: W. Endter, 1644. Reprinted, New York, 1979.

Muir, Lynette R. "The Mass on the Medieval Stage." *Comparative Drama* 23 (1989): 316–30.

Muldoon, James, ed. *Varieties of Religious Conversion in the Middle Ages*. Gainesville: University of Florida Press, 1997.

Mullaney, Steven. *The Place of the Stage: License, Play, and Power in Renaissance England*. Chicago: University of Chicago Press, 1988.

Müller, Joel. *Teshuvot Geonei Mizrah u-Ma'arav*. Berlin, 1888.

———. *Teshuvot Hakhmei Zarfat ve-Lotir*. Vienna, 1881.

Müller, Jorg R. "Sexual Relationships between Christians and Jews in Medieval Germany according to Christian Sources." *Iggud: Selected Essays in Jewish Studies* 2 (2005): 19–32.

Mundill, Robin R. "Clandestine Crypto-Camouflaged Usurer or Legal Merchant? Edwardian Jewry, 1275–90." *Jewish Culture and History* 3, no. 2 (2000): 73–97.

———. *England's Jewish Solution: Experiment and Expulsion, 1262–1290*. Cambridge: Cambridge University Press, 1998.

———. *The King's Jews: Money, Massacre, and Exodus in Medieval England*. London: Continuum, 2010.

Munro, D. C. "The Speech of Pope Urban II at Clermont, 1096." *American Historical Review* 11 (1905): 231–42.

Münz-Manor, Ophir. "Carnivalesque Ambivalence and the Christian Other in Aramaic Poems from Byzantine Palestine." In *Jews in Byzantium: Dialectics of Minority and Majority Cultures*, edited by Robert Bonfil et al., 829–43. Leiden: Brill, 2012.

———. "Nozrim ve-Nazrut be-Sifrut ha-Piyyut: Bein Yizzugim Tippologiyyim li-(Y)zuggim Meforashim." In *Ot Le-Tovah: Pirqei Mehqar Mugashim Le-Professor Tovah Rozen. Mi-Kan* [*Journal for Hebrew and Israeli Literature and Culture*] 11 (2012): 43–56.

Murphy, Rhodes. "Sürgün." In *Encyclopedia of Islam*, edited by P. Bearman et al., 12:767. 2nd ed. Leiden: Brill, 1960–2007.

Narin van Court, Elisa Marie. "Critical Apertures: Medieval Anti-Judaism and Middle English Narrative." PhD diss., University of California, Berkeley, 1994.

———. "The Hermeneutics of Supersession: The Revision of the Jews from the B Text to the C Text of *Piers Plowman*." *Yearbook of Langland Studies* 10 (1996): 43–87.

———. "The Siege of Jerusalem and Augustinian Historians Writing about Jews in Fourteenth-Century England." *Chaucer Review* 29, no. 3 (1995): 227–48. Reprinted in Sheila Delany, ed., *Chaucer and the Jews: Sources, Contexts, Meanings*. New York: Routledge, 2002.

———. "Socially Marginal, Culturally Central: Representing Jews in Late Medieval English Literature." *Exemplaria* 12, no. 2 (2000): 293–326.

Narkiss, Bezalel. *Hebrew Illuminated Manuscripts*. New York: Macmillan, 1969.

Narkiss, Bezalel, and Aliza Cohen-Mushlin. "The Illumination of the Worms Mahzor: Description and Iconographical Study." In *Mahzor Worms*, edited by Malachi Beit-Arie, 79–89. Vaduz, 1985.

Neis, Rachel. "'Their Backs toward the Temple, and Their Faces toward the East': The Temple and Toilet Practices in Rabbinic Palestine and Babylonia." *Journal for the Study of Judaism* 43 (2012): 328–68.

Nelson, Benjamin. *The Idea of Usury: From Tribal Brotherhood to Universal Otherhood*. 1949. 2nd enlarged ed. Chicago: University of Chicago Press, 1969.

Neubauer, Adolf. *Mediaeval Jewish Chronicles and Chronological Notes*. 2 vols. Oxford: Clarendon Press, 1887–95.

Neubauer, Adolf, and R. Driver. *The Fifty-Third Chapter of Isaiah*. 2 vols. New York: Ktav, 1969.

Neusner, Jacob. *The Idea of Purity in Ancient Judaism*. Leiden: Brill, 1973.

Neusner, Jacob, and Ernest S. Frerichs, eds. *"To See Ourselves as Others See Us": Christians, Jews, and "Others" in Late Antiquity*. Chico, CA: Scholars Press, 1985.

Newman, Barbara. *Medieval Crossover: Reading the Secular against the Sacred*. Notre Dame, IN: Notre Dame University Press, 2013.

———. "The Passion of the Jews of Prague: The Pogrom of 1389 and the Lessons of a Medieval Parody." *Church History* 81, no. 1 (March 2012): 12–26.

Newman, Hillel I. "At Cross Purposes: The Ritual Execution of Haman in Late Antiquity." In *Between Personal and Institutional Religion: Self, Doctrine, and Practice in Late Antique Eastern Christianity*, edited by Brouria Bitton-Ashkelony and Lorenzo Perrone, 311–36. Turnhout: Brepols, 2013.

———. "The Death of Jesus in the 'Toledot Yeshu' Literature." *Journal of Theological Studies* 50, no. 1 (April 1999): 59–79.

Newman, Paul B. *Growing Up in the Middle Ages*. Jefferson, NC: McFarland, 2007.

Neyrinck, Axelle. "Richard of Pontoise, the 'Holy Innocent' of Paris." *Histoire Urbaine* 60, no. 1 (January 2021): 51–69.

Nichols, Anne. "The Croxton Play of the Sacrament: A Re-reading." *Comparative Drama* 22 (1988–89): 117–37.

Nicht in einem Bett: Juden und Christen in Mittelalter und Frühneuzeit. Vienna: Institut für Geschichte der Juden in Oesterreich, 2005.

Niesner, Manuela. "Wer mit juden well disputiren." *Deutschprachige Adversus-Judaeus-Literatur des 14. Jahrhunderts*. Tübingen: Mohr Siebeck, 2005.

Nirenberg, David. *Aesthetic Theology and Its Enemies: Judaism in Christian Painting, Poetry, and Politics*. Waltham, MA: Brandeis University Press, 2015.

——. *Anti-Judaism: The Western Tradition*. New York: W. W. Norton, 2013.

——. "Christian Love, Jewish 'Privacy,' and Medieval Kingship." In *Center and Periphery: Studies on Power in the Medieval World in Honor of William Chester Jordan*, edited by Katherine L. Jansen, G. Geltner, and Ann E. Lester, 25–37. Leiden: Brill, 2013.

——. *Communities of Violence: Persecution of Minorities in the Middle Ages*. 1996. Updated edition, Princeton, NJ: Princeton University Press, 2015.

——. "Conversion, Sex, and Segregation: Jews and Christians in Medieval Spain." *American Historical Review* 107 (October 2002): 1065–93. Reprinted in David Nirenberg, *Neighboring Faiths: Christianity, Islam, and Judaism in the Middle Ages and Today*. Chicago: University of Chicago Press, 2014.

——. "Deviant Politics and Jewish Love: Alfonso VIII and the Jewess of Toledo." *Jewish History* 21 (2007): 15–41.

——. "Enmity and Assimilation: Jews, Christians and Converts in Medieval Spain." *Common Knowledge* 9 (2003): 137–55.

——. "Epilogue: A Brief History of Jewish Enmity." In *The Passion Story: From Visual Representation to Social Drama*, edited by Marcia Kupfer, 217–34. University Park: Penn State University Press, 2008.

——. "Figures of Thought and Figures of Flesh: 'Jews' and 'Judaism' in Late Medieval Spanish Poetry and Politics." *Speculum* 81 (2006): 398–426. Reprinted in David Nirenberg, *Neighboring Faiths: Christianity, Islam, and Judaism in the Middle Ages and Today*. Chicago: University of Chicago Press, 2014.

——. "Love between Muslim and Jew: A Triangular Affair." In *Jews, Muslims, and Christians in and around the Crown of Aragon: Essays in Honour of Elena Lourie*, edited by Harvey J. Hames, 127–55. Leiden: Brill, 2004. Reprinted in David Nirenberg, *Neighboring Faiths: Christianity, Islam, and Judaism in the Middle Ages and Today*. Chicago: University of Chicago Press, 2014.

——. "Mass Conversion and Genealogical Mentalities: Jews and Christians in Fifteenth-Century Spain." *Past and Present* 174 (February 2002): 3–41. Reprinted in David Nirenberg, *Neighboring Faiths: Christianity, Islam, and Judaism in the Middle Ages and Today*. Chicago: University of Chicago Press, 2014.

——. "Muslim-Jewish Relations in the Fourteenth-Century Crown of Aragon." *Viator* 24 (1993): 249–68.

——. "Muslims in Christian Iberia 1000–1526: Varieties of Experience." In *The Medieval World*, edited by Peter Linehan and Janet Nelson, 60–76. London: Routledge, 2001.

——, ed. *Neighboring Faiths: Christianity, Islam, and Judaism in the Middle Ages and Today*. Chicago: University of Chicago Press, 2014.

——. "The Rhineland Massacres of Jews in the First Crusade: Memories Medieval and Modern." In *Medieval Concepts of the Past: Ritual, Memory, Historiography*, edited by Gerd Althoff, Johannes Fried, and Patrick J. Geary, 279–309. Cambridge: Cambridge University Press, 2002.

———. "Shakespeare's Jewish Questions." *Renaissance Drama* 38 (2010): 77–113.

———. "Spanish 'Judaism' and 'Christianity' in an Age of Mass Conversion." In *Rethinking European Jewish History*, edited by Jeremy Cohen and Moshe Rosman, 149–72. Oxford: Littman Library of Jewish Civilization, 2009.

———. "Was There Race before Modernity? The Example of 'Jewish Blood' in Late Medieval Spain." In *The Origins of Racism in the West*, edited by Miriam Eliav-Feldon, Benjamin Isaac, and Joseph Ziegler 232–64. Cambridge: Cambridge University Press, 2009. Reprinted in David Nirenberg, *Neighboring Faiths: Christianity, Islam, and Judaism in the Middle Ages and Today*. Chicago: University of Chicago Press, 2014.

Nisse, Ruth. *Jacob's Shipwreck: Diaspora, Translation, and Jewish-Christian Relations in Medieval England*. Ithaca, NY: Cornell University Press, 2017.

———. "'Your Name Will No Longer Be Aseneth': Apocrypha, Anti-Martyrdom, and Jewish Conversion in Thirteenth-Century England." *Speculum* 81, no. 3 (2006): 734–53.

Noam, Vered. "Another Look at the Rabbinic Conception of Gentiles from the Perspective of Impurity Laws." In *Judaea-Palaestina, Babylon and Rome: Jews in Antiquity*, edited by Benjamin Isaac and Yuval Shahar, 89–110. Tübingen: Mohr Siebeck, 2012.

Noble, Thomas F. X., and John Van Engen, eds. *European Transformations: The Long Twelfth Century*. Notre Dame, IN: Notre Dame University Press, 2012.

Noonan, John. *The Scholastic Analysis of Usury*. Cambridge, MA: Harvard University Press, 1957.

Nothaft, C. Philipp P. "Duking It Out in the Arena of Time: Chronology and the Christian-Jewish Encounter (1100–1600)." *Medieval Encounters* 22 (2016): 213–35.

Novak, David. *The Election of Israel: The Idea of the Chosen People*. Cambridge: Cambridge University Press, 1995.

———. "Gentiles in Rabbinic Thought." In *The Cambridge History of Judaism IV: The Late Roman-Rabbinic Period*, edited by Steven T. Katz, 647–62. Cambridge: Cambridge University Press, 2006.

———. *The Image of the Non-Jew in Judaism: An Historical and Constructive Study of the Noahide Laws*. New York: Mellen Press, 1983.

———. *The Image of the Non-Jew in Judaism: The Idea of Noahide Law*. Edited by Matthew Lagrone. Portland, OR: Littman Library of Jewish Civilization, 2011.

———. "The Origin of the Noahide Laws." In *Perspectives on Jews and Judaism: Essays in Honor of Wolfe Kelman*, edited by Arthur A. Chiel, 301–10. New York: Rabbinical Assembly, 1978.

Novikoff, Alex J. *The Medieval Culture of Disputation: Pedigogy, Practice, and Performance*. Philadelphia: University of Pennsylvania Press, 2013.

———. "The Middle Ages." In *Antisemitism: A History*, edited by Albert S. Lindemann and Richard S. Levy, 63–78. Oxford: Oxford University Press, 2010.

O'Brian, Darren. *The Pinnacle of Hatred: The Blood Libel and the Jews*. Jerusalem: Magnes Press, 2011.

Ocker, Christopher. "Anti-Judaism and Anti-Semitism." In *Oxford Encyclopedia of Martin Luther*, edited by Derek Nelson and Paul Hinlicky. New York: Oxford University Press, 2017.

———. "Contempt for Jews and Contempt for Friars in Late Medieval Germany." In *Friars and Jews in the Middle Ages and Renaissance*, edited by Steven McMichael and Susan E. Myers, 119–46. Leiden: Brill, 2004.

———. "German Theologians and the Jews in the Fifteenth Century." In *Jews, Judaism and the Reformation in Sixteenth-Century Germany*, edited by Dean Phillip Bell and Stephen G. Burnett, 33–65. Leiden: Brill, 2006.

———. "Ritual Murder and the Subjectivity of Christ: A Choice in Medieval Christianity." *Harvard Theological Review* 91, no. 2 (April 1998): 153–92.

Ocker, Christopher, with Kevin Madigan. "After Beryl Smalley: Thirty Years of Medieval Exegesis, 1984–2013." *Journal of the Bible and Its Reception* 2 (2015): 87–130.

Odo of Tournai. "A Disputation with the Jew, Leo, concerning the Advent of Christ, the Son of God." In *On Original Sin*, translated by Irven M. Resnick, 85–98. Philadelphia: University of Pennsylvania Press, 1994.

Oehme, Annegret. *The Knight without Boundaries: Yiddish and German Arthurian Wigalois Adaptations*. Leiden: Brill, 2022.

Oesterley, Hermann, ed. *Gesta Romanorum*. 1872. Reprinted, Hildesheim: Olms, 1963.

Offenberg, Sara. "Beauty and the Beast: On a Doe, a Devilish Hunter, and Jewish-Christian Polemics." *AJS Review* 44, no. 2 (November 2020): 269–85.

———. *Illuminated Piety: Pietistic Texts and Images in the North French Hebrew Miscellany*. Los Angeles: Cherub Press, 2013.

———. "Jacob the Knight in Ezekiel's Chariot: Imagined Identity in a Micrography Decoration of an Ashkenazic Bible." *AJS Review* 40, no. 1 (April 2016): 1–16.

———. "A Jewish Knight in Shining Armour: Messianic Narrative and Imagination in Ashkenazic Illuminated Manuscripts." *University of Toronto Journal of Jewish Thought* 4 (2014): 1–14.

———. "Staging the Blindfold Bride: Between Medieval Drama and Piyyut Illumination in the Levy Mahzor." In *Resounding Images: Medieval Intersections of Art, Music, and Sound*, edited by Susan Boynton and Diane J. Reilly, 281–94. Turnhout: Brepols, 2015.

Oliger, L[ivarius]. "Liber exemplorum fratrum minorum saeculi XIII." *Antonianum* 2 (1927): 203–76.

Olszowy-Schlanger, Judith. "Juifs et chrétiens à Troyes au Moyen Age: la pratique du prêt sur gages à travers les manuscrits de Saint-Etienne." *La vie en Champagne* 42 (2005): 44–49.

———. "The Money Language: Latin and Hebrew in Jewish Legal Contracts from Medieval England." In *Studies in the History of Culture and Science: A Tribute to Gad Freudenthal*, edited by Resianne Fontaine et al., 233–50. Leiden: Brill, 2011.

Ophir, Adi, and Ishay Rosen-Zvi. *Goy: Israel's Multiple Others and the Birth of the Gentile*. Oxford: Oxford University Press, 2018.

Osier, Jean-Pierre. *L'Evangile du ghetto*. Paris: Berg, 1984.

Ottenheijm, Eric. "Martyrdom as a Contested Practice in Ancient Judaism." In *Contesting Religious Identities: Transformations, Disseminations and Mediations*, edited by Bob Becking, Anne-Marie Korte, and Lucien van Liere, 219-39. Leiden: Brill, 2017.

Owen-Hughes, Diane. "Distinguishing Signs: Ear-rings, Jews and Franciscan Rhetoric in the Italian Renaissance City." *Past and Present* 112 (1986): 3-59.

Pagden, Anthony, ed. *The Idea of Europe from Antiquity to the European Union*. Cambridge: Cambridge University Press, 2002.

Pagels, Elaine. *The Origin of Satan*. New York: Random House, 1995.

———. "The Social History of Satan, the 'Intimate Enemy': A Preliminary Sketch." *Harvard Theological Review* 84, no. 2 (April 1991): 105-28.

Pakter, Walter. "De his qui foris sunt: The Teachings of the Medieval Civil and Canon Lawyers concerning the Jews." PhD diss., Johns Hopkins University, 1974.

———. *Medieval Canon Law and the Jews*. Abhandlungen zur Rechtswissenschaftlichen Grundlagenforschung 68. Ebelsbach: Gremer, 1988.

Panitz, Esther L. *The Alien in Their Midst: Images of Jews in English Literature*. Rutherford, NJ: Fairleigh Dickenson University Press, 1981.

Panxhi, Lindsey Zachary. "Hoc Est Corpus Meum: The Eucharist in Twelfth-Century Literature." PhD diss., University of Arkansas, 2016.

Parkes, James. *Antisemitism*. London: Valentine, Mitchell, 1963.

———. *The Conflict of the Church and the Synagogue*. London: Soncino, 1934.

———. *The Jew in the Medieval Community*. London: Soncino Press, 1938.

Partner, Nancy. *Serious Entertainments: The Writing of History in Twelfth-Century England*. Chicago: University of Chicago Press, 1977.

Patterson, Lee. "Introduction: Critical Historicism and Medieval Studies." In *Literary Practice and Social Change in Britain, 1380-1530*, edited by Lee Patterson, 1-14. Berkeley: University of California Press, 1990.

———, ed. *Literary Practice and Social Change in Britain, 1380-1530*. Berkeley: University of California Press, 1990.

———. "'The Living Witnesses of Our Redemption': Martyrdom and Imitation in Chaucer's Prioress's Tale." *Journal of Medieval and Early Modern Studies* 31, no. 1 (2001): 507-60.

———. *Negotiating the Past: The Historical Understanding of Medieval Literature*. Madison: University of Wisconsin Press, 1987.

———. "On the Margin: Postmodernism, Ironic History, and Medieval Studies." *Speculum* 65, no. 1 (January 1990): 87-107.

Patton, Pamela Anne. *Art of Estrangement: Redefining Jews in Reconquest Spain*. University Park: Penn State University Press, 2012.

———, ed. *Envisioning Others: Race, Color, and the Visual in Iberia and Latin America*. Leiden: Brill, 2016.

Paulus, Simon. *Die Architektur der Synagoge im Mittelalter: Überlieferung und Bestand*. Petersberg, Germany: M. Imhof, 2007.

Pelikan, Jaroslav. *Christian Tradition: A History of the Development of Doctrine*. 5 vols. Chicago: University of Chicago Press, 1971-89.

Pennington, Kenneth. "Gratian and the Jews." *Bulletin of Medieval Canon Law* 31 (2014): 111–24.
Perez, Alvaraz Rosa. "Next-Door Neighbors: Aspects of Judeo-Christian Cohabitation in Medieval France." In *Urban Space in the Middle Ages and the Early Modern Age*, edited by Albrecht Classen, 309–30. Berlin: Walter de Gruyter, 2009.
Perryman, Judith, ed. *The King of Tars*. Heidelberg: Winter, 1980.
Peter Alfonsi. *Dialogue against the Jews*. Translated by Irven M. Resnick. Washington, DC: Catholic University of America Press, 2014.
Peter the Venerable. *Adversus Judeorum inveteratam duritiem*, edited by Yvonne Friedman. Corpus Christianorum Continuatio Medievalis. Turnhout: Brepols, 1985.
——. *Against the Inveterate Obduracy of the Jews*. Translated by Irven M. Resnick. Washington, DC: Catholic University of America Press, 2013.
——. *The Letters of Peter the Venerable*. Edited by Giles Constable. 2 vols. Cambridge, MA: Harvard University Press, 1967.
Peters, Edward, ed. *The First Crusade: The Chronicle of Fulbert of Chartres and Other Source Materials*. 2nd ed. Philadelphia: University of Pennsylvania Press, 1971.
Pflaum, Heinz. "Les scènes de juifs dans la littérature dramatique du moyen âge." *Revue des études juives* 89 (1930): 111–34.
Pick, Lucy K. *Conflict and Coexistence: Archbishop Rodrigo and the Muslims and Jews in Medieval Spain*. Ann Arbor: University of Michigan Press, 2004.
Pigg, Daniel F. "Refiguring Martyrdom: Chaucer's Prioress and Her Tale." *Chaucer Review* 29, no. 1 (1994): 65–73.
Plamper, Jan. *The History of Emotions: An Introduction*. Translated by Keith Tribe. Oxford: Oxford University Press, 2015.
Poliakov, Léon. *The Aryan Myth: A History of Racist and Nationalist Ideas in Europe*. Translated by Edmund Howard. New York: Basic Books, 1971.
——. *The History of Antisemitism*. Translated by Richard Howard. 4 vols. New York: Vanguard Press, 1965.
——. *Jewish Bankers and the Holy See: From the Thirteenth to the Seventeenth Century*. Translated by Miriam Kochan. London: Routledge and K. Paul, 1977.
Porat, Dina. *The Fall of a Sparrow: The Life and Times of Abba Kovner*. Translated by Elizabeth Yuval. Stanford, CA: Stanford University Press, 2010.
——. *Nakam: The Holocaust Survivors Who Sought Full-scale Revenge*. Translated by Mark L. Levinson. Stanford, CA: Stanford University Press, 2023.
Price, Merrall Llewelyn. "Englishness/Jewishness/Otherness: Teaching English National Identity." In *Jews in Medieval England: Teaching Representations of National Identities*, edited by Miriammne Ara Krummel and Tison Pugh, 37–52. New York: Palgrave Macmillan, 2018.
——. "Medieval Antisemitism and the Excremental Libel." In *Jews in Medieval Christendom: Slay Them Not*, edited by Kristine T. Utterback and Merrall L. Price, 177–88. Leiden: Brill, 2013.
——. "Sadism and Sentimentality: Absorbing Antisemitism in Chaucer's Prioress." *Chaucer Review* 43, no. 2 (2008): 197–214.

Przybilski, Martin. "Konversion als Form und Möglichkeit des Kontaktes und Austausches zwischen Juden und Christen im europäischen Mittelalter." In *Konversion in Räume des Judischen Geschichte*, edited by Martin Przybilski and Martin Schapkow, 5–20. Wiesbaden: Harrassowitz, 2013.

Przybilski, Martin, and Carsten Schapkow, eds. *Konversion in Räume des Jüdischen Geschichte*. Wiesbaden: Reichert, 2014.

Pseudo-Kodinos. *Narratio de aedificatione templi sanctae sophiae in scriptore originum Constantinipolitanum*. Leipzig: T. Praeger, 1901.

Rabinowitz, Louis. *The Herem Hayyishub: A Contribution to the Medieval Economic History of the Jews*. London: E. Goldston, 1945.

———. *Jewish Merchant Adventurers: A Study of the Radanites*. London: E. Goldston, 1948.

Rabinowitz, Zvi Meir. *Mahzor Piyyutei R. Yannai*. 2 vols. Jerusalem: Mosad Bialik, 1985–87.

Ramey, Lynn T. *Black Legacies: Race and the European Middle Ages* Gainesville: University Press of Florida, 2014.

Rankin, Oliver Shaw, ed. *Jewish Religious Polemic*. 1956. Reprinted, New York: Ktav, 1970.

Raspe, Lucia. "The Black Death in Jewish Sources: A Second Look at 'Mayse Nissim.'" *Jewish Quarterly Review* 94, no. 3 (2004): 471–89.

———. "Jerusalem am Rhein: Anfänge jüdischen Lebens in Deutschland im Mittelalter." In *Innere Räume—äußere Zäune: Jüdische Alltag im Rheingebiet im Spätmittelalter und in der Frühen Neuzeit*, edited by Ludolf Pelizaeus, 13–28. Mainz: Verein für Sozialgeschichte Mainz, 2010.

———. "Jewish Saints in Medieval Germany: A Contradiction of Terms?" *Frankfurter Judaistiche Beiträge* 31 (2004): 75–90.

———. *Jüdische Hagiographie im mittelalterlichen Aschkenas*. Tübingen: Mohr Siebeck, 2006.

———. "'The Lord Was with Them, and They Were Not Found Out': Jews, Christians and the Veneration of Saints in Medieval Ashkenaz." *Jewish History* 30, no. 1–2 (June 2016): 43–59.

———. "Payyetanim as Heroes of Medieval Folk Narrative: The Case of R. Shimon b. Yishaq of Mainz." In *Jewish Studies between the Disciplines*, edited by Klaus Hermann, Margarete Schlüter, and Giuseppe Veltri, 354–71. Leiden: Brill, 2003.

———. "Props of Memory, Triggers of Narration: Time and Space in Medieval Jewish Historiography." In *The Making of Memory in the Middle Ages*, edited by Lucie Doležalová, 309–27. Leiden: Brill, 2010.

———. "Sacred Space, Local History, and Diasporic Identity: The Graves of the Righteous in Medieval and Early Modern Ashkenaz." In *Jewish Studies at the Crossroads of Anthropology and History*, edited by Ra'anan S. Boustan, Oren Kosansky, and Marina Rustow, 147–63, 370–79. Philadelphia: University of Pennsylvania Press, 2011.

———. "Die SchUM-Gemeinden in der narrativen Überlieferung aus Mittelalter und früher Neuzeit." In *Die SchUM-Gemeinden. Speyer—Worms—Mainz auf dem*

Weg zum Welterbe, edited by Generaldirektion Kulturelles Erbe Rheinland-Pfalz, 313–26. Regensburg: Schnell and Steiner, 2013.

———. "Yuzpa Shammes and the Narrative Tradition of Medieval Worms." In *Jüdische Kultur in den SchUM-Städten: Literatur—Theater—Musik*, edited by Karl E. Grözinger, 99–118. Jüdische Kultur, Band 26. Wiesbaden: Harrassowitz, 2014.

Ravid, Benjamin. "The Forced Baptism of Jews in Christian England: An Introductory Overview." In *Christianizing Peoples and Converting Individuals*, edited by Guyda Armstrong and Ian N. Woods, 157–67. Turnhout: Brepols, 2000.

Ray, Jonathan. *After Expulsion: 1492 and the Making of Sephardic Jewry*. New York: NYU Press, 2013.

———. *The Sephardic Frontier: The "Reconquista" and the Jewish Community in Medieval Iberia*. Ithaca, NY: Cornell University Press, 2006.

Rees-Jones, Sarah, and Sethina Watson, eds. *Christians and Jews in Angevin England: The York Massacre of 1190, Narratives and Contents*. Rochester, NY: Boydell and Brewer, 2013.

Reif, Stefan C. "The Early History of Jewish Worship." In *The Making of Jewish and Christian Worship*, edited by Paul F. Bradshaw and Lawrence A. Hoffman, 109–36. Notre Dame, IN: Notre Dame University Press, 1991.

———. "The Early Liturgy of the Synagogue." In *The Cambridge History of Judaism*. Vol. 3, *The Early Roman Period*, edited by William Horbury, W. D. Davies, and John Sturdy, 326–57. Cambridge: Cambridge University Press, 1999.

Reif, Stefan C., Andreas Lehnardt, and Avriel Bar-Levav, eds. *Death in Jewish Life: Burial and Mourning Customs among Jews of Europe and Nearby Communities*. Berlin: Walter De gruyter, 2014.

Reiner, Avraham (Rami). "Bible and Politics: A Correspondence between Rabbennu Tam and the Authorities of Champagne." In *Entangled Histories: Knowledge, Authority, and Jewish Culture in the Thirteenth Century*, edited by Elisheva Baumbarten, Ruth Mazo Karras, and Katelyn Mesler, 59–72. Philadelphia: University of Pennsylvania Press, 2016.

———. *Rabbeinu Tam: Parshanut, Halakhah, Pulmus*. Ramat Gan: University of Bar-Ilan Press, 2021.

Rembaum, Joel. "The Influence of *Sefer Nestor HaKomer* on Medieval Jewish Polemics." *Proceedings of the American Academy for Jewish Research* 45 (1978): 155–85.

Rendsburg, G. A. "The Egyptian Sun-God Ra in the Pentateuch." *Henoch* 10 (1988): 3–15.

———. "Word Play in Biblical Hebrew: An Ecclectic Collection." In *Puns and Pundits: Word Play in the Hebrew Bible and in Ancient Near Eastern Literature*, edited by Scott B. Noegel, 137–62. Bethesda, MD: CDL Press, 2000.

———. "Wordplay in the Bible." *Vetus Testamentum* 38, no. 3 (1988): 354–56.

Renna, Thomas. "The Jews in the *Golden Legend*." In *Christian Attitudes toward the Jews in the Middle Ages: A Casebook*, edited by Michael Frassetto, 137–50. New York: Routledge, 2007.

Resnick, Irven M. "Conversion from the Worst to the Best: The Relationship between Medieval Judaism, Islam and Christianity." In *Contesting Inter-Religious Conversion in the Medieval World*, edited by Yaniv Fox and Yosi Yisraeli, 197–209. New York: Routledge, 2017.

——. "The Jews' Badge." In *Jews and Muslims under the Fourth Lateran Council*, edited by Marie-Thérèse Champagne and Irven M. Resnick, 65–79. Turnhout: Brepols, 2018.

——. *Marks of Distinction: Christian Perceptions of Jews in the High Middle Ages*. Washington, DC: Catholic University of America Press, 2012.

——. "Medieval Roots of the Myth of Jewish Male Menses." *Harvard Theological Review* 93, no. 3 (July 2000): 241–63.

——. "Odo of Tournai and the Dehumanization of Medieval Jews: A Reexamination." *Jewish Quarterly Review* 98 (2008): 471–84.

——. "Ps.-Albert the Great on the Physiognomy of Jesus and Mary." *Mediaeval Studies* 64, no. 1 (2002): 217–40.

——. "Race, Anti-Jewish Polemic, Arnulf of Seéz, and the Contested Papal Election of Anaclet II (A. D. 1130)." In *Jews in Medieval Christendom: "Slay Them Not,"* edited by Kristine T. Unterback and Merrall Llewelyn Price, 45–70. Leiden: Brill, 2013.

Reuter, Fritz, and Ulrike Schäfer, eds. and trans. *Wundergeschichten aus Warmaisa. Juspa Schammes, sein ma'aseh nissim und das jüdische Worms im 17. Jahrhundert*. Worms: Kultur und Veranstaltungs GmbH, 2005.

Reuther, Rosemary Radford. "The *Adversus Judaeos* Tradition in the Church Fathers: The Exegesis of Christian Anti-Judaism." In *Essential Papers on Judaism and Christianity in Conflict: From Late Antiquity to the Reformation*, edited by Jeremy Cohen, 174–89. New York: NYU Press, 1991.

——. *Faith and Fratricide: The Theological Roots of Anti-Semitism*. New York: Seabury Press, 1974.

Rex, Richard. "Chaucer and the Jews." *Modern Language Quarterly* 45 (1984): 107–22.

Richard, Jeffrey. *Sex, Dissidence, and Damnation: Minority Groups in the Middle Ages*. New York: Routledge, 1991.

Richardson, H. G. *The English Jewry under Angevin Kings*. London: Methuen, 1960.

Richardson, Peter. "The Beginnings of Christian Anti-Judaism, 70–c. 235." In *The Cambridge History of Judaism IV: The Late Roman-Rabbinic Period*, edited by Steven T. Katz, 244–58. Cambridge: University of Cambridge Press, 2006.

Ridley, Florence. *The Prioress and the Critics*. Berkeley: University of California Press, 1965.

Riemer, Nathaniel. "Juden und Christen und Juspa Schammes' Mayse Nissim und das Selbstverständniss der Wormser Jüdischen Gemeinde als Aschkenasisches 'Jerusalem' in einer dieseitigen, fragilen Gemeinde." In *Jüdische Kultur in den SchUM-Städten: Literatur—Theater—Musik*, edited by Karl E. Grözinger, 119–36. Jüdische Kultur, Band 26. Wiesbaden: Harrassowitz, 2014.

Riess, Frank. "From Aachen to Al-Andalus: The Journey of Deacon Bodo (823–876)." *Early Medieval Europe* 13, no. 2 (2005): 131–57.

———. *The Journey of Deacon Bodo from the Rhine to the Quadalquivir: Apostasy and Conversion to Judaism in Early Medieval Europe*. New York: Routledge, 2019.
Riley-Smith, Jonathan. *The Crusades: A Short History*. New Haven, CT: Yale University Press, 1987.
———. "The First Crusade and the Persecution of the Jews." In *Persecution and Toleration*, edited by W. J. Shields, 51–72. Studies in Church History 21. Oxford: Ecclesiastical History Society, 1984.
Riley-Smith, Louise, and Jonathan Riley-Smith, eds. *The Crusades: Idea and Reality, 1095–1274*. London: Edward Arnold, 1981.
Rist, Rebecca. *Popes and Jews 1095–1291*. Oxford: Oxford University Press, 2015.
Rives, James B. *Religion in the Roman Empire*. Oxford: Blackwell, 2007.
Robert, Ulysse. *Les signes d'infamie au moyen âge: juifs, sarrasins, heretiques, lepreux, cagots, et filles publiques*. Paris, 1891.
Robert of Torigni. *Chronicle*. Edited by Richard Howlett. In *Chronicles of the Reigns of Stephen, Henry II, and Richard I*, 4:250–51. Rolls Series 82. London, 1884–89.
Roblin, Michel. *Les Juifs de Paris*. Paris: Editions A. et J. Picard et Cie., 1952.
Roemer, Nils. *German City, Jewish Memory: The Story of Worms*. Waltham, MA: Brandeis University Press, 2010.
———. "Turning Defeat into Victory: *Wissenschaft des Judentums* and the Martyrs of 1096." *Jewish History* 13, no. 2 (1999): 65–80.
Rohrbacher, Stefan. "The Charge of Deicide: An Anti-Jewish Motif in Medieval Christian Art." *Journal of Medieval History* 17, no. 4 (1991): 297–321.
Rohrbacher, Stefan, and Michael Schmidt. *Judenbilder: Kulturgeschichte antijudischer Mythen und antisemitischer Vorurteile*. Reinbeck bei Hamburg: Rowohlt, 1991.
Rokeah, David. *Justin Martyr and the Jews*. Leiden: Brill, 2002.
Rokéah, Zefirah Entin. "The Church, the State, and the Jews in Medieval England." In *Antisemitism through the Ages*, edited by Shmuel Almog, 99–125. Oxford: Pergamon Press, 1988.
———. "Drawings of Jewish Interest in Some Thirteenth-Century English Public Records." *Scriptorium* 26, no. 1 (1972): 55–62.
———. "The Jewish Church-Robbers and Host Desecrators of Norwich (ca. 1285). *Revue des études juives* 141 (1982): 331–62.
———. "Money and the Hangman in Late 13th-Century England: Jews, Christians, and Coinage Offenses Alleged and Real." *Jewish Historical Studies* 31 (1990): 83–109; 32 (1993): 159–218.
Romain, Jonathan. "River Jews: Medieval Jews along the Thames as a Microcosm of Anglo-Jewry." *Jewish Historical Studies* 43 (2011): 21–24.
Roos, Lena. "Cross-dressing among Medieval Ashkenazi Jews: Confirming Challenged Group Borders." *Nordisk Judaistik. Scandinavian Jewish Studies* 28, no. 2 (2017): 4–22.
———. *"God Wants It!": The Ideology of Martyrdom of the Hebrew Crusade Chronicles and Its Jewish and Christian Background*. Turnhout: Brepols, 2006.

Roscher, Wilhelm. "The Status of the Jews in the Middle Ages Considered from the Standpoint of Commercial Policy." Translated by Solomon Grayzel. *Historia Judaica* 6 (1964): 13–26.

Rose, Christine. "The Jewish Mother-in-Law: Synagoga and the Man of Laws Tale." In *Chaucer and the Jews: Sources, Contexts, Meanings*, edited by Sheila Delany, 3–24. New York: Routledge, 2002.

Rose, E[mily] M. "Crusades, Blood Libels, and Popular Violence." In *The Cambridge Companion to Antisemitism*, edited by Steven T. Katz, 194–212. Cambridge: Cambridge University Press, 2022.

———. *The Murder of William of Norwich: The Origins of the Blood Libel in Medieval Europe.* Oxford: Oxford University Press, 2015.

———. "Royal Power and Ritual Murder: Notes on the Expulsion of the Jews from the Royal Domain of France, 1182." In *Center and Periphery Studies on Power in the Medieval World in Honor of William Chester Jordan*, edited by Katherine L. Jansen, G. Geltner, and Ann E. Lester, 51–63. Leiden: Brill, 2013.

Rosen, Tova. "Love and Race in a Thirteenth-Century Romance in Hebrew, with a Translation of the Story of Maskil and Peninah by Jacob ben El'azar." *Florilegium* 23, no. 1 (2006): 155–72.

Rosenfeld, Abraham. *The Authorized Kinot for the Ninth of Av.* London: C. Labworth, 1965.

Rosenthal, Judah. "Anti-Christian Polemic in Rashi on the Bible." In *Rashi, Torato v-Ishiyuto*, edited by Shimon Federbush, 45–54 [Hebrew]. New York: World Jewish Congress, 1958.

———. *Mehqarim u-Meqorot.* 2 vols. Jerusalem: Reuven Maas, 1967.

———. "Peirush Rashi 'al Shir ha-Shirim." In *The Samuel K. Mirsky Jubilee Volume*, edited by Simon Bernstein and Gershon A. Churgin, 130–88. New York: Va'd ha-Yoveil, 1958.

Rosenthal, Judith. "Introduction to Anti-Judaism, Fantasy and Medieval Literature." *Medieval Encounters* 5, no. 3 (1999): 358–63.

———. "Margerie Kempe and Medieval Anti-Judaic Ideology." *Medieval Encounters: Jewish, Christian and Muslim Cultures in Conference and Dialogue* 5, no. 3 (2000): 409–20.

Rosenwein, Barbara H., ed. *Anger's Past: The Social Uses of an Emotion in the Middle Ages.* Ithaca, NY: Cornell University Press, 1998.

———. "Feudal War and Monastic Peace: Cluniac Liturgy as Ritual Aggression." *Viator* 2 (1971): 129–57.

———. *A Short History of the Middle Ages.* 5th ed. Toronto: University of Toronto Press, 2018.

Rosenwein, Barbara H., and Riccardo Cristiani. *What Is the History of Emotions?* Cambridge, UK: Polity Press, 2018.

Rosenwein, Barbara H., and Lester K. Little. "Social Meaning in the Monastic and Mendicant Spiritualities." *Past and Present* 63 (1974): 4–32.

Rosenzweig, Claudia. "The Jewish Knight, the Jewish Princess, and the Sceptical Reader: Some Remarks on Realism and Fictionality in the Yiddish Bovo D'Antona."

In *Early Modern Yiddish Poetry*, edited by Shlomo Berger, 7–25. Amsterdam: Menasseh ben Israel Institute, 2009.

Roth, Cecil, ed. *The Dark Ages: Jews in Christian Europe, 711–1096*. World History of the Jewish People, second series. Vol. 2, *The Medieval Period*. New Brunswick, NJ: Rutgers University Press, 1966.

———. "Economic Life and Population Movements." In *The Dark Ages: Jews in Christian Europe, 711–1096*, edited by Cecil Roth, 2:13–48. New Brunswick, NJ: Rutgers University Press, 1966.

———. "The Feast of Purim and the Origins of the Blood Accusation." *Speculum* 8, no. 4 (1933): 520–26.

———. *History of the Jews in England*. 3rd ed. Oxford: Clarendon Press, 1978.

———. *The Jewish Contribution to Civilization*. New York: Harper and Brothers, 1938.

———. "Marranos and Racial Antisemitism: A Study in Parallels." *Jewish Social Studies* 2, no. 3 (July 1940): 239–48.

———. "The Medieval Conception of the Jew: A New Interpretation." In *Essays and Studies in Memory of Linda R. Miller*, edited by Israel Davidson, 171–90. New York: Jewish Theological Seminary, 1938.

Roth, Norman. *Daily Life of the Jews in the Middle Ages*. Westport, CT: Greenwood Press, 2005.

Roth, Pinchas. "Mourning Murderers in Medieval Jewish Law." In *Medieval and Early Modern Murder: Legal, Literary, and Historical Contexts*, edited by Larissa Tracey, 77–95. Woodbridge, UK: Boydell Press, 2018.

Rothkrug, Lional. "The 'Odour of Sanctity' and the Hebrew Origins of Christian Relic Veneration." *Historical Reflections/Réflexions Historiques* 8, no. 2 (Summer 1981): 95–142.

Rotman, David. "Monsters, Metamorphosis, and Intra-Community Conflict in the Tales of Rabbi Judah the Pious." In *Jüdische Kultur in den SchUM-Städten: Literatur—Musik—Theater*, edited by Karl E. Grözinger, 83–98. Jüdische Kultur, Band 26. Wiesbaden: Harrassowitz, 2014.

Rovang, Paul R. "Hebraizing Arthurian Romance: The Jewish Knight, the Jewish Princess, and the Sceptical [*sic*] Reader: Some Remarks on Realism and Fictionality in the Yiddish Bovo D'Antona." In *Early Modern Yiddish Poetry*, edited by Shlomo Berger, 3–9. Amsterdam Yiddish Symposium 3. Amsterdam: Menasseh ben Israel Institute, 2009.

———. "Hebraizing Arthurian Romance: The Originality of 'Melech Artus.'" *Arthuriana* 19, no. 2 (Summer 2009): 3–9.

Rowe, Nina. *The Jew, the Cathedral and the Medieval City: Synagoga and Ecclesia in the Thirteenth Century*. Cambridge: Cambridge University Press, 2011.

———. "Other." *Studies in Iconography* 33 (2012): 131–44.

Rubens, Alfred. *A History of Jewish Costume*. New York: Crown, 1967.

Rubin, Miri. *Cities of Strangers: Making Lives in Medieval Europe*. Cambridge: Cambridge University Press, 2020.

———. *Corpus Christi: The Eucharist in Late Medieval Culture*. Cambridge: Cambridge University Press, 1991.

———. "Desecration of the Host: The Birth of an Accusation." In *Christianity and Judaism*, edited by Diana Wood, 169–85. Studies in Church History 29. Oxford: Blackwell, 1992.

———. "*Ecclesia* and *Synagoga*: The Changing Meanings of a Powerful Pairing." In *Conflict and Religious Conversation in Latin Christendom: Studies in Honour of Ora Limor*, edited by Israel Jacob Yuval and Ram Ben-Shalom, 55–86. Turnhout: Brepols, 2014.

———. "The Eucharist and the Construction of Medieval Identities." In *Culture and History 1350–1600: Essays on English Communities, Identities, and Writing*, edited by David Aers, 43–63. Detroit: Wayne State University Press, 1992.

———. "Europe Remade: Purity and Danger in Late Medieval Europe." *Transactions of the Royal Historical Society* 11, 6th series (2001): 101–24.

———. *Gentile Tales: A Narrative Tale of the Assault on Late Medieval Jews*. New Haven, CT: Yale University Press, 1999.

———. "Imagining the Jew: The Late Medieval Eucharistic Discourse." In *In and Out of the Ghetto*, edited by R. Po-chia Hsia and Hartmut Lehman, 177–208. Cambridge: Cambridge University Press, 1995.

———. "Jews and Anti-Judaism in Christian Religious Literature." In *The Cambridge Companion to Antisemitism*, edited by Steven T. Katz, 232–47. Cambridge: Cambridge University Press, 2022.

———. *Mother of God: A History of the Virgin Mary*. New Haven, CT: Yale University Press, 2009.

———. "Norwich: 1144: Origins and Afterlives." In *The Medieval Roots of Antisemitism: Continuities and Discontinuities from the Middle Ages to the Present Day*, edited by Jonathan Adams and Cordelia Hess, 257–64. New York: Routledge, 2018.

———. "The Passion of Mary: The Virgin and the Jews in Medieval Culture." In *The Passion Story: From Visual Representation to Social Drama*, edited by Marcia Kupfer, 53–66. University Park: Penn State University Press, 2008.

———. "Rudolph of Schlettstadt, O.P.: Reporter of Violence, Writer on Jews." In *Christ among the Medieval Dominicans: Representations of Christ in the Texts and Images of the Order of Preachers*, edited by Kent Emery Jr. and Joseph Wawrykow, 283–92. Notre Dame, IN: University of Notre Dame Press, 1998.

Rustow, Marina. *Heresy and the Politics of Community: The Jews of the Fatimid Caliphate*. Ithaca, NY: Cornell University Press, 2008.

Saelemaekers, Monika. "Can Halakhic Texts Talk History? The Example of Sefer Or Zarua (MS Ros. 3, CA 1300 CE)." *Zutot* 6, no. 1 (2009): 17–23.

Samuel, Maurice. *The Great Hatred*. New York: Knopf, 1940.

Sanders, E. P. *Jewish and Christian Self-Definition*. 3 vols. London: SCM Press, 1980–82.

———. *Paul and Palestinian Judaism: A Comparison of Patterns of Religion*. Philadelphia: Fortress Press, 1977.

Sansy, Danièle. "Marquer la différence: l'imposition de la rouelle aux XIIIe et XIVe siècles." *Médiévales* 41 (2001): 15–36.
Saperstein, Marc. "Christians and Jews: Some Positive Images." *Harvard Theological Review* 79 (1986): 236–46.
———. "Medieval Christians and Jews: A Review Essay." *Shofar* 8, no. 4 (1990): 1–10.
Sartre, Jean-Paul. *Anti-Semite and Jew: An Exploration of the Etiology of Hate*. Translated by George J. Becker. New York: Schocken Books, 1948.
Satlow, Michael. *Judaism and the Economy: A Sourcebook*. New York: Routledge, 2019.
Scarry, Elaine. *The Body in Pain: The Making and Unmaking of the World*. Oxford: Oxford University Press, 1985.
Schacter, Jacob J., ed. *Judaism's Encounter with Other Cultures: Rejection or Integration?* Northvale, NJ: Jason Aronson, 1997.
Schäfer, Peter. "Agobard's and Amulo's *Toledot Yeshu*." In *Toledot Yeshu ("The Life Story of Jesus") Revisited: A Princeton Conference*, edited by Peter Schäfer, Michael Meerson, and Yaacov Deutsch, 27–48. Tübingen: Mohr Siebeck, 2011.
———. *Jesus in the Talmud*. Princeton, NJ: Princeton University Press, 2007.
———. "Jesus' Origin, Birth, and Childhood according to the *Toledot Yeshu* and the Talmud." In *Judaea-Palaestina, Babylon and Rome: Jews in Antiquity*, edited by Benjamin Isaac and Yuval Shahar, 139–61. Tübingen: Mohr Siebeck, 2012.
———. "Jews and Gentiles in Yerushalmi Avodah Zara." In *The Talmud Yerushalmi and Graeco-Roman Culture*, edited by Peter Schäfer, 3:335–52. Tübingen: Mohr Siebeck, 2002.
———. *Judeophobia: Attitudes toward the Jews in the Ancient World*. Cambridge, MA: Harvard University Press, 1997.
Schäfer, Peter, Michael Meerson, and Yaacov Deutsch, eds. *Toledot Yeshu ("The Life Story of Jesus") Revisited: A Princeton Conference*. Tübingen: Mohr Siebeck, 2011.
Schechter, Solomon. "Jewish Saints in Medieval Germany." In *Studies in Judaism*, 1–24. Third Series. Philadelphia: Jewish Publication Society, 1924.
Schedel, Hermann. *Liber Chronicorum* [*The Nuremberg Chronicle*]. Nuremberg: Anton Koberger, 1493.
Scheiber, Alexander. "Ein aus arabischer Gefangenschaft befreiter christlicher Proselyt in Jerusalem." *Hebrew Union College Annual* 39 (1968): 163–73.
Schiffmann, Sara. "Die Urkunden für die Juden von Speyer 1090 und Worms 1157." *Zeitschrift für die Geschichte der Juden* 2 (1930–31): 28–39.
Schlauch, Margaret. "The Allegory of the Church and the Synagogue." *Speculum* 14 (1939): 448–64.
Schmitt, Jean-Claude. *Conversion of Herman the Jew: Autobiography, History, and Fiction in the Twelfth Century*. Translated by Alex J. Novikoff. Philadelphia: University of Pennsylvania Press, 2010.
———. "Die autobiographische Fiktion: Hermann des Juden Bekehrung." Trier: Kleine Schriften des Arye-Maimon-Instituts, 2000.
———. "La question des images dans les debats entre juifs et chrétiens au XIIe siècle." In *Spannungen und Widersprüche: Gedenkschrift für František Graus*, 245–54. Sigmaringen, Germany: J. Vorbecke Verlag, 1992.

———. *Raison des gestes dans l'Occident médiéval*. Paris: Gallimard, 1990.

Schnitzler, Norbert. "Contra naturam—Sexuelle devianz und christlich-jüdische Koexistenz im Mittelalter." In *Wechselseitige Wahrnehmung der Religionen im Spätmittelalter und in der Frühen Neuzeit I.: Konzeptionelle Grundfragen und Fallstudien (Heiden, Barbaren, Juden)*, edited by Ludger Grenzmann et al., 251–81. Berlin: Walter de Gruyter, 2006.

Schoeck, Richard J. "Chaucer's Prioress: Mercy and Tender Heart." *Bridge: A Yearbook of Judaeo-Christian Studies* 2 (1956): 239–55.

Schoenfeld, Devorah. *Isaac on Jewish and Christian Altars: Polemic and Exegesis in Rashi and the Glossa Ordinaria*. New York: Fordham University Press, 2013.

Schofer, Jonathan Wyn. *Confronting Vulnerability: The Body and the Divine in Rabbinic Ethics*. Chicago: University of Chicago Press, 2010.

Schorsch, Ismar. "The Myth of Sephardic Supremacy." *Leo Baeck Yearbook* 34, no. 1 (January 1989): 47–66.

Schreckenberg, Heinz. *Die Christlichen Adversus-Judaeos-Texte (13.-20. Jh.)*. Frankfurt am Main: P. Lang, 1994.

———. *Die Christlichen Adversus-Judaeos-Texte (11.-13. Jh.)*. 3rd ed. Frankfurt am Main: P. Lang, 1997.

———. *Die christlichen Adversus-Judaeos-Texte und ihr literarisches und historisches Umfeld (1.-11. Jh.)*. 3rd ed. Frankfurt am Main: P. Lang, 1995.

———. *The Jews in Christian Art: An Illustrated History*. New York: Continuum, 1996.

———. *Die Juden in der Kunst Europas: Ein historischer Bildatlas*. Göttingen: Vandenhoeck und Ruprecht, 1996.

Schultz, Margarete. "The Blood Libel: A Motif in the History of Childhood." *Journal of Psychohistory* 15 (1986): 1–24.

Schütte, Sven, Marianne Gechter, and Astrid Bader. *Von der Ausgrabung zum Museum: Kölner Archäologie zwischen Rathaus und Praetorium: Ergbnisse und Materialien 2006-2012*. Cologne: Archëologische Zone, 2012.

Schwartz, Stuart B. *All Can Be Saved: Religious Tolerance and Salvation in the Iberian Atlantic World*. New Haven, CT: Yale University Press, 2008.

———. *Blood and Boundaries: The Limits of Religious and Racial Exclusion in Early Modern Latin America*. Waltham, MA: Brandeis University Press, 2020.

Schwarzfuchs, Simon. *Études sur l'origine et le développement du rabbinat au moyen âge*. Paris, 1957.

———. "The Expulsion of the Jews from France (1306)." *Jewish Quarterly Review* 57 (1967): 482–89.

———. "France and Germany under the Carolingians." In *The Dark Ages: Jews in Christian Europe, 711-1096*, edited by Cecil Roth, 2:122–42. New Brunswick, NJ: Rutgers University Press, 1966.

———. "France under the Early Capets." In *The Dark Ages: Jews in Christian Europe, 711-1096*, edited by Cecil Roth, 2:143–61. New Brunswick, NJ: Rutgers University Press, 1966.

———. "Hishtalsheluto shel Herem ha-Yishuv: Re'iyyah Mi-Zavit Aheret." In *Sefer Yovel li-Shelomo Simonsohn: Qovez Mehqarim le-Toledot ha-Yehudim bimei ha-Beinayuim u-va-Renasans*, edited by Daniel Carpi et al., 105–17. Ramat Aviv: Tel Aviv University, Faculty of Humanities, Chaim Rosenberg School of Jewish Studies, 1993.

Scott, James C. *Domination and the Arts of Resistance: Hidden Transcripts*. New Haven, NJ: Yale University Press, 1990.

———. "Protest and Profanation: Agrarian Revolt and the Little Tradition." *Theory and Society* 4, no. 1 (1977): 1–38; 4, no. 2 (1977): 211–46.

———. *Weapons of the Weak: Everyday Forms of Peasant Resistance*. New Haven, CT: Yale University Press, 1985.

Seabourne, Gwen. *Royal Regulation of Loans and Sales in Medieval England: "Monkish Superstition and Civil Tyranny."* Woodbridge, UK: Boydell Press, 2003.

Seasonwein, Johanna G. "The Nursing Queen: Sculptures of the Virgo Lactans in Late Medieval France." PhD diss., Columbia University, 2010.

Sed-Rajna, Gabrielle. "The Illustrations of the Kaufman Mishneh Torah." *Journal of Jewish Art* 6 (1979): 64–77.

Sefer ha-Asufot. Former Hebrew MS Montefiore 115. Privately owned.

Seiferth, Wolfgang S. *Synagogue and Church in the Middle Ages: Two Symbols in Art and Literature*. New York: Frederick Ungar, 1970.

Septimus, Bernard. "Hispano-Jewish Views of Christendom and Islam." In *Iberia and Beyond: Hispanic Jews between Cultures: Proceedings of a Symposium to Mark the 500th Anniversary of the Expulsion of Spanish Jewry*, edited by Bernard Dov Cooperman, 43–65. Newark: University of Delaware, 1998.

———. "'Tahat Edom ve-Lo Tahat Yishmael': Gilgulo shel Ma'amar." *Zion* 47, no. 2 (1982): 103–11.

Sewell, John. "The Son Rebelled and So the Father Made Man Alone: Ridicule and Boundary Maintenance in the *Nizzahon Vetus*." In *Laughter in the Middle Ages and Early Modern Times*, edited by Albrecht Classen, 295–324. Berlin: Walter de Gruyter, 2010.

Shachar, I. *The Judensau: A Medieval Anti-Jewish Motif and Its History*. London: Warburg Institute, 1974.

Shagrir, Iris. "The Parable of the Three Rings: A Revision of Its History." *Journal of Medieval History* 23, no. 2 (1997): 163–77.

Shagrir, Iris, and Netta Amir. "The Persecution of the Jews in the First Crusade: Liturgy, Memory and Nineteenth-Century Visual Culture." *Speculum* 92, no. 2 (April 2017): 405–28.

Shahar, Uri. "Inspecting the Pious Body: Christological Morphology and the Ritual-Crucifixion Allegation." *Journal of Medieval History* 41, no. 1 (2015): 21–40.

Shain, Milton. *Antisemitism*. London: Bowerdean, 1998.

Shakespeare, William. *The Merchant of Venice*. In *The Riverside Shakespeare*, edited by G. Blakemore Evans, 284–319. Boston: Houghton Mifflin, 1997.

Shalev-Eyni, Sarit. "The Aural-Visual Experiences in the Ashkenazi Ritual Domain of the Middle Ages." In *Resounding Images in Medieval Intersections of Art, Music, and Sound*, edited by Susan Boynton and Diane J. Reilly, 189–204. Turnhout: Brepols, 2015.

———. "The Bared Breast in Medieval Ashkenazi Ilumination: Cultural Connotations in a Heterogeneous Society." *Different Visions: A Journal of New Perspectives on Medieval Art* 5 (August 2014): 1–39.

———. "Between Carnality and Spirituality: A Cosmological Vision of the End at the Turn of the Fifth Jewish Millennium." *Speculum* 90, no. 2 (April 2015): 458–82.

———. "Iconography of Love: Illustrations of Bride and Bridegroom in Ashkenazi Prayer Books of the Thirteenth and Fourteenth Centuries." *Studies in Iconography* 26 (2005): 27–57.

———. "Iti Mi-Levanon Kallah." *Rimonim* 6–7 (1999): 6–20.

———. *Jews among Christians: Hebrew Book Illumination from Lake Constance*. Turnhout: Brepols, 2010.

———. "Martyrdom and Sexuality: The Case of Eleventh-Century *Piyyut* for Hanukkah, and Its Visual Interpretation in the Sixteenth Century." In *Conflict and Religious Conversation: Religious Encounters in Latin Christendom*, edited by Israel Yuval and Ram Ben-Shalom, 91–108. Cultural Encounters in Late Antiquity and the Middle Ages 17. Turnhout: Brepols, 2014.

———. "Panehah ha-Enoshiyot shel ha-Torah ve-Emunat Yemei ha-Beinayim." *Zion* 73 (2008): 139–71.

———. "Purity and Impurity: Naked Women Bathing in Jewish and Christian Art." In *Between Judaism and Christianity: Art Historical Essays in Honor of Elisheva (Elisabeth) Revel-Neher*, edited by Katrin Kogman-Appel and Mati Meyer, 191–213. Leiden: Brill, 2009.

———. "Reconstructing Jerusalem in the Jewish Liturgical Realm: The Worms Synagogue and Its Legacy." In *Visual Constructs of Jerusalem*, edited by Bianca Kühnel, Galit Noga-Banai, and Hanna Vorholt, 161–70. Turnhout: Brepols, 2014.

Shapiro, James. *Shakespeare and the Jews*. New York: Columbia University Press, 1997.

Shapiro, Marc. "Torah Study on Christmas Eve." *Journal of Jewish Thought and Philosophy* 8 (1999): 319–53.

Shapiro, Susan E. "Écriture judaïque: Where Are the Jews in Western Discourse?" In *Displacements: Cultural Identity in Question*, edited by Angelika Bammer, 182–201. Bloomington: Indiana University Press, 1994.

Sharf, Andrew. *Byzantine Jewry from Justinian to the Fourth Crusade*. New York: Schocken Books, 1971.

———. "Byzantine Jewry in the Seventh Century." *Byzantinische Zeitschrift* 48 (1955): 103–15.

———. *Jews and Other Minorities in Byzantium*. Ramat Gan: Bar-Ilan University Press, 1995.

Shatzmiller, Joseph. "Les Angevins et les juifs de leurs états: Anjou, Naples et Provence." In *L'État angevin: Pouvoir, culture et société entre XIIIe et XIVe siècle*, 289–300. Rome: Nella Sede del Instituto Palazzo Borromini, 1998.

———. "Church Articles: Pawns in the Hands of Jewish Moneylenders." In *Wirtschaftsgeschichte der mittelalterlichen Juden: Fragen und Einschätzungen*, edited by Michael Toch, 93–102. Munich: R. Oldenbourt, 2008.

———. "Converts and Judaizers in the Early Fourteenth Century." *Harvard Theological Reveiw* 74 (1981): 63–77.

———. *Cultural Exchange: Jews, Christians, and Art in the Medieval Marketplace*. Princeton, NJ: Princeton University Press, 2013.

———. *La deuxième controverse de Paris: un chapitre dans la polémique untre juifs et chrétiens au moyen âge*. Paris-Louvain: Editions E. Peeters, 1994.

———. "Doctors and Medical Practice in Germany around the Year 1200: The Evidence of *Sefer Hasidim*." *Journal of Jewish History* 33, no. 1-2 (1982): 583–93.

———. *Fromme Juden und christlich-höfische Ideale im Mittelalter*. Trier: Kleine Schriften des Arye Maimon-Instituts 10, 2008.

———. "L'Inquisition et les juifs au Provence au XIIIᵉ siècle." *Provence historique* 23 (1974): 327–38.

———. "Jewish Converts to Christianity in Medieval Europe 1200–1500." In *Cross-Cultural Convergences in the Crusader Period: Essays Presented to Aryeh Grabois on His Sixty-fifth Birthday*, edited by Michael Goodich, Sophia Menache, and Sylvia Schein, 296–318. New York: Peter Lang, 1995.

———. "Jews, Pilgrimage and the Christian Cult of Saints: Benjamin of Tudela and His Contemporaries." In *After Rome's Fall: Narrators and Sources of Early Medieval History—Essays Presented to Walter Goffert*, edited by Alexander Callander Murray, 337–47. Toronto: University of Toronto Press, 1998.

———. "Mi-Giluyehah shel ha-Antisheimiyut bi-mei ha-Beinayim: Ha'ashamat ha-Yehudim be-Hillul ha-Zelav." In *Studies in the History of the Jewish People and the Land of Israel* 5, edited by B. Oded, 159–73. Haifa: University of Haifa Press, 1980.

———. "Rabbi Isaac Ha-Cohen of Manosque and His Son Rabbi Peretz: The Rabbinate and Its Professionalization in the Fourteenth Century." In *Jewish History: Essays in Honour of Chimen Abramsky*, edited by Ada Rapoport-Albert and Steven J. Zipperstein, 61–83. London: Peter Halban, 1988.

———. *Shylock Revisited: Jews, Moneylending, and Medieval Society*. Berkeley: University of California Press, 1990.

———. "*Tumultus et Rumor in Synagoga*: An Aspect of the Social Life of Provençal Jews in the Middle Ages." *AJS Review* 2 (1977): 225–55.

———. "*Tumultus et Rumor in Synagoga*: Suite d'une enquête." *Provence Historique* 49:195–96 (January–June 1999): 451–59.

Shea, Jennifer. "Adgar's *Gracial* and Christian Images of Jews in Twelfth-Century Vernacular Literature." *Journal of Medieval History* 33 (2007): 181–96.

Shepkaru, Shmuel. "Death Twice Over: Dualism of Metaphor and Realia in 12th-Century Hebrew Crusading Accounts." *Jewish Quarterly Review* 93 (2002): 217–56.

———. "From After Death to Afterlife: Martyrdom and Its Recompense." *AJS Review* 24:1 (1999): 1–44.

———. *Jewish Martyrs in the Pagan and Christian Worlds*. Cambridge: Cambridge University Press, 2006.

Shereshevsky, Esra. *Rashi: The Man and His World*. New York: Sepher-Hermon Press, 1982.

Sherwood, Jessie. "A Convert of 1096: Guillaume, Monk of Flaix, Converted from the Jew." *Viator* 39 (2008): 1–22.

———. "Jewish Conversion from the Sixth to the Twelfth Century." PhD diss., University of Toronto, 2006.

———. "Rebellious Youth and Pliant Children: Jewish Converts in Adolescentia." In *Medieval Life Cycles: Continuity and Change*, edited by Isabelle Cochelin and Karen Smyth, 183–209. Turnhout: Brepols, 2013.

Shinan, Avigdor, ed. *Oto ha-Ish: Yehudim Mesaprim 'al Yeshu*. Tel Aviv: Yedi'ot Aharonot, 1999.

Shoham-Steiner, Ephraim. "An Almost Tangible Presence: Some Thoughts on Material Purity among Medieval European Jews." In *Discourses of Purity in Transcultural Perspective (300–1600)*, edited by Matthias Bley, Nikolas Jaspert, and Stefan Köck, 54–74. Leiden: Brill, 2015.

———. "'And in Most of Their Business Transactions They Rely on This': Some Reflexions on Jews and Oaths in the Commercial Arena in Medieval Europe." In *On the Word of a Jew: Religion, Reliability and the Dynamics of Trust*, edited by Nina Caputo and Mitchell B. Hart, 36–61. Bloomington: Indiana University Press, 2019.

———. "Clinging to a Jewish Saint in a Time of Growing Turmoil: Appropriating the Figure of Rabbi Judah the Pious in Late Fifteenth-Century Jewish Folktales from Regensburg." *Medieval Encounters* 28, no. 4 (January 2022): 336–67.

———. "'For a Prayer in That Place Would Be Most Welcome': Jews, Holy Shrines, and Miracles—A New Approach." *Viator* 37 (2006): 369–95.

———. "The Humble Sage and the Wandering Madman: Madness and Madmen in an Exemplum from *Sefer Hasidim*." *Jewish Quarterly Review* 96, no. 1 (Winter 2006): 38–49.

———, ed. *Intricate Interfaith Networks: Quotidian Jewish-Christian Contacts in the Middle Ages*. Studies in the History of Daily Life (800–1600) 5. Turnhout: Brepols, 2016.

———. *Jews and Crime in Medieval Europe*. Detroit: Wayne State University Press, 2020.

———. "Jews and Healing at Medieval Saints' Shrines: Participation, Polemics and Shared Cultures." *Harvard Theological Review* 103, no. 1 (January 2010): 111–29.

———. "Making a Living in Early Medieval Ashkenaz." In *Jüdische Kultur in den SchUM-Städten: Literatur—Musik—Theater*, edited by Karl E. Grözinger, 65–82. Jüdische Kultur, Band 26. Wiesbaden: Harrassowitz, 2014.

———. "Pharaoh's Bloodbath: Medieval European Jewish Thoughts about Leprosy Disease and Blood Therapy." In *Jewish Blood: Reality and Metaphor in Jewish History, Religion, and Culture*, edited by Mitchell B. Hart, 99–115. New York: Routledge, 2009.

———. "'This Should Not Be Shown to a Gentile': Medico-Magical Texts in Medieval Franco-German Rabbinic Manuscripts." In *Bodies of Knowledge: Cultural Interpretations of Illness and Medicine in Medieval Europe*, edited by Sally Crawford and Christina Lee, 53–59. Oxford: BAR Publishing, 2010.

———. "The Virgin Mary, Miriam, and Jewish Reactions to Marian Devotion in the High Middle Ages." *AJS Review* 37, no. 1 (April 2013): 75–91.

———. "Vitam finivit infelicem: Madness, Conversion, and Adolescent Suicide among Jews in Late Twelfth-Century England." In *Jews in Medieval Christendom: Slay Them Not*, edited by Kristine T. Utterback and Merrall Llewelyn Price, 71–90. Leiden: Brill, 2013.

Shoham-Steiner, Ephraim, and Elisabeth Hollender. "Beyond the Rabbinic Paradigm." *Jewish Quarterly Review* 111, no. 3 (Spring 2021): 236–64.

Shoulson, Jeffrey S. *Fictions of Conversion: Jews, Christians, and Cultures in Early Modern England*. Philadelphia: University of Pennsylvania Press, 2013.

Shyovitz, David I. *A Remembrance of His Wonders: Nature and the Supernaural in Medieval Ashkenaz*. Philadelphia: University of Pennsylvania Press, 2017.

———. "Was Judah he-Hasid the 'Author' of *Sefer Hasidim*?" *Jewish History* 34, no. 1–2 (2021): 31–35.

Sicroff, Albert A. *Les controverses des statuts de 'pureté de sang' en Espagne du XVe au XVIIe siècle*. Paris: Didier, 1960.

Sifre: A Tannaitic Commentary on the Book of Deuteronomy. Translated from the Hebrew with an introduction by Reuven Hammer. New Haven, CT: Yale University Press, 1986.

Sifrei Devarim. Edited by Louis Finkelstein. New York: Jewish Theological Seminary, 1969.

Signer, Michael. "King/Messiah: Rashi's Exegesis of Psalm 2." *Prooftexts* 3, no. 3 (1983): 273–78.

Signer, Michael, and Jon Van Engen, eds. *Jews and Christians in Twelfth-Century Europe*. Notre Dame, IN: Notre Dame University Press, 2000.

Silberstein, Laurence J., ed. *The Other in Jewish Thought and History: Constructions of Jewish Culture and Identity*. New York: NYU Press, 1994.

Silver, Zachary. "The Excommunication of Mordecai Kaplan." *American Jewish Archives Journal* 62, no. 1 (2010): 21–48.

Simms, Norman. "The Unspeakable Agony of Kiddush Ha-shem: Forced Jewish Infanticide during the First and Second Crusades." *Medieval History Journal* 3, no. 2 (2000): 337–62.

Simon, Marcel. "Christian Antisemitism." In *Essential Papers on Judaism and Christianity in Conflict from Late Antiquity to the Reformation*, edited by Jeremy Cohen, 131–73. New York: NYU Press, 1991.

———. *Verus Israel: A Study of the Relations between Christians and Jews in the Roman Empire (AD 135–425)*. 1st French ed., 1948. London: Littman Library of Jewish Civilization, 1996.

Simonsohn, Shlomo. *The Apostolic See and the Jews: Documents: 492–1404*. Pontifical Institute of Medieval Studies and Texts 94. Toronto: Pontifical Institute of Mediaeval Studies, 1988.

———. "Some Well-Known Jewish Converts during the Renaissance." *Revue des études juives* 148 (1989): 17–52.

Sinanoglou, Leah. "The Christ Child as Sacrifice: A Medieval Tradition and the Corpus Christi Play." *Speculum* 48 (1973): 491–509.

Sirat, Colette. "Looking at Latin Books, Understanding Latin Texts: Different Attitudes in Different Jewish Communities." In *Hebrew to Latin to Hebrew: The Mirroring of Two Cultures in the Age of Humanism*, edited by Giulio Busi, 7–22. Berlin: Institut für Judaistik, Freie Universität Berlin, 2006.

———. "Notes sur la circulation des livres entre juifs et chrétiens au Moyen Age." In *Du copiste au collectionneur. Mélanges d'histoire des textes et des bibliothèques en l'honneur d'André Vernet, Bibliologia* (Elementa ad librorum studia pertinentia) 18, edited by D. Nebbiai-Dalla Guarda and J.-F. Genest, 383–403. Turnhout: Brepols, 1999.

Skinner, Patricia, ed. *Jews in Medieval Britain: Historical, Literary and Archaeological Perspectives*. Rochester, NY: Boydell Press, 2012.

———. "Viewpoint: Confronting the 'Medieval' in Medieval History: The Jewish Example." *Past and Present* 181 (November 2003): 219–47.

Smail, Daniel Lord. *Imaginary Cartographies*. Ithaca, NY: Cornell University Press, 1999.

Smalley, Beryl. *The Study of the Bible in the Middle Ages*. Oxford: Oxford University Press, 1942.

Smith, Anthony D. *Chosen Peoples: Sacred Sources of National Identity*. Oxford: Oxford University Press, 2011.

Smith, Emma. "Was Shylock Jewish?" *Shakespeare Quarterly* 64, no. 2 (Summer 2013): 188–219.

Smith, Hannah. "Jews, Monks and Martyred Children: The Development of Ritual Murder Narratives in Twelfth and Thirteenth Century England." Master's thesis, University of Canterbury at Christchurch, New Zealand, 2017.

Smith, Jonathan Z. *To Take Place: Toward a Theory in Ritual*. Chicago: University of Chicago Press, 1987.

Smith, Morton. "The Gentiles in Judaism 125 BCE–CE 66." In *The Cambridge History of Judaism*. Vol. 3, *The Early Roman Period*, edited by William Horbury, W. D. Davies, and John Sturdy, 192–249. Cambridge: Cambridge University Press, 1999.

Soloveitchik, Haym. "Dialectics, Scholasticism, and the Origins of the Tosafot." In *Collected Essays: Volume II*, by Haym Soloveitchik, 23–28. Oxford: Littman Library of Jewish Civilization, 2014.

———. "Halakhah, Hermeneutics, and Martyrdom in Medieval Ashkenaz." *Jewish Quarterly Review* 94 (2004): 77–108, 278–99.

———. "Religious Law and Change: The Medieval Ashkenazi Example." *AJS Review* 12 (1987): 205–21.

Sorkin, David. *Jewish Emancipation: A History across Five Centuries*. Princeton, NJ: Princeton University Press, 2019.

Southern, Richard W. *Anselm and His Biographer: A Study of Monastic Life and Thought, 1059–c. 1130*. Cambridge: Cambridge University Press, 1963.

———. *The Making of the Middle Ages*. New Haven, CT: Yale University Press, 1953.

———. *Medieval Humanism and Other Studies*. Oxford: Blackwell, 1970.

———. "St. Anselm and Gilbert Crispin, Abbot of Westminster." *Medieval and Renaissance Studies* 3 (1954): 78–115.

———. *Western Society and the Church in the Middle Ages*. Harmondsworth, UK: Penguin Books, 1970.

———. *Western Views of Islam in the Middle Ages*. Cambridge, MA: Harvard University Press, 1962.

Soyer, François. *Medieval Antisemitism?* York: Arc Humanities Press, 2019.

Spence, Sarah. "Text of the Body: Abelard and Guibert de Nogent." In *Texts and the Self in the Twelfth Century*, edited by Sarah Spence, 55–84. Cambridge: Cambridge University Press, 1996.

Spicer, Andrew, and Sarah Hamilton, eds. *Defining the Holy: Sacred Space in Medieval and Early Modern Europe*. Aldershot, UK: Ashgate, 2005.

Spiegel, Gabrielle M. "Memory and History: Liturgical Time and Historical Time." *History and Theory* 41, no. 2 (May 2002): 149–62.

Spitzer, Leo. "Review of *Die religiöse Disputation in der europäischen Dichtung des Mittelalters: I. Der allegorische Streit zwischen Synagoge und Kirche* by Hiram Pflaum." *Speculum* 13, no. 3 (July 1938): 356–60.

Spitzer, Shlomo. "She'eilot u-Teshuvot Rabbeinu Yehudah he-Hasid be-'Inyanei Teshuvah." In *Sefer ha-Zikaron li-khvodo u-le-Zikhron shel R. Shmuel Barukh Werner*, edited by Yosef Asher Buksboim, 199–205. Jerusalem: Makhon Yerushalayim, 1996.

Stacey, Robert C. "'Adam of Bristol' and Tales of Ritual Crucifixion in Medieval England." In *Christians and Jews in Angevin England: The York Massacre of 1190 Narratives and Texts*, edited by Sarah Rees Jones and Sethina Watson, 1–15. York: York Medieval Press, 2013.

———. "Anti-Semitism and the Medieval English State." In *The Medieval State: Essays Presented to James Campbell*, edited by J. R. Maddicott and D. M. Palliser, 163–77. London: Hambledon Press, 2000.

———. "The Conversion of Jews to Christianity in Thirteenth-Century England." *Speculum* 67, no. 2 (1992): 263–83.

———. "Crusades, Martyrdoms, and the Jews of Norman England, 1096–1190." In *Juden und Christen zur Zeit der Kreuzzüge*, edited by Alfred Haverkamp, 233–51. Vorträge und Forschungen 47. Sigmaringen: Jan Thorbecke Verlag, 1999.

———. "The English Jews under Henry III." In *The Jews in Medieval Britain: Historical, Literary and Archaeological Perspectives*, edited by Partricia Skinner, 41–54. Rochester, NY: Boydell Press, 2003.

———. "From Ritual Crucifixion to Host Desecration: Jews and the Body of Christ." *Jewish History* 12, no. 1 (Spring 1998): 11–28.

———. "History, Religion, and Medieval Antisemitism: A Response to Gavin Langmuir." *Religious Studies Review* 20, no. 2 (April 1994): 95–101.

———. "Jewish Lending and the Medieval English Economy." In *A Commercialising Economy: England 1086–to c. 1300*, edited by Richard H. Britnell and Bruce M. S. Campbell, 78–101. Manchester: Manchester University Press, 1995.

———. "Jews and Christians in Twelfth-Century England: Some Dynamics of a Changing Relationship." In *Jews and Christians in Twelfth-Century Europe*, edited by Michael A. Signer and John Van Engen, 340–54. Notre Dame, IN: Notre Dame University Press, 2001.

———. "King Henry III and the Jews." In *Jews in Medieval Christendom: "Slay Them Not,"* edited by Kristine T. Utterback and Merrall Llewelyn Price, 117–27. Leiden: Brill, 2013.

———. "The Massacres of 1189–90 and the Origins of the Jewish Exchequer, 1189–1226." In *Christians and Jews in Angevin England: The York Massacre of 1190 Narratives and Texts*, edited by Sarah Rees Jones and Sethina Watson, 106–24. York: York Medieval Press, 2013.

———. "Parliamentary Negotiation and the Expulsion of the Jews from England." *Thirteeth-Century England*, edited by Michael Prestwich, R. H. Britnell, and Robin Frame, 6:77–101. Rochester, NY: Boydell Press, 1997.

———. "Royal Taxation and the Social Structure of Medieval Anglo-Jewry: The Tallages of 1239–1242." *Hebrew Union College Annual* 56 (1985): 175–249.

———. "1240–60: A Watershed in Anglo-Jewish Relations?" *Historical Research* 41, no. 145 (June 1988): 135–50.

Starr, Joshua. *The Jews in the Byzantine Empire: 641–1204*. Athens: Verlag der Byzantinisch-Neugriechischen Jahrbücher, 1939.

———. "The Mass Conversion of Jews in Southern Italy (1290–1293)." *Speculum* 21, no. 2 (1946): 203–11.

Stein, Siegfried. "The Development of the Jewish Law on Interest from the Biblical Period to the Expulsion of the Jews from England." *Historia Judaica* 17, no. 1 (1955): 3–40.

———. "A Disputation on Moneylending between Jews and Gentiles in Me'ir ben Simeon's *Milhemeth Miswah* (Narbonne, 13th-Cent.)." *Journal of Jewish Studies* 10 (1959): 45–61.

———. "Laws of Interest in the Old Testament." *Journal of Theological Studies* 4 (1953): 161–70.

Steiner, Emily. *Reading Piers Plowman*. Cambridge: Cambridge University Press, 2013.

Steiner, Richard. "'Iqvot Leshoniyim shel Soharim Yehudim mei-Arzot ha-Islam be-Mamlakhah ha-Frankit." *Leshoneinu* 73, no. 3–4 (2011): 347–70.

Steinová, Evina. "The Correspondence of Pablo Alvaro with Eleazar: A Rare Sample of Judeo-Christian Dispute from the 9th Century." *Canonicity and Authority* (2010): 1–37.

Stemberger, Günter. "The Impact of Paganism and Christianity." In *The Oxford Handbook of Jewish Daily Life in Roman Palestine*, edited by Catherine Hezser, 503–20. Oxford: Oxford University Press, 2010.

Stern, David, and Mark Mirsky, eds. *Rabbinic Fantasies: Imaginative Narratives from Classical Hebrew Literatures*. New Haven, CT: Yale University Press, 1998.

Stern, Fritz R. *The Politics of Cultural Despair: A Study in the Rise of the German Ideology*. Berkeley: University of California Press, 1961.

Stevenson, Joseph, trans. *The Chronicles of Robert de Monte*. London: Church Historians of England, 1856. Reprinted, Llanerch Publishers, 1991.

Stocking, Rachel L. *Bishops, Councils, and Consensus in the Visigothic Kingdom, 589–633*. Ann Arbor: University of Michigan Press, 2000.

Stone, Carole. "Anti-Semitism in the Miracle Tales of the Virgin." *Medieval Encounters* 5, no. 3 (1999): 364–74.

Stone, Linda M. A. *"Slay Them Not": Twelfth-Century Christian-Jewish Relations and the Glossed Psalms*. Leiden: Brill, 2019.

Stoudt, Debra L. "Parallels between Jewish and Christian Mystical Experience in Medieval Germany." In *German Literature between Faiths: Jew and Christian at Odds and in Harmony*, edited by Peter Meister, 39–51. Oxford: Peter Lang, 2004.

Stow, Kenneth R. "Agobard of Lyons and the Medieval Conception of the Jew." *Conservative Judaism* 29 (1974): 58–65. Reprinted in Kenneth R. Stow, *Popes, Church, and Jews: Confrontation and Response*. Aldershot, UK: Ashgate, 2007.

———. *Alienated Minority: The Jews of Medieval Latin Europe*. Cambridge, MA: Harvard University Press, 1992.

———. "The Church and the Jews: St. Paul to Pius IX." In *Atlante del Cristianesimo*, edited by Roberto Usconi, 1–70. Turin: UTET, 2006. Revised in Kenneth R. Stow, *Popes, Church, and Jews: Confrontation and Response*. Aldershot, UK: Ashgate, 2007.

———. "Conversion, Apostasy, and Apprehensiveness: Emicho of Flonheim and the Fear of Jews in the Twelfth Century." *Speculum* 76 (2001): 911–33. Reprinted in Kenneth R. Stow, *Popes, Church, and Jews: Confrontation and Response*. Aldershot, UK: Ashgate, 2007.

———. "The Cruel Jewish Father: From Martyrdom to Murder." In *Studies in Medieval Social and Intellectual History: Festschrift in Honor of Robert Chazan*, edited by David Engel, Lawrence Schiffman, and Elliot Wolfson, 245–78. Leiden: Brill, 2012.

———. "Expulsion Italian Style: The Case of Lucio Ferraris." *Jewish History* 3 (1988): 51–63.

———. "Hatred of the Jews or Love of the Church: Papal Policy toward the Jews in the Middle Ages." In *Antisemitism through the Ages*, edited by Shmuel Almog, 71–90. Oxford: Pergamon Press, 1988.

———. *Jewish Dogs: An Image and Its Interpreters. Continuity in the Jewish-Christian Encounter*. Stanford, CA: Stanford University Press, 2006.

———. "Papal and Royal Attitudes toward Jewish Lending in the Thirteenth Century." *AJS Review* 6 (1981): 161–84. Reprinted in Kenneth R. Stow, *Popes, Church, and Jews: Confrontation and Response*. Aldershot, UK: Ashgate, 2007.

———. *Popes, Church and Jews in the Middle Ages: Confrontation and Response*. Aldershot, UK: Ashgate, 2007.

Strack, Hermann. *Jew and Human Sacrifice: Human Blood and Jewish Ritual, an Historical and Sociological Inquiry*. New York: Bloch, 1909.

Strang, David, and Sarah A. Soule. "Diffusion in Organizations and Social Movements: From Hybrid Corn to Poison Pills." *Annual Review of Sociology* 24 (1998): 265–90.

Straus, Raphael. "'The Jewish Hat' as an Aspect of Social History." *Jewish Social Studies* 4 (1942): 59–72.

Strickland, Debra Higgs. "Antisemitism in Medieval Art." In *The Cambridge Companion to Antisemitism*, edited by Steven T. Katz, 248–70. Cambridge: Cambridge University Press, 2022.

———. "The Jews, Leviticus, and the Unclean in Medieval English Bestiaries." In *Beyond the Yellow Badge: Anti-Judaism and Antisemitism in Medieval and Early Modern Visual Culture*, edited by Mitchell B. Merback, 203–32. Leiden: Brill, 2007.

———. *Saracens, Demons, and Jews: Making Monsters in Medieval Art*. Princeton, NJ: Princeton University Press, 2003.

Stroll, Mary. *The Jewish Pope: Ideology and Politics in the Papal Schism of 1130*. Leiden: Brill, 1987.

Stroumsa, Gedaliahu G. "From Anti-Judaism to Antisemitism in Early Christianity?" In *Contra Iudaeos: Ancient and Medieval Polemics between Christians and Jews*, edited by Ora Limor and Guy G. Stroumsa, 1–26. Tübingen: Mohr Siebeck, 1996.

———. "Religious Contacts in Byzantine Palestine." *Numen* 36, no. 1 (June 1989): 16–42.

Sturges, Robert S., ed. and trans. *Aucassin and Nicolette: A Facing-Page Edition and Translation*. East Lansing: Michigan State University Press, 2015.

Swartz, Michael D. "'Like the Ministering Angels': Ritual and Purity in Early Jewish Mysticism and Magic." *AJS Review* 19, no. 2 (1994): 135–67.

———. "Three-Dimensional Philology: Some Implications of the *Synopse zur Hekhalot Literatur*." In *Envisioning Judaism: Studies in Honor of Peter Schäfer on the Occasion of his Seventieth Birthday*, edited by Ra'anan S. Boustan et al., 1:529–50. Tübingen: Mohr Siebeck, 2013.

Sweeney, Eileen C. "Abelard and the Jews." In *Rethinking Abelard: A Collection of Critical Essays*, edited by Babette S. Hellemans, 37–50. Leiden: Brill, 2014.

Synan, Edward A. *The Popes and the Jews in the Middle Ages*. New York: Macmillan, 1965.

Szermach, Paul E. Introduction to *Aspects of Jewish Culture in the Middle Ages*, edited by Paul E. Szermach, ix–xxi. Albany: SUNY Press, 1979.

Szpiech, Ryan. *Conversion and Narrative: Reading and Religious Authority in Medieval Polemic*. Philadelphia: University of Pennsylvania Press, 2013.

Tabory, Joseph. "The Benedictions of Self-Identity and the Changing Status of Women and of Orthodoxy." *Kenishta: Studies of the Synagogue World* 1 (2001): 107–38.

Taitz, Emily. *The Jews of Medieval France: The Community of Champagne*. Westwood, CT: Greenwood Press, 1994.

Talgam, Rina. *Mosaics of Faith: Floors of Pagans, Jews, Samaritans, Christians, and Muslims in the Holy Land*. Jerusalem: Yad Ben-Zvi Press, 2014.

Talmage, Frank. *Apples of Gold in Settings of Silver: Studies in Medieval Jewish Exegesis and Polemics*. Edited by Barry Dov Walfish. Toronto: Pontifical Institute of Medieval Studies, 1999.

———, ed. *Disputation and Dialogue: Readings in the Jewish-Christian Encounter*. New York: Ktav, 1975.

Tannahill, Reay. *Flesh and Blood: A History of the Cannibal Complex*. London: Abacus, 1996.

Tanner, Norman P. *Decrees of the Ecumenical Councils*. 2 vols. Washington, DC: Georgetown University Press, 1990.

Tarantul, Elijahu. "Das 'Buch der Frommen' im Spannungsfeld zwischen der Mündlichkeit und der Schriftlichkeit." *Aschkenas* 15, no. 1 (2005): 1–23.

Tartakoff, Paola. *Between Christian and Jew: Conversion and Inquisition in the Medieval Crown of Aragon: 1250–1391*. Philadelphia: University of Pennsylvania Press, 2012.

———. "Conversion and Return to Judaism in High and Late Medieval Europe: Christian Perceptions and Portrayals." In *Contesting Inter-Religious Conversion in the Medieval World*, edited by Yaniv Fox and Yosi Yisraeli, 177–94. New York: Routledge, 2017.

———. *Conversion, Circumcision, and Ritual Murder in Medieval Europe*. Philadelphia: University of Pennsylvania Press, 2019.

———. "Of Purity, Piety, and Plunder: Jewish Apostates and Poverty in Medieval Europe." In *Bastards and Believers: Jewish Converts and Conversion from the Bible to the Present*, edited by Theodor Dunkelgrün and Paweł Maciejko, 75–88, 298–305. Philadelphia: University of Pennsylvania Press, 2020.

———. "Testing Boundaries: Jewish Conversion and Cultural Fluidity in Medieval Europe: c. 1200–1391." *Speculum* 90, no. 3 (July 2015): 728–62.

Ta-Shma, Israel. *Ha-Tefillah ha-Ashkenazit ha-Qedumah*. Jerusalem: Magnes, 2003.

Tellenbach, Gerd. *Church, State and Christian Society at the Time of the Investiture Contest*. Oxford: B. Blackwell, 1940.

Teter, Magda. *Blood Libel: On the Trail of an Anti-Semitic Myth*. Cambridge, MA: Harvard University Press, 2020.

———. *Christian Supremacy: Reckoning with the Roots of Antisemitism and Racism*. Princeton, NJ: Princeton University Press, 2023.

Thomas of Monmouth. *The Life and Miracles of St. William of Norwich by Thomas of Monmouth*. Edited and translated by Augustus Jessopp and Montague Rhodes James. Cambridge: Cambridge University Press, 1896. Reprinted 2011.

———. *The Life and Passion of William of Norwich*. Edited by Miri Rubin. New York: Penguin Classics, 2015.

Thornton, T.C.G. "Christian Understandings of the Birkath Ha-Minim in the Eastern Roman Empire." *Journal of Theological Studies* 38 (1987): 419–31.

———. "The Crucifixion of Haman and the Scandal of the Cross." *Journal of Theological Studies* 37 (1986): 419–26.

———. "Trees, Gibbits, and Crosses." *Journal of Theological Studies* 23 (1972): 130–31.

Thorpe, Lewis. *The Journey through Wales and a Description of Wales by Gerald of Wales*. Harmondsworth, UK: Penguin, 1978.

Thräde, Klaus. "Jakob und Esau." In *Reallexikon für Antike und Christentum*, edited by Theodor Klauser et al., 14: 1118–1217. 26 vols. Stuttgart: A. Hiersmann, 1994.

Thurn, David H. "Economic and Ideological Exchange in Marlowe's 'Jew of Malta.'" *Theater Journal* 46, no. 2 (May 1994): 157–70.

Timm, Erika. "Ein neu entdeckter literarischer Text in hebräischen Lettern aus der Zeit vor 1349." *Zeitschrift für deutsches Altertum und deutsche Literatur* 142, no. 4 (2013): 417–43.

———. "Zur Frühgeschichte der jüdischen Erzählungsprosa. Eine neuaufgefundene Maise-Handschrift." *Beiträge zur deutschen Sprache und Literatur* 117 (1995): 243–80.

Timmer, David E. "Biblical Exegesis in the Jewish-Christian Controversy in the Early Twelfth Century." *Church History* 58, no. 3 (September 1989): 309–21.

———. "The Religious Significance of Judaism for Twelfth-Century Monastic Exegesis: A Study of the Thought of Rupert of Deutz, c. 1070–1129." PhD diss., Notre Dame University, 1983.

Tinkle, Theresa. "Exegesis Reconsidered: The Fleury 'Slaughter of Innocents' and the Myth of Ritual Murder." *Journal of English and Germanic Philology* 102, no. 2 (April 2003): 211–43.

Toch, Michael. *The Economic History of European Jews: Late Antiquity and Early Middle Ages*. Études sur le judaïsme médiéval, 56. Leiden: Brill, 2013.

———. "Fear, Terror and Its Alternatives: The Case of Medieval Jews." In *Por Política, Terror Social*, edited by Flocel Sabaté, 67–75. Lleida, Spain: Pagès editors, 2013.

———. "The Formation of a Diaspora: The Settlement of Jews in the Medieval German Reich." *Aschkenas* 7, no. 1 (1997): 55–78.

———. "Geldleiher und sonst nichts? Zur wirschaftslichen Tätigkeit der Juden im deutchen Sprachraum des Spätmittelalters." *Tel Aviver Jahrbuch fur deutsche Geschichte* 22 (1993): 117–26.

———. *Die Juden im mittelalterlichen Reich*. Enzyklopädie deutscher Geschichte 44. Munich: Oldenbourg Press, 2003.

———. "Siedlungsstruktur der im Wandel vom Mittelalter zur Neuzeit." In *Juden in der christlichen Umwelt während des späten Mittelalters*, edited by Alfred Haverkamp and Franz-Josef Ziwes, 29–30. Berlin: Duncker, 1992.

———. "Die Wirtschaftsgeschichte der Juden im Mittelalter: Stand, Aufgaben und Möglichkeiten der Forschung." *Wiener Jahrbuch für jüdische Geschichte und Museumswesen* 4 (1999–2000): 9–24.

Tolan, John. *England's Jews: Finance, Violence, and the Crown in the Thirteenth Century*. Philadelphia: University of Pennsylvania Press, 2023.

———. "The First Imposition of a Badge on European Jews: The English Royal Mandate of 1218." In *The Character of the Christian-Muslim Encounter: Essays in Honor of David Thomas*, edited by Douglas Pratt et al., 145–66. Leiden: Brill, 2015.

———. "Of Milk and Blood: Innocent III and the Jews, Revisited." In *Jews and Christians in Thirteenth-Century France*, edited by Elisheva Baumgarten and Judah D. Galinsky, 139–49. New York: Palgrave Macmillan, 2015.

———. "Royal Policy and Conversion of Jews to Christianity in Thirteenth-Century Europe." In *Contesting Inter-Religious Conversion in the Medieval World*, edited by Yaniv Fox and Yosi Yisraeli, 96–111. New York: Routledge, 2017.

———. *Saracens: Islam in the Medieval European Imagination*. New York: Columbia University Press, 2002.

———. *Sons of Ishmael: Muslims through European Eyes in the Middle Ages*. Gainesville: University of Florida Press, 2008.

Tomasch, Sylvia S. "Judecca, Dante's Satan, and the *Dis*-placed Jew." In *Text and Territory: Geographical Imagination in the European Middle Ages*, edited by Sylvia Tomasch and Sealy Gilles, 247–67. Philadelphia: University of Pennsylvania Press, 1998.

———. "Postcolonial Chaucer and the Virtual Jew." In *The Postcolonial Middle Ages*, edited by Jeffrey Jerome Cohen, 243–60. New York: St. Martin's Press, 2000.

Tomasch, Sylvia S., and Scott D. Westrem, eds. *Text and Territory: Geographical Imagination in the European Middle Ages*. Philadelphia: University of Pennsylvania Press, 1998.

Tomlinson, Julia. "The Missing Accusation: The Circumcision Case of Odard and the Legacy of St William of Norwich." *Saeculum Undergraduate Academic Journal* 12, no. 1 (2017): n.p.

Torrell, Jean-Pierre. "Les juifs dans l'oeuvre de Pierre le Vénérable." *Cahiers de civilization médiéval* 30, no. 4 (1987): 339–46.
Tovey, d'Blossiers. *Anglo-Judaica, or, the History and the Antiquities of the Jews of England*. London, 1738.
Trachtenberg, Joshua. *The Devil and the Jews: The Medieval Conception of the Jew and Its Relation to Modern Anti-Semitism*. 1943. Reprinted, Philadelphia: Jewish Publication Society of America, 1983.
Tractatus adversus Judaeum. In *Thesaurus Novus Anecdotorum*, edited by Edmond Martène and Durand, vol. 5, col. 1567. Paris, 1717.
Trautner-Kromann, Hanne. *Shield and Sword: Jewish Polemics against Christianity and Christians in France and Spain from 1100–1500*. Tübingen: Mohr Siebeck, 1993.
Trial of the Talmud, 1240. Hebrew texts translated by John Friedman. Latin texts translated by Jean Connell Hoff. Historical essay by Robert Chazan. Toronto: Pontifical Institute of Mediaeval Studies, 2012.
Turner, Victor, and Edith Turner. *Image and Pilgrimage in Christian Culture*. New York: Columbia University Press, 1978.
Uebel, Michael. "Unthinking the Monster: Twelfth-Century Responses to Saracen Alterity." In *Monster Theory: Reading Culture*, edited by Jeffrey Jerome Cohen, 264–91. Minneapolis: University of Minnesota Press, 1996.
Ullendorff, Edward. "The Bawdy Bible." *Bulletin of the School of Oriental and African Studies* 42, no. 3 (1979): 425–56.
Urbach, Ephraim Elimelekh. *Ba'alei ha-Tosafot*. 2 vols. Jerusalem: Mosad Bialik, 1980.
——. "Goy, Nokhri, ve-'Aqum." In *Mehqarim be-Mada'ei ha-Yahadut*, edited by Moshe David Heer and Jonah Frankel, 2:520–28. Jerusalem: Magnes Press, 1998.
——. "Hilekhot 'Avodah Zarah ve-ha-Metzi'ut ha-arkhiologit ve-ha-historit ba-me'ah ha-Sheniyah u-va-Me'ah ha-Shelishit." *Eretz Yisrael* 5 (1958): 189–205. Reprinted in Ephraim Elimelekh Urbach, *Mei-'Olamam shel Hakhamim: Qovetz Mehqarim*. Jerusalem: Magnes Press, 1988.
Utterback, Kristine T. "*Conversi* Revert: Voluntary and Forced Return to Judaism in the Early Fourteenth Century." *Church History* 64 (1995): 16–28.
Utterback, Kristine T., and Merrall L. Price, eds. *Jews in Medieval Christendom: "Slay Them Not."* Leiden: Brill, 2013.
Valk, Jonathan. "Crime and Punishment: Deportation in the Levant in the Age of Assyrian Hegemony." *Bulletin of the American Schools of Oriental Research* 384 (2020): 77–103.
Valles, Margot Behrend. "Judaized Romance and Romanticized Judaization: Adaptation into Hebrew and Early Yiddish Chivalric Literature." PhD diss., Indiana University, 2013.
Van Bekkum, W. Jac. "Anti-Christian Polemics in Hebrew Liturgical Poetry (*Piyyut*) of the Sixth and Seventh Centuries." In *Early Christian Poetry: A Collection of Essays*, edited by J. Den Boeft and A. Hilhorst, 297–309. Leiden: Brill, 1993.
Vauchez, André. "Antisémitisme et canonisation populaire: Saint werner ou vernier d. 1287 enfant martyr et patron des vignerons." *Comtes-rendus des séances de l'Academie des inscriptions et belles-lettres* 126, no. 1 (1982): 65–79.

———. "Saints and Pilgrimages: New and Old." In *The Cambridge History of Christianity. Christianity in Western Europe: c. 1100–c. 1500*, edited by Miri Rubin and Walter Simons, 4:324–39. Cambridge: Cambridge University Press, 2009.

———. *The Spirituality of the Medieval West: The Eighth to the Twelfth Century*. Kalamazoo, MI: Cistercian Press, 1993.

Vincent, Nicholas. "Jews, Poitevins, and the Bishop of Winchester." In *Christianity and Judaism*, edited by Diana Wood, 119–32. Studies in Church History 29. Oxford: Blackwell Publishers, 1992.

———. "Two Papal Letters on the Wearing of the Jewish Badge, 1221 and 1229." *Jewish Historical Studies* 34 (1994–96): 209–24.

Visscher, Eva de. *Reading the Rabbis: Christian Hebraism in the Writings of Herbert of Bosham*. Leiden: Brill, 2014.

Vose, Robin J. E. *Dominicans, Muslims, and Jews in the Medieval Crown of Aragon*. Cambridge: Cambridge University Press, 2009.

Wachtel, David. "The Ritual and Liturgical Commemoration of Two Medieval Persecutions." Master's thesis, Columbia University, 1995.

Wagenaar-Nolthenius, Helene. "Der Planctus Iudei und der Gesang jüdischer Märtyrer in Blois Anno 1171." In *Mélanges offerts à René Crozet*, edited by Pierre Gallais and Yves-Jean Riou, 2:881–85. Poitiers: Société d'études médiévales, 1966.

Walzer, Michael, Menachem Lorberbaum, and Noam J. Zohar, eds. *The Jewish Political Tradition*. 3 vols. New Haven, CT: Yale University Press, 2000–2018.

Ward, Benedicta. *Miracles and the Medieval Mind: Theory, Record, and Event, 1000–1215*. Philadelphia: University of Pennsylvania Press, 1987.

Warner, Marina. *Alone of All Her Sex: The Myth and the Cult of the Virgin Mary*. New York: Alfred A. Knopf, 1976.

Warnock, Robert G. "The Arthurian Tradition in Hebrew and Yiddish." In *King Arthur through the Ages*, edited by Valerie M. Legorio and Mildred Leake Day, 1:189–208. New York: Garland, 1990.

———. "Widwilt." In *The New Arthurian Encyclopedia*, edited by Norris J. Lacy, 512–13. Chicago: St. James Press, 1991.

Wasserman, Mira Beth. "The Humanity of the Talmud: Reading for Ethics in Bavli 'Avoda Zara." PhD diss., University of California, Berkeley, 2014.

———. *Jews, Gentiles and Other Animals: The Talmud after the Humanities*. Philadelphia: University of Pennsylvania Press, 2017.

Wasyliw, Patricia Healy. *Martyrdom, Murder, and Magic: Child Saints and Their Cults in Medieval Europe*. Berlin: Peter Lang, 2008.

Waugh, Scott, L., and Peter D. Diehl, eds. *Christendom and Its Discontents: Exclusion, Persecution, and Rebellion, 1000–1500*. Cambridge: Cambridge University Press, 1996.

Weber, Paul. *Geistliches Schauspiel und Kirchliche Kunst in ihrem Verhältnis, erlautert an einer Ikonographie der Kirche und Synagoga*. Stuttgart: Ebner und Seubert, 1894.

Weeda, Claire. "Ethnic Stereotyping in Twelfth-Century Paris." In *Difference and Identity in Francia and Medieval France*, edited by Meredith Cohen and Justine Firnhaber-Baker, 115–38. Farnham, UK: Ashgate, 2010.

Weijers, Olga. *In Search of the Truth: A History of Disputation Techniques from Antiquity to Early Modern Times*. Studies in the Faculty of Arts, History and Influence. Turnhout: Brepols, 2014.

Weinfeld, Moshe. *Deuteronomy and the Deuteronomic School*. Winona Lake, IN: Eisenbrauns, 1992.

———. *Ha-Liturgiyah ha-Yehudit ha-Qedumah: mei-ha-Sifrut ha-Mizmorit ve-'ad ha-Tefillot bi-Megillot Qumran u-ve-Sifrut Hazal*. Jerusalem: Magnes Press, 2004.

Weinhouse, Linda. "Faith and Fantasy: The Texts of the Jews." *Medieval Encounters* 5, no. 3 (1999): 391–408.

Weissberger, Barbara. "Motherhood and Ritual Murder in Medieval Spain and England." *Journal of Medieval and Early Modern Studies* 39, no. 1 (2009): 7–30.

Weissman, Susan. *Final Judgement and the Dead in Medieval Jewish Thought*. London: Littman Library of Jewish Civilization, 2020.

Wenzel, Edith. "Alt-Jiddish oder Mittelhochdeutsch?" In *Greuzen und Greuzüberschreitungen: Kulturelle Beziehungen zwischen Juden und Christen im Mittelalter*. Part of *Aschkenas: Zeitschrift für Geschichte und Kultur der Juden* 14, no. 1 (2004): 31–50.

Wheatley, Edward. "'Blind' Jews and Blind Christians: Metaphorics of Marginalisation in Medieval Europe." *Exemplaria* 14, no. 2 (October 2002): 351–82.

Wickham, Chris. *Medieval Europe: From the Breakup of the Western Roman Empire to the Reformation*. New Haven, CT: Yale University Press, 2016.

Wieder, Naftali. "Be'etya shel Gimatria Anti-notzrit ve-Anti-islamit." *Sinai* 76 (1975): 1–14.

Wiedl, Birgit. "Anti-Jewish Polemics in Business Documents from Late Medieval Austria." *Medieval Worlds* 7 (2018): 61–79.

———. "Host on the Doorstep: Perpetrators, Victims and Bystanders in an Alleged Host Desecration in Fourteenth-Century Austria." In *Crime and Punishment in the Middle Ages and Early Modern Age*, edited by Albrecht Classen and Connie Scarborough, 299–346. Berlin: Walter de Gruyter, 2011.

———. "Jews and the City: Parameters of Jewish Life in Late Medieval Austria." *Urban Space in the Middle Ages and the Early Modern Age*, edited by Albrecht Classen, 273–308. Berlin: Walter de Gruyter, 2009.

———. "Laughing at the Beast: The Judensau: Anti-Jewish Propaganda and Humor from the Middle Ages to the Early Modern Period." In *Laughter in the Middle Ages and Early Modern Times*, edited by Albrecht Classen, 325–64. Berlin: Walter de Gruyter, 2010.

Wilken, Robert L. *John Chrysostom and the Jews*. Berkeley: University of California Press, 1983.

William of Malmesbury. *Gesta regum Anglorum, atque Historia*. Edited by Thomas Duffus Hardy. Novella. 2 vols. London, 1840.

William of Tyre. *Chronicon*. Edited by Georg Heinrich Pertz. In MGH SS 1. Hannover, 1826.

———. *Chronicon*. Edited by Robert B. C. Huygens. Turnhout: Brepols, 1986.

———. *Historia Rerum in Partibus Transmarinis Gestarum*. RHC, 1–4. Paris, 1894–95.

———. *A History of Deeds Done beyond the Sea*. Translated by Emily A. Babcock and A. C. Krey. New York: Columbia University Press, 1943.
Williams, A. Lukyn. *Adversus Judaeos: A Bird's-Eye View of Christian Apologiae until the Renaissance*. New York: Macmillan, 1935.
Williams, Benjamin. "*Glossa Ordinaria* and *Glossa Hebraica*: Midrash in Rashi and the *Ordinaria*." *Traditio* 71 (2016): 179–201.
Williamson, Beth. "The Virgin Lactans and the Madonna of Humility in Italy, Metz and Avignon in the Thirteenth and Fourteenth Centuries." PhD diss., London University, 1996.
Wind, Edgar. "The Crucifixion of Haman." *Journal of the Warburg Institute* 1 (1937): 245–48.
Winer, Rebecca Lynn. "Conscripting the Breast: Lactation, Slavery and Salvation in the Realms of Aragon and Kingdom of Majorca, c. 1250–1300." *Journal of Medieval History* 34, no. 2 (2008): 164–84.
———. *Women, Wealth, and Community in Perpignan, c. 1250–1300: Christians, Jews, and Enslaved Muslims in a Medieval Mediterranean Town*. Aldershot, UK: Ashgate, 2006.
Winges, Scott. "Temple of Impiety: The Politics of Restitution in the Aftermath of the Destruction of the Callinicum Synagogue." https://www.researchgate.net/publication/332764026.
Wischnitzer, Rachel. *The Architecture of the European Synagogue*. Philadelphia: Jewish Publication Society of America, 1964.
Wise, Sherry Lynn. "Cursed Companions: The Literary Representation of Jews in the Medieval and Early Modern Periods in England." PhD diss., York University, 2017.
Wistrich, Robert S. *Anti-Semitism: The Longest Hatred*. New York: Pantheon, 1991.
———. *A Lethal Obsession: Anti-Semitism from Antiquity to the Global Jihad*. New York: Random House, 2010.
Wood, Charles T. "The Doctor's Dilemma: Sin, Salvation and the Menstrual Cycle in Medieval Thought." *Speculum* 56 (1981): 710–27.
Wood, Diana, ed. *Christianity and Judaism*. Studies in Church History 29. Oxford: Blackwell, 1992.
Worthen, Jeremy F. *The Internal Foe: Judaism and Anti-Judaism in the Shaping of Christian Theology*. Newcastle upon Tyne: Cambridge Scholars Publishing, 2009.
Yarrow, Simon. *Saints and Their Communities*. New York: Oxford University Press, 2006.
Yassif, Eli. "Local Identity: Spatial Consciousness and Social Tensions in Hebrew Legends from Medieval Ashkenaz." In *Jüdische Kultur in Den SchUM-Städten: Literatur—Musik—Theater*, edited by Karl-Erich Grözinger, 39–54. Jüdische Kultur, Band 26. Wiesbaden: Harrassowitz, 2014.
———. *Me'ah Sippurim Haser Ehud*. Tel Aviv: Tel Aviv University Press, 2013.
———. "Storytelling and Meaning: Theory and Practice of Narrative Variants." In *("The Life Story of Jesus") Revisited: A Princeton Conference*, edited by Peter Schaäfer, Michael Meerson, and Yaacov Deutsch, 101–35. Tübingen: Mohr Siebeck, 2011.
Yerushalmi, Yosef Hayim. *Antisemitism: The Iberian and the German Model*. Leo Baeck Memorial Lecture. New York: Leo Baeck Institute, 1982. Reprinted in

David M. Mayers and Alexander Kaye, eds., *The Faith of Fallen Jews: Yosef Hayim Yerushalmi and the Writing of Jewish History*. Waltham, MA: Brandeis University Press, 2014.

———. "The Inquisition and the Jews of France in the Time of Bernard Gui." *Harvard Theological Review* 63 (1970): 317–76.

———. "Medieval Jewry: From Within and from Without." In *Aspects of Jewish Culture in the Middle Ages*, edited by Paul E. Szermach, 1–26. Albany: SUNY Press, 1979.

Yuval, Israel Jacob. "All Israel Have a Portion in the World to Come." In *Redefining First-Century Jewish and Christian Identities: Essays in Honor of Ed Parish Sanders*, edited by Fabian E. Udoh, Susannah Heschel, and Mark A. Chancey, 114–38. Notre Dame, IN: Notre Dame University Press, 2008.

———. "Christianity in the Talmud and Midrash: Parallelomania or Parallelophobia?" In *Transforming Relations: Essays on Jews and Christians throughout History—in Honor of Michael A. Signer*, edited by Franklin T. Harkins, 50–74. Notre Dame, IN: Notre Dame University Press, 2010.

———. *Hakhamim be-Doram*. Jerusalem: Magnes, 1988.

———. "Ha-Neqam ve-ha-Qelalah, ha-Dam ve-ha-'alilah; mei-'alilot Qedoshim le-'alilot ha-Dam." *Zion* 58, no. 1 (1993): 33–90.

———. "Heilige Städte, heilige Gemeinden—Mainz as Jerusalem Deutschlands." In *Jüdische Gemeinden und Organisationsformen von der Antike bis zur Gegenwart*, edited by Robert Jütte and Abraham Kustermann, 91–101. Vienna: Böhle Verlag, 1996.

———. "Jews and Christians in the Middle Ages: Shared Myths, Common Language." In *Demonizing the Other: Antisemitism, Racism, Xenophobia*, edited by Robert S. Wistrich, 88–107. Amsterdam: Harwood, 1999.

———. "The Orality of Jewish Oral Law: From Pedagogy to Ideology." In *Judaism, Christianity, and Islam in the Course of History: Exchange and Conflicts*, edited by Lothar Gall and Dietmar Willoweit. 237–60. Munich: Oldenbourg Verlag, 2011.

———. "'They Tell Lies; You Ate the Man': Jewish Reactions to Ritual Murder Accusations." In *Religious Violence between Christians and Jews: Medieval Roots, Modern Perspectives*, edited by Anna Sapir Abulafia, 86–106. New York: Palgrave, 2002.

———. *Two Nations in Your Womb: Perceptions of Jews and Christians in Late Antiquity and the Middle Ages*. Berkeley: University of California Press, 2006.

Yuval, Israel J., and Ram Ben-Shalom, eds. *Conflict and Religious Conversation in Latin Christendom: Studies in Honour of Ora Limor*. Cultural Encounters in Late Antiquity and the Middle Ages 17. Turnhout: Brepols, 2014.

Zafran, Eric M. "An Alleged Case of Image Desecration by the Jews and Its Representation in Art: The Virgin of Cambron." *Journal of Jewish Art* 2 (1975): 62–71.

———. "The Iconography of Anti-Semitism." PhD diss., Art Institute, New York University, 1973.

Zfatman, Sara. *Rosh va-Rishon: Yissud Manhigut ve-Sifrut Yisrael*. Jerusalem: Magnes, 2010.

———. *Shivhei Rabbi Shmuel ve-Rabbi Yehudah Hasid*. Jerusalem: Magnes, 2020.

Ziegler, Joseph. "Physiognomy, Science, and Proto-Racism: 1200–1500." In *The Origins of Racism in the West*, edited by Miriam Eliav-Feldon, Benjamin Isaac, and Joseph Ziegler, 181–99. Cambridge: Cambridge University Press, 2009.

Zimmer, Eric. "Tiqqunei ha-Guf bi-She'at ha-Tefillah." *Sidra* 5 (1989): 89–130.

Zimmermann, Moshe. *Wilhelm Marr: The Patriarch of Anti-Semitism*. New York: Oxford University Press, 1986.

Ziolkowski, Jan M. "Avatars of Ugliness in Medieval Literature." *Modern Language Review* 79 (1984): 1–20.

——, ed. *Obscenity: Social Control and Artistic Creation in the European Middle Ages*. Cultures, Beliefs, and Traditions 4. Leiden: Brill, 1998.

Zitter, Emmy Stark. "Anti-Semitism in Chaucer's Prioress's Tale." *Chaucer Review* 25, no. 4 (1991): 277–84.

Žižek, Slavoj. *The Plague of Fantasies*. London: Verso, 1997.

Zuckerman, Arthur J. *A Jewish Princedom in Feudal France, 768–900*. New York: Columbia University Press, 1972.

Zunz, Leopold. *Die Synagogale Poesie des Mittelalters*. 1855. 2nd ed. Frankfurt am Main: Aron Freimann, 1920. Reprinted, Hildesheim: Georg Olms Verlag, 1967.

——. *Zur Geschichte und Literatur*. Berlin, 1845.

INDEX

Aaron of Lincoln, 173, 183, 209n41
Aaron the Devil, 148
Abelard, Peter, 12, 67
Abraham of Berkhamstead, 229n78
Abraham's covenant with God, 7–8, 9
Abulafia, Anna, 72, 191, 192–93
Abun family, 23
Adam of Bristol, 122, 222n64
Adams, Jonathan, 194
agency: in acting out without risk, 98; on both sides in Christian-dominated culture, 197; in Jewish assertiveness, 3; in post-1096 liturgical poetry, 217n69; of tenth-century Jewish community leaders, 22; of unmarried Jewish daughters, 185
Agobard of Lyon, 71
Aisenberg, Edna, 161
Akiba, martyred rabbi, 130
Albert of Aachen, 59, 61–62
Alexander II (pope), 50, 54, 131
Alfonsi, Peter, 162
Alfonso VI of Castile, 45
Alfonso X of Castile, 148, 161
Almohads, 70, 169
Amir, Netta, 215n32
Amnon of Mainz, 103–4
Amulo of Lyon, 71
Anacletus II (Jewish pope), 168
Anselm of Canterbury, 79–80
anti-Judaism: Langmuir's usage of, 191–92; misleading uses of, 191–94; Nirenberg's sense of, 190; relieving church of responsibility, 192, 247n21
antisemitism: modern coinage of the term, 189, 246n1; terminological issues about, 190–94; three-part structure of, 18, 196–98
antisemitism, medieval: directed at Jews not Judaism, 4; in dynamic and mutually reinforcing process, 65; increased by Jews' assertiveness, 3–4, 13; in new ways between 800 and 1500, 2, 4; recycled by postmodern forms of nativism, 199; three-part structure of, 18, 196–98; transformed into modern categories, 17–18, 196–98
antisemitism, modern: as antimodern movement, 248n34; Arendt's distinction from religious Jew-hatred, 190–91; blood libel and, 125, 187; concerned above all with power, 194, 195–96; contemporary in United States, 198–99; medieval sources of stereotypes in, 194; racist, 17, 189, 190–91, 192, 193, 194, 197–99, 248n34; of Shakespeare's audience, 187; teleological vs. contextual, 189–90, 192; three-part structure of, 18, 196–98; as transformation of medieval categories, 17–18, 196–98
apostates: insulting names given to, 73, 168; in story about blood libel, 123–24. *See also* converts to Christianity
apostolic age, 41, 42, 43, 44
apostolic poverty, 17, 43, 177
Aragon, Kingdom of: conversion to Christianity in, 166
architecture, holy, 76–78
Arendt, Hannah, 190
Ashkenaz, 2, 205n5; beginnings of, 23; bias for Sepharad over, 206n13; foundation legend of, 36
assertiveness of Jews, 2, 3–4, 197; about chosenness, 13, 14, 64; after attacks of 1096, 14–15, 16, 64, 65; bodily excretion and, 90; Christians' defensive reactions to, 16, 18, 65, 192, 197; clashing with Christian reformers, 14; downplayed for fear of blaming the victims, 206n15; in dynamic and mutually reinforcing process, 65; influencing Christians' view of themselves, 206n15; as knights with Christians as servants, 86; making Christian authorities more antisemitic, 3–4, 13;

assertiveness of Jews (*continued*)
  power in Christian society and, 18; in
  resistance to role of servitude, 45–46.
  See also insulting Christianity; latrine
  blasphemy
atonement, vicarious, by Jewish martyrs,
  60, 167
Aucassin and Nicolette, 149–50
Augustine, 10–11; denying Jewish idolatry, 207n17; on Jacob and Esau, 134, 207n26; on Jews as blind witnesses, 10, 152; on Jews as servants or slaves, 208n32; on Jews to be part of Christian society, 10, 17; on Jews to be scattered and subordinated, 10, 11; on not killing Jews, 11, 132

Ba'al-Pe'or, 91–92, 97
Babylonian Jewish practice: Ashkenaz claim of superiority over, 40; German Jewish claim of superiority over, 37; replaced by Italian practice in Mainz, 35. *See also* Baghdad, Abbasid
Babylonian rabbinic masters: not followed by R. Gershom, 25; transfer of learning to the West, 32, 37–40
Babylonian Talmud, 69; on spitting in the synagogue, 95. *See also* Talmud
Baghdad, Abbasid: Ashkenazic mysticism from, 37; international Jewish merchants from, 21; Mainz in relationship to Jewish leadership in, 38; rabbinic authority in Córdoba and, 30, 31–32; rabbinic masters in, 24. *See also* Babylonian Jewish practice
Bale, Anthony, 120, 229n1
baptism: forced, 55, 57, 60–61, 62–63, 130; of Jesus, 83; Jews believed immune to efficacy of, 169; killings and suicides to avoid at all costs, 139, 165; parents trying to prevent, 165; spiritual and physical effects of, 167, 169; traits of Jewish men unchanged by, 141, 167; trying to undo, 104. *See also* conversion to Christianity
Barabas, 182–85, 187, 191, 194–95, 197.
  See also *Jew of Malta*
bar mitzvah, 165

Baron, Salo, 129, 191, 205n6
Barukh ben Isaac, 56
Barzilay, Tzafrir, 125
Baumgarten, Elisheva, 143
beards, 145–46, 148, 149, 162, 237n24; of older Jewish men, 145–46, 237n23
beauty: Christian idealization of, 149–51; collective identity and, 141; conversion to Christianity and, 149–51, 159; falseness of ecclesia and, 155; Jewish sin and exile affecting, 155–60; of Jewish women, 16, 160–61, 162, 184–85, 238n44; new standard in mid-thirteenth century, 162, 239nn67–68; of synagoga and ecclesia, 151, 152, 169, 238n44. *See also* cultural aesthetics; physical appearance
Benedictine monasteries: house of Cluny, 43, 128; revival of martyred Christian saints, 108–9; in rivalry for local child martyr saint, 110; values of, 43.
  See also de Torigni, Robert; Guibert, Abbot of Nogent
Benedictine monks: interested in new saints and their cults, 127–28, 135; ritual murder idea among, 15, 108–9, 115, 120, 122, 126, 128, 132. *See also* Thomas of Monmouth
Benjamin b. Zerah, 238n47
Benjamin of Tudela, 33
Ben-Sasson, Haim Hillel, 217n60
Berger, David, 84, 127, 193, 221n48
Bernard of Clairvaux, 128, 131–33, 135, 136, 242n94
Bible. *See* Hebrew Bible; New Testament; Old Testament
Biddick, Kathleen, 179
binary of inverted hierarchy: Christian reform movements and, 42, 44, 213n1; contemporary antisemitism and, 198, 199; imagined Jew and, 7, 18, 170, 171, 178; in structure of medieval and modern antisemitism, 196–97
Bitton-Jackson, Livia, 185
Black Death, and well poisoning accusation, 125, 232n44
Bloch, Marc, 43
Blois, 112, 116–20, 121, 122, 135, 136, 230n5

blood libel, 15, 123–25, 127, 163, 232n47; Jewish men's alleged need for blood and, 240n69; modern accusations of, 125, 187; persisting after expulsions, 178–79
Blumenkranz, Bernhard, 162
Boccaccio, Giovanni, 67
bodily appearance. *See* physical appearance
bodily excretion vs. the holy: for Christians, 89; for Jews, 89, 90–91, 92–93, 225n21. *See also* feces
bodily fluids, life-giving in Judaism, 90
body of Christ: accusations of Jews' assaults on, 170; belief in real presence in the host, 125, 127; changing meanings of, 122–23; harmed by imagined Jew, 15–16. *See also* Eucharist; host
body studies, 90
Book of Margery Kempe, 180
Boyarin, Daniel, 224n11
boys, Jewish: initiation into Torah learning, 15, 105–7, 165, 229n86; motif of cruel Jewish father and, 130; under thirteen years of age, 164; vulnerable to conversion, 15, 16, 107, 165, 229n86, 241n78
Breuer, Mordecai, 74
Byzantine Christians, and armed pilgrimage, 41, 46
Byzantine Empire, 2–3, 30, 206n11
Byzantine Jewry, 23; piyyutim of, 69, 72

Caesarius of Heisterbach, 82, 100, 104, 161, 165, 185
Calixtus II (pope), 45
Calonymos, 33
cannibalism, ritual, 123–25, 232n47
canon 68, 142–43, 145, 147–49, 162, 185
Cantimpré, Thomas de, 163
Carolingian Empire: charters of protection (*tuitio*) for Jewish merchants, 20–21, 35; protecting Jewish local self-rule, 29
Caviness, Madeline, 240n68
Champagne, County of, 28–29, 36, 133
Charlemagne: canonized by Frederick Barbarossa, 36–37; Christian uses of legend of, 36–37; crowned Roman emperor by pope in 800, 11, 30, 32; foundation legends based on, 14, 21, 29, 32–37, 38; using Italian models for reforms, 35
Charles II of Anjou, 176
Charles the Great. *See* Charlemagne
charters, communal, 21, 29
charters of protection (*tuitio*), 13, 29, 45
Chaucer, Geoffrey, 68, 227n51. See also *Prioress's Tale*
Chazan, Robert, 189, 192–93, 194–95
children: vulnerable to conversion, 165, 241n78. *See also* boys, Jewish
chosenness: ancient theological assumptions about, 5–6, 207nn23–24; anti-Christian polemic and, 153; in binary of inverted hierarchy, 18, 170, 178, 196–97; Christian claim of, 71; Christians' difficulty in understanding Jews and, 13; Christian supersessionism and, 9, 65; in confrontation between two religious cultures, 3–5; Crusaders taunting Jews about, 9; Jewish assertiveness about, 13, 14, 64; Paul on letter vs. spirit and, 8–9
Christianitas, 42
Christianity: becoming central religious identity, 11; bodily elimination vs. the holy in, 90; as "foreign worship" (*'avodah zarah*), 4, 13, 27, 194, 206n16, 211n39; imagined, 15, 51; Jewish contempt for, 53–54, 64, 65, 194, 198 (*see also* insulting Christianity; latrine blasphemy); viewed by Jews as bodily elimination, 91
Christians: Barabas's hatred for, 184; charging interest to other Christians, 185; early modern acts of revenge against, 182; hating Jews, not Judaism, 178, 191, 198; needing images of the Jew as their opposite, 90; not hated by Jews, 194, 198
Church of the Holy Sepulcher, 46, 48, 72, 220n37
circumcision: accusation about forced act of, 122; argument with a monk about, 83; first-generation conversion and, 168; of Jesus, 83; as Jewish male mark of distinction, 163, 165, 167; Jews gathered for feast of, 129

clothing, 141–45; canon 68 to distinguish Jews and Muslims, 142–43, 145, 147–49, 162, 185; collective identity asserted by, 141, 148, 162; of Jews in some neighborhoods today, 142; with mixture of linen and wool, 143, 144–45

Cohen, Jeremy, 58, 102–3, 104, 179, 191

coin clipping, 94, 121

collective prophecy, 49, 56

Cologne, Germany: archaeology of Jewish quarter in, 85, 210n3; attacks of 1096 in, 64; Jewish settlement in, 20, 22

communal boards, 28

communal leaders, 28

communion. *See* Eucharist

confessing to rabbis, 12

contextual view, of premodern anti-Jewish behavior, 189–90, 191–92

conversion to Christianity: adult Jewish men and, 16, 18, 140, 141, 149, 161; attack on Rabbeinu Jacob in hope of, 133; beauty acquired by means of, 149–51; forced on Shylock, 183, 184, 186, 187; forcible, 51, 57, 215n33; forcible in 1096, 145, 167–68; fruitless if Jews weren't rational, 166–67; gender and age in likelihood of, 161, 165, 241n78; of Jewish daughters, 185; Jews' resistance to, 3, 169; mass conversions in fifteenth-century Spain, 75, 166; of one's children, 206n16; permanent Jewish identity and, 17, 18, 167–69, 197, 241n89; pressure based on Jesus as foretold messiah, 75; private debates on, 82; after seeing bleeding host, 125; synagogue represented as, 152; temporary, 62, 217n62; three days to decide, 103–4; voluntary, 164–66 (*see also* converts to Christianity); young boys' vulnerability to, 15, 16, 107, 165, 229n86, 241n78; of young Jewish men, 165, 241n78. *See also* baptism

converts to Christianity: claiming Jews crucified a wax Jesus figure, 234n77; continued Jewish identity of, 168; Judah-Hermannus, 80, 165; in Paris Talmud trial of 1240, 75. *See also* apostates

Córdoba: caliph emerging despite caliph in Baghdad, 30, 37; challenge to rabbinic authority in Baghdad, 31–32, 33, 37; Christian martyrs in, 108; R. Moses displacing local authority in, 32, 37, 40

covenant with God: in Exodus, 5, 6; Justin Martyr on, 9; Paul on, 6–9

Crispin, Gilbert, 79–80

cross: carried by rabbi so he wouldn't be killed, 145; insulted, 126; *Sefer Hasidim* on not using utensils with, 224n11; sitting on, 97; spitting on, 95; trampled on, 95–96; urinating on, 95–97

Croxton Play of the Sacrament, 180, 244n45

crucifixion. *See* Passion

Crusaders: attack on Rabbeinu Jacob by, 133–35; blamed by Christian chroniclers, 61–64, 130; in mobs of 1096, 14, 16; Würzburg ritual murder accusation and, 113–15, 117, 122

Crusades: Jews as internal enemy and, 18, 197; sin of usury and, 17. *See also* First Crusade; Second Crusade; Eighth Crusade

Cuffel, Alexandra, 90

cultural aesthetics, 16, 140–41, 149, 167, 236n2. *See also* physical appearance

Dahan, Gilbert, 179, 191

David, *nasi* signifying descent from, 33, 38

David and Goliath, 85

debates, Jewish-Christian, 75–76; Christian efforts to prevent, 80–81; danger of conversion in, 82; in private encounters, 79–84

Despres, Denise, 141, 179, 186

de Torigni, Robert, 119–21, 126, 135, 231n31

Deuteronomy, Book of: Jews as chosen people in, 5–6; nocturnal emission and, 225n14; on spitting at refusal of levirate marriage, 94

Dimitrovsky, Haim Zalman, 224n11

dirges, Hebrew liturgical, 71, 235n99

disguised great scholar, 38–40, 212n60, 213n64

Disputation of Barcelona, 75

Donin, Nicholas, 75

Dorin, Rowan, 172–73

Easter: blood libel connected to, 123, 240n69; ritual murder accusations claimed to be at, 108, 109, 112, 115, 116, 117, 119–20, 126

ecclesiastical objects: Christians prohibited from pawning, 235n109; as collateral or forfeited property, 88, 101; Jews accused of abusing, 87–88, 101, 120

Edward I of England, 175–76, 177

Eidelberg, Shlomo, 99

Eighth Crusade, 175

Einbinder, Susan, 165

Ekkehard of Aura, 63

elder serving the younger, 105. *See also* Esau and Jacob

Eleanor of Aquitaine, 116–17, 128

Eleazar ben Judah of Worms, 34–38, 138

Eleazar Hazan of Speyer, 34

Eliezer bar Nathan, 52, 56, 92, 220n29

Elijah of Norwich, 243n25

elites, Jewish regional, 14, 21, 23, 30. *See also* foundation legends

Elizabeth of Hungary, Saint, 110–11

Emicho of Flonheim, 49, 63–64, 214n28, 216n50

England: as "Ashkenaz," 2, 205n5; assimilation into other Jewish communities from, 171; communal charters issued in, 21; conversions to Christianity in, 164, 166; distinctive clothing for Jews in, 148; expulsion of Jews from, 172, 173, 176–77, 184, 229n1; a few Jews remaining in, 178; imagined Jew spread by empire of, 171; Jewish moneylenders in, 173, 175–76; protection of Jewish local self-rule in, 29; ritual murder accusations in, 121, 127–28, 135, 185, 222n64; royal reactions to usury in, 174–76. *See also* Benedictine monasteries

English literature, 178–79, 180; antisemitic, 17, 172; beautiful Jewish women in, 161; imagined Jew in, 171–72; late medieval and early modern, 180–84; medieval conversion stories, 150–51; medieval poetry of Elijah of Norwich, 243n25. *See also* Barabas; *Jew of Malta* (Marlowe); *Merchant of Venice* (Shakespeare); *Prioress's Tale* (Chaucer); Shylock

Ephraim of Bonn, 95, 113–15, 117–18, 131–35

Esau, piyyutim with Rome personified as, 69

Esau and Jacob: Augustine on, 134, 207n26; Jews as knights and, 84; Paul's interpretation of, 7, 178; rabbis' interpretation of, 7, 134; right order and, 45; ritual murder accusation and, 134

esoteric traditions, transferred from Babylonia, 34, 37

Eucharist: belief in real presence of Christ in, 100, 123; blood libel and, 15–16, 123–25; in consolidation of Christian identity, 126–27; Jewish countereucharistic rite, 15, 105–7, 165, 229n86; Jewish "enemy within" and, 15–16; Jewish insulting of, 100–105; Jewish understanding of, 104–5; negated by elimination from the body, 104; receptivity to ritual murder accusation and, 126–27; required once a year on Easter, 142; spiritualized and not excreted, 106–7, 229n84; taken by Christian wet nurses, 89. *See also* body of Christ; host

Eugenius III (pope), 128

Europa, in Greek mythology, 29, 32

Europe, formation of, 2–3, 11; real and imagined Jewish populations in, 18–19; two phases of, 43–44

Exodus, Book of, 5, 6

expulsion of foreign Christian moneylenders, 172, 186

expulsion of Jews, 171–72; from Anjou, 176; from England, 172, 173, 176–77, 184, 229n1; group expulsions and, 172, 177; imagined Jew persisting after, 17, 178; motives for, 17, 172–78, 213n1; by Philip Augustus, 122, 172, 174; by Philip IV and later French kings, 176–77, 243n27; ritual murder accusation and, 122, 231n33; vision of ideal Christian society and, 172, 176, 177

falconry, 85
farting, 97–99, 227n51, 227n57
feces: associated with Christianity by Jews, 87, 92, 225n15; associated with Jews by Christians, 87, 89; idolatry and Jesus equated with, 91; not impure in Judaism, 90; place of worship upstairs from, 91; in worship of idol Ba'al-Pe'or, 91–92. *See also* bodily excretion vs. the holy
feudal ages, 43
First Crusade: Albert of Aachen's history of, 61–62; Christian criticism of Crusaders in, 60–64, 130; Crusader speeches in, 72; intensifying rival claims to chosenness, 21; Jews as "enemy within" at time of, 9, 14–15, 18, 41, 127, 170–71, 197; Jews resisting Christian triumphalism and, 9; knights offered atonement for sins, 48, 54, 58; never getting to Jerusalem, 58–59, 61–62, 232n39; Pope Urban's speech of 1095 and, 47–49; as the will of God, 48–49, 54, 56–57, 216n52. *See also* riots of 1096
"foreign worship" ('*avodah zarah*'): Christianity as, 4, 13, 27, 194, 206n16, 211n39; Eucharist as, 100. *See also* idolatry
foundation legends, 14, 21, 29–40; based on Charlemagne, 14, 21, 29, 32–37, 38; as claim over community in the East, 30–33; as claim over neighboring community in the West, 30, 32–37; historical approaches to, 30, 35–36; of Jewish elite of Muslim Spain, 31–32; reality of settlement in Mainz and, 35; three claims in each story, 30–31
four captives, story of, 31–32, 37, 40, 212n57
Fradenburg, Louise O., 193
France: assimilation into other Jewish communities from, 171, 177; conversion to Christianity in, 164; expelled English Jews arriving in, 176–77; expulsion of Jews from, 122, 172, 174, 176–77, 243n27; failed effort to convert Jews in, 176; group expulsions from, 172–73; Jewish usury attacked in revolutionary period of, 187. *See also* Narbonne; northern France
Frankel, Jonathan, 187
Frederick Barbarossa, 36–37
Frederick II of German Empire, 124
Freedman, Paul, 160–61
French language, 12
French literature, 149–50, 179, 244n35
Fulda, blood libel at, 123–24

Gay, Peter, 5
German Empire: as "Ashkenaz," 2, 14, 205n5; communal charters issued in, 21; competing with Philip Augustus, 36–37; conversion to Christianity in, 164; Crusader mobs of 1096 in, 14, 16; distinctive clothing for Jews in, 148; host desecration libel leading to violence in, 125; Jewish local self-rule protected in, 29; modern German lethal antisemitism and, 190, 198; popes vying with emperors of, 44–45; tenth-century establishment of Jewish communities in, 22–28. *See also* Mainz
Germanic kingdoms, 11. *See also* Charlemagne
Gershom b. Judah, 24–27, 28, 40
Gilman, Sander, 236n9
Glassman, Bernard, 179
Gloucester. *See* Harold of Gloucester
God: allegorical representation of, 154–55; in interpretations of Song of Songs, 155; Joseph Official on restoration of beauty by, 158–59
Goldin, Simha, 107, 165
Goldstein, Julie, 107
Goliaths, Jewish knights as, 85
Gow, Andrew, 193
Gower, John, 67–68
Graetz, Heinrich, 205n6
Grayzel, Solomon, 102–3
great scholar in disguise, motif of, 38–40, 212n60, 213n64
Greenberg, Moshe, 207n20, 227n57
Gregoire, Abbé, 187
Gregorian reform, 41, 42
Gregory, Bishop of Tours, 20

Gregory I (pope), 167
Gregory IX (pope), 124–25
Gregory VII (pope), 42, 44, 45, 46–47
Gui, Bernard, 104
Guibert, Abbot of Nogent, 54, 88, 100, 147

Hagar, 7, 178
hair coverings, in Jewish women, 142
Halbertal, Moshe, 100
Halivni, David Weiss, 237n23
Haman figures, hanged or burned on Purim, 129, 234n77
Harold of Gloucester, 110, 112, 116, 119–20, 127, 129
Harris, Manford, 84
hats: in allegorical representation of God, 155; on Jewish men, 142, 146, 148, 149, 162
Haverkamp, Alfred, 164
Hear, O Israel (*shema yisrael*), 59–60, 72
Hebrew Bible: binary of inverted hierarchies in, 196–97; as both Jewish and Christian book, 207n20; Christian ignorance about Judaism and, 134; directly applied by R. Gershom, 25; Justin Martyr's use of, 9; Paul's use of, 6–7; replies to Christian arguments based on, 73; rite for Jewish boys and, 105–7; on showing contempt by spitting, 94; studied with French interpreter, 12; wordplay denigrating pagan religion in, 68–69. *See also* Torah
Hebrew chronicles: anti-Christian insults in, 65, 70–72, 74, 77, 139–40; Christianity associated with bodily waste in, 92; Crusade and Jerusalem in, 214n26; Crusader motives in, 51–54; Crusaders accused of abusing Torah scrolls, 224n8; farting in, 98–99; Jewish martyrs of 1096 and, 51–52, 56–60, 71; on martyrdom as will of God, 56–57; spitting at a cross in, 95; by survivors who temporarily converted, 217n62; women in, 58, 153. *See also* Mainz Anonymous; martyrs, Jewish; Solomon bar Samson chronicle
Hebrew liturgical dirges, 71, 235n99

Hebrew writings: illustrated with knights in combat, 15; imitating Gothic script of Christian scribes, 12
Heng, Geraldine, 172
Henry II of England, 119
Henry III of England: antiusury policy of, 174–75; conversion efforts under, 164, 166, 168; execution and arrest of Jews by, 181; laws to implement canon 68 and, 148; moneylender with close ties to, 173; politicization of ritual murder idea and, 112, 121, 126; trampling on a cross and, 95–96
Henry IV of England, 29, 46–47, 55
Henry of Winchester, 168
hermeneutical Jew, 179
Hess, Cordelia, 194
hierarchy: of Jacob and Esau, 84; between pietists and Christians, 81–82, 138; in religious buildings, 76; reversed by Christian wet nurse, 105. *See also* binary of inverted hierarchy; right order
Higden, Ranulph, 89
Hildebrand, 42
Hillaby, Joe, 112
Hillel, disguised in Jerusalem, 38
Holocaust, 2, 189, 194
Horowitz, Elliott, 99
Hosea, criticizing Jeroboam, 69
host: believed to contain real body of Christ, 125, 127; latrine blasphemy and, 1; stories about bleeding of, 125. *See also* Eucharist
host desecration accusation, 16, 125–26, 180, 181, 192
Hugh of Lincoln, 93, 109, 121, 129, 180, 181, 185
Hushiel, father of Rabbenu Hananel, 31–32

Iberia: Alexander II on protecting the Jews in, 54; Almohads in, 70, 169; distinctive clothing for Jews in, 148; emigration into Ottoman Empire from, 171; Muslims ruling areas of, 3; purity of blood laws in, 169, 197; rabbinic leaders succeeding geonim in Baghdad, 31–32; ritual murder idea appearing in, 129; Sephardi Jewish communities of, 23, 212n59. *See also* Córdoba

Ibn Daud, Abraham, 31–33, 37, 38–39, 212n57
idolatry: equated with feces, 91; Eucharist as form of, 100; Jewish animosity toward Christianity and, 4, 59, 64, 71, 89, 206n16; Jews seen as practicing, 207n17; Judah the Pious on Christianity as, 74; latrine blasphemy and, 87; as rabbinic view of Christianity, not Christians, 66, 86, 211n39; in worship of idol Ba'al-Pe'or, 91–92. *See also* "foreign worship" (*'avodah zarah*); paganism
imagined Christianity, 15, 51
imagined Jew: binary of inverted hierarchy and, 7, 18, 170, 171, 178; as Christians' inverted self-image, 178; as cultural construction, 141, 177–78; dangerous new forms of, 108; emergence of, 51; as "enemy within," 9, 14, 15, 17, 18, 51; explosion of terms for, 179–80; before expulsion from England, 229n1; harming "body of Christ," 15–16; indistinguishable in appearance from Christians, 145, 162; Marlowe's and Shakespeare's unrealistic versions of, 195; as opposite of Christian beliefs and rituals, 130; persisting into modern world, 171, 188; physical appearance of, 140–41, 149; as reciprocal of Christian in early modern times, 181–82; remaining after expulsion, 17, 79; ritually crucifying a Christlike martyr boy, 127; three elements of, 18, 169–70, 196–98; transition between medieval and modern images of, 182
Incarnation: Anselm's defense of, 79; arguments for Jews to use against, 82–83; Christian polemics on, 75; putting God in bodily filth, 92
Innocent III (pope): blood libel and, 124; canon 68 on distinctive clothing and, 143, 148, 151; Christian wet nurses and, 1, 88–89, 100, 101–4, 105; synagogues higher than churches and, 76
Innocent IV (pope), 124
insulting Christianity: acting-out form of, 84; in affirming Jewish identity, 45–46; in bilingual Hebrew/Latin contracts, 73; even when complimenting Christians, 66, 219n6; in piyyutim of Byzantine Palestine, 69–70; in private encounters, 79–84, 222n64; in quotations of reported speech, 77; by renaming apostates, 73; after riots of 1096, 64, 218n90; two sources most filled with, 139–40; by wordplay in Hebrew Bible and Talmud, 68–69. *See also* assertiveness of Jews
insulting Jews, while complimenting behavior, 67–68
intermarriage, increased, 198–99
investiture controversy, 44, 47
inward acculturation, selective, 12, 153, 208n39, 209n41
Isaac, 7, 8, 9, 133–34, 178
Isaac, Jules, 189
Isaac bar Eleazar, 117
Isaac b. Joseph of Corbeil, 66
Isaac son of Elyakim, 95
Ishmael, 7, 178
Ishmaelites, 126, 131–32. *See also* Muslims
Islam, 3, 90, 206n14. *See also* Muslims
Israel: chosen in Deuteronomy, 5–6; Christians' claim to be chosen and, 6, 10; iconography of synagoga and, 151–52; Jacob known as, 7; Justin Martyr on Christians as, 9; Paul on covenant between God and, 6, 7, 9; Rashi on apparent rejection of, 156; in Song of Songs, 152, 153–54
Ivanhoe (Scott), 161

Jacob: in biblical story on appearances, 160; Paul on, 7, 8, 9. *See also* Esau and Jacob
Jacob b. Meir (Rabbeinu Tam): attacked by two Crusaders, 224n8; on conversion to Christianity in France, 164; on insulting name for apostate, 73; near crucifixion of, 133–35, 154; on not selling items for Eucharist, 100; on taking interest from Christian borrowers, 173
Jacobus de Voragine, 110
Jerusalem: Crusaders failing to reach, 58–59, 61–62, 232n39; defenders of Masada after 70 CE and, 57; First

Crusade and, 14, 41; Paul on, 7; Seljuk Turks in, 46; symbolically replicated in Europe, 59. See also Temple in Jerusalem

Jesus: as Christ Child, 127–28; equated with feces, 91, 92; Haman figures understood as, 129, 234n77; in hell in boiling excrement, 92, 104; impermissible medical remedies connected to, 139; Jewish saints compared to, 107; mocking language about, 69, 70, 72; Rabbeinu Jacob in role of, 134, 135; spat on in New Testament, 94; Talmud on Messiah and, 75. See also body of Christ; Passion

Jewish-Christian relations, 3–5; in business dealings, 13, 14, 19, 21, 25–27, 41, 42, 45; cooperating in a violent society, 44; each with an inverted virtual other, 89–90, 178, 196–97, 224n12; increased with urban growth, 40, 42, 43, 44; responsa of Meshullam b. Qalonimos on, 23–24; social rivalries among Jews and, 26; symmetry and asymmetry in, 4, 178; in tenth-century migration and settlement, 22; turning point of 1096 in, 51. See also assertiveness of Jews; chosenness; power

Jewish communities: charter of privileges granted to, 29; economic competition in, 28; governed by elders, 22, 28, 29; with legal decisions by religious judges or rabbis, 28; local autonomy of, 24, 28–29; self-governing as recognized by Christian rulers, 3, 22, 45; two forms of leadership in, 27–28. See also settlement of Jews in Christian West

Jewish identity, permanence of, 17, 18, 167–69, 170, 197, 198, 241n89

Jewish merchants: fluid boundary between moneylenders and, 173; ma'arufia of, 24, 25; in northern Christian lands, 22; as rabbis in period of first settlement, 28

Jewish merchants, international: Barabas as, 183; bringing commodities from China, 21; Carolingian charters of protection for, 20–21, 29; R. Gershom's ruling against polygyny and, 25; settling in northern Christian lands, 22

Jew of Malta (Marlowe), 17, 161. See also Barabas

Jews: allowed to live in Christian society, 6, 7, 10, 11; appearing different from Christians, 16, 142–49; as assets for developing economies, 13; to be scattered and subordinated, 10–11; as blind witnesses according to Augustine, 10, 152; claimed not to be rational, 166–67, 193; as "enemies of God," 8–9; as fourth medieval civilization, 2–3, 11, 206n11; hiring Christian servants and wet nurses, 88–89, 101, 138 (see also wet nurses, Christian); inward acculturation of, 12, 153, 208n39, 209n41; medieval demographic and culture areas of, 23; treated as pagans, 4. See also boys, Jewish; imagined Jew; men, Jewish; women, Jewish

Jews as "enemy within," 197; alleged rites and, 107, 108; Christian reform and, 42; imagined Jew and, 9, 14, 15, 17, 18, 51; knights on way to Jerusalem and, 49–50, 51, 53–54; latrine blasphemy and, 88; Pauline idea developing into, 177; Pope Urban II and, 50; urban expansion and, 46; well-poisoning accusation and, 125. See also expulsion of Jews; riots of 1096

Jews as killers of Christ: anti-Jewish riots of 1189 and, 136; Christian mob incited by Radulph and, 132; Crusaders' vengeance for, 50, 52–53, 88, 215n33; priest offering the Eucharist and, 127; punished with exile for, 10, 182; religious zeal against nearby enemies and, 41; reversed in attack on Rabbeinu Jacob, 133–34, 135; suffering imposed as a result of, 132, 136, 182

John Paul II, 208n32
Johnson, Willis, 131
Jones, Michael, 191
Jordan, William Chester, 64, 165, 187
Joseph b. Nathan Official, 73, 96, 157–59
Joseph story in Egypt, 212n59
Josephus Flavius, 205n8

Judah ha-Kohen, 28–29
Judah-Hermannus, 80, 165
Judah the Pious: as author of *Sefer Hasidim*, 66, 138; esoteric traditions and, 34; on excretion of Hebrew letters, 107; "foreign worship" (*'avodah zarah*) and, 206n16; migration from Speyer to Regensburg, 212n52; on religious debates with Christians, 82; Samuel the father of, 133, 137; in story about blood libel, 123–24; on suicide, 97, 226n38. *See also* pietist Jews; *Sefer Hasidim*
Judaism: alleged double standard of morality in, 248n34; Christians paying little attention to, 4; Christians' theological need for, 191; European and even Christianized, 12; life-giving bodily fluids in, 90
Julius Aronius, 234n77
Justinian, 76–77

Katz, Jacob, 138, 224n10, 248n34
Kedar, Benjamin, 63, 172
King of Tars, 150, 152, 159
knights, Christian. *See* Crusaders; riots of 1096
knights, Jewish, 84–86; in dreams of Judah Herman, 165; efforts to make effeminate, 163
Kovner, Abba, 184
Kruger, Steven, 179
Krummel, Miriamni Ara, 179–80

Langland, William, 67
Langmuir, Gavin, 189, 191–93, 248n37
Last Supper, 126–27
Latin Christian Europe, 3, 42
latrine blasphemy, 1–2, 15, 87, 93–94; asymmetry between Jews and Christians in, 224n10; Christian leaders' reactions to, 87–89; Christian wet nurses and, 89, 100, 102, 105; by farting, 97–99; Incarnation and, 92; of killing a Christian and putting the body in a latrine, 93, 181, 226n33; showing contempt for the cross, 95–97. *See also* assertiveness of Jews
Lavezzo, Kathy, 179

Lehnhertz, Andreas, 146
Leo III (pope), 11, 32
Leo IX (pope), 42
lepers, and well poisoning accusation, 125
levirate marriage, 94, 98
Levy, Richard S., 194
Levy Mahzor, 152–55
Licoricia of Winchester, 173
Lieberman, Saul, 224n11
Lipmann Mühlhausen, Yom Tov, 159
Lipton, Sara, 146, 148, 161, 162, 236n9
literature. *See* English literature; French literature; romance literature
Little, Lester K., 43
Lopez, Roderigo, 187
Louis the Pious, 21, 29, 71
Louis VII of France, 1, 87, 116, 118–19, 120, 122, 128
Louis IX of France, 148, 172, 175, 176, 240n68
Luther, Martin, 187

ma'arufia, 24, 25, 26
Machiavelli, Niccolò, 182
Mainz: attacks of 1096 in, 55–56, 63, 64, 165; autonomous local governance and, 24, 28–29; Charlemagne as claimed founder in, 14, 32, 33–36; elite Jewish families of, 23; as Jerusalem in Ashkenazic trope, 212n59; Jewish settlement in, 22; Rabbeinu Gershom b. Judah in, 24–27; Speyer charter for Jews fleeing fire in, 29; story claiming superiority over Babylonia, 37–40; symbolically rebuilding the Temple in, 59, 214n26
Mainz Anonymous, 52, 55, 56, 58, 216n51, 220n29
Makhir, in Narbonnese foundation legend, 33
Malkiel, David, 215n33
Manesse Codex, 146
manna, not excreted, 107
Margalit, Avishai, 100
Marlowe, Christopher. *See* Barabas; *Jew of Malta*
Marr, Wilhelm, 189
Marranos, 183, 186
Martyr, Justin, 6, 9

INDEX [357]

martyrs, Jewish: burned in Blois, 118, 119, 121. *See also* martyrs of 1096

martyr saints, Christian: allegedly explaining child mortality, 109, 110, 230n8; anti-Jewish violence and, 109–10; Benedictines interested in identifying, 135; performing miracles, 109, 111, 113–16, 119, 121, 136; ritual murder accusation and, 108, 109, 113, 127–28; smelling sweet, 136. *See also* ritual murder accusations; saints, Christian

martyrs of 1096: in acts of religious defiance and superiority, 139; ambivalence imputed to, 217n62; assertive acts of loyalty to Judaism, 59–60; to avoid forcible baptism of their children, 165, 215n33; benediction to be recited by, 217n60; Christian accusations supposedly explained by, 130–31; Christian chroniclers blaming Crusaders for, 61–64, 130; criticism of, 57; crying out *Hear, O Israel*, 59–60; after fasting for three days, 104; Hebrew chronicles and, 51–52, 56–60, 71; hierarchical boundaries and right order in, 138; insulting Christianity in moment of death, 72; Judah the Pious on suicide and, 97; piyyutim directed at adolescent students and, 229n86; precedents for, 57; rituals of assertiveness in, 57–60; vicarious atonement and, 60, 167; will of God and, 49, 56–57, 216n51; women's roles in, 58, 59, 61–62, 153

Mary: coronation of, 153; as dark haired, 163; growth of cult of, 127–28; insulting references to, 74, 221n48; Jewish assertiveness and, 58; latrine blasphemy and, 92; mocked in attack on New Testament, 70; as nursing mother, 105, 229n78; in piyyut based on Song of Songs, 154–55; symbolically replaced by real Jewish women, 155

Mary stories: with cruel Jewish father, 127, 130; *Prioress's Tale* as, 121, 180–81

Masada, 57

Matthew Paris, 93–94, 95, 121–22, 181, 232n47

medieval historians: not seeing Jewish culture and society, 206n111; seeing Jews as victims, 2, 205nn6–7

Meir of Rothenburg, 164, 185

Melito of Sardis, 208n30

men, Jewish: age as factor in conversion of, 165; allegedly bleeding monthly or annually, 163, 240n69; beards and, 145–46, 148, 162, 237nn23–24; conversion to Christianity and, 16, 18, 140, 141, 149, 161; dark and ugly in Christian judgment, 160–63; distinctive appearance from mid-thirteenth century, 162, 163–64; handsome in view of Jews, 166; hats of, 142, 146, 148, 149, 162; impediments to conversion of, 166–70; mid-thirteenth-century increase in conversion efforts, 163–64, 166, 197; older men, 145–46, 163–64; permanent physical features of, 16, 141, 165, 169–70, 171. *See also* boys, Jewish

Mendes, Doña Gracia, 183

menstrual blood, 157, 158, 160

menstruation: ascribed to Jewish men, 163, 240n69; Gentiles having sexual relations during, 160; language mocking Mary and, 70

Merchant of Venice (Shakespeare), 17, 161. *See also* Shylock

merchants. *See* Jewish merchants

Meshullam ben Qalonimos, 23–24, 34, 37–40, 212n59

Messiah, Christian claim based on Talmud, 75

messianic times, Jews' different appearance in, 159

migration of Jews: from central Europe eastward, 171; into Christian West, 3, 11–12, 21; from Iberia into Ottoman Empire, 171

minhag, 23

minhag avoteinu, 23

Mirrer, Louise, 161

Mishnah: on acts involving excretions, 91; directly applied by R. Gershom, 25, 27; on doing business with idolators, 100; on spitting in the synagogue, 95; on worshiping an idol by defecation, 91–92

Mizrahi Jewry, 23
moneylenders: foreign Christian, 172, 186, 195; Jewish, 186, 232n44. *See also* usury
Morrison, Susan, 181
Moses bar Qalonimos, 32, 34–35, 38, 40
Moses ben Nachman (Nachmanides), 75
Muslims: distinctive clothing of, 142–43, 236n6; effects of conversion to Christianity in, 169; ruling parts of what became Europe, 3. *See also* Ishmaelites; Islam
mysticism, Ashkenazic, 34, 37

Narbonne: Charlemagne as claimed founder in, 14, 32–33; Jews' early settlement in, 20
nasi, 33, 38, 39
Nasi, Don Joseph, 183
Nathan Official, 83–84, 96
Nathan the Pious, 32, 38
Nazi regime. *See* Holocaust; racist antisemitism
Nelson, Benjamin, 184
Nestor ha-Komer polemic, 70, 73
Newman, Barbara, 136
New Testament: attacked in *Toledot Yeshu*, 70; Passion accounts in, 134; Paul's letters in, 6–9; on showing contempt by spitting, 94; usury forbidden in, 174; verbal denigation of, 69, 73–74. *See also* Paul
Nirenberg, David, 122, 190
Nizzahon Vetus: on appearance of Gentiles vs. Jews, 159–60; blood libel and, 123; insulting language in, 73–74, 77–78; preparing Jews to confront Christians, 83–84; sitting on a cross in, 97
northern France: as "Ashkenaz," 2, 205n5; German Jewish battle for authority in, 36; imagined Jew as dangerous usurer in, 177, 244n29; rabbinic contacts with far-off centers, 24
Norwich: accusation of forced circumcision in, 122. *See also* William of Norwich
nose: Christian ideal of, 149, 150; Jewish, 149, 163, 236n9

Novikoff, Alex, 194
Numbers, Book of: on manna not excreted, 107; on pagan cult Ba'al-Pe'or, 91

Odo of Cambrai, 92
Offenburg, Sara, 84
Old Testament: coming of Jesus and, 191; in tablets held by synagoga, 152; usury forbidden in, 174
Ottoman Empire, 3; blood libel accusations in, 187; Iberian Jewry emigrating into, 171; Marlowe's Barabas and, 182, 183; population transfers within borders of, 172
Ovadiah the Proselyte, 53–54, 88

Pablo Christiani, 75
paganism: Augustine's defense of Christianity and, 10; Christians treating Jews as followers of, 4; Christians viewing Islam as, 46, 214n19; gradually becoming Christianized, 11; Jews viewing Christianity as, 12, 15, 51, 92, 178, 194. *See also* idolatry
Paris debate in 1270s, 75
Paris Talmud trial of 1240, 75
Parkes, James, 179, 189
Passion: attack on Rabbeinu Jacob as reversal of, 133–35; attacks of 1096 as vengeance for, 128; Christians killing Jews as reversal of, 132, 133; idea of reenactment of, 135; Latin narratives with reversal of, 136; reenacted in the Eucharist, 15, 126, 127, 134; in synagoga and ecclesia, 151. *See also* Jews as killers of Christ; ritual murder accusations
Passio of Prague in 1389, 136
Passover: blood libel connected to, 123; in no relation to Blois, 118; piyyut for Sabbath preceding, 153–54, 238n47; ritual cannibalism and, 124
Paul, 6–9; Augustine's theological policy and, 10; binary of inverted hierarchy and, 171; on Israel of flesh and spirit, 197; on Jewish servitude, 7, 10, 11, 14; on Jews as enemies of God, 8–9; on Jews as enemies of the Gospel, 177; on Jews as potential converts, 41, 169; on Jews to be part of Christian society, 6,

7, 17, 174; on letter vs. spirit, 8–9; parable of wild olive tree, 8, 10, 152
permanent Jewish identity, 17, 18, 167–69, 170, 197, 198, 241n89
Peter the Venerable, 1, 87, 128
Philip Augustus: Frederick Barbarossa's propaganda against, 36; latrine blasphemy and, 88; ritual murder accusations and, 112, 120–21, 122, 126, 231n33; temporarily expelling Jews in 1182, 122, 172, 174
Philip III, 175
Philip IV, 176, 177
physical appearance, 16, 142–49; collective identity asserted by, 141, 148; Jews denying permanence of, 166; of Jews in some neighborhoods today, 142. *See also* beauty; clothing; cultural aesthetics
Pierleoni candidate for papacy, 168, 242n94
Piers Plowman, 180
pietist Jews, 137–40; hierarchical sense of exclusivity among, 137–38; Jewish knights critiqued by, 84–85; Judah the Pious's group of, 74, 137; Mainz foundation legend from, 34, 212n52; major figures in circle of, 138; on need to make difficult choices, 137; opposed to using Christian building materials, 222n63; postures toward Christians, 138–40; religious debates with Christians, 81; ritual for young boys, 15, 105–7, 165, 229n86; Samuel traveling to see Rabbeinu Jacob, 133; on scatological worship of idols, 97. *See also* Judah the Pious; *Sefer Hasidim*
piyyutim, 69–70, 72, 220n29; based on Song of Songs, 153–54, 238n47; directed at adolescent Tosafist students, 229n86
poems, liturgical. *See* piyyutim
polemical handbooks: on accusation that Jews are dark and ugly, 157–59; anti-Christianity language in, 70, 73–74; with arguments for Jews to use, 82–84; imagined critique of Speyer Cathedral, 77–78; on Jews' appearance, 159–60. See also *Nizzahon Vetus*
Poliakov, Léon, 189

polygyny, 25
Pontoise, 118–21, 122, 135, 231n33, 232n47
popes: against active efforts to convert, 166; asserting right order, 14; denying blood libel, 124–25; as early Europe became Christianized, 11; Gregorian reform originating with, 41, 42; Jewish, 168; opposed to Christian servants in Jewish homes, 138; Pierleoni candidate for papacy, 168, 242n94; protecting Jews that acted subordinate, 45; public burning of Talmud in Paris of 1242, 75; railing against Christian wet nurses, 101; vying with emperors for supremacy, 44–45. *See also* Innocent III; Urban II
power: in binary of inverted hierarchy, 18; of Christians in confrontation with Jews, 3, 197; insult language attributed to Christians and, 77; modern antisemitism concerned with, 194, 195–96; right order and, 14, 45; in worlds of Barabas and Shylock, 184–85
prayer, Jewish rules about, 92–93
Price, Merrall, 181
Prioress's Tale (Chaucer), 17, 93, 121, 180–81, 193
protean Jew, 179, 186
Protestants, in conflict with Catholics, 244n31
Prynne, William, 185
puns. *See* wordplay
Purim, 129, 234n77
purity in Judaism, 90. *See also* bodily excretion vs. the holy
purity of blood laws in Iberia, 169, 197

Qallir, 69
Qalonimos, Rabbi of Lucca, 38, 39; *responsa* of, 23; surviving riots of 1096, 36
Qalonimos b. Judah, 60
Qalonimos b. Meshullam, 55–56
Qalonimos family, 23; asserting authority in northern France, 36; as intellectual elite in Ashkenaz, 40; with member in court of Frederick Barbarossa, 37; migration from Italy, 34; nearly wiped out in 1096, 36. *See also* Meshullam ben Qalonimos

Qalonimos of Bacharach, 95
Qalonimos of Speyer, 77–78

rabbinate, paid, 28
race, in medieval Europe, 166, 169
Rachel, in Hebrew Crusade chronicles, 58, 155
racist antisemitism, 17, 189, 190–91, 192, 193, 194, 197–99, 248n34
Radulph, 131–32
Rashi of Troyes: on dark appearance as temporary state of sin, 156–57, 160; dialectic Talmud analysis and, 36; on farting in Ezekiel 8:17, 99; as French interpreter of Bible and Talmud, 12; as grandfather of Rabbeinu Tam, 134; Jewish images of knights and, 85; on Jews as God's chosen people, 6; names of Christian saints and, 221n41; on permanence of Jewish status, 167; on piyyut of romance between God and Israel, 154; verbal insult based on Hebrew Bible and, 69; on worshiping an idol by defecation, 91
Rava, on spitting in the synagogue, 95
Raymond Martini, 71
reform movements, Christian: critical of extreme violence, 42–43; Crusade as extension of, 47; Gregorian reform in, 41, 42; Jewish servitude and, 45; money and credit in, 16–17; reasserting hierarchical superiority, 42, 44. *See also* right order
Resnick, Irven, 162
Rex, Richard, 68
Rhineland, 23; riots of 1096 as location of, 51; Talmud analysis in, 36. *See also* Mainz
Richard I, coronation riots in 1189, 136, 232n39
Richard of Devizes, 122, 136, 232n39, 232n47
Richard of Pontoise, 118–21, 122, 135, 231n33, 232n47
right order, 14, 44–45; assertive claims acted out in 1096 and, 64; Christian criticism of Crusaders and, 60–64; Christian servants in Jewish homes and, 138; ecclesiastical superiority over kings and, 14; Jewish servitude as, 45, 52; Jews attempting to restore, 55–56; Jews' protected place in Christian society and, 55; Jews' subordinate presence as, 61; keeping away from Christians and, 16; martyrs of 1096 having sense of, 138; pietists' social boundaries with Christians and, 138–39; violated by hiring Christian servants and wet nurses, 103, 105; violated by Turks in Jerusalem, 41, 46. *See also* hierarchy; reform movements, Christian
Rigord, 88, 101, 120–21, 231n33, 232n47
Riley-Smith, Jonathan, 49–50
riots of 1096, 14, 51–52; armed resistance in Mainz, 55–56; assertiveness of Jews after, 14–15, 16, 64, 65; Crusader motives in, 50–55, 215n33; German vs. French Jewish authority after, 36; Hebrew liturgical dirges about, 71, 235n99; insult language associated with, 73; Latin chronicles mentioning, 61; not tied to ritual murder accusation, 128; Rabbi Qalonimos the Elder as survivor of, 34, 36; Worms remembrances of, 235n99. *See also* First Crusade; Hebrew chronicles; martyrs of 1096
riots of 1146, 131–32, 136
riots of 1189, 136, 232n39
riots of 1391 in Spain, 166
ritual baths, 12, 78
ritual cannibalism, 123–25, 232n47
ritual murder accusations, 15, 113–22; aimed at Jew as enemy within, 170; appearing quickly in France and Germany, 129; claimed to be at Easter, 108, 109, 112, 115, 116, 117, 119–20, 126; claimed to be revenge for Jewish suffering, 132, 136, 181, 182; confused interpretation of Purim and, 129; explanations inspired by Jewish practices, 129–31; guilt over Christian behavior and, 131, 132, 136; as idea beginning in mid-twelfth century, 109–10, 120, 122, 126, 128, 135; as idea in modern England, 185; Jewish behavior in 1096 and, 130–31, 218n75; latrines in, 93, 111; motives for acceptance of, 126–29; as narrative idea preceding the cases, 122;

persisting after expulsions, 178–79; plausible if Jewish fathers could kill their daughters, 185; politicization of, 109, 112–13, 121, 122; saint making and, 107, 116, 127–28, 135; spread of idea of, 112, 230n12; usually boys, 111, 230n11; of violent Esau against innocent Jacob, 134. *See also* Benedictine monasteries; Benedictine monks; martyr saints, Christian; Passion

Robert of Bury St. Edmonds, 110

Robert of Reims, 48

romance literature, Judaized versions of, 12, 84, 85

Roman Empire: formation of Europe and, 2–3, 11; Jewish settlement in late antiquity, 20; Jews as survivors of, 3

Rome, Christians blamed for sack of, 10

Rose, E. M., 116

Rosenthal, Judah, 82–83

Rosenwein, Barbara, 43

Roth, Cecil, 129

Rubin, Miri, 104, 126, 169, 229n77

Rüdiger, bishop of Speyer, 29

Rupert of Deutz, 80

saints, Christian: Jews competing with, 107; replaced with pejorative terms, 73, 74, 221n41; reviving children who were found dead, 110–11; smelling sweet, 109, 118. *See also* martyr saints, Christian

saints, Jewish, 107, 118, 136, 137; posture of superiority toward Christians and, 139; Rabbeinu Tam as, 134, 135

Salimbene de Adam, 225n19

Sampson son of Samuel of Northampton, 84

Samuel, disguise and recognition of, 212n60, 213n64

Samuel b. Qalonimos the Elder, 133, 137–38

Samuel the Pious, 34, 133

Santiago (St. James) de Compostela, 108

Sarah, 7, 178

Schachter, Hannah Teddy, 146

Schechter, Solomon, 137

Scott, James C., 98

Second Crusade: forced converts in decade prior to, 167; Jews seen as immediate threat and, 128; preached by Radulph, 131–32; propaganda for, 53, 115; religious enthusiasm for, 15, 113, 128; spitting on crucified Jesus and, 95; Würzburg murder and, 113, 115, 122

Sefer Hasidim, 5, 207n19; anti-Christian expressions in, 74, 139–40, 220n37; on beards, 145–46, 147; on clothing that Christians can identify, 143, 147–48, 162; on clothing with forbidden mixtures, 148; code of love in, 84; on danger of blasphemous gestures, 96–97; on disguising Jewish identity, 143–45; on farting near holy objects, 98; on not taking interest even from Christians, 173; on not using bowl or cup with cross, 224n11; on not using names of Christian saints, 220n37; personal honor of Jewish knights and, 84–85; postures of superiority toward Christians in, 138–40; on private debates with Christians, 81–82; on separating the holy from bodily excretions, 90–91, 225n19; socioreligious utopian program of, 138; on spitting in the synagogue, 95; on women's disguise as a man or Christian, 147. *See also* Judah the Pious

Sefer Zekhirah, 113, 131, 135

Seljuk Turks, 41, 46, 48, 54–55

semen, 90, 92, 100

Sephardi Jewish communities, 23, 212n59

servitude, Jewish: Paul on, 7, 10, 11, 14; Pope Alexander II and, 50; resistance to role of, 45–46; as right order, 45, 52

settlement of Jews in Christian West, 20–22; compared to foundation legends, 35; early period of cooperation with Christians, 13, 21–22; limited by founding families, 28. *See also* Jewish communities

sexual mixing: canon 68 requiring distinctive clothing and, 142–43, 145, 162, 185; common between Jews and Christians in medieval Europe, 185; death penalty in thirteenth-century Castile and, 148; expulsion from Anjou for, 176; indistinguishable appearances and, 140–41; Jewish father's rage about, 185

sexual thoughts, while sitting in latrine, 225n19
sha'atnez (mixture of linen and wool), 143, 144–45
Shagrir, Iris, 215n32
Shakespeare, William. See *Merchant of Venice*; Shylock
Shatzmiller, Joseph, 177, 220n37
Shavuot (Pentecost): attack on Rabbeinu Jacob in, 133; rite for Jewish boys and, 106, 165, 229n83; suicide of Yom Tov on eve of, 165
Shemariah b. R. Elhanan, 31–32
Shephatiah, 76–77
Shylock, 173, 182–87, 194–95, 197. See also *Merchant of Venice*
Simcha ha-Kohen, 59
Simon ben Isaac of Würzburg, sister of, 95
Simon of Trent, 123
Sir Gawain and the Green Knight, 180
skin color, 149, 150, 155–60, 162, 169, 240n68
Solomon bar Samson chronicle: anti-Christian epithets in, 71–72, 74, 220n29; on armed resistance, 55–56; building of the Temple and, 77; on fasting for three days before martyrdom, 104; physical signs of censorship in, 72, 220n32; praising religious loyalty of forced converts, 167–68; on speeches of Crusaders, 53; viewing Mainz as Jerusalem, 232n39; will of God and, 216n51; women's roles in, 58
Song of Roland, 46, 236n6
Song of Songs, 150, 152–54, 155–58, 160, 238n47
Southern, Richard W., 43, 79, 192
Spain, Christian: communal charters issued in, 21; fifteenth-century conversion of Jews in, 75, 166; Narbonnese Jewry's foundation legend and, 33; protection of Jewish local self-rule in, 29
Spain, Muslim. See Iberia
Spain, Roman and Visigothic, 20
Speyer charter, 29, 55
spitting, 94–95; on a cross, 95
Stacey, Robert, 18, 176, 192, 248n37

stereotypes of the "Jew," 18, 179, 186, 194–96
Stern, Fritz, 248n34
Stroumsa, Guy, 193
Sukkot, 138–39
supersessionism, Christian, 9, 65
synagoga and ecclesia, 151–52; beautiful, 152, 159, 160, 238n44; blindfold in, 152–53, 154, 155, 159, 160; crownless Jew in, 153; iconography of defeat in, 151–52; *Levy Mahzor* and, 152–53; no longer similar in later Middle Ages, 169; similarly dressed, 162; symbolic reversal of Christian meaning, 152–55; as women representing Jews and Christians of both genders, 151
synagogues: Christian builder of, 74; with Christian materials and architecture, 12, 78; higher than churches, 76

Taitz, Emily, 223n79
Talmud: on answering a dullard, 81; anti-Christian insults in, 75; Babylonian, 69, 95; Christian ignorance about, 134; communal legal decisions and, 28; in debates between Jews and Christians, 75; dialectical analysis of, 36; directly applied by R. Gershom, 25; on "foreign worship" (*'avodah zarah*), 27; on goods engulfed in a river, 26–27; on Jesus in hell in boiling excrement, 92, 104; motif of great scholar in disguise, 38; on New Testament, 74; on permanence of Jewish status, 167; pietist Jews' teachings conflicting with, 137; preventing conversions by students of, 165; Rabbeinu Tam as great glossator of, 134; studied with French interpreter, 12; studied with French scholastic commentators, 12, 208n39; wordplay denigrating pagan religion in, 68–69; on worshiping an idol by defecation, 91; wreaths or crowns of Jewish brides in, 153. See also Tosafist (Talmud glossator)
taxes: for Christian authorities, 28; collected by Jews in Roman Empire, 20
teleological view, of modern Jew hatred, 189–90, 192

Tellenbach, Gerd, 44
Temple in Jerusalem, 76–78, 158–59
Teter, Magda, 187
Theobold, 132
Theodoros, 33
Thibaut V, Count of Blois, 112, 116–17, 118, 119, 126
Thomas of Becket, Saint, 108
Thomas of Monmouth: imagining choosing of a victim, 196; imagining putting a body in latrine, 93, 111; never having heard of 1096, 130–31; possibly influenced by Würzburg murder, 116; *Prioress's Tale* compared to, 181; reenactment of the Passion and, 133, 135; revenge for Jewish suffering and, 132, 136, 181, 182. *See also* William of Norwich
three days, in ritual and folklore, 103–4
Toch, Michael, 191
Toledot Yeshu (Life of Jesus), 70, 72, 74
Tomasch, Sylvia, 179
Torah: Christians accused of abusing scrolls, 89, 133, 134, 224n8, 224n10; initiation of young boys into, 15, 105–7, 165, 229n86; *Sefer Hasidim* on answering a Christian about, 81–82; *Sefer Hasidim* on separation from bodily excretions, 90–91, 225n19; Shavuot and, 165; Talmud on answering a Christian about, 81. *See also* Hebrew Bible
Tosafist (Talmud glossator): adolescent students of, 229n86; Rabbeinu Tam as, 134; on ritual homicide, 57
Tovey, D'Blossier, 95–96
Trachtenberg, Joshua, 179, 189, 191
transfer of authority (*translatio imperii*), 30, 32, 36
transfer of learning (*translatio studii*), 30, 31, 32, 36, 38–39
transubstantiation, 100, 123, 192. *See also* Eucharist

urban expansion in Christian Europe: in eleventh and twelfth centuries, 22, 27, 46; increasing contact between Jews and Christians, 40, 42, 43, 44; religious issues about credit and, 173

Urban II (pope): on atonement for sins, 48, 54–55; on categories of holy vs. polluted, 51; First Crusade and, 14, 47–49, 214n26; on Muslim enemy in Spain, 50; not distinguishing between Muslims and nearby Jews, 131; not motivating ritual murder accusation, 128
usury: expulsion of Jews from European states and, 173; by foreign Christians, 17, 174–75; in image of Jews after expulsions, 178–79; Jews as dangerous enemy within and, 177; local Jewish merchants and, 17; Martin Luther's attack on Jews for, 187; not practiced only by Jews, 173; seen as danger to Christian society, 167; temporal and ecclesiastical rulers acting to control, 17, 44, 174–77. *See also* moneylenders

violence: acting out against Christian symbols and, 89; Christian reform movements and, 42–44; of knights attacking one another, 48; toward Christian attackers, 59
violence, anti-Jewish: after alleged ritual murder, 109–10, 113, 115, 116, 117, 121, 230n5; antisemitism as much more than, 189, 193, 246n4; blood libel and, 125; for disruption of right order, 55; host desecration libel and, 125
Virgin Mary. *See* Mary
Visigothic Spain, 20
Vitry, Jacques de, 229n84, 240n69
von Trimberg, Süsskind, 146

Wagenseil, Johann Christian, 71
wandering Jew, 179
well-poisoning libel, 16, 125, 167, 177, 232n44
the West: as Christian Europe, 3; formed by Rome, Germanic customs, and Christianity, 11; Nirenberg's "anti-Judaism" and, 190. *See also* Europe, formation of
wet nurses, Christian: acceptable to pietists, 138; accused of expressing milk into latrine, 1, 88–89, 100, 101–2, 104–5; violating popes' idea of right order, 45, 101

white supremacists, 198
wild olive tree, parable of, 8, 10, 152
William of Malmesbury, 81
William of Norwich, 93, 110, 111–13, 115–16, 119–20, 126, 127. *See also* Thomas of Monmouth
William of Tyre, 64
William Rufus, King of England, 81
William the Breton, 232n47
will of God: First Crusade and, 48–49, 54, 56–57, 216n52; martyrs of 1096 and, 49, 56–57, 216n51
Winchester. *See* Richard of Devizes
women, Jewish: in allegory of Song of Songs, 152–56; beautiful, 16, 160–61, 162, 184–85, 238n44; Christian idealization of beauty and, 149; disguised as a Christian or nun, 147; disguised as a man, 145–46, 147; likeliness of conversion, 165, 169; in medieval illuminations, 142; not to perform ritual acts in public, 164; sexual attractiveness of, 161, 239n59. *See also* synagoga and ecclesia
wordplay: denigrating pagan religion, 68–69; insulting Christianity, 73
Worms: Eleazar ben Judah of, 34–38, 138; Jews going to saints' tombs in, 136, 235n99
Würzburg murder, 113–17, 119, 126, 128, 136, 230n5

Yannai, 69
Yiddish, 12; earliest preserved passage of, 85; stories about Judah the Pious in, 123
Yohanan, 69
Yom Tov of England, 95, 165, 226n38
Yuval, Israel, 116, 130, 218n75, 230n5, 234n80

Zfatman, Sara, 212n57, 212n59
Zunz, Leopold, 69–70

A NOTE ON THE TYPE

THIS BOOK has been composed in Miller, a Scotch Roman typeface designed by Matthew Carter and first released by Font Bureau in 1997. It resembles Monticello, the typeface developed for The Papers of Thomas Jefferson in the 1940s by C. H. Griffith and P. J. Conkwright and reinterpreted in digital form by Carter in 2003.

Pleasant Jefferson ("P. J.") Conkwright (1905–1986) was Typographer at Princeton University Press from 1939 to 1970. He was an acclaimed book designer and AIGA Medalist.

GPSR Authorized Representative: Easy Access System Europe - Mustamäe tee 50, 10621 Tallinn, Estonia, gpsr.requests@easproject.com

www.ingramcontent.com/pod-product-compliance
Lightning Source LLC
Chambersburg PA
CBHW011951150426
43195CB00019B/2893